The Eternal Vision

Bill Sykes is Chaplain of University College, Oxford. For over thirty years he also led Reflection Groups for undergraduate and postgraduate students, using his ever-growing collection of quotations from the Bible and from spiritual writers through the ages.

The Eternal Vision

The Ultimate Collection of
Spiritual Quotations

Compiled by
William Sykes

HENDRICKSON PUBLISHERS

Hendrickson Publishers, Inc.
P. O. Box 3473
Peabody, Massachusetts 01961-3473

ISBN 1-56563-910-3

First published in 2002 by the Canterbury Press Norwich
(a publishing imprint of Hymns Ancient & Modern Limited,
a registered charity)
St Mary's Works, St Mary's Plain,
Norwich, Norfolk, NR3 3BH

www.scm-canterburypress.co.uk

Hendrickson Publishers edition reprinted by
arrangement with the Canterbury Press.

Hendrickson Publishers edition first printing — January 2003

Printed in Great Britain

CONTENTS

CONTENTS

FOLLOWING THE STURDY PILGRIM:

A Preface for Sceptics

(The rest of you can skip this bit)

A quarter of a century ago, a young priest named Bill Sykes suffered a crisis of faith. There's not much news in that, I suppose. It's the sort of thing young priests are probably supposed to do, or at least the smart ones are anyway. The usual answers are either to hobble emptily along in the chosen career or go into another line of work. I see some of these types in my classes as law students from time to time. But this particular fellow was a tad different.

Whether it was having grown up with the same name as a Dickens character or having chased about the countryside as a Gurkha officer, some spark kept the young Reverend Sykes on a quest to find and restore what he'd lost. This quest took him years of experience, study and conversation, but it has ended in success. That last bit must be unsurprising to you, who are holding this book and so have an idea where we're headed; this book is the record of that quest.

I happened to join Bill on his trail, quite literally, about ten years ago. I was one of those most absurd of creatures, an American graduate student in Oxford University. Bill was our college chaplain and also one of the most ardent supporters of the college rugby club. Through one role or the other we saw a good bit of each other and even began a daily trundle, a jog of a mile or occasionally two we'd take each morning, during the frequent breaks from which we would cure the ills of the world. So I learned quite a bit about Bill's programmes of group study, in which he'd bring small gangs of students to his quarters and, over tea and biscuits (cookies to us Americans), the students would read, think, and wrangle with a topic drawn by one of the group from a cornucopia of ideas that he'd collected while working out his own views of God, man, life and all that.

Strange as this sounds to me now, these meetings were immensely popular. Despite the cynicism and loftiness of the average Oxford student, we showed up in droves to read Bill's stuff and to talk about it. It seems he'd hit not just one nerve but a whole tangle of them.

In the years since I've left England, Bill has somewhat improved on that 'stuff'. Far from the old black binders and topic lists pasted onto cardboard, he's worked and refined, expanded and trimmed. Most importantly, he's allowed more and more of his personal journey to show through the readings.

The result is this wonderful volume, rewrought from six earlier tomes and with a breadth of concern for the fears and obstacles, as well as the triumphs and quiet satisfactions, that we all face. The readings are drawn not just from the Christian testaments and canons but also from a wide field of saints and more than a few sinners. They are prefaced, in each topic, by one of Bill's encounters with the problem enshrined by the heading.

I find, after having given many copies of his early books to friends and still keeping my own around, that the books grow fresher as I grow older. A favourite trick is to grab one just before my midnight snack and read a chapter at random. My goal, of course, is to become sufficiently wrapped up in the chapter to skip the snack. It actually works occasionally. More often I have the snack anyway and then find myself moved to reverie by the chapter, and then I'll read another chapter.

Some years ago, prefacing one of Bill's earlier books, I wrote that Bill had grappled with our demons, that is, the doubts and fears that haunt the dark hours of our lives. Since then, I've had many occasions to look again at his works and question my words. I was correct but incomplete. Bill has grappled with our demons, but he has also seen our strengths. I was wrong, as youth often is, to be too distracted by his sharing of his battles with doubt and fear. He shares as much of his wonder at grace and faith. In both endeavours and in the countless shades of our spiritual lives between them, I commend to you the fun of sharing the trail with Bill Sykes.

Steve Sheppard is a lawyer and law professor teaching at the University of Arkansas.

INTRODUCTION

At the age of thirty, having just completed a busy four-year curacy at Bradford Cathedral, I became aware of being spiritually bankrupt. In my next job I was fortunate in being appointed chaplain to University College, London, which gave me an opportunity for renewal. Shortly after arriving in my new location someone recommended two anthologies: *A Year of Grace* and *From Darkness to Light* – both by the publisher Victor Gollancz. I found these books enormously helpful. On another visit to what was now my favourite bookshop, I jocularly asked the elderly assistant which, in her opinion, was the best book in the shop. She immediately said the book she would recommend was out of stock, but would I like to borrow her own copy? I declined as I did not know her very well, but asked if I could order a copy? 'Yes,' she said, 'provided you are prepared to wait for six weeks. The book is an American publication. We shall have to import it.' As it happened I was due to go to New York soon so she gave me the address of a bookshop where I might find a copy of the book in question: *The Choice Is Always Ours* – by Dorothy Berkley Phillips.

As soon as I opened *The Choice . . .* I realized I had been looking for this book unconsciously for ten years. Pondering over its contents led to the emergence of what I would describe as *The Eternal Vision*. The starting-point is the Genesis story of the creation of humanity. In this story God is depicted as fashioning and shaping the first man in his own image and likeness, and the last thing he does is breathe into the man, and he becomes a living being. I took this to mean that God breathed something of his own nature into humans giving them something akin to a divine potential. The other truth which comes out of this story is that what was fashioned and shaped in the image and likeness of God was taken from the dust of the earth, so that as well as our having something akin to a divine potential we are at one and the same time earthy and creaturely. I would like to add 'and rightly so' as I see a value in the earthy and creaturely – a potential source of energy and dynamism.

If we want to see *The Eternal Vision* fully worked out in a life we go to the Gospels – to the person of Jesus Christ. As he went through life he discovered something of the presence of 'the Father' in the depths of himself and was able to say to his disciples: 'Do you not believe that I am in the Father and the Father is in me? The words that I say to you I do not speak on my own; but the Father who dwells in me does his works. Believe that I am in the Father and the Father is in me'. A brief look through the Gospels also reveals he discovered in himself the full range of the gifts of the Holy Spirit, wisdom, counsel (guidance), understanding, knowledge, fear (in the sense of awe and reverence), power and the spirit of the Lord. This in turn led to the full development of the fruits of the Holy Spirit in the experience of his short life: love, joy, peace, patience, kindness, goodness, faithfulness, gentleness and self-control. We can also find divine attributes in his personality, such as life, light, truth, hope, grace and glory. Lastly he brought about an inner integration of the divine with the carthy and creaturely, becoming a whole full-blooded dynamic person – very God and very Man. Later he was recognized as 'the image of the invisible God', and 'the *second Adam*'.

We find in the epistles a valuable insight coming from the pen of St Paul. He discovered that what Christ had experienced in his life, we can also experience in some measure in our lives. Some time after his conversion on the road to Damascus, Paul wrote in his epistle to the Galatians: 'it is no longer I who live, but it is Christ who lives in me'. And he followed this up in another epistle with: 'For in him the whole fullness of deity dwells bodily, and you have come to fulness of life in him'. The result of this means we can expect to experience something of the Father, the Son and the Holy Spirit in our lives. This includes the gifts and fruits of the Holy Spirit already mentioned as well as those divine attributes – life, light, truth, hope, grace and glory. Thus we can say *The Eternal Vision* is deeply rooted in both the Old and the New Testaments, and in the depths of ourselves.

The Eternal Vision expands enormously when we consider the spiritual experience of the last two thousand years. We start with the spiritual writings of theologians and the spiritual experience of the saints. We move on to a whole range of people we normally consider to have been inspired, i.e. 'breathed into' – as in the Genesis story of the creation of humanity. This opens up *The Eternal Vision* to the spiritual experience and insight of poets, playwrights, novelists, philosophers, scientists, historians, politicians, economists, psychologists, statesmen, artists and musicians. In the last thirty years I have had an exciting time rounding up insights, thoughts and experiences form the writings of these 'inspired' men and women. Over a period of time I have arranged these findings in 230 topics. These have been published in five books: *Visions of Faith, Visions of Hope, Vision of Love, Visions of Grace* and *Visions of Glory*. Of *Visions of Grace*, a critic wrote rather amusingly: 'If there is a shortage of wisdom in the world it is because . . . Bill Sykes has used it all up in this book.' *The Eternal Vision* is an attempt to extract the heart and core of these five books and to bring the findings together in one volume. All told I have selected 122 of the more important topics and have tried to go for the shorter quotations, hoping these will be easier to understand, and more economical as regards time.

How then can we use the material in *The Eternal Vision*? First and foremost I use this book for growing in *The Eternal Vision* and in moving towards becoming a whole person. The underlying technique used in this book is reflection – a simple form of meditation and contemplation. Reflection involves pondering and mulling over the contents in *The Eternal Vision*. In reflection we are encouraged to think with our minds as far as they will go. In reflection, we make use of our instincts and intuitions (feelings), by looking carefully at the quotations and working out what we *feel about* them. In reflection we use our imaginations, again as far as they will go. In reflection we use our experiences of life so far, which are a considerable resource. In reflection we make use of 'lateral thinking' and 'vertical thinking' – the latter bringing in the important spiritual dimension. A good description of reflection comes from the Book of Common Prayer, from a Collect intended for the scriptures, but also relevant here: 'Grant that we may in such wise hear them, read, mark, learn, and inwardly digest them.' In reflection great use is made of silence, allowing for the evolution of a 'listening form of prayer'. Reflection on the contents of *The Eternal Vision* is an excellent way of fostering 'the daily increase' and a valuable follow-up for confirmation. There is enough material here to last a lifetime. Perhaps the most valuable thing I have done is use this material to stimulate the keeping of a spiritual journal. Often I take a short phrase and with the aid of a pen and paper spend a whole hour just reflecting on that phrase and recording the findings in my spiritual journal (diary). One undergraduate using this simple technique confided in me: 'Through reflection I have discovered I have a mind that can think'. I know of many hundreds of people who have benefited from the practice of reflection and my hope is *The Eternal Vision* will stimulate thousands of other people to take up the practice of reflection.

Twenty-four years ago I was elected to be Chaplain Fellow of University College. Oxford – having been chaplain to University College, London, for nine years. Since coming to Oxford I have used the material of *The Eternal Vision* for 'reflection groups' in college. These groups have been very popular, and for many years in term-time, I have had about thirty different reflection groups meeting each week in my room. These reflection groups are voluntary and there are on average three or four undergraduates in a group. The same is true for postgraduate groups. We arrange to meet at a mutually convenient time and each reflection group lasts for an hour. We begin with a cup of tea, coffee, hot chocolate or orange juice, according to taste, and also have on hand a big tin of Hobnob biscuits. My observation over the years is that undergraduates love Hobnobs. In practice anyone can dig in during the hour and help themselves. A list of 160 topics is circulated and each participant is encouraged to choose a topic. After three or four minutes we share the titles of the topic we have chosen and select one of these topics by consensus. The material is then circulated and silent reflection begins. My most recent practice is to ask each person in the group to select the three quotations they consider to be the best. Some undergraduates make use of clip-boards and pens. Others are content to concentrate solely on the material. The period of reflection lasts for about twenty-five minutes, until the halfway stage is reached. As convenor (or enabler or facilitator), I then start the discussion part of the reflection group. First of all I ask if they have managed to get through all the material. Then I ask the person whose topic we have chosen the following question: 'Was there any particular reason for choosing this topic?' Usually there is a reason. My next question, partly depending on the answer, is: 'Did you find anything that was helpful?' This means we usually start on a positive note. The same applies when we share the choice of the best three quotations. We end promptly on the hour, as time is precious in an eight-week term. This also means we can start the next reflection group on time.

My experience of reflection groups is that they are non-threatening and open to a wide variety of participants. In our reflection groups we have Roman Catholics, members of the Church of England, Methodists, United Reformed Church members, the occasional Quaker, Jews, Hindus, Muslims, Buddhists, atheists and agnostics, and a wide vareity of people with no fixed allegiance. The groups vary a great deal. One year we had a group of brilliant sportsmen, several of whom had represented their countries at an international level. There was another group in which each member had a first-class degree. On the other hand a reflection group can have just one person as well as myself, and that person might be going through a difficult time. We use the material in *The Eternal Vision* to work through the difficulties and to put that person in touch with his or her inner resources. The pattern of the reflection group I have mentioned seems to work well in a college setting. Different patterns may develop in other locations and these are to be welcomed and encouraged. Two reactions have reached my ears from our undergraduates. For many the reflection group is their most enjoyable and valuable hour of the week. I never mention this to tutors because in their eyes there is only one valuable hour of the week – their tutorials. The second is that for one person, taking part in a reflection group was the most valuable thing he did in Oxford.

I am very much aware that in *The Eternal Vision* I have only selected one third of the material used in *Visions of Faith*, *Visions of Hope*, *Visions of Love*, *Visions of Grace* and *Visions of Glory*. If anyone dips into *The Eternal Vision* and wants to go further, one or more copies of the five books can be obtained from me at the following address: The Revd Bill Sykes, University College, Oxford, OX1 4BH; telephone (01865) 277763; e-mail william.sykes@univ.ox.ac.uk or fax (01865) 276790.

I hope you enjoy the contents of *The Eternal Vision*. If used well, the book acts as a skeleton or framework of faith. Lots of clues are given but it allows the person reflecting freedom to put his or her own flesh and blood on that skeleton or framework. This is an attempt to get to the heart and core of spirituality, making it readily available for a wide variety of people at the beginning of this twenty-first century.

I

ACCEPTANCE

*A**cceptance – favourable reception, approval, belief*

At the age of ten I had a firm conviction that there was one job I would never do – that of being a priest. In my teens, in the midst of a very active life, I became aware of a growing faith. This led to a commitment in my early twenties and a conviction that from now on, whatever happened, I was going to lead a Christian life. What particularly stimulated me was a quiet but encouraging awareness of the Holy Spirit. At the time I was wrestling with what to do in life. While pondering over various possibilities I was suddenly challenged by the thought that if my Christian faith was so important to me, perhaps instead of just living it I ought to be actively engaged in spreading it? A chord had been struck and a state of acceptance reached. Over the years I have also been aware of another area of acceptance. At one level there is an acceptance of the worst life can throw at you, and at another level, facing disaster in the most creative way possible. Another form of acceptance is being accepted by God and by other people. There are, therefore, several sides to acceptance.

The beloved of the Lord rests in safety – the High God surrounds him all day long – the beloved rests between his shoulders.
Deuteronomy 33.12

But to all who received him, who believed in his name, he gave power to become children of God.
John 1.12

It is so, it cannot be otherwise.
Anon

We must accept finite disappointment, but we must never lose infinite hope.
Martin Luther King, in Coretta Scott King, *The Words of Martin Luther King*

The will of God . . . cannot be simply that we accept the situations of life but must be rather that we go through them and emerge from them.

John S. Dunne, *The Reasons of the Heart*

You often try to run away from your life, but you're wasting your time. If you sincerely believe that your life is worthwhile and necessary, then you will have accepted it.

Michel Quoist, *With Open Heart*

He who is in a state of rebellion cannot receive grace, to use the phrase of which the Church is so fond – so rightly fond, I dare say – for in life as in art the mood of rebellion closes up the channels of the soul, and shuts out the airs of heaven.

Oscar Wilde, *De Profundis*

The self-accepting person has a realistic appraisal of his resources combined with appreciation of his own worth; assurance about standards and convictions of his own without being a slave to the opinions of others; and realistic assessment of limitations without irrational self-reproach.

Arthur T. Jersild, *The Psychology of Adolescence*

To accept a person does not mean that I deny his defects, that I gloss over them or try to explain them away. Neither does acceptance mean to say that everything the person does is beautiful and fine. Just the opposite is true. When I deny the defects of the person, then I certainly do not accept him. I have not touched the depth of that person. Only when I accept a person can I truly face his defects . . .

Peter G. van Breemen SJ, *As Bread that Is Broken*

There liveth no man on earth who may always have rest and peace without troubles and crosses, with whom things always go according to his will; there is always something to be suffered here, turn which way you will. And as soon as you are quit of one assault, perhaps two will come in its place. Wherefore yield thyself willingly to them, and seek only that true peace of the heart, which none can take away from thee, that thou mayest overcome all assaults.

Theologia Germanica

I am accepted by God as I am – *as I am*, and not as I should be . . . He loves me with my ideals and disappointments, my sacrifices and my joys, my successes and my failures. God is himself the deepest Ground of my being. It is one thing to know I am accepted and quite another thing to realize it. It is not enough to have but just once touched the love of God. There is more required to build one's life on God's love. It takes a long time to believe that I am accepted by God as I am.

Peter G. van Breemen SJ, *As Bread that Is Broken*

Out of evil, much good has come to me. By keeping quiet, repressing nothing, remaining attentive, and by accepting reality – taking things as they are, and not as I wanted them to be – by doing all this, unusual knowledge has come to me, and unusual powers as well, such as I could never have imagined before. I always thought that when we accepted things they overpowered us in some way or other. This turns out not to be true at all, and it is only by accepting them that one can assume an attitude toward them.

    Richard Wilhelm and C.G. Jung (extract from a former patient), *The Secret of the Golden Flower*

One of the deepest needs of the human heart is the need to be appreciated. Every human being wants to be valued . . . Every human being craves to be accepted, accepted for what he is . . . When I am not accepted, then something in me is broken . . . Acceptance means that the people with whom I live give me a feeling of self-respect, a feeling that I am worthwhile.

    They are happy that I am who I am. Acceptance means that I am welcome to be myself. Acceptance means that though there is need for growth, I am not forced. I do not have to be the person I am not!

    Peter G. van Breemen SJ, *As Bread that Is Broken*

Sometimes . . . a wave of light breaks into our darkness, and it is as though a voice were saying: 'You are accepted.' *You are accepted*, accepted by that which is greater than you, and the name of which we do not know. Do not ask for the name now; perhaps you will find it later. Do not try to do anything now; perhaps later you will do much. Do not seek for anything; do not perform anything; do not intend anything. *Simply accept the fact that you are accepted!* If that happens to us, we experience grace.

    Paul Tillich, *The Shaking of the Foundations*

Each one of us is born with many potentialities. But unless they are drawn out by the warm touch of another's acceptance, they will remain dormant. Acceptance liberates everything that is in me. Only when I am loved in that deep sense of complete acceptance can I become myself. The love, the acceptance of other persons, makes me the unique person that I am meant to be. When a person is appreciated for what he *does*, he is not unique; someone else can do the same work perhaps better than the other. But when a person is loved for what he *is*, then he becomes a unique and irreplaceable personality.

    Peter G. van Breemen SJ, *As Bread that Is Broken*

See also Contentment, Freedom, Obedience, Patience, Understanding

2

ACTION

*A*ction *– process of acting, exertion, of energy or influence, as men of action, thing done, act*

In *The Devils of Loudun*, Aldous Huxley comes out with this challenging sentence: 'A man of prayer can do more in a single year than another can accomplish in a whole lifetime.' In retrospect, the early years of my life were taken up in action. I loved all sorts of sport – rugby, hockey, cricket and golf – and played them to the full. In my late teens I was called up for National Service and commissioned into the Gurkhas. After 'Malaya' I went to Balliol for three years, ending with a university expedition to Nepal, followed by training at theological college, and a four-year curacy in Bradford. By the time I was thirty I was feeling the strain. Fortunately I had a colleague – Father Simon Holden of the Community of the Resurrection, Mirfield – who introduced me to the passive side of life, to the life of prayer. The result has been an emergence of a balance between the active life and the passive life.

Now begin the work, and the Lord be with you.
  1 Chronicles 22.16

So let us not grow weary in doing what is right, for we will reap at harvest time, if we do not give up.
  Galatians 6.9

What you theoretically know, vividly realize.
  Francis Thompson, 'Shelley'

Perform every action as though it were your last.
  Marcus Aurelius, *The Meditations of Marcus Aurelius*

Pray, with *humility*; and do, with *diligence*.
  Benjamin Whichcote, *Moral and Religious Aphorisms*

Action springs not from thought, but from a readiness for responsibility.
    Dietrich Bonhoeffer, *Letters and Papers from Prison*

There is nothing like active work for relieving and steadying the mind.
    A.C. Benson, *Letters of Dr A.C. Benson to M.E.A.*

In our era, the road to holiness necessarily passes through the world of action.
    Dag Hammarskjöld, *Markings*

No man can read the Gospels without being impressed with the immense activity of Christ.
    Henry Ward Beecher, *Proverbs from Plymouth Pulpit*

Christians are living in this sinful world and must bear its burden, they may not steal away from the battlefield.
    Nicolas Berdyaev, *Christianity and Class War*

The worst of partialities is to withhold oneself, the worst ignorance is not to act, the worst lie is to steal away.
    Charles Péguy, *Basic Verities*

Enlarging insight depends on expansion due to exercise; vision on action, on acting up to the limit of what has been glimpsed.
    Anon

He who is morally active does not exert himself in vain, for much more of the seed falls on fertile ground than the Gospel all too modestly estimates in the parable of the sower.
    Johann Wolfgang von Goethe, in Ludwig Curtius, *Wisdom and Experience*

Why stand we here trembling around
Calling on God for help, and not ourselves, in whom God dwells
Stretching a hand to save the falling Man?
    William Blake, 'Jerusalem'

All passion becomes strength when it has an outlet from the narrow limits of our personal lot in the labour of our right arm, the cunning of our right hand, or the still, creative activity of our thought.
    George Eliot, *Adam Bede*

No one need search for a programme of action or a crusade. The world and suffering humanity create the agenda for those who have eyes for human misery, ears for the stories of oppression and degradation and hearts to respond to the distress of our human family.

Basil Hume OSB, *To Be a Pilgrim*

> 'Tis God gives skill,
> But not without men's hands: He could not make
> Antonio Stradivari's violins
> Without Antonio.
>> George Eliot, 'Stradivarius'

These two lives, action and contemplation, instead of excluding each other, call for each other's help, implement and complete each other. Action, to be productive, has need of contemplation. The latter, when it gets to a certain degree of intensity, diffuses some of its excess on the first. By contemplation the soul draws directly from the heart of God the graces which the active life distributes.

Mother Teresa, in Brother Angelo Devananda, *Jesus, the Word to Be Spoken*

He would have urged all Christians to fulfil their duties in a world that still belongs to God despite its sin and shame. But equally firmly he would have declared that no scheme for social betterment, no international organization, no political or ecclesiastical reform can in themselves heal the wounds of humanity. In one way only can men be saved, by ridding their hearts of the selfishness that hides from them the knowledge of the love of God.

Florence Higham, said of F.D. Maurice, in *Frederick Denison Maurice*

Seen with the eyes of the social historian, this three years' activity as a social revolutionary is the life of Jesus in its impact upon human history. What makes it unique is the scope of the vision which it embodies, and his profound insight into the conditions demanded for its accomplishment. The teaching of Jesus is not something separable from his life; it is the expression of the understanding which grew out of his life. Theory and practice are there completely unified. The one interprets and expounds the other. It is the fusion of insight and action that makes the life of Jesus the religious life *par excellence* . . .

John Macmurray, *Creative Society*

Two methods exist, of aiming at human improvement, – by adjusting circumstances without and by addressing the affections within; by creating facilities of position, or by developing force of character; by mechanism or by mind. The one institutional and systematic, operating on a large scale; reaching individuals circuitously and at last; the other is personal and moral, the influence of soul on soul, life creating life, beginning in the regeneration of the individual and spreading thence over communities; the one, in short, reforming from the circumference to the centre, the other from the centre to the circumference. And in comparing these it is not difficult to show the superior triumphs of the latter, which was the method of Christ and Christianity.

James Martineau, *Endeavours After the Christian Life: Discourses*

See also Discipleship, Kingdom of God, Progress, Service, Work

3

ADORATION

*A*doration – regarding with the utmost respect and affection: worshipping as a deity; reverence

We had a tragedy in college. One of our retired Fellows had a daughter with a tumour on the brain. She was married with a two-year-old son. The surgeon had operated on her several times, but was unable to remove the roots of the tumour. He feared he might irretrievably damage her speech and eyesight, some considerable time before she died, which sadly seemed inevitable. I was visiting her in hospital after one of these operations. I had only been there a short time when there was a knock on the door and in came her son – along with other members of the family. He quickly made his way to her bedside and looked adoringly into her eyes. Contact was made and suddenly they gave each other a look of sheer delight and wonder – the look reserved for a person greatly loved and adored. This was one of the most beautiful sights I have ever seen, and gave me a valuable insight into adoration.

～

O come, let us worship and bow down, let us kneel before the Lord, our Maker!
  Psalm 95.6

And all of us, with unveiled faces, seeing the glory of the Lord as though reflected in a mirror, are being transformed into the same image from one degree of glory to another; for this comes from the Lord, the Spirit.
  2 Corinthians 3.18

We adore in order to love, to absorb into our own beings the being of God.
  Kenneth Leech, *True Prayer*

This is adoration: not a difficult religious exercise, but an attitude of the soul.
  Evelyn Underhill, *The Love of God*

If we would understand Divine things, we must cultivate an attitude of humble adoration. Whoever does not begin by kneeling down, runs every possible risk.

> Ernest Hello, *Life, Science, and Art*

Nothing is more needed by humanity today, and by the church in particular, than the recovery of a sense of 'beyondness' in the whole of life to revive the springs of wonder and adoration.

> John V. Taylor, *The Go-Between God*

> It is a beauteous evening, calm and free,
> The holy time is quiet as a Nun
> Breathless with adoration.
>> William Wordsworth, 'It is a Beauteous Evening'

Man is most truly himself, as the Eastern Church well knows, not when he toils but when he adores. And we are learning more and more that all innocent joy in life may be a form of adoration.

> Vida D. Scudder, *The Privilege of Age*

What I cry out for, like every being, with my whole life and all my earthly passions, is something very different from an equal to cherish: it is for a God to adore . . .

The more man becomes man, the more will he become prey to a need, a need that is always more explicit, more subtle and more magnificent, the need to adore.

> Pierre Teilhard de Chardin, *Le Milieu Divin*

But 'to adore' (Lat: ad-orare) is 'to pray toward . . .'. It is to go out of oneself, to commune with a Reality larger, deeper, purer than one's own being. Adoration is an enhancement of one's being, though paradoxically this comes about through going out of oneself.

> John Macquarrie, *Paths in Spirituality*

To adore . . . means to lose oneself in the unfathomable, to plunge into the inexhaustible, to find peace in the incorruptible, to be absorbed in defined immensity, to offer oneself to the fire and the transparency, to annihilate oneself in proportion as one becomes more deliberately conscious of oneself, and to give one's deepest to that whose depth has no end.

> Pierre Teilhard de Chardin, *Le Milieu Divin*

To worship is to quicken the conscience by the holiness of God, to feed the mind with the truth of God, to purge the imagination by the beauty of God, to open the heart to the love of God, to devote the will to the purpose of God. All this is gathered up in that emotion which most cleanses us from selfishness because it is the most selfless of all emotions – adoration.

   William Temple, *The Hope of a New World*

Adoration is a rejoicing in what we believe God is in himself, in the more that he must be that we cannot understand; it is reaching out to this in love and longing, wanting to know and prove as much of this as is permitted here on earth, going to that rim of experience where something tells you to turn back to life because this is as far as you can go in wonder at the devastating richness of life. The rest we may hope to know after death, but it is not for now.

   J. Neville Ward, *The Use of Praying*

Worship is essentially an act of adoration, adoration of the one true God in whom we live and move and have our being. Forgetting our little selves, our petty ambitions, our puny triumphs, our foolish cares and fretful anxieties, we reach out towards the beauty and majesty of God. The religious life is not a dull, grim drive towards moral virtues, but a response to a vision of greatness . . . The pattern prayer given by our Lord offers us the clue to right worship. It begins and ends with words of adoration.

   Thomas F. Green, *Preparation for Worship*

Adoration is the first and greatest of life's responses to its spiritual environment; the first and most fundamental of spirit's movements towards Spirit, the seed from which all other prayer must spring. It is among the most powerful of the educative forces which purify the understanding, form and develop the spiritual life. As we can never know the secret of great art or music until we have learned to look and listen with a self-oblivious reverence, acknowledging a beauty that is beyond our grasp – so the claim and loveliness remain unrealized, till we have learned to look, to listen, to adore.

   Evelyn Underhill, *The Golden Sequence*

The essence of adoration . . . is something far deeper and more demanding than the most ardent praise. It asks for our whole being; and it is rooted in the will. In the words of a French writer: 'you must be convinced that you go to adoration not to receive but to give, and, further, to give often without seeing what you are giving. You go to this act of worship to give your whole being to God in the dark.

And you need to realize what these words mean of obscure faith, sometimes of suffering, and always of love.'
  Olive Wyon, *On the Way*

For Christian experience, the life and person of Christ stand apart as the greatness of these self-revelations; the perfect self-expression of the Holy in human terms, and the supreme school and focus of man's adoring prayer. For here the Invisible God, by the most wonderful of His condescensions, discloses His beauty and attraction – the brightness of His glory and the express image of His person – in a way that is mercifully adapted to our limitations, and meets us on our own ground. Therefore the events of Christ's life – alike the most strange and the most homely – are truly 'mysteries'. They contain far more than they reveal.
  Evelyn Underhill, *The Golden Sequence*

See also Love, Music, Transformation, Wonder, Worship

4

ANXIETY

Anxiety – uneasiness, concern, solicitous desire (for a thing, to do)

When I was young I went through several periods of anxiety. A close friend recommended a book to me by Dale Carnegie. The title of this book was *How to Stop Worrying and Start Living.* He observed far too many people lived in the future and were caught up in fears and anxieties. He drew our attention to the design of a modern liner. Many of these were now equipped with heavy steel partition doors. If a liner was holed, the doors could seal off the damaged part and enable the liner to stay afloat. He suggested we discipline ourselves to live 'in watertight compartments'. I also read *The Power of Positive Thinking* by Norman Vincent Peale. I used to have a problem with anxiety in taking exams. In revision time fear would set in and I would almost talk myself into failure. Having read this book, I suddenly realized it was possible to adopt a more positive approach and gently talk myself in to passing exams. Later I found 'positive thinking' a valuable help in all areas of life and an antidote to anxiety. Somewhere in my reading I have picked up the phrase 'wise forethought' as a help in facing anxiety. Writing out solutions to problems and anxieties has also been a great help. The daily time of quiet has proved invaluable.

∽

Cast your burden on the Lord, and he will sustain you.
  Psalm 55.22

Humble yourselves therefore under the mighty hand of God, so that he may exalt you in due time. Cast all your anxieties on him, because he cares for you.
  1 Peter 5.6–7

Cast all your cares on God; that anchor holds.
  Alfred, Lord Tennyson, 'Enoch Arden'

He has not learned the lesson of life who does not every day surmount a fear.

    Ralph Waldo Emerson, *Letters and Social Aims, Addresses*

It is a help to have something to do, and not to creep about in a dim fatiguing dream of anxiety.

    A.C. Benson, *Extracts from the Letters of Dr A.C. Benson to M.E.A.*

Anxiety, fear, ill-fated desire are signatures on the human face. Suffering and anxious care are written there.

    Henry Ward Beecher, *Proverbs from Plymouth Pulpit*

I know well the feeling of being all tense with business and worry. The only cure is the old one – 'whenever you have too much to do, don't do it'.

    A.C. Benson, *Extracts from the Letters of Dr A.C. Benson to M.E.A.*

Anxiety is the rust of life, destroying its brightness and weakening its powers. A childlike and abiding trust in Providence is its best preventive and remedy.

    Author unknown

Anxiety usually comes from strain, and strain is caused by too complete a dependence on ourselves, on our own devices, our own plans, our own idea of what we are able to do.

    Thomas Merton, *No Man Is an Island*

The peril of certain troubles is that although they prevent consecutive thinking, they stimulate a tumultuous activity round a fixed point. Then ensues rapid, monstrous diseased growth.

    Mark Rutherford, *Last Pages from a Journal*

If what we have we receive as a gift, and if what we have is to be cared for by God, and if what we have is available to others, then we will possess freedom from anxiety.

    Richard Foster, *The Celebration of Discipline*

If we are relieved from serious care we are not necessarily relieved from cares. A crowd of small, impertinent worries torment me which I should not notice if I were in real trouble.

    Mark Rutherford, *Last Pages from a Journal*

In our age everything has to be a 'problem'. Ours is a time of anxiety because we have willed it to be so. Our anxiety is not imposed on us by force from outside. We impose it on our world and upon one another from within ourselves.

Thomas Merton, *Thoughts in Solitude*

Let us put all our worries to God, squarely, and then, having told him everything, so that he should know them from us, we should drop them, leave them to him. Now that he is in the know, it is no longer any of our concern: we can freely think of him.

Anthony Bloom, *The Essence of Prayer*

This bewilderment – this confusion as to who we are and what we should do – is the most painful thing about anxiety. But the positive and hopeful side is that just as anxiety destroys our self-awareness, so awareness of ourselves can destroy anxiety. That is to say, the stronger our consciousness of ourselves, the more we can take a stand against and overcome anxiety.

Rollo May, *Man's Search for Himself*

The release of anxiety is to turn cares into prayers. If we feel anxious about somebody, ill or in danger or need, that anxiety does no good to us or to them. But if that anxiety is turned into a prayer, it widens and enriches our spiritual life, it turns a thought which is depressing into a thought which is uplifting, and it helps the person we are praying for.

Geoffrey Harding, in George Appleton, *Journey for a Soul*

. . . if God has you, then He has your yesterdays and your tomorrows. He has your yesterdays and forgives all that has been amiss in them; He has your tomorrows and will provide grace and power to meet them. But only as they come. He will not provide for what is not yet here. His grace is like manna – when kept over for the next day, it spoiled. It had to be eaten day by day.

E. Stanley Jones, *Growing Spiritually*

While there is always need of wise forethought and due reference to the demands of the future, these have yet nothing in common with mere anxieties and worries which are disintegrating and fret away all the pure gold in life. Worry is simply lack of faith in God. 'For your heavenly Father knoweth what things ye have need of before ye ask Him.' Only in peace of spirit can any true achievement be won.

Lilian Whiting, *Lilies of Eternal Peace*

Annihilation of this swarm of petty invading cares by adoration! They possess and distract, not by their inherent strength but through the absence of a dominant power. The lover is absorbed in the desire to be with his mistress and keeps his appointment with her, breaking all hindrances like threads. Who shall deliver me from the body of this death? The answer was not difficult to St Paul, but how is it with me?

Mark Rutherford, *Last Pages from a Journal*

'Anxiety and misgiving,' wrote Fénelon, 'proceed solely from love of self. The love of God accomplishes all things quietly and completely; it is not anxious or uncertain. The spirit of God rests continually in quietness. Perfect love casteth out fear. It is in forgetfulness of self that we find peace. Happy is he who yields himself completely, unconsciously, and finally to God. Listen to the inward whisper of His Spirit and follow it – that is enough; but to listen one must be silent, and to follow one must yield.'

Lilian Whiting, *The Life Radiant*

See also Courage, Faith, Grace, Hope, Trust

5

ART

Art – skill applied to imitation and design, as in painting, etc., of artistic design, etc., thing in which skill may be exercised

At theological college, we were each assigned a pastoral task. I was a member of a team which went to an experimental boarding school for boys with problems. We used to go there twice a week – on a Wednesday evening and a Sunday morning. The school had a mid-term break. There was one boy who had no home to go to so we invited him to come and stay in college. As you can imagine, he was soon bored stiff. One of our team knew he had an artistic streak so bought him brushes and paints, and offered him a wall in his room, for a mural. For the next forty-eight hours this fourteen-year-old boy was thoroughly engrossed. When we were eventually allowed in we were completely taken aback by what we saw. What he had produced was a magnificent picture of the nativity. It was the work of a genius. Where had this artistic 'gift' come from? Is this another consequence of the 'divine inbreathing' of the Genesis story of the creation of human beings? Some of the quotations are suggesting this.

I have filled him with divine spirit, with ability, intelligence, and knowledge in every kind of craft, to devise artistic designs, to work in gold, silver, and bronze, in cutting stones for setting, and in carving wood, in every kind of craft.

   Exodus 31.3–5

. . . and there are varieties of activities, but it is the same God who activates all of them in everyone.

   1 Corinthians 12.6

Nature is a revelation of God; Art a revelation of man.

   Henry Wadsworth Longfellow, 'Hyperion'

Fine art is that in which the hand, the head, and the *heart* of man go together.

   John Ruskin, *The Two Paths*

[16]

Every artist dips his brush in his own soul, and paints his own nature into his pictures.

Henry Ward Beecher, *Proverbs from Plymouth Pulpit*

The Fine Arts once divorcing themselves from *truth*, are quite certain to fall mad, if they do not die.

Thomas Carlyle, *Latter-Day Pamphlets*

True art, is the desire of a man to express himself, to record the reactions of his personality to the world he lives in.

Amy Lowell, *Tendencies in Modern American Poetry*

The art which is grand and yet simple is that which presupposes the greatest elevation both in artist and in public.

Henri Frédéric Amiel, *Amiel's Journal*

The artist, of whatever kind, is a man so much aware of the beauty of the universe that he must impart the same beauty to whatever he makes.

A. Clutton Brock, *The Ultimate Belief*

All true Art is the expression of the soul. The outward forms have value only in so far as they are the expression of the inner spirit of man.

Mohandas K. Gandhi, in C.F. Andrews, *Mahatma Gandhi's Ideas*

Painting is an art, and art is not vague production, transitory and isolated, but a power which must be directed to the improvement and refinement of the human soul.

Wassily Kandinsky, *Concerning the Spiritual in Art*

To draw a moral, to preach a doctrine, is like shouting at the north star. Life is a vast and awful business. The great artist sets down his vision of it and is silent.

Ludwig Lewisohn, *The Modern Drama*

All great art is the work of the whole living creature, body and soul, and chiefly of the soul. But it is not only *the work* of the whole creature, it likewise *addresses* the whole creature.

John Ruskin, *The Stones of Venice*

The man who has honesty, integrity, the love of inquiry, the desire to see beyond, is ready to appreciate good art. He needs no one to give him an art education; he is already qualified.

Robert Henri, *The Art Spirit*

Art is the gift of God, and must be used
Unto His glory. That in Art is highest
Which aims at this.
> Henry Wadsworth Longfellow, 'Michel Angelo'

Not everything has a name. Some things lead us into a realm beyond words. Art thaws even the frozen, darkened soul, opening it to lofty spiritual experience. Through Art we are sometimes sent – indistinctly, briefly – revelations not to be achieved by rational thought.
> Alexander Solzhenitsyn, *One Word of Truth: The Nobel Speech in Literature*

A picture, however admirable the painter's art, and wonderful his power, requires of the spectator a surrender of himself, in due proportion with the miracle which has been wrought. Let the canvas glow as it may, you must love with the eye of faith, or its highest excellence escapes you.
> Nathaniel Hawthorne, *The Marble Faun*

Art is the true and happy science of the soul,
exploring nature for spiritual influences,
as doth physical science for comforting powers,
advancing so to a sure knowledge with life progress.
> Robert Bridges, 'The Testament of Beauty'

But the artist appeals to that part of our being which is not dependent on wisdom; to that in us which is a gift and not an acquisition – and, therefore more permanently enduring. He speaks to our capacity for delight and wonder, to the sense of mystery surrounding our lives; to our sense of pity, and beauty, and pain.
> Joseph Conrad, *The Nigger of the 'Narcissus'*

When the artist is alive in any person, whatever his kind of work may be, he becomes an inventive, searching, daring, self-expressing creature. He becomes interesting to other people. He disturbs, upsets, enlightens, and he opens ways for a better understanding. Where those who are not artists are trying to close the book, he opens it, shows there are still more pages possible.
> Robert Henri, *The Art Spirit*

Upon the whole it seems to me, that the object and intention of all the Arts is to supply the natural imperfection of things, and often to gratify the mind by realizing and embodying what never existed but in the imagination.

It is allowed on all hands, that facts, and events, however they may bind the historian, have no dominion over the poet or the painter. With us, history is made to bend and conform to this great idea of art. And why? Because these arts, in their highest province, are not addressed to the gross senses; but to the desires of the mind, to that spark of divinity which we have within . . .

Sir Joshua Reynolds, *Sir Joshua Reynolds' Discourses*

See also Beauty, Literature, Music, Poetry, Truth

6

ASPIRATION

A spiration – drawing of breath; desiring earnestly – for or after

I think I have always been susceptible to aspiration. A special time of aspiration was a visit to Oxford at the age of fifteen. On looking at the colleges and the university buildings I was suddenly fired with a burning desire to study in Oxford. From then onwards I worked hard at my studies, and was delighted some years later to get a place at Balliol. A smaller aspiration, which bore fruit later, was watching the coronation on television, and seeing the Gurkhas for the first time. Later I saw them again, taking part in an Edinburgh Tattoo. When I came to do National Service, I soon became aware of a burning desire to serve with them, and was greatly privileged to be with them in Singapore. What is the difference between inspiration and aspiration? Inspiration is an inward influence, a divine inbreathing – as in the Genesis story of the creation. Aspiration is more of an outward influence, as in the two instances cited above.

How lovely is your dwelling-place, O Lord of hosts! My soul longs, indeed faints for the courts of the Lord; my heart and my flesh sing for joy to the living God.
> Psalm 84.1–2

. . . he breathed on them, and said to them, 'Receive the Holy Spirit.'
> John 20.22

My . . . aspirations are my only friends.
> Henry Wadsworth Longfellow, 'The Masque of Pandora'

> Thou, who canst *think* as well as *feel*.
> Mount from the earth. aspire! aspire!
> > William Wordsworth, 'Devotional Incitements'

By aspiring to a similitude of God in goodness or love, neither man nor angel ever transgressed, or shall transgress.

    Francis Bacon, *The Advancement of Learning*

A good man, through obscurest aspriotion,
Has still an instinct of the one true way.

    Johann Wolfgang von Goethe, *Faust*

It's not a matter of chasing sensations, but welcoming those which come to us legitimately, and directing them towards the goals we aspire to.

    Michel Quoist, *With Open Heart*

And thou my mind aspire to higher things:
Grow rich in that which never taketh rust.

    Sir Philip Sidney, 'Leave Me, O Love'

An aspiration is a joy for ever, a possession as solid as a landed estate, a fortune which we can never exhaust and which gives year by year a revenue of pleasurable activity.

    Robert Louis Stevenson, *Familiar Studies of Men and Books, Virginibus Puerisque, Selected Poems*

Enflam'd with the study of learning, and the admiration of virtue; stirr'd up with high hopes of living to be brave men, and worthy patriots, dear to God, and famous to all ages.

    John Milton, *Of Education*

By the word soul, or psyche, I mean that inner consciousness which aspires. By prayer I do not mean a request for anything preferred to a deity; I mean soul-emotion, intense aspiration.

    Richard Jefferies, *The Story of My Heart*

The sensual man is at home in worldliness because he has no higher aspiration. The spiritual man, however much attracted to worldliness, cannot be at home in the world of sense because he is groping towards the world of spirit.

    Hubert van Zeller, *Considerations*

It is true, no doubt . . . that many persons 'go through life' without being consciously aware of their high endowment, they accumulate 'things', live in their outside world, 'make good' . . . but . . . the *push for the beyond* is always there in us . . .

　　Rufus M. Jones, in H. Loukes, *The Quaker Contribution*

But I do hold to a something more, far higher than the actual human, something to which it is human to aspire and to seek to translate into life individual and communal; this something translates itself to me best as the Holy Spirit.

　　Stephen MacKenna, *Journal and Letters*

> For rigorous teachers seized my youth,
> And purged its faith, and trimmed its fire,
> Showed me the high, white star to Truth,
> There bade me gaze, and there aspire.
>
> 　　Matthew Arnold, 'Stanzas from the Grande Chartreuse'

> It was my duty to have loved the highest:
> It surely was my profit had I known:
> It would have been my pleasure had I seen.
> We needs must love the highest when we see it.
>
> 　　Alfred, Lord Tennyson, 'Idylls of the King, Guinevere'

The religious spirit is in us. It preceded the religions, and their task as well as that of the prophets, of the initiated, consists in releasing, directing, and developing it. This mystical aspiration is an essentially human trait. It slumbers at the bottom of our souls awaiting the event, or the man capable, in the manner of an enzyme, of transforming it into true mysticism, into faith.

　　Lecomte du Nöuy, *Human Destiny*

All religions, arts and sciences are branches of the same tree. All these aspirations are directed toward ennobling man's life, lifting it from the sphere of mere physical existence and leading the individual toward freedom. It is no mere chance that our older universities have developed from clerical schools. Both churches and universities – insofar as they live up to their true function – serve the ennoblement of the individual. They seek to fulfil this great task by spreading moral and cultural understanding, renouncing the use of brute force.

　　Albert Einstein, *Out of My Later Years*

No aspiring soul, . . . has not at some time bowed in worship before the wonder, mystery and beauty of the world. The glorious forms and colours of sunset and dawn; the ripple of moonlight on the surface of some quiet lake; the majesty of mountain peaks; and the quaintly flowing music of mountain streams, remind every lover of Nature that God is not apart from His world, but can be found hidden there as the very Spirit of it all – 'Beauty Itself among beautiful things'. The beauty is there for all to see, but men dwell in the shadows of their own creation and their eyes are blind to it.

Raynor C. Johnson, *A Pool of Reflections*

See also Experience, Inspiration, Revelation, Vision, Wonder

7

AWARENESS

*A*wareness – a condition of knowing

In the latter reaches of a nine-year period as chaplain to University College London, I was invited to join a group consisting of the Director of the Health Centre (a psychiatrist), two GPs from the health centre, and the student counsellor. We met once a fortnight. We took it in turns to present a student problem. If it was my turn I would put before the others all the material facts about the student and the problem, except his or her name – observing confidentiality. We would then try to solve the problem using our different skills and experience. At the end of the hour's session, I would leave the health centre, feeling my awareness had increased fourfold. As a consequence there was now a real possibility of solving the problem. Reflection Groups and using this anthology on an individual basis, work on the same principle, with the aim of increasing our awareness.

O Lord, you have searched me and known me. You know when I sit down and when I rise up; you discern my thoughts from far away.
  Psalm 139.1

Be alert at all times.
  Luke 21.36

The seership of a poet's heart, the insight that is given to faith.
  Edward Bellamy, *Looking Backwards*

How another sees you depends on how you see him. Respect him, and he will respect you.
  Michel Quoist, *With Open Heart*

The only way to get our values right is to see, not the beginning, but the end of the way, to see things, not only in the light of time, but in the light of eternity.

William Barclay, *The Gospel of Matthew*

The inability to see into ourselves often manifests itself in a certain coarseness and clumsiness. One can be brazen, rude and even dishonest without being aware of it.

Eric Hoffer, *The Passionate State of Mind*

Be quite sure that you will never have the unclouded vision of God here in this life. But you may have the awareness of him, if he is willing by his grace to give it you.

The Cloud of Unknowing

He [Jesus] was not concerned with advice about conduct, but with the exposure of motive, penetrating the inner heart's secrets with the two-edged sword of his inescapable insight.

F.R. Barry, *The Relevance of Christianity*

When thou lookest upon the Imperfections of others, allow one Eye for what is Laudable in them, and the balance they have from some excellency, which may render them considerable.

Sir Thomas Browne, *Christian Morals*

If we had a keen vision and feeling of all ordinary human life, it would be like hearing the grass grow and the squirrel's heart beat, and we should die of that roar which lies on the other side of silence. As it is, the quickest of us walk about well wadded with stupidity.

George Eliot, *Middlemarch*

Another lesson I learned was that the intensity of prayer is not measured by time, but by the reality and depth of one's awareness of unity with God. I learned to look on prayer not as a means of influencing the Creator in my favour, but as an awareness of the presence of God – everywhere.

Margaret Bondfield, *What Life Has Taught Me*

If we do not understand our fellow creatures we shall never love them. And it is equally true, that if we do not love them we shall never understand them. Want of charity, want of sympathy, want of good feeling and fellow-feeling – what does it, what can it breed but endless mistakes and ignorances, both of men's characters and men's circumstances.

Charles Kingsley, *Daily Thoughts*

The person who never notices the person next to him can never move beyond and see the 'incognito' Christ in him. Busyness can lead pastors to miss seeing those they meet: people can be a hindrance in a carefully-planned schedule for the day, since they are so unpredictable and time-consuming. And simply to be noticed, recognized as a person, transforms the day for many people.

Frank Wright, *The Pastoral Nature of the Ministry*

Whoever really loves will use a magnifying glass to see the small and hidden details of another's need. I will be able to see that he has cold feet and I can move him nearer the fire; that he is deaf and I must speak closer to his ear; that a secret anxiety torments him; that he longs for a good word; and many more such things which usually lie, seemingly hidden, under the surface of our lives.

Helmut Thielicke, *I Believe – The Christian's Creed*

While we are immersed in our own thoughts we cannot recognize the reality of other people's needs, we do not see the other person at all as he is; all we see is a being who is or is not meeting our requirements. For this reason most domestic dissension is a battle between ghosts. Neither husband nor wife is loving or hating the real other, only an illusion, a projection of his or her personal wishes or resentments.   J. Neville Ward, *The Use of Praying*

I learned . . . that to condemn others is a grave mistake, since hatred, and even the wrong kind of criticism, is an evil which recoils upon its author and poisons every human relationship.

That does not mean we should be blind to the weaknesses or wickedness of others, any more than to our own, but that we should learn to look at them as the limitations of birth and circumstance, limitations which it is our duty to help them to rise above. In this I have found that example and service are more helpful than advice or preaching.   Margaret Bondfield, *What Life Has Taught Me*

Our most important task is to become aware of the fact that our new conscious-ness of space no longer admits the traditional imagery by which we represent to ourselves our encounter with God. At the same time, we must also recognize that this traditional imagery *was never essential to Christianity*. We must recover the New Testament awareness that our God does not need a temple (Acts 7.47–53) or even a cathedral. The New Testament teaches in fact that God has one indestructible temple: which is man himself (1 Cor. 3.17). To understand that God is present in the world in man is in fact no new or radical idea. It is, on the contrary, one of the most elementary teachings in the New Testament.

Thomas Merton, *Conjectures of a Guilty Bystander*

See also Belief, Education, Listening, Understanding

8

BEAUTY

Beauty – combination of qualities, as shape, proportion, colour, in human face or form, or in other objects, that delight the sight; combined qualities, delighting the other senses, the moral sense, or the intellect

I have been conscious of beauty as far back as I can remember. In childhood I quickly discovered the beauty of nature in a garden – in the flowers, the trees, and the shrubs. After this I became aware of the beauty of the seasons – snow in winter, crocuses and daffodils in springtime, the sun, sea and sky in summer, and the rich hues of autumn. Travel opened up fresh vistas of beauty, especially in the mountains of the Himalayas, Africa and the Alps. Dawn and dusk are also constant reminders of the beauty of the world. For many people today, beauty is seen as something outside us, not only in nature, but in music, poetry and art, and in the beauty of another person. However, we seem to have lost the awareness of beauty present in the depths of our being, and rarely do we become the beauty we feel after and long for.

And let the beauty of the Lord our God be upon us.

Psalm 90.17 (AV)

Finally, beloved, whatever is true, whatever is honourable, whatever is just, whatever is pure, whatever is pleasing, whatever is commendable, if there is any excellence and if there is anything worthy of praise, think about these things.

Philippians 4.8

He has a daily beauty in his life.

William Shakespeare, *Othello*

Beauty may be said to be God's trade mark in creation.

Henry Ward Beecher, *Proverbs from Plymouth Pulpit*

Nothing in human life, least of all religion, is ever right until it is beautiful.
Harry Emerson Fosdick, *As I See Religion*

This world is the world of wild storm kept tame with the music of beauty.
Rabindranath Tagore, *Stray Birds*

The hours when the mind is absorbed by beauty are the only hours when we really live.
Richard Jefferies, *Pageant of Summer*

I want to help you to grow as beautiful as God meant you to be when he thought of you first.
George Macdonald, *The Marquis of Lossie*

Though we travel the world over to find the beautiful, we must carry it with us, or we find it not.
Ralph Waldo Emerson, *Essays and Representative Men*

When you reach the heart of life you shall find beauty in all things, even in the eyes that are blind to beauty.
Kahlil Gibran, *Sand and Foam*

It is part and parcel of every man's life to develop beauty in himself. All perfect things have in them an element of beauty.
Henry Ward Beecher, *Proverbs from Plymouth Pulpit*

Every bit of beauty in this world, the beauty of man, of nature, of a work of art, is a partial transfiguration of this world, a creative break-through to another.
Nicolas Berdyaev, *Christian Existentialism*

Flowers, shade, a fine view, a sunset sky, joy, grace, feeling, abundance, and serenity, tenderness, and song, – here you have the element of beauty.
Henri Frédéric Amiel, *Amiel's Journal*

Physical beauty is the sign of an interior beauty, a spiritual and moral beauty which is the basis, the principle, and the unity of the beautiful.
Friedrich Schiller, *Essays, Aesthetical and Philosophical*

I feel more and more that the instinct for beauty (spiritual and moral as well as natural) is the most trustworthy of all instincts, and the surest sign of the nearness of God.
A.C. Benson, *Extracts from the Letters of Dr A.C. Benson to M.E.A.*

Spirit of BEAUTY, that dost consecrate
With thine own hues all thou dost shine upon
Of human thought or form – where art thou gone?
> Percy Bysshe Shelley, 'Hymn to Intellectual Beauty'

Man comes into life to seek and find his sufficient beauty, to serve it, to win and increase it, to fight for it, to face anything and dare anything for it, counting death as nothing so long as the dying eyes still turn to it.
> H.G. Wells, *The History of Mr Polly*

There comes a moment in life . . . when moral beauty seems more urgent, more penetrating, than intellectual beauty; when all that the mind has treasured must be bathed in the greatness of soul, lest it perish in the sandy desert, forlorn as the river that seeks in vain for the sea.
> Maurice Maeterlinck, *Wisdom and Destiny*

But a celestial brightness – a more ethereal beauty –
Shone on her face and encircled her form, when, after confession,
Homeward serenely she walked with God's benediction upon her.
When she had passed, it seemed like the ceasing of exquisite music.
> Henry Wadsworth Longfellow, 'Evangeline, Part the First'

Man is so inclined to concern himself with the most ordinary things, while his mind and senses are so easily blunted against impressions of beauty and perfection, that we should use all means to preserve the capacity of feeling them . . . Each day we should at least hear one little song, read one good poem, see one first-rate picture, and if it can be arranged, utter some sensible remarks.
> Johann Wolfgang von Goethe, *Wilhelm Meister's Year of Apprenticeship*

Spirit of Beauty, whose sweet impulses,
Flung like the rose of dawn across the sea,
Alone can flush the exalted consciousness
With shafts of sensible divinity –
Light of the World, essential loveliness.
> Alan Seeger, 'An Ode to Natural Beauty'

I believe that there is nothing lovelier, deeper, more sympathetic, more rational, more manly, and more perfect than the Saviour; I say to myself with jealous love that not only is there no one else like Him, but that there could be no one. I would say even more: If anyone could prove to me that Christ is outside the truth, and if the truth really did exclude Christ, I should prefer to stay with Christ and not with truth . . . There is in the world only one figure of absolute beauty: Christ. That infinitely lovely figure, is as a matter of course, an infinite marvel.

Fyodor Dostoyevsky, *Letters of Fyodor Michailovitch Dostoyevsky to His Family and Friends*

See also Art, Literature, Music, Poetry, Truth

9

BELIEF

Belief – trust or confidence (in); acceptance of Christian theology; thing believed, religion, opinion, intuition

Mark Rutherford, in this section, encourages us to struggle earnestly to increase our beliefs. 'Every addition to these', he writes, 'is an extension of life both in breadth and depth.' My belief started off as a belief in God the creator. In my teens I went one stage further and found I could assent to a belief in the contents of a creed. In my early twenties belief focused mainly on the person of Jesus Christ and the Holy Spirit. At the age of thirty a big step forward was taken when I came to believe in 'the God within' – something of the Father, Son, and the gifts and fruits of the Holy Spirit. A constant unfolding of belief has led to an extension of life both in breadth and depth. The results are to be found in this anthology. *The Eternal Vision* acts as a skeleton or framework of belief, but enables us to put our own flesh and blood on them through the practice of reflection.

Believe in the Lord your God and you will be established; believe his prophets
  2 Chronicles 20.20

I believe; help my unbelief!
  Mark 9.24

Belief makes the mind abundant.
  W.B. Yeats, in Samuel H. Miller, *The Great Realities*

He does not believe, that does not live according to his Belief.
  Thomas Fuller, *Gnomologia*

When I believe, I am no longer a mere man, I am already a son of God.
  Carlo Carretto, *Summoned by Love*

Believe that life *is* worth living, and your belief will help create the fact.
   William James, *The Will to Believe*

In the world of today the crisis of Christianity is essentially a crisis of belief.
   F.R. Barry, *Secular and Supernatural*

Belief consists in accepting the affirmations of the soul; unbelief, in denying them.
   Ralph Waldo Emerson, *Essays and Representative Men*

But we ought to struggle earnestly to increase our beliefs. Every addition to these is an extension of life both in breadth and depth.
   Mark Rutherford, *Last Pages from a Journal*

So, once again, you chose for yourself – and opened the door to chaos. The chaos you become whenever God's hand does not rest upon your head.
   Dag Hammarskjöld, *Markings*

Firstly I believe in the reality of God as the centre of human aspiration and history. What I believe about man, made in the image of God, derives first and foremost from what I believe about God.
   David Sheppard, *Bias to the Poor*

That all things are possible to him who *believes*, that they are less difficult to him who *hopes*, they are more easy to him who *loves*, and still more easy to him who perseveres in the practice of these three virtues.
   Brother Lawrence, *The Practice of the Presence of God*

I believe in Jesus Christ, in whom I get a picture of God within the limits of my comprehension. Upon Him rests the whole fabric of my life. He alone holds it together in form and purpose, and without Him it would disintegrate.
   Hugh Redwood, *Residue of Days*

We all know people who tell us they cannot believe what cannot be proved. Of course it is not true. Of course they do in fact believe a great deal that they cannot prove – concerning the trustworthiness of their friends, for example.
   William Temple, *The Hope of a New World*

We have only to believe. And the more threatening and irreducible reality appears, the more firmly and desperately must we believe. Then, little by little, we shall see the universal horror unbend, and then smile upon us, and then take us in its more than human arms.

Pierre Teilhard de Chardin, *Le Milieu Divin*

There comes a time when we have to believe where we cannot prove, and to accept where we cannot understand. If, even in the darkest hour, we believe that somehow there is a purpose in life, and that somehow that purpose is love, then even the unbearable becomes bearable, and even in the darkness there is still a glimmer of light.

William Barclay, *The Gospel of John*

There is nothing that so sanctifies the heart of man, that keeps us in such habitual love, prayer and delight in God: nothing that so kills all the roots of evil in our nature, that so renews and perfects all our virtues, that fills us with so much love, goodness, and good wishes to every creature as this faith that God is always present in us with His Light and Holy Spirit.

William Law, in Stephen Hobhouse, *Selected Mystical Writings of William Law*

One thing, however, which the apologist must always have in mind is that the debate between belief and unbelief is by no means merely a debate between himself who believes and another who disbelieves. It is also in large part a debate within himself, who both believes and disbelieves, and who must ever continue to pray humbly, 'Lord, I believe; help thou mine unbelief.'

John Baillie, *Invitation to Pilgrimage*

And so I accept God, and I accept him not only without reluctance, but, what's more, I accept his divine wisdom and purpose – which are completely beyond our comprehension. I believe in the underlying order and meaning of life. I believe in the eternal harmony into which we are all supposed to merge one day. I believe in the Word to which the universe is striving, and which itself was 'with God' and which was God, and, well, so on and so forth, *ad infinitum*.

Fyodor Dostoyevsky, *The Brothers Karamazov*

As one who has put God to the test in peace and war, who has let himself go on Jesus, who has tried the way of love and the path of prayer, I am not the less definite here. I believe in God. I believe in the love of God. I believe He lived, and died, and rose again. I believe in mercy, I believe in judgement.

These are not opinions with me. These are convictions. By these I steer. Respecting this chart, I am confident of coming in safety to the haven under the hill.

W.E. Sangster, *These Things Abide*

I believe in one God, the creator of the universe. That he governs it by his Providence. That he ought to be worshipped. That the most acceptable service we can render to him is doing good to his other children. That the soul of man is immortal, and will be treated with justice in another life respecting its conduct in this. These I take to be the fundamental points in all sound religion, and I regard them as you do in whatever sect I meet with them. As to Jesus of Nazareth, my opinion of whom you particularly desire, I think the system of morals and his religion as he left them to us, the best the world saw or is like to see.

Benjamin Franklin, *The Private Correspondence of B. Franklin 1753–90*

See also Acceptance, Commitment, Faith, Obedience, Trust

I O

BLESSEDNESS

Blessedness – happiness, enjoyment of divine favours

It took me some thirty-six years to understand the mystery of blessedness. The insight came through a rereading of the Genesis story of the creation of humanity. In that story God is depicted as fashioning and shaping Adam in his own image and likeness, and the last thing he did was breathe into Adam and for him to become a living being. I have taken this to mean that all of us have an enormous source of life in the depths of ourselves. If we want to see this fully worked out in a life we can go to the person of Jesus Christ – recognized in scripture as 'the image of the invisible God'. During his life he found something of the 'Father's' presence in the depths of himself – as well as the gifts and fruits of the Holy Spirit. In this he experienced blessedness and discovered true 'happiness; enjoyment of divine favours'. We too can find this source of happiness and divine favour in ourselves through reflection, meditation and contemplation.

The Lord bless you and keep you; the Lord make his face to shine upon you, and be gracious to you; the Lord lift up his countenance upon you, and give you peace.

Numbers 6.24–26

And God is able to provide you with every blessing in abundance, so that by always having enough of everything, you may share abundantly in every good work.

2 Corinthians 9.8

Blessed is he who has found his work; let him ask no other blessedness.

Thomas Carlyle, *Past and Present*

There is in man a HIGHER than Love of Happiness: he can do without Happiness, and instead thereof find Blessedness.

Thomas Carlyle, *Sartor Resartus*

He is blessed who is assured that the animal is dying out in him day by day, and the divine being established.

Henry David Thoreau, *Walden*

> Amid my list of blessings infinite,
> Stand this the foremost, 'That my heart has bled.'

Edward Young, *Night Thoughts*

But blessedness comes to the man who, in spite of failures and failings, still clutches to him the passionate love of the highest.

William Barclay, *The Gospel of Matthew*

The soul of man can by recognizing God draw Him into its narrow boundaries, but also by love to Him itself expand into the Infinite – and this is blessedness on earth.

John Burchhardt, *The Civilization of the Renaissance in Italy*

There is nothing that is a greater blessing in a community than a man who is known to be an honest, truth-speaking man, and who is kind and genial and cheerful everywhere and at all times.

Henry Ward Beecher, *Proverbs from Plymouth Pulpit*

Blessings, we enjoy daily. And for most of them, because they be so common, most men forget to pay their praises: but let not us; because it is a sacrifice so pleasing to Him that made that sun and us, and still protects us, and gives us flowers, and showers, and stomachs, and meat, and content, and leisure.

Izaak Walton, *The Compleat Angler*

God is present in a silent way always. A certain hidden element or hiding element then is in the Divine Mind. God's blessings steal into life noiselessly. They are neither self-proclaiming nor even self-announcing.

Henry Ward Beecher, *Proverbs from Plymouth Pulpit*

All the great works and wonders that God has ever wrought or shall ever work in or through the creatures, or even God Himself with all His goodness, so far as these things exist or are done outside of me, can never make me blessed, but only in so far as they exist and are done and loved, known, tasted and felt within me.

Theologia Germanica

The first Beatitude is very properly first. 'Blessed are the poor in spirit'. This means: Blessed is he who knows that he is not wise and good and strong enough to make himself good, and who therefore relies wholly upon God to give him that positive righteousness which alone is sufficient. The man in Christ is not distinguished by the absence of evil in him, but by the dominant and overmastering presence in him of the good which comes from God.

Carroll E. Simcox, *The Promises of God*

The Spirit of Love, wherever it is, is its own Blessing and Happiness, because it is the Truth and Reality of God in the Soul; and therefore is in the same Joy of Life, and is the same Good to itself, everywhere, and on every Occasion . . .

Would you know the Blessing of all Blessings, it is this God of Love dwelling in your Soul, and killing every Root of Bitterness, which is the Pain and Torment of every earthly selfish Love.

William Law, *The Spirit of Love and the Spirit of Prayer*

Life indeed must be measured by thought and action, not by time. It certainly may be, and ought to be, bright, interesting, and happy; and, according to the Italian proverb, 'if all cannot live on the Piazza, everyone may yet feel the sun'.

If we do our best; if we do not magnify trifling troubles; if we look resolutely, I do not say at the bright side of things, but at things as they really are; if we avail ourselves of the manifold blessings which surround us; we cannot but feel that life is indeed a glorious inheritance.

Sir John Lubbock, *The Pleasures of Life*

Magnificent weather. The morning seems bathed in happy peace, and a heavenly fragrance rises from mountain and shore; it is as though a benediction were laid upon us . . . One might believe oneself in a church – a vast temple in which every being and every natural beauty has its place. I dare not breathe for fear of putting the dream to flight, – a dream traversed by angels . . . In these heavenly moments the cry of Pauline rises to one's lips. 'I feel! I believe! I see!' All the miseries, the cares, the vexations of life, are forgotten; the universal joy absorbs us; we enter into the divine order, and into the blessedness of the Lord.

Henri Frédéric Amiel, *Amiel's Journal*

Things worth remembering:
The value of time,
The success of perseverance,
The pleasure of working,
The dignity of simplicity,
The worth of character,
The improvement of talent,
The influence of example,
The obligation of duty,
The wisdom of economy,
The virtue of patience,
The joy of originating,
The power of kindness.
    Anon

See also Grace, Fulfilment, Happiness, Joy, Serenity

CHARACTER

Character – moral strength, back-bone; reputation, good reputation; description of person's qualities

I have always been influenced by people of character. Two biographies, both by George Seaver, have been about men of character, and have influenced me a great deal. The first was *Edward Wilson of the Antarctic* – the life story of the doctor, zoologist and artist, on Scott's expedition to the Antarctic. Although Scott was the official leader, the qualities of Edward Wilson's character exercised a quiet but decisive influence on the members of the expedition. The second was *Albert Schweitzer: The Man and His Mind.* Here was portrayed the character of a man with four doctorates, in philosophy, theology, music and medicine, who went on to found and run a mission hospital in a remote part of equatorial West Africa. He was described as a man of moral strength, with impressive qualities. Character continues to be an important influence in our day and age.

～

For as he thinketh in his heart, so is he.
    Proverbs 23.7 (AV)

Do you not know that you are God's temple and that God's Spirit dwells in you?
    1 Corinthians 3.16

This above all: to thine own self be true.
    William Shakespeare, *Hamlet*

An honest man's the noblest work of God.
    Alexander Pope, *An Essay on Man*

Happiness is not the end of life, character is.
    Henry Ward Beecher, *Life Thoughts*

A talent is formed in stillness, a character in the world's torrent.

Johann Wolfgang von Goethe, *Torquato Tasso*

Character is higher than intellect . . . A great soul will be strong to live, as well as strong to think.

Ralph Waldo Emerson, *Society and Solitude: Letters and Social Aims: Addresses*

Religion is only another word for character, and it is developed in man. Religious education is a growth, and requires time.

Henry Ward Beecher, *Proverbs from Plymouth Pulpit*

Let us be true: this is the highest maxim of art and of life, the secret of eloquence and of virtue, and of all moral authority.

Henri Frédéric Amiel, *Amiel's Journal*

[Jesus] – the most innocent, the most benevolent, the most eloquent and sublime character that ever has been exhibited to man.

Thomas Jefferson, *The Writings of Thomas Jefferson*

In Christ was comprehended the fullest conception of greatness and nobleness of character. Every idea of true manhood is in Him.

Henry Ward Beecher, *Proverbs from Plymouth Pulpit*

Friends, suffering, marriage, environment, study and recreation are influences which shape character. The strongest influence, if you are generous enough to yield to it, is the grace of God.

Hubert van Zeller, *Considerations*

There is no sight more beautiful than a character which has been steadfastly growing in every direction, and has come to old age rich and ripe.

Henry Ward Beecher, *Proverbs from Plymouth Pulpit*

Character cannot be developed in ease and quiet. Only through experiences of trial and suffering can the soul be strengthened, vision cleared, ambition inspired and success achieved.

Helen Keller, *Helen Keller's Journal*

There is no point so critical of Christian character as the power to maintain love toward all men – not a love of personal attraction, but a love of benevolence, that begets a willingness to bear with them and work for them.

Henry Ward Beecher, *Proverbs from Plymouth Pulpit*

The character I admire is a character that is a rod of iron to itself and a well-spring of tenderness and pity for others; a character that forces itself to be happy in itself, blames no one but itself, and compels itself to clear away obstacles from the path to happiness for every organism it encounters.

John Cowper Powys, *Autobiography*

People's characters are tested in three ways: by the circumstances in which they live, by the people whom they meet, and by the experience of their own failure. Their characters are tested by the degree in which these things draw forth from them love and not bitterness, a humble penitence and dependence upon God and not despair.

Father Andrew SDC, *A Gift of Light*

Our characters are shaped by our companions and by the objects to which we give most of our thoughts and with which we fill our imaginations. We cannot always be thinking even about Christ, but we can refuse to dwell on any thoughts which are out of tune with Him. We can, above all, quite deliberately turn our minds towards Him at any time when those thoughts come in.

William Temple, *Christian Faith and Life*

Supreme and tremendous energy and positiveness enter into the spiritual delineation of Christian character. Intense virtues and self-denials, bearing yokes, bearing the cross, sacrificing, crucifying, are enjoined.

Henry Ward Beecher, *Proverbs from Plymouth Pulpit*

It is the character only of a good man to be able to deny and disown himself, and to make a full surrender of himself unto God; forgetting himself, and minding nothing but the will of his Creator; triumphing in nothing more than in his own nothingness, and in the allness of the Divinity. But indeed this, his being nothing, is the only way to be all things; this, his having nothing, the truest way of possessing all things.

John Smith the Platonist, *Select Discourses*

Now these mental and moral possessions are their own reward. They cannot, like earthly possessions, be taken away from us. For those who know what they are worth, the world is a much brighter place than for those who think that a man's life consisteth in the abundance of the things which he possesseth. The man whose 'mind to him a kingdom is' does not complain much of the injustices of life. Still less does the true Christian complain. He has found the joy that no man taketh from him. This world is not a bad place in his eyes, because he finds it full of love and beauty and wisdom.

W.R. Inge, *Personal Religion and the Life of Devotion*

The crown and glory of life is character. It is the noblest possession of a man, constituting a rank in itself, and an estate in the general good-will; dignifying every station, and exalting every position in society. It exercises a greater power than wealth, and secures all the honour without the jealousies of fame. It carries with it an influence which always tells; for it is the result of proved honour, rectitude, and consistency – qualities which, perhaps more than any other, command the general confidence and respect of mankind. Character is human nature in its best form. It is moral order embodied in the individual.

Samuel Smiles, *Self-Help*

See also Friendship, Integrity, Mystics, Saints, Wholeness

12

CHEERFULNESS

Cheerfulness – being contented, in good spirits, hopeful, animating, pleasant; being willing, not reluctant

The Gurkhas are noted for their cheerfulness. On jungle patrols my platoon sergeant, Sgt Nandaraj, would come and see me shortly after we had bivouacked for the night. With nostrils twitching and eyes twinkling, he would give me his latest *sungur* (wild pig) report. He had just reconnoitred the area, and knew exactly where the wild pigs were. He was extremely keen to ambush them and supplement our basic army rations. On another occasion we were by the sea, and manoeuvres were over by 4 pm. The Gurkhas went off crabbing, again to supplement their *bhat* (curry). That night Sgt Major Kabiram dug his fingers into the curry, and pulled out a huge crab's claw. In broken English he said, 'Ah, this afternoon, you ate me; now, I eat you.' With that he stuffed the claw into his mouth, crunched the contents and scoffed the lot. With the Gurkhas, cheerfulness, linked with loyalty, made them excellent soldiers and companions.

~

A cheerful heart is a good medicine, but a downcast spirit dries up the bones.
Proverbs 17.22

I have said this to you, so that in me you may have peace. In the world you face persecution. But take courage; I have conquered the world!
John 16.33

Continual cheerfulness is a sign of wisdom.
Thomas Fuller, *Gnomologia*

That which befits us . . . is cheerfulness and courage.
Ralph Waldo Emerson, *Essays and Representative Men*

Health and cheerfulness mutually beget each other.

Joseph Addison, *The Works of Joseph Addison*

And so of cheerfulness, or a good temper – the more it is spent, the more of it remains.

Ralph Waldo Emerson, *The Conduct of Life, Nature, and Other Essays*

A happy, joyful spirit spreads joy everywhere; a fretful spirit is a trouble to ourselves and to all around us.

Anon

> A merry heart goes all the day,
> Your sad tires in a mile-a.

William Shakespeare, *The Winter's Tale*

A cheerful temper, joined with innocence, will make beauty attractive, knowledge delightful, and wit good-natured.

Joseph Addison, *The Works of Joseph Addison*

In my long illness, the people who helped me most were those who took for granted that I should behave with apparent cheerfulness and courage.

A.C. Benson, *Extracts from the Letters of Dr A.C. Benson to M.E.A.*

Cheerfulness, it would appear, is a matter which depends fully as much as on the state of things within, as on the state of things without, and around us.

Charlotte Brontë, *Shirley*

Good nature is worth more than knowledge, more than money, more than honour, to the persons who possess it, and certainly to everybody who dwells with them, in so far as mere happiness is concerned.

Henry Ward Beecher, *Proverbs from Plymouth Pulpit*

Mirth is like a flash of lightning, that breaks through in a gloom of clouds and glitters for a moment; cheerfulness keeps up a kind of day-light in the mind, and fills it with a steady and perpetual serenity.

Joseph Addison, *The Works of Joseph Addison*

Cheered by the presence of God, I will do at the moment, without anxiety, according to the strength which he shall give me, the work that his providence assigns me. I will leave the rest; it is not my affair.

François de la M. Fénelon, in Mrs Follen, *Extracts from the Writings of Fénelon*

The men whom I have seen succeed best in life have always been cheerful and hopeful men, who went about their business with a smile on their faces, and took the changes and chances of this mortal life like men, facing rough and smooth alike as it came, and so found the truth of the old proverb 'that good times and bad times and all times pass over'.

Charles Kingsley, *Daily Thoughts*

Use your sense of humour. Laugh about things. Laugh at the absurdities of life. Laugh about yourself and about your own absurdity.

We are all of us infinitesimally small and ludicrous creatures within God's universe. You have to be serious, but never be solemn, because if you are solemn about anything there is the risk of you becoming solemn about yourself.

Michael Ramsey, in Margaret Duggan, *Through the Year with Michael Ramsey*

Thy soul was like a Star, and dwelt apart:
Thou hadst a voice whose sound was like the sea:
Pure as the naked heavens, majestic, free,
So didst thou travel on life's common way,
In cheerful godliness.

William Wordsworth, 'London'

Be brave! Let us remain aware of our task and not grumble, a solution will come . . . I know what I want, I have a goal, an opinion, I have a religion and love. Let me be myself, and then I am satisfied. I know that I'm a woman with inward strength and plenty of courage.

If God lets me live . . . I shall not remain insignificant, I shall work in the world and for mankind!

And now I know that first and foremost I shall require courage and cheerfulness!

Anne Frank, *The Diary of Anne Frank*

I believe that God will help us to forget things, the memory of which would do us harm, or rather that He will enable us to remember only so much of them as will be for our good, and we, ourselves, not emotionally overwhelmed . . .

The pain endured. The lesson learned. Let it now be forgotten! Face the future with courage, cheerfulness, and hope. Give God the chance and He will make you forget all that it would be harmful to remember.

W.E. Sangster, *Westminster Sermons*

See also Happiness, Holiness, Joy, Kindness, Thanksgiving

13

CHRISTIAN

Christian – an adherent of Christianity

I grew up thinking I was a Christian because I had been baptized as an infant and confirmed at the age of sixteen. Within a few weeks of arriving in Oxford I burnt my boats and made a firm commitment to the person of Jesus Christ. I now felt that in following Christ lay the very essence of being a Christian. Six busy years passed by and I found myself in a crisis. Intuitively I felt something was radically wrong. It was at this stage I discovered the book *The Choice Is Always Ours*, by Dorothy Berkley Phillips. This brilliant anthology enabled me to find 'the God within' – that in the depths of our being we can discover something of the presence of the Father, the Son, and the gifts and fruits of the Holy Spirit. At last I had found what I had been looking for. I now think of a Christian as a person who experiences the richness of divine life in the depths of his or her being and lives by it.

You are the salt of the earth.
> Matthew 5.13

Yet if any one of you suffers as a Christian, do not consider it a disgrace, but glorify God because you bear this name.
> 1 Peter 4.16

A Christian is the highest style of man.
> Edward Young, *Night Thoughts*

O noble testimony of the soul by nature Christian!
> Tertullian, *The Writings of Tertullian*

Those who reject Christian beliefs, cannot count on keeping Christian morals.
  Sir Richard Livingstone, *On Education*

If a man cannot be a Christian in the place where he is, he cannot be a Christian anywhere.
  Henry Ward Beecher, *Life Thoughts*

The greatest of all blessings, as it is the most ennobling of all privileges, is to be indeed a Christian.
  Samuel Taylor Coleridge, *Letters of Samuel Taylor Coleridge*

It doesn't take much of a person to be a Christian, but it takes all there is of him – person and possessions.
  E. Stanley Jones, *Growing Spiritually*

The only absolute for the Christian is love, and on *that* you have got to be prepared to take *unconditional* stands and say, 'Here I stand, I can no other' (sic).
  John A.T. Robinson, *The Roots of a Radical*

The ultimate criterion of a person's Christian spirit is not theory but practice: not how he thinks of teachings, dogmas, interpretations, but how he acts in ordinary life.
  Hans Küng, *On Being a Christian*

The life of every Christian on earth has in it much that is mysterious. It is aiming at an awful grandeur which has never been unveiled. God carries in His bosom the full ideal. We know it not.
  Henry Ward Beecher, *Proverbs from Plymouth Pulpit*

When the imitation of Christ does not mean to live a life like Christ, but to live your life authentically as Christ lived his, then there are many ways and forms in which a man can be a Christian.
  Henri J.M. Nouwen, *The Wounded Healer*

. . . That simplicity which was usually found in the primitive Christians, who were (as most Anglers are) quiet men, and followers of peace; men that were so simply-wise, as not to sell their Consciences to buy riches.
  Izaak Walton, *The Compleat Angler*

To live Christ is not to screw oneself up to great heights of moral endeavour and self-sacrifice. It is to accept, to accept what God says is possible for us. This is the achievement, the only achievement for a Christian, to become open to what God offers and what God can do.

Henry McKeating, *God and the Future*

Not only do I leave the door open for the Christian message, but I consider it of central importance for Western man. It needs, however, to be seen in a new light, in accordance with the changes wrought by the contemporary spirit. Otherwise, it stands apart from the times, and has no effect on man's wholeness.

C.G. Jung, *Memories, Dreams, Reflections*

He only is a Christian in fact in whom Christ dwelleth, liveth and hath His being, in whom Christ hath arisen as the eternal ground of the soul. He only is a Christian who has this high title in himself, and has entered with mind and soul into that Eternal Word which has manifested itself as the life of our humanity.

Rufus M. Jones, *Spiritual Reformers in the 16ᵗʰ and 17ᵗʰ Centuries*

What originality Christianity admits! A man may be a Christian and yet lose nothing of that which is truly original in him. Nay, more, it provokes originality, just as the polishing of a pebble brings out the beauty and definiteness of its structure. I can call to mind people whom I knew forty or fifty years ago . . . who had become *individual* through their religion.

Mark Rutherford, *Last Pages from a Journal*

He [Sebastian Franck] is especially interesting and important as an exponent and interpreter of a religion based on inward authority because he unites, in an unusual manner, the intellectual ideals of the Humanist with the experience and attitude of the Mystic. In him we have a Christian thinker who is able to detach himself from the theological formulations of his own and of earlier times, and who could draw, with a breadth of mind and depth of insight, from the wells of the great original thinkers of all ages, and who, besides, in his own deep and serious soul could feel the inner flow of central realities.

Rufus M. Jones, *Spiritual Reformers in the 16ᵗʰ and 17ᵗʰ Centuries*

Christians are, or should be, the pioneers of the new humanity which God is bringing into being through Christ, for they are already experiencing in themselves the renewal which God intends for all his creation. Christ is not only 'the first born among a large family of brothers', but he is also in relation to mankind as a whole 'a second Adam'. In Christ, God made a new and fresh beginning and its success is assured by the victory which Christ, 'the second

Adam', achieved over evil. Those who are inspired by his spirit and live in his way are the prototype of a new re-ordered humanity.

David Brown, *God's Tomorrow*

See also Acceptance, Commitment, Compassion, Love, Service

14

CHURCH

Church – building for public Christian worship; body of all Christians, organized Christian society, clergy or clerical profession

I was listening recently to an American at a summer school in Oxford. He was telling me that although he had a spiritual awareness he found organized religion boring. As far as I could tell he was being thoroughly honest and voicing what a large number of people felt. I remember trying to tackle this problem in my early twenties. A group of us got together and used to meet for an hour a week, trying to work out the aim and the function of the church. We were greatly helped by Ernest Southcott's book *The Parish Comes Alive*. The author, a parish priest, recorded his experiences at Halton, Leeds. As I recall it, when he first went there he found the church services, dull, boring and sterile. He felt the congregation was going through the motions of worship with little inner conviction. He tackled this at two levels. First, he formed a number of house churches which used to meet in the parish during the week. Second, the life generated by these house churches was fed into the corporate life of the church. Inner conviction was rediscovered and the parish did indeed come alive.

∽

Unless the Lord builds the house, those who build it labour in vain.
  Psalm 127.1

. . . strive to excel in them for building up the church.
  1 Corinthians 14.12

The maintenance of powerful benevolence is more vital to the Christian church than dogmatic systems.
  Henry Ward Beecher, *Proverbs from Plymouth Pulpit*

. . . the church is itself a mystery which opens on to the 'ineffable riches of Christ', which we must accept in their totality.

Cardinal Suenens, *A New Pentecost?*

A humiliated and defenceless church must go out into a hostile world to re-discover the God-man in the least of his brethren.

Paul Oestreicher, Introduction to Hans Jürgen Schultz, *Conversion to the World*

There must be vitality, elasticity, variety, and liberty in church life, or it will fail for the most part in the great ends for which it was established.

Henry Ward Beecher, *Proverbs from Plymouth Pulpit*

. . . it belongs to the very life of the people of God that it must accept again and again to have its life renewed by a new confrontation with its Lord and his holy will.

W.A. Visser 'T Hooft, *The Renewal of the Church*

The church exists to proclaim the good news of where true humanity is to be found and to exemplify in the midst of this present world what growth towards maturity in Christ means.

Daniel Jenkins, *Christian Maturity and the Theology of Success*

Jesus never required membership of a church as a condition of entry into God's kingdom. The obedient acceptance of his message and the immediate and radical submission to God's will sufficed.

Hans Küng, *On Being a Christian*

The Church has a right to edify itself by the gifts of all its members. Nothing is more striking than the latent and undeveloped power in the Church to-day.

Henry Ward Beecher, *Proverbs from Plymouth Pulpit*

The Church is most true to its own nature when it seeks nothing for itself, renounces power, humbly bears witness to the truth but makes no claim to be the *possessor* of truth, and is continually dying in order that it may live.

J.H. Oldham, *Life Is Commitment*

A Church without hope has nothing to offer anyone. It is just a collection of demoralized individuals so concerned about their own survival that they haven't the freedom to offer society the Gospel in its power and comprehensiveness.

Colin Morris, *The Hammer of the Lord*

The great problem of the Church (and therefore of its theologians) is to establish or re-establish some kind of vital contact with that enormous majority of human beings for whom the Christian faith is not so much unlikely as irrelevant and uninteresting.

H.E. Root, in A.R. Vidler, *Soundings*

It is not permissable to designate as 'unchurched' those who have become alienated from organized denominations and traditional creeds. In living among these groups for half a generation I learned how much of the latent Church there is within them.

Paul Tillich, *On the Boundary*

The Church must take care that in trying to build bridges across to the secularized modern world, it does not abandon the bridgehead on the Christian side and find itself left with nothing to communicate and nothing distinctively Christian to contribute.

F.R. Barry, *Secular and Supernatural*

Without contemplation and interior prayer the Church cannot fulfil her mission to transform and save mankind. Without contemplation, she will be reduced to being the servant of cynical and worldly powers, no matter how hard her faithful may protest that they are fighting for the Kingdom of God.

Thomas Merton, *Contemplative Prayer*

It is the Church of the saints and martyrs and prophets, who have been the lights of the world in their several generations, that has the demand upon your allegiance – not the Church which has been corrupted by wealth and worldly power. But the true Church is embedded in the existing Churches – you will not find it elsewhere.

Alec R. Vidler, *God's Demand and Man's Response*

If we manage to be clever and busy about all else – contemporary problems and contemporary tasks, even the meeting of other great and real human ends, but are silent or ineffective about the mystery of the soul's communion with God, then the greatest riches offered to the Church are lost and its ultimate distinctiveness from all other associations has gone.

Norman Goodall, *The Local Church*

The Church is the community of the Spirit, not as having a monopoly of the Spirit, but as having been called into existence by God and entrusted with the word and the sacraments. In the Church there should be going on in a concentrated way the work of the Spirit, which in a diffuse way is going on throughout creation. When the Church is truly the Church it is introducing a new dimension into the social situation, thus giving hope for an eventual transformation.

George Appleton, *Journey for a Soul*

Within the strange, sprawling, quarrelling mass of the churches, within their stifling narrowness, their ignorance, their insensitivity, their stupidity, their fear of the senses and of truth, I perceive another Church, one which really is Christ at work in the world. To this Church men seem to be admitted as much as by a baptism of the heart as of the body, and they know more of intellectual charity, of vulnerability, of love, of joy, of peace, than most of the rest of us. They have learned to live with few defences and so conquered the isolation which torments us. They do not judge, especially morally; their own relationships make it possible for others to grow.

Monica Furlong, *With Love to the Church*

See also God, Holy Spirit, Jesus Christ, Kingdom of God, Saints

COMMITMENT

Commitment – act of committing or being committed; dedication or obligation to particular action or cause, etc.

I can remember my initial act of commitment very clearly. The occasion was a Sunday morning in Oxford during my first year as an undergraduate. I went along to a church service, little knowing what lay in store for me that day. The preacher was Cuthbert Bardsley, the then Bishop of Coventry. I remember very little of the sermon, but what impressed me was the man himself. Here was someone vitally alive and radiant, living the Christian life in the power of the Spirit. This was the quality of life I had unconsciously been looking for. At the end of the service I went forward, along with a few others, to take a step of commitment. The bishop then spoke to us gently and gave us his blessing. I remember feeling at the time a vital step had been taken in life, and was now looking forward to the future with a mixture of feelings, of awe and excitement, and of fear and trepidation.

Commit your way to the Lord; trust in him, and he will act.
  Psalm 37.5

And every one who has left houses or brothers or sisters or father or mother or children or lands, for my name's sake, will receive a hundredfold, and inherit eternal life.
  Matthew 19.29

The words he spoke, the deeds he performed, the demands he raised confronted people with a final decision. Jesus left no one neutral. He himself had become the great question.
  Hans Küng, *On Being a Christian*

If we are to be in Christ new creatures, we must show that we are so, by having new ways of living in the world. If we are to follow Christ, it must be in our common way of spending every day.

William Law, *A Serious Call to a Devout and Holy Life*

The most sovereign act of an independent person is to give the one thing he owns – himself. Then God gives the most precious thing He owns – Himself. Then we are filled with the Holy Spirit.

E. Stanley Jones, *Mastery*

. . . the self is not lost when it is surrendered to Christ. It is lost in a higher will, redeemed from a self-centred will, and found again in obedience to that higher will. So it all ends in self-affirmation. The self is not cancelled – it is heightened.

E. Stanley Jones, *The Word Became Flesh*

I leaped headlong into the Sea, and thereby have become better acquainted with the Soundings, the quicksands, & the rocks, than if I had stayed upon the green shore, and piped a silly pipe, and took tea & comfortable advice.

John Keats, *The Letters of John Keats*

The death by which we enter into life is not an escape from reality but a complete gift of ourselves which involves a total commitment to reality. It begins by renouncing the illusory reality which created things acquire when they are seen only in their relation to our own selfish interests.

Thomas Merton, *Thoughts in Solitude*

He [Jesus] provoked a final *decision*, but not a yes or no to a particular title, to a particular dignity, a particular office, or even to a particular dogma, rite or law. His message and community raised the question of the aim and purpose to which a man will ultimately direct his life. Jesus demanded a final decision for God's cause and man's.

Hans Küng, *On Being a Christian*

Either we must confess our blindness and seek the opening of our eyes; or else we must accept the light and walk by it. What we may not do, yet all strive to do, is to keep our eyes half open and live by half the light. That kind of sight holds us to our sin and our sin to us. But the only way of avoiding it is to look with eyes wide open upon ourselves and the world as the full light reveals it; but this is the surrender of faith, and pride resists it.

William Temple, *Readings in St John's Gospel*

The one thing he [Jesus] seems to have condemned utterly was evasion of choice. The man in the parable who was afraid to risk his bag of gold and brought it back uninvested and uncommitted was flung out into the dark. To choose is to commit yourself. To commit yourself is to run the risk of failure, the risk of sin, the risk of betrayal. Jesus can deal with all those, for forgiveness is his métier. The only thing he can do nothing with is the refusal to be committed. Even Judas should do quickly whatever he chooses to do and be responsible.

John V. Taylor, *The Go-Between God*

There are some commitments that need a lifetime to be fulfilled. The commitment of baptism, which is simply the special Christian expression of the general commitment to become a truly human person along the way of transcendence; to be a loyal and reliable friend, in season and out of season; to be a good husband or wife, father or mother, to make a success of marriage and family; to be devoted to a vocation, whether it be that of priest or scientist or nurse or farmer; these all need a lifetime, and even at the end of a lifetime there is more to be done.

John Macquarrie, *In Search of Humanity*

Father Raymond tells the charming story of a little child whose mother was teaching him to pray. When he got to the part, 'Lord, I surrender everything to thee, everything I own,' he abruptly broke off and whispered to himself, 'except my baby rabbit.'

All of us have our baby rabbits. Sometimes it is an ugly thing, sometimes beautiful, sometimes large, sometimes small; but we are more attached to it than to anything else. But this is the thing that God asks of us and that he touches upon when we sincerely ask guidance of him. God does not, however, ask us to seek out our neighbour's little rabbits.

Paul Tournier, *Escape from Loneliness*

The terrible thing, the almost impossible thing is to hand over your whole self – all your wishes and precautions – to Christ. But it is far easier than what we are all trying to do instead. For what we are trying to do is to remain what we call 'ourselves', to keep personal happiness as our great aim in life, and yet at the same time to be 'good'. We are all trying to let our mind and heart go their own way – centred on money or pleasure or ambition – and hoping, in spite of this, to behave honestly and chastely and humbly. And that is exactly what Christ warned us you could not do. As He said, a thistle cannot produce figs. If I am a field that contains nothing but grass-seed, I cannot produce wheat . . . If I want to produce wheat, the change must go deeper than the surface. I must be ploughed up and re-sown.

C.S. Lewis, *Mere Christianity*

I had gone a-begging from door to door in the village path, when thy golden chariot appeared in the distance like a gorgeous dream and I wondered who was this King of all kings! . . . The chariot stopped where I stood. Thy glance fell on me and thou camest down with a smile. I felt that the luck of my life had come at last. Then of a sudden thou didst hold out thy right hand and say, 'What hast thou to give me?' Ah, what a kingly jest was it to open thy palm to a beggar to beg! I was confused and stood undecided, and then from my wallet I slowly took out the least little grain of corn and gave it thee.

But how great my surprise when at the day's end I emptied my bag on the floor to find a least little grain of gold among the poor heap. I bitterly wept and wished that I had had the heart to give thee my all.

Rabindranath Tagore, *Gitanjali*

See also Belief, Cross, Faith, Obedience, Trust

16

COMPASSION

Compassion – pity inclining one to spare or help

I was in my chaplain's office in London. The phone rang one Sunday morning – after the early service. It was a student asking for help. He had come across a young man in a semi-conscious state, suffering from drug abuse. Could I come over and lend a hand? I drove over to where he was – in Holborn. Initial fears were quickly confirmed. We were both out of our depth! Fortunately I knew an Anglican priest nearby, an unusual man – a qualified psychiatric nurse, with a specialized knowledge of drugs. He was free to come and lend a hand. From the moment he arrived I saw 'compassion' in action. The young man quickly realized he was in the presence of an expert. Communication immediately took place. The names and quantities of drugs were taken and noted. An atmosphere of pity and sympathy predominated. The priest then showed the depth of his compassion by taking him to his home and looking after him there.

~

The Lord is good to all, and his compassion is over all he has made.
Psalm 145.9

As God's chosen ones, holy and beloved, clothe yourselves with compassion, kindness, lowliness, meekness, and patience. Bear with one another and, if one has a complaint against another, forgiving each other; as the Lord has forgiven you, so you also must forgive.
Colossians 3.12–13

What value has compassion that does not take its object in its arms?
Antoine de Saint-Exupéry, *The Wisdom of the Sands*

Christianity taught us to care. Caring is the greatest thing, caring matters most.
Baron Friedrich von Hügel, *Letters to a Niece*

Compassion was the chief and, perhaps, the only law of all human existence.

Fyodor Dostoyevsky, *The Idiot*

Jesus does not regard in Judas his enmity, but the order of God, which He loves, and admits, since He calls him friend.

Blaise Pascal, *Pensées*

Our tragedy is not that we suffer but that we waste suffering. We waste the opportunity of growing into compassion.

Mary Craig, *Blessings*

Compassion is born when we discover in the centre of our own existence not only that God is God and man is man, but also that our neighbour is really our fellow man.

Henri J.M. Nouwen, *The Wounded Healer*

Jesus *found him*. The man did not find Jesus; Jesus found him. That is the deepest truth of Christian faith; Jesus found me. Our fellowship with Him is rooted in His compassion.

William Temple, *Readings in St John's Gospel*

Compassion is not a simple feeling-state but a complex emotional attitude toward another, characteristically involving imaginative dwelling on the condition of the other person, an active regard for his good, a view of him as a fellow human being, and emotional responses of a certain degree of intensity.

L. Blum, in James F. Childress and John Macquarrie, *A New Dictionary of Christian Ethics*

Let us not underestimate how hard it is to be compassionate. Compassion is hard because it requires the inner disposition to go with others to the place where they are weak, vulnerable, lonely, and broken. But this is not our spontaneous response to suffering. What we desire most is to do away with suffering by fleeing from it or finding a quick cure for it.

Henri J.M. Nouwen, *The Way of the Heart*

Compassion is one of the emotions or attitudes with an emotional component, that are altruistic or other regarding. Compassion presupposes sympathy, is close to both pity and mercy, and leads to acts of beneficence – the Samaritan 'showed mercy on' the victim and 'took care of him'. Compassion is often an expression of love or *agape*.

James F. Childress, in James F. Childress and John Macquarrie, *A New Dictionary of Christian Ethics*

The root of the matter is a very simple and old-fashioned thing, a thing so simple that I am almost ashamed to mention it, for fear of the derisive smile with which wise cynics will greet my words. The thing I mean – please forgive me for mentioning it – is love, Christian love, or compassion. If you feel like this, you have a motive for existence, a guide in action, a reason for courage, an imperative necessity for intellectual honesty.

Bertrand Russell, *The Impact of Science on Society*

The Son of God was seen
Most glorious, in him all his Father shone
Substantially express'd, and in his face
Divine compassion visibly appear'd.
Love without end, and without measure Grace.

John Milton, 'Paradise Lost'

Compassion is probably the only antitoxin of the soul. Where there is compassion even the most poisonous impulses are relatively harmless. One would rather see the world run by men who set their hearts on toys but are accessible to pity than by men animated by lofty ideals whose dedication makes them ruthless. In the chemistry of man's soul, almost all noble qualities – courage, honour, hope, faith, duty, loyalty, etc. – can be transmuted into ruthlessness. Compassion alone stands apart from the continuous traffic between good and evil proceeding within us.

Eric Hoffer, *The Passionate State of Mind*

But to share with Christ his passion, his crucifixion, his death, means to accept unreservedly all these events, in the same spirit as he did, that is, to accept them in an act of free will, to suffer together with the man of sorrows, to be there in silence, the very silence of Christ, interrupted only by a few decisive words, the silence of real communion; not just the silence of pity, but of compassion, which allows us to grow into complete oneness with the other so that there is no longer one and the other, but only one life and one death.

Anthony Bloom, *Living Prayer*

I don't know what has caused me to read so many articles lately on the subject of 'compassion', but I think we, as Co-workers, are faced with compassion when we are with the poor and the lonely and the dying. Compassion asks us to go where it hurts, to enter into places of pain, to share in brokenness, fear, confusion and anguish. Compassion challenges us to cry out with those in misery, to mourn with those who are lonely, to weep with those in tears. Compassion requires us to be weak with the weak, vulnerable with the vulnerable, and powerless with the powerless. Compassion means full immersion in the conditions of being human. When we look at compassion in this way, it becomes clear that something more is involved than a general kindness.

A co-worker, in Kathryn Spink, *A Chain of Love*

See also Awareness, Kindness, Love, Saints, Understanding

17

CONTEMPLATION

Contemplation – gazing upon; viewing mentally

As far back as I can remember I have always had a contemplative side to my nature. When I was nearing the end of National Service I took some leave and spent a quiet day on the beach at Port Dixon, near Penang, northern Malaya (as it was then). I took very little with me – a swimming costume, a towel and some food – and finding a secluded spot, spent the whole day on the beach, doing absolutely nothing at all. At first numerous thoughts and feelings came to the surface. I listened to the ebbing of the sea, and began to muse over the early part of my life. Precious truths and insights came to the surface. New ideas took root. I felt this was my first real experience of contemplation. Now I try to spend a day on the beach every year, and contemplate.

Be still, and know that I am God!
   Psalm 46.10

Pray in the Spirit at all times in every prayer and supplication.
   Ephesians 6.18

Contemplatives are not useful, they are only indispensable.
   Ernest Dimnet, *What We Live By*

What we plant in the soil of contemplation we shall reap in the harvest of action.
   Meister Eckhart, in Franz Pfeiffer, *Meister Eckhart*

Mystical theology, the secret science of God, which spiritual men call contemplation.
   St John of the Cross, *The Complete Works of St John of the Cross*

All civil mankind have agreed in leaving one day for contemplation against six for practice.

Ralph Waldo Emerson, *Miscellaneous Pieces*

The peace of the contemplative is at once the most beautiful and the most fruitful act of man.

Stephen MacKenna, *Journal and Letters*

A Church which starves itself and its members in the contemplative life deserves whatever spiritual leanness it may experience.

Michael Ramsey, *Canterbury Pilgrim*

> When Contemplation, like the night-calm felt
> Through earth and sky, spreads widely, and sends deep
> Into the soul its tranquillizing power.
>
> William Wordsworth, 'Prelude'

More than anything else, it is the loving contemplation of its Maker that causes the soul to realize its own insignificance, and fills it with holy fear and true humility, and with abundant love to our fellow Christians.

Lady Julian of Norwich, *Revelations of Divine Love*

Contemplation means rest, suspension of activity, withdrawal into the mysterious interior solitude in which the soul is absorbed in the immense and fruitful silence of God and learns something of the secret of His perfections less by seeing than by fruitful love.

Thomas Merton, *Elected Silence*

In popular usage the word can indicate either thinking about some object or gazing upon some object. In Christian spirituality it is the latter meaning that is uppermost: thinking about God gives place to a simple, loving, looking towards him, and this is contemplation.

Richard Harries, in Alan Richardson and John Bowden, *A New Dictionary of Christian Theology*

All contemplative life on earth implies penance as well as prayer, because in contemplation there are always two aspects: the positive one, by which we are united to God in love, and the negative one, by which we are detached and separated from everything that is not God. Without both these elements there is no real contemplation.

Thomas Merton, *The Waters of Silence*

[63]

I think there is a place both inside and outside of religion for a sort of contemplation of the Good, not just by dedicated experts but by ordinary people: an attention which is not just the planning of particular good actions but an attempt to look right away from self towards a distant transcendent perfection, a source of uncontaminated energy, a source of *new* and quite undreamt-of-virtue.

Iris Murdoch, *The Sovereignty of Good Over Other Concepts*

For not, surely, by deliberate effort of thought does a man grow wise. The truths of life are not discovered by us. At moments unforeseen, some gracious influence descends upon the soul, touching it to an emotion which, we know not how, the mind transmutes into thought. This can happen only in a calm of the senses, a surrender of the whole being to passionless contemplation. I understand, now, the intellectual mood of the quietist.

George Gissing, *The Private Papers of Henry Rycroft*

Contemplation is the state of union with the divine Ground of all being. The highest prayer is the most passive. Inevitably; for the less there is of self, the more there is of God. That is why the path to passive or infused contemplation is so hard, and, for many, so painful – a passage through successive or simultaneous Dark Nights, in which the pilgrim must die to the life of sense as an end in itself, to the life of private and even of traditionally hallowed thinking and believing, and finally to the deep source of all ignorance and evil, the life of the separate, individualized will.

Aldous Huxley, *The Perennial Philosophy*

Contemplation is the highest expression of man's intellectual and spiritual life. It is that life itself, fully awake, fully active, fully aware that it is alive. It is spiritual wonder. It is spontaneous awe at the sacredness of life, of being. It is gratitude for life, for awareness and for being. It is a vivid realization of the fact that life and being in us proceed from an invisible, transcendent and infinitely abundant Source. Contemplation is, above all, awareness of the reality of that Source. It *knows* the Source, obscurely, inexplicably, but with a certitude that goes both beyond reason and beyond simple faith. For contemplation is a kind of spiritual vision to which both reason and faith aspire, by their very nature, because without it they must always remain incomplete.

Thomas Merton, *New Seeds of Contemplation*

The contemplation of God – and contemplative prayer is, I believe, not necessarily an advanced state but something accessible to us very backward Christians – the waiting upon God in quietness can be our greatest service to the world if in our apartness the love for people is on our heart. As Aaron went into the holy of holies wearing a breastplate with jewels representing the twelve tribes upon it, so the Christian puts himself deliberately into the presence of God with the needs and sorrows of humanity upon his heart. And he does this best not by the vocal skill with which he informs the Deity about the world's needs but by the simplicity of his own exposure to God's greatness and the world's need.

Michael Ramsey, 'The Idea of the Holy and the World Today' in *Spirituality for Today*

Poetry, music and art have something in common with the contemplative experience. But contemplation is beyond aesthetic intuition, beyond art, beyond poetry. Indeed, it is beyond philosophy, beyond speculative theology. It resumes, transcends and fulfils them all, and yet at the same time it seems, in a certain way, to supersede and to deny them all. Contemplation is always beyond our own knowledge, beyond our own light, beyond systems, beyond explanations, beyond discourse, beyond dialogue, beyond our own self. To enter into the realm of contemplation one must in a certain sense die: but this death is in fact the entrance into a higher life. It is a death for the sake of life, which leaves behind all that we can know or treasure as life, as thought, as experience, as joy, as being.

Thomas Merton, *New Seeds of Contemplation*

See also Listening, Meditation, Prayer, Thinking, Wonder

18

CONTENTMENT

Contentment – being in a state of satisfaction, well pleased – originally it meant, bounded (in desires by what one has)

I had the good fortune to go to Kenya to stay with some friends during a summer vacation. We went to stay on a farm on the slopes of Mount Kenya. The farm was vast, specializing in the cultivation of wheat. The farmhouse, built to overlook the farm included a magnificent view of Mount Kenya. This alone was impressive. What was more striking was the farmer, his wife and family. They all had about them an air of contentment. Here they were, living in the heart of Africa, at an altitude of 8,000 feet. The climate was well-nigh perfect. All the time they were close to nature, living an outdoor life. Here was a contentment rarely to be found elsewhere. How do we find contentment?

The lines have fallen for me in pleasant places; yea, I have a goodly heritage.
Psalm 16.6

. . . for I have learned to be content with whatever I have. I know what it is to have little, and I know what it is to have plenty. In any and all circumstances I have learned the secret of being well-fed and of going hungry, of having plenty and of being in need. I can do all things through him who strengthens me.
Philippians 4.11–13

A contented mind is a continual feast.
English proverb

The noblest mind the best contentment has.
Edmund Spenser, 'The Faerie Queene'

A mind content, both Crown and Kingdom is.
> Robert Greene, 'Farewell to Folly'

Great wealth and content seldom live together.
> Thomas Fuller, *Gnomologia*

Content will never dwell but in a meek and quiet soul.
> Izaak Walton, *The Compleat Angler*

We only see in a lifetime a dozen faces marked with the peace of a contented spirit.
> Henry Ward Beecher, *Proverbs from Plymouth Pulpit*

How seldom a face in repose is a face of serene content.
> W.E. Sangster, *The Secret of Radiant Life*

To be content with little is difficult; to be content with much, impossible.
> Old proverb

The rarest feeling that ever lights the human face is the contentment of a loving soul.
> Henry Ward Beecher, *Proverbs from Plymouth Pulpit*

> Content is Wealth, the Riches of the Mind;
> And happy He who can that Treasure find.
> John Dryden, 'The Wife of Bath, Her Tale'

. . . nobody who gets enough food and clothing in a world where most are hungry and cold has any business to talk about 'misery' . . .
> C.S. Lewis, *They Stand Together*

In order to be content men must also have the possibility of developing their intellectual and artistic powers to whatever extent accord with their personal characteristics and abilities.
> Albert Einstein, *Out of My Later Years*

Those who face that which is actually before them, unburdened by the past, undistracted by the future, these are they who live, who make the best use of their lives; these are those who have found the secret of contentment.
> Alban Goodier SJ, *The School of Love*

To be content with a little is greater than to possess the world, which a man may possess without being so. Lay up my treasure! What matters where a man's treasure is whose heart is in the Scriptures? There is the treasure of the Christian.

Henry Fielding, *Joseph Andrews*

My crown is in my heart, not on my head;
Not deck'd with diamonds and Indian stones,
Nor to be seen: my crown is call'd content;
A crown it is that seldom kings enjoy.

William Shakespeare, *King Henry VI*

Content and discontent should run in and out of each other in every true man's life. Every man should have a generous discontent with what he has attained, and strive to go upward; and yet every one should be so much the master of himself as to refuse to be disquieted by his environments.

Henry Ward Beecher, *Proverbs from Plymouth Pulpit*

For not that, which men covet most, is best,
Nor that thing worst, which men do most refuse;
But fittest is, that all contented rest
With that they hold: each hath his fortune in his brest.

Edmund Spenser, 'The Faerie Queene'

How calm and quiet a delight
It is alone, to read, and meditate, and write,
By none offended, nor offending none;
To walk, ride, sit, or sleep at one's own ease,
And pleasing a man's self, none other to displease!

Charles Cotton, 'The Retirement'

To live content with small means; to seek elegance rather than luxury, and refinement rather than fashion; to be worthy, not respectable, and wealthy, not rich; to study hard, to think quietly, talk gently, act frankly; to listen to stars and birds, to babes and sages, with open heart; to bear all cheerfully, do all bravely, await occasions, hurry never. In a word, to let the spiritual, unbidden and unconscious, grow up through the common. This is to be my symphony.

William E. Channing, *A Series of Miscellaneous Illustrated Cards*

Let us be contented with what has happened to us and thankful for all we have been spared. Let us accept the natural order in which we move. Let us reconcile ourselves to the mysterious rhythm of our destinies, such as they must be in this world of space and time. Let us treasure our joys but not bewail our sorrows. The glory of light cannot exist without its shadows. Life is a whole, and good and ill must be accepted together. The journey has been enjoyable and well worth making – once.

Winston S. Churchill, *Thoughts and Adventures*

See also Joy, Peace, Serenity, Thanksgiving, Trust

19

COURAGE

Courage – bravery, boldness, ability to nerve oneself to a venture

In recent years we have had several physically handicapped undergraduates in college. All of them have had something in common, namely, a quiet courageous approach to life. This has caused me to think about the nature of their courage. I found some clues in the words of Cardinal Manning. He wrote in *Pastime Papers*: 'the Italians call it *Coraggio*, or greatness of heart; the Spaniards, *Corage*; the French, *Courage*, from whom we have borrowed it. And we understand it to mean manliness, bravery, boldness, fearlessness, springing not from a sense of physical power, or from insensibility to danger or pain, but from the moral habit of self-command, with deliberation, fully weighing present dangers, and clearly foreseeing future consequences, and yet in the path of duty advancing unmoved to its execution.' This fits in roughly with my observations. Somehow they have found an inner strength which carries them beyond their various disabilities.

Be strong and of good courage; be not frightened, neither be dismayed; for the Lord your God is with you wherever you go.
  Joshua 1.9

Keep alert, stand firm in your faith, be courageous, be strong. Let all that you do be done in love.
  1 Corinthians 16.13–14

Great things are done more through courage than through wisdom.
  German proverb

. . . but there is a higher sort of courage, the bravery of self-control.
  Thomas Bailey Aldrich, *The Stillwater Tragedy*

It requires moral courage to grieve; it requires religious courage to rejoice.

Søren Kierkegaard, *The Journals of Søren Kierkegaard*

Courage is the ba‿ic virtue for everyone so long as he continues to grow, to move ahead.

Rollo May, *Man's Search for Himself*

The Courage we desire and prize is not the Courage to die decently, but to live manfully.

Thomas Carlyle, *Boswell's Life of Johnson*

Courage is sustained, not only by prayer, but by calling up anew the vision of the goal.

A.D. Sertillanges OP, *The Intellectual Life*

The greatest virtue in life is real courage, that knows how to face facts and live beyond them.

D.H. Lawrence, *The Selected Letters of D.H. Lawrence*

Courage is what it takes to stand up and speak; courage is also what it takes to sit down, and listen.

Anon

The most precious thing about Jesus is the fact that he is not the great discourager, but the great encourager.

William Barclay, *The Gospel of Matthew*

One has to be courageous not to let oneself be carried along by the world's march; one needs faith and will-power to go cross-current.

Carlo Carretto, *Letters from the Desert*

Courage is not simply *one* of the virtues but the form of every virtue at the testing point, which means at the point of highest reality.

C.S. Lewis, in Cyril Connelly, *The Unquiet Grave*

The stout heart is also a warm and kind one. Affection dwells with Danger, all the holier and lovelier for such stern environment.

Thomas Carlyle, *Corn-Law Rhymes*

People talk about the courage of condemned men walking to the place of execution: sometimes it needs as much courage to walk with any kind of bearing towards another person's habitual misery.

Graham Greene, *The Heart of the Matter*

Courage is required not only in a person's occasional crucial decision for his own freedom, but in the little hour-to-hour decisions which place the bricks in the structure of his building of himself into a person who acts with freedom and responsibility.

Rollo May, *Man's Search for Himself*

Life, willing to surpass itself, is the good life, and the good life is courageous life. It is the life of the 'powerful soul' and their 'triumphant body' whose self-enjoyment is virtue. Such a soul banishes everything cowardly; it says: 'bad – that is cowardly'.

Paul Tillich, *The Courage to Be*

The world seems somehow so made as to suit best the adventurous and courageous, the men who, like Nelson, wear all their stars, like Napoleon's marshals their most splendid uniforms, not that they may be less but more conspicuous and incur greater dangers than their fellows.

W. MacNeile Dixon, *The Human Situation*

We must accept our existence as far as it is possible; everything, even the unheard of, must be possible there. That is fundamentally the only courage which is demanded of us; to be brave in the face of the strangest, most singular and most inexplicable things that can befall us.

Rainer Maria Rilke, *Letters to a Young Poet*

The affirmation of one's essential being in spite of desires and anxieties creates joy . . . it is the happiness of a soul which is 'lifted above every circumstance'. Joy accompanies the self-affirmation of our essential being in spite of the inhibitions coming from the accidental elements in us. Joy is the emotional expression of the courageous Yes to one's own being.

Paul Tillich, *The Courage to Be*

Courage is far more common than is commonly supposed, and it belongs as much, and more, to the ordinary events of life than to the spectacular. Every man who lives in intimate contact with other people, especially the unprivileged people, is amazed at the quiet bravery of obscure folk. To those who have eyes to see, there is evidence of courage on every hand.

W.E. Sangster, *These Things Abide*

Strange is the vigour of a brave man's soul. The strength of his spirit and his irresistible power, the greatness of his heart and the height of his condition, his mighty confidence and contempt of danger, his true security and repose in himself, his liberty to dare and do what he pleaseth, his alacrity in the midst of fears, his invincible temper, are advantages which make him master of fortune. His courage fits him for all attempts, renders him serviceable to God and man, and makes him the bulwark and defence of his king and country.

Thomas Traherne, *The Way to Blessedness*

See also Aspiration, Cheerfulness, Commitment, Faith, Ideals

CROSS

Cross – stake (usually with traverse bar) used by the ancients for crucifixion, especially that on which Christ was crucified; Christian religion; trial, affliction, annoyance

I wonder if we place too much emphasis on the historical cross of Christ, and not enough on taking up our cross daily and following Christ I am fond of Jesus' teaching, that unless a grain of wheat falls into the earth and dies, it remains alone; but if it dies it bears much fruit. This parable contains a vital truth for understanding one of the mysteries of the cross. The grain of wheat, of course, does not wholly die when sown. The outer case perishes, but this lets in the nutrients of the soil, stimulating growth from the centre. Roots grow downward and the stem grows upwards, seeking sun, warmth and rain. Growth continues until the grain is ripe – and plentiful. Apply this parable now to the human scene. Our self-centredness, like the outer case of the grain of wheat, has to perish in order for the divine in the depths of our being to grow and flourish. This is what I mean by taking up our cross daily and following Christ. It is a painful process, but in it lies the secret of life.

Then Jesus told his disciples, 'If any want to become my followers, let them deny themselves and take up their cross and follow me. For those who want to save their life will lose it, and those who lose their life for my sake will find it.'

Matthew 16.24–25

I have been crucified with Christ; and it is no longer I who live, but it is Christ who lives in me. And the life I now live in the flesh I live by faith in the Son of God, who loved me and gave himself for me.

Galatians 2.20

It is the crushed grape that yields the wine.

Anon

The way to God is the way of the Cross. Christ Himself is the pattern and His way of Life is the typical way for all who would find God.

Rufus M. Jones, *Spiritual Reformers in the 16th and 17th Centuries*

All the activity of man in the works of self-denial has no good in itself, but is only an entrance for the one only Good, the light of God, to operate upon us.

William Law, in Stephen Hobhouse, *Selected Mystical Writings of William Law*

It is the triumph over one's own nature that means full victory; for when a man has himself under control so that every desire submits to reason and reason submits to me, then he is really victorious over self, and is master of the world.

Thomas à Kempis, *The Imitation of Christ*

Except the seed die . . . It has to die in order to liberate the energy it bears within it so that with this energy new forms may be developed. So we have to die in order to liberate a *tied up* energy, in order to possess an energy which is free and capable of understanding the true relationship of things.

Simone Weil, *Gravity and Grace*

The Way of the Cross winds through our towns and cities, our hospitals and factories, and through our battlefields; it takes the road of poverty and suffering in every form. It is in front of these new Stations of the Cross that we must stop and meditate and pray to the suffering Christ for strength to love him enough to act.

Michel Quoist, *Prayers of Life*

'Our kingdom go' is the necessary and unavoidable corollary of 'Thy Kingdom come'. For the more there is of self, the less there is of God. The divine fullness of life can be gained only by those who have deliberately lost the partial, separative life of craving and self-interest, of egocentric thinking, feeling, wishing, and acting.

Aldous Huxley, *The Perennial Philosophy*

[How could Christ die for our sins?] This is the hardest thing for people to realize intellectually. You can tell them about it, but I believe the experience of Christ's death, the freedom from sin, can only be experienced personally. You can hear about it and know about it, but I think this is the gap across which a person has to leap by experience or by faith.

George Reindorp, in Gerald Priestland, *Priestland's Progress*

Batter my heart, three-person'd God; for you
As yet but knocke, breathe, shine, and seeke to mend;
That I may rise, and stand, o'erthrowe mee, and bend
Your force, to breake, blowe, burn and make me new.

John Donne, 'Holy Sonnets, XIV'

Therefore we should make ourselves poor, that we may fundamentally die, and in this dying be made alive again. Therefore Christ said, 'Unless the grain of corn fall into the ground and die it cannot bring forth fruit. But if it die it bringeth forth much fruit.' So also is it in truth. Whoso wisheth to have all the fruit of life must suffer all manner of death . . . And whoso doth not entirely die cannot either fully live.

John Tauler, *The Following of Christ*

The Cross was not a transaction. It was the culmination of this mighty Love, for 'here on the cross hung God and man' – God's Love springing forth in a soul strong enough to show it in its full scope. But let no person think he can 'cover himself with the purple mantle of Christ's sufferings and death', and so win his salvation: 'Thou thyself', he says, 'must go through Christ's whole journey, and enter wholly into His process.'

Rufus M. Jones, *Spiritual Reformers in the 16th and 17th Centuries*

The Christ of God was not then first crucified when the Jews brought him to the Cross; but Adam and Eve were his first real Murderers; for the Death which happened to them, in the Day that they did eat of the earthly Tree, was the Death of the Christ of God, or the Divine Life in their Souls. For Christ had never come into the World as a Second Adam to redeem it, had he not been originally the Life and Perfection, and Glory of the First Adam.

William Law, in Sidney Spencer, *The Spirit of Prayer and the Spirit of Love*

We Christians often use the words 'Christ died to save us from our sins'. He shows us the limitless measure of God's love and that draws our hearts to him. He makes known to us God's forgiveness, not only in his teaching, but by the fact of his own forgiveness of those who brought him to the cross. There is something more which it is difficult to describe – he works within us, assuring us of God's forgiveness, changing our hearts towards sin and selfishness, and sharing his risen life so that sin, though it may attack us, need find no entry.

George Appleton, *Journey for a Soul*

Are you willing to be sponged out, erased, cancelled, made nothing?
Are you willing to be made nothing, dipped into oblivion?
If not, you will never really change. The phoenix renews her youth only when she
    is burnt,
burnt alive, burnt down to hot and flocculent ash.
Then the small stirring of a new and small bub in the nest with strands of down
    like floating ash
Shows us that she is renewing her youth like the eagle, immortal bird.
    D.H. Lawrence, 'Phoenix'

See also Humility, Selfishness, Suffering, Temptation, Transformation

DEATH

*D*eath – dying, end of life, ceasing to be, annihilation, want of spiritual life

I remember a teacher at primary school telling us time was valuable. 'Every minute of your life is precious,' she said. 'One day you will die, so never waste time. Make the most of your life, and then you will be happy.' She had such a determined look in her eyes I took these words to heart and have lived by them ever since. My teenage years were very full as a consequence. I had also taken on board some advice from my parents that you only get out of life what you are prepared to put into it. I was still not satisfied. Something vital was missing. A book by Ralph Waldo Trine, *In Tune with the Infinite*, opened my eyes to the spiritual dimension. Through reflection I began to discover a new quality and value of life. From time to time I was given brief moments of 'eternal life'. In them I experienced feelings of joy, freedom, harmony and wholeness. The fear of death was transcended. When I die, I hope to enter more fully a dimension I have already experienced. Death is then seen as a culmination, not an annihilation.

By the sweat of your face you shall eat bread until you return to the ground, for out of it you were taken; you are dust, and to dust you shall return.

Genesis 3.19

In my Father's house there are many dwelling-places. If it were not so, would I have told you that I go to prepare a place for you? And if I go and prepare a place for you, I will come again and will take you to myself, so that where I am, there you may be also.

John 14.2–3

A good life has a peaceful death.

French Proverb

As a well-spent day brings happy sleep, so life well used brings happy death.

> Leonardo da Vinci, *The Notebooks of Leonardo da Vinci*

Death helps us to see what is worth trusting and loving and what is a waste of time.

> J. Neville Ward, *Five for Sorrow, Ten for Joy*

To die is poignantly bitter, but the idea of having to die without having lived is unbearable.

> Erich Fromm, *Man for Himself*

Do not seek death. Death will find you. But seek the road which makes death a fulfilment.

> Dag Hammarskjöld, *Markings*

Death's stamp gives value to the coin of life; making it possible to buy with life what is truly precious.

> Rabindranath Tagore, *Stray Birds*

Walking with God . . . means walking through death. It means living with death behind one rather than ahead of one.

> John S. Dunne, *The Reasons of the Heart*

People who love life and love giving to it and receiving from it do not find themselves particularly perturbed about death.

> J. Neville Ward, *Friday Afternoon*

The only religious way to think of death is as part and parcel of life; to regard it, with the understanding and with the emotions, as the inviolable condition of life.

> Thomas Mann, *The Magic Mountain*

I have a feeling that there probably is some fellowship and communion of like-minded people beyond death, which can begin here – and that our jealous and exclusive friendships and alliances rather hinder it. But it is all a very big subject!

> A.C. Benson, *Extracts from the Letters of Dr A.C. Benson to M.E.A.*

It makes it possible for us to rest in the certainty that the end of life on earth is not the end of life, that the haunting fragility of things has a meaning, that love is given for eternity, that no accident in these dimensions of time and space can prevent the accomplishment of the ends for which men and women with minds and hearts have come into existence

Norman Goodall, *The Local Church*

On the day when death will knock at thy door what wilt thou offer to him? Oh, I will set before my guest the full vessel of my life – I will never let him go with empty hands.

All the sweet vintage of all my autumn days and summer nights, all the earnings and gleanings of my busy life will I place before him at the close of my days when death will knock at my door.

Rabindranath Tagore, *Gitanjali*

The Lord does not promise that anyone who keeps His word shall avoid the physical incident called death; but that if his mind is turned towards that word it will not pay any attention to death; death will be to it irrelevant. It may truly be said that such a man will not 'experience' death, because, though it will happen to him, it will matter to him no more than the fall of a leaf from a tree under which he might be reading a book.

William Temple, *Readings in St John's Gospel*

Our attitude to all men would be Christian if we regarded them as though they were dying, and determined our relation to them in the light of death, both of their death and our own. A person who is dying calls forth a special kind of feeling. Our attitude to him is at once softened and lifted on to a higher plane. We then can feel compassion for people whom we did not love. But every man is dying. I too am dying and must never forget about death.

Nicolas Berdyaev, *The Destiny of Man*

People who believe that death is part of God's purpose, one of the forms of his caring, can take their time over life. There being a message of beginning or deepening in every ending, their sufferings are worth working through with considerable care. They are not going to miss or lose anything that matters. And there is never any reason for ceasing to love, even for loving less, since every moment, every experience, brings God with it and the possibility of deeper communion with life.

J. Neville Ward, *Friday Afternoon*

It was not physical life and physical death of which Jesus was thinking. He meant that, for the man who fully accepted Him, there is no such thing as death. Death had lost its finality. The man who enters into fellowship with Jesus has entered into a fellowship which is independent of time. The man who accepts Jesus has entered into a relationship with God which neither time nor eternity can sever. Such a man goes, not from life to death, but from life to life. Death is only the introduction to the nearer presence of God.

William Barclay, *The Gospel of John*

The death of someone we love is always shattering. To love is to carry another within oneself, to keep a special place in one's heart for him or her. This spiritual space is nourished by a physical presence; death, then, tears out a part of our own heart. Those who deny the suffering of death have never truly loved; they live in a spiritual illusion.

To celebrate death, then, is not to deny this laceration and the grief it involves, it is to give space to live it, to speak about it, and even to sing of it. It is to give mutual support, looking the reality in the face and placing all in the Heart of God in deep trust.

Jean Vanier, *Man and Woman He Made Them*

See also Anxiety, Depression, Doubt, Grief, Loneliness, Resurrection

22

DEPRESSION

Depression – a psychological state of extreme low spirits characterized by a sense of hopelessness and despair

A medical student dropped in to see me. He was normally a bright and cheerful person, competent in his studies and a gifted musician but now he was going through a period of depression. I listened to him carefully, gave him a short quotation, and suggested he get a pen and paper, and write down all his thoughts as he pondered over these words. He was to come and see me in an hour's time. Two hours went by and then he returned, back to his usual cheerful self. 'Do you know,' he exclaimed, 'I have just had my very first thoughts ever! For a long time I have been learning facts and more facts. I reckon that is what has been depressing me. But today, for the very first time in my life, I've discovered I have a mind that can think. I got so absorbed I forgot about the time. Now at least I can live.' How often external pressures depress us, and dampen down our precious inner resources.

Why are you cast down, O my soul, and why are you disquieted within me? Hope in God; for I shall again praise him, my help and my God.
Psalm 43.5

. . . God, who consoles the downcast.
2 Corinthians 7.6

Despair gives courage.
Sir Walter Scott, *The Heart of Midlothian*

Darkness is more productive of sublime ideas than light.
Edmund Burke, *Burke's Works*

Half the spiritual difficulties that men and women suffer arise from a morbid state of health.

>Henry Ward Beecher, *Proverbs from Plymouth Pulpit*

Into each life some rain must fall,
Some days must be dark and dreary.

>Henry Wadsworth Longfellow, 'The Rainy Day'

I believe there is a way out of dark experiences though one cannot see it, and that all the suffering does not come in vain.

>A.C. Benson, *Extracts from the Letters of Dr A.C. Benson to M.E.A.*

Resolve to be thyself; and know that he,
Who finds himself, loses his misery!

>Matthew Arnold, 'Self-Dependence'

More people are destroyed by unhappiness than by drink, drugs, disease, or even failure. There must be something about sadness which attracts or people would not accept it so readily into their lives.

>Hubert van Zeller, *Considerations*

For there is no despair so absolute as that which comes with the first moments of our first great sorrow, when we have not yet known what it is to have suffered and be healed, to have despaired and to have recovered hope.

>George Eliot, *Adam Bede*

The severely self-rejecting adolescent is his own enemy. He has taken unto himself all the unkindness of his heredity and all the harshness of his environment, and then has added something more: everything is his fault and he is no good.

>Arthur T. Jersild, *The Psychology of Adolescence*

The human being cannot live in a condition of emptiness for very long: if he is not growing *toward* something, he does not merely stagnate; the pent-up potentialities turn into morbidity and despair, and eventually into destructive activities.

>Rollo May, *Man's Search for Himself*

It is one of the secrets of Nature in its mood of mockery that fine weather lays a heavier weight on the minds and hearts of the depressed and the inwardly tormented than does a really bad day with the dark rain snivelling continuously and sympathetically from a dirty sky.

>Muriel Spark, *Territorial Rights*

Then black despair,
The shadows of a starless night, was thrown
Over the world in which I moved alone.
    Percy Bysshe Shelley, 'The Revolt of Islam: Dedication: To Mary'

That Jesus fought despair and triumphed we know from his prayers on the cross
which began with 'My God, why have you forsaken me?' and ended with 'Into
your hand, Lord, I commend my spirit.' However near we come to despair, we
have this precedent to refer to.
    Hubert van Zeller, *Considerations*

I can enjoy feeling melancholy, and there is a good deal of satisfaction about
being thoroughly miserable, but nobody likes a fit of the blues. Nevertheless,
everybody has them; notwithstanding which, nobody can tell why. There is no
accounting for them. You are just as likely to have one on the day after you have
come into a large fortune, as on the day after you have left your new silk umbrella
in the train.
    Jerome K. Jerome, *Idle Thoughts of an Idle Fellow*

Sometimes I battle with depression. I never know all the reasons for this 'dark
pit', as it seems to me. Some of it may be hurt pride. Sometimes it is obviously
exhaustion, physical, mental, emotional and spiritual. At times, when I am tired
and strained, I can get angry over an incident that may be quite trivial in itself;
and then I get angry with myself for getting angry. As I suppress both forms of
anger, depression is the result. I am then even more difficult to live with than
usual. I do not want people to get too near to me, but I hope very much that they
will not go too far away either.
    David Watson, *You Are My God*

When the heart is hard and parched up, come upon me with a shower of mercy.
When grace is lost from life, come with a burst of song.
When tumultuous work raises its din on all sides shutting me out from beyond,
    come to me, my lord of silence, with thy peace and rest.
When my beggarly heart sits crouched, shut up in a corner, break open the door,
    my king, and come with the ceremony of a king.
When desire blinds the mind with delusion and dust, O thou holy one, thou
    wakeful, come with thy light and thy thunder.
    Rabindranath Tagore, *Gitanjali*

A vague feeling of anguish is prowling around in me like a caged beast, immobilizing my energies and concentration. The feeling has no shape and I don't know what to call it. I am its prisoner. I've got to shake it off. I need all my energy at the moment, at every moment, if I'm to live my life in its fullness. But I won't be free of it until I've let the bad feeling wash over me, then faced it without fear, grabbed it with both hands and offered it to God who can bring new life out of sin.

I can understand the awful pain of those who are suffering from depression. It's a paralysing of one's whole being, while others whisper: He should pull up his socks! Control himself! But the trouble is *he can't*. It's an ordeal, one of the worst. He needs drugs, perhaps. But he also needs someone always to be there, patient, sensitive, to help him set free the little pieces of life which are stagnating in him, polluting his source.

Michel Quoist, *With Open Heart*

See also Healing, Loneliness, Perseverance, Suffering, Transformation

23

DISCIPLESHIP

Discipleship – one who attends upon another for the purpose of learning from him/her – includes practice as well as theory; learning by doing

When I first went to Bradford Cathedral as a curate I had a brief chat with one of my colleagues. I was keen to find out how best to operate in this new environment. His advice was: observe the provost closely and learn all you can from him. He likened this to an apprenticeship, in which one learned from an experienced old hand. At theological college the emphasis had been mainly on theory, on the academic side of things. In that rarefied atmosphere we had studied the Bible, doctrine, church history, ethics and worship. Now the time had come for practical application, under the watchful eye of the provost. I did as he suggested. Looking back over the four-year curacy, the 'apprenticeship' was in reality a valuable period of discipleship. Theory and practice were carefully brought together.

You shall speak to him and put the words in his mouth; and I will be with your mouth and with his mouth, and will teach you what you shall do.

    Exodus 4.15

Come to me, all you that are weary and are carrying heavy burdens, and I will give you rest. Take my yoke upon you, and learn from me; for I am gentle and humble in heart, and you will find rest for your souls. For my yoke is easy, and my burden is light.

    Matthew 11.28–30

When the body is most disciplined, the mental and the spiritual faculties are most alert.

    William Barclay, *The Gospel of Matthew*

The commandment of absolute truthfulness is really only another name for the fulness of discipleship.

    Dietrich Bonhoeffer, *The Cost of Discipleship*

Christ cannot be followed unless a man gives the benefit of his gifts and attainments to the whole community.

    Henry Ward Beecher, *Proverbs from Plymouth Pulpit*

We are called to represent Christ spontaneously and with incalculable consequences in the pedestrian obscurity of everyday life.

    Hans Jürgen Schultz, *Conversion to the World*

In dealing with ourselves inner genuineness, with our fellows utter goodwill, with God perfect confidence – that, in brief, is discipleship to Jesus.

    Harry Emerson Fosdick, *The Hope of a New World*

For though our Saviour's passion is over, his compassion is not. That never fails his humble sincere disciples. In him they find more than all they lose in the world.

    William Penn, *Fruits of Solitude*

When we fail in our discipleship it is always for one of two reasons; either we are not trying to be loyal, or else we are trying in our own strength and find that it is not enough.

    William Temple, *Readings in St John's Gospel*

We know by doing. Take up thy cross, lift it up yourself on your own shoulder, stagger under it, go on with it, and your intellect will be enriched with what no books could give.

    Mark Rutherford, *Last Pages from a Journal*

God in Jesus Christ enters the human battles for existence and wholeness, and exerts his power to redeem men. The disciple is called to enter into this decisive issue – not merely 'decide' about it, but participate in it.

    John J. Vincent, *Secular Christ*

On one occasion three would-be disciples came to Jesus and offered their discipleship with reservations or delays. He warned them that discipleship involved hardship, with total, immediate and life-long commitment (Luke 9.57–62). When we begin to follow we shall soon realize that more is needed, and if we are honest enough or rash enough to ask 'What do I still lack?' he will unerringly put his finger on the one thing we are least ready to surrender.

George Appleton, *Journey for a Soul*

There is a kind of Church-worker for whom our age even more urgently calls, and on whom the life and example of Christ set more immediately the seal of discipleship – the man who, to the glory of God and for the good of his fellows, does honest work of the everyday sort.

Archibald C. Craig, *University Sermons*

He prepared His disciples for a change after the critical moment was passed; with the Cross and Resurrection His Kingdom would have come with power, and they were no longer to be apart from the world, bringing to it *ab extra* the divine act of redemption which is itself the revelation of God, but were to carry its power into the world as leaven that should leaven the whole lump.

William Temple, *Citizen and Churchman*

The Christian who reads, in these verses (Luke 14.25–35), of the price of discipleship will see that, if he is to take the divine words seriously, he must learn not to be too much 'entangled in the affairs of this life', whether human affairs or relationships, or personal and material things. He must learn to think of these as things that he can do without, including life itself. No one knows what he may be called upon one day to face or to do in loyalty to his profession as a Christian disciple – especially in a world as dangerous and uncertain as that in which our lives are cast. The man who is bogged down by worldly ties and considerations will find obedience much harder if God should call him one day to do some sacrificial act.

J.R.H. Moorman, *The Path to Glory*

Every disciple knows that the aim of his life is to grow like his Lord. To achieve this he will study the earliest records of the divine life lived among men. He will want to get back behind the words to their meaning, behind the actions to the mind and character which inspired those actions. He will be eager to enter into intimate touch with him who promised to be with men and to live within the inmost being of each man. So with the outer study and the inner communion he will come to understand and acquire something of the mind of Christ.

George Appleton, *Journey for a Soul*

We are summoned to a new level of identification. We are summoned to be disciples, and so to a discipline. A disciple is a learner and his discipline is the training whereby he learns. To learn the way of the cross is the hardest thing of all, and the training by which we are to advance in this learning is provided for us by the discipline of prayer and worship. Those who disparage prayer and worship and imagine that without these one can achieve some kind of instant Christianity do not know what they are talking about. They understand neither the weakness of our humanity nor the depth of the richness of the spiritual maturity into which Christ is calling us.

John Macquarrie, *Paths in Spirituality*

The price of discipleship, . . . is to be willing to give up everything if occasion should demand it, and, in the meanwhile, to live as men 'looking for their Lord', with loins girt and lamps burning, ready for action when the word is given. Discipleship, is, or may be, a very costly thing. It may cost us all we have. In this passage [Luke 14.25–35] therefore, Jesus introduces a fourth condition, and that is that we should not go into it except with our eyes wide open. He does this in the form of three little parables, those of the tower builder who carefully surveys his material; the warrior-king who closely considers his chances of success; and the salt, which, if it cannot last out, goes bad.

Jesus bids us count the cost of discipleship. Can we face it? Is it going to be too much for us? Dare we risk failure and be cast out?

J.R.H. Moorman, *The Path to Glory*

See also Action, Christian, Growing, Obedience, Service

24

DIVINITY

Divinity – theology; being divine, Godhood

One of our undergraduates was helped in her understanding of the Christian faith by some words of Meister Eckhart in this section. 'The seed of God is in us. Given an intelligent farmer and a diligent fieldhand, it will thrive and grow up to God whose seed it is, and accordingly its fruit will be God-nature. Pear seeds grow into pear trees; nut seeds into nut trees, and God-seed into God!' Through these words she was able to understand baptism (and confirmation) as a cleansing and *a spiritual rebirth*. She then considered the words of the confirmation service; that 'she may . . . daily increase in your Holy Spirit more and more, until she comes to your everlasting Kingdom'. She worked out spiritual rebirth, initiated in baptism and confirmation, needed to grow in prayer, as in reflection. She now came to understand divinity as a 'divine life', rather than 'a divine science', and she was gradually changed by it.

His divine power has given us everything needed for life and godliness, through the knowledge of him who called us by his own glory and goodness. Thus he has given us, through these things, his precious and very great promises, so that through them you may escape from the corruption that is in the world because of lust, and may become participants in the divine nature. For this very reason, you must make every effort to support your faith with goodness, and goodness with knowledge, and knowledge with self-control, and self-control with endurance, and endurance with godliness, and godliness with mutual affection, and mutual affection with love.

2 Peter 1.3–7

We know that we are God's children.

1 John 5.19

The mystery of a Person, indeed, is ever divine, to him that has a sense for the Godlike.

    Thomas Carlyle, *Sartor Resartus*

> There's a divinity that shapes our ends,
> Rough-hew them how we will.
>   William Shakespeare, *Hamlet*

The essential truth . . . is that man is under an absolute mandate to express divinity in his own nature and in his whole life.

    F. Ernest Johnson, *The Social Gospel Re-Examined*

> The seeds of godlike power are in us still;
> Gods we are, bards, saints, heroes, if we will!
>   Matthew Arnold, *Written in Emerson's Essays*

He is divinely favoured who may trace a silver vein in all the affairs of life, see sparkles of light in the gloomiest scenes, and absolute radiance in those which are bright.

    Henry Ward Beecher, *Proverbs from Plymouth Pulpit*

Were I indeed to define divinity, I should rather call it a *divine life*, rather than a *divine science*; it being something rather to be understood by a spiritual sensation, than by any verbal description.

    John Smith the Platonist, *Select Discourses*

There is a power in the soul untouched by time and flesh, flowing from the Spirit, remaining in the Spirit, altogether spiritual. In this power is God, ever verdant, flowering in all the joy and glory of his actual self.

    Meister Eckhart, in Franz Pfeiffer, *Meister Eckhart,* translated by C. de B. Evans

That only which we have within, can we see without. If we meet no gods, it is because we harbour none. If there is grandeur in you, you will find grandeur in porters and sweeps. He only is rightly immortal, to whom all things are immortal.

    Ralph Waldo Emerson, *The Conduct of Life, Nature and Other Essays*

Divinity is essentially the first of the professions, because it is necessary for all at all times; law and physic are only necessary for some at some times. I speak of them, of course, not in their abstract existence, but in their applicability to man.

    Samuel Taylor Coleridge, *Table Talk of Samuel Taylor Coleridge*

The soul may rise through all earthly influences into such a susceptible spiritual condition that the throb and impulse of the Divine nature shall fall upon our souls and give us an abiding state of wisdom, of peace, of rest, and of joy in the Holy Ghost.

Henry Ward Beecher, *Proverbs from Plymouth Pulpit*

To the poet, to the philosopher, to the saint, all things are friendly and sacred, all events profitable, all days holy, all men divine. For the eye is fastened on the life, and slights the circumstance. Every chemical substance, every plant, every animal in its growth, teaches the unity of cause, the variety of appearance.

Ralph Waldo Emerson, *Essay on History*

. . . it takes a divine man to exhibit anything divine, Socrates, Alfred, Columbus, Wordsworth, or any other brave preferrer of the still small voice within to the roar of the populace – a thing very easy to speak and very hard to do for twenty-four hours. The rest are men potentially, not actually, now only pupas or tadpoles – say rather quarries of souls, heroes that shall be, seeds of gods.

Ralph Waldo Emerson, *Journals*

'All divinity is love, or wonder', John Donne wrote in one of his poems. No phrase could better express the intense religious life of the group of spiritual poets in England who interpreted in beautiful, often immortal, form this religion of the spirit, this glowing consciousness that the world and all its fulness is God's and that eternity is set within the soul of man, who never is himself until he finds his Life in God.

Rufus M. Jones, *Spiritual Reformers in the 16th and 17th Centuries*

I think it might be said not (with Voltaire) that we invent our gods, but that we carry them with us and inside us.

Cutting across the differences in doctrines between the great world religions – of Moses and Jesus, of Lao-tzu and Buddha, of Confucius and Mohammed – there remains the truth that God is what man finds that is divine in himself. God is the best way man can behave in the ordinary occasions of life, and the farthest point to which man can stretch himself.

Max Lerner, *The Unfinished Country*

The Scriptures say of human beings that there is an outward man and, along with him, an inner man. To the outward man belong those things that depend on the soul but are connected with the flesh and blended with it, and the co-operative functions of the several members such as the eye, the ear, the tongue, the hand, and so on. The Scripture speaks of all this as the old man, the earthy man, the outward person, the enemy, the servant. Within us all is the other person, the inner man, whom the Scripture calls the new man, the heavenly man, the young person, a friend, the aristocrat . . . The seed of God is in us. Given an intelligent farmer and a diligent fieldhand, it will thrive and grow up to God whose seed it is, and accordingly its fruit will be God-nature. Pear seeds grow into pear trees; nut seeds into nut trees, and God-seed into God!

Meister Eckhart, *Meister Eckhart*, translated by Raymond B. Blakney

See also God, Holy Spirit, Incarnation, Jesus Christ, Mystics

25

DOUBT

Doubt – feeling of uncertainty about something, undecided state of mind, inclination to disbelieve; uncertain state of things, lack of full proof or clear indication

At theological college we had a quiet day taken by the then Archbishop of York, Stuart Blanch. He was giving us some advice about coping with doubt, and told us of a recent experience. It was summertime. In the evening he was taking his dog for a walk in his grounds, and they came across a hedgehog on the lawn. The dog had never seen a hedgehog before and joyfully bounded up to explore. The hedgehog, sensing danger, curled itself into a ball, and the dog got its nose badly pricked. With a great howl of pain the dog tucked its tail between its legs and headed off for the security of the bushes. The next evening there was a repeat performance. This time the dog was more circumspect. He approached the hedgehog slowly, stopping six feet in front of it, observing it carefully. After a while he turned on his heels, tail high, and bounded off to the bushes. The archbishop made the point the dog was unable to understand the hedgehog but felt he could still enjoy life, not knowing all the answers. He wondered if this had something to tell us about living creatively with doubt.

Among those nations you shall find no ease, no resting-place for the sole of your foot. There the Lord will give you a trembling heart, failing eyes, and a languishing spirit. Your life shall hang in doubt before you; night and day you shall be in dread, with no assurance of your life.

   Deuteronomy 28.65–66

So the other disciples told him, 'We have seen the Lord.' But he said to them, 'Unless I see the mark of the nails in his hands, and put my finger in the mark of the nails, and my hand in his side, I will not believe.'

   John 20.25

Honest doubt is suspended judgment.

A.R. Orage, *On Love*

Feed your faith, and your doubts will starve to death.

Anon

All fanaticism is a strategy to prevent doubt from becoming conscious.

H.A. Williams CR, *The True Wilderness*

If we are sensible, we will not doubt God, we will doubt our world and we will doubt ourselves.

Agnes Sanford, *The Healing Light*

> Modest doubt is call'd
> The beacon of the wise.
>
> William Shakespeare, *Troilus and Cressida*

To doubt is to live, to struggle, to struggle for life and to live by struggle . . . A faith which does not continue to doubt is a dead faith.

Miguel de Unamuno, *The Agony of Christianity*

When we say: 'Yes, I doubt, but I do believe in God's love more than I trust my own doubts', it becomes possible for God to act.

Anthony Bloom, *The Essence of Prayer*

If Christ has grappled our hearts to Himself at all, then it were surely wise to trust His certainties and not our own doubts, however persistent.

Herbert H. Farmer, *The Healing Cross*

I refused to allow myself to accept any of it in my heart, because I was afraid of a headlong fall, but I was hanging in suspense which was more likely to be fatal than a fall.

St Augustine, *Confessions*

If a man will begin in certainties, he shall end in doubts; but if he will be content to begin with doubts, he shall end in certainties.

Francis Bacon, *The Advancement of Learning*

There are the shadows of doubts and uncertainties. Sometimes the way ahead is far from being clear. Sometimes we feel like people groping among the shadows with nothing firm to cling to.

William Barclay, *The Gospel of John*

> Our doubts are traitors,
> And make us lose the good we oft might win,
> By fearing to attempt.
>
> William Shakespeare, *Measure for Measure*

Enthusiasm for the universe, in knowing as well as in creating, also answers the question of doubt and meaning. Doubt is the necessary tool of knowledge. And meaninglessness is no threat so long as enthusiasm for the universe and for man as its centre is alive.

Paul Tillich, *The Courage to Be*

> For nothing worthy proving can be proven,
> Nor yet disproven: wherefore thou be wise,
> Cleave ever to the sunnier side of doubt,
> And cleave to Faith beyond the forms of Faith!
>
> Alfred, Lord Tennyson, 'The Ancient Sage'

But this is an age not of faith, but of cathartic doubt, and unless everything can, potentially at least, be questioned, then there is a kind of betrayal of the spirit of the times. It seems possible that doubt *is* our search for meaning, and that whatever refuses this painful path has cut itself off from our search for life.

Monica Furlong, *The End of Our Exploring*

There is an increasing number of people to whom everything they are doing seems futile. They are still under the spell of the slogans which preach faith in the secular paradise of success and glamour. But doubt, the fertile condition of all progress, has begun to beset them and has made them ready to ask what their real self-interest as human beings is.

Eric Fromm, *Man for Himself*

Doubt and perplexity will often be the lot of travellers on this life's journey. Beyond the questions arising in our daily thought and conduct are those greater difficulties which seem to stop our progress and to render existence an insoluble riddle. Doubt has many sources. It may be true that some could find the origin of their doubts in an unwillingness to face their moral condition and obey the demands of duty. But at the present day, doubt frequently arises from a sense that received dogmas do not correspond with the facts of life or with the moral values which our truest insight reveals. In other cases there may be not so much per-plexity and doubt as an exhilarating spirit of inquiry and exploration driving a man forward on the quest for truth for himself and all men.

Christian Faith and Practice in the Experience of the Society of Friends

See also Faith, Growing, Guidance, Hope, Thinking

26

EDUCATION

Education – bringing up (young persons); giving intellectual and moral training; development of character or mental powers

A quotation about higher education suggests we are in danger of producing intellectual giants who remain spiritual and emotional pygmies. Over the years I have been impressed with the intellectual qualities of our fellows, postgraduates, and undergraduates. However I sometimes wonder if we are too one-sided in our system of education. The emphasis tends to be mainly on developing critical and analytical skills, and the power of reason and the intellect. Reflection Groups are an attempt to educate the 'whole' person. They are based on the original meaning of the Latin word *educere* – to draw out, lead out – and concentrate on developing latent gifts and talents. A typical Reflection Group meets for an hour a week, chooses a topic, mulls over the contents in silence and then talks it through. Much is learned from the other members of the group. The intellectual content is still present, but the spiritual and moral contents are also there, and development of character takes place unconsciously. The Reflection Group thus makes its contribution in the academic institution aiming to educate the whole person, body, mind and spirit.

～

I will instruct you and teach you the way you should go; I will counsel you with my eye upon you.
   Psalm 32.8

About the middle of the festival Jesus went up into the temple and began to teach. The Jews were astonished at it, saying, 'How does this man have such learning, when he has never been taught?'
   John 7.14–15

Learning is its own exceeding great reward.
   William Hazlitt, *The Plain Speaker*

Deep verst in books and shallow in himself.

   John Milton, *Paradise Regain'd*

Education has for a chief object the formation of character.

   Herbert Spencer, *Social Statics*

The direction in which education starts a man will determine his future life.

   Plato, *The Republic of Plato*

To be what we are, and to become what we are capable of becoming, is the only end of life.

   Robert Louis Stevenson, *Familiar Studies of Men and Books, Virginibus Puerisque*

. . . he is perfectly educated who is taught all the will of God concerning him, and enabled, through life, to execute it.

   Thomas Arnold, *Sermons*

Finally, education, alone, can conduct us to that enjoyment which is, at once, best in quality and infinite in quantity.

   Horace Mann, *Lectures and Reports on Education*

A child is not educated who has not physical education, social education, intellectual education, industrial education, professional education, spiritual education.

   Henry Ward Beecher, *Proverbs from Plymouth Pulpit*

The task of religious education is to fashion a religious lifestyle, and to nurture in people that creative spirit of love that will help them to grow up and live wisely without a rule-book.

   Roy Stevens, *On Education and the Death of Love*

Education: by that I understand not merely the imparting of knowledge, but the drawing out of the powers of the mind, spirit, and body; the evoking of a reverence for the truth, and the use of the imagination in its pursuit.

   Michael Ramsey, in Margaret Duggan, *Through the Year with Michael Ramsey*

Education . . . is the leading of human souls to what is best, and making what is best out of them; and these two objects are always attainable together, and by the same means; the training which makes men happiest in themselves, also makes them most serviceable to others.

   John Ruskin, *The Stones of Venice*

Education ought to teach how to be in love always and what to be in love with. The great things of history have been done by the great lovers, by the saints and men of science and artists; and the problem of civilization is to give every man a chance of being a saint, a man of science, or an artist.

A. Clutton Brock, *The Ultimate Belief*

An education which is not religious is atheistic; there is no middle way. If you give to children an account of the world from which God is left out, you are teaching them to understand the world without reference to God. If He is then introduced, He is an excrescence. He becomes an appendix to His own creation.

William Temple, *The Hope of a New World*

One person who has mastered life is better than a thousand persons who have mastered only the contents of books, but no one can get anything out of life without God. If I were looking for a master of learning, I should go to Paris to the colleges where the higher studies are pursued, but if I wanted to know about the perfection of life, they could not tell me there.

Meister Eckhart, *Meister Eckhart*, translated by Raymond B. Blakney

. . . the modern educationalist is forever pointing out that *educere* means to lead forth, or to draw out, a student's potentiality, as opposed to the old-style education that was content to stuff a head full of presumed facts. If there is any analogy with spiritual direction, then it is very up-to-date indeed, for this has always been its aim; to develop innate gifts and graces.

Martin Thornton, *Spiritual Direction*

Ordinary, secular education, as it deals only with the comprehensible, puts the pupil in a wrong position. He has to do with nothing which may not be mastered, and becomes insensible to that which is beyond. Worse – he is affected only by reasons which appeal to his understanding, by what is immediate, and his conduct is not governed, as it so often should be, by that which is intangible, shadowy, and remote.

Mark Rutherford, *Last Pages from a Journal*

The development of general ability for independent thinking and judgment should always be placed foremost, not the acquisition of special knowledge. If a person masters the fundamentals of his subject and has learnt to think and work independently, he will surely find his way and besides will be better able to adapt himself to progress and changes than the person whose training principally consists in the acquiring of detailed knowledge.

Albert Einstein, *Out of My Later Years*

Most people live, whether physically, intellectually, or morally, in a very restricted circle of their potential being. They *make use* of a very small portion of their possible consciousness, and of their soul's resources in general, much like a man who, out of his whole bodily organism, should get into the habit of using and moving only his little finger. Great emergencies and crises show us how much greater our vital resources are than we had supposed.

William James, *The Letters of William James*

See also Growing, Intellect, Knowledge, Mind, Thinking

27

ETERNAL LIFE

*E*ternal life – existing always, without end or usually beginning; a quality and value of life; endless life after death; being eternal

I once had the good fortune to meet George Appleton in his home in Oxford, where he had settled down in retirement. His writings had always appealed to me; that is why so many of them have been included. One of his contributions on eternal life has been particularly helpful. He describes eternal life as 'a quality of life, the kind of life which Jesus had, human life permeated by the grace and love of God . . . Jesus taught his disciples they could have eternal life now, the perfection of which will come in the dimension beyond death.' I feel he gets right to the heart of the matter in these few words. If we want to know more about this quality of life we can go to the Gospels, and see for ourselves a life permeated by the grace and love of God. As we read, we might become aware of this grace and love of God welling up inside us, and experience eternal life for ourselves. One of the great joys of Christianity is to experience moments of eternal life in this present life, and thus have an assurance of eternal life in the future.

~

The eternal God is a dwelling-place, and underneath are the everlasting arms.
　　Deuteronomy 33.27

But those who drink of the water that I will give them will never be thirsty. The water that I will give will become in them a spring of water gushing up to eternal life.
　　John 4.14

We feel and know that we are eternal.
　　Benedict Spinoza, *Spinoza's Ethics and De Intellectus Emendatione*

Time is eternity; and we live in eternity now.
　　Herman Melville, *Mardi*

The truest end of life is to know the life that never ends.

William Penn, *Fruits of Solitude*

The noise of the moment scoffs at the music of the Eternal.

Rabindranath Tagore, *Stray Birds*

To have the sense of the eternal in life is a short flight for the soul. To have had it, is the soul's vitality.

George Meredith, *Diana of the Crossways*

> But felt through all this fleshly dresse
> Bright *shoots* of everlastingnesse.
>
> Henry Vaughan, *Silex Scintillans*

Every creative act of ours in relation to other people – an act of love, of pity, of help, of peacemaking – not merely has a future but is eternal.

Nicolas Berdyaev, *The Destiny of Man*

If there is a God and a future life, then there is truth and goodness, and man's highest happiness consists in striving to attain them.

Leo Tolstoy, *War and Peace*

Eternal life is the life of God, and to have eternal life is to share the life of God. Here we are at the very heart of the matter. Eternal life is nothing less than God's life.

William Barclay, *The Plain Man Looks at the Apostles' Creed*

It is eternity now. I am in the midst of it. It is about me in the sunshine; I am in it, as the butterfly floats in the light-laden air. Nothing has to come: it is now. Now is eternity; now is the immortal life.

Richard Jefferies, *The Story of My Heart*

Any one who feels the full significance of what is involved in knowing the *truth* has a coercive feeling that Eternity has been set within us, that our finite life is deeply rooted in the all-pervading Infinite.

Rufus M. Jones, *Spiritual Reformers in the 16th and 17th Centuries*

Eternal life is not a gift as something out of the hand of God, like a sceptre, or like a coronet. It is a gift as education is; something wrought patiently and long in a man. It is a gift as the sunlight is to the flowers – an influence which enters into them and fashions them.

Henry Ward Beecher, *Proverbs from Plymouth Pulpit*

If a man once knows the Spirit within him, the source of all his aspiration after holiness, as indeed the Spirit of Jesus Christ, and if he knows this Spirit of Jesus Christ within himself as none other than the Spirit of the Eternal and Almighty God, what more can he want? *This is the eternal life.*

William Temple, *Readings in St John's Gospel*

The eternal life is not the future life; it is life in harmony with the true order of things, – life in God. We must learn to look upon time as a movement of eternity, as an undulation in the ocean of being. To live, so as to keep this consciousness of ours in perpetual relation with the eternal, is to be wise; to live, so as to personify and embody the eternal, is to be religious.

Henri Frédéric Amiel, *Amiel's Journal*

Jesus did not promise to men simply life after death, but a quality of life now. He promised us eternal life, the sharing of God's life, participation in his own risen life. He said that he had come to give men abundant life – sufficient to keep the body in health and strength, to illuminate and guide the mind, to bring peace to the heart. If we have that life within us now, we shall not worry about our last migration into the spiritual world, for we shall know a good deal about it already.

George Appleton, *Journey for a Soul*

Religion, in its fullest development, essentially requires, not only this our little span of earthly years, but a life beyond. Neither an Eternal Life that is already fully achieved here below, nor an Eternal Life already to be begun and known solely in the beyond, satisfies these requirements. Only an Eternal Life already begun and truly known in part here, though fully to be achieved and completely to be understood hereafter, corresponds to the deepest longings of man's spirit as touched by the prevenient Spirit, God.

Friedrich von Hügel, *Eternal Life*

Now there are some things we all know, but we don't take'm out and look at'm very often. We all know that *something* is eternal. And it ain't houses and it ain't names, and it ain't earth, and it ain't even the stars . . . everybody knows in their bones that *something* is eternal, and that something has to do with human beings. All the greatest people ever lived have been telling us that for five thousand years, and yet you'd be surprised how people are always losing hold of it. There's something way down deep that's eternal about every human being.

Thornton Wilder, *Our Town*

Now let us take the idea of *eternal life*. It is far better to speak of *eternal* life than to speak of *everlasting* life. The main idea behind eternal life is not simply that of duration. It is quite clear that a life which went on for ever could just as easily be hell as heaven. The idea behind eternal life is the idea of a certain quality of life, a certain kind of life. What kind of life? There is only one person who can properly be described by this adjective eternal (*aionios*) and that one person is God. Eternal life is the kind of life that God lives; it is God's life.

William Barclay, *The Gospel of John*

See also Awareness, Freedom, Hope, Life, Time

28

EXPERIENCE

Experience – personal observation of or involvement with fact, event, etc.; knowledge of skill based on this; event that affects one

This topic is not about experience of life in general but of experience of 'God' in particular. I am very fond of St Augustine's 'experience' of God, recorded in his *Confessions*. He writes of Beauty – 'at once so ancient and so new' – and after a long search discovers this Beauty as something within himself. It takes him many years to find this Beauty, as he was outside himself, searching elsewhere. He concludes, 'You were with me, but I was not with you.' His experience of Beauty was deeply convincing. With me the penny finally dropped when I discovered Beauty in the depths of myself, and was able to experience this at first hand. Beauty, of course, is only one aspect of this 'inner presence'. There are many others – Father, Son, Holy Spirit and the gifts and fruits of the Holy Spirit. Experience of this kind is crucial in our quest for faith. Through it we reach an inner conviction of mind, heart and spirit, at one with our deepest intuitions and instincts.

‿

I have acquired great wisdom . . . and my mind has had great experience of wisdom and knowledge.

Ecclesiastes 1.16

. . . though indeed he is not far from each one of us. For 'In him we live and move and have our being.'

Acts 17.27–28

Never, 'for the sake of peace and quiet', deny your own experience or convictions.

Dag Hammarskjöld, *Markings*

So much of the Gospel as has been reproduced in a living form in Christian people's experience is what the world needs more than almost anything else.
  Henry Ward Beecher, *Proverbs from Plymouth Pulpit*

All authentic religion originates with mystical experience, be it the experience of Jesus, of the Buddha, or Mohammed, of the seers and prophets of the *Upanishads*.
  William Johnston, *The Inner Eye of Love*

The notes of religious experience that ring out of the soul are notes gladder than marriage-bells. Religion is real if it is experimental. Religion is glorious, and experimental religion is the most glorious of all.
  Henry Ward Beecher, *Proverbs from Plymouth Pulpit*

His emphasis is always . . . upon the native divine possibilities of the soul, upon the fact of a spiritual environment in immediate correspondence and co-operation with the soul, and upon the necessity of personal and inward experience as the key to every gate of life.
  Rufus M. Jones, *Spiritual Reformers in the 16th and 17th Centuries*

By religious experience we ought to mean an experience which is religious through and through – an experiencing of all things in the light of the knowledge of God. It is this, and not any moment of illumination, of which we may say that it is self-authenticating; for in such an experience all things increasingly fit together in a single intelligible whole.
  William Temple, *Thoughts on Some Problems of the Day*

He who receives Christ *experiences* something, but he hardly notices it. The wonder of the new life, the joy of forgiveness, and the liberation from fear keep him looking constantly to this figure from whom streams of living water flow into his life, reclaiming the desert of his lost heart and working the miracle of a new beginning.
  Helmut Thielicke, *I Believe: The Christian's Creed*

A creed is always the result and fruit of many minds and many centuries, purified from all the oddities, shortcomings, and flaws of individual experience. But for all that, the individual experience, with its very poverty, is immediate life, it is the warm red blood pulsating today. It is more convincing to a seeker after truth than the best tradition.
  C.G. Jung, in Jolande Jacobi, *Psychological Reflections*

The significant features of the experience are the consciousness of fresh springs of life, the release of new energies, the inner integration and unification of personality, the inauguration of a sense of mission, the flooding of the life with hope and gladness, and the conviction, amounting in the mind of the recipient to certainty, that God is found as an environing and vitalizing presence.

Rufus M. Jones, *Spiritual Reformers in the 16th and 17th Centuries*

. . . strain every nerve in every possible way to know and experience yourself as you really are. It will not be long, I suspect, before you have a real knowledge and experience of God as he is. Not as he is in himself, of course, for that is impossible to any save God; and not as you will in Heaven, both in body and soul. But as much as is now possible for a humble soul in a mortal body to know and experience him . . . and as much as he will permit.

The Cloud of Unknowing

He comes to us as One unknown, without a name, as of old, by the lake-side, He came to those men who knew Him not. He speaks to us the same word: 'Follow thou me!' and sets us to the tasks which He has to fulfil for our time. He commands. And to those who obey Him, whether they be wise or simple, He will reveal Himself in the toils, the conflicts, the sufferings which they shall pass through in His fellowship, and, as an ineffable mystery, they shall learn in their own experience Who He is.

Albert Schweitzer, *The Quest of the Historical Jesus*

People today are not prepared to take their faith from the tradition in which they were born, nor from other people. They want to deduce it from their own experience of life. They do not need theories, but the experience which will be the source of their own interpretation. They are suspicious of anything which seems to escape from life into theory, from experience into doctrine, or from the thing itself into talk about it. The method they want to follow is the inductive one rather than the deductive.

George Appleton, *Journey for a Soul*

Science has never discovered any 'God', epistemological criticism proves the impossibility of knowing God, but the psyche comes forward with the assertion of the experience of God. God is a psychic fact of immediate experience, otherwise there would never have been any talk of God. The fact is valid in itself, requiring no non-psychological proof and inaccessible to any form of non-psychological criticism. It can be the most immediate and hence the most real of experiences, which can be neither ridiculed nor disproved. Only people with a poorly developed sense of fact, or who are obstinately superstitious, could deny this truth.

C.G. Jung, *The Structure and Dynamics of the Psyche*

Religious experience is absolute. It is indisputable. You can only say that you have never had such an experience, and your opponent will say: 'Sorry, I have.' And there your discussion will come to an end. No matter what the world thinks about religious experience, the one who has it possesses the great treasure of a thing that has provided him with a source of life, meaning and beauty and that has given him a new splendour, to the world and to mankind. He has *pistis* and peace. Where is the criterium by which you could say that such a life is not legitimate, that such experience is not valid and thus such *pistis* is mere illusion? Is there, as a matter of fact, any better truth about ultimate things than the one that helps you to live?

C.G. Jung, *Psychology and Religion*

See also Finding God, Fulfilment, Inner Life, Presence, Revelation

FAITH

Faith – strong belief, especially in the Christian faith; things believed; loyalty, trustworthiness

When I was ordained, I had a fear about the future. I would be keen and enthusiastic for the first years of ministry and then would end up going through the motions. As it happened my faith came to a grinding halt after only four years. A new way beckoned forward through the discovery of *The Choice Is Always Ours* – an anthology compiled by Dorothy Berkley Phillips. This remarkable book opened up to me a new vision of faith of enormous dimensions. At first I had to be content with a skeleton of faith, but for the last twenty-five years I have been collecting material and putting flesh and blood on it. This vision of faith is founded on the Bible and the writings of many theologians, but includes the insights from poets, novelists, playwrights, philosophers, historians, scientists, politicians, economists, statesmen, psychologists, artists and musicians. With this vision of faith goes the practice of reflection. In reflection we mull over the contents of this anthology. After thirty-seven years of ministry I am still keen and enthusiastic about faith, learning something new day by day.

∽

Though they do not see me with bodily eyes, yet with the spirit they will believe the things I have said.
2 Esdras 1.37

For we walk by faith, not by sight.
2 Corinthians 5.7

Reason saw not till *Faith* sprung the Light.
John Dryden, 'Religio Laici'

We live in an age which asks for faith, pure faith, naked faith, mystical faith.
William Johnston, *The Inner Eye of Love*

Relying on God has to begin all over again every day as if nothing had yet been done.

C.S. Lewis, *Letters of C.S. Lewis*

Faith is kept alive in us, and gathers strength, from practice more than from speculation.

Joseph Addison, *The Works of Joseph Addison*

To abandon religion for science is merely to fly from one region of faith to another.

Giles and Melville Harcourt, *Short Prayers for the Long Day*

Faith is a kind of winged intellect. The great workmen of history have been men who believed like giants.

Charles H. Parkhurst, *The Pattern and the Mount and Other Sermons*

It is neither *necessary*, nor indeed *possible*, to understand any matter of Faith; farther than it is Revealed.

Benjamin Whichcote, *Moral and Religious Aphorisms*

Faith in Christ was not primarily a matter of doctrinal or intellectual belief, but a way of life, a following, an allegiance.

Said of Edward Wilson, in George Seaver, *Edward Wilson of the Antarctic*

The life of faith is a continually renewed victory over doubt, a continually renewed grasp of meaning in the midst of meaninglessness.

Lesslie Newbigin, *Honest Religion for Secular Man*

It is faith that is expected of you and honest living, not profound understanding and deep knowledge of the mysteries of God.

Thomas à Kempis, *The Imitation of Christ*

Faith is a certitude without proofs . . . Faith is a sentiment, for it is a hope, it is an instinct, for it precedes all outward instruction.

Henri Frédéric Amiel, *Amiel's Journal*

Nothing in life is more wonderful than faith – the one great moving force which we can neither weigh in the balance nor test in the crucible.

Sir William Osler, *Aphorisms from His Bedside Teachings and Writings*

Religious faith does not consist in supposing that there is a God. It consists in personal trust in God rising to personal fellowship with God.

William Temple, *Basic Convictions*

The only faith that wears well and holds its colour in all weathers is that which is woven of conviction and set with the sharp mordant of experience.

J.R. Lowell, *My Study Windows*

Like all human knowledge, the knowledge of faith is also fragmentary. Only when faith remains aware of this does it remain free from arrogance, intolerance and false zeal.

Hans Küng, *On Being a Christian*

To have faith is to meet the world with the conviction that in spite of all its ambiguities and its downright evils, there can be discerned in it the reality of love and a ground of hope.

John Macquarrie, *Paths in Spirituality*

Proofs are the last thing looked for by a truly religious mind which feels the imaginative fitness of its faith and knows instinctively that, in such a manner, imaginative fitness is all that can be required.

George Santayana, *Interpretations of Poetry and Religion*

> One in whom persuasion and belief
> Had ripened into faith, and faith become
> A passionate intuition.
>
> William Wordsworth, 'The Excursion'

That man is perfect in faith who can come to God in the utter dearth of his feelings and his desires, without a glow or an inspiration, with the weight of low thoughts, failures, neglects, and wandering forgetfulness, and say to him, 'Thou art my refuge, because thou art my home.'

George Macdonald, *Unspoken Sermons*

How do we stand in respect of our use of the watch-tower of Faith? Are we so busy on the ground floor that we take it for granted, and seldom go upstairs? It is true that those stairs are dark and steep; but if we never make the effort, never ascend to the soul's summit, we remain something less than human.

Evelyn Underhill, in John Stobbart, *The Wisdom of Evelyn Underhill*

The creeds are not objects of faith; they are expressions of a faith of which Christ is the object, and in regard to all such personal relationships there is scope for at least a great width of intellectual movement as we seek more and more perfectly to understand and to interpret the character with which we are confronted.

William Temple, *The Preacher's Theme Today*

. . . it is only by living completely in this world that one learns to believe . . . This is what I mean by worldliness – taking life in one's stride, with all its duties and problems, its successes and failures, its experiences and helplessness. It is in such a life that we throw ourselves utterly into the arms of God and participate in his sufferings in the world and watch with Christ in Gethsemane. That is faith, that is *metanoia*, and that is what makes a man and a Christian.

Dietrich Bonhoeffer, *Letters and Papers from Prison*

See also Belief, Commitment, Experience, Mystics, Trust

FINDING GOD

Finding God – the search, discovery and coming to a personal knowledge of God

William Law wrote one of the greatest religious treatises in the English language – *The Spirit of Prayer*. In this book he encourages us to find God by searching the deepest and most central part of our souls. There we shall discover the Light and Spirit of God, and so come to a personal knowledge of God. This approach rings true to my own experience. Early in life, I discerned something of God the creator in the creation. Several years later in the Gospels I was confronted by the person of Jesus Christ. In my early twenties I experienced something of the Holy Spirit. However these manifestations were mainly seen to be outside myself, and so lacked conviction. What ultimately proved decisive was the search suggested by William Law which led to the discovery of the Light and Spirit of God within me, and so to a personal knowledge of God. Reflecting on this material may help us to find God. We put ourselves in a position where God can find us, and expose ourselves to 'the gift of faith'.

O that I knew where I might find him, that I might come even to his dwelling!
  Job 23.3

Search, and you will find.
  Matthew 7.7

Humble recognition of what your nature is will lead more surely to God than profound searching for knowledge.
  Thomas à Kempis, *The Imitation of Christ*

People are generally better persuaded by the reasons which they have themselves discovered than by those which have come into the mind of others.
  Blaise Pascal, *Pensées*

None of the formal arguments for the existence of God really convince. The proof lies in hints and dreams which are not expressible by human language.

    Mark Rutherford, *Last Pages from a Journal*

There is only one 'place' to look for God and that is in one's own soul, there is only one 'region' in which to find heaven or hell, and that is in the nature and character of the person's own desire and will.

    Rufus M. Jones, *Spiritual Reformers in the 16th and 17th Centuries*

> I found Him in the shining of the stars,
> I marked Him in the flowering of His fields
> But in His ways with men I find Him not.
>
>   Alfred, Lord Tennyson, 'The Passing of Arthur'

To discover God is not to discover an idea but to discover oneself. It is to awake to that part of one's existence which has been hidden from sight and which one has refused to recognize. The discovery may be very painful; it is like going through a kind of death. But it is the one thing which makes life worth living.

    Bede Griffiths OSB, *The Golden String*

Thy hand be on the latch to open the door at his first knock.

    Shouldst thou open the door and not see him, do not say he did not knock, but understand that he is there, and wants thee to go out to him. It may be he has something for thee to do for him. Go and do it, and perhaps thou wilt return with a new prayer, to find a new window in thy soul.

    George Macdonald, *Unspoken Sermons*

The French religious writer Père Jean de Caussade insisted, in one of his discussions of Christian prayer, that we are to find God 'in the sacrament of the present moment'. That is, we are to find him when we are confronted with the demands of life, given the opportunity to make our response to those demands, and enabled to labour responsibly for God in the place where we are.

    Norman Pittenger, *The Christian Situation Today*

The longer one travels toward the city he seeks the nearer and nearer he comes to the goal of his journey; exactly so is it with the soul that is seeking God. If he will travel away from himself and away from the world and seek only God as the precious pearl of his soul, he will come steadily nearer to God, until he becomes one spirit with God the Spirit; but let him not be afraid of mountains and valleys on the way, and let him not give up because he is tired and weary, *for he who seeks finds*.

Rufus M. Jones, *Spiritual Reformers in the 16ᵗʰ and 17ᵗʰ Centuries*

. . . How did I come to Him? He alone knows. I groped for Him and could not find Him. I prayed to Him unknown and He did not answer . . . Then, one day, He was there again . . . It should be an occasion, I knew. One should be able to say: 'This was the time, the place, the manner of it. This was my conversion to religion. A good man spoke to me and I became good. I saw creation in the face of a child and I believed.' It was not like that at all. He was there. I knew He was there, and that He made me and that He still loved me . . . I never understood till this moment the meaning of the words 'The gift of faith'.

Morris West, *The Devil's Advocate*

For this turning to the Light and Spirit of God within Thee, is thy *only true* turning unto God, there is no other way of finding Him but in that Place where he dwelleth in Thee. For though God be everywhere present, yet He is only present to Thee in the deepest, and most central Part of thy Soul. Thy natural *Senses* cannot possess God, or unite Thee to Him, nay thy inward Faculties of *Understanding, Will,* and *Memory*, can only reach after God, but cannot be the *Place* of his Habitation in Thee. But there is a *Root*, or *Depth* in Thee, from whence all these Faculties come forth, as Lines from a *Centre*, or as Branches from the Body of the Tree.

William Law, in Sidney Spencer, *The Spirit of Prayer*

Experiencing God. An indescribable embrace, dazzling, breathtaking. A certainty, a sureness that wipes out months and years of searching, thinking, doubts and discussion. Oh, yes, you can reason on the subject of God, but 'knowing' him (being born to him) is a different matter altogether!

I need to write down these moments of life – real life, not the superficial daily spectacle that passes for life. I'm trembling. I fear that words may turn out to be obstacles.

A few minutes, and I'm drunk with light. I don't know anything any more. I just feel very peaceful.

Michel Quoist, *With Open Heart*

Many persons, Christians and non-Christians, whose thought has been influenced by a particular philosophy and by modern scientific attitudes, profess themselves no longer able to admit the concept of God as presented by the Church. Any facet of the human personality that has been projected upon this concept, must, they feel, be stripped away. They go so far as to speak of idols. Others even maintain that we can neither say anything nor can we know anything about God. Now in so far as this demand to clarify and advance in the knowledge of God is legitimate and possible, it must be recognized that the contemplatives who have been able to translate their experiences of the divine into human language, give us the loftiest and the purest possible concept of God.

René Voillaume, *The Need for Contemplation*

See also Divinity, Experience, God, Holy Spirit, Jesus Christ

3 1

FREEDOM

Freedom – personal liberty, non-slavery; independence; liberty of action, right to do; power of self-determination, independence of fate or necessity, freedom of speech and religion, from fear and want

It was two o'clock on a Monday afternoon. I began my weekly visiting on the wards of the Bradford Royal Infirmary. The man in the first bed was rather anxious about a pending operation. We chatted briefly about his condition, the doctors and nurses on the ward, and the likely outcome of the operation. I tried to give him some reassurance and moved on to the next patient. Here was a man of a very different disposition – blunt and direct – a typical Yorkshireman. 'They are not very intelligent in here, padre,' he started off apologetically, 'take, for instance, the man you have just been talking to. He came in yesterday, and tried to make conversation with me. 'I've worked for thirty-five years for such-and-such a firm,' he said. 'Really,' I replied, 'you might just as well have been a cabbage.' He hasn't spoken to me since. He was proud of the fact that he had worked so long for one firm. I don't think of it in that way at all. With those sort of people there is no get-up-and-go, no initiative, and certainly no freedom.' I wonder if most of us settle down too quickly – in our work, in getting married, and in having families – at the cost of our freedom.

❧

Out of my distress I called on the Lord; the Lord answered me and set me in a broad place.
  Psalm 118.5

And you will know the truth, and the truth will make you free.
  John 8.32

So free we seem, so fettered fast we are!
  Robert Browning, 'Andrea del Sarto'

Anything is free when it spontaneously expresses its own nature to the full in activity.

John Macmurray, *Freedom in the Modern World*

Christianity promises to make men free; it never promises to make them independent.

W.R. Inge, *The Philosophy of Plotinus*

Every man has freedom to do all that he wills, provided he infringes not the equal freedom of any other man.

Herbert Spencer, *Social Statics*

Freedom has always been an expensive thing. History is fit testimony to the fact that freedom is rarely gained without sacrifice and self-denial.

Martin Luther King, in Coretta Scott King, *The Words of Martin Luther King*

The freedom of the heart from all that is other than God is needful if it is to be preoccupied with the love of Him and the direct experience of Him.

Al-Ghazali, *Al-Ghazali, The Mystic*

The hope of the world is still in dedicated minorities. The trailblazers in human, academic, scientific, and religious freedom have always been in the minority.

Martin Luther King, in Coretta Scott King, *The Words of Martin Luther King*

God has laid upon man the duty of being free, of safeguarding freedom of spirit, no matter how difficult that may be, or how much sacrifice and suffering it may require.

Nicolas Berdyaev, *The Fate of Man in the Modern World*

All creation is for [God] a communication of his very being, that is, he can only create free beings. He can only call into existence beings that he calls upon to make themselves.

Louis Lavelle, in Paul Foulquié, *Existentialism*

When freedom is not an inner idea which imparts strength to our activities and breadth to our creations, when it is merely a thing of external circumstance, it is like an open space to one who is blindfolded.

Rabindranath Tagore, *Creative Unity*

If we would have a living thing, we must give that thing some degree of liberty –
even though liberty brings with it risk. If we would debar all liberty and all risk,
then we can have only the mummy and the dead husk of the thing.

Edward Carpenter, *Love's Coming-of-Age*

Men were invited to hear; but none was compelled to listen or to respond. For
that is the law of the New Birth. Initiation is free from constraint, because freedom
is of the essence of the Spirit-begotten life and the faith which accompanies it.

L.S. Thornton CR, *The Common Life in the Body of Christ*

The coming of the Son of God and the Messiah in His power and glory as the
King of the world and as a conqueror would have been the end of the freedom of
the human spirit and the realization of the Kingdom of God by means of necessity
and compulsion.

Nicolas Berdyaev, *Freedom and the Spirit*

The price of freedom for all musicians, both composers and interpreters, is
tremendous control, discipline and patience; but perhaps not only for musicians.
Do we not all find freedom to improvise, in all art, in all life, along the guiding
lines of discipline?

Yehudi Menuhin, *Theme and Variations*

You shall be free indeed when your days are not without a care and your nights
without a want and a grief.

But rather when these things girdle your life and yet you rise above them
named and unbound.

Kahlil Gibran, *The Prophet*

> Yes! To this thought I hold with firm persistence;
> The final word of all that's wise and true:
> He only earns his freedom and existence,
> Who daily conquers them anew.
>
> Johann Wolfgang von Goethe, *Faust*

Be sure that if you offer your freedom to God – whether it is a question of time or
affection or place or anything else – He will take it, He will take it, and you will
no longer be free *in the same way*. But He will give you a far greater liberty
instead. You will be free with the liberty of the children of God.

Hubert van Zeller, *Praying while You Work*

Freedom in Christ is not freedom to do what I like, but freedom to be what I am meant to be. It is freedom from all the chains which hold me back from being my true self. It is freedom from all imposed limitations and external pressures. It is to share in Christ's freedom to do God's will, and then to help others find a similar freedom.

George Appleton, *Journey for a Soul*

It may now be very easily conceived what is human freedom, which I define to be this: it is, namely, a firm reality which our understanding acquires through direct union with God, so that it can bring forth ideas in itself, and effects outside itself, in complete harmony with its nature; without, however, its effects being subjected to any external causes, so as to be capable of being changed or transformed by them.

Benedict Spinoza, *Short Treatise on God, Man, and His Well-Being*

See also Eternal Life, Grace, Joy, Power, Presence

32

FRIENDSHIP

Friendship – the state of being a friend; association of persons as friends; a friendly intimacy, conformity, affinity, correspondence, aptness to unite

Friendship is very important in all stages of life but particularly so with young people. At the beginning of an academic year with a fresh intake there is always a frenetic rush to make new friends. For some undergraduates this is their first time away from home. A few suffer acutely from homesickness and it takes them time to settle down in a new environment. Most experience bouts of loneliness during their three or four years at university. The learning process involves hours and hours of reading on one's own, and this inevitably cuts people off from one another. Stress and strain inevitably take their toll. Friendship is thus extremely important in this situation. In this arena I have found some words of Ralph Waldo Emerson helpful: 'The only way to have a friend is to be one.'

Faithful friends are a sturdy shelter: whoever finds one has found a treasure.
    Ecclesiasticus 6.14

I do not call you servants any longer, because the servant does not know what the master is doing; but I have called you friends, because I have made known to you everything that I have heard from my Father.
    John 15.15

I am wealthy in my friends.
    William Shakespeare, *Timon of Athens*

Be a friend to thy self, and others will be so too.
    Thomas Fuller, *Gnomologia*

A friend may well be reckoned the masterpiece of nature.
   Ralph Waldo Emerson, *Essays*

To be a strong hand in the dark to another in the time of need.
   Hugh Black, *Friendship*

The essence of friendship is entireness, a total magnanimity and trust.
   Ralph Waldo Emerson, *Essays*

Friendship . . . is an union of spirits, a marriage of hearts, and the bond thereof virtue.
   William Penn, *Reflections and Maxims, Relating to, the Conduct of Human Life*

Friendship requires great communication between friends. Otherwise, it can neither be born nor exist.
   St Francis de Sales, *Introduction to the Devout Life*

To experience God's presence in earthly friendship and to be friendliness oneself – that is the dialectic which rules the good man's life.
   Ladislaus Boros, *Hidden God*

Nor do I question for a moment that Affection is responsible for nine-tenths of whatever solid and durable happiness there is in our natural lives.
   C.S. Lewis, *The Four Loves*

A true friend unbosoms freely, advises justly, assists readily, adventures boldly, takes all patiently, defends courageously, and continues a friend unchangeably.
   William Penn, *Reflections and Maxims, Relating to, the Conduct of Human Life*

Fortunate people manage to gather two or three friends on their journey through life. Others speak loosely of having hosts of friends, but what they mean is that they have a lot of pleasant acquaintances.
   Robert Standish, *The Big One Got Away*

That friendship may be at once fond and lasting, there must not only be equal virtue on each part, but virtue of the same kind; not only the same end must be proposed, but the same means must be approved by both.
   Samuel Johnson, *The Rambler*

Like everyone else I feel the need of relations and friendship, of affection, of friendly intercourse, and I am not made of stone or iron, so I cannot miss these things without feeling, as does any other intelligent and honest man, a void and deep need. I tell you this to let you know how much good your visit has done me.

Vincent van Gogh, *Dear Theo: An Autobiography of Vincent van Gogh*

To be honest, to be kind – to earn a little, and to spend a little less, to make upon the whole a family happier for his presence, to renounce when that shall be necessary and not be embittered, to keep a few friends, but these without capitulation – above all, on the same grim condition, to keep friends with himself – here is a task for all that a man has of fortitude and delicacy.

Robert Louis Stevenson, *Across the Plains*

We pine for a friend to whom we can unbosom our thoughts and emotions and we are disappointed. We think only of ourselves in our discontent. Ought we not to think a little of others and allow some small consideration to the possibility of doing good? The friendship which proceeds from unselfishness will be firmer and more intimate than that which is, after all, mere selfishness refined.

Mark Rutherford, *Last Pages from a Journal*

> I dream'd in a dream I saw a city invincible to the attacks
> of the whole of the rest of the earth,
> I dream'd that was the new city of Friends,
> Nothing was greater there than the quality of robust love, it led the rest,
> It was seen every hour in the actions of the men of that city,
> And in all their looks and words.
>
> Walt Whitman, 'I Dream'd in a Dream'

The end of friendship is a commerce the most strict and homely that can be joined; more strict than any of which we have experience. It is for aid and comfort through all the relations and passages of life and death. It is fit for serene days, and graceful gifts, and country rambles, but also for rough road, and hard fare, shipwreck, poverty and persecution. It keeps company with the sallies of the wit and the trances of religion. We are to dignify to each other the daily needs and offices of man's life, and embellish it by courage, wisdom and unity.

Ralph Waldo Emerson, *Essay on Friendship*

The truest kind of friendship is what we call spiritual friendship. We should desire it for its own intrinsic worth and for the way it reaches into the human heart, rather than for any external reason or because it might bring any worldly advantage.

The spiritual friendship that exists between people of integrity springs out of their common attitude to life, their shared moral outlook and the kind of activities they engage in – in other words, it consists of mutual agreement in matters human and divine, combined with goodwill and practical loving concern.

Aelred of Rievaulx, *De spiritu amicitia*

See also Character, Kindness, Relationships, Trust, Understanding

33

FULFILMENT

Fulfilment – develop fully one's gifts and character

This may seem far-fetched but a key to an understanding of fulfilment lies in some words of Etty Hillesum: 'I thank You for the sense of fulfilment I sometimes have; that fulfilment is after all nothing but being filled with You.' This fits in with the vision behind this book. As a consequence of the divine inbreathing in the Genesis story of the creation of humans, and the life of Christ, we are able to find something of this divine life in the depths of our being – Father, Son, Holy Spirit – and the gifts and fruits of the Holy Spirit. Seen from this perspective the parables of the pearl of great price, the treasure buried in a field, and faith as a grain of mustard seed begin to make sense. How then do we develop fully our gifts and character and feel a sense of fulfilment? I have found the practice of reflection helpful. In reflection we draw to the surface something of that rich resource of divine life from the depths of our being. The outcome is an experience of fulfilment.

He died at a good old age, full of days, riches, and honour.
  1 Chronicles 29.28

For this reason I bow my knees before the Father, from whom every family in heaven and on earth takes its name. I pray that, according to the riches of his glory, he may grant that you may be strengthened in your inner being with power through his Spirit, and that Christ may dwell in your hearts through faith, as you are being rooted and grounded in love. I pray that you may have the power to comprehend, with all the saints, what is the breadth and length and height and depth, and to know the love of Christ that surpasses knowledge, so that you may be filled with all the fullness of God.
  Ephesians 3.14–19

None save God can fill the perfect whole.
P.J. Bailey, *Festus*

Happiness lies in the fulfilment of the spirit through the body.
Cyril Connolly, *The Unquiet Grave*

Thou crossest desert lands of barren years to reach the moment of fulfilment.
Rabindranath Tagore, *Stray Birds*

We must make the choices that enable us to fulfil the deepest capacities of our real selves.
Thomas Merton, *No Man Is an Island*

It is by losing himself in the objective, in inquiry, creation and craft, that a man becomes something.
Paul Goodman, *The Community of Scholars*

The moment one is on the side of life 'peace and security' drop out of consciousness. The only peace, the only security, is in fulfilment.
Henry Miller, *The Wisdom of the Heart*

When we rejoice in our fullness, then we can part with our fruits with joy.
Rabindranath Tagore, *Stray Birds*

The truth is that all of us attain the greatest success and happiness possible in this life whenever we use our native capacities to their fullest extent.
Smiley Blanton, *Love or Perish*

Nothing is unthinkable, nothing impossible to the balanced person, provided it arises out of the needs of life and is dedicated to life's furthest developments.
Lewis Mumford, *The Conduct of Life*

To me there is something completely and satisfyingly restful in that stretch of sea and sand, sea and sand and sky – complete peace, complete fulfillment.
Anne Morrow Lindbergh, *Bring Me a Unicorn*

God is good, and He wishes a fulfilment for beings in the universe that they may also enjoy bliss and become Sons – that they may enter into the psychology of the Being who created the World.
A.R. Orage, *On Love*

I think people ought to fulfil sacredly their desires. And this means fulfilling the deepest desire, which is a desire to live unhampered by things which are extraneous, a desire for pure relationships and living truth.

> D.H. Lawrence, *Letter to Catherine Caswell*

In order to reach the deepest levels of relationship to God one has to put imagination to work and to start upon the daring venture of seeking a God who is loving beyond any experience we have and fulfilling in a way that few of us have ever dreamed of.

> Morton T. Kelsey, *The Other Side of Silence*

To be capable of giving and receiving mature love is as sound a criterion as we have for the fulfilled personality. But by that very token it is a goal gained only in proportion to how much one has fulfilled the prior condition of becoming a person in one's own right.

> Rollo May, *Man's Search for Himself*

The greatness of the work of the fulfiller, as compared with the work of the destroyer, is indicated by the faculties and qualities which it requires. Destruction calls for nothing but hatred and vigour. Fulfilment calls for sympathy, intelligence, patience and hope.

> Phillips Brooks, *Twenty Sermons*

As long as anyone believes that his ideal and purpose is outside him, that it is above the clouds, in the past or in the future, he will go outside himself and seek fulfillment where it can not be found. He will look for solutions and answers at every point except the one where they can be found – in himself.

> Erich Fromm, *Man for Himself*

We and God have business with each other; and in opening ourselves to his influence our deepest destiny is fulfilled. The universe, at those parts of which our personal being constitutes, takes a turn genuinely for the worse or for better in proportion as each one of us fulfils or evades God's demands.

> William James, *The Varieties of Religious Experience*

> The social, friendly honest man,
> Whate'er he be,
> 'Tis he, fulfils great Nature's plan,
> And none but *he*.
>
> Robert Burns, 'Second Epistle to J. Lapraik'

Give me fulness of life like to the sea and the sun, to the earth and the air; give me fulness of physical life, mind equal and beyond their fulness; give me a greatness and perfection of soul higher than all things; give me my inexpressible desire which swells in me like a tide – give it to me with all the force of the sea.

My heart has been lifted the higher towards perfection of soul . . . Fulness of physical life ever brings to me a more eager desire of soul-life.

Richard Jefferies, *The Story of My Heart*

See also Blessedness, Ideals, Joy, Love, Wholeness

34

GLORY

Glory – exalted renown, honourable fame; resplendent majesty, beauty, or magnificence, imagined unearthly beauty; state of exaltation, prosperity, etc.; circle of light round head or figure of deity or saint, aureole, halo

I have a firm conviction that the divine glory first and foremost can be found in ourselves. If we want to see this fully worked out in a life, we go to the Gospels – to the person of Jesus Christ. In the Prologue of John's Gospel we find the words: 'And the Word became flesh and lived among us, and we have seen his glory, the glory as of a father's son, full of grace and truth.' Jesus went one stage further and spelt out the implications of this verse in a crucial passage later on in John's Gospel: 'The glory that you have given me I have given them, so that they may be one as we are one, I in them and you in me, that they may become completely one.' In my early twenties I came across someone who had entered into this heritage, and whose features radiated the glory of God. This meeting with glory was to change the whole course of my life.

The heavens are telling the glory of God; and the firmament proclaims his handiwork.

Psalm 19.1

For it is the God who said, 'Let light shine out of darkness', who has shone in our hearts to give the light of the knowledge of the glory of God in the face of Christ. But we have this treasure in clay jars.

2 Corinthians 4.6

God! glory in His goodness.

Henry Ward Beecher, *Proverbs from Plymouth Pulpit*

The glory of God is a living Man (i.e. a man fully alive).

    St Irenaeus, *Five Books of St Irenaeus Against Heresies*

That is what gives Him the greatest glory – the achieving of great things through the weakest and most improbable means.

    Thomas Merton, *The Sign of Jonas*

When one candle is lighted . . . we light many by it, and when God hath kindled the Life of His glory in one man's Heart he often enkindles many by the flame of that.

    Rufus M. Jones, *Spiritual Reformers in the 16th and 17th Centuries*

What is the freedom of the godly man? Being absolutely nothing to and wanting absolutely nothing for himself but only the glory of God in all his works.

    Meister Eckhart, in Franz Pfeiffer, *Meister Eckhart*, translated by C. de B. Evans

To live and work for the glory of God cannot remain an idea about which we think once in a while. It must become an interior, unceasing doxology.

    Henri J.M. Nouwen, *The Way of the Heart*

There is the supreme truth that the glory of God lies in His compassion, and that God never so fully reveals His glory as when He reveals His pity.

    William Barclay, *The Gospel of John*

The glory of love is its unaccountability: it is not something rendered proportionately – such and such an excellence, so much regard for it – but is rather a divine overflow.

    Mark Rutherford, *Last Pages from a Journal*

God does all for his *own* glory, by communicating good out of himself; *not* by looking for anything from his creatures; our duty is not for His sake: our duty is our perfection and happiness.

    Benjamin Whichcote, *Moral and Religious Aphorisms*

Every energetic person wants something they can count as 'glory'. There are those who get it – film stars, famous athletes, military commanders, and even some few politicians, but they are a small minority, and the rest are left to day dreams.

    Bertrand Russell, *Authority and the Individual*

Sound, sound the clarion, fill the fife!
To all the sensual world proclaim,
One crowded hour of glorious life
Is worth an age without a name.

Anon in Sir Walter Scott, *Old Mortality*

It is to God that all glory must be referred. This glory is the end of the Divine work . . . If God adopts us as His children; if He realizes this adoption through the grace of which the plenitude is in His Son Jesus, if He wills to make us partakers in Christ's eternal inheritance, it is for the exaltation of His glory.

D. Columba Marmion, *Christ the Life of the Soul*

The principle that governs the universe 'became flesh and dwelt among us and we beheld His glory', and the impression was as of something that shone through Him from beyond – 'glory as of an Only Begotten Son from a Father'; of One who perfectly represented something and who is perfectly united with it.

William Temple, *Christian Faith and Life*

As we become forgetful of ourselves and entirely filled with His glory, the glory of His righteousness and love, we become transformed into His image . . . from glory to glory and because we are more like Him, we shall do something that is far more truly His will than what we might have planned out for ourselves in an eager and perhaps impatient generosity.

William Temple, *Basic Convictions*

I believe God gives a glory to every period of life. I believe that the people who are wise – the people who live with Him – learn now to take the glory from each succeeding age. If you ask those people – those who have really learned the secret – at any stage of their life, 'What is the most glorious period of their life?' they will always say: 'Now! Now!'

W.E. Sangster, *Westminster Sermons*

To God be the glory. Think how Jesus lived, prayed, worked, suffered, all to the *greater* glory of God. He sought always the Father's glory. His pure ambition was the glory of God and the Kingdom of God. Pre-eminently Jesus could have said: 'to thee, O Father, be the glory for ever and ever: Amen.' 'I seek not mine own glory, but the glory of him that sent me.' All was done to the Father's greater glory.

Eric Symes Abbott, *The Compassion of God and the Passion of Christ*

[132]

A man does not direct all his actions to the glory of God by forming a conception in his mind, or stirring up a strong imagination upon any action, that that must be for the glory of God: it is not thinking of God's glory that is glorifying of Him . . .

We rather glorify God by entertaining the impressions of His glory upon us, than by communicating any kind of glory to Him. Then does a good man become the tabernacle of God, wherein the divine Shechinah does rest, and which the Divine glory fills, when the frame of his mind and life is wholly according to that idea and pattern which he receives from the mount.

John Smith the Platonist, *Select Discourses*

See also Grace, Light, Presence, Saints, Transformation

35

GOD

God – Supreme Being, Creator and Ruler of the universe, often the Lord God, Almighty God, God the Father, Son, Holy Ghost, Persons of the Trinity

I think I have always had an intuitive awareness of God. As a child I was most acutely aware of this while gardening or out at play in the woods and fields. At university I went through a phase where I came to believe all we can know about God is to be found in the person of Jesus Christ. Three books, *A Year of Grace, From Darkness to Light* (both by Victor Gollancz) and *The Choice Is Always Ours* by Dorothy Berkley Phillips, revealed to me something of the breadth and length, and height and depth of God. These books directed my gaze beyond the historical Jesus, to the experiences of God enjoyed by many people down the ages. From there I was encouraged to look within – for the presence of God in my own soul. The penny dropped. The wealth I found is beyond description. To 'know' God we have to experience him in ourselves. Some form of contemplation is crucial.

❧

God said to Moses, 'I AM WHO I AM.'
Exodus 3.14

And I heard a loud voice from the throne saying, 'See, the home of God is among mortals. He will dwell with them; they will be his peoples, and God himself will be with them.'
Revelation 21.3

God isn't a think; He's a feel.
Joyce Grenfell, *In Pleasant Places*

God is not an optional extra, He's an absolute must.
A girl of fourteen

God! Thou art love! I build my faith on that.
    Robert Browning, 'Paracelsus V'

The Divine Essence itself is Love and Wisdom.
    Emanuel Swedenborg, *The Divine Love and Wisdom*

The Father is our ground and origin, in which we begin our being and our life.
    John of Ruysbroeck, *The Adornment of Spiritual Marriage*

[God is] . . . someone present in the quick of being . . . in existence as it exists, in the fibre, in the pulse of the world.
    Dennis Potter, *The Other Side of the Dark*

Our best conceptions, our truest ideals, our highest moods – even these interpret God but imperfectly to us. We see through a glass darkly.
    Henry Ward Beecher, *Proverbs from Plymouth Pulpit*

I will tell you, Scholar, I have heard a grave Divine say, that God has two dwellings; one in heaven, and the other in a meek and thankful heart.
    Izaak Walton, *The Compleat Angler*

. . . there is still a way in which God can be called 'transcendent'. It is not that God is beyond all human experience. It is, rather, that the experience is inexhaustible, that further insight is always possible.
    John S. Dunne, *The Reasons of the Heart*

True Religion never finds itself out of the Infinite Sphere of Divinity and wherever it finds Beauty, Harmony, Goodness, Love, Ingenuity, Wisdom, Holiness, Justice, and the like, it is ready to say: *Here is God*.
    Rufus M. Jones, *Spiritual Reformers in the 16th and 17th Centuries*

I should like to speak of God not only on the borders of life but at its centre, not in weakness but in strength, not, therefore, in man's suffering and death but in his life and prosperity . . . God is the beyond in the midst of life.
    Dietrich Bonhoeffer, *Letters and Papers from Prison*

. . . an inner flooding of the life with a consciousness of God, a rational apprehension of the soul's inherent relation to the Divine, and a transforming discovery of the meaning of life through the revelation in Christ, which sets all one's being athrob with love and wonder.
    Rufus M. Jones, *Spiritual Reformers in the 16th and 17th Centuries*

[135]

... to say that God is Love is to say that God is the living, active, dynamic, cease-lessly desiring reality who will not let go until he has won the free response of his creation – and won this response, not by the employment of methods other than love, but by the indefatigable quality of his loving.

  Norman Pittenger, *Christology Reconsidered*

Every man, though he realizes that he was conceived by a bodily father in his mother's womb, is conscious also that he has within him a spirit that is free, intel-ligent, and independent of the body. That eternal spirit proceeding from the infi-nite, is the origin of all and is what we call God.

  Leo Tolstoy, *A Confession, the Gospel in Brief, and what I Believe*

We know that God is everywhere; but certainly we feel His presence most when His works are on the grandest scale spread before us; and it is the unclouded night-sky, where His worlds wheel their silent course, that we read clearest His infinitude, His omnipotence, His omniscience.

  Charlotte Brontë, *Jane Eyre*

There is something in men which compels them instinctively to rebel against an irrational universe and which will not allow them to conceive of a Divine Being except as One who is the sum total, and much more, of everything they, in their highest moments, feel to be most beautiful and good and true.

  F.C. Happold, *Mysticism*

> A voice is in the wind I do not know;
> A meaning on the face of the high hills,
> Whose utterance I cannot comprehend.
> A something is behind them: that is God.
>   George Macdonald, 'Without and Within'

The Word 'God' is used in most cases as by no means a term of science or exact knowledge, but a term of poetry and eloquence, a term *thrown out*, so to speak, at a not fully grasped object of the speaker's consciousness, a *literary* term, in short; and mankind mean different things by it as their consciousness differs.

  Matthew Arnold, *Literature and Dogma*

We can never know God by seeking to grasp and manipulate him, but only by let-ting him grasp us. We know him not by taking him into our possession (which is absurd) but by letting ourselves be possessed by him, by becoming open to his infinite being which is within us and above us and around us.

  John Macquarrie, *Paths in Spirituality*

As yet, no race has been discovered without some word for what is not-visible, not-finite, not-human, for something super human and divine ... To my mind the historical proof of the existence of God, which is supplied to us by the history of the religions of the world, has never been refuted, and cannot be refuted.

F. Max Muller, *Anthropological Religion*

See also Divinity, Finding God, Holy Spirit, Incarnation, Jesus Christ

36

GOODNESS

Goodness – virtue; positive or comparative excellence; benevolence, kindness, generosity; what is good in a thing, its essence or strength

John's Gospel gives a clue on the nature of 'good' and 'goodness'. In a certain passage Jesus described himself as 'the good shepherd'. The good shepherd was a tough character, carrying a heavy burden of responsibility. He spent endless days in the mountains looking after the village flock. Often this involved sleepless nights, keeping a vigilant eye on the sheep, protecting them from wild animals, thieves and robbers, sometimes laying down his life for the sheep. For Jesus 'good' and 'goodness' were not passive concepts, but meant activity and costly involvement, right in the thick of life. As followers we are expected to live in like manner: 'The good man out of the treasure of his heart produces good.' Perhaps this is another consequence of the divine inbreathing of the Genesis story of the creation of humanity.

God saw everything that he had made, and indeed, it was very good.
Genesis 1.31

I am the good shepherd. The good shepherd lays down his life for the sheep.
John 10.11

Be good yourself, and the world will be good.
Hindu proverb

Nature meant me to be, on the whole, a good man.
Charlotte Brontë, *Jane Eyre*

To be good is to be in harmony with one's self.

Oscar Wilde, *The Picture of Dorian Gray*

Good nature is one of the richest fruits of Christianity.

Henry Ward Beecher, *Proverbs from Plymouth Pulpit*

Goodness is a special kind of truth and beauty. It is truth and beauty in human behaviour.

H.A. Overstreet, *The Enduring Quest*

[Goodness] needeth not to enter into the soul, for it is there already, only it is unperceived.

Theologia Germanica

Goodness is something so simple: always to live for others, never to seek one's own advantage.

Dag Hammarskjöld, *Markings*

> I am larger, better than I thought,
> I did not know I held so much goodness.
>
> Walt Whitman, 'Song of the Open Road'

Loving-kindness is the better part of goodness. It lends grace to the sterner qualities of which this consists.

W. Somerset Maugham, *The Summing Up*

> Look around the Habitable World, how few
> Know their own Good; or knowing it, pursue.
>
> John Dryden, 'The Satires of Juvenal'

Good in a strong many-compounded nature is of slower growth than any other mortal thing, and must not be forced.

George Meredith, *The Ordeal of Richard Feverel*

> Good is no good, but if it be spend:
> God giveth good for none other end.
>
> Edmund Spenser, 'The Shepherd's Calendar: May'

In his love he clothes us, enfolds and embraces us; that tender love completely surrounds us, never to leave us. As I saw it he is everything that is good.

Lady Julian of Norwich, *Revelation of Divine Love*

How God is a true, simple, perfect Good, and how He is a Light and a Reason and all virtues, and how what is highest and best, that is, God, ought to be most loved by us.

    Theologia Germanica

> Good, the more
> Communicated, more abundant grows.
>   John Milton, 'Paradise Lost'

Anyone who proposes to do good must not expect people to roll stones out of his way, but must accept his lot calmly if they even roll a few more upon it.

    Albert Schweitzer, *Out of My Life and Thought*

Goodness as a fruit of the Divine Spirit is raining satisfaction and happiness upon all around us, not studying our own welfare; a fountain out of which all the time flow streams of delight for others.

    Henry Ward Beecher, *Proverbs from Plymouth Pulpit*

There is but one unconditional commandment, which is that we should seek incessantly, with fear and trembling, so to vote and to act as to bring about the very largest total universe of good which we can see.

    William James, *The Will to Believe*

By desiring what is perfectly good, even when we don't quite know what it is and cannot do what we would, we are part of the divine power against evil – widening the skirts of light and making the struggle with darkness narrower.

    George Eliot, *Middlemarch*

But my life now, my whole life, independently of anything that can happen to me, every minute of it is no longer meaningless as it was before, but has a positive meaning of goodness with which I have power to invest it.

    Leo Tolstoy, *Anna Karenina*

Good men are not those who now and then do a good act, but men who join one good act to another. It is men, the whole tendency of whose lives is the production of good things, kind things, right things.

    Henry Ward Beecher, *Proverbs from Plymouth Pulpit*

It should be part of our private ritual to devote a quarter of an hour every day to the concentration of the good qualities of our friends. When we are not *active*, we fall back idly upon defects, even of those whom we most love.

Mark Rutherford, *Last Pages from a Journal*

He [John Smith the Platonist] lived in a continuous enjoyment of God and perpetually drew nearer to the Centre of his soul's rest and always stayed God's time of advancement. His spirit was absorbed in the business and employment of becoming perfect in his art and profession – which was the art *of being a good man*.

Rufus M. Jones, *Spiritual Reformers in the 16th and 17th Centuries*

See also Holiness, Integrity, Kindness, Mystics, Saints

37

GRACE

Grace – unmerited favour of God, divine regenerating, inspiring and strengthening influence, condition (also state of grace) of being so influenced; divinely given talent

Once a year the Gurkhas celebrate a big religious festival called Dashera. On the final night the whole battalion gathers together and there is feasting, singing, dancing, sketches and role playing, throughout the night. At ten o'clock the following morning the battalion's weapons are assembled, and a specially selected Gurkha officer (noted for his strength) beheads a bullock – usually in one stroke of a double-handed kukri. The blood of the bullock is then sprinkled over the weapons – a blessing for the coming year. I arrived at the battalion during Dashera, and was intrigued by this ceremony. I particularly enjoyed watching one of the Gurkha dancers. He was brilliant. His sense of rhythm and timing was perfect, and he made it look so easy. The only word to describe his dancing was *graceful*. I can still see him dancing in my mind's eye, forty years after the event. This is only one manifestation of *grace* and there are many others. I still value the simple definition of grace I learnt as a child – 'God's love in action.' The older I get the more I value God's grace.

❧

The Lord make his face to shine upon you, and be gracious to you.
   Numbers 6.25

From his fullness we have all received, grace upon grace.
   John 1.16

. . . God gives us grace, but leaves it to us to become new creatures.
   Anthony Bloom, *The Essence of Prayer*

God gives His gifts where He finds the vessel empty enough to receive them.
   C.S. Lewis, *Williams and the Arthuriad*

The greater the perfection to which a soul aspires, the more dependent it is upon divine grace.

Brother Lawrence, *The Practice of the Presence of God*

Christian graces are natural faculties which have blossomed under the influence of divine love.

Henry Ward Beecher, *Proverbs from Plymouth Pulpit*

> Grace was in all her steps, Heav'n in her Eye,
> In every gesture dignitie and love.
>
> John Milton, 'Paradise Lost'

. . . he discovered the central significance of the new birth through a creative work of Grace within.

Rufus M. Jones, *Spiritual Reformers in the 16th and 17th Centuries*

And when grace comes and your soul is penetrated by the spirit, you shouldn't pray or exert yourself, but remain passive.

John Osborne, *Luther*

The chief characteristic of the new people of God gathered together by Jesus is their awareness of the boundlessness of God's grace.

Joachim Jeremias, *New Testament Theology*

. . . it clearly seems that man by grace is made like unto God, and a partaker in His divinity, and that without grace he is like unto the brute beasts.

Blaise Pascal, *Pensées*

The power of grace always remains God's power but it becomes operative in man and thus fulfils, sustains, and renews human nature.

Daniel D. Williams, in James F. Childress and John Macquarrie, *A New Dictionary of Christian Ethics*

It is not only through the qualities of native strength that God can work. Quite equally and more conspicuously He can make our weakness the opportunity of His grace.

William Temple, *Readings in St John's Gospel*

Grace is not something other than God, imparted by Him; it is the very Love of God (which is Himself) approaching and seeking entry to the soul of man.

William Temple, *Nature, Man and God*

If you knew how to annihilate self-interest and cast out all affection for the created world, then I would come, and my grace would well up abundantly within you.

Thomas à Kempis, *The Imitation of Christ*

This gift is from God and not of man's deserving. But certainly no one ever receives such a great grace without tremendous labour and burning desire.

Richard of Saint-Victor, *Selected Writings on Contemplation*

Do you know that sentence from a prayer – 'Give us grace to bear both our joys and our sorrows lightly'? It is so perfectly true and brave and sensible, and is often in my mind.

A.C. Benson, *Extracts from the Letters of Dr A.C. Benson to M.E.A.*

Let nobody presume upon his own powers for such exaltation or uplifting of the heart or ascribe it to his own merits. For it is certain that this comes not from human deserving but is a divine gift.

Richard of Saint-Victor, *Selected Writings on Contemplation*

Grace strikes us when we are in great pain and restlessness. It strikes us when we walk through the dark valley of a meaningless and empty life. It strikes us when we feel that our separation is deeper than usual.

Paul Tillich, *The Shaking of the Foundations*

Grace, *charis*, in its Greek religious usage means 'divine gift' or 'favour'. Thus a 'grace' was a quality or power usually bestowed by the gods, a quality that could be exhibited by a mortal. The English word 'graceful' reflects this meaning.

Daniel D. Williams, in James F. Childress and John Macquarrie, *A New Dictionary of Christian Ethics*

O Lord, I need your grace so much if I am to start anything good, or go on with it, or bring it to completion. Without grace, I have no power to do anything – but nothing is beyond my powers, if your grace gives strength to me.

Thomas à Kempis, *The Imitation of Christ*

No one is suddenly endowed with all graces, but when God, the source of all grace, helps and teaches a soul, it can attain this state by sustained spiritual exercises and wisely ordered activity. For without His especial help and inner guidance no soul can reach a state of perfection.

Walter Hilton, *The Ladder of Perfection*

If and when a horror turns up you will then be given Grace to help you. I don't think one is usually given it in advance. 'Give us our daily bread' (not an annuity for life) applies to spiritual gifts too; the little *daily* support for the *daily* trial. Life has to be taken day by day and hour by hour.

C.S. Lewis, *Letters of C.S. Lewis*

By 'grace' we do not mean some magical power of God forcibly intervening in the events of history or in the inner life of man. We mean rather a humble presence. Grace is God's presence and solidarity with his creatures in their strivings. God is not a distant figure presiding in the skies, but one who stands with his creation, to strengthen and encourage whatever is affirmative in it.

John Macquarrie, *The Humility of God*

See also Contemplation, Contentment, Divinity, Freedom, Serenity

38

GREATNESS

Greatness – of remarkable ability, genius, intellectual or practical qualities, loftiness or integrity of character

At school we undertook a study of Napoleon. Recently I came across a record of Napoleon's 'Conversation with General Bertrand at St Helena'. To my delight I discovered Napoleon himself had made some interesting remarks on greatness. He is recorded as having said several great men: 'Alexander, Caesar, Charlemagne and myself founded empires. But on what did we rest the creations of our genius? Upon force. Jesus Christ alone founded his empire upon love; and at this hour, millions of men would die for him.' He added: 'everything in Christ astonishes me. His spirit overawes me, and his will confounds me . . . the nearer I approach, the more carefully I examine, everything is above me; everything remains grand, – of a grandeur which overpowers'. In the life of Jesus we find all the qualities mentioned in the dictionary definition of greatness – remarkable ability, genius, intellectual and practical qualities, and a loftiness or integrity of character. His greatness continues to inspire those of us who worship him.

Look, the Lord our God has shown us his glory and greatness.
  Deuteronomy 5.24

I pray that the God of our Lord Jesus Christ, the Father of glory, may give you a spirit of wisdom and revelation as you come to know him, so that, with the eyes of your heart enlightened, you may know what is the hope to which he has called you, what are the riches of his glorious inheritance among the saints, and what is the immeasurable greatness of his power for us who believe, according to the working of his great power.
  Ephesians 1.17–19

Great Hopes make great Men.
> Thomas Fuller, *Gnomologia*

Great souls care only for what is great.
> Henri Frédéric Amiel, *Amiel's Journal*

It is a rough road that leads to the heights of greatness.
> Seneca, *Epistulae Morales*

Great men are the guide-posts and landmarks in the state.
> Edmund Burke, *Speeches and Letters on American Affairs*

Nothing great or new can be done without enthusiasm.
> Dr Harvey Cushing, in *Dialogues of Alfred North Whitehead*

All great gifts are one-sided and pretty well exclude the others.
> Theodor Haecker, *Journal in the Night*

There is never any easy way to greatness; greatness is always the product of toil.
> William Barclay, *The Gospel of Matthew*

[Jesus] was clear that He had come 'not to make life easy, but to make men great'.
> William Barclay, *The Gospel of Matthew*

No great man lives in vain. The History of the world is but the Biography of great men.
> Thomas Carlyle, *Sartor Resartus*

Some are born great, some achieve greatness,
And some have greatness thrust upon 'em.
> William Shakespeare, *Twelfth Night*

There is a great man who makes every man feel small. But the real great man is the man who makes every man feel great.
> G.K. Chesterton, *Charles Dickens*

Very rarely something may emerge complete and perfect in a flash, but far oftener greatness is the result of long labour and constant attention to detail.
> William Barclay, *The Gospel of Matthew*

Great truths are portions of the soul of man;
Great souls are portions of Eternity.
J.R. Lowell, 'Sonnet No. 6'

Man's Unhappiness, as I construe, comes of his Greatness; it is because there is an Infinite in him, which with all his cunning he cannot quite bury under the Finite.
Thomas Carlyle, *Sartor Resartus*

Greatness after all, in spite of its name, appears to be not so much a certain size as a certain quality in human lives. It may be present in lives whose range is very small.
Phillips Brooks, *Sermons*

And I smiled to think God's greatness flowed around our incompleteness, –
Round our restlessness, His rest.
E.B. Browning, 'Rhyme of the Duchess May'

Greatness is a spiritual condition worthy to excite love, interest, and admiration and the outward proof of possessing greatness is that we excite love, interest, and admiration.
Matthew Arnold, *Sweetness and Light*

If a man is great in the spiritual elements, he is great everywhere else; but if he is small there, he is small everywhere else. Not animalhood, but manhood, must be measured.
Henry Ward Beecher, *Proverbs from Plymouth Pulpit*

Great men are the true men, the men in whom Nature has succeeded. They are not extraordinary – they are in the true order. It is the other species of men who are not what they ought to be.
Henri Frédéric Amiel, *Amiel's Journal*

All things that we see standing accomplished in the world are properly the outer material result, the practical realization and embodiment, of Thoughts that dwelt in the Great Men sent into the world.
Thomas Carlyle, *Sartor Resartus*

The heights by great men reached and kept
Were not attained by sudden flight,
But they, while their companions slept,
Were toiling upward in the night.
    Henry Wadsworth Longfellow, 'The Ladder of St Augustine'

See also Courage, Inspiration, Integrity, Jesus Christ, Saints

39

GRIEF

Grief – deep or violent sorrow caused by loss or trouble; keen or bitter regret or remorse

As a college chaplain I have come across a special form of grief, caused by the untimely death of young people. This leaves me feeling deeply upset and sorrowful. Sometimes I feel guilty and regret not having cared enough for that person when alive. Often I experience a sense of injustice, and feel angry the young person in question never had a chance to find fulfilment in life. I also experience feelings of inadequacy in dealing with grief-stricken parents. Keeping busy and occupied helps us cope with grief, provided we don't overdo it. Talking about feelings with relatives and friends acts as a valuable safety-valve. A good aid is a Cruse publication entitled *All in the End Is Harvest*, edited by Agnes Whitaker. This book contains experiences of those who have known grief at first hand, and helps us in our time of sorrow. (Cruse is a national organization for the bereaved and their children.)

Be gracious to me, O Lord, for I am in distress; my eye wastes away from grief, my soul and body also.
   Psalm 31.9

Blessed are those who mourn, for they will be comforted.
   Matthew 5.4

Grief is itself a med'cine.
   William Cowper, 'Charity'

See how Time makes all griefs decay.
   Adelaide Anne Proctor, *Life in Death and Death in Life*

To weep is to make less the depth of grief.
   William Shakespeare, *King Henry VI*

Time and thinking tame the strongest grief.
   English proverb

Those who have known real grief seldom seem sad.
   Benjamin Disraeli, *Endymion*

For grief once told brings somewhat back of peace.
   William Morris, 'Prologue, The Wanderers'

In mourning let grief suffice as its highest expression.
   Confucius, *The Analects of Confucius*

Someone has called bereavement 'loving in a new key'.
   J. Neville Ward, *Friday Afternoon*

Every man is a solitary in his griefs. One soon finds that out.
   Norman Douglas, *An Almanac*

Passionate grief does not link us with the dead but cuts us off from them.
   C.S. Lewis, *A Grief Observed*

In the great complication or grief, only the saint can 'see life steadily and see it whole'.
   J. Neville Ward, *Friday Afternoon*

It is dangerous to abandon oneself to the luxury of grief; it deprives one of courage, and even the wish for recovery.
   Henri Frédéric Amiel, *Amiel's Journal*

You cannot prevent the birds of sorrow from flying over your head, but you can prevent them from building nests in your hair.
   Chinese proverb

When we lose one we love, our bitterest tears are called forth by the memory of hours when we loved not enough.
   Maurice Maeterlinck, *Wisdom and Destiny*

Grief is near-sighted, and holds its trouble close up; but love is long-sighted, and looks at them in all points of view.

    Henry Ward Beecher, *Proverbs from Plymouth Pulpit*

One must go on living, in spite of anything tragic that may happen – and it's useless to break one's heart over troubles.

    A.C. Benson, *Extracts from the Letters of Dr A.C. Benson to M.E.A*

To spare oneself from grief at all cost can be achieved only at the price of total detachment, which excludes the ability to experience happiness.

    Erich Fromm, *Man for Himself*

I value sympathy in bereavement, because it seems – I won't say to *replace* the affection taken away, but to remind one that love is still there.

    A.C. Benson, *Extracts from the Letters of Dr A.C. Benson to M.E.A*

> No bond
> In closer union knits two human hearts
> Than fellowship in grief.
>
>   Robert Southey, *Joan of Arc and Minor Poems*

Grief is beautiful, as in winter ice-clad trees are beautiful when the sun shines upon them, but it is dangerous. Ice breaks many a branch, and so many persons are bowed down and crushed by their afflictions.

    Henry Ward Beecher, *Proverbs from Plymouth Pulpit*

Do you imagine that it is in a fit of absent-mindedness that God has afflicted you? We have so much to learn, and grief must be our master. It is only through suffering that we can hope to come to self-knowledge.

    Mary Craig, *Blessings*

> But grief should be the instructor of the wise;
> Sorrow is knowledge: they who know the most
> Must mourn the deepest.
>
>   Lord Byron, *Manfred*

The thought of death leaves me perfectly calm for I am fully convinced that our spirit is absolutely indestructible: it is something that works on from eternity to eternity, it is like the sun which only seems to sink judged by our earthly eyes and in reality never sinks at all but shines without ceasing.

    Johann Wolfgang von Goethe, *To Eckermann*

People often say, 'My mother was such a good woman: why should she have suffered?' or 'My boy was such a fine boy: why should he have died?' It is a very natural thing to say, but when we find ourselves saying it we should look at Jesus crowned with thorns, holiest of all, loveliest of all, and yet suffering more than all. His whole life, as He lived it amongst the people of His time, was a beauty and a glory, a flame of love passing by, and yet He was crucified.

Father Andrew SDC, *A Gift of Light*

See also Compassion, Cross, Death, Depression, Suffering

40

GROWING

Growth – increasing in size, height, quality, degree, power etc., advancing to maturity, reaching full size

When I was being prepared for confirmation at the age of sixteen, the school chaplain told us our main aim in life was 'to glorify God and enjoy him for ever'. This did not mean much to me at the time. God was somehow put over as being 'out there' miles away beyond the clouds. 'Glorifying God' suggested an attitude of worship, with hands upraised towards the heavens. I was somehow meant to enjoy this for ever, but I was unable to enjoy it at all.

Years later I was trying to work out what our main aim in life is, in a practical and realistic way. I remember looking at a flower, observing it carefully, and suddenly realizing that if it unfolded, blossomed, bloomed, flourished and then died, nobody would be particularly upset because it had achieved in what it set out to do. It had actually succeeded in growing to its highest level of development and expression. I wondered if there was a lesson here for human life. Could it be that our main aim in life is to grow a soul (a character or a personality) which is us at our highest level of development and expression – so that we become most truly and fully ourselves? But do not most of us get stunted in our growing and never reach our wholeness?

⁓

Happy are those whose strength is in you . . . They go from strength to strength.
  Psalm 84.5, 7

The kingdom of heaven is like a mustard seed that someone took and sowed in his field; it is the smallest of all the seeds, but when it has grown it is the greatest of shrubs and becomes a tree.
  Matthew 13.31–32

Big oaks from little acorns grow.
  Anon

Why stay we on the earth unless to grow?
>   Robert Browning, 'Cleon'

If only I may grow: firmer, simpler – quieter, warmer.
>   Dag Hammarskjöld, *Markings*

No life is spoiled but one whose growth is arrested.
>   Oscar Wilde, *The Picture of Dorian Gray*

Men never grow up into manhood as an acorn grows into an oak-tree. Men come to it by re-birth in every faculty, again, and again, and again.
>   Henry Ward Beecher, *Proverbs from Plymouth Pulpit*

> All growth that is not towards God
> Is growing to decay.
>> George Macdonald, 'Within and Without'

Only love enables humanity to grow, because love engenders life and it is the only form of energy that lasts forever.
>   Michel Quoist, *With Open Heart*

There is in the universe a provision by which men are helped by the Divine Spirit. God inspires us to the Christian life, and helps to the development of its graces.
>   Henry Ward Beecher, *Proverbs from Plymouth Pulpit*

There is little hope for us until we become tough-minded enough to break loose from the shackles of prejudice, half-truths, and downright ignorance.
>   Martin Luther King, in Coretta Scott King, *The Words of Martin Luther King*

To regret one's own experience is to arrest one's own development. To deny one's own experience is to put a lie into the lips of one's own life. It is no less than a denial of the soul.
>   Oscar Wilde, *De Profundis*

I never allow principles to carry me far enough. I do not think that in this I am peculiar. I notice that in the gardens of most men are nothing but arrested buds. How rare it is to see the fully developed flower!
>   Mark Rutherford, *Last Pages from a Journal*

If your roots are firmly planted, be sure you know what you're doing before pulling them up and moving on. A plant always suffers when transplanted; it needs time to grow more roots and time to develop before it can bear any fruit.

Michel Quoist, *With Open Heart*

A child-like man is not a man whose development has been arrested; on the contrary, he is a man who has given himself a chance of continuing to develop long after most adults have muffled themselves in the cocoon of middle-aged habit and convention.

Aldous Huxley, *Music at Night*

Omnipotence as a divine attribute comes to meaning in organic growth. The tree does not develop first at this point, and then at the other. *All over* it proceeds to perfection. So should the growth of character be, and so it is when it is divinely prompted.

Mark Rutherford, *Last Pages from a Journal*

. . . we need some means by which in time the Eternal grows real, the invisible shines through the seen, God becomes a speaking Presence, conscience is quickened, resources are deepened and hope is renewed, until one hears the trumpets of the soul again and is adequate for life!

Harry Emerson Fosdick, *Successful Christian Living*

To grow is to emerge gradually from a land where our vision is limited, where we are seeking and governed by egotistical pleasure, by our sympathies and antipathies, to a land of unlimited horizons and universal love, where we will be open to every person and desire their happiness.

Jean Vanier, *Community and Growth*

I would finally just like to advise you to grow through your development quietly and seriously; you can interrupt it in no more violent manner than by looking outwards, and expecting answer from outside to questions which perhaps only your innermost feeling in your most silent hour can answer.

Rainer Maria Rilke, *Letters to a Young Poet*

The hope is not in our own efforts to love. It is not in psychoanalysis which tries to throw light on the knots and blocks of our life, nor in a more equitable reorganization of the political and economic structures which have their effects on our personal lives. All this is perhaps necessary. But true growth comes from God, when we cry to him from the depths of the abyss to let his Spirit penetrate us. Growth in love is a growth in the Spirit. The stages through which we must pass in order to grow in love are the stages through which we must pass to become more totally united to God.

Jean Vanier, *Community and Growth*

See also Contemplation, Holy Spirit, Ideals, Meditation, Transformation

4 1

GUIDANCE

Guidance – guiding, being guided, advice on problems

I was greatly helped on guidance by Edward Wilson, the doctor on Scott's expedition to the Antarctic. In George Seaver's book, *Edward Wilson of the Antarctic*, the biographer describes how Wilson kept a journal. His practice was to go through the Gospels over a period of years. Often the meaning was obvious, but when this was not so, he would work out his own interpretations and record these in his 'spiritual diary'. Over the years he was conscious of being guided. This practice appealed to me so I started keeping a journal. Following Edward Wilson, I began with the Gospels, and later moved on to the material in this compilation. What evolved was a listening form of prayer out of which came guidance. The rationale is that if God is within us, he might want to guide us. So I look carefully at the material and listen, with a pen in my hand, recording what is presented to me in the journal. Sometimes we need to be reminded that counsel (guidance) is one of the gifts of the Holy Spirit.

I will put my law within them, and I will write it on their hearts; and I will be their God, and they shall be my people.

Jeremiah 31.33

If you love me, you will keep my commandments. And I will ask the Father, and he will give you another Advocate, to be with you for ever. This is the Spirit of truth, whom the world cannot receive, because it neither sees him nor knows him. You know him, because he abides with you, and he will be in you.

John 14.15–17

Let me think that there is one among those stars that guides my life through the dark unknown.

Rabindranath Tagore, *Stray Birds*

We are not meant to live solely by intellectual convictions, we are meant more and more to open ourselves to the Spirit.

Basil Hume OSB, *Searching for God*

> God shall be my hope,
> My stay, my guide, and lantern to my feet.
>
> William Shakespeare, *King Henry VI*

There is a spirit that works within us, and develops a power in us that teaches us how to accomplish what we will, and guides us by its inspiration to successful results.

Henry Ward Beecher, *Proverbs from Plymouth Pulpit*

Guidance does not end when calamity begins. In every situation He meets us and out of every situation He can lead us to a greener pasture and a sphere of wider use.

W.E. Sangster, *God Does Guide Us*

> From thee, great God, we spring, to thee we tend,
> Path, motive, guide, original and end.
>
> Samuel Johnson, Motto for *The Rambler*

I don't think some decisions are made by the reasoning faculties, but by some instinct. One *knows* what one can do and what one cannot do, when the time arrives.

A.C. Benson, *Extracts from the Letters of Dr A.C. Benson to M.E.A.*

For a time will come when your innermost voice will speak to you, saying: 'This is *my* path; here I shall find peace. I will pursue this path, come what may.'

Grace Cooke, *Spiritual Unfoldment*

God is not a Person of caprice. If we can venture at all on belief in His detailed guidance, we can believe also that the conditions of our life are known to Him, and that He will direct us in such circumstances as we find ourselves.

W.E. Sangster, *God Does Guide Us*

> And I will place within them as a guide,
> My umpire *Conscience*, who if they will hear,
> Light after light well us'd they shall attain,
> And to the end persisting, safe arrive.
>
> John Milton, 'Paradise Lost'

We do not need to be very old to look back on life and see that things that we thought were disasters worked out to our good; things that we thought were disappointments worked out to greater blessings. We can look back, and we can see a guiding and a directing hand in it and through it all.

William Barclay, *The Letter to the Romans*

If I am to learn to want what God wants, the way to do it is not to disown the inmost desires of my heart, but rather deliberately to spread them out before God – to face with all the honesty I can achieve the real truth about my desires, to wrestle with the sham of professing desires which are not really mine, and *then* to pray.

John Burnaby, in A.R. Vidler, *Soundings*

> I give you the end of a golden string:
> Only wind it into a ball,
> It will lead you in at Heaven's Gate
> Built in Jerusalem's wall.
>
> William Blake, *Epigrams, Verses, and Fragments for the Note Book*

Over and over again it will happen that if a man, having thought out such a problem to the best of his ability, will then lay the whole matter in the hands of God, and genuinely desire that God's Will shall be done in his life and not his own, he will become perfectly clear what that will is. Over and over again that happens.

William Temple, *Christian Faith and Life*

It is the chief object of prayer and of a seclusion of heart from outward things, that we should be brought to attend to the guidance of this tender Guide, and be wholly in His power, and according to His will. No human plans or forms can help in this matter – they only hinder. The soul must be as the clay – formless and passive in the hand of the potter. This Hand of love forms us according to His own heart.

Gerhard Tersteegen, in Frances Bevan, *Sketches of the Great in the Land*

Jesus promised that his Spirit would guide his disciples into all truth, both truth of mind and direction of life. There can be no hesitation in the choice between what is good and what is evil, what is loving and what is selfish, what is true and what is false. Sometimes, however, the choice is between two goods or between two paths neither of which is completely good. How do we seek the Spirit's guidance?

George Appleton, *Journey for a Soul*

I have nothing to say at the finish except that if one wants a permanent rock in life and goes deep enough for it, it is difficult for historical events to shake it. There are times when we can never meet the future with sufficient elasticity of mind, especially if we are locked in the contemporary systems of thought. We can do worse than remember a principle which both gives us a firm Rock and leaves us with the maximum elasticity for our minds: the principle: Hold to Christ, and for the rest remain totally uncommitted.

Herbert Butterfield, *Christianity and History*

See also Holy Spirit, Listening, Obedience, Prayer, Thinking

42

HAPPINESS

Happiness – (of person or circumstance) lucky, fortunate, contented with one's lot

When I was young, the one thing I wanted out of life was happiness. At school, happiness came by way of achievement, getting through exams, involvement in sport, and friendships. In National Service, happiness came through a sense of adventure, an involvement with the Gurkhas, and travel. There was the long sea voyage in the troopship the *Empire Fowey* via Gibraltar, the Suez Canal, Aden (now South Yemen), Ceylon (Sri Lanka), and finally Singapore. This led to new experiences in Malaya (Malaysia), Hong Kong and Sarawak. At university, happiness came primarily through being in Oxford with many opportunities for learning, sport and friendship. I began to realize how lucky and fortunate I had been so far in life. I then did a lot of thinking about the future. I was not going to pursue happiness as an end in itself, but fulfilment. There have been many ups and downs working as a priest but also precious moments of happiness and fulfilment.

❧

Happy is everyone who fears the Lord, who walk in his ways. You shall eat the fruit of the labour of your hands; you shall be happy, and it shall go well with you.
   Psalm 128.1–2

Happiness lies more in giving than in receiving.
   Acts 20.35 (NEB)

There is no duty we so much underrate as the duty of being happy.
   Robert Louis Stevenson, *Virginibus Puerisque*

The happy person is he who is striving to actualize his potentialities.
   A.R. Orage, *On Love*

Happiness is more than anything that serene, secure, happy freedom from guilt.

　Henrik Ibsen, *Rosmersholm*

Happiness is neither without us nor within us. It is in God, both without us and within us.

　Blaise Pascal, *Pensées*

Happiness . . . must be something solid and permanent, without fear and without uncertainty.

　Samuel Johnson, *The History of Rasselas*

In every part and corner of our life, to lose oneself is to be gainer; to forget oneself is to be happy.

　Robert Louis Stevenson, *Memories and Portraits*

Look inwards, for you have a lasting fountain of happiness at home that will always bubble up if you will but dig for it.

　Marcus Aurelius, *The Meditations of Marcus Aurelius*

The happy people are those who are producing something; the bored people are those who are consuming much and producing nothing.

　W.R. Inge, in Sir James Marchant, *The Wit and Wisdom of Dean Inge*

We are to give our heart to God that he may make it happy, with a happiness which stretches its capacity to the full.

　Gordon S. Wakefield, in *A Dictionary of Christian Spirituality*

The largest proportion of the happiness experienced among men on earth has been derived from social relationships.

　Henry Ward Beecher, *Proverbs from Plymouth Pulpit*

I have come to know happy individuals, by the way, who are happy only because they are whole. Even the lowliest, provided he is whole, can be happy and in his own way perfect.

　Johann Wolfgang von Goethe, *Wisdom and Experience*

. . . there is a secret belief amongst some men that God is displeased with man's happiness; and in consequence they slink about creation, ashamed and afraid to enjoy themselves.

　Arthur Helps, *Companions of My Solitude*

If you will be true to the best of yourself, fearing and desiring nothing, but living up to your nature, standing boldly by the truth of your word, and satisfied therewith, then you will be a happy man.

Marcus Aurelius, *The Meditations of Marcus Aurelius*

There is certainly no greater happiness, than to be able to look back on a life usefully and virtuously employed, to trace our own progress in existence, by such tokens as excite neither shame nor sorrow.

Samuel Johnson, *The Rambler*

The monastery is a school – a school in which we learn from God how to be happy. Our happiness consists in sharing the happiness of God, the perfection of His unlimited freedom, the perfection of His love.

Thomas Merton, *Elected Silence*

A loving heart, a genuine sympathy, a pure, unadulterated taste, a life that is not scorched by dissipation or wasted by untimely hours, a good, sound body and a clear conscience, ought to make any man happy.

Henry Ward Beecher, *Proverbs from Plymouth Pulpit*

It is not our level of prosperity that makes for happiness but the kinship of heart to heart and the way we look at the world. Both attitudes lie within our power, so that a man is happy so long as he chooses to be happy and no one can stop him.

Alexander Solzhenitsyn, *Cancer Ward*

And happiness . . . what is it? I say it is neither virtue nor pleasure nor this thing nor that, but simply *growth*. We are happy when we are growing. It is this primal law of all nature and the universe, and literature and art are the cosmic movements in the conscious mind.

J.B. Yeats, *Letters to His Son, W.B. Yeats and Others*

If we were to ask the question: 'What is human life's chief concern?' one of the answers we should receive would be: 'It is happiness.' How to gain, how to keep, how to recover happiness, is in fact for most men at all times the secret motive of all they do, and of all they are willing to endure.

William James, *The Varieties of Religious Experience*

Is not making others happy the best happiness? To illuminate for an instant the depths of a deep soul . . . is to me a blessing and a precious privilege. There is a sort of religious joy in helping to renew the strength and courage of noble minds. We are surprised to find ourselves the possessors of a power of which we are not worthy, and we long to exercise it purely and seriously.

Henri Frédéric Amiel, *Amiel's Journal*

When I looked outside right into the depth of nature and God, then I was happy, really happy . . . so long as I have that happiness here, the joy in nature, health and a lot more besides, all the while one has that, one can always recapture happiness.

Riches can all be lost, but that happiness in your own heart can only be veiled, and it will still bring you happiness again, as long as you live. As long as you can look fearlessly up into the heavens, as long as you know that you are pure within and that you will still find happiness.

Anne Frank, *The Diary of Anne Frank*

See also Blessedness, Cheerfulness, Contentment, Fulfilment, Joy

43

HEALING

Healing – restoring (person, wound), to health, cure (person of disease); (of wound) become sound or whole; health-giving; conducive to moral or spiritual welfare

An experience of 'healing' affected me greatly. It occurred in a hospital in Bradford, West Yorkshire, while visiting as a part-time hospital chaplain. I knocked on the door of a single room and got a rather feeble 'come in'. I found 'Douglas' in an extremely weak condition. He had just undergone major surgery, in which his bowels had been removed, and a catheter fitted. He was in pain and weary, and just wanted to die. The meeting was short. He asked me: 'Do you believe in faith healing?' I told him I did when I felt the circumstances were right. 'Could you please lay hands on me and pray?' I did so, and then took my leave as he was in such a weak condition. The next day he seemed a little stronger and we had a five minute conversation ending with the laying on of hands. I saw him regularly during the next few weeks, and he made a remarkable recovery. On my last visit he said: 'Do you realize you've got the gift of healing in your hands? Whenever you lay hands on my head and pray it is as if an electric shock goes right through my body. I'm convinced it has played a major part in healing me.' From time to time we need to be reminded that Jesus 'healed' people, and still does so, through others gifted in this way.

❧

. . . for I am the Lord who heals you.
> Exodus 15.26

Jesus went throughout Galilee, teaching in their synagogues and proclaiming the good news of the kingdom and curing every disease and every sickness among the people.
> Matthew 4.23

Stress has replaced disease as the problem of the day.
> GP in Birmingham, in *Faith in the City*

HEALING

The crickets sing, and man's o'er-labour'd sense
Repairs itself by rest.
　　William Shakespeare, *Cymboline*

God is Himself a vast medicine for man. It is the heart of God that carries restoration, inspiration, aspiration, and final victory.
　　Henry Ward Beecher, *Proverbs from Plymouth Pulpit*

A bodily disease, which we look upon as whole and entire within itself, may, after all, be but a symptom of some ailment in the spiritual part.
　　Nathaniel Hawthorne, *The Scarlet Letter*

. . . it remains eternally true that we can never be right physically until we are right spiritually, that health in body and peace with God go hand in hand.
　　William Barclay, *The Gospel of Matthew*

Psychosomatic illnesses are illnesses of the soul transmitted to the body; a sick spirit and a healthy body inevitably come into conflict and finally break down.
　　Michel Quoist, *With Open Heart*

There is a healing curative nature forever outworking from the Divine Mind upon ours, although we may not co-operate voluntarily upon His will.
　　Henry Ward Beecher, *Proverbs from Plymouth Pulpit*

The exercise of prayer, in those who habitually exert it, must be regarded by us doctors as the most adequate and normal of all the pacifiers of the mind and calmers of the nerves.
　　William James, *On Faith and Morals*

It is the infinite, overflowing, swelling impulse of the Divine nature to cure souls of their diseases; to augment that which is good in them; to develop them; to equip them; to perfect them.
　　Henry Ward Beecher, *Proverbs from Plymouth Pulpit*

Look to your health: and if you have it, praise God, and value it next to a good conscience; for health is the second blessing that we mortals are capable of; a blessing that money cannot buy; and therefore value it, and be thankful for it.
　　Izaak Walton, *The Compleat Angler*

The basic idea of inner healing is simply this: that Jesus, who is the same yesterday, today, and forever, can take the memories of our past and (1) *Heal* them from the wounds that still remain and affect our present lives; and (2) *Fill* with his love all these places in us that have been empty for so long, once they have been healed and drained of the poison of past hurts and resentment.

    Francis MacNutt, *Healing*

I find great occasion for alarm in very much of that modern practice of psychotherapy from which no doubt we are also going to gain great benefits. But in some of this practice there is a strong suggestion that all we have to do is somehow to become at peace with ourselves, to restore an internal harmony, to become, as they like to say, fully integrated. And I want to ask, about what centre? – with what manner of self is my whole being to be harmonized?

    William Temple, *The Preacher's Theme Today*

    I am not a mechanism, an assembly of various sections.
    And it is not because the mechanism is working wrongly, that I am ill.
    I am ill because of wounds to the soul, to the deeper emotional self
    and the wounds to the soul take a long, long time, only time can help
    and patience, and a certain difficult repentance
    long, difficult repentance, realization of life's mistake, and freeing oneself
    from the endless repetition of the mistake
    which mankind at large has chosen to sanctify.

      D.H. Lawrence, 'Healing'

The paralysed man (Mark 2.1–12) could not get free from a feeling of guilt and was healed by the word of forgiveness. The paralysed man at the Sheep Gate (John 5.2–9) was asked 'Do you want to be healed?' inferring that he preferred to escape from the responsibilities of daily life. The man who called himself Legion (Mark 5.1–20) had his many divisions unified in the acceptance of Christ's authority and encouragement. Many of our troubles are spiritual and will not be healed by treating the physical symptoms but only by tackling the spiritual causes – fear of failure, fear of ridicule, anxiety, frustrated irritation, escapism, inner division, feelings of guilt for which we are not humble enough or wise enough to accept God's forgiveness.

    George Appleton, *Journey for a Soul*

Let us open ourselves to the healing, forgiving Spirit of Jesus. Let us open up all the pains of the past, the wounds that came from the moment of conception –

wanted or unwanted – and from the months we were carried in our mother's womb; the wounds from our early childhood when we felt rejected or stifled, unloved in our being and unrecognized in our gifts; the wounds coming from all the failures of the past; our incapacity to love and give life, the people we have hurt because of our sinfulness, pride or fears, and the barriers we have built around our vulnerability.

Let us allow the healing, forgiving Spirit of Jesus to penetrate our whole being, and lead us to wholeness. Then will rise from that very darkness a new understanding of others.

Jean Vanier, *The Broken Body*

See also Acceptance, Grace, Holiness, Salvation, Wholeness

44

HOLINESS

Holiness – consecrated, sacred; belonging to, commissioned by, devoted to, God; of high moral excellence

One of my earliest childhood memories was being taken to a church by my godmother. It must have been just before Christmas, for we went off to see the baby Jesus in the crib. I remember it was dark inside the church and she hushed me to be quiet. In a spirit of awe and reverence we peeped into the manger. A light shone on the baby Jesus. There was a quiet atmosphere of holiness about the whole scene. It made a deep impression on me. Years later I remember the same feeling of holiness listening to a sermon, preached by a bishop. I can't remember a word he said now, but I can remember his face. It was radiant and energetic. There was something sacred permeating his being. I was never argued into accepting the Christian faith but I was won over by the sight of holiness.

Worship the Lord in holy splendour.
    1 Chronicles 16.29

. . . and be renewed in the spirit of your minds, and clothe yourselves with the new self, created according to the likeness of God in true righteousness and holiness.
    Ephesians 4.23–24

There is no true Holiness, without Humility
    Thomas Fuller, *Gnomologia*

Real holiness has a fragrance about it which is its own advertisement.
    Father Andrew SDC, *The Way of Victory*

There is nothing holier, in this life of ours, than the first consciousness of love, – the first fluttering of its silken wings.
    Henry Wadsworth Longfellow, 'Hyperion'

That the Inward man by the Light of Grace, through possession and practice of a holy life, is to be acknowledged and live in us.

Rufus M. Jones, *Spiritual Reformers in the 16ᵗʰ and 17ᵗʰ Centuries*

A true love to God must begin with a delight in his holiness, and not with a delight in any other attribute: for no other attribute is truly lovely without this.

Jonathan Edwards, *A Treatise Concerning Religious Affections*

Let the remembrance of all the glory wherein I was created make me more serious and humble, more deep and penitent, more pure and holy before Thee.

Thomas Traherne, *Centuries*

Holiness means living within the divine perspective. It comes from attention to God – on your knees in prayer; and it comes from obedience to God – on your feet in action.

Hugh Montefiore, *Sermons from Great St Mary's*

Jesus wants us to be holy as his Father is. We can become very great saints if we only want to. Holiness in not the luxury of the few, but a simple duty for you and for me.

Mother Teresa, in Brother Angelo Devanando, *Jesus, the Word to Be Spoken*

> We cannot reach our Saviour's puritie,
> Yet are we bid, *Be holy e'en as He.*
> In both let's do our best.
>
> George Herbert, 'Lent'

No one can resist the argument of holiness, brought in a personified form before him, in its gentleness, in its sweetness, in its aspiration, in its love, in all its blossoms and fruits of peace and joy.

Henry Ward Beecher, *Proverbs from Plymouth Pulpit*

Holiness . . . in men, is their dei-formity; likeness to God in goodness, righteousness, and truth. Such real holiness sanctifies the subject by its presence: and where that is, the person is made pure, good, righteous.

Benjamin Whichcote, *Moral and Religious Aphorisms*

The way of holiness was by the gift of the Holy Spirit, and the common use of the word 'saint' waited on the outpouring of the Spirit. The outpouring of the Spirit was the Birthday of the Christian Church.

W.E. Sangster, *The Pure in Heart*

The measure of your holiness is proportionate to the goodness of your will. Consider then how good your will is, and the degree of your holiness will be clear to you. For every one is as holy, as he is good of heart.

John of Ruysbroeck, *The Seven Steps of the Ladder of Spiritual Love*

Holiness is the goal of every Christian. 'Holy' means 'set apart for God'. A holy person is not gloomy and unnatural, but 'whole' and therefore happy. That is why holiness, whenever we see it in others, is always attractive.

Hugh Montefiore, *Confirmation Notebook*

He that sees the beauty of holiness, or true moral good, sees the greatest and most important thing in the world, which is the fulness of all things, without which all the world is empty . . . Unless this is seen, nothing is seen that is worth the seeing; for there is no other true excellency or beauty.

Jonathan Edwards, *A Treatise Concerning Religious Affections*

It doesn't matter, he is holy, his heart contains the secret of a renewal for all, the power which will finally establish truth on earth, and all will be holy, and will love each other, and there will be no more rich nor poor, exalted nor humbled, but all men will be as the children of God and the real kingdom of Christ will come.

Fyodor Dostoyevsky, *The Brothers Karamazov*

All human love is a holy thing, the holiest thing in our experience. It is the chief mode of initiation into the mysteries of the divine life, the most direct point of contact with the nature of the Creator. 'He prayeth best who loveth best.' Pure affection 'abides' in a sense in which nothing else abides. It is rooted in the eternal, and cannot be destroyed by any of the changes and chances of mortal life.

W.R. Inge, *Speculum Animae*

It is not to the clever folk, nor even to the scientific folk, that the empire over souls belongs, but to those who impress us as having conquered nature by grace, as having passed through the burning bush, and as speaking, not the language of human wisdom, but that of the divine will. In religious matters it is holiness which gives authority; it is love, or the power of devotion and sacrifice, which goes to the heart, which moves and persuades.

Henri Frédéric Amiel, *Amiel's Journal*

See also Beauty, Blessedness, Healing, Saints, Wholeness

45

HOLY SPIRIT

Holy Spirit – third Person of the Trinity, God as spiritually active, sevenfold gift of the Spirit: counsel, wisdom, understanding, knowledge, fear (awe, reverence), might (power) and the spirit of the Lord. Also the fruits of the Spirit – love, joy, peace, patience, kindness, goodness, faithfulness, gentleness, self-control

In my last year as an undergraduate I was trying to work out what to do in life. A friend had given me a book for a birthday present, *Margaret* by James Davidson Ross. I remember reading this book on a train journey from the West Country to London. Margaret was a teenage girl. She was smitten by cancer. The way she faced up to her ordeal, dying at such a young age, convinced me of the reality of the Holy Spirit. In her short life there was ample evidence of God spiritually alive and active. My feelings at the time were summed up by the words of Goethe in this section: 'The spirit, alive and gifted, focusing with practical intent on the most immediate concerns, is the finest thing on earth.' The way ahead opened up. I wanted to dedicate myself to the finest things on earth, to the work of the Holy Spirit. The gifts and fruits of the Holy Spirit are open to all and our spiritual heritage.

∽

I will put my spirit within you, and you shall live.
Ezekiel 37.14

When he had said this, he breathed on them and said to them, 'Receive the Holy Spirit.'
John 20.22

The simple fact is that the world is too busy to give the Holy Spirit a chance to enter in.
William Barclay, *The Gospel of John*

Spiritual experience is the supreme reality in man's life: in it the divine is not proven, it is simply shown.

  Nicolas Berdyaev, *Christian Existentialism*

The Divine Spirit works along the line of a man's own thinking power, along the channel of a man's own motive power, and wakes up in the man that which was in him.

  Henry Ward Beecher, *Proverbs from Plymouth Pulpit*

He was an ideal pastor and true shepherd of his flock – loving them and being beloved by them. His ministry was fresh and vital, and made his hearers *feel* the presence and power of the Spirit of God.

  Rufus M. Jones, *Spiritual Reformers in the 16ᵗʰ and 17ᵗʰ Centuries*

A spiritual life is simply a life in which all that we do comes from the centre, where we are anchored in God: a life soaked through and through by a sense of His reality and claim, and self-given to the great movement of His will.

  Evelyn Underhill, in John Stobbart, *The Wisdom of Evelyn Underhill*

. . . the Church's real business is the nurture of men and women in life's final meaning, the provision – the mediation – of resources for living in the power and grace and serenity (serenity amidst toil and sacrifice) of the Holy Spirit of God.

  Norman Goodall, *The Local Church*

Spirit is no less real than matter, and the spiritual values of truth, goodness, and beauty no mere creations of finite minds, but abiding characteristics of that reality in the apprehension of which all minds capable of apprehending it find their satisfaction.

  C.G.J. Webb, *Religious Experience*

The true goal of the spiritual life is such a oneness with God that He is in us and we in Him, so that the inner joy and power take our outer life captive and draw us away from the world and its 'pictures' and make it a heartfelt delight to do all His commandments and to suffer anything for Him.

  Rufus M. Jones, *Spiritual Reformers in the 16ᵗʰ and 17ᵗʰ Centuries*

. . . spirituality is the basis and foundation of human life . . . It must underlie everything. To put it briefly, man is a spiritual being, and the proper work of his mind is to interpret the world according to his higher nature, and to conquer the material aspects of the world so as to bring them into subjection to the spirit.

  Robert Bridges, *The Spirit of Man*

Holy Spirit . . . was hardly recognized as distinct from the Word until the Word was uttered in a new fullness of expression, as Christians believe, in the historical Person, Jesus of Nazareth. That fuller objective self-manifestation of the divine called forth a new potency of responsive aspiration to which, as an experienced fact, was given the name Holy Spirit.

    William Temple, *Nature, Man and God*

From the beginning, the Spirit of God has been understood as God in the midst of men, God present and active in the world, God in his closeness to us as a dynamic reality shaping the lives and histories of men. The Spirit, in this sense, is not something other than God, but God in that manner of the divine Being in which he comes closest, dwells with us, acts upon us.

    John Macquarrie, *Paths in Spirituality*

The Holy Ghost is . . . the manifest Energy of God in the world. He is, moreover, the indwelling Strengthener who enables man to live righteously in God's sight; the Guide who leads us into truth; the Revealer of the truths of God; the Consoler in our distresses; the Encourager in our tribulations. Our Lord in His promise of the special coming of the Spirit stresses His personal and loving attributes.

    Carroll Simcox, *Living the Creed*

My own attempt to understand the Holy Spirit has convinced me He is active in precisely those experiences that are very common – experiences of recognition, sudden insight, an influx of awareness when you wake up and become alive to something. It may be another person, or a scientific problem, and suddenly the penny drops. Every time a human being cries 'Ah! I see it now!', that's what I mean by the Holy Spirit.

    John V. Taylor, in Gerald Priestland, *Priestland's Progress*

But if a man here on earth is enlightened with the Holy Ghost from the fountain of Jesus Christ, so that the spirits of nature, which signify the Father, are kindled in him, then there ariseth such a joy in his heart, and it goeth forth into all his veins, so that the whole body trembleth, and the soulish animal spirit triumpheth, as if it were in the holy Trinity, which is understood only by those who have been its guests in that place.

    Jacob Boehme, *The Aurora*

No person will ever reach a stage of earthly life in which the spur of the flesh is eradicated, and so no person can be infallibly certain that he is beyond sin, but when Christ is inwardly united to the soul and His Spirit dwells in us and reigns in us and we are risen in soul, spirit, and mind with Him, then we no longer live after the flesh, or according to its thrust and push, and share His life and partake of the conquering power of His Spirit.

Rufus M. Jones, *Spiritual Reformers in the 16ᵗʰ and 17ᵗʰ Centuries*

Spirituality of life is an achievement as well as a gift. It is not a mere negation, a sentimental attitude that ignores and eludes all the just claims of the great realities of human existence, but it is intellectual and moral energy raised to the highest degree; it is an absolute persistence in well-doing; it is justice and gentleness; it is consideration and good judgment and discriminating appreciation and love.

Spirituality of life is, indeed, life raised to the highest power.

Lilian Whiting, *Lilies of Eternal Peace*

See also Divinity, God, Jesus Christ, Mystics, Presence

46

HOPE

*H*ope – *expectation and desire combined (of thing, of doing, that); feeling of trust*

I remember a programme on TV. A young woman, whose baby son had disappeared some years ago while they were on holiday on a Greek island, was being interviewed. She still hoped he would be found and that they would be reunited. There was something inside her which gave her hope. An important verse of scripture is: 'May the God of hope fill you with all joy and peace in believing, so that you may abound in hope by the power of the Holy Spirit.' One of God's attributes is 'hope'. As a consequence of the divine inbreathing a seed or a spark of this 'God of hope' resides in the depths of our being. This can be catalysed and brought to life. When we reflect and contemplate on the contents of this topic the source of hope already in us can come alive so that 'by the power of the Holy Spirit we may abound in hope'. The odds were stacked against Jesus, but he was rooted and grounded in hope, and went out to transform the world. His work continues, and we are invited to play our part – in hope.

Let your steadfast love, O Lord, be upon us, even as we hope in you.
  Psalm 33.22

Blessed be the God and Father of our Lord Jesus Christ! By his great mercy he has given us a new birth into a living hope through the resurrection of Jesus Christ from the dead, and into an inheritance that is imperishable, undefiled, and unfading, kept in heaven for you.
  1 Peter 1.3–4

. . . entertain him with hope . . .
  William Shakespeare, *The Merry Wives of Windsor*

Hope in action is charity, and beauty in action is goodness.

    Miguel de Unamuno, *The Tragic Sense of Life in Men and in Peoples*

The ability to hope is the greatest gift that God could make to man.

    Carlo Carretto, *Summoned by Love*

Hope is itself a species of happiness, and, perhaps, the chief happiness which this world affords.

    Samuel Johnson, *Boswell's Life of Johnson*

Ah! If man would but see that hope is from within and not from without – that he himself must work out his own salvation.

    H. Rider Haggard, *She*

Optimism means faith in men, in the human potentiality; hope means faith in God in His omnipotence.

    Carlo Carretto, *The Desert in the City*

> To hope till Hope creates
> From its own wreck the thing it contemplates.
>   Percy Bysshe Shelley, 'Prometheus Unbound'

Hope is the best possession. None are completely wretched but those who are without hope; and few are reduced so low as that.

    William Hazlitt, *Characteristics*

The virtue of hope is an orientation of the soul towards a transformation after which it will be wholly and exclusively love.

    Simone Weil, *Gateway to God*

Hope is lived, and it comes alive, when we go outside of ourselves and, in joy and pain take part in the lives of others. It becomes concrete in open community with others.

    Jürgen Moltmann, *The Open Church*

> Hope springs eternal in the human breast:
> Man never is, but always to be blest.
>   Alexander Pope, 'An Essay on Man'

Anything that is found to stimulate hope should be seized upon and made to serve. This applies to a book, a film, a broadcast, or a conversation with someone who can impart it.

Hubert van Zeller, *Considerations*

Christian Hope is the consecration of desire, and desire is the hardest thing of all to consecrate. That will only happen as you begin to think how lovely the life according to Christ is.

William Temple, *Christian Faith and Life*

'Hope', says St Thomas Aquinas, 'is a divinely infused quality of the soul, whereby with certain trust we expect those good things of the life eternal which are to be attained by the grace of God.'

W.R. Inge, *Personal Religion and the Life of Devotion*

He is a God who does not make empty promises for the hereafter nor trivilize the present darkness, futility and meaninglessness, but who himself in the midst of darkness, futility and meaninglessness invites us to the venture of hope.

Hans Küng, *On Being a Christian*

Oh, how good a thing it is that the great God who has placed us in this world – where amid so much that is beautiful, there still exists vast bestowal among men of grief, disappointment, and agony – has planted in our bosoms the great sheet-anchor, Hope.

Walt Whitman, *The Early Poems and the Fiction*

Hope to the last . . . Always hope; . . . Never leave off hoping; . . . Don't leave a stone unturned. It's always something to know you've done the most you could. But don't leave off hoping, or it's no use doing anything. Hope, hope, to the last!

Charles Dickens, *Nicholas Nickleby*

Hope is a completely confident expectation; that sureness and certitude with which the awakened soul aims at God and rests in God. It is the source of that living peace, that zest and alertness, that power of carrying on, which gives its special colour to the genuine Christian life.

Evelyn Underhill, in John Stobbart, *The Wisdom of Evelyn Underhill*

For if you find hope in the ground of history, you are united with the great prophets who were able to look into the depth of their times, who tried to escape it, because they could not stand the horror of their visions, and who yet had the strength to look to an even deeper level and there to discover hope.

Paul Tillich, *The Shaking of the Foundations*

Every blade of grass, each leaf, each separate floret and petal, is an inscription of hope. Consider the grasses and the oaks, the swallows, the sweet blue butterfly – they are one and all a sign and token showing before our eyes earth made into life . . . my hope becomes as broad as the horizon afar, reiterated by every leaf, sung on every bough, reflected in the gleam of every flower. There is so much for us yet to come, as much to be gathered, and enjoyed. Not for you or me, now, but for our race, who will ultimately use this magical secret for their happiness.

Richard Jefferies, *The Pageant of Summer*

See also Faith, Grace, Ideals, Inner Life, Kingdom of God

47

HUMILITY

Humility – the faculty of being humble, or having a lowly opinion of oneself; meekness, lowliness, humbleness; the opposite of pride or haughtiness

William Temple once wrote: 'The source of humility . . . is the habit of realizing the presence of God.' We have a good illustration of this in the experience of John the Baptist. When Jesus started baptizing people, John's disciples questioned his authority which led John to say: 'He must increase, I must decrease.' We, too, in our day, must develop a habit of realizing the presence of God in our lives, and in humility adopt John the Baptist's words. To the outsider this looks ridiculous, but to the adherent humility is the gateway to that more abundant life Jesus came to bring.

He leads the humble in what is right, and teaches the humble his way.
  Psalm 25.9

. . . unless you change and become like children, you will never enter the kingdom of heaven. Whoever becomes humble like this child is the greatest in the kingdom of heaven.
  Matthew 18.3–4

True humility is contentment.
  Henri Frédéric Amiel, *Amiel's Journal*

Show yourselves humble in all things.
  Thomas à Kempis, *The Imitation of Christ*

Humility like darkness reveals the heavenly lights.
  Henry David Thoreau, *Walden*

An humble able man is a jewel worth a kingdom.
> William Penn, *Fruits of Solitude*

Humility . . . is the groundwork of Christian virtues.
> Charlotte Brontë, *Jane Eyre*

The Churches must learn humility as well as teach it.
> George Bernard Shaw, *The Complete Bernard Shaw Prefaces*

All paths open up before me because I walk in humility.
> Johann Wolfgang von Goethe, *Wisdom and Experience*

The humble man, because he sees himself as nothing, can see other things as they are.
> Iris Murdoch, *The Sovereignty of Good Over Other Concepts*

In itself, humility is nothing else but a true knowledge and awareness of oneself as one really is.
> *The Cloud of Unknowing*

We must learn to detach ourselves from all that is capable of being lost, to bind ourselves absolutely only to what is absolute and eternal.
> Henri Frédéric Amiel, *Amiel's Journal*

> He that is humble, ever shall
> Have God to be his Guide.
>> John Bunyan, *The Pilgrim's Progress*

There must be feelings of humility, not from nature, but from penitence, not to rest in them, but to go on to greatness.
> Blaise Pascal, *Pensées*

> True humility,
> The highest virtue, mother of them all.
>> Alfred, Lord Tennyson, 'The Holy Grail'

You will find Angling to be like the virtue of humility, which has a calmness of spirit, and a world of other blessings attending upon it.
> Izaak Walton, *The Compleat Angler*

The Holy Ghost flows into the soul as fast as she is poured forth in humility and so far as she has gotten the capacity. He fills all the room he can find.

Meister Eckhart, in Franz Pfeiffer, *Meister Eckhart*, translated by C. de B. Evans

The humble are not those who are most troubled by their own defects and dwell upon them. True humility is begotten by the worship of superiority, and chiefly by the worship of God.

Mark Rutherford, *Last Pages from a Journal*

Humility is a head-on quality – not a dragging, miserable, mean feeling. It is not mortified pride. It is one of the noblest and one of the most resplendent of all the experiences of the soul.

Henry Ward Beecher, *Proverbs from Plymouth Pulpit*

> Fast and pray,
> That so perchance the vision may be seen
> By thee and those, and all the world be heal'd.
>
> Alfred, Lord Tennyson, 'The Holy Grail'

Let us acquiesce. Let us take our bloated nothingness out of the path of the divine circuits. Let us unlearn our wisdom of the world. Let us lie low in the Lord's power, and learn that truth alone makes rich and great.

Ralph Waldo Emerson, *Spiritual Laws*

Now I find hidden somewhere away in my nature something that tells me that nothing in the whole world is meaningless, and suffering least of all. That something hidden away in my nature, like a treasure in a field, is Humility.

Oscar Wilde, *De Profundis*

I shall recommend humility to you, as highly proper to be made the constant subject of your devotions . . . earnestly desiring you to think no day safe, or likely to end well, in which you have not . . . called upon God to carry you through the day, in the exercise of a meek and lowly spirit.

William Law, *A Serious Call to a Devout and Holy Life*

> If thou wouldst become a pilgrim on the path
> Of love
> The first condition is
> That thou become as humble as dust
> And ashes.
>
> Al-Ansari, 'The Invocations of Sheikh Abdullah Ansari of Herat'

I believe the first test of a truly great man is his humility. I do not mean, by humility, doubt of his own power, or hesitation in speaking his opinions; but a right understanding of the relation between what *he* can do and say and the rest of the world's sayings and doings. All the great men not only know their business, but usually know that they know it, and are not only right in their main opinions, but usually know that they are right in them; only, they do not think much of themselves on that account.

John Ruskin, *Modern Painters*

See also Acceptance, Cross, Guidance, Obedience, Salvation

48

IDEALS

Ideals – one's highest conceptions; things embodying an idea; things existing only in idea; the visionary, relating to, consisting of, ideas; perfect types; actual things as standards for imitation

My ideals are in this book and have been collected from a wide variety of sources. The foundation is made up of many verses from the Bible, culminating in the Gospels and Epistles. To these have been added ideals coming from poets, playwrights, novelists, philosophers, theologians, historians, scientists, artists, musicians, statesmen, politicians, economists, and psychologists. Albert Schweitzer advises us: 'Grow into your ideals, so that life can never rob you of them. If all of us could become what we were at fourteen, what a different place the world would be!' In the practice of reflection, meditation and contemplation we mull over the contents of this book and grow into our ideals.

❧

Mark the blameless, and behold the upright, for there is posterity for the peaceable.
Psalm 37.37

The kingdom of heaven is like treasure hidden in a field, which someone found and hid; then in his joy he goes and sells all that he has and buys that field. Again, the kingdom of heaven is like a merchant in search of fine pearls; on finding one pearl of great value, he went and sold all that he had and bought it.
Matthew 13.44–46

An ideal is often but a flaming vision of reality.
Joseph Conrad, *Chance*

To be happy one must have an ideal and strive to live up to it.
George Moore, *Evelyn Innes*

The Christian ideal has not been tried and found wanting. It has been found difficult; and left untried.

G.K. Chesterton, *What's Wrong with the World*

The Ideal is in thyself, the Impediment too is in thyself: thy condition is but the stuff thou art to shape that same Ideal out of.

Thomas Carlyle, *Sartor Resartus*

Even a rich man is sad if he has no ideals. He may try to hide his sadness from himself and from others, but his efforts only make him sadder still.

Yevgeny Yevtushenko, *A Precocious Autobiography*

It is hard for a man to take the ideals of honour, and truth, and rectitude, and plough through life with them. It breeds conflicts with himself and with all others.

Henry Ward Beecher, *Proverbs from Plymouth Pulpit*

The highest flights of charity, devotion, trust, patience, bravery to which the wings of human nature have spread themselves have been flown for religious ideals.

William James, *The Varieties of Religious Experience*

It is the very ideal of true manhood not to be suppressed. A man should lay it down in his mind, when he begins life, 'I am, and I will be, superior to my circumstances.'

Henry Ward Beecher, *Proverbs from Plymouth Pulpit*

If one advances confidently in the direction of his dreams, and endeavours to live the life which he has imagined, he will meet with a success unexpected in common hours.

Henry David Thoreau, *Walden*

The most consummate ideal that men have ever known, or felt, or thought, is the ideal of one who is supreme and sovereign, guiding nature and in it Providence.

Henry Ward Beecher, *Proverbs from Plymouth Pulpit*

For the idealist living wholly with people occupied with the concrete, existence is not merely lonely, but fatiguing. It is as though he or she were for ever talking a foreign language.

L. Falconer, in M.G. Ostle, *The Note Books of a Woman Alone*

Christ's ideal of manhood is power in the head, and power in the heart, and art in the hand, with the humiliation of love, and carried down to the lowest and meanest, if thereby they may be helped.

Henry Ward Beecher, *Proverbs from Plymouth Pulpit*

Every ideal affirms that, in some sense, our supernatural environment is more truly active than the world of our apprehension, and is always offering itself as a world to be possessed and not to be created.

John Oman, *The Natural and the Supernatural*

The ideal, after all, is truer than the real: for the ideal is the eternal element in perishable things: it is their type, their sum, their *raison d'etre*, their formula in the book of the Creator, and therefore at once the most exact and most condensed expression of them.

Henri Frédéric Amiel, *Amiel's Journal*

'The kingdom of heaven is like a merchant seeking precious pearls.' Yes, we have promised great things but greater things are promised us. Be faithful to Christ and pray for perseverance. Remember to say to yourself, 'I have been created for greater things.' Never stoop lower than the ideal. Let nothing satisfy you but God.

Mother Teresa, in Brother Angelo Devananda, *Jesus, the Word to Be Spoken*

Religion cannot remain on the level of ideas alone. Religion must be an expression. It must be an incarnation in the real world of an ideal that is of supreme import to the individual of belief. Religion not only has to be worth living for, it has to be worth living. Faith on a theoretical level is a fossilized faith if it only remains on that level.

Harry James Cargas, *Encountering Myself*

In reverence for life my knowledge passes into existence . . . My life carries its own meaning in itself. This meaning lies in my living out the highest idea which shows itself in my will-to-live, the idea of reverence for life. With that as a starting-point I give value to my own life and to all the will-to-live which surrounds me, I persevere in activity, and I produce values.

Albert Schweitzer, *The Philosophy of Civilization*

The ideals which have lighted my way, and time after time have given me new courage to face life cheerfully, have been Kindness, Beauty, and Truth. Without the sense of kinship with men of like mind, without the occupation with the objective world, the eternally unattainable in the field of art and scientific endeavour, life would have seemed to me empty. The trite objects of human efforts – possessions, outward success, luxury – have always seemed to me contemptible.

Albert Einstein, *Ideas and Opinions*

There is something more in man than is apparent in his ordinary consciousness, something which frames ideals and thoughts, a finer spiritual presence, which makes him dissatisfied with mere earthly pursuits. The one doctrine that has the longest intellectual ancestry is the belief that the ordinary condition of man is not his ultimate being, that he has in him a deeper self, call it breath or ghost, soul or spirit. In each being dwells a light which no power can extinguish, an immortal spirit, benign and tolerant, the silent witness in his heart. The greatest thinkers of the world unite in asking us to know the self.

Sir Sarvepalli Radhakrishnan, *Eastern Religions and Western Thought*

See also Beauty, Character, Goodness, Integrity, Truth

49

IMAGE OF GOD

Image of God – man's original nature, made in the image and likeness of God, fully worked out in the life of Christ

In the second chapter of the book of Genesis we read that God formed the first human of dust from the ground, and breathed into his nostrils the breath of life; and Adam became a living being. Initially the man of dust was earthy and creaturely, but once God breathed into his nostrils the breath of life, this man had also something akin to a divine potential. If we wish to see this fully worked out in a life we go to the Gospels, to the person of Jesus Christ. As he went through life he discovered something of the Father in himself, as well as the full range of the gifts and fruits of the Holy Spirit. At the same time he accepted the earthy and creaturely side of his nature, bringing about an inner integration, and thereby becoming a whole person. Paul acknowledged Jesus as the image of the invisible God and recognized the implications for us: 'Just as we have born the image of the man of dust, so shall we also bear the image of the man of heaven.'

$$\backsim$$

– then the Lord God formed man from the dust of the ground, and breathed into his nostrils the breath of life; and the man became a living being.

Genesis 2.7

And all of us, with unveiled faces, seeing the glory of the Lord as though reflected in a mirror, are being transformed into the same image from one degree of glory to another; for this comes from the Lord, the Spirit.

2 Corinthians 3.18

When God made man the innermost heart of the Godhead was put into man.

Meister Eckhart, in Franz Pfeiffer, *Meister Eckhart*, translated by C. de B. Evans

You never know yourself till you know more than your body. The Image of God is not seated in the features of your face, but in the lineaments of your Soul.

Thomas Traherne, *Centuries*

The God-image in man was not destroyed by the Fall but was only damaged and corrupted ('deformed'), and can be restored through God's grace.

C.G. Jung, *Aion*

If we take Adam as a type of the natural man, and ask in whose image he was created, we are told that it was in God's image. Man alone has mind, intelligence, reason, and a nature destined to be ennobled through the Incarnation.

Father Andrew SDC, *Meditations for Every Day*

. . . 'moulded into the image of his Son' (Romans 8.29). Let us gaze upon this adorable Image, remain always with His radiance, that He may impress Himself upon us. Then let us do everything in the same disposition as our Holy Master.

Sister Elizabeth of the Trinity, *Spiritual Writings*

The greatest of painters only once painted a mysteriously divine child; he couldn't have told how he did it, and we can't tell why we feel it to be divine. I think there are stores laid up in our human nature that our understandings can make no complete inventory of.

George Eliot, *Mill on the Floss*

. . . they all proclaimed that deep in the central nature of man – an inalienable part of Reason – there was a Light, a Word, an Image of God, something permanent, reliable, universal, and unsundered from God himself. They all knew that man is vastly more than 'mere man'.

Rufus M. Jones, *Spiritual Reformers in the 16ᵗʰ and 17ᵗʰ Centuries*

. . . 'Honour all men'. Every man should be honoured as God's image, in the sense in which Novalis says – that we touch Heaven when we lay our hand on a human body! . . . The old Homeric Greeks I think, felt that, and acted up to it, more than any nation. The Patriarchs too seem to have had the same feeling . . .

Charles Kingsley, *Daily Thoughts*

The Difference then of a good and a bad Man does not lie in this, that the one wills that which is good, and the other does not, but solely in this, that the one concurs with the living inspiring Spirit of God within him, and the other resists it, and is and can be *only chargeable* with Evil, because he resists it.

William Law, *The Spirit of Love*

'Let us make man in OUR image.' Such is man's height and depth and breadth and mystery. He has not come from one principle or distinction of the Divine Nature, but out of all principles. Man is the image of the whole Deity. There is in him a sanctuary, for the Father, and for the Son, and for the Holy Ghost. 'We will make our abode with him.'

John Pulsford, *Quiet Hours*

I have often said before that there is an agent in the soul, untouched by time and flesh, which proceeds out of the Spirit, and which remains forever in the Spirit and is completely spiritual. In this agent God is perpetually verdant and flowering with all the joy and glory that is in him. Here is joy so hearty, such inconceivably great joy that no one can ever fully tell it . . . God glows and burns without ceasing, in all his fullness, sweetness, and rapture.

Meister Eckhart, *Meister Eckhart*, translated by Raymond B. Blakney

The image of God in man is the conformity of the human soul, understanding, spirit, mind, will, and all internal and external bodily and spiritual powers with God and the Holy Trinity and with all divine qualities, virtues, wills, and characteristics. This is indicated in the decision of the Holy Trinity: Let us make man in our image after our likeness; and let him have dominion over the fish of the sea, and over the birds of the air, and over the cattle, and over all the earth (Gen. 1.26).

Johann Arndt, *True Christianity*

How do we detect this spark within us? I imagine that it is different in each person, which would not be surprising since every person is unique. I think it has something to do with a longing deep down within us. We long to know and possess the good, or the good that we see in a great number of persons and objects which fall within our experience. In the end we discover that the pursuit of truth and goodness leads us to long for truth and goodness in their absolute form. This absolute truth and this absolute goodness we call God.

Basil Hume OSB, *To Be a Pilgrim*

. . . the secret impulse out of which kindness acts is an instinct which is the noblest part of ourselves, the most undoubted remnant of the image of God, which was given us at the first. We must therefore never think of kindness as being a common growth of our nature, common in the sense of being of little value. It is the nobility of man. In all its modifications it reflects a heavenly type. It runs up into one, and it is human because it springs from the soul of man just at the point of where the divine image was graven deepest.

F.W. Faber, *Spiritual Writings*

See also Divinity, Holy Spirit, Imagination, Jesus Christ, Presence

50

IMAGINATION

Imagination – imagining, mental faculty forming images of external objects not present to the senses; creative faculty of the mind

Late one evening an undergraduate popped in to see me. He was looking shaken. He had been to see a film called *The Shining* and it had affected him greatly. I listened carefully and promised to go and see the film with him the following evening. The film was absorbing. We returned to my rooms to talk it through. I knew my undergraduate friend was reputed to have 'a Rolls Royce mind', but now I witnessed a powerful imagination in action. He quickly revealed to me the underlying plot, not immediately obvious to a casual film-goer like myself. He then slipped his imagination into top gear and made scores and scores of connections. We must have gone on for two or three hours – an exciting and stimulating experience. Not surprisingly he went into television when he graduated. In the many programmes he has produced, he has continued to make excellent use of his imagination.

⌒

For God speaks in one way, and in two, though people do not perceive it. In a dream, in a vision of the night, when deep sleep falls on mortals, while they slumber on their beds, then he opens their ears.

Job 33.14–16

Do not be conformed to this world, but be transformed by the renewing of your minds, so that you may discern what is the will of God – what is good and acceptable and perfect.

Romans 12.2

Imagination is the eye of the soul.

Joseph Joubert, *Pensées and Letters*

There is no power on earth like imagination . . .

> Laurens van der Post, *Venture to the Interior*

The great instrument of moral good is the imagination.

> Percy Bysshe Shelley, *A Defence of Poetry*

Faith means a sanctified imagination, or the imagination applied to spiritual things.

> Henry Ward Beecher, *Proverbs from Plymouth Pulpit*

There are no days in life so memorable as those which vibrated to some stroke of the imagination.

> Ralph Waldo Emerson, *The Conduct of Life, Nature, and Other Essays*

It is the marriage of the soul with Nature that makes the intellect fruitful, that gives birth to imagination.

> Henry David Thoreau, *The Journal of Henry D. Thoreau*

Imagination grows by exercise and contrary to common belief is more powerful in the mature than in the young.

> W. Somerset Maugham, *The Summing Up*

Meditation, experience of life, hope, charity, and all the emotions – out of these the imaginative reason speaks.

> J.B. Yeats, *Letters to His Son, W.B. Yeats and Others*

For God hath made you able to create worlds in your own mind which are more precious unto Him than those which He created.

> Thomas Traherne, *Centuries*

Only in men's imagination does every truth find an effective and undeniable existence. Imagination, not invention, is the supreme master of art as of life.

> Joseph Conrad, *A Personal Record*

What is it that we ask of our ideal audience? It is imagination. And is not all our writing a profession of belief in the powers of the imagination?

> Katherine Mansfield, in Anthony Alpers, *Katherine Mansfield*

The imagination is the secret and marrow of civilization. It is the very eye of faith. The soul without imagination is what an observatory would be without a telescope.

> Henry Ward Beecher, *Proverbs from Plymouth Pulpit*

'What is imagination?' asks Rider Haggard in the midst of his narratives. And he answers: 'Perhaps it is a shadow of the intangible truth, perhaps it is the soul's thought!'

Henry Miller, *The Books in My Life*

But how entirely I live in my imagination; how completely depend upon spurts of thought, coming as I walk, as I sit; things churning up in my mind and so making a perpetual pageant, which is to be my happiness.

Virginia Woolf, *A Writer's Diary*

When the pioneer in science sends forth the groping fingers of his thoughts, he must have a vivid intuitive imagination, for new ideas are not generated by deduction, but by an artistically creative imagination.

Max Planck, in F.C. Happold, *Religious Faith and Twentieth-Century Man*

He realized in the entire sphere of human relations that imaginative sympathy which in the Sphere of Art is the sole secret of creation. He understood the leprosy of the leper, the darkness of the blind, the fierce misery of those who live for pleasure, the strange poverty of the rich.

Oscar Wilde, *De Profundis*

. . . I cannot tell you how strongly I feel that the kind of imagination which the gods have given me is more than imagination! In fact almost all the power we call 'imagination' may come from an actual tapping of some great reservoir of planetary, if not cosmic, experience.

John Cowper Powys, *Autobiography*

Imagination is distinct from the mere dry faculty of reasoning. Imagination is creative – it is an immediate intuition; not a logical analysis – we call it popularly a kind of inspiration. Now imagination is a power of the heart: – Great thoughts originate from a large heart: – a man must have a heart, or he never could create.

F.W. Robertson, *Sermons*

If I were asked what has been the most powerful force in the making of history, you would probably adjudge of unbalanced mind were I to answer, as I should have to answer, metaphor figurative expression. It is by imagination that men have lived; imagination rules all our lives. The human mind is not, as philosophers would have you think, a debating hall, but a picture gallery. Around it hang our similes, our concepts.

W. MacNeile Dixon, *The Human Situation*

The imagination – the divinest of mental faculties – is God's self in the soul. All our other faculties seem to me to have the brown touch of earth on them but this one carries the very livery of heaven. It is God's most supernal faculty, interpreting to us the difference between the material and the immaterial, and the difference between the visible and the invisible; teaching us how to take material and visible things and carry them up into the realm of the invisible and the immaterial, and how to bring down immaterial and invisible things, and embody them in visible and material symbols; – and so being God's messenger and prophet, standing between our soul and God's.

Henry Ward Beecher, *Royal Truths*

See also Aspiration, Experience, Image of God, Inspiration, Vision

INCARNATION

Incarnation – embodiment in flesh, especially in human form; living type (of quality); the incarnation of God in Christ

For many years I have been going to Mürren, a village high up in the Swiss Alps, to take services at the 'English Church' during the Christmas and New Year period. One of the main services is Midnight Communion on Christmas Eve. In the short address I usually speak about the mystery of the incarnation. At one level we are celebrating the historical birth of Jesus at Bethlehem. At another level we are celebrating a birth at the present time. A way of understanding this comes through some words of Angelus Silesius:

> Christ could be born
> A thousand times in Galilee –
> But all in vain
> Until he is born in me.

Discovering this simple verse led me to a deeper understanding of Christmas and the mystery of the incarnation. There is a line in the carol 'O Little Town of Bethlehem' which almost makes the same point 'Be born in us today.' How important the incarnation is, both historically and today.

∽

In the beginning was the Word, and the Word was with God, and the Word was God . . . And the Word became flesh and lived among us, and we have seen his glory, the glory as of a father's only son, full of grace and truth.

John 1.1, 14

Those who love me will keep my word, and my Father will love them, and we will come to them and make our home with them.

John 14.23

By virtue of the Creation and still more, of the Incarnation, *nothing* here below is *profane* for those who know how to see.

    Pierre Teilhard de Chardin, *Le Milieu Divin*

God became man to turn creatures into sons: not simply to produce better men of the old kind but to produce a new kind of man.

    C.S. Lewis, *Mere Christianity*

Everyone has, inside himself . . . what shall I call it? A piece of good news! Everyone is . . . a very great, very important character.

    Ugo Betti, *The Burnt Flower-Bed*

The Word of God, Jesus Christ our Lord: Who for His immense love's sake was made that which we are, in order that He might perfect us to be what He is.

    St Irenaeus, *Five Books of St Irenaeus*

God so united Himself to us and us to Him, that the descent of God to the human level was at the same time the ascent of man to the divine level.

    St Leo, in F.C. Happold, *Religious Faith and Twentieth-Century Man*

Christianity does mean getting down to actual ordinary life as the medium of the Incarnation, doesn't it, and our lessons in that get sterner, not more elegant as times goes on.

    Evelyn Underhill, *The Letters of Evelyn Underhill*

God incarnated himself in Jesus Christ. Many people spend their time denying his incarnation. They search the sky and miss him right here on earth, where he is to be found in their daily lives.

    Michel Quoist, *With Open Heart*

At this time . . . the renewal of Christianity depends solely on accepting the Incarnation in all its fulness. For without the realization of God's love for the world, we can love neither the world nor God.

    Alan W. Watts, *Behold the Spirit*

As it is, there is one road, and one only, well secured against all possibility of going astray and this road is provided by one who is himself both God and man. As God, he is the goal; as man, he is the way.

    St Augustine, *City of God*

Prayer then is the interiorizing of the Incarnation. The Word is to become enfleshed in me. Bethlehem is here. So Christmas Day is to become all days, and the adoration of Emmanuel, God with us, must be a daily and continuous event.

    Kenneth Leech, *True Prayer*

The real difficulty which prevents people from believing in the Virgin Birth is not want of evidence, but belief in a 'closed universe', and the impossibility of miracles. But he who believes this, cannot believe in the Incarnation, and therefore cannot be a Christian at all.

    C.B. Moss, *The Christian Faith*

The soul of a monk is a Bethlehem where Christ comes to be born – in the sense that Christ is born where His likeness is re-formed by grace, and where His Divinity lives, in a special manner, with His Father and His Holy Spirit, by charity, in this 'new incarnation', this 'other Christ'.

    Thomas Merton, *Elected Silence*

True religion . . . is a reception and assimilation of the Life of God within the soul of man which is predisposed by its fundamental nature to the influx and formative influence of the Spirit of God, who is the environing Life and inner atmosphere of all human spirits; '*Spiritual Life comes from God's breath within us and from the formation of Christ within the soul.*'

    Rufus M. Jones, *Spiritual Reformers in the 16th and 17th Centuries*

'Man is the true Shekinah' – the visible presence, that is to say, of the divine. We are far too apt to limit and mechanize the great doctrine of the Incarnation which forms the centre of the Christian faith. Whatever it may mean, it means at least this – that in the conditions of the highest human life we have access, as nowhere else, to the inmost nature of the divine.

    A.S. Pringle-Pattison, *The Idea of God*

Once the Creator Spirit became involved in matter and in developing life, once the spirit of man was created in the likeness of the divine Spirit, it would seem natural that he should become fully incarnate in a person, not only to manifest the divine life but also to be the prototype of human life. The union of the divine and human in Jesus speaks of the hope of man sharing in the divine life.

    George Appleton, *Journey for a Soul*

The incarnation is a proclamation that 'the All-great is the All-loving too' – a doctrine which few, I think, accept who do not believe in the Incarnation of the Son of God in Christ.

And if, with the Church of the Creeds and Fathers, we accept something like the Logos-doctrine already held by St Paul and briefly summarized by St John, we have the most inspiring thought that the laws of the universe, in their deepest meaning, are the expression of the character of the creating and sustaining Word who became flesh and tabernacled among us in the person of Jesus of Nazareth. I need not dwell on the consecration of the whole of nature which follows from this belief . . .

W.R. Inge, *Speculum Animae*

The Incarnation was not an isolated event, wonderful though it would have been if it was that and nothing more. It was the beginning of something new, perhaps rather the manifestation of something which had never been recognized, but which could now happen in a fully conscious and effective way. The Spirit of God, incarnate fully and supremely in Jesus, wishes to indwell every man, not only as an immanent force, but as an invited, personal guest.

George Appleton, *Journey for a Soul*

See also Divinity, Inner Life, Jesus Christ, Presence, Transformation

52

INFLUENCE

Influence – affecting character and destiny of persons; action insensibly exercised upon, ascendancy, moral power (over, with persons, etc.); thing, person, exercising power

There are certainly some very important institutional influences at work in our lives – home, school, higher education, state, Church, work, marriage, the media, and so on. Looking back over my life, I can see there have been many institutional forces at work which have helped to mould and fashion me. These institutions, however, are made up of vast numbers of individual people, and I know that hundreds of men, women, and children, have influenced me at various stages of my life. Books have exerted an incalculable influence on me; so have the difficulties and tragedies I have been through. Other people's experiences of life have been invaluable. Lastly the grace of God has influenced me. This sometimes comes to me in quiet times of reflection and exercises an influence over the whole of life.

O Lord, the God of Abraham, Isaac, and Israel, our ancestors, keep for ever such purposes and thoughts in the hearts of your people, and direct their hearts towards you.

1 Chronicles 29.18

. . . he died, but through his faith he still speaks.

Hebrews 11.4

In every relationship lies a possibility of influence.

André Gide, *The Journals of André Gide*

Your influence, your life, your all, depends on prayer.

Forbes Robinson, *Letters to His Friends*

Every throb of our spirit that answers to spiritual things is caused by the influence of God.

Henry Ward Beecher, *Proverbs from Plymouth Pulpit*

Blessed influence of one true loving human soul on another!

George Eliot, *Scenes of Clerical Life, Janet's Repentance*

A teacher affects eternity; he can never tell where his influence stops.

Henry Adams, *The Education of Henry Adams*

God must act and pour in as soon as he finds that you are ready.

Meister Eckhart, *Meister Eckhart*, translated by Raymond B. Blakney

The very point of power in the church of Christ is the personal influence of Christian lives.

Henry Ward Beecher, *Proverbs from Plymouth Pulpit*

It is certain, that either wise bearing or ignorant carriage is caught, as men take diseases, one of another, therefore, let men take heed of their company.

William Shakespeare, *II King Henry IV*

The secret of his influence lay in a self-discipline that was as habitual as most men's habits are, an inner culture of mind and heart and will that gave his life a poise, so that he could not be untrue either to himself or his fellow-men.

George Seaver (said of Edward Wilson) in *Edward Wilson of the Antarctic*

Except by the personal influence of God's nature on ours, we cannot reach our higher manhood.

Henry Ward Beecher, *Proverbs from Plymouth Pulpit*

When we think about the people who have given us hope and have increased the strength of our soul, we might discover that they were not the advice givers, warners or moralists, but the few who were able to articulate in words and actions the human condition in which we participate and who encouraged us to face the realities of life.

Henri J.M. Nouwen, *Reaching Out*

The older we grow, the more we understand our own lives and histories, the more we shall see that the spirit of wisdom is the spirit of love, that the true way to gain influence over our fellow-men is to have charity towards them. That is a hard lesson to learn; and all those who learn it generally learn it late; almost . . . too late!

Charles Kingsley, *Daily Thoughts*

'Tis the same with human beings as with books. All of us encounter, at least once in our life, some individual who utters words that make us think for ever. There are men whose phrases are oracles; who condense in a sentence the secrets of life; who blurt out an aphorism that forms a character or illustrates an existence. A great thing is a great book; but greater than all is the talk of a great man.

Benjamin Disraeli, *Coningsby*

Certainly religion has lost its extensive control over other fields: it has less and less direct influence – on science, education, politics, law, medicine, social service. But can we conclude from all this that the influence of religion on the life of the individual and of society as a whole has declined? Instead of the former extensive control and guardianship, it may now have a more extensive and indirect moral influence.

Hans Küng, *On Being a Christian*

Any man or woman, in any age and under any circumstances, who will, can live the heroic life and exercise heroic influences.

It is of the essence of self-sacrifice, and therefore of heroism, that it should be voluntary; a work of supererogation, at least, towards society and man; an act to which the hero or heroine is not bound by duty, but which is above though not against duty.

Charles Kingsley, *Daily Thoughts*

If the sublime fire of infused love burns in your soul, it will inevitably send forth throughout the Church and the world an influence more tremendous than could be estimated by the radius reached by words or by example. St John of the Cross writes: 'A very little of this pure love is more precious in the sight of God and of greater profit to the Church, even though the soul appear to be doing nothing, than are all other works put together.'

Thomas Merton, *Elected Silence*

The spirit and character which is already advanced in constant creativeness, in wide compassion and unceasing illumination, knowing what life means and how to attain that meaning – such a spirit not only influences those among whom it is – but its influence spreads radioactively, telepathetically, and the limits of its force cannot be set, because the source on which it is drawing is itself illimitable. Being, therefore, is all, and doing merely the symptom and sign of being, as body is the appearance of spirit.

Anon

We can influence and direct others as we desire their good, but only when they are convinced, with the shrewd sense that all creatures have, that our motives are clean, our statements true, that we do seek their good, and not our advancement and elevation as their essential benefactors. All of us are individual spirits created to evolve into a common union. If we have made ourselves to grow, so that we are advanced some stages beyond the average intensity of individualism, we can directly influence those who wish to grow, and who are feeling the natural need to grow, in that direction.

Anon

See also Character, Greatness, Integrity, Power, Service

53

INNER LIFE

Inner life – interior, internal, humanity's soul or mind, spirit

After I had taken a step of faith in my early twenties I began to keep a 'quiet time' each day. In the evening, just before going to bed, I would read a passage of scripture, and think it through with the aid of a pen and paper. Shortly afterwards I began collecting verses from the Bible and short phrases from elsewhere, to be used as a resource for the quiet time. One of these phrases from the Psalms became a great favourite: 'Be still, and know that I am God'. I would spend a few minutes mulling over this phrase, so that it became a part of my inner life. In retrospect the practice of a quiet time was invaluable and formed the basis of my inner life. Later on I collected material on a larger scale, and this eventually led to the forming of this compilation. The contents of this book are mainly about the inner life. With the practice of reflection, this material can be used to foster the 'quiet time' and so promote the growth of the inner life.

I have heard of you that a spirit of the gods is in you, and that enlightenment, understanding, and excellent wisdom are found in you.

Daniel 5.14

I pray that, according to the riches of his glory, he may grant that you may be strengthened in your inner being with power through his Spirit, and that Christ may dwell in your hearts through faith . . .

Ephesians 3.16

The man who has no inner life is the slave of his surroundings.

Henri Frédéric Amiel, *Amiel's Journal*

It is wonderful how a time away, especially abroad, changes all one's views of life from within.

A.C. Benson, *Extracts from the Letters of Dr A.C. Benson to M.E.A.*

. . . the inner life is the only means whereby we may oppose a profitable resistance to circumstance.

Henri Frédéric Amiel, *Amiel's Journal*

The important matter was the increase of this inward life, the silent growth of this kingdom of God in the hearts of men, the spread of this invisible Church.

Rufus M. Jones, *Spiritual Reformers in the 16ᵗʰ and 17ᵗʰ Centuries*

We must revolutionize this system of life, that is based on *outside* things, money, property, and establish a system of life which is based on *inside* things.

D.H. Lawrence, *The Letters of D.H. Lawrence*

God does not die on the day when we cease to believe in a personal deity, but we die on the day when our lives cease to be illumined by the steady radiance, renewed daily, of a wonder, the source of which is beyond all reason.

Dag Hammarskjöld, *Markings*

. . . he turned more and more, as time went on, toward interior religion, the cultivation of an inner sanctuary, the deepening of the mystical roots of his life, and the perfection of a religion of inner and spiritual life.

Rufus M. Jones, *Spiritual Reformers in the 16ᵗʰ and 17ᵗʰ Centuries*

There is in most of us a lyric germ or nucleus which deserves respect; it bids a man ponder, or create; and in this dim corner of himself he can take refuge and find consolations which the society of his fellow-creatures does not provide.

Norman Douglas, *An Almanac*

The life of Jesus was a calm. It was a life of marvellous composure. The storms were all about it, tumult and tempest, tempest and tumult, waves breaking over Him all the time . . . But the inner life was a sea of glass. It was a life of perfect composure . . . the great calm is there.

Henry Drummond, *The Greatest Thing in the World*

Part of the discipline of the Christian's spiritual life is designed to bring the insights and the inspiration of the inner life to bear on his conduct in the outer life, in his relations with his fellows and his responsibilities towards his family and his country.

Christopher Bryant SSJE, *Jung and the Christian Way*

He, within,
Took measure of his soul, and knew its strength,
And by that silent knowledge, day by day,
Was calmed, ennobled, comforted, sustained.
  Matthew Arnold, 'Mycerinus'

Such practice of inward orientation, of inward worship and listening, is no mere counsel for special religious groups, for small religious orders, for special 'interior souls,' for monks retired in cloisters. This practice is the heart of religion. It is the secret, I am persuaded, of the inner life of the Master of Galilee. He expected this secret to be freshly discovered in everyone who would be his follower.
  Thomas Kelly, *A Testament of Devotion*

He that thus seeks shall find; he shall live in truth, and that shall live in him; it shall be like a stream of living waters issuing out of his own soul; he shall drink of the waters of his own cistern, and be satisfied; he shall every morning find this heavenly manna lying upon the top of his own soul, and be fed with it to eternal life; he will find satisfaction within, feeling himself in conjunction with truth, though all the world should dispute against him.
  John Smith the Platonist, *Select Discourses*

I have nothing to give to another; but I have a duty to open him to his own life, to allow him to be himself – infinitely richer and more beautiful than he could ever be if I tried to enrich and shape him only from the outside. All is *within* him because the source lies in his heart of hearts. But so many obstacles prevent it from surfacing! I must be the one to help it spring forth and smash the concrete around him, and in him. I must be the one to help him dig and search, and dig some more, to find the source. And from that source, life will spring.
  Michel Quoist, *With Open Heart*

The divine mystery of this infinite God is revealed and discovered in the hearts of the sons of men, whom He hath chosen: and He hath given us, to enjoy and possess in us a measure of that fulness that is in Himself, even a measure of the same Love and Life, of the same Mercy and Power, and of the same divine Nature . . . These things ye know, if ye be born from above, and if the immortal birth live in you, and you be constant in the faith, then are you heirs through it, of the everlasting inheritance of eternal life . . . and all are yours, because you are Christ's, and he is God's, and you have the Father and the Son.
  Edward Burroughs, *The Memorable Works of a Son of Thunder and Consolation*

And many a man carries within him an inheritance of incalculable worth, who is not aware of his immense resources. The richest things are ever hidden from common gaze. The things of God are neither entrusted to the brute, nor to 'the brutish man.' The sensual man can have very little perception of the soul's immortality, for the life to which he has abandoned himself is not immortal. His is the false life, the life that is not lawful *for a man* to live, and there is no eternity which will be any comfort to him. Eternity will most rigorously punish him. But there is no man who reverently, wisely, and perseveringly cultivates his own spiritual life, who is not rewarded far beyond his thoughts.

John Pulsford, *Quiet Hours*

See also Blessedness, Grace, Inspiration, Mystics, Presence

54

INSPIRATION

Inspiration – drawing in of breath; divine influence, sudden happy idea; inspiring principle

In the Genesis story of the creation of humanity, God is depicted as fashioning and shaping humans in his own image and likeness, and the last thing he does is breathe into humans and they become living beings – that is, fundamentally 'inspired'. Consider for a moment those we think of being inspired – William Shakespeare, Mozart, Shelley and the scientist Marie Curie. What were the sources of their inspiration? Was it environment, hereditary, or something deeper – a gift of God perhaps? I came across an interesting observation of inspiration some years ago. An American, a former member of University College came to visit me. In the conversation which followed he said, 'You know, Bill, I have come to realize Oxford is a very spiritual place. I think *the Spirit is in the walls*.' I knew exactly what he meant. Oxford is an inspirational place. The Spirit is, indeed, in the walls.

But truly it is the spirit in a mortal, the breath of the Almighty, that makes for understanding. It is not the old that are wise, nor the aged that understand what is right. Therefore I say, 'Listen to me; let me also declare my opinion.'
   Job 32.8–10

Now we have received not the spirit of the world, but the Spirit that is from God, so that we may understand the gifts bestowed on us by God. And we speak of these things in words not taught by human wisdom but taught by the Spirit, interpreting spiritual things to those who are spiritual.
   1 Corinthians 2.12–13

When a man has given up the one fact of the inspiration of the Scriptures, he has given up the whole foundation of revealed religion.
   Henry Ward Beecher, *Proverbs from Plymouth Pulpit*

Inspiration will always sing; inspiration will never explain.

    Kahlil Gibran, *Sand and Foam*

Spirit gives meaning to his [man's] life, and the possibility of the greatest development.

    C.G. Jung, in Jolande Jacobi, *Psychological Reflections*

The soul may be so inspired by the Divine Spirit as to be certified of its relationship to God.

    Henry Ward Beecher, *Proverbs from Plymouth Pulpit*

An inspiration – a long deep breath of the pure air of thought – could alone give health to the heart.

    Richard Jefferies, *The Story of My Heart*

Christ reformed man by inspiring the love of goodness, as well as by hatred of evil. He controlled the passions by the inspiration of the moral sentiments.

    Henry Ward Beecher, *Proverbs from Plymouth Pulpit*

Perpetual Inspiration, therefore, is in the Nature of the Thing as necessary to a Life of Goodness, Holiness, and Happiness, as perpetual Respiration of the Air is necessary to animal life.

    William Law, *The Spirit of Love*

It is the man who puts the vigour and enthusiasm which God inspires into the life that now is who will be fitted for the world that is to come. 'Having done all, stand.'

    Henry Ward Beecher, *Proverbs from Plymouth Pulpit*

The authority of the inspired scriptures resides, not in an intrusive control of the writing process, nor in an error-free presentation, but in a reliable expression of the faith in the unique period of its earliest gestation.

    James Tunstead Burtchaell CSC, in Alan Richardson and John Bowden, *A New Dictionary of Christian Theology*

There is in human life very little spiritual inspiration; very little that men can get from each other; very little that they can get from society; very little that they can get from laws and institutions. Its source is above us.

    Henry Ward Beecher, *Proverbs from Plymouth Pulpit*

And do we not all agree to call rapid thought and noble impulse by the name of inspiration? After our subtlest analysis of the mental process, we will still say . . . that our highest thoughts and our best deeds are all given to us.

    George Eliot, *Adam Bede*

Those divinely possessed and inspired have at least the knowledge that they hold some greater thing within them though they cannot tell what it is; from the movements that stir them and the utterances that come from them they perceive the power, not themselves, that moves them.

    Plotinus, *The Enneads*

God should be in the Christian's soul, in his living consciousness, vital, active, fiery. He should inspire him and fill him with admiration. His God should be one that loves him, inspires him, rebukes him, punishes him, wounds him, heals him, and rejoices him – one whose arms and whose bosom he feels.

    Henry Ward Beecher, *Proverbs from Plymouth Pulpit*

To dare to listen to that inspiration from within which voices the ultimate reality of one's own being requires an act of faith which is rare indeed. When the conviction is borne in upon one that anything which is put together, or made up, has no ultimate reality and so is certain to disintegrate, one turns to one's own final reality in the faith that it and it alone can have any virtue or any value.

    Esther Harding, *Women's Mysteries*

The artist's inspiration may be either a human or a spiritual grace, or a mixture of both. High artistic achievement is impossible without at least those forms of intellectual, emotional and physical mortification appropriate to the kind of art which is being practised. Over and above this course of what may be called professional mortification, some artists have practised the kind of self-naughting which is the indispensable pre-condition of the unitive knowledge of the divine Ground. Fra Angelico, for example, prepared himself for this work by means of prayer and meditation.

    Aldous Huxley, *The Perennial Philosophy*

The uninitiated imagine one must await inspiration in order to create. That is a mistake. I am far from saying that there is no such thing as inspiration; quite the opposite. It is found as a driving force in every kind of human activity, and is in no wise peculiar to artists. But that force is only brought into action by an effort, and that effort is work. Just as appetite comes by eating, so work brings inspiration, if inspiration is not discernible at the beginning. But it is not simply inspiration that counts; it is the result of inspiration – that is, the composition.

Igor Stravinsky, *An Autobiography*

It is by long obedience and hard work that the artist comes to unforced spontaneity and consummate mastery. Knowing that he can never create anything on his own account, out of the top layers, so to speak, of his personal consciousness, he submits obediently to the workings of 'inspiration'; and knowing that the medium in which he works has its own self-nature, which must not be ignored or violently overridden, he makes himself its patient servant and, in this way, achieves freedom of expression. But life is also an art, and the man who would become a consummate artist in living must follow, on all the levels of his being, the same procedure as that by which the painter or the sculptor or any other craftsman comes to his own more limited perfection.

Aldous Huxley, *The Perennial Philosophy*

See also Art, Aspiration, Literature, Music, Poetry

55

INTEGRITY

Integrity – wholeness; soundness; uprightness, honesty, purity

Shortly after returning from our expedition to Nepal someone recommended a book entitled *Edward Wilson of the Antarctic* by George Seaver. Edward Wilson was the doctor on Scott's expedition to the Antarctic in 1910. He was a man of deep religious convictions. He had an intense love of the countryside and was a sensitive artist, committing to paper what he observed in nature. In the pages of this book I was confronted with the finest character I have ever come across. Throughout his life he was solid and dependable. Scott wrote of him as being shrewdly practical, intensely loyal and quite unselfish. He knew and understood people, more deeply than most. He had a quiet sense of humour and was modest and unassuming in his relationships. Always discreet and tactful, he was also kind and friendly. He was a man of many parts – a skilful doctor as well as a zoologist. His courage and bravery were outstanding features of his character. In short, he was a man of the utmost integrity.

~

The integrity of the upright guides them.
  Proverbs 11.3

. . . by purity, knowledge, patience, kindness, holiness of spirit, genuine love, truthful speech, and the power of God; with the weapons of righteousness for the right hand and for the left; in honour and dishonour, in ill repute and good repute. We are treated as impostors, and yet are true.
  2 Corinthians 6.6–8

Integrity is the noblest possession.
  Latin proverb

Nothing endures but personal qualities.
  Walt Whitman, 'Song of the Broad-Axe'

What stronger breastplate than a heart untainted!
  William Shakespeare, *II King Henry VI*

Rather than love, than money, than fame, give me truth.
  Henry David Thoreau, *Walden*

Each man needs to develop the sides of his personality which he has neglected.
  Alexis Carrel, *Reflections on Life*

Man's main task in life is to give birth to himself, to become what he potentially is. The most important product of his efforts is his own personality.
  Erich Fromm, *Man for Himself*

. . . the individual needs to be in constant struggle with his environment if he is to develop to his highest capacity. Hard conditions of life are indispensable to bringing out the best in human personality.
  Alexis Carrel, *Reflections on Life*

A cultivation of the powers of one's own personality is one of the greatest needs of life, too little realized even in these assertive days, and the exercise of the personality makes for its most durable satisfactions.
  Randolph Bourne, *Youth and Life*

One whose greatest power lay in unfolding the love of God by speech and action, and in helping individual men and women to find the meaning and the glory, the purpose and the joy of life, in that surrender to the all-pervading presence of God which for him gave each the character of heaven.
  G.A. Studdert Kennedy, *By His Friends*

The only drama that really interests me and that I should always be willing to depict anew is the debate of the individual with whatever keeps him from being authentic, with whatever is opposed to his integrity, to his integration. Most often the obstacle is within him. And all the rest is merely accidental.
  André Gide, *The Journals of André Gide*

One person with integrity, even living the most private life, affects the entire behaviour of the universe. That is God's promise, and it is among modern psychology's great lessons. But the converse is also true. So with each of us empowered with this awesome ability, will we dare be less than as fully Christians as we can?

Harry James Cargas, *Encountering Myself*

The present state of the world calls for a moral and spiritual revolution, revolution in the name of personality, of man, of every single person. This revolution should restore the hierarchy or values, now quite shattered, and place the value of human personality above the idols of production, technics, the state, the race or nationality, the collective.

Nicolas Berdyaev, *The Fate of Man in the Modern World*

Integrity originally means wholeness. The leader who can attain within himself a unity or wholeness of drive and outlook will possess integrity. The acquiring of this quality is thus no little thing, and the process requires no minor adjustments. It is a major problem of the whole life philosophy and character of the individual. It is a question of the leader's capacity to be loyal to the basic demand for loyalty itself.

Ordway Tead, *The Art of Leadership*

If we could adapt ourselves more to the life of God within us we would be more able to adapt ourselves to the will of God as expressed all about us. We are unyielding in outward things only because we have not fully yielded to inward ones. The integrated soul, the man who has broken down the barriers of selfishness and is detached from his own will, is ready to meet every circumstance however suddenly presented and however apparently destructive, fortuitous, unreasonable, and mad.

Hubert van Zeller, *Leave Your Life Alone*

By integrity I do not mean simply sincerity or honesty; integrity rather according to the meaning of the word as its derivation interprets it – entireness – wholeness – soundness: that which Christ means when He says, 'If thine eye be single or sound, thy whole body shall be full of light.'

This integrity extends through the entireness or wholeness of the character. It is found in small matters as well as great; for the allegiance of the soul to truth is tested by small things rather than by those which are more important.

F.W. Robertson, *Sermons*

Let your actions speak; your face ought to vouch for your speech. I would have virtue look out of the eye, no less apparently than love does in the sight of the beloved. I would have honesty and sincerity so incorporated with the constitution, that it should be discoverable by the senses, and as easily distinguished as a strong breath, so that a man must be forced to find it out whether he would or no . . . In short, a man of integrity, sincerity, and good-nature can never be concealed, for his character is wrought into his countenance.

Marcus Aurelius, *The Meditations of Marcus Aurelius*

What do we mean when we speak of a man of integrity? One who will be true to the highest he knows; who will never betray the truth or trifle with it; one who will never make a decision from self-regarding motives; one who will never yield to the persuasion of friends or the pressure of critics unless either conforms to his own standards of right and wrong; one who will face the consequences of his attitudes, decisions and actions, however costly they may be; one who will not be loud in self-justification, but quietly confident and humbly ready to explain.

George Appleton, *Journey for a Soul*

See also Character, Relationships, Saints, Truth, Wholeness

56

INTELLECT

Intellect – faculty of knowing and reasoning; understanding; persons collectively, of good understanding

While chaplain to University College, London, I was fortunate in being a member of a group that went on a tour of the east coast of America. Several of us had a special interest in student counselling and took every opportunity to meet experts in this field. At Baltimore we visited a downtown hospital. This hospital was going through a difficult time, financially and administratively, and had just called in a 'high-flyer' from Harvard to sort out these problems. We met him for a few minutes and he gave a brief analysis of the situation. He then went on to give an outline of the proposals to rescue the hospital. He was brilliant – a man of enormous intellect. His clear lucid mind had immediately identified the causes of the problems. Not only did he understand them in full, but at one and the same time, thought out practical ways to resolve them – a true intellectual in action.

～

Wise warriors are mightier than strong ones, and those who have knowledge than those who have strength.

Proverbs 24.5

Therefore prepare your minds for action.

1 Peter 1.13

But only to our intellect is he incomprehensible: not to our love.

The Cloud of Unknowing

Logic does not help you to appreciate York Minister, or Botticelli's Primavera, and mathematics give no useful hints to lovers.

W. MacNeile Dixon, *The Human Situation*

The greater intellect one has, the more originality one finds in men. Ordinary persons find no difference between men.

Blaise Pascal, *Pensées*

It is always the task of the intellectual to 'think otherwise'. This is not just a perverse idiosyncrasy. It is an absolutely essential feature of a society.

Harvey Cox, *The Secular City*

When Man has arrived at a certain ripeness of intellect any one grand and spiritual passage serves him as a starting-post towards all 'the two-and-thirty Palaces'.

John Keats, *Letter to J.H. Reynolds*

The mind will never unveil God to man. God is only found at a certain point on the road of experience. He speaks to man through his heart and when that happens man knows, and he never again questions the love of God.

Grace Cooke, *Spiritual Unfoldment*

We must shut the eye of sense, and open that brighter eye of our understandings, that other eye of the soul, (as the philosopher calls our intellectual faculty,) . . . which indeed all have, but few make use of.

John Smith the Platonist, *Select Discourses*

How often does the weak will obscure the clear call of conscience by resort to intellectual 'difficulties'! Some of these are real enough but some are sheer self-protection against the exacting claim of the holy love of God.

William Temple, *Readings in St John's Gospel*

The uncertainty, however, lies always in the intellectual region, never in the practical. What Paul cares about is plain enough to the true heart, however far from plain to the man whose desire to understand goes ahead of his obedience.

George Macdonald, *Unspoken Sermons*

There is a moral faith which is a virtue – faith in a friend, for example. Is there not an intellectual faith which is a virtue, which holds fast when proof fails? I believe there is such an intellectual faith and that it is a sign of strength.

Mark Rutherford, *Last Pages from a Journal*

We should not pretend to understand the world only by the intellect; we apprehend it just as much by feeling. Therefore the judgement of the intellect is, at best, only the half of truth, and must, if it be honest, also come to an understanding of its inadequacy.

    C.G. Jung, *Psychological Types*

To cultivate the man of intellect is not enough, for stillness is a quality of the whole man . . . Each man must discover the perfect tension of his being – in action or solitude, in love or asceticism, in philosophy or faith – by continual adjustments of thought and experience.

    Charles Morgan, *The Fountain*

All these intellectual attitudes would have short shrift if Christianity had remained what it was, a communion, if Christianity had remained what it was, a religion of the heart. This is one of the reasons why modern people understand nothing of true, real Christianity, of the true, real history of Christianity and what Christendom really was.

    Charles Péguy, *Basic Verities*

But intellectual acceptance even of correct doctrine is not by itself vital religion; orthodoxy is not identical with the fear or the love of God. This fact of the inadequacy of the truest doctrine is a warning that to argue syllogistically from doctrinal formula is to court disaster. The formula may be the best possible; yet it is only a label used to designate a living thing.

    William Temple, *Nature, Man and God*

> The longest way to God
> the indirect
> lies through the intellect
> Here is my journey's end
> and here its start.
>
>   Angelus Silesius, 'Of the Inner Light and Enlightenment'

The intellectual is constantly betrayed by his own vanity. God-like, he blandly assumes that he can express everything in words; whereas the things one loves, lives, and dies for are not, in the last analysis, completely expressible in words. To write or to speak is almost inevitably to lie a little. It is an attempt to clothe an intangible in a tangible form; to compress an immeasurable into a mold. And in the act of compression, how Truth is mangled and torn.

    Anne Morrow Lindbergh, *The Wave of the Future*

Western civilization is distinguished by its worship of the intellect. Yet there is no reason to give intellect pride of place over feeling. It is obviously wrong to classify young people by examinations in which the moral and organic values have no place. To make thought itself the goal of thought is a kind of mental perversion. Intellect and sexual activity alike should be exercised in a natural way. The function of the intellect is not to satisfy itself but to contribute, along with the other organic and mental functions, to the satisfaction of the individual's total needs.

Alexis Carrel, *Reflections on Life*

See also Education, Knowledge, Mind, Philosophy, Thinking

57

JESUS CHRIST

Jesus Christ – the name Jesus refers to the person Jesus of Nazareth as known from historical research; Christ refers to the 'Messiah', or 'Lord's anointed' of Jewish prophecy, now applied to Jesus as fulfilling this prophecy; image or picture of Jesus

Jesus Christ is important to me because he worked out in his person what is meant by humanity being made in the image and likeness of God. As he went through life he discovered the presence of the Father in himself. At the height of his ministry he was able to say to his disciples: 'Whoever has seen me has seen the Father . . . Do you not believe that I am in the Father and the Father in me?' He also discovered in himself the full range of the gifts and fruits of the Holy Spirit. In the epistles, the apostle Paul recognized that what Christ had experienced we can all in some measure also experience. He points out that 'in him the whole fullness of deity dwells bodily', and states what this means for us 'and you have come to fullness in him'. I like J.S. Whale's observation: 'the man Christ Jesus has the decisive place in man's ageless relationship with God. He is what God means by "Man". He is what man means by "God".'

〜

'If you know me, you will know my Father also; from now on you do know him and have seen him.' Philip said to him, 'Lord, show us the Father, and we will be satisfied.' Jesus said to him, 'Have I been with you all this time Philip, and you still do not know me? Whoever has seen me has seen the Father. How can you say, "Show us the Father?" Do you not believe that I am in the Father and the Father is in me? The words that I say to you I do not speak on my own; but the Father who dwells in me does his works. Believe me that I am in the Father and the Father is in me; but if you do not, then believe me because of the works themselves.'

John 14.7–11

. . . that is, Christ himself, in whom are hidden all the treasures of wisdom and knowledge.

Colossians 2.2–3

Jesus is not a figure in a book; He is a living presence.

William Barclay, *The Gospel of Matthew*

Jesus did not come into the world to make life easy; he came to make men great.

Anon

As Man alone, Jesus could not have saved us; as God alone, he would not; Incarnate, he could and did.

Malcolm Muggeridge, *Jesus, the Man who Lives*

We need the personal allegiance of love to Christ – such a presentation of Him through the imagination of our minds as will draw forth the soul's enthusiasm and secret life.

Henry Ward Beecher, *Proverbs from Plymouth Pulpit*

If we refuse the invitation of Christ, some day our greatest pain will be, not in the things we suffer, but in the realization of the precious things we have missed, and of which we have cheated ourselves.

William Barclay, *The Gospel of Matthew*

He does not say 'No man knoweth God save the Son'. That would be to deny the truth of the Old Testament revelation. What he does say is that He alone has a deeper secret, the essential Fatherhood of the Sovereign Power.

D.S. Cairns, *The Riddle of the World*

Two thousand years ago, there was One here on this earth who lived the grandest life that ever has been lived yet, a life that every thinking man, with deeper or shallower meaning, has agreed to call Divine.

F.W. Robertson, *Lectures and Addresses*

When criticism has done its worst, the words and acts of our Lord which remain are *not* those of 'a good and heroic man', but of one deliberately claiming unique authority and insight, and conscious of a unique destiny.

Evelyn Underhill, *The Letters of Evelyn Underhill*

Christ in us and we in Him! Why should the activity of God and the presence of the Son of Man within us not be real and observable? Every day I am thankful to God that I have been allowed to experience the reality of the Divine Image within me.

C.G. Jung, in F.C. Happold, *Religious Faith and Twentieth-Century Man*

His is easily the dominant figure in history . . . A historian without any theological bias whatever should find that he simply cannot portray the progress of humanity honestly without giving a foremost place to a penniless teacher from Nazareth.

H.G. Wells, in William Barclay, *The Gospel of Matthew*

Look on our divinest Symbol: on Jesus of Nazareth, and his Life . . . and what followed therefrom. Higher has the human Thought not yet reached . . . a Symbol of quite perennial infinite character; whose significance will ever demand to be anew inquired into, and anew made manifest.

Thomas Carlyle, *Sartor Resartus*

> But the Wind of heav'n
> bloweth where it listeth, and Christ yet walketh the earth,
> and talketh still as with those two disciples once
> on the road to Emmaus.
>
> Robert Bridges, 'The Testament of Beauty'

If you accept that Jesus is the revelation and manifestation of the Father, then you are a follower of Christ and so a Christian. If you move from that to asking in what sense is Christ God, then I would think you have to come in the end to making that act of faith which is recorded of St Thomas the Doubtful: 'My Lord and my God'.

Basil Hume OSB, in Gerald Priestland, *Priestland's Progress*

What was Christ's life? Not one of deep speculations, quiet thoughts, and bright visions, but a life of fighting against evil; earnest, awful prayers and struggles within, continued labour of body and mind without; insult, and danger, and confusion, and violent exertion, and bitter sorrow. This was Christ's life. This was St Peter's, and St James's, and St John's life afterwards.

Charles Kingsley, *Daily Thoughts*

Christ's communion with His Father was the life-centre, the point of contact with Eternity, whence radiated the joy and power of the primitive Christian flock: the classic example of a corporate spiritual life. When the young man with great possessions asked Jesus, 'What shall I do to be saved?' Jesus replied in effect, 'Put aside all lesser interests, strip off unrealities, and come, give yourself the chance of catching the infection of holiness from Me!'

Evelyn Underhill, in John Stobbart, *The Wisdom of Evelyn Underhill*

Unless we know Christ experimentally so that 'He lives within us spiritually, and so that all which is known of Him in the Letter and Historically is truly done and acted in our souls – until we experimentally verify all we read of Him – the Gospel is a mere tale to us.' It is not saving knowledge to know that Christ is born in Bethlehem but to know that He is born in us. It is vastly more important to know experimentally that we are crucified with Christ than to know historically that He died in Jerusalem many years ago, and to feel Jesus Christ risen again within you is far more operative than to have 'a notional knowledge' that He rose on the third day . . . here is a Christ indeed, a real Christ who will do thee some good.

Rufus M. Jones, *Spiritual Reformers in the 16th and 17th Centuries*

See also Character, Divinity, God, Holy Spirit, Image of God

5 8

JOY

Joy – pleasurable emotion due to well-being or satisfaction; the feeling or state of being highly pleased; exultation of spirit, gladness, delight

I wonder if joy can be seen as another illustration of the Genesis story of the creation of humanity. In that story a seed or a spark of the divine joy is 'breathed into' human beings. Jesus was no stranger to joy. He found joy in the depths of his own being and wished to extend this to his disciples. In John's Gospel he is recorded as having said to them: 'I have said these things to you so that my joy may be in you, and that your joy may be complete.' We remember the 'good and faithful servant' was bidden to 'enter into the joy of your master'. Joy has not been a stranger to our experience during the last two thousand years. Many of us are able to sympathize with those words of Samuel Taylor Coleridge: 'Joy rises in me, like a summer's morn.'

❧

You show me the path of life. In your presence there is fullness of joy; in your right hand are pleasures for evermore.

Psalm 16.11

But now I am coming to you, and I speak these things in the world so that they may have my joy made complete in themselves.

John 17.13

Joy rises in me, like a summer's morn.

Samuel Taylor Coleridge, 'A Christmas Carol'

But the fulness of joy is in God's immediate presence.

Richard Baxter, *The Saints' Everlasting Rest*

Every joy, great or small, is akin and always a refreshment.
> Johann Wolfgang von Goethe, *The Practical Wisdom of Goethe*

Life in the dimension of Spirit is a mystery rooted in the joy of being.
> John Main OSB, in Clare Hallward, *The Joy of Being*

These little thoughts are the rustle of leaves: they have their whisper of joy in my mind.
> Rabindranath Tagore, *Stray Birds*

The joy which a man finds in his work and which transforms the tears and sweat of it into happiness and delight – that joy is God.
> Harry Williams CR, *The True Wilderness*

Joy is prayer – Joy is strength – Joy is love . . . A joyful heart is the normal result of a heart burning with love.
> Mother Teresa, in Malcolm Muggeridge, *Something Beautiful for God*

> How good is man's life, the mere living! how fit to employ
> All the heart and soul and the senses for ever in joy!
> > Robert Browning, 'Saul'

This glory and honour wherewith man is crowned ought to affect every person that is grateful, with celestial joy: and so much the rather because it is every man's proper end and sole inheritance.
> Thomas Traherne, *Centuries*

Joy is the sentiment that is born in a soul, conscious of the good it possesses. The good of our intelligence is truth; the more this truth is abundant and luminous, the deeper is our inward joy.
> D. Columba Marmion, *Christ in His Mysteries*

The Christian joy and hope do not arise from an ignoring of the evil in the world, but from facing it at its worst. The light that shines for ever in the Church breaks out of the veriest pit of gloom.
> William Temple, *Readings in St John's Gospel*

Our faith is faith in what the synoptic gospels call 'the Kingdom of God' and the Kingdom of God is simply God's power enthroned in our hearts. This is what makes us light of heart and it is what Christian joy is all about.
> John Main OSB, *Moment of Christ*

If a man has sought first and chiefly the soul's treasure – goodness, kindness, gentleness, devoutness, cheerfulness, hope, faith, and love – he will extract more joy from the poorest furniture and outfitting of life than otherwise he would get from the whole world.

Henry Ward Beecher, *Proverbs from Plymouth Pulpit*

'To be a joy-bearer and a joy-giver says everything,' she wrote, 'for in our life, if one is joyful it means that one is faithfully living for God, and that *nothing else counts*; and if one gives joy to others one is doing God's work; with joy without and joy within, all is well . . . I can conceive no higher way.'

Janet Erskine Stuart, in Maud Monahan, *Life and Letters of Janet Erskine Stuart*

At first the Lark, when she means to rejoice, to cheer herself and those that hear her; she then quits the earth, and sings as she ascends higher into the air, and having ended her heavenly employment, grows then mute, and sad, to think she must descend to the dull earth, which she could not touch, but for necessity.

Izaak Walton, *The Compleat Angler*

Joy is the affect which comes when we use our powers. Joy, rather than happiness, is the goal of life, for joy is the emotion which accompanies our fulfilling our natures as human beings. It is based on the experience of one's identity as a being of worth and dignity, who is able to affirm his being, if need be, against all other beings and the whole organic world.

Rollo May, *Man's Search for Himself*

'The fruit of the spirit is love – joy.' So the opaque Christian is a slander on God. The thing which the church has been so much afraid of – joy, cheerfulness, hopefulness, gentleness, sweetness, overflowing manhood – this is one of the fruits of the Spirit. Love and joy are put first.

Henry Ward Beecher, *Proverbs from Plymouth Pulpit*

Joy; the Greek word is *chara*, and the characteristic of this word is that it most often describes that joy which has a basis in religion, and whose real foundation is God . . . It is not the joy that comes from earthly things or cheap triumphs; still less is it the joy that comes from triumphing over someone else in rivalry or competition. It is a joy whose basis is God.

William Barclay, *The Letters to the Galatians and Ephesians*

There are some people who have the quality of richness and joy in them and they communicate it to everything they touch. It is first of all a physical quality; then it is a quality of spirit. With such people it makes no difference if they are rich or poor; they are really always rich because they have such wealth and vital power within them that they give everything interest, dignity, and a warm colour.

Thomas Wolfe, *The Web and the Rock*

See also Cheerfulness, Freedom, Fulfilment, Happiness, Transformation

59

KINDNESS

Kindness – the quality or habit of being kind; kind feeling; affection, love

If someone were to ask me what has been the greatest influence in my life, I would have to say – kindness. When I went into the army to do National Service, we were first of all put through basic training. Towards the end of this I was recommended to attend a WOSB – a War Office Selection Board. If I passed this hurdle I would go to Mons Officer Cadet School in Aldershot for four months' training. After that, all being well, I would be commissioned. I remember going to a very cold barracks in a remote part of Hampshire. For three days we were put through a series of tests. I was then summoned to see the colonel. My papers were laid out before him. 'I notice your eyesight is not A1. Regulations restrict you to the Pay Corps or the Pioneer Corps.' He looked at me intently. 'How keen are you to go into the infantry?' I looked him straight in the eye and said, 'Very keen, Sir.' He said, 'Okay, we'll see what we can do.' His act of kindness changed the whole course of my life. I ended up in the 2nd Gurkhas.

～

Blessed be the Lord: for he has wondrously shown his steadfast love to me.
   Psalm 31.21

But love your enemies, do good, and lend, expecting nothing in return. Your reward will be great, and you will be children of the Most High; for he is kind to the ungrateful and the wicked.
   Luke 6.35

A kind word is like a spring day.
   Russian proverb

Kind hearts are more than coronets.
   Alfred, Lord Tennyson, 'Lady Clara Vere de Vere'

Kindnesses, like grain, grow by sowing.
> Proverb

Kindliness in judgement is nothing less than a sacred duty.
> William Barclay, *The Gospel of Matthew*

What wisdom can you find that is greater than kindness?
> Jean Jacques Rousseau, *Emile or Education*

There is a grace of kind listening, as well as a grace of kind speaking.
> F.W. Faber, *Spiritual Conferences*

Kindness is the principle of tact, and respect for others the first condition of
savoir-vivre.   Henri Frédéric Amiel, *Amiel's Journal*

> The heart benevolent and kind
> The most resembles GOD.
> > Robert Burns, 'A Winter Night'

Gentleness as the fruit of the Spirit is a strong man's treating all men with lenity,
and kindness, and forbearance, and patience.
> Henry Ward Beecher, *Proverbs from Plymouth Pulpit*

My feeling is that there is nothing in life but refraining from hurting others, and
comforting those that are sad.
> Olive Schreiner, *The Letters of Olive Schreiner*

Life is short, and we have never too much time for gladdening the hearts of those
who are travelling the dark journey with us. Oh, be swift to love, make haste to
be kind!
> Henri Frédéric Amiel, *Amiel's Journal*

> On that best portion of a good man's life,
> His little, nameless, unremembered, acts
> Of kindness and of love.
> > William Wordsworth, 'Lines Composed a few Miles Above Tintern Abbey'

I have had that curiously *symbolic* and reassuring pleasure, of being entertained
with overflowing and simple kindness by a family of totally unknown people – an
adventure which always brings home to me the goodwill of the world.
> A.C. Benson, *Extracts from the Letters of Dr A.C. Benson to M.E.A.*

True kindness presupposes the faculty of imagining as one's own the suffering and joy of others. Without imagination, there can be weakness, theoretical or practical philanthropy, but not true kindness.

André Gide, *Pretexts, Reflections on Literature and Morality*

I expect to pass through this world but once; any good thing therefore that I can do, or any kindness that I can show to any fellow-creature, let me do it now; let me not defer or neglect it, for I shall not pass this way again.

Attributed to Stephen Grellet

Kind thoughts are rarer than either kind words or kind deeds. They imply a great deal of thinking about others. This in itself is rare. But they imply also a great deal of thinking about others without the thoughts being criticisms. This is rarer still.

F.W. Faber, *Spiritual Conferences*

Let the weakest remember – let the humblest . . . remember, that in his daily course he can, if he will, shed around him almost a heaven. Kindly words, sympathizing attentions, watchfulness against wounding men's sensitiveness – these cost very little, but they are priceless in their value. Are they not . . . almost the stable of our daily happiness? From hour to hour, from moment to moment, we are supported, blest, by small kindnesses.

F.W. Robertson, *Sermons*

Be kind and merciful. Let no one ever come to you without leaving better and happier. Be the living expression of God's kindness – kindness in your face, kindness in your eyes, kindness in your smile, kindness in your warm greeting. In the slums we are the light of God's kindness to the poor. To children, to the poor, all who suffer and are lonely, give always a happy smile. Give them not only your care but also your heart. Because of God's goodness and love every moment of our life can be the beginning of great things. Be open, ready to receive and you will find him everywhere. Every work of love brings a person face to face with God.

Mother Teresa, in Kathryn Spink, *In the Silence of the Heart*

And it is here that the saints serve us yet again. Kindness recovers all its apostolic quality in them. In the saint it is never sentimental; never divorced from reality; never undisciplined; never evasive. On the other hand, it is ever-present: never excluded by their concern for God's holiness; never driven away by any pride in their own virtue. The cheapening of the word in the world, and the neglect of this grace in the sanctuary, are both corrected in the saint. He reveals kindness *as a fruit of the Spirit*. He shows it grounded in the nature of God. It flows directly from his faith. It is supernatural love disclosing itself in costly affection towards his fellow-men . . . That is why it has a robustness and pertinacity unknown to the sentimental kindness of the world . . .

    W.E. Sangster, *The Pure in Heart*

See also Awareness, Compassion, Grace, Love, Neighbour

60

KINGDOM OF GOD

Kingdom of God – the central theme of the teaching of Jesus, involving an understanding of his own person and work

In the process of growing in faith, I have come to discover something of the kingdom of God in the depths of my being. At one level this has come through baptism, with the spiritual rebirth of the Father, the Son and the Holy Spirit. In the course of prayer one has become aware of the 'presence' of the gifts and fruits of the Holy Spirit. I have also been greatly helped by commentators who point out 'the kingdom of God is within you' can also mean 'the kingdom of God is among you'. My experience has been that when the kingdom of God 'within you' becomes a living reality, it is as though scales are removed from our eyes, and we are able to see the kingdom of God 'among you' – in other people, in the processes of nature and creation, in other faiths, in work, and in the international scene as a whole. It is then that a phrase of the Lord's Prayer not only enables us to understand the person and work of Jesus, but calls us, too, to the kingdom of God – 'Thy kingdom come . . . on earth as it is in heaven.'

∽

But strive first for the kingdom of God and his righteousness, and all these things will be given to you as well.

Matthew 6.33

The time is fulfilled, and the kingdom of God has come near; repent, and believe in the good news.

Mark 1.15

This life, this kingdom of God, this simplicity of absolute existence, is hard to enter. How hard? As hard as the Master of salvation could find words to express the hardness.

George Macdonald, *Unspoken Sermons*

To keep alive the sense of wonder, to live in unquestioning trust, instinctively to obey, to forgive and forget – that is the childlike spirit, and that is the passport to the Kingdom of God.

William Barclay, *The Gospel of Luke*

The outer world, with all its phenomena, is filled with divine splendour, but we must have experienced the divine within ourselves, before we can hope to discover it in our environment.

Rudolf Steiner, *Knowledge of the Higher Worlds*

This Kingdom of God is now within us. The Grace of the Holy Spirit likewise shines forth and warms us, distils a multitude of fragrances in the air around us, and pervades our senses with heavenly delight, flooding our hearts with inexpressible joy.

Seraphim of Sarov, in G.P. Fedotov, *A Treasury of Russian Spirituality*

'The Kingdom of God is within you' – it is written in the very constitution of our being. The laws of the Kingdom are the laws of our being, stamped within our very selves, therefore inescapable. When you revolt against them, you revolt against yourself.

E. Stanley Jones, *Mastery*

As a matter of fact, that is the one business of man on earth – to co-operate with the divine power. All the activities of life – commercial, industrial, economic, social, political – should be, in their real nature, this co-operation with the divine power for the advancement of humanity.

Lilian Whiting, *Lilies of Eternal Peace*

The kingdom of God, which the Christian wishes to share with others, involves the individual and the community of faith in a process of looking back to the life and ministry of Jesus, in a deep commitment to the present where the kingdom is to be more clearly recognized and established, and in a longing for the future when all obstacles to the kingdom have been removed and the beauty and perfection of God's love is experienced in all its glory.

Trevor Beeson, *An Eye for an Ear*

The Kingdom of God is something within you which has the power of growth like a seed; something that you discover almost accidentally; something that you are searching for, and of whose value you become more confident and excited as the search proceeds, and you discover truer, lovelier things which are constantly being surpassed; something for which you have to give everything you have, no less yet no more, including the earlier finds with which you were once so completely delighted.

George Appleton, *Journey for a Soul*

We are at the beginning of the end of the human race. The question now before it is whether it will use for beneficial purposes or for purposes of destruction the power which modern science has placed in its hands. So long as its capacity for destruction was limited, it was possible to hope that reason would set a limit to disaster. Such an illusion is impossible today, when its power is illimitable. Our only hope is that the Spirit of God will strive with the spirit of the world and will prevail.

Albert Schweitzer, in E.N. Mozley, *The Theology of Albert Schweitzer*

To discover the Kingdom of God exclusively within oneself is easier than to discover it, not only there, but also in the outer world of minds and things and living creatures. It is easier because the heights within reveal themselves to those who are ready to exclude from their purview all that lies without. And though this exclusion may be a painful and mortificatory process, the fact remains that it is less arduous than the process of inclusion, by which we come to know the fullness as well as the heights of spiritual life.

Aldous Huxley, *The Perennial Philosophy*

Modern faith finds the beginning of the Kingdom of God in Jesus and in the Spirit which came into the world with him. We no longer leave the fate of mankind to be decided at the end of the world. The time in which we live summons us to new faith in the Kingdom of God.

We are no longer content, like the generations before us, to believe in the Kingdom that comes of itself at the end of time. Mankind today must either realize the Kingdom of God or perish. The very tragedy of our present situation compels us to devote ourselves in faith to its realization.

Albert Schweitzer, in E.N. Mozley, *The Theology of Albert Schweitzer*

The Kingdom of God was the main subject of the early preaching of Jesus. He claimed that in himself the Kingdom had drawn near, was in operation, and he called to men to accept this fact in faith and to change their attitudes, behaviour and world view. Many of his parables dealt with the meaning of the Kingdom, as if he were wanting to ensure that those who could not at first understand would remember one vivid human story, and that one day the penny would drop. He wanted everyone to share the treasure that he had brought.

George Appleton, *Journey for a Soul*

The miracle must happen in us before it can happen in the world. We dare not set our hope on our own efforts to create the conditions of God's Kingdom in the world. We must indeed labour for its realization. But there can be no Kingdom of God in the world without the Kingdom of God in our hearts. The starting-point is our determined effort to bring every thought and action under the sway of the Kingdom of God. Nothing can be achieved without inwardness. The Spirit of God will only strive against the spirit of the world when it has won its victory over that spirit in our hearts.

Albert Schweitzer, in E.N. Mozley, *The Theology of Albert Schweitzer*

Why did the idea of the Kingdom of God have no significance in the early church? It was closely connected with the expectation of the end of the world. And when hope of the coming of the end of the world had faded, the idea of the Kingdom of God lost its force as well. So it came about that the creeds were not at the same time preoccupied with the idea of redemption. Only after the reformation did the idea gradually arise that we men and women in our own age must so understand the religion of Jesus that we endeavour to make the Kingdom of God a reality in this world. It is only through the idea of the Kingdom of God that religion enters into relationship with civilization.

Albert Schweitzer, in Charles H. Joy, *An Anthology*

See also Church, Incarnation, Inner Life, Presence, Transformation

61

KNOWLEDGE

*K*nowledge – *the sum of what is known, as every branch of knowledge, personal knowledge, knowledge of God*

Last week I went into All Souls for lunch, and spotted the portrait of one of my heroes – Sir Sarvepalli Radhakrishnan. He has been a Fellow of All Souls, but more importantly was at one time President of India. In this introductory paragraph, I include a short passage from his book, *Indian Philosophy*, as it has something important to say about knowledge. 'Knowledge,' he wrote, 'is not something to be packed away in some corner of our brain, but what enters into our being, colours our emotion; haunts our soul, and is as close to us as life itself. It is the overmastering power which through the intellect moulds the whole personality, trains the emotions and disciplines the will.'

Wise words indeed. However nowadays we tend to concentrate on the first phrase of his passage, and pack away the contents of a degree course in some corner of our brain. By and large we ignore that overmastering power which through the intellect moulds the whole personality, trains the emotions and disciplines the will. Who would see to this in a modern-day university anyway? So, for some students, a university education is a disappointment and produces low performance.

⮑

Talk no more so very proudly, let not arrogance come from your mouth; for the Lord is a God of knowledge . . .

1 Samuel 2.3

I want their hearts to be encouraged and united in love, so that they may have all the riches of assured understanding and have the knowledge of God's mystery, that is, Christ himself, in whom are hidden all the treasures of wisdom and knowledge.

Colossians 2.2–3

Knowledge is the action of the soul.

Ben Jonson, *Explorata: or, Discoveries*

Knowledge comes, but wisdom lingers.

Alfred, Lord Tennyson, 'Locksley Hall'

To know is not to prove, nor to explain. It is to accede to vision.

Antonio de Saint-Exupéry, *Flight to Arras*

To know yourself is to realize that you're at once unique and multiple.

Michel Quoist, *With Open Heart*

But those who know do not theorize, they merely bear witness to what they have seen and experienced.

Kathleen Raine, *Defending Ancient Springs*

> Knowledge is proud that he has learn'd so much;
> Wisdom is humble that he knows no more.
>
> William Cowper, 'The Task'

To *know*, to get into the truth of anything, is ever a mystic act, – of which the best Logics can but babble on the surface.

Thomas Carlyle, *Sartor Resartus*

I see more and more that the knowledge of one human being, such as love alone can give, and the apprehension of our own private duties and relations, is worth more than all the book learning in the world.

Charles Kingsley, *Daily Thoughts*

What then can give rise to a true spirit of peace on earth? Not commandments and not practical experience. Like all human progress, the love of peace must come from knowledge. All living knowledge as opposed to academic knowledge can have but one object. This knowledge may be seen and formulated by thousands in a thousand different ways, but it must always embody one truth. It is the knowledge of the living substance in us, in each of us, in you and me, of the secret magic, the secret godliness that each of us bears within him.

Hermann Hesse, *If the War Goes on*

We do well to gather in every available fact which biology or anthropology or psychology can give us that throws light on human behaviour, or on primitive cults, or on the richer subjective and social religious functions of full-grown men. But the interior insight got from religion itself, the rich wholeness of religious experience, the discovery within us of an inner nature which defies description and baffles all plumb-lines, and which *can draw out of itself more than it contains,* indicate that we here have dealings with a type of reality which demands for adequate treatment other methods of comprehension than those available to science.

Rufus M. Jones, *Spiritual Reformers in the 16th and 17th Centuries*

The Indian mind has never been content to know 'about God'; it has always sought to know God. And here there is no separation between subject and object. To 'realize' God is to experience his presence, not in the imagination or in the intellect but in the ground of the soul from which all human faculties spring. This is the knowledge which the Upanishads were intended to impart, the knowledge of the Self, the Knower, which is the subject not the object of thought, the ground alike of being and of thought. To realize God in this way is to discover one's true self.

Bede Griffiths OSB, in Peter Spink, *The Universal Christ*

There has long been a distinction between two types of knowledge. There is the knowledge of things created, and this exerts a proper attraction on most of us. There is, more importantly, self-knowledge which, unfortunately, does not attract us nearly as much. Knowledge of that which is outside ourselves is very important and becomes a problem only when we make that the goal of our journey in life. It complements, in a very important way, self-knowledge but must be held in balance so as not to crowd out our search for the true interior of our beings. For it is deep within ourselves that the meaning of the universe is to be found.

Harry James Cargas, *Encountering Myself*

But the greatest error . . . is the mistaking or misplacing of the last or furthest end of knowledge. For men have entered into a desire of learning and knowledge, sometimes upon a natural curiosity and inquisitive appetite; sometimes to entertain their minds with variety and delight; sometimes for ornament and reputation; and sometimes to enable them to victory of wit and contradiction; and most times for lucre and profession; and seldom sincerely to give a true account of their gift of reason to the benefit and use of men: as if there were sought in knowledge a couch whereupon to rest a searching and restless spirit; or a terrace for a wandering and variable mind to walk up and down with a fair prospect; . . . and not a rich storehouse for the glory of the Creator and the relief of man's estate.

Francis Bacon, *The Advancement of Learning*

The message the mystics have for us is that while there is indeed a very real world 'out there', there is a more real world within each of us. What the meaning of this cosmic centre is, each must learn, individually. I am the living text for me and the only text. I cannot learn the lesson from what another has experienced or has written. Some can help me on the periphery, but the heart of the matter is in the heart of my soul. To ignore the truth from the Messenger is to put ourselves outside the *community of individuals* who are the true seekers, who are willing to wrestle and struggle with the difficulties that self-knowledge implies to gain the freedom and light that self-knowledge promises.

Harry James Cargas, *Encountering Myself*

See also Education, Listening, Meditation, Thinking, Wisdom

62

LEADERSHIP

*L*eadership – direction given by going in front, example, encouragement by doing thing

During my time of National Service we were given some training on 'leadership' at Mons Officer Cadet School in Aldershot. Here we were given a technique for exercising leadership in the field. First of all we had to 'make an appreciation of the situation'. This enabled us to identify our aim and objective. We then considered factors to be taken into account. Having made an appreciation of the situation, identified our aim and objective, and worked out our strategy, we were now be in a position to give clear, concise orders, and take group action. We were then able to exercise effective practical leadership. Leadership is costly. Leadership skills are increasingly needed in modern society.

❧

You should also look for able men among all the people, men who fear God, are trustworthy, and hate dishonest gain.
  Exodus 18.21

. . . the greatest among you must become like the youngest, and the leader like one who serves. For who is greater, the one who is at table, or the one who serves it? Is it not the one at the table? But I am among you as one who serves.
  Luke 22.26–27

A leader must have but one passion: for his work and his profession.
  André Maurois, *The Art of Living*

The real leader has no need to lead – he is content to point the way.
  Henry Miller, *The Wisdom of the Heart*

In the simplest terms, a leader is one who knows where he wants to go, and gets up and goes.

John Erskine, *The Complete Life*

Many leaders are in the first instance executives whose primary duty is to direct some enterprise or one of its departments or sub-units . . .

It remains true that in every leadership situation the leader has to possess enough grasp of the ways and means, the technology and processes by means of which the purposes are being realized, to give wise guidance to the directive effort *as a whole* . . .

Ordway Tead, *The Art of Leadership*

There are men, who, by their sympathetic attractions, carry nations with them, and lead the activity of the human race.

Ralph Waldo Emerson, *The Conduct of Life, Nature, and Other Essays*

> He that would govern others, first should be
> The master of himself.
>
> Philip Massinger, *The Bondman*

No man is great enough or wise enough for any of us to surrender our destiny to. The only way in which any one can lead us is to restore to us the belief in our own guidance.

Henry Miller, *The Wisdom of the Heart*

In general the principle underlying success at the co-ordinative task has been found to be that *every special and different point of view in the group affected* by the major executive decisions should *be fully represented by its own exponents when decisions are being reached.* These special points of view are inevitably created by the differing outlooks which different jobs or functions inevitably foster. The more the leader can know at first hand about the technique employed by all his group, the wiser will be his grasp of all his problems . . .

Ordway Tead, *The Art of Leadership*

People think of leaders as men devoted to service, and by service they mean that these men serve their followers . . . The real leader serves truth, not people.

J.B. Yeats, *Letters to His Son, W.B. Yeats and Others*

Good leaders are aware of both their strengths and weaknesses. They are not afraid to admit to the latter. They know how to find support and are humble enough to ask for it. There is no perfect leader who has all the gifts necessary for good leadership.

    Jean Vanier, *Community and Growth*

However dedicated men may be, the success of their work inevitably depends on the quality of their leaders. I am convinced that the key to leadership lies in the principle: 'He that is greatest among you, let him be as the younger and he that is chief, as he that doth serve.' Leadership should not bring privileges, but duties.

    Sir John Glubb, *The Fate of Empires and Search for Survival*

> We that had loved him so, followed him, honoured him,
> Lived in his mild and magnificent eye,
> Learned his great language, caught his clear accents,
> Made him our pattern to live and to die!
>
>   Robert Browning, 'The Lost Leader'

Leaders must take great care of those who have been given responsibility in the community and who for one reason or another (health, tiredness, lack of certain qualities, etc.) cannot exercise it well. Sometimes they must be relieved of their responsibility; in other cases, the leader must be more demanding and encourage them to do better. Much wisdom is needed here.

    Jean Vanier, *Community and Growth*

The leader also must recognize that his job is more demanding than the average. Strength literally goes out from him. Leading is hard work. It usually requires more average working hours than are given by others. It often requires sustained, concentrated effort; it requires occasional emergency demands which must be able to draw on physical reserves of strength and endurance. By his enthusiasm the leader makes unusual demands upon himself. Leading means a generous lavishing of energy which is abnormally taxing.

    Ordway Tead, *The Art of Leadership*

A leader of his people, unsupported by any outward authority; a politician whose success rests neither upon craft nor the mastery of technical devices, but simply on the convincing power of his personality; a victorious fighter who has always scorned the use of force; a man of wisdom and humility, armed with resolve and inflexible consistency, who has devoted all his strength to the uplifting of his people and the betterment of their lot; a man who has confronted the brutality of Europe with the dignity of the simple human being, and thus at all times risen superior. Generations to come, it may be, will scarce believe that such a one as this ever in flesh and blood walked upon this earth.

Albert Einstein (written of Mahatma Gandhi), *Ideas and Opinions*

Organizations tend to put a premium upon a display of sheer activity or busyness and upon constant physical presence on the job. Yet the values which leadership peculiarly demands are not cultivated by a flurry of constant action. More thoughtfulness, more chance for meditation, for serenity, for using one's imagination, for developing one's total personal effectiveness and poise, for being more straightforwardly human with one's associates – these are required. And these values flourish where there is physical well-being. People who are going to lead have to be rested and fresh; they need time to think about the aims and the problems of their organization. And their working schedules should allow for this.

Ordway Tead, *The Art of Leadership*

See also Awareness, Character, Influence, Integrity, Power

63

LIFE

Life – period from birth to death, birth to the present time, or present time to death; energy, liveliness, vivacity, animation; vivifying influence, active part of existence

At the age of twenty-four I was at the crossroads of life. I was soon to sit 'Schools' (the Oxford name for Finals) for a law degree, and make a choice of career. I thought carefully about going into the family firm of lawyers. The material rewards were promising. As I was musing over this possibility, I discerned a certain selfishness of outlook. I was thinking primarily of myself and my own comfort and security. About this time I made a spiritual commitment – to live the Christian *life* at all costs. I had just come to see the spiritual dimension as the most important thing in life. Before long an inner voice challenged my integrity: 'Come on, Bill, if living this Christian spiritual life is so important to you, shouldn't you be actively engaged in spreading it?' A vital question had been asked. Money, comfort and status were set aside as I made a bid for life itself.

$\backsim$

– then the Lord God formed man from the dust of the ground, and breathed into his nostrils the breath of life; and the man became a living being.

Genesis 2.7

Let anyone who is thirsty come to me, and let the one who believes in me drink. As the scripture has said, 'Out of the believer's heart shall flow rivers of living water.'

John 7.38

Creative life is always on the yonder side of convention.

C.G. Jung, in Jolande Jacobi, *Psychological Reflections*

The secret of life is to be found in life itself; in the full organic, intellectual and spiritual activities of our body.

Alexis Carrel, *Reflections on Life*

Is life so wretched? Isn't it rather your hands which are too small, your vision which is muddied? You are the one who must grow up.

Dag Hammarskjöld, *Markings*

To live as fully, as completely as possible, to be happy and again to be happy is the true aim and end of life. 'Ripeness is all.'

Llewelyn Powys, *Impassioned Clay*

After all it is those who have a deep and real inner life who are best able to deal with the 'irritating details of outer life'.

Evelyn Underhill, *The Letters of Evelyn Underhill*

What makes our lives worthwhile is stretching towards God who is love and truth. That we reach out beyond our capacity is at once our pain, our adventure, our hope.

Hubert van Zeller, *Considerations*

Life, as Christianity has always taught, as all clear-eyed observers have known, is a perilous adventure, and a perilous adventure for men and nations it will, I fear and believe, remain.

W. MacNeile Dixon, *The Human Situation*

The web of our life is of a mingled yarn, good and ill together; our virtues would be proud if our faults whipp'd them not, and our crimes would despair if they were not cherish'd by our virtues.

William Shakespeare, *All's Well that Ends Well*

The true spiritual goal of life is the formation of a rightly fashioned will, the creation of a controlling personal love, the experience of a guiding inward Spirit, which keep the awakened soul steadily approximating the perfect Life which Christ has revealed.

Rufus M. Jones, *Spiritual Reformers in the 16ᵗʰ and 17ᵗʰ Centuries*

People are always blaming their circumstances for what they are. I don't believe in circumstances. The people who get on in this world are the people who get up and look for the circumstances they want, and, if they can't find them, make them.

George Bernard Shaw, *Mrs Warren's Profession*

You have striven so hard, and so long, to *compel* life. Can't you slowly change, and let life slowly drift into you. Surely it is even a greater mystery and preoccupation even than willing, to let the invisible life steal into you and slowly possess you.

    D.H. Lawrence, *The Selected Letters of D.H. Lawrence*

A woman . . . recalls on one occasion when, as a girl, she complained of her hardships, and her mother, who was of pioneer stock, turned on her. 'See here,' said the mother, 'I have given you life; that is about all I will ever be able to give you – life. Now stop complaining and do something with it.'

    Harry Emerson Fosdick, *On Being a Real Person*

Human life is the expression of a spiritual existence, which we know has its glory in spiritual values and in spiritual beauty. 'In the way of righteousness is life', not in the way of riches or prosperity or health or happiness, but in the way of righteousness which is revealed to be nothing else than the purity of love.

    Father Andrew SDC, *The Way of Victory*

Not a May-Game is this man's life; but a battle and a march, a warfare with principalities and powers. No idle promenade through fragrant orange-groves and green flowery spaces, waited on by coral Muses and rosy Hours: it is a stern pilgrimage through burning sandy solitudes, through regions of thick-ribbed ice.

    Thomas Carlyle, *Past and Present*

If you don't know what man was made for, neither do you know what man can do. You don't know the heights to which he can rise, the fullness of living of which he is capable or the happiness which can come his way. The whole thing means a tremendous difference here and now, the difference of knowing what life really can be.

    R.L. Smith, 'Life Made Possible by the Gospel' in Paul Rowntree Clifford, *Man's Dilemma and God's Answer*

I want to prepare you, to organize you for life, for illness, for crisis, and death . . . Live all you can – as complete and full a life as you can find – do as much as you can for others. Read, work, enjoy – love and help as many souls – do all this. Yes – but remember: Be alone, be remote, be away from the world, be desolate. Then you will be near God.

    Frederick von Hügel, *Letters to a Niece*

We come fully to life only in meeting one another . . . and because we do come fully to life in that meeting we appear to have met not only one another but also

God. We appear to have met God in one another, to have addressed God, to have been stirred with a breath of God. Yet that breath is not a breath of immortality but a breath of eternal life.

John S. Dunne, *The Reasons of the Heart*

A man contains all that is needful to his government within himself. He is made a law unto himself. All real good or evil that can befall him must be from himself . . . The purpose of life seems to be to acquaint a man with himself. He is not to live to the future as described to him, but to live to the real future by living the real present. The highest revelation is that God is in every man.

Ralph Waldo Emerson, *The Heart of Emerson's Journals*

See also Blessedness, Eternal Life, Fulfilment, Love, Wholeness

64

LIGHT

*L*ight – *mental illumination, elucidation, enlightenment, vivacity in a person's face, especially the eyes, illumination of the soul by divine truth*

At Bradford Cathedral we devised a special service for the feast of the Epiphany. The format consisted of lessons, carols and anthems, celebrating the manifestation of Christ (the light of the world) to the Gentiles. Once everyone was in place, all the lights were switched off and the service started in darkness – symbolic of a world without the light of Christ. Gradually as the service progressed, lights were switched on. By the end of the service the cathedral was bathed in light. As I recall there was a particular sequence in the readings. The service began with the three wise men seeking the baby Jesus – a light to lighten the Gentiles. The main focus then was on Christ 'the Light of the World'. More lights were switched on, with the words: 'You are the light of the world.' When all the lights had been switched on, we were dismissed with the words: 'Let your light shine before others, so that they may see your good works and give glory to your Father who is in heaven.' The sequence of the service mirrored my own journey of faith – of finding light through the person of Jesus Christ.

❧

Indeed, you are my lamp, O Lord, the Lord lightens my darkness.

2 Samuel 22.29

I am the light of the world. Whoever follows me will never walk in darkness but will have the light of life.

John 8.12

Open your heart to the influence of the light, which, from time to time, breaks in upon you.

Samuel Johnson, *The History of Rasselas*

> Of the great world of light that lies
> Behind all human destinies.
>
> Henry Wadsworth Longfellow, 'To a Child'

A man should learn to detect and watch that gleam of light which flashes across his mind from within, more than the lustre of the firmament of bards and sages.

Ralph Waldo Emerson, *Self-Reliance*

I am aware of something in myself *whose shine is my reason.* I see clearly that something is there, but what it is I cannot understand. But it seems to me, that, if I could grasp it, I should know all truth.

Meister Eckhart, *Meister Eckhart*, translated by Raymond B. Blakney

The 'Depth of God within the Soul', the Inner Light, is the precious Pearl, the never-failing Comfort, the Panacea for all diseases, the sure Antidote even against death itself, the unfailing Guide and Way of all Wisdom.

Rufus M. Jones, *Spiritual Reformers in the 16th and 17th Centuries*

What is that light whose gentle beams now and again strike through to my heart, causing me to shudder in awe yet firing me with their warmth? I shudder to feel how different I am from it; yet in so far as I am like it, I am aglow with its fire.

St Augustine, *Confessions*

> Hast never come to thee an hour,
> A sudden gleam divine, precipitating, bursting all these bubbles,
>   fashions, wealth?
> These eager business aims – books, politics, art, amours,
> To utter nothingness?
>
> Walt Whitman, 'Hast Never Come to Thee an Hour'

. . . I thought the Light of Heaven was in this world: I saw it possible, and very probable, that I was infinitely beloved of Almighty God, the delights of Paradise were round about me, Heaven and earth were open to me, all riches were little things; this one pleasure being so great that it exceeded all the joys of Eden.

Thomas Traherne, *Centuries*

> And I said to the man who stood at the gate of the year:
> 'Give me a light that I may tread safely into the unknown.'
> And he replied: 'Go out into the darkness and put your hand into
>   the hand of God.
> That shall be to you better than light and safer than a known way.'
>
> Louise M. Haskins, 'God Knows'

There is a light in man which shines into his darkness, reveals his condition to him, makes him aware of evil and checks him when he is in the pursuit of it; gives him a vision of righteousness, attracts him towards goodness, and points him infallibly toward Christ from whom the Light shines. The light is pure, immediate, and spiritual. It is of God, in fact it is God immanently revealed.

Rufus M. Jones, *Spiritual Reformers in the 16ᵗʰ and 17ᵗʰ Centuries*

The doctrine of Christ in every man, as the indwelling Word of God, the Light who lights every one who comes into the world, is no peculiar tenet of the Quakers, but one which runs through the whole of the Old and New Testaments, and without which they would both be unintelligible, just as the same doctrine runs through the whole history of the Early Church for the first two centuries, and is the only explanation of them.

Charles Kingsley, *Daily Thoughts*

The world may be in darkness but this should not upset us. Christ is the light of the world. If we bring this truth into the context of our own experience we must know that light inaccessible has invited us to enter into this light. He has asked us not merely to reflect it but to *be* it. Otherwise his words 'you are the light of the world, the city seated on a hill, the salt of the earth' are no more than an oratorical flourish. Jesus did not go in for oratorical flourishes.

Hubert van Zeller, *Consideratiions*

The supreme experience of his life – and one of the most remarkable instances of 'illumination' in the large literature of mystical experiences – occurred when Boehme was twenty-five years of age, some time in the year 1600. His eye fell by chance upon the surface of a polished pewter dish which reflected the bright sunlight, when suddenly he felt himself environed and penetrated by the Light of God, and admitted into the innermost ground and centre of the universe. His experience, instead of waning as he came back to normal consciousness, on the contrary deepened.

Rufus M. Jones, *Spiritual Reformers in the 16ᵗʰ and 17ᵗʰ Centuries*

Jesus said: 'He who follows me will not walk in darkness, but he will have the light of life.' The phrase *the light of life* means two things. In the Greek it can mean, either, the light which issues from the source of life, or, the light which gives life to men. In this passage it means both things. Jesus is the very light of God come among men; and Jesus is the light which gives men life. Just as the flower can never blossom when it never sees the sunlight, so our lives can never flower with the grace and beauty they ought to have until they are irradiated with the light and presence of Jesus Christ.

William Barclay, *The Gospel of John*

I do not believe that we can put into anyone ideas which are not in him already. As a rule there are in everyone all sorts of good ideas, ready like tinder. But much of this tinder catches fire, or catches it successfully, only when it meets some flame or spark from outside, i.e., from some other person. Often, too, our own light goes out, and is rekindled by some experience we go through with a fellow-man. Thus we have each of us cause to think with deep gratitude of those who have lighted the flames within us. If we had before us those who have thus been a blessing to us, and could tell them how it came about, they would be amazed to learn what had passed over from their life into ours.

Albert Schweitzer, *Memoirs of Childhood and Youth*

See also Beauty, Grace, Inspiration, Revelation, Vision

65

LISTENING

L istening – make effort to hear something, hear person speaking with attention; give ear to or now usually to (person or sound or story)

I was prepared for confirmation by our school chaplain. As part of our preparation we were taught how to say our prayers. I used his method for several years, until I gradually became aware of the importance of *listening*. I realized that in my prayer-life I was doing all the talking, almost telling God what to do. If God was indeed, in some mysterious way, in the depths of my being, then perhaps I ought to be taking a humbler approach and listen to him instead of speaking. It was just possible he might have something important to say to me. So I started *listening*. At first I found it very difficult. I would sit down in my room in a comfortable chair and try to listen. Soon I would get very restless and fidgety. A breakthrough came when I took up a pen and paper, and started writing – eventually leading to keeping a spiritual diary. I now go through the contents of *The Eternal Vision*, *listening* carefully, and recording insights which come to me in times of quiet. The emerging form of *listening prayer* has become a vital source of guidance. This book can be used to encourage the practice of *listening*.

Incline your ear, and come to me; listen, so that you may live.
   Isaiah 55.3

Then a cloud overshadowed them, and from the cloud there came a voice. 'This is my Son, the Beloved; listen to him!'
   Mark 9.7

Give us grace to listen well.
   John Keble, *The Christian Year*

Listen for the meaning beneath the words.
Anon

He [God] cannot be seen, but he can be listened to.
Martin Buber, *I and Thou*

By listening it is possible to bring a man's soul into being.
Anon, heard on the radio

Listen, my heart, to the whispers of the world with which it makes love to you.
Rabindranath Tagore, *Stray Birds*

The more faithfully you listen to the voice within you, the better you will hear what is sounding outside.
Dag Hammarskjöld, *Markings*

Difficult as it is really to listen to someone in affliction, it is just as difficult for him to know that compassion is listening to him.
Simone Weil, *Waiting on God*

Basically the answer is simple, very simple. We need only listen to what Jesus has told us. It's enough to listen to the Gospel and put into practice what it tells us.
Carlo Carretto, *Letters from the Desert*

How can you expect to keep your powers of hearing when you never want to listen? That God should have time for you, you seem to take as much for granted as that you cannot have time for Him.
Dag Hammarskjöld, *Markings*

I've become, re-become, a sceptic: with however a deepened spiritual sense, more of a Listener, a deeper sense of the possibilities of something stirring, emerging, from There Back-of-things.
Stephen MacKenna, *Journal and Letters*

Before we can hear the Divine Voice we must shut out all other voices, so that we may be able to listen, to discern its faintest whisper. The most precious messages are those which are whispered.
Mark Rutherford, *More Pages from a Journal*

If we knew how to listen to God, we should hear him speaking to us. For God does speak. He speaks in his Gospel; he speaks also through life – that new Gospel to which we ourselves add a page each day.

Michel Quoist, *Prayers of Life*

The boy Samuel was told by Heli to pray: 'Speak, Lord, for your servant listens.' He was not instructed to say: 'Listen, Lord, for your servant speaks.' If we listened more we would learn more about spirit and truth . . . and in turn would be better able to worship in spirit and in truth.

Hubert van Zeller, *Considerations*

And when, as happens more and more here, people bring their problems to me, I know that that is no compliment to my learning. It is better than that. It is a recognition on their part that I am free to listen to them, that I am open to them, that I am in some sort a free man.

Dan Billany and David Dowie, *The Cage*

Most of us in our praying, devote far less time and attention to 'waiting upon God' – to the listening side of prayer – than we devote to the incessantly active and vocal form of praying that most of us indulge in. We ought . . . to give more time to listening to God than we do to speaking to Him.

Dr Cyril H. Powell, *Secrets of Answered Prayer*

There are different kinds of listening. There is the listening of criticism; there is the listening of resentment. There is the listening of superiority; there is the listening of indifference. There is the listening of the man who only listens because for the moment he cannot get the chance to speak. The only listening that is worth while is the listening which listens and learns. There is no other way to listen to God.

William Barclay, *The Gospel of John*

If he didn't tell you what was on his mind it was because he didn't feel he could.

You think he was afraid. In a way that's true, but if he was afraid, it was because you weren't really inviting, you weren't 'empty' enough, loving enough, to receive him. Listening isn't easy! And yet, I'm fairly sure that people are overflowing with words, and in allowing them to express themselves, we allow them a measure of release, and a chance to become themselves again.

Michel Quoist, *With Open Heart*

Listening to oneself is so difficult because this art requires another ability, rare in modern man: that of being alone with oneself . . .

Listening to the feeble and indistinct voice of our conscience is difficult also because it does not speak to us directly but indirectly and because we are often not aware that it is our conscience which disturbs us. We may feel only anxious (or even sick) for a number of reasons which have no apparent connection with our conscience.

Erich Fromm, *Man for Himself*

The most difficult and decisive part of prayer is acquiring this ability to listen. Listening is no passive affair, a space when we happen not to be doing or speaking. Inactivity and superficial silence do not necessarily mean that we are in a position to listen. Listening is a conscious, willed action, requiring alertness and vigilance, by which our whole attention is focused and controlled. Listening is in this sense a difficult thing. And it is decisive because it is the beginning of our entry into a personal and unique relationship with God, in which we hear the call of our own special responsibilities for which God has intended us. Listening is the aspect of silence in which we receive the commission of God.

Mother Mary Clare SLG, *Encountering the Depths*

See also Awareness, Contemplation, Guidance, Meditation, Prayer

66

LITERATURE

Literature – literary culture; realm of letters, writings of country or period; writings whose value lies in beauty of form or emotional effect

I once went on a camping holiday with my young sister on the continent. Our ultimate destination was a beach in what was then Yugoslavia but we planned to take our time over the journey, visit places of interest en route, and read as we went along. We crossed the Channel and soon got into a leisurely routine. We enjoyed a brief sojourn in Paris. In Switzerland we camped in the Lauterbrunnen valley and visited the high-altitude village of Mürren. By now we were both deeply absorbed in novels and for me Tolstoy's *Anna Karenina* was compulsive reading. Various times during the day were set aside for books. As we approached Venice we faced a mini-crisis. We had read all our books. Luck was on our side and we replenished our supplies in Venice. After a couple of days we moved on to Yugoslavia and camped near a beach. The next few days were spent sun-bathing, swimming and reading. On this holiday I discovered something of the truth of Carlyle's words: 'Literature is the Thought of thinking Souls.'

Seek and read from the book of the Lord.
   Isaiah 34.16

But as for you, continue in what you have learned and firmly believed, knowing from whom you learned it, and how from childhood you have known the sacred writings that are able to instruct you for salvation through faith in Christ Jesus.
   2 Timothy 3.14–15

Works of fiction are just as wholesome as anything else, if they are read wholesomely.
   Henry Ward Beecher, *Proverbs from Plymouth Pulpit*

Great literature is simply language charged with meaning to the utmost possible degree.

Ezra Pound, *How to Read*

. . . something that was greater than Jefferies's books – the spirit that led Jefferies to write them.

E.M. Forster, *Howard's End*

The Bible stands alone in human literature in its elevated conception of manhood, in character and conduct.

Henry Ward Beecher, *Proverbs from Plymouth Pulpit*

Can anything be called a book unless it forces the reader by one method or another, by contrast or sympathy, to discover himself?

Norman Douglas, *An Almanac*

. . . a true work of art . . . is an analysis of experience and a synthesis of the findings into a unity that excites the reader.

Rebecca West, *Ending in Earnest*

Literature is rather an image of the spiritual world, than of the physical, is it not? – of the internal, rather than the external.

Henry Wadsworth Longfellow, *Kavanagh*

He [Shakespeare] was the man who of all Modern, and perhaps Ancient Poets, had the largest and most comprehensive soul.

John Dryden, *Essay of Dramatic Poesy*

I tell him prose and verse are alike in one thing – the best is that to which went the hardest thoughts. This also is the secret of originality, also the secret of sincerity.

J.B. Yeats, *Letters to His Son, W.B. Yeats and Others*

Those writers are to be valued above all others who lay hold of us and gently transform us into a new world, closing communication with the world in which we live.

Mark Rutherford, *Last Pages from a Journal*

Books are the treasured wealth of the world and the fit inheritance of generations and nations . . . Their authors are a natural and irresistible aristocracy in every society, and, more than kings or emperors, exert an influence on mankind!

Henry David Thoreau, *Walden*

Of all literary pleasures, the reading of a poem is the highest and purest. Only pure lyric poetry can sometimes achieve the perfection, the ideal form wholly permeated by life and feeling, that is otherwise the secret of music.

Hermann Hesse, in Volker Michels, *Reflections*

It is a marvel of literature that the most profound conceptions of the sin and guilt of mankind are the subject matters of a sacred literature more cheerful and hopeful, more invigorating and comforting, than any that has ever existed.

Henry Ward Beecher, *Proverbs from Plymouth Pulpit*

It is chiefly through books that we enjoy intercourse with superior minds, and these invaluable means of communication are in the reach of all. In the best books, great men talk to us, give us their most precious thoughts, and pour their souls into ours. God be thanked for books. They are the voices of the distant and the dead, and make us heirs of the spiritual life of past ages. Books are the true levellers. They give to all, who will faithfully use them, the society, the spiritual presence of the best and greatest of our race.

William E. Channing, *Self-Culture*

There are some books, when we close them; one or two in the course of our life, difficult as it may be to analyse or ascertain the cause: our minds seem to have made a great leap. A thousand obscure things receive light; a multitude of indefinite feelings are determined. Our intellect grasps and grapples with all subjects with a capacity, a flexibility and a vigour before unknown to us. It masters questions hitherto perplexing, which are not even touched or referred to in the volume just closed. What is this magic? It is the spirit of the supreme author, by a magnetic influence blending with our sympathising intelligence, that directs and inspires it.

Benjamin Disraeli, *Coningsby*

Just as words have two functions – information and creation – so each human mind has two personalities, one on the surface, one deeper down. The upper personality has a name. It is called S.T. Coleridge, or William Shakespeare, or Mrs Humphry Ward. It is conscious and alert, it does things like dining out, answering letters, etc., and it differs vividly and amusingly from other personalities. The lower personality is a very queer affair. In many ways it is a perfect fool, but without it there is no literature, because, unless a man dips a bucket down into it occasionally he cannot produce first-class work. There is something general about it. Although it is inside S.T. Coleridge, it cannot be labelled with his name. It has something in common with all other deeper personalities, and the mystic will assert that the common quality is God, and that here, in the obscure recesses of our being, we near the gates of the Divine . . . What is so wonderful about great literature is that it transforms the man who reads it towards the condition of the man who wrote, and brings to birth in us also the creative impulse. Lost in the beauty where he was lost, we find more than we ever threw away, we reach what seems to be our spiritual home, and remember that it was not the speaker who was in the beginning but the Word.

E.M. Forster, *Anonymity, An Enquiry*

See also Imagination, Revelation, Thinking, Understanding, Wisdom

67

LONELINESS

*L*oneliness – dejection at the consciousness of being alone; having a feeling of solitariness, dreariness

Some years ago I went on sabbatical leave. A friend kindly lent me a farmhouse cottage in a remote hamlet on the Cumbrian fells. The nearest village was three miles away. At first I greatly enjoyed the peace and quiet, and being able to work without anyone making demands on me was a great privilege. After a few weeks a feeling of loneliness crept up on me, and I was missing people. I was feeling extremely isolated and dejected. I remember one morning bemoaning the fact I had a voice and no one to talk to, eyes and no one to look at, only scores of sheep in the surrounding fields. Loneliness is a great source of human suffering today and afflicts both young and old alike. The breakdown of society and the competitive nature of living bring about feelings of isolation difficult to combat. One antidote to loneliness is an acquisition of wholeness in which we become happy in ourselves, and learn to relate well with those around us.

❧

Turn to me, and be gracious to me, for I am lonely and afflicted. Relieve the troubles of my heart, and bring me out of my distress.

Psalm 25.16–17

In the morning, while it was still very dark, he got up and went out to a deserted place, and there he prayed.

Mark 1.35

> The quiet and exalted thoughts
> Of loneliness.
> William Wordsworth, 'Prelude'

Pray that your loneliness may spur you into finding something to live for, great enough to die for.

    Dag Hammarskjöld, *Markings*

The deepest need of man . . . is the need to overcome his separateness, to leave the prison of his aloneness.

    Erich Fromm, *The Art of Loving*

When one does give one's heart over to the loneliness of God . . . one does actually experience a transformation of loneliness into love.

    John S. Dunne, *The Reasons of the Heart*

Does not all creativity ask for a certain encounter with our loneliness, and does not the fear of this encounter severely limit our possible self-expression.

    Henri J.M. Nouwen, *Reaching Out*

> And lifting up my eyes, I found myself
> Alone, and in a land of sand and thorns.
>   Alfred, Lord Tennyson, 'The Holy Grail'

Loneliness is bred of a mind that has grown earthbound. For the spirit has its homeland, which is the realm of the meaning of all things.

    Antoine de Saint-Exupéry, *The Wisdom of the Sands*

We are born helpless. As soon as we are fully conscious we discover loneliness. We need others physically, emotionally, intellectually; we need them if we are to know anything, even ourselves.

    C.S. Lewis, *The Four Loves*

Our language has wisely sensed those two sides of man's being alone. It has created the word 'loneliness' to express the pain of being alone. And it has created the word 'solitude' to express the glory of being alone.

    Paul Tillich, *The Eternal Now*

The knowledge of the ever-present Christ can reach down into the hidden depths and assure lonely modern man that he is not alone. More than that; it can draw him out of his loneliness to the rediscovery of the human race.

    Stephen Neill, *The Church and Christian Union*

It is true, 'loneliness is not the sickness unto death', but when there is no passing over, no entering into the lives of others, then the longing in loneliness becomes something dark at work in our lives, something 'evil and lonely', a nightmare of soul, a 'heart of darkness'.

John S. Dunne, *The Church of the Poor Devil*

Children, adolescents, adults, and old people are in growing degree exposed to the contagious disease of loneliness in a world in which a competitive individualism tries to reconcile itself with a culture that speaks about togetherness, unity, and community as the ideals to strive for . . .

Henri J.M. Nouwen, in Robert Durback, *Seeds of Hope*

When loneliness is haunting me with its possibility of being a threshold instead of a dead end, a new creation instead of a grave, a meeting place instead of an abyss, then time loses its desperate clutch on me. Then I no longer have to live in a frenzy of activity, overwhelmed and afraid for the missed opportunity.

Henri J.M. Nouwen, *Reaching Out*

I never know what people mean when they complain of loneliness.

To be alone is one of life's greatest delights, thinking one's own thoughts, doing one's own little jobs, seeing the world beyond and feeling oneself uninterrupted in the rooted connection with the centre of all things.

D.H. Lawrence, *Loneliness*

The roots of loneliness are very deep and cannot be touched by optimistic advertisement, substitute love images, or social togetherness. They find their food in the suspicion that there is no one who cares and offers love without conditions, and no place where we can be vulnerable without being used.

Henri J.M. Nouwen, in Robert Durback, *Seeds of Hope*

We are always being told that no man is an island, but are not most of us islands? Desert islands at that. Each man has his empty shore of sand, his jungle thicket, his struggle for survival. Left to himself he deals with whatever habitation there is as best he can. But the point is that if he has faith in the presence and providence of God he is not left to himself.

Hubert van Zeller, *Considerations*

Lonely is not a synonym for *alone*. The word *lonely* connotes isolation and dejection, a missed absence of companions when it is applied to persons. The root of *alone*, however, is in two words: *all one*. This means the opposite of isolation and dejection. The emphasis is not on the *one* but on the *wholly one*. It means complete by oneself.

Harry James Cargas, *Encountering Myself*

Essentially loneliness is the knowledge that one's fellow human beings are incapable of understanding one's condition and therefore are incapable of bringing the help most needed. It is not a question of companionship – many are ready to offer this and companionship is certainly not to be despised – but rather one of strictly sharing, of identifying. No two human beings can manage this, so to a varying extent loneliness at times is the lot of all.

Hubert van Zeller, *Considerations*

See also Inner Life, Longing, Presence, Transformation, Wholeness

68

LONGING

*L*onging – *yearn, wish vehemently, for thing to do*

Kenya is a beautiful country. On a short visit I went to Treetops, and stayed up all night to watch wild animals come to the salt lick and waterhole. After dusk the area around Treetops is spotlighted, so there is an excellent view of animals coming to seek refreshment. During the night a number of gazelles came to drink water, and I was reminded of the words of the psalmist: 'As a deer longs for flowing streams, so my soul longs for you, O God.'

This set me off thinking about longing. I recalled to mind my youth. I saw this as a time of life of intense longing – for meaning, for purpose, for companionship, for a spouse, for sporting achievement, for success, for a career, for money, for security – for God perhaps? St Augustine took me one stage further in: 'You have made us for yourself and our hearts find no peace until they rest in you.' I wonder if we have something akin to a homesickness, namely 'a God-sickness', in our longing. This I take to be a longing for the divine, best satisfied by experiencing the presence of God.

⤳

As a deer longs for flowing streams, so my soul longs for you, O God.
Psalm 42.1

For the creation waits with eager longing for the revealing of the children of God.
Romans 8.19

This longing is for the one who is felt in the dark, but not seen in the day.
Rabindranath Tagore, *Stray Birds*

In every man's bosom there is that which at times longs for something better and purer than he is.
Henry Ward Beecher, *Proverbs from Plymouth Pulpit*

[265]

The thing we long for, that we are
For one transcendent moment.

J.R. Lowell, 'Longing'

But it [longing] is also there, playing its part in the despair and the sorrowing and the regrets and the remorse. Sadly it seems that this yearning can become misdirected into channels which lead to drugs or drink or other excesses for excitement to assuage the longing when it has not been recognized for what it is.

There are countless ways in which the longing can be expressed, by poets and painters, musicians and dancers, and by so many of those whose talent is for living and loving in awe and worship.

Perhaps the whole of life is concerned with this yearning. Nothing can be left out, but it carries us on into death and beyond when we dare hope that we shall come face to face with the source of all our longing.

Elizabeth Bassett, *The Bridge Is Love*

None but God can satisfy the longings of an immortal soul;
that, as the heart was made for Him, so He only, can fill it.

Richard Chevenix Trench, *Notes on the Parables of Our Lord*

Men turn to prayer in the extremity of their fears, or anxieties, or helplessness before the perils of their day, and of all human existence. But they also turn to prayer because of the almost universal and unquenchable yearning they have for God, and for that fullness of life to be found in knowing, loving and serving Him.

John L. Casteel, *Rediscovering Prayer*

He found God in solitude, 'the source and reason of all joy', but he still felt, even after he had found God, an unfulfilled longing for intimacy. It was an undifferentiated longing that did not know whether it longed for God or for a human being. It was dark and unknowing like the heart of a leopard, fierce and violent like the heart of a lion, cold and unloving like the heart of a wolf.

John S. Dunne, *The Reasons of the Heart*

I once heard Professor Jung say: 'Always follow your longing and it will lead you to God, even if at the beginning it seems to turn another way.' I followed this principle with my patients and it has proved sound. If I follow a person's deepest longing, although it may seem to lead to human love, to amusement, or to other things, as we go deeper, following the thread of that longing, we come to the inner life, to the sanctuary of the Divine.

Anon

This longing, this love has, we believe, undoubtedly been implanted in us by God; and as the eye naturally demands light and vision and our body by its nature desires food and drink, so our mind cherishes a natural and appropriate longing to know God's truth and to learn the causes of things.

Now we have not received this longing from God on the condition that it should not or could not ever be satisfied; for in that case the 'love of truth' would appear to have been implanted in our mind by God the Creator to no purpose, if its gratification is never to be accomplished

 Origen, in G.W. Butterworth, *Origen on First Principles*

The promise of it [of longing] is there in our love for another person. In the glory of a sunrise or sunset, the silver path of the moon on the sea, the sad haunting cry of sea-birds, the touching protective courage of a wild thing for its young or its mate. In the mountains and the streams, in the flowers and the forests, in the suffering and sorrows of mankind as well as in the joys and the laughter. This longing is all bound up with memories too, it carries its light like a will-o-the-wisp through the scents and sounds and sights which suddenly bring back to us the magical moments when we were very young and in love with life.

 Elizabeth Basset, *The Bridge Is Love*

In saying: 'I know who I am' Don Quixote said: 'I know what I will be!' That is the hinge of all human life: to know what one wills to be. Little ought you to care who you are; the urgent thing is what you will to be. The being that you are is but an unstable, perishable being, which eats of the earth and which the earth some day will eat; what you will to be is the idea of you in God, the Consciousness of the universe; it is the divine idea of which you are the manifestation in time and space. And your longing impulse toward the one you will to be is only homesickness drawing toward your divine home. Man is complete and upstanding only when he would be more than man.

 Miguel de Cervantes Saavedra, *The Life of Don Quixote and Sancho*

Life is a search for this 'something', a search for something or someone to give meaning to our lives, to answer the question, who am I, why am I here, what is the purpose of my life?

I believe that this great need we all feel is caused by a longing which cannot be satisfied by the usual goals we set ourselves in this journey of life. Even when they have been achieved they so often fall short of our hopes and expectations. The longed-for objective is not something which can be possessed, it cannot be held or kept, can only be fleetingly glimpsed as it comes and goes.

It can only be hinted at, referred to obliquely, indescribable in words, it can only be felt, and all we know of it is that it is what we are looking for.

Elizabeth Bassett, *The Bridge Is Love*

If there was one that I could trust and love and be so bound up with that he or she could share with me and understand my joys and my love, and my passion for beauty, for colour, for form, for pure joy in nature, – if he or she could enter into my thoughts and feel with me, – if my sorrow, my pain, my doubts, my unspoken thoughts and hopes and fancies and longings – my life and my love – if only – If I could find such a one, shouldn't I bring every joy, every delight, every pain, every sorrow, every passion, every love to be shared and to open the whole before that one: I know that I should: but there exists not the person on earth with whom lies the power of even to a small extent feeling with me in one of the smallest of my joys. Now and again one can truly say that one has felt with another, in joy or pain, in love or sorrow. But it is only now and again, and for years the heart hungers in between.

Edward Wilson, in George Seaver, *Edward Wilson of the Antarctic*

See also Aspiration, Eternal Life, Finding God, Love, Relationships

69

LOVE

*L*ove – *warm affection, attachment, liking, or fondness. In its deepest expression, a self-sacrificial form of love as exemplified in the life of Christ*

If we want to see 'Love' fully worked out in a life we can go to the person of Jesus Christ. At the height of his ministry he came out with his greatest command: 'You shall love the Lord your God with all your heart, and with all your soul, and with all your mind, and with all your strength . . . You shall love your neighbour as yourself.' I imagine Jesus was speaking out of his own experience. Here was someone who was prepared to love God with all his inner being: heart, soul, mind and strength. This was to be balanced with an outer love to neighbour (which included everyone in the immediate vicinity) and was further balanced by a true and genuine love of himself. In John's Gospel he confirmed the source of his love: 'As the Father has loved me, so have I loved you; abide in my love. If you keep my commandments, you will abide in my love, just as I have kept my Father's commandments and abide in his love.' The two commandments were simplified into one: 'I give you a new commandment that you love one another. Just as I have loved you, you also should love one another.' Jesus lived out this 'new commandment' to the very end.

∽

. . . you shall love your neighbour as yourself.
   Leviticus 19.18

I give you a new commandment, that you love one another. Just as I have loved you, you also should love one another.
   John 13.34

Whoever lives true life, will love true love.
   E R. Browning, 'Aurora Leigh'

By love may He be gotten and holden; but by thought never.
  The Cloud of Unknowing

We are all born for love . . . It is the principle of existence and its only end.
  Benjamin Disraeli, *Sybil or the Two Nations*

The great tragedy of life is not that men perish, but that they cease to love.
  W. Somerset Maugham, *The Summing Up*

The highest love of all finds its fulfilment not in what it keeps, but in what it gives.
  Father Andrew SDC, *Seven Words from the Cross*

> You give but little when you give of your possessions.
> It is when you give of yourself that you truly give.
>   Kahlil Gibran, *The Prophet*

The greatest thing that can happen to any human soul is to become utterly filled with love; and self-sacrifice is love's natural expression.
  William Temple, *Christian Faith and Life*

For even as love crowns you so shall he crucify you. Even as he is for your growth so is he for your pruning.
  Kahlil Gibran, *The Prophet*

There is no surprise more magical than the surprise of being loved; it is God's finger on man's shoulder.
  Charles Morgan, *The Fountain*

We should take pains to be polite to those whom we love. Politeness preserves love, is a kind of sheath to it.
  Mark Rutherford, *More Pages from a Journal*

Love it is – not conscious – that is God's regent in the human soul, because it can govern the soul as nothing else can.
  Henry Ward Beecher, *Proverbs from Plymouth Pulpit*

Nothing is sweeter than love, nothing stronger, nothing higher, nothing broader; nothing is more lovely, nothing richer, nothing better in heaven or in earth.
  Thomas à Kempis, *The Imitation of Christ*

Love to God is the slowest development to mature in the soul. No man ever learned to love God with all his heart, and his neighbour as himself, in a day.

Henry Ward Beecher, *Proverbs from Plymouth Pulpit*

All noble qualities feed and exalt Love. They in turn are by Love fed and exalted. Love, even as a *passion*, derives singular strength from its alliance with them.

Mark Rutherford, *Last Pages from a Journal*

When you love you should not say, 'God is in my heart', but rather, 'I am in the heart of God.' And think not you can direct the course of love, for love, if it finds you worthy, directs your course.

Kahlil Gibran, *The Prophet*

Love . . . is the supreme badge of any true Christianity, and the traits of the beatitudes in a person's life are a surer evidence that he belongs in Christ's family, than is the fact that he holds current opinions on obscure questions of belief.

Rufus M. Jones, *Spiritual Reformers in 16th and 17th Centuries*

Love is eager, sincere and kind; it is glad and lovely; it is strong, patient and faithful; wise, long-suffering and resolute; and it never seeks its own ends, for where a man seeks his own ends, he at once falls out of love.

Thomas à Kempis, *The Imitation of Christ*

Would'st thou learn thy Lord's meaning in these things? Learn it well: Love was His meaning. Who shewed it thee? Love. What shewed He thee? Love. Wherefore shewed it He? For Love. Hold thee therein and thou shalt learn and know more in the same.

Lady Julian of Norwich, *Revelations of Divine Love*

Love all God's creation, the whole of it and every grain of sand. Love every leaf, every ray of God's light! Love the animals, love the plants, love everything. If you love everything, you will perceive the divine mystery in things. And once you have perceived it, you will begin to comprehend it ceaselessly more and more every day.

Fyodor Dostoyevsky, *The Brothers Karamazov*

To make Love the ruling power of my life, the only power. To be kind, gentle, considerate and unselfish, to let nothing stand in the way of doing everyone a good turn, never to consider myself and my own feelings, but only other people's.

To put myself out to any extent for the sake of others, especially for the sake of those who are not attractive.

Edward Wilson, in George Seaver, *The Faith of Edward Wilson*

Existence will remain meaningless for you if you yourself do not penetrate into it with active love and if you do not in this way discover its meaning for yourself. Everything is waiting to be hallowed by you; it is waiting for this meaning to be disclosed and to be realized by you . . . Meet the world with the fullness of your being and you shall meet God. If you wish to believe, love!

Martin Buber, in Aubrey Hodes, *Encounter with Martin Buber*

See also Friendship, Longing, Marriage, Relationships, Saints

MARRIAGE

Marriage – the relation between married persons – intimate union

A young couple came to see me for marriage preparation. At the time I prepared couples for marriage by going through the wedding service, drawing out the meaning in considerable detail. On this particular occasion we were still on the first page when a terrific row broke out between the couple. A fundamental difference had surfaced which resulted in the 'bride' storming out of the room, and their relationship was at an end. Fortunately there was a happy outcome – both married different spouses later on. As a result of this experience I changed my way of preparing couples for marriage. I now lend them a copy of about fifty quotations on my 'Marriage material' and encourage them to reflect on 'Marriage' in their own time. In this way they can share their hopes and aspirations on marriage, and develop their unique relationship. My hope is having reflected on 'Marriage' they will continue the practice of reflection on other topics and deepen and widen their relationship.

It is not good that the man should be alone; I will make a helper as his partner.
  Genesis 2.18

But from the beginning of creation, 'God made them male and female.' 'For this reason a man shall leave his father and mother and be joined to his wife, and the two shall become one flesh.' So they are no longer two, but one flesh. Therefore what God has joined together, let no one separate.
  Mark 10.6–9

Never marry but for love; but see that thou lovest what is lovely.
  William Penn, *Fruits of Solitude*

None can be eternally united who have not died for each other.
  Coventry Patmore, *The Rod, the Root and the Flower*

Being married is something that takes everything you've got.
  Henry Ibsen, *The League of Youth*

Love is a glass which shatters if you hold it too tightly or too loosely.
  Russian proverb

But the highest form of affection is based on full sincerity on both sides.
  Thomas Hardy, *Jude the Obscure*

Love does not cause suffering: what causes it is the sense of ownership, which is
love's opposite.
  Antoine de Saint-Exupéry, *The Wisdom of the Sands*

Suitability helps the security of a marriage, but spirituality, by calling for mutual
self-sacrifice, ensures it.
  Hubert van Zeller, *Considerations*

Life has taught us that love does not consist in gazing at each other but in looking outward together in the same direction.
  Antoine de Saint-Exupéry, *Wind, Sand and Stars*

It is an essential condition for the proper choice of partners that both should be
on the same plane of existence.
  Count Hermann Keyserling, *The Book of Marriage*

Love is a recent discovery and requires a new law. Easy divorce is the vulgar solution. The true solution is some undiscovered security for true marriage.
  Coventry Patmore, *The Rod, the Root and the Flower*

Seldom, or perhaps never, does a marriage develop into an individual relationship smoothly and without crises; there is no coming to consciousness without
pain.
  C.G. Jung, *Contributions to Analytical Psychology*

The most precious gift that marriage gave me was this constant impact of something very close and intimate yet all the time unmistakably other, resistant – in a
word, real.
  C.S. Lewis, *A Grief Observed*

Unless marriage is thought of in terms of supernatural vocation even the natural side of it will be incomplete. The material and physical will outweigh the natural and spiritual.

Hubert van Zeller, *Considerations*

For the rest let him attend to his work, be glad in it, love his wife, be glad in her, bring up his children with joyfulness, love his fellow men, rejoice in life.

Søren Kierkegaard, *Training in Christianity*

If love be not thy chiefest motive, thou will soon grow weary of a married state, and stray from thy promise, to search out thy pleasures in forbidden places.

William Penn, *Fruits of Solitude*

As man is essentially a dynamic, aspiring, evolutionary being, marriage can bring fulfilment only inasmuch as it intensifies life. Wherever it causes diminution it fails in its purpose.

Count Hermann Keyserling, *The Book of Marriage*

Marriage is a terrifying responsibility. Marriage is a unique wholeness and completeness and having a best friend to confide in, to hurt, a friend who will understand, argue, fight, but still make love and be friends.

A young housewife

Love is not getting, but giving; not a wild dream of pleasure, and a madness of desire – oh, no, love is not that – it is goodness, and honour, and peace, and pure living – yes, love is that; and it is the best thing in the world, and the thing that lives longest.

Henry Van Dyke, *Little Rivers*

The fulfilment of marriage is that joy in which each lover's true being is flowering because its growth is being welcomed and unconsciously encouraged by the other in the infinite series of daily decisions which is their life together.

J. Neville Ward, *Five for Sorrow, Ten for Joy*

Affection, companionship, common interests, mutual respect and enduring devotion: these are the temporal elements in a good marriage. Temporal elements have their eternal dimension.

Hubert van Zeller, *Considerations*

The joy of going through life hand in hand with the comrade of one's choice, sharing one another's burdens, stimulating one another's courage, doubling one another's sagacity, buckling on one another's armour, wearing one another's laurels and easing one another's pain.

W.C. Willoughby, *Race Problems in the New Africa*

The essence of a good marriage is respect for each other's personality combined with that deep intimacy, physical, mental, and spiritual, which makes a serious love between man and woman the most fructifying of all human experiences. Such love, like everything else that is great and precious, demands its own morality, and frequently entails a sacrifice of the less to the greater, but such sacrifice must be voluntary, for where it is not, it will destroy the very basis of the love for the sake of which it is made.

Bertrand Russell, *Marriage and Morals*

See also Friendship, Kindness, Love, Relationships, Trust

71

MEDITATION

*M*editation *– the verb means to plan mentally, design; exercise the mind in contemplation on (upon) a subject, thinking about or reflecting on something spiritual or religious*

I began meditation at theological college. We had an official quiet time each day, before breakfast, lasting for half an hour. When the weather was fine I used to go to the nearby university parks and walk down to the river. I used sentences from the psalms such as – 'Be still and know that I am God!' – and repeated this phrase quietly to myself as I strolled around the parks. The beauty of nature added another dimension to the meditation. When the weather was bad I stayed in my room, and carried out the same exercise, seated in a chair. My practice of meditation developed slowly. I carefully searched the scriptures and noted suitable phrases for meditation. Later I made a collection of short phrases and sentences from a wide selection of sources. I then began to keep a spiritual diary or journal. With the aid of a pen and clipboard I would write out thoughts and feelings that came to the surface in meditation. My hope is others will benefit from the valuable practice of meditation.

I will meditate on your precepts, and fix my eyes on your ways.
    Psalm 119.15

The good person out of the good treasure of the heart produces good . . . for it is out of the abundance of the heart that the mouth speaks.
    Luke 6.45

Our duty is not primarily to strive and to brace up our wills, but primarily to fasten our attention upon the divine love, that it may do its own work upon us and within us.
    William Temple, *The Preacher's Theme Today*

The art of meditation may be exercised at all hours, and in all places, and men of genius, in their walks, at table, and amidst assemblies, turning the eye of the mind upwards, can form an artificial solitude; retired amidst a crowd, calm amidst distraction, and wise amidst folly.

Isaac Disraeli, *Literary Character of Men of Genius*

A man will be effective to the degree that he is able to concentrate! Concentration is not basically a mode of *doing* but above all a mode of being.

We meditate to find, to recover, to come back to something of ourselves we once dimly and unknowingly had and have lost without knowing what it was or where or when we lost it.

Lawrence LeShan, *How to Meditate*

In meditative prayer, one thinks and speaks not only with the mind and lips, but in a certain sense with one's *whole being*. Prayer is not then just a formula of words or a series of desires springing up in the heart – it is the orientation of our whole body, mind and spirit to God in silence, attention, and adoration. All good meditative prayer is a *conversion of our entire self to God*.

Thomas Merton, *Thoughts in Solitude*

Mental prayer, by way of meditation, is very easy, even to the meanest capacities; it requires nothing but a good will, a sincere desire of conversing with God, by thinking of him, and loving him. In effect, the great business of mental prayer is *thinking* and *loving*; and who is there that can even live without *thinking* and *loving*?

Richard Challenor, in Gordon S. Wakefield, *A Dictionary of Christian Spirituality*

After having placed yourself in the presence of God, by an act of loving faith, you must read something which is substantial, and stop gently upon it; not that you may reason, but only to fix your mind, remembering that the principal exercise ought to be the [practice of the presence] of God, and that the subject should serve more to stay your mind than to employ your reason.

Madame Guyon, *A Method of Prayer*

The purpose of meditation is not to achieve an academic exercise in thinking; it is not meant to be a purely intellectual performance, nor a beautiful piece of thinking without further consequences; it is meant to be a piece of straight thinking under God's guidance and Godwards, and should lead us to draw conclusions about how to live.

Anthony Bloom, *Living Prayer*

Unless one takes time to turn inward and be silent, meditation and the spiritual quest will not get very far. We seldom find God in a hurry, or in bits and pieces of reflection on a day of busy activity. I am told that Dr Jung once remarked: 'Hurry is not *of* the Devil, it *is* the Devil.' There is simply no better way to keep ourselves out of relationship with God than by simply having no time for Him, having no time to look within in meditation.

Morton T. Kelsey, *The Other Side of Silence*

People need to discover their own self-identity. Many go to drugs, not to forget the miseries of life, but to discover its secrets, to explore an inner life of identity, liberation and happiness. The mystics tell us that this experience can be gained from some discipline of meditation, entering into silence, stilling the activity of the mind, allowing feelings and intuitions to rise from the depths of our being.

George Appleton, *Journey for a Soul*

Meditative prayer is not an intellectual exercise in which we reflect about theological propositions. In meditation we are not *thinking* about God at all, nor are we thinking of His Son, Jesus, nor of the Holy Spirit. In meditation we seek to do something immeasurably greater; we seek to *be with* God, to *be with* Jesus, to *be with* his Holy Spirit, not merely to think about them.

John Main OSB, in Clare Hallward, *The Joy of Being*

Living things need an appropriate climate in order to grow and bear fruit. If they are to develop to completion, they require an environment that allows their potential to be realized. The seed will not grow unless there is soil that can feed it, light to draw it from, warmth to nurture and moisture that unlocks its vitality. Time is also required for its growth to unfold . . .

Meditation is the attempt to provide the soul with a proper environment in which to grow and to become.

Morton T. Kelsey, *The Other Side of Silence*

Meditation is a way of liberation from all fear. Fear is the greatest impediment to fullness of life. The wonder of the vision proclaimed by Jesus is that the great power of love which dispels fear is the power that we make contact with in the depths of our own being. The power of love is the energy that sweeps all before it. What we need to understand and what we need to proclaim if we are going to proclaim the Christian message to the world is that in prayer we begin to live fully from the life force that is set free in our inmost being and that life force is love because it is God.

John Main OSB, *Moment of Christ*

Meditation is a channel for the continuous reconstitution of the self, to prepare it that it may move into the new . . . The entire nervous system and the vital processes rest as in deep sleep, while there is a condition of alert attention in the mind, a listening to the world of being. We are then open to the qualities of the Higher Self, which essentially are peace, love, gentleness, courage and joy.

While these fill the soul, there is simply no room for the negative qualities of the lower self, which include remorse, regret, disappointment, anger, resentment for things past, and fear, anxiety and doubt about the future. These negative emotions cannot enter, any more than darkness can remain in a room when we switch on the light.

George Trevelyan, *A Vision of the Aquarian Age*

One of the main purposes of meditation is to expose us to the reality of the Father in such a way that we can become the kind of people who are able to love. His life radiating through us cleanses, heals and transforms us. Then we can truly love in the way that Jesus asked of us. He did not tell us that we are His followers when we are great at meditating and religious activities, but only when we love one another as He loved us. This is the ultimate criterion of our lives, which can be fully realized only as we turn inward and open ourselves to God.

Morton T. Kelsey, *The Other Side of Silence*

See also Contemplation, Guidance, Listening, Revelation, Transformation

MIND

M *ind – direction of thoughts or desires; way of thinking and feeling, seat of consciousness; thought, volition, and feeling; person as embodying mental qualities*

I was delighted with my rooms at Balliol. There were old and had a medieval feel about them. Sadly, they no longer exist. I had only been in residence a few days when I learnt they had once been occupied by a famous person – William Temple, a former Archbishop of Canterbury. Here was a man who impressed me with the sheer quality of his mind. He went on to be a lecturer in philosophy at Queen's College, Oxford, and wrote a major work, *The Creative Mind*. Later he combined his philosophy with theology, and became one of the most influential thinkers in the Church of England in recent times. 'You shall love the Lord your God . . . with all your mind'. What a challenge for us to use our minds. 'Let the same mind be in you that was in Christ Jesus'. What a command. 'Be transformed by the renewal of your minds'. What potential. The quotations which follow have been gathered from great minds of earlier generations. Reflection is a way to develop our minds on these lines.

∽

For the human heart and mind are deep.
  Psalm 64.6

You shall love the Lord your God . . . with all your mind.
  Mark 12.30

But the essential thing is to put oneself in a frame of mind which is close to that of prayer.
  Henri Matisse, in Françoise Gilot and Carlton Lake, *Life with Picasso*

The centre of nature is in the human mind. The meaning of the outward world is not in itself but in us.
  Henry Ward Beecher, *Proverbs from Plymouth Pulpit*

The mind of man is capable of anything – because everything is in it, all the past as well as all the future.

Joseph Conrad, *Heart of Darkness*

The mind grows always by intercourse with a mind more mature than itself. That is the secret of all teaching.

William Temple, *Christian Faith and Life*

It is the mind that maketh good or ill,
That maketh wretch or happy, rich or poor.

Edmund Spenser, 'The Faerie Queene'

The Divine Mind does not think for us, or in spite of us, but works in us to think, and to will, and to do.

Henry Ward Beecher, *Proverbs from Plymouth Pulpit*

Thinkers sometimes look on doers with pity. Things are always easier and more attractive in the mind . . .

Michel Quoist, *With Open Heart*

Few of us . . . make the most of our minds. The body ceases to grow in a few years; but the mind, if we will let it, may grow almost as long as life lasts.

Sir John Lubbock, *The Pleasures of Life*

Our minds are finite, and yet even in these circumstances of finitude we are surrounded by possibilities that are infinite, and the purpose of human life is to grasp as much as we can out of that infinitude.

Alfred North Whitehead, in Lucien Price, *Dialogues of Alfred North Whitehead*

Christ presents to the mind a better, wider, deeper, and more correct theory and conception of what God is than can be derived from nature or philosophy or any of the analogies of human life or human experience.

Henry Ward Beecher, *Proverbs from Plymouth Pulpit*

The truth of things is what they are in the mind of God, and it is only when we act according to the mind of God that we are acting in accordance with the truth, in accordance with reality. Everything else is making a mistake.

William Temple, *Basic Convictions*

The life of Christ is not simply a thing written. It is a thing lived. My sanctification lies in re-living this life in the context of my own life. It lies in identifying myself with the mind of Christ which is primarily the mind of love.

Hubert van Zeller, *Considerations*

Man is distinguished from the animals by possessing, among other things, a conscious mind, with the ability to think, reason, remember, imagine, understand and express himself. He is not just mind, nor is mind just a machine that he uses. It is a vital part of man's personality but not the whole of it. It needs to be brought under the inspiration and guidance of God.

George Appleton, *Journey for a Soul*

No man is changed till his mind is changed. We do most of our living within. Our deeds express our thoughts. It is into our minds that Christ must come if He is to come into our lives. From our minds, He will shape our character, discipline our will and control our bodies.

W.E. Sangster, *The Secret of Radiant Life*

It is a hard thing for a man to take such an instrument as the human mind and keep it in tune with itself, and also keep it in accord with other minds, with their different temperaments, and in all their varying moods, and under all their trials and swayings, and warpings and biasings.

Henry Ward Beecher, *Proverbs from Plymouth Pulpit*

There is a certain paradox in the human situation. God gave man a mind, and it is man's duty to use that mind to think to the very limits of human thought. But it is also true that there are times when that mind can only go so far, and, when that limit is reached, all that is left is to accept and to adore.

William Barclay, *The Letter to the Romans*

This is a plea for the use of the whole mind, intellectual and emotional, detached and involved; for only when the whole mind is alive can imagination work and creatively operate. And the trouble is that so many institutions formally connected with education and with morality behave as if they had, at best, only half a mind.

Roy Stevens, *Education and the Death of Love*

The mind of man is meant to be a microcosm of the mind of God. This was shown supremely, in terms of a human life, in Jesus Christ. We therefore need to study the records of that divine and human life, recognizing the faith of the writers but reaching back as far as possible to the life itself. Also, by communion with the ever-living, ever-present Christ, we can experience direct, intuitive contact and illumination.

George Appleton, *Journey for a Soul*

See also Intellect, Knowledge, Thinking, Truth, Wisdom

73

MONEY

Money – current coin; property viewed as convertible into money; coin in reference to its purchasing power

I remember reading a book – *Miracle on the River Kwai*. This book was a grim account of life in a prisoner of war camp in the Second World War. When POWs were dying (of wounds, fever, dysentery, malnutrition and the like) they were moved to a special hut and left to die. There were hardly any survivors. A Scottish minister, the author of the book, rounded up some able-bodied men and began to care for the sick and the dying. With the help of prayer, nursing and friendship, lives were saved. For those caught up in this healing work this was the *Miracle on the River Kwai*. The author, encouraged by what he had experienced, went home at the end of the war with high hopes for the future. Soon, however, he saw a return to the conditions which had existed before the war. He came to see men were separated by *economic competition*. He recognized the love of money was indeed a root of all evil. Is this still true today?

∽

The lover of money will not be satisfied with money; nor the lover of wealth, with gain. This also is vanity.

Ecclesiastes 5.10

But those who want to be rich fall into temptation and are trapped by many senseless and harmful desires that plunge people into ruin and destruction. For the love of money is a root of all kinds of evil, and in their eagerness to be rich some have wandered away from the faith and pierced themselves with many pains.

1 Timothy 6.9–10

To have money is a fear, not to have it a grief.
George Herbert, *Outlandish Proverbs*

Great Wealth and Content seldom live together.
Thomas Fuller, *Gnomologia*

The dangers gather as the treasures rise.
Samuel Johnson, *The Vanity of Human Wishes*

He who multiplies Riches multiplies Cares.
Benjamin Franklin, *Poor Richard's Almanack*

Riches are gotten with pain, kept with care, and lost with grief.
Thomas Fuller, *Gnomologia*

Money – money, like everything else – is a deception and a disappointment.
H.G. Wells, *Kipps*

There is nothing that makes men rich and strong but that which they carry inside of them.
Henry Ward Beecher, *Proverbs from Plymouth Pulpit*

Is there no prosperity other than commercial? It is surely time to have done with this utilitarian nonsense.
Norman Douglas, *An Almanac*

> Ill fares the land, to hastening ills a prey,
> Where wealth accumulates, and men decay.
> Oliver Goldsmith, 'The Deserted Village'

The commerce of the world is conducted by the strong; and usually it operates against the weak.
Henry Ward Beecher, *Proverbs from Plymouth Pulpit*

Whenever money is the principal object of life with either man or nation, it is both got ill, and spent ill; and does harm both in the getting and spending.
John Ruskin, *The Crown of Wild Olives*

We can hardly respect money enough for the blood and toil it represents. Money is frightening. It can serve or destroy man.
Michel Quoist, *Prayers of Life*

Money is human happiness in the abstract: he, then, who is no longer capable of enjoying human happiness in the concrete devotes himself utterly to money.

Arthur Schopenhauer, in W.H. Auden, *A Certain World*

We are prone to judge success by the index of our salaries or the size of our automobiles, rather than by the quality of our service and our relationship to humanity.

Martin Luther King, in Coretta Scott King, *The Words of Martin Luther King*

. . . money-getting men, men that spend all their time first in getting, and next in anxious care to keep it; men that are condemned to be rich, and then always busy or discontented.

Izaak Walton, *The Compleat Angler*

I saw that . . . where the heart was set on greatness, success in business did not satisfy the craving; but that commonly with an increase of wealth, the desire of wealth increased.

John Woolman, *The Journal of John Woolman*

Strong as is money and invincible, yet, in the long run, ideas are mightier than money. Tyrannies are overthrown by ideas. Armies are defeated by ideas. Nations, and Time itself, are overmatched by ideas.

Henry Ward Beecher, *Proverbs from Plymouth Pulpit*

Riches are a slow poison, which strikes almost imperceptibly, paralyzing the soul at the moment when it seems healthiest. They are thorns which grow with the grain and suffocate it right at the moment when corn is beginning to shoot up.

Carlo Carretto, *Letters from the Desert*

For forty years he had fought against economic fatality. It was the central ill of humanity, the cancer which was eating into its entrails. It was there that one must operate; the rest of the healing process would follow.

Arthur Koestler, *Darkness at Noon*

Money as money is not evil. It speeds on errands of mercy, and lends itself to a thousand philanthropies. It feeds the hungry, clothes the naked, and succours men who are tempted to suicide. It is the insensate love of riches which is the perilous thing.

W.E. Sangster, *He Is Able*

The two things which, of all others, most want to be under a strict rule, and which are the greatest blessings both to ourselves and others, when they are rightly used, are our time and our money. These talents are continual means and opportunities of doing good.

William Law, *A Serious Call to a Devout and Holy Life*

We have not driven home upon men His clear intuition that though, if wealth comes, it ought to be accepted and used as an opportunity, yet it must be recognized as rather a snare to the spiritual life than an aim which the Christian may legitimately set before himself to pursue.

William Temple, *Christian Faith and Life*

See also Happiness, Freedom, Pride, Temptation, Worldliness

74

MORALS

M orals – concerned with the distinction between right and wrong

I have tried to work out why I behave the way I do. Looking back, I am aware of several strands which have influenced me in my behaviour. First of all, there is home, and the upbringing of one's parents. Second, there is school, and for me, National Service and going to university. In these institutions I reached important stages of life – working out my own values – and conscious of coming into being as a person in my own right. Third, there has been the influence of the media. However, the most important influence for me has been an evolving Christian faith. As a foundation there is the Bible and the person of Jesus Christ. Then there are the findings of theology, broadly construed, and the tradition of the church down the ages. An important influence here has been the recorded experience of the saints over the last two thousand years, still being collected, and the object of reflection. And lastly there is conscience, in constant need of education for fresh truth. And dare one end this section without mentioning the influence of 'grace' and the Holy Spirit?

Do what is right and good in the sight of the Lord, so that it may go well with you . . .
    Deuteronomy 6.18

Blessed are those who hunger and thirst after righteousness, for they will be filled.
    Matthew 5.6

Men are great in proportion as they are moral.
    Henry David Thoreau, *The Journal of Henry D. Thoreau*

Morality is often grace working out into a noble life-form.
    Henry Ward Beecher, *Proverbs from Plymouth Pulpit*

[289]

Morality, when vigorously alive, sees farther than intellect.
> J.A. Froude, *Short Stories on Great Subjects*

Conduct is three-fourths of our life and its largest concern.
> Matthew Arnold, *Literature and Dogma*

If your morals make you dreary, depend upon it they are wrong.
> Robert Louis Stevenson, *Across the Plains*

Half at least of all morality is negative and consists in keeping out of mischief.
> Aldous Huxley, *The Doors of Perception*

A right moralist is a great and good man; but, for that reason, he is rarely to be found.
> William Penn, *Fruits of Solitude*

Morality without spirituality has no roots. It becomes a thing of custom, transient, and optional.
> Henry Ward Beecher, *Proverbs from Plymouth Pulpit*

Without civic morality communities perish; without personal morality their survival has no value.
> Bertrand Russell, *Authority and the Individual*

His [Jesus'] system of morality was the most benevolent and sublime probably that has been ever taught.
> Thomas Jefferson, *The Writings of Thomas Jefferson*

The moral man is he that loves God above all, and his neighbour as himself: which fulfils both tables at once.
> William Penn, *Fruits of Solitude*

The whole spectrum about morality is an effort to find a way of living which men who live it will instinctively feel is good.
> Walter Lippman, *A Preface to Politics*

So far, about morals, I know only that what is moral is what you feel good after and what is immoral is what you feel bad after . . .
> Ernest Hemingway, *Death in the Afternoon*

The ultimate foundation for morality is that immorality doesn't work, it doesn't pay off. It doesn't lighten the burden of living. It increases it.

    Norman Vincent Peale, *Man, Morals and Maturity*

The Christian moral standard is, after all, not a code which has to be defended against the attacks of a forward generation: it is an insight to be achieved.

    F.R. Barry, *The Relevance of Christianity*

> The real immorality, as far as I can see it
> Lies in forcing yourself or somebody else
> Against all your deeper instincts and your intuition.
>   D.H. Lawrence, 'Immorality'

Jesus Christ takes as man a place alike in the realms of ethics and of faith. He gives to us the moral standard of life, the ethical ideal; He discloses the culminating power of the religious consciousness, for He is, in the deep harmony of his relationship with God, the mystic ideal also.

    William Boyd Carpenter, *The Witness to the Influence of Christ*

The great secret of morals is love; or a going out of our own nature, and an identification of ourselves with the beautiful which exists in thought, action, or person, not our own. A man, to be greatly good, must imagine intensely and comprehensively; he must put himself in the place of another and of many others; the pains and pleasures of his species must become his own.

    Percy Bysshe Shelley, *A Defence of Poetry*

We can offer this summary of moral obligation: Your being is personal; live as a person in fellow-membership with all others who, being personal, are your fellow-members in the community of persons. Strive to grow in fullness of personality, in width and depth of fellowship; and seek to draw the energy for this from that to which you and all things owe their origin, the Personal Love which is Creator and Sustainer of the world.

    William Temple, *Nature, Man and God*

The standard of morals is the mind of Christ; that is our great principle if we are Christian. It will not help you at once to solve each particular problem; it will give you a touchstone. As you seek to live in the constant companionship of Christ, you will find yourself knowing ever more fully what your duty is in accordance with His mind. Your moral authority is not a principle, but a Person. It is the mind of Christ.

    William Temple, *Christian Faith and Life*

The things that will destroy us are:
Politics without principle;
Pleasure without conscience;
Wealth without work;
Knowledge without character;
Business without morality;
Science without humanity;
and Worship without sacrifice.
    Anon

See also Awareness, Life, Neighbour, Relationships, Selfishness

7 5

MUSIC

*M*usic – *art of combining sounds with a view to beauty of form*
and expression of emotion; sounds so produced

I wonder if in *music* we can see another variant and consequence of what it means to be made in the image and likeness of God, and of the divine inbreathing. A seed or a spark of the divine is planted in the depths of our being. Some people, with a sensitive and intuitive ear for sound, might experience this as music. Take, for instance, a composer such as Beethoven. In the depths of the night, or out for a walk in the forest he becomes aware of a tune or harmony. Slowly a symphony takes form. Later a conductor comes along with an orchestra (whose members are also made in the image and likeness of God) and they put on a concert. The audience, with a feel for music, enjoy the performance. Dare we say – that something akin to a divine performance has taken place? It is no accident that music plays such an important part in worship in a church. But why restrict it to a church building? Music is everywhere.

∽

It is good to give thanks to the Lord, to sing praises to your name, O Most High; to declare your steadfast love in the morning, and your faithfulness by night, to the music of the lute and the harp, to the melody of the lyre.

Psalm 92.1–3

. . . but be filled with the Spirit, as you sing psalms and hymns and spiritual songs among yourselves, singing and making melody to the Lord in your hearts.

Ephesians 5.18–19

Organ playing . . . is the manifestation of a will fitted with a vision of eternity.

C.M. Widor, in Charles R. Joy, *Music in the Life of Albert Schweitzer*

MUSIC

> Who hears music, feels his solitude
> People at once.
>> Robert Browning, 'Balaustion's Adventure'

The soul continues as an instrument of God's harmony, a tuned instrument of divine joy for the Spirit to strike on.
> William Law, in Stephen Hobhouse, *Selected Mystical Writings of William Law*

See deep enough, and you see musically; the heart of Nature *being* everywhere music, if you can only reach it.
> Thomas Carlyle, *Sartor Resartus*

. . . music is a higher revelation than all wisdom and philosophy, the wine which inspires one to new generative processes.
> Ludwig von Beethoven in *Thayer's Life of Beethoven*

The language of tones belongs equally to all men, and that melody is the absolute language in which a musician addresses every heart.
> Richard Wagner, *Beethoven*

God makes every man happy who knows how to play upon himself. Every man is full music; but it is not every man who knows how to bring it out.
> Henry Ward Beecher, *Proverbs from Plymouth Pulpit*

> When music sounds, gone is the earth I know,
> And all her lovely things even lovelier grow.
>> Walter de la Mare, 'Music'

There was no instrument that was ever struck that has such music as every faculty of the human soul has in it. God never makes anything else so beautiful as man.
> Henry Ward Beecher, *Proverbs from Plymouth Pulpit*

Who is there that, in logical words, can express the effect music has on us? A kind of inarticulate unfathomable speech, which leads us to the edge of the Infinite, and lets us for moments gaze into that!
> Thomas Carlyle, *Sartor Resartus*

For even that vulgar and Taverne Musicke, which makes one merry, another mad, strikes me into a deepe fit of devotion, and a profound contemplation of the first Composer; there is something in it of Divinity more than the eare discovers.
> Sir Thomas Browne, *Religio Medici*

[294]

I lost myself in a Schubert Quartet at the end of a Crowndale Road concert, partly by ceasing all striving to understand the music, partly by driving off intruding thoughts, partly feeling the music coming up inside me, myself a hollow vessel filled with sound.

    Joanna Field, *A Life of One's Own*

[Music] is a principal means of glorifying our merciful Creator, it heightens our devotion, it gives delight and ease to our travails, it expelleth sadness and heaviness of spirit, preserveth people in concord and amity, allayeth fierceness and anger; and lastly, is the best physic for many melancholy diseases.

    Henry Peacham, *The Compleat Gentleman*

Musical training is a more potent instrument than any other, because rhythm and harmony find their way into the secret places of the soul, on which they mightily fasten, imparting grace, and making the soul graceful of him who is rightly educated, or ungraceful of him who is ill-educated.

    Plato, *The Republic of Plato*

. . . I came gradually to see that music and poetry were perhaps closer kin than I had at first realized. I came gradually to see that beyond the music of both arts there is an essence that joins them – an area where the meanings behind the notes and the meaning beyond the words spring from some common source.

    Aaron Copeland, *Music and Imagination*

For his part, Henri Bergson was interested in Casals' subjective reactions to music – what did he feel when he was playing the music of Bach or Beethoven? Casals tried to explain that if he was satisfied after a good performance . . . he had a special feeling, an almost physical sensation that could be likened to carrying inside himself a weight of gold.

    H.L. Kirk, *Pablo Casals. A Biography*

Now, what is music? This question occupied me for hours before I fell asleep last night. Music is a strange thing. I would almost say it is a miracle. For it stands halfway between thought and phenomenon, between spirit and matter, a sort of nebulous mediator, like and unlike each of the things it mediates – spirit that requires manifestation in time, and matter that can do without space. We do not know what music is.

    Heinrich Heine, in Jacques Barzun, *Pleasures of Music*

A patient once said to S., 'I sometimes have the feeling that God is right inside me, for instance when I hear the St Matthew Passion.' And S. said something like: 'At such moments you are completely at one with the creative and cosmic forces that are at work in every human being.' And these creative forces are ultimately part of God, but you need courage to put that into words.

Etty Hillesum, *A Diary, 1941–43*

See also Art, Beauty, Literature, Poetry, Wonder

76

MYSTICS

Mystics, mysticism – a type of religion which puts the emphasis on immediate awareness of relation with God, on direct and immediate awareness of divine presence; religion in its most acute, intense and living stage

I like this definition of mystics and mysticism. The words have given me an insight into the character and personality of Jesus Christ. I now feel to be in a much better position to understand his life and work. The same applies to St Paul. Many people down the ages have spoken of an immediate awareness of relation with God. In prayer and contemplation they found rich resources of divine life welling up in themselves. The great mystical poets George Herbert and John Donne found their inspiration in a direct and immediate consciousness of the divine. The composer, Ralph Vaughan Williams, was influenced by the mystics and mysticism. The artist Fra Angelico used to meditate before painting, and attributed his genius to a divine source. According to our definition, mysticism is religion in its most acute, intense and living stage. Long ago, Henri Frédéric Amiel claimed we had lost the mystical sense. Perhaps this helps us to understand why today the church is struggling in our day and age. A rediscovery of mysticism might well bring about a much-needed regeneration.

∽

Now there was a great wind, so strong that it was splitting the mountains and breaking rocks in pieces before the Lord, but the Lord was not in the wind; and after the wind an earthquake, but the Lord was not in the earthquake; and after the earthquake a fire, but the Lord was not in the fire; and after the fire a sound of sheer silence.

1 Kings 19.11–12

I became its servant according to God's commission that was given to me for you, to make the word of God fully known, the mystery that has been hidden throughout the ages and generations but has now been revealed to his saints.

Colossians 1.25–26

We have lost the mystical sense, and what is religion without mysticism?
  Henri Frédéric Amiel, *Amiel's Journal*

The ultimate gift of conscious life is a sense of the mystery that encompasses it.
  Lewis Mumford, *The Conduct of Life*

. . . mysticism is wisdom and knowledge that is found through love; it is loving knowledge.
  William Johnston, *The Inner Eye of Love*

For the mystics, the great aim of all religious experience is the vision of God and union with him.
  William Barclay, *The Letters to the Corinthians*

The mystics are not only themselves an incarnation of beauty, but they reflect beauty on all who with understanding approach them.
  Havelock Ellis, *Selected Essays*

'Mysticism' . . . the simple childlike intercourse of the believing soul with God, by no effort of the mind, but by the working of the Holy Spirit.
  Gerhard Tersteegen, in Frances Bevan, *Sketches of the Quiet in the Land*

. . . by love, by the willing loss of self, we realize our true nature and become partakers in the being of God. The ego may be said to represent a stage in a spiritual process. By breaking out of its shell we can be born again, into a boundless freedom. That is the doctrine implied in all mystical philosophy.
  Gerald Bullett, *The English Mystics*

Other faiths have their mystics but only in Jesus, I believe, can we find such spontaneous and personal communion with God combined with such a passionate ethical concern for humanity. Both awareness of God and awareness of the world attain their zenith in him.
  John V. Taylor, *The Go-Between God*

The typical mystic is the person who has a certain first-hand experience and knowledge of God through Love; and the literature of mysticism tells us, or tries to tell us, what the finite human spirit has come to know through love of the relation between the little half-made spirit of man and the Infinite Spirit of God.
  Evelyn Underhill, in John Stobbart, *The Wisdom of Evelyn Underhill*

The highest thought . . . is ineffable; it must be felt from one person to another but cannot be articulated. All the most essential and thinking part of thought is done without words. It is not till doubt and consciousness enter that words become possible. Our profoundest and most important convictions are unspeakable.

Samuel Butler, in Gerald Bullett, *The English Mystics*

The problem of mysticism is to endow the mind and will of man with a supernatural experience of God as He is in Himself and, ultimately, to transform a human soul into God by a union of love. This is something that no human agency can perform or merit or even conceive by itself. This work can be done only by the direct intervention of God.

Thomas Merton, *The Waters of Silence*

'In the time of the philosophers,' he [Al-Ghazzali] writes, 'as at every period, there existed some of these fervent mystics. God does not deprive this world of them, for they are its sustainers.' It is they who, dying to themselves, become capable of perpetual inspiration and so are made the instruments through which divine grace is mediated to those whose unregenerated nature is impervious to the delicate touches of the Spirit.

Aldous Huxley, *The Perennial Philosophy*

That which makes Christian mysticism so rich, deep, life-giving, and beautiful is the Christian doctrine of the nature and action of God. It is different because it is based upon the Incarnation, the redemptive self-giving of the Eternal Charity. The Christian mystic tries to continue in his own life Christ's balanced life of ceaseless communion with the Father and the lonely service to the crowd.

Evelyn Underhill, in John Stobbart, *The Wisdom of Evelyn Underhill*

It is a central idea of mysticism that there is a way to God through the human soul. The gate to Heaven is thus kept, not by St Peter or by any other saint of the calendar; it is kept by each individual person himself as he opens or closes within himself the spiritual circuit of connection with God. The door into the Eternal swings within the circle of our own inner life, and all things are ours if we learn how to use the key that opens, for 'to open' and 'to find God' are one and the same thing.

Rufus M. Jones, *Spiritual Reformers in the 16ᵗʰ and 17ᵗʰ Centuries*

The most beautiful and most profound emotion we can experience is the sensation of the mystical. It is the sower of all true science. He to whom this emotion is a stranger, who can no longer wonder and stand wrapt in awe, is as good as dead. To know that what is impenetrable to us really exists, manifesting itself as the highest wisdom and the most radiant beauty which our dull faculties can comprehend only in their most primitive forms – this knowledge, this feeling is at the centre of true religiousness.

Albert Einstein, in Lincoln Barnett, *The Universe and Dr Einstein*

Mysticism keeps men sane. As long as you have mystery you have health; when you destroy mystery you create morbidity. The ordinary man has always been sane because the ordinary man has always been a mystic. He has permitted the twilight. He has always had one foot in earth and the other in fairyland. He has always left himself free to doubt his gods; but (unlike the agnostic of to-day) free also to believe in them. He has always cared more for truth than for consistency. If he saw two truths that seemed to contradict each other, he would take the two truths and the contradiction along with them.

G.K. Chesterton, *Orthodoxy*

See also Divinity, Holiness, Holy Spirit, Inner Life, Saints

77

NEIGHBOUR

Neighbour – dweller in the same street or district, or one having claims on others' friendliness

Somewhere I have come across a description of a neighbour as 'anyone close by in need'. Within half an hour of being ordained there was a knock on the clergy house door, and there was a young woman with a baby in her lap, 'close by in need' – of money and food.

This was the start of coming close to hundreds of people in need during the last thirty-seven years of ministry. Some have been destitute men and women in need of food and sustenance. Others have been sick, physically, mentally and spiritually, in need of healing. Another group have been the elderly and the infirm, in need of care. I also have taken on individuals with special needs. I remember trying to help a young 'drop-out' over a three-year period, and he was followed by another man, with serious psychological problems, whom I saw regularly for fifteen years. As a college chaplain I have been confronted by almost every student problem imaginable. Being resident in college means being exposed and vulnerable throughout a term to neighbours – i.e. 'anyone close by in need'.

∽

Do not plan harm against your neighbour who lives trustingly beside you.
Proverbs 3.29

In everything do to others as you would have them do to you; for this is the law and the prophets.
Matthew 7.12

You cannot love a fellow-creature fully till you love God.
C.S. Lewis, *The Great Divorce*

All is well with him, who is beloved of his neighbours.
George Herbert, *Outlandish Proverbs*

The love of our neighbour is the only door out of the dungeon of self.
George Macdonald, *Unspoken Sermons*

We are made *one for another*; and each is to be a Supply to his Neighbour.
Benjamin Whichcote, *Morals and Religious Aphorisms*

Those who are all things to their neighbours cease to be anything to themselves.
Norman Douglas, *An Almanac*

The good neighbour looks beyond the external accidents and discerns those inner qualities that make all men human, and therefore, brothers.
Martin Luther King, *Strength to Love*

We cannot be sure if we are loving God, although we may have good reasons for believing that we are, but we can know quite well if we are loving our neighbour.
St Teresa of Avila, *Interior Castle*

Each man can learn something from his neighbour; at least he can learn this – to have patience with his neighbour, to live and let live.
Charles Kingsley, *Daily Thoughts*

A man must not choose his neighbour; he must take the neighbour that God sends him . . . The neighbour is just the man who is next to you at the moment, the man with whom any business has brought you into contact.
George Macdonald, *Unspoken Sermons*

But it is His long-term policy, I fear, to restore to them a new kind of self-love – a charity and gratitude for all selves, including their own; when they have really learned to love their neighbours as themselves, they will be allowed to love themselves as their neighbours.
C.S. Lewis, *The Screwtape Letters*

Jesus, however, is not interested in universal, theoretical or poetical love . . . It is a love, not of man in general, of someone remote, with whom we are not personally involved, but quite concretely love of one's immediate neighbour . . . *anyone who wants me here and now.*
Hans Küng, *On Being a Christian*

We must . . . not mix ourselves up uninvited in other people's business. On the other hand we must not forget the danger lurking in the reserve which our practical daily life forces upon us. We cannot possibly let ourselves get frozen into regarding everyone we do not know as an absolute stranger.

Albert Schweitzer, *Memoirs of Childhood and Youth*

The ultimate measure of a man is not where he stands in moments of comfort and convenience, but where he stands at times of challenge and controversy. The true neighbour will risk his position, his prestige, and even his life for the welfare of others. In dangerous valleys and hazardous pathways, he will lift some bruised and beaten brother to a higher and more noble life.

Martin Luther King, in Coretta Scott King, *The Words of Martin Luther King*

Strive to love your neighbours actively and indefatigably. And the nearer you come to achieving this love, the more convinced you will become of the existence of God and the immortality of your soul. If you reach the point of complete self-lessness in your love of your neighbours, you will most certainly regain your faith and no doubt can possibly enter your soul. This has been proved. This is certain.

Fyodor Dostoyevsky, *The Brothers Karamozov*

The remarkable thing is that we really love our neighbour as ourselves: we do unto others as we do unto ourselves. We hate others when we hate ourselves. We are tolerant towards others when we tolerate ourselves. We forgive others when we forgive ourselves. We are prone to sacrifice others when we are ready to sacrifice ourselves.

It is not love of self but hatred of self which is at the root of all the troubles that afflict the world.

Eric Hoffer, *The Passionate State of Mind*

True neighbourliness must begin within our own psychological attitudes. I must accept my neighbour for what he is, I must let him be himself, respect his 'isness' and self-understanding. I must not impose my pattern on him or exploit him for my own purposes. I must be interested in him as a person, so that our relation-ship will encourage mutual development in maturity. I must be ready to take initiatives, to engage in adventures of understanding and friendship.

George Appleton, *Journey for a Soul*

Today there is an inescapable duty to make ourselves the neighbour of every man, no matter who he is, and if we meet him, to come to his aid in a positive way, whether he is an aged person abandoned by all, a foreign worker despised without reason, a refugee, an illegitimate child wrongly suffering for a sin he did not commit, or a starving human being who awakens our conscience by calling to mind the words of Christ: 'As you did it to one of the least of these my brothers, you did it to me' (Mt 25.40).

Vatican Council 11, *The Conciliar and Post Conciliar Documents*

See also Friendship, Image of God, Other Faiths, Relationships, Self

78

OBEDIENCE

Obedience – obeying the will of God; doing God's will rather than doing one's own

One of the authors who has helped me to understand 'obedience' is Victor Gollancz. In an excerpt in *From Darkness to Light* he wrote: 'I dislike talk about obeying God, as if he were some Stalin or Hitler; I cannot think that he wants me to obey him; what he wants, I think, is that I should learn to cooperate, quietly and in complete freedom, with his blessed and blessing will, that will of his which I discover deep in my own heart as my will also – as the best, essential me – and which, discovering it also deep in the heart of everything else, I find to be not only vaster, but also saner and more fruitful of life and peace and joy, than the self-regarding wilfulness that would deceive me with its appearance of leading me to my goal, but would in fact cut me off, if it had its way, from my birthright of unity with all things.' I have quoted this almost verbatim as it coincides with what I have experienced. I don't think God wants me to obey him as some Stalin or Hitler – but prefers quiet cooperation.

❧

Teach me your way, O Lord.
　　Psalm 27.11

Everyone then who hears these words of mine and acts on them will be like a wise man who built his house on rock. The rain fell, the floods came, and the winds blew and beat on that house, but it did not fall, because it had been founded on rock.
　　Matthew 7.24–25

Obedience is the key to every door.
　　George Macdonald, *The Marquis of Lossie*

If within us we find nothing over us we succumb to what is around us.

P.T. Forsyth, *Positive Preaching and the Modern Mind*

The 'obedience' of Jesus is not simply submission, but real striving, cooperation, activity.

John J. Vincent, *Secular Christ*

God does not desire that we should abound in spiritual lights, but that in all things we should submit to His will.

Henry Suso, in St Alphonus de Liguori, *On Conformity with the Will of God*

Had he done as the Master told him, he would soon have come to understand. Obedience is the opener of eyes.

George Macdonald, *Unspoken Sermons*

Men should find their hearts with a sense of fidelity, of generosity, and of obedience to God, and then let God take care of the result.

Henry Ward Beecher, *Proverbs from Plymouth Pulpit*

We can only have power if we are obedient. If we are disobedient, all power falls from us, because we are living in our own strength, in our own way.

Father Andrew SDC, *A Gift of Light*

. . . there are various paths to Christian obedience. The essential point, however, is that this obedience can only be measured by its commitment to the world.

Paul Oestreicher, in Hans Jürgen Schultz, *Conversion to the World*

There is but one single faculty in the whole roll of the soul's faculties to which every one in the nature of man consents to be obedient. This is the faculty of LOVE.

Henry Ward Beecher, *Proverbs from Plymouth Pulpit*

If a man does not keep pace with his companions, perhaps it is because he hears a different drummer. Let him step to the music which he hears, however measured or far away.

Henry David Thoreau, *Walden*

In practical terms obedience is in line with the very root of the word which suggests 'listening to' – listening to the will of God by listening *to* each other and listening *with* each other to its varied manifestations.

Sister Madeleine OSA, *Solitary Refinement*

'If,' said a Celtic saint of the ninth century, 'If a man does his own will he walks with a shadow on the heart, but if with Christ's power in thee, thou doest God's will, thou shalt walk in a circle of light.'

    Alistair MacLean, *The Quiet Heart*

So many people need to learn that Obedience must often come before Faith; that it is by going on patiently obeying the commandments of God and the teaching of Christ that faith will come to them; that faith is neither something to which they are entitled nor something which is either given or withheld, but something which has to be earned by a life of discipline and obedience. It is really no good saying: 'I find it so difficult to believe' when we are doing little or nothing to build up faith by using the means of grace which God has provided for us and by bringing our lives under the control of his will.

    J.R.H. Moorman, *The Path to Glory*

Jesus lays hold on the individual and summons him to *obedience to God,* who is to embrace his whole life. These are simple, transparent, liberating appeals, dispensing with arguments from authority or tradition but providing examples, signs, tokens, for transforming one's life.

    Hans Küng, *On Being a Christian*

Obedience is a complicated act of virtue, and many graces are exercised in one act of obedience. It is an act of humility, of mortification and self-denial, of charity to God, of care of the public, of order and charity to ourselves and all our society, and a great instance of a victory over the most refractory and unruly passions.

    Jeremy Taylor, *Holy Living*

God . . . lays claim not to half the will, but the whole. He demands not only external acts which can be observed and controlled, but also internal responses which cannot be controlled or checked. He demands man's heart. He wants not only good fruits, but the good tree: not only action but being; not something, but myself – and myself wholly and entirely.

    Hans Küng, *On Being a Christian*

We have no code of rules that can only be obeyed in the circumstances of their origin, no scheme of thought which can only be understood in the terms in which it was first conceived, but a Person to whom we can be loyal in all circumstances whatever, with that infinite flexibility and delicacy of adjustment which are compatible with a loyalty that remains absolute and unalterable.

    William Temple, *Thoughts on Some Problems of the Day*

And if we are to practise obedience we can scarcely do better than begin with the three commands which Jesus gave to Peter in the boat. 'Thrust out a little from the land'; do not allow yourself to become earthbound, your life dominated by things of this world; . . . And then 'launch out into the deep' and explore the depths of God's love; consider his nature, his goodness, his strength; let the thought of his majesty and of his tender mercy and compassion flow into your heart; learn to be alone with him in the deep. And then 'Let down your nets for a draught'; learn to accept what God gives of his grace, his peace, his strength; spread your nets wide for that miraculous draught of all that your soul can need.

J.R.H. Moorman, *The Path to Glory*

See also Belief, Commitment, Discipleship, Guidance, Humility

79

OTHER FAITHS

*O*ther faiths – the relationship of Christianity to Judaism, Islam, Buddhism, Hinduism, etc.

Three things have altered the way I look at people of other faiths. The first is the Genesis story of the creation of humanity. In this story God is depicted as fashioning and shaping humans in his own image and likeness, and the last thing he does is breathe into the first man, and he becomes a living being. This means all men and women, irrespective of race, creed, caste and colour, have something of the divine latent in them. The second is a passage by William Barclay: 'There are many ways to God. God has His own secret stairway into every heart. God fulfils Himself in many ways; and no man, and no Church, has a monopoly of the truth of God.' The third is a passage by Mahatma Gandhi: 'After long study and experience I have come to these conclusions that: 1) all religions are true; 2) all religions have some error in them; 3) all religions are almost as dear to me as my own Hinduism. My veneration for other faiths is the same as for my own faith. Consequently, the thought of conversion is impossible . . . Our prayer for others ought never to be: "God! give them the light thou has given to me!" But: "Give them all the light and truth they need for their highest development."' My attitude is to be loyal to the truths of Christ, and open to truths of God to be found in people of other faiths, and from different backgrounds.

❧

I have other sheep that do not belong to this fold.

John 10.16

Now among those who went up to worship at the festival were some Greeks. They came to Philip, who was from Bethsaida in Galilee, and said to him, 'Sir, we wish to see Jesus.'

John 12.20–21

As all men are alike (tho' infinitely various),
So all Religions &, as all similars, have one source,
The true Man is the source, he being the Poetic Genius.

William Blake, 'All Religions Are One'

. . . we believe we may speak not only of the unknown God of the Greeks but also of the *hidden Christ of Hinduism* – hidden and unknown and yet present and at work because he is not far from any one of us.

Raimundo Panikkar, *The Unknown Christ of Hinduism*

The humble, meek, merciful, just, pious, and devout souls, are everywhere of one religion; and when death has taken off the mask, they will know one another, though the diverse liveries they wear have made them strangers.

William Penn, *Fruits of Solitude*

The Church has never declared that the Judeo-Christian religion was alone in possessing revealed Scriptures, sacraments, and supernatural knowledge about God. It has never declared that there was no affinity at all between Christianity and the mystical traditions of countries other than Israel.

Simone Weil, *Gateway to God*

If we believe in God as Creator we must surely think of him as wanting to make an impact on all, through their history, their experience, their prophets. We believe that he is the source of all truth, goodness and love, so where we see signs of these we must surely believe that he has been active.

George Appleton, *Journey for a Soul*

In Jesus we see mirrored and perfectly revealed the Cosmic Being, the principle of the Godhead active in all history.

The Cosmic Christ may be seen working in and through the Israelites and speaking through the patriarchs and prophets. In like manner the same Cosmic Being may be seen moving in and through all the great religions in every age.

Bede Griffiths OSB, in Peter Spink, *The Universal Christ*

'But the Jews, the Mohammedans, the Confucians, the Buddhists – what of them?' he put to himself the dilemma that had threatened him before. 'Can those hundreds of millions of human beings be deprived of that greatest of blessings without which life has no meaning?' he pondered, but immediately pulled himself up. 'But what is it that I want to know?' he said to himself. 'I am asking about the relation to the Deity of all the different religions of mankind.'

Leo Tolstoy, *Anna Karenina*

Our purpose is to take God and his love to the poorest of the poor, irrespective of their ethnical origin or the faith that they profess. Our discernment of all is not the belief but the necessity. We never try to convert those who receive to Christianity but in our work we bear witness to the love of God's presence and if Catholics, Protestants, Buddhists or agnostics become for this better men – simply better – we will be satisfied. Growing up in love they will be nearer to God and will find him in his goodness.

Mother Teresa, in Kathryn Spink, *In the Silence of the Heart*

Once some blind men chanced to come near an animal that someone had told them was an elephant. They were asked what the elephant was like. The blind men began to feel its body. One of them said the elephant was like a pillar; he had touched only its leg. Another said it was like a winnowing-fan; he had touched only its ear. In this way the others, having touched its tail or belly, gave their different versions of the elephant. Just so, a man who has seen only one aspect of God limits God to that alone. It is his conviction that God cannot be anything else.

Sri Ramakrishna, *Ramakrishna: Prophet of New India*

People of other faiths are our spiritual neighbours in the journey of life and in the search for spiritual dimensions and values. The outgoing Christian mission has made them neighbours and has stimulated them to examine their own religious traditions. The ease of travel and the development of trade brings them to our countries, so they are now physical as well as spiritual neighbours. Their presence makes them our neighbours, as well as their interest in religious questions. We have to interpret the second great commandment in our attitude towards them.

George Appleton, *Journey for a Soul*

The Holy Spirit is at work in all creation and within all humanity, drawing all men and all things to unity in Christ, that is, into his mystical Body.

The realization of this unity begins within ourselves. From the depths of our being we learn with Christ to say 'Abba, Father'. It is there that we touch the source from which all life flows.

At the surface level of the various religions there are great diversity, differences and separation to unity, from contradiction to oneness and from diversity to convergence. In every human being the Holy Spirit is present and at work. Even when ignored or denied the Spirit is moving, and drawing towards unity in Christ.

Bede Griffiths OSB, in Peter Spink, *The Universal Christ*

There have been times when the Christian Church has rightly claimed to have an exclusive role. This was particularly so in its beginnings. If Christianity had not claimed to be the final and only true revelation in its own Mediterranean world and refused to become merely one of the many religions of that world, it could never have become the inspiration of European civilization. Those days are now past. The Spirit of God is moving in the world, leading men into a wider vision, which does not destroy but fulfils and is in part contained within all the earlier partial visions. Christianity, and this is true of all higher religions, is now called upon, within the divine economy, to become universal, not by each religion ceasing to be itself, or watering down its own particular revelation, not by an attempt to iron out differences at the intellectual level, so that all may be lost in some nebulous World Faith, but by each seeing itself within the other, by each becoming incarnate within the other.

F.C. Happold, *The Journey Inwards*

See also Awareness, Humility, Listening, Love, Neighbour

80

PATIENCE

Patience – calm endurance of pain or any provocation; perseverance

In 1968 I went to Nigeria for six months, looking after All Saints Church, Jericho, Ibadan. I soon discovered Nigerians have a different concept of time from ours. This came home to me officiating at a wedding. The service was scheduled to start at 11.00am. At 10.55am hardly anyone had arrived. At 12.00 noon about half the guests had arrived and I was beginning to get impatient. At 1.00pm the bride and her father arrived, as did the bridegroom and the best man. The bridesmaids, however, were still not to be seen. I started the wedding at 1.30pm and the service ended an hour later. While the couple were proceeding down the aisle after the final blessing, six beautifully dressed bridesmaids arrived – supposedly for the start of the service. Amidst much laughter and hilarity we set off for the reception. I learnt a great deal about patience in my six months in Nigeria. As I have gone through life I value more and more my 'apprenticeship' in patience.

Be still before the Lord, and wait patiently for him.
   Psalm 37.7

But as for that in the good soil, these are the ones who, when they hear the word, hold it fast in an honest and good heart, and bear fruit with patient endurance.
   Luke 8.15

Possess your soul with patience.
   John Dryden, 'The Hind and the Panther'

Calumnies are answer'd best with silence.
   Ben Jonson, *Volpone*

One of the principal parts of faith is patience.
  George Macdonald, *Weighed and Wanting*

Patience and application will carry us through.
  Thomas Fuller, *Gnomologia*

I worked with patience, which means almost power.
  E.B. Browning, 'Aurora Leigh'

Endurance is nobler than strength, and patience than beauty.
  John Ruskin, *The Two Paths*

Sorrow and silence are strong, and patient endurance is godlike.
  Henry Wadsworth Longfellow, 'Evangeline'

This impatience or strenuousness is the white man's characteristic, and his curse.
  Norman Douglas, *An Almanac*

Patience is not passive; on the contrary, it is active; it is concentrated strength.
  Anon

> Endurance is the crowning quality,
> And patience all the passion of great hearts.
>   J.R. Lowell, 'Columbus'

One moment of patience may ward off great disaster, one moment of impatience may ruin a whole life.
  Chinese proverb

I know how unbearable is suspense of mind, to have to face a situation which one cannot alter or even affect, and have to wait.
  A.C. Benson, *Extracts from the Letters of Dr A.C. Benson to M.E.A.*

People are always talking of perseverance, and courage, and fortitude, but patience is the first and worthiest part of fortitude – and the rarest too.
  John Ruskin, *Ethics of the Dust*

I can see that patience is essential in this life, for there is much that goes against the grain. Whatever I do to ensure my peace, I find that fighting and suffering are inevitable.
  Thomas à Kempis, *The Imitation of Christ*

To be silent, to suffer, to pray, when there is no room for outward action, is an acceptable offering to God. A disappointment, a contradiction, an injury received and endured for God's sake, are of as such value as a long prayer.

François de la M. Fénelon, *Spiritual Thoughts for Busy People*

Let patience have her perfect work. Statue under the chisel of the sculptor, stand steady to the blows of his mallet. Clay on the wheel, let the fingers of the divine potter model you at their will. Obey the Father's lightest word; hear the Brother who knows you, and died for you.

George Macdonald, *Unspoken Sermons*

> I do oppose
> My patience to his fury, and am armed
> To suffer with a quietness of spirit
> The very tyranny and rage of his.
>
> William Shakespeare, *The Merchant of Venice*

Patience and diligence, like faith, remove mountains. Never give out while there is hope; but hope not beyond reason, for that shows more desire than judgment. It is a profitable wisdom, to know when we have done enough; much time and pains are spared, in not flattering ourselves against probabilities.

William Penn, *Fruits of Solitude*

Someone has said that the secret of patience is 'doing something else in the meantime'. The 'something else' the saints do is to dwell on the use God can make even now of the trials which beset them. 'Let me receive them with patient meekness' they seem to say 'and perhaps by this means, God will polish His Jewel.'

W.E. Sangster, *The Pure in Heart*

Patience is the most difficult thing of all and the only thing that is worth learning. All nature, all growth, all peace, everything that flowers and is beautiful in the world depends on patience, requires time, silence, trust, and faith in long-term processes which far exceed any single lifetime, which are accessible to the insight of no one person, and which in their totality can be experienced only by peoples and epochs, not by individuals.

Hermann Hesse, in Volker Michels, *Reflections*

We must wait for God, long, meekly, in the wind and wet, in the thunder and the lightning, in the cold and the dark. Wait, and He will come. He never comes to those who do not wait. He does not go their road. When He comes, go with Him, but go slowly, fall a little behind; when He quickens His pace, be sure of it, before you quicken yours. But when He slackens, slacken at once. And do not be slow only, but silent, very silent, for He is God.

F.W. Faber, *Growth in Holiness*

See also Acceptance, Hope, Kindness, Obedience, Perseverance

81

PEACE

Peace – freedom from, cessation of war, freedom from civil disorder, quiet tranquillity, mental calm, bring person, oneself, back into friendly relations

I can clearly remember the end of the Second World War. For the first time for several years we experienced peace. There was an immediate lessening of tension everywhere and a great communal sense of relief. At last we could relax and start enjoying life again. At a more personal level, twenty years later, I recall a visit to the Bradford Royal Infirmary. There I met a man in one of the wards. He was dying of cancer and knew it. I was struck by his appearance. He had a calm, serene disposition and quiet demeanour. He had come to terms with the fact that he was shortly to die, and I was impressed by his faith and peace of mind. He was troubled by a row in the ward between a patient and a nurse. This had somehow tarnished the atmosphere, so he went to considerable trouble to sort it out. He was delighted with the outcome, especially as the peaceful atmosphere of the ward was restored. Peace is supremely important and many of us can be instruments of peace, wherever we are. Peace is one of the fruits of the Spirit, and is its own reward.

Those of steadfast mind you keep in peace – in peace because they trust in you.
   Isaiah 26.3

Peace I leave with you, my peace I give to you. I do not give to you as the world gives. Do not let not your hearts be troubled, and do not let them be afraid.
   John 14.27

Peace is always beautiful.
   Walt Whitman, 'The Sleepers'

Where there is peace, God is.
>   George Herbert, *Outlandish Proverbs*

You touched me, and I am inflamed with love of your peace.
>   St Augustine, *Confessions*

> Peace,
> The central feeling of all happiness.
>> William Wordsworth, 'The Excursion'

Peace comes not by establishing a calm outward setting so much as by inwardly surrendering to whatever the setting.
>   Hubert van Zeller, *Leave Your Life Alone*

Live in peace yourself and then you can bring peace to others – a peaceable man does more good than a learned one.
>   Thomas à Kempis, *The Imitation of Christ*

I am a child of peace and am resolved to keep the peace for ever and ever, with the whole world, inasmuch as I have concluded it at last with my own self.
>   Johann Wolfgang von Goethe, *Wisdom and Experience*

People are always expecting to get peace in heaven; but you know whatever peace they get there will be ready made. Whatever making of peace *they* can be blest for, must be on earth here.
>   John Ruskin, *The Eagle's Nest*

The more a man gives up his heart to God, to his vocation and to men, forgetful of himself and of that which belongs to him – the greater poise he will acquire, until he reaches peace, quiet, joy – the apanage of simple and humble souls.
>   Father Yelchaninov, in G.P. Fedotov, *A Treasury of Russian Spirituality*

A soul divided against itself can never find peace. Peace cannot exist where there are contrary loyalties. For true peace there has to be psychological and moral harmony. Conscience must be at rest.
>   Hubert van Zeller, *Considerations*

When people are praying for peace, the cause of peace is being strengthened by their very act of prayer, for they are themselves becoming immersed in the spirit of peace, and committed to the cause of peace.
>   John Macquarrie, *The Concept of Peace*

To thee, O God, we turn for peace . . . but grant us too the blessed assurance that nothing shall deprive us of that peace, neither *ourselves*, nor our foolish, earthly desires, nor my wild longings, nor the anxious craving of my heart.

Søren Kierkegaard, *The Journals of Søren Kierkegaard*

In India the great example of the power of peace was seen in Mahatma Gandhi whose inner peace influenced the whole nation. Work for peace must first of all be a work within ourselves.

Bede Griffiths OSB, in Peter Spink, *The Universal Christ*

Calm soul of things! make it mine
To feel amid the city's jar,
That there abides a peace of thine,
Man did not make and cannot mar!

Matthew Arnold, 'In Kensington Gardens'

No man has touched the essential characteristics of Christianity, and no man has entered into the interior spirit of Christianity, who has not reached to a certain extent that peace which Christ said He gave to His disciples, and which at times they declared to be past all understanding.

Henry Ward Beecher, *Proverbs from Plymouth Pulpit*

Children, that peace which is found in the spirit and inner life is well worth our care, for in that peace lies the satisfaction of all our wants. In it the Kingdom of God is discovered and His righteousness is found. This peace a man should allow nothing to take from him, whatever betide, come weal or woe, honour or shame.

John Tauler, *The History and Life of the Reverend Doctor John Tauler*

There is an experience of being in pure consciousness which gives lasting peace to the soul. It is an experience of the Ground or Depth of being in the Centre of the soul, an awareness of the mystery of being beyond sense and thought, which gives a sense of fulfilment, of finality, of absolute truth.

Bede Griffiths OSB, *Return to the Centre*

In the Bible the word *peace*, *shalom*, never simply means the absence of trouble. Peace means everything which makes for our highest good. The peace which the world offers us is the peace of escape, the peace which comes from the avoidance of trouble, the peace which comes from refusing to face things. The peace which Jesus offers us is the peace of conquest. It is the peace which no experience in life can ever take from us. It is the peace which no sorrow, no danger, no suffering can make less. It is the peace which is independent of outward circumstances.

William Barclay, *The Gospel of John*

See also Acceptance, Contemplation, Contentment, Grace, Presence

82

PERSEVERANCE

Perseverance – a steadfast pursuit of an aim, constant persistence

I met a young disabled woman. She had come to University College, London, to do a postgraduate degree in librarianship. After a week or so she told me about herself. She had been born with cerebral palsy. Her father had left home when she was very young and had not been seen by her since. She decided to get stuck into life, and got through her O and A levels at school. She made a successful application to Exeter University and managed to get an honours degree. Disaster struck again. In her early twenties she was involved in a serious car accident, which left her more disabled than ever. Life then became a constant struggle to survive. She had now arrived in London to get a further qualification. She was not finding it easy. London provided her with peculiar problems of its own. The course was academic and demanding. It required all her powers of perseverance. She was involved in another car crash. Her persistence was rewarded when she got her qualification and a job as a librarian. She has persisted in her job ever since, but recently has had to take early retirement. Perseverance and endurance have definitely played an important part in her life.

The way of the Lord is a stronghold for the upright.
Proverbs 10.29

Pray in the Spirit at all times in every prayer and supplication. To that end keep alert and always persevere . . .
Ephesians 6.18

Some strains are bearable and even bracing, but others are deadly.
A.C. Benson, *Extracts from the Letters of Dr A.C. Benson to M.E.A*

No great cause is ever lost or ever won. The battle must always be renewed and the creed restated.

John Buchan, *Montrose*

> Perseverance, dear my lord,
> Keeps honour bright.
>
> William Shakespeare, *Troilus and Cressida*

Life should be a voluntary overcoming of difficulties, those met with and those voluntarily created, otherwise it is just a dice-game.

A.R. Orage, *On Love*

> Attempt the end, and never stand to doubt;
> Nothing's so hard, but search will find it out.
>
> Robert Herrick, 'Hesperides: Seek and Find'

I often wish there were some index or inward monitor showing me when I had not reached the limit of my power of resistance and endurance in trouble. Sometimes, I dare say, I fancy I can hold out no longer when, in reality, I am nowhere near falling.

Mark Rutherford, *Last Pages from a Journal*

To endure is greater than to dare; to tire out hostile fortune; to be daunted by no difficulty; to keep heart when all have lost it; to go through intrigue spotless; to forego even ambition when the end is gained – who can say this is not greatness?

William Makepeace Thackeray, *The Virginians*

There remain times when one can only endure. One lives on, one doesn't die, and the only thing that one can do, is to fill one's mind and time as far as possible with the concerns of other people. It doesn't bring immediate peace, but it brings the dawn nearer.

A.C. Benson, *Extracts from the Letters of Dr A.C. Benson to M.E.A.*

For me at least there came moments when faith wavered. But there is the great lesson and the great triumph if you keep the fire burning until, by and by, out of the mass of sordid details there comes some result, be it some new generalization or be it a transcending spiritual repose.

Oliver Wendell Holmes, in Max Lerner, *The Mind and Faith of Justice Holmes*

The years should temper a man like steel, so that he can bear more and more and emerge more and more the conqueror over life. In the nature of things we must grow weaker in body, but in the divine nature of things we must grow ever stronger in the faith which can endure the slings and arrows of life, and not fail.

William Barclay, *The Letters to Timothy and Titus*

Exasperation at not being able to do a thing *uninterruptedly*; and I am more and more convinced that nothing good is achieved without a long perseverance, without applying one's effort for some time in the same direction. It is a matter of patient selection, analogous to that exercised by good horticulturalists.

André Gide, *The Journals of André Gide*

We live in a very beautiful world; but few good things are to be had in it without hard work. It is not a world in which any one can expect to be prosperous if he is easily discouraged. Perseverance – earnest, steady perseverance – is necessary to success. This is no drawback. Good, solid work is as necessary to peace of mind as it is for the health of the body; in fact the two are inseparable.

Right Hon. Lord Avebury, *Essays and Addresses*

The value of such moral teaching lies in a man learning what others have experienced and what he too may expect of life. Whatever happens to him, he will realize that he is meeting the common lot of mankind and not a peculiar fate, fortunate or unfortunate. Even if this knowledge does not help us to escape sorrows, it shows us how to endure them and, perhaps, how to conquer them.

Johann Wolfgang von Goethe, in Emil Ludwig, *The Practical Wisdom of Goethe*

Life makes many an attempt to take away our faith. Things happen to us and to others which baffle our understanding; life has its problems to which there seems no solution and its questions to which there seems no answer; life has its dark places where there seems to be nothing to do but hold on. Faith is always a *victory*, the victory of the soul which tenaciously maintains its clutch on God.

William Barclay, *The Letters to the Corinthians*

Disraeli the elder held that the secret of all success consisted in being master of your subject, such mastery being attainable only through continuous application and study. Hence it happens that the men who have most moved the world have been not so much men of genius, strictly so called, as men of intense mediocre abilities, untiring workers, persevering, self-reliant and indefatigable; not so often the gifted, of naturally bright and shining qualities, as those who have applied themselves diligently to their work, in whatever line that might lie.

Samuel Smiles, *Self-Help*

He [Paul] begins with one triumphant word of the Christian life – *endurance (hupomone)*. It is untranslatable. It does not describe the frame of mind which can sit down with folded hands and bowed head and let a torrent of troubles sweep over it in passive resignation. It describes the ability to bear things in such a triumphant way that it transfigures them . . . It is the courageous and triumphant ability to pass the breaking-point and not to break and always to greet the unseen with a cheer. It is the alchemy which transmutes tribulation into strength and glory.

William Barclay, *The Letters to the Corinthians*

Another important value in an abundance of energy should be mentioned. The *ability to persevere* in the face of discouragement and disappointment and the possession of *courage* to face strong opposition are both qualities which mark successful leaders. And both of these qualities are fed at their roots by an endowment of energy. Probably no single corroding influence eats away perseverance and courage so much as fatigue and bodily unfitness. Both the buoyancy of the outlook and the constancy of the effort of all of us derive from forces not primarily of the mind but of the body.

Ordway Tead, *The Art of Leadership*

See also Action, Courage, Discipleship, Hope, Patience

83

PHILOSOPHY

Philosophy – love of wisdom or knowledge, especially that which deals with ultimate reality, or with the most general causes – principles of things, study of principles of human action or conduct; system of conduct of life

At university the study of philosophy has become a very exacting academic discipline, far removed from the ordinary person. I have been greatly helped by some words of Lord Byron which he wrote in his poem, 'Childe Harold's Pilgrimage', of 'that untaught innate philosophy'. This was fortified in turn by some words of a former Dean of St Paul's – W.R. Inge. In his book *Outspoken Essays* he wrote that 'philosophy means thinking things out for oneself'. I wonder if we can make yet another link here with the Genesis story of the creation of humanity and of the divine inbreathing; that as a natural consequence of this we have inside us something of 'that untaught innate philo-sophy'. If ordinary people can get hold of this, then they may be given confidence to go one stage further and 'think things out for themselves'. We might then get an increase in the 'love of wisdom or knowledge', and an enrichment of our corporate life. *The Eternal Vision* provides us with some thought-provoking material and the practice of reflection, whether in groups or on an individual basis, a way in which we too can think things out for ourselves.

❧

Can you find out the deep things of God? Can you find out the limit of the Almighty?

Job 11.7

My speech and my proclamation were not with plausible words of wisdom, but with a demonstration of the Spirit and of power.

1 Corinthians 2.4

The example of good men is visible philosophy.
  English proverb

Any genuine philosophy leads to action and from action back again to wonder, to the enduring fact of mystery.
  Henry Miller, *The Wisdom of the Heart*

Philosophical knowledge is a spiritual act, where not only the intellect is active, but the whole of man's spiritual power, his emotions and his will.
  Nicolas Berdyaev, *Christian Existentialism*

For philosophy is the study of wisdom, and wisdom is the knowledge of things divine and human; and their causes. Wisdom is therefore queen of philosophy.
  Clement of Alexandria, *The Miscellanies*

The maxims and statements of Christ were the very roots of philosophy. We have never, under any moral philosophy, come up to the maxims and root-teachings of the Lord Jesus Christ.
  Henry Ward Beecher, *Proverbs from Plymouth Pulpit*

The philosophy of six thousand years has not searched the chambers and magazines of the soul. In its experiments, there has always remained, in the last analysis, a residium it could not resolve.
  Ralph Waldo Emerson, *Essays and Representative Men*

Philosophies of life, when they are widely believed, also have a very great influence on the vitality of a community. The most widely accepted philosophy of life at present is that what matters most to a man's happiness is his income. This philosophy, apart from other demerits, is harmful because it leads men to aim at a result rather than an activity, an enjoyment of material goods in which men are not differentiated, rather than a creative impulse which embodies each man's individuality . . .
  Bertrand Russell, *Principles of Social Reconstruction*

To be a philosopher is not merely to have subtle thoughts, nor even to found a school, but so to love wisdom as to live according to its dictates, a life of simplicity, independence, magnanimity, and trust.
  Henry David Thoreau, *Walden*

'Come unto me . . . and I will give you rest'; it is not Philosophy that can estimate the right of the Speaker to issue that invitation or to make that promise; that right can be proved or disproved only by the experiment of life.

William Temple, *Nature, Man and God*

The philosophy which is so important in each of us is not a technical matter; it is our more or less dumb sense of what life honestly and deeply means. It is only partly got from books; it is our individual way of just seeing and feeling the total push and pressure of the cosmos.

William James, *Pragmatism*

Theology, which is the science of Religion, starts from the Supreme Spirit and explains the world by reference to Him. Philosophy starts from the detailed experience of men, and seeks to build up its understanding of that experience by reference to that experience alone.

William Temple, *Nature, Man and God*

Most people in England think of a philosopher as one who talks in a difficult language about matters which are of interest only to philosophers. But Philosophy is concerned with what must interest every human being, with the nature of man and the nature of the universe. Every man is born a philosopher, but often the philosopher is suppressed in him by the hand-to-mouth thinking needed for the struggle for life.

A. Clutton Brock, *The Ultimate Belief*

The world has need of a philosophy, or a religion, which will promote life. But in order to promote life it is necessary to value something other than mere life. Life devoted only to life is animal, and without any real human value, incapable of preserving men permanently from weariness and the feeling that all is vanity. If life is to be fully human it must serve some end which seems, in some sense, outside human life, some end which is personal and above mankind, such as God or truth or beauty.

Bertrand Russell, *Principles of Social Reconstruction*

The highest triumphs of philosophy are possible only to those who have achieved in themselves a purity of soul. This purity is based upon a profound acceptance of experience, realized only when some point of hidden strength within man, from which he can not only inspect but comprehend life, is found. From this inner source the philosopher reveals to us the truth of life, a truth which mere intellect is unable to discover. The vision is produced almost as naturally as a fruit from a flower out of the mysterious centre, where all experience is reconciled.

Sir Sarvepalli Radhakrishnan, *Indian Philosophy*

Those who best promote life do not have life for their purpose. They aim rather at what seems like a gradual incarnation, a bringing into our human existence of something eternal, something that appears to imagination to live in a heaven remote from strife and failure and the devouring jaws of Time. Contact with this eternal world – even if it be only a world of our imagining – brings a strength and a fundamental peace which cannot be wholly destroyed by the struggles and apparent failures of our temporal life. It is this happy contemplation of what is eternal that Spinoza calls the intellectual love of God. To those who have once known it, it is the key of wisdom.

Bertrand Russell, *Principles of Social Reconstruction*

See also Intellect, Mind, Thinking, Truth, Wisdom

84

POETRY

Poetry – art, work, of the poet; elevated expression of elevated thought or feeling in metrical form; quality (in any thing) that calls for poetical expression

I was intrigued to see a young poet in action. He was a student at University College, London, and lived in our chaplaincy house. From time to time he would stay up late at night. This was when he was feeling lucid and receptive. He found his best poems came in the early hours of the morning, when it was quiet and there were no distractions. It seemed as though the source of his inspiration was in the deep centre of his being, though he did have a finely-tuned mind and a vivid imagination. All these faculties were used in the writing of his poems. The cost was great. I would see him the following morning, ashen white, haggard, and exhausted, though there was usually a twinkle in his eyes. I wonder if the poet taps into the same reservoir of 'inspiration' as the artist, musician, playwright, etc., but it comes out in a unique form of expression.

My heart overflows with a goodly theme; I address my verses to the king; my tongue is like the pen of a ready scribe.

Psalm 45.1

. . . so that they would search for God and perhaps grope for him and find him – though indeed he is not far from each one of us. For 'In him we live and move and have our being'; as even some of your own poets have said, 'For we too are his offspring.'

Acts 17.27–28

The true poet is a solitary, as is man in his great moments.

J.B. Yeats, *Letters to His Son, W.B. Yeats and Others*

Poetry is the record of the best and happiest moments of the happiest and best minds.

   Percy Bysshe Shelley, *A Defence of Poetry*

Poetry, therefore, we will call *musical Thought*. The Poet is he who *thinks* in that manner.

   Thomas Carlyle, *Sartor Resartus*

Poetry is divine because it is the voice of the personality – this poor captive caged behind the bars.

   J.B. Yeats, *Letters to His Son, W.B. Yeats and Others*

Let us therefore deem the glorious art of Poetry a kind of medicine divinely bestowed upon man.

   John Keble, *Lectures on Poetry*

All that is best in the great poets of all countries is not what is national in them, but what is universal.

   Henry Wadsworth Longfellow, *Kavanagh*

Poets deal with what I call ultimate human nature – descending into the depths.

   J.B. Yeats, *Letters to His Son, W.B. Yeats and Others*

The poet enters into himself in order to create. The contemplative enters into God in order to be created.

   Thomas Merton, *New Seeds of Contemplation*

Most people do not believe in anything very much and our greatest poetry is given us by those who do.

   Cyril Connolly, in Stephen Spender, *The Making of a Poem*

[Poetry] was ever thought to have some participation of divineness, because it doth raise and erect the mind.

   Francis Bacon, *The Advancement of Learning*

Poetry should be great and unobtrusive, a thing which enters into one's soul, and does not startle it or amaze it with itself, but with its subject.

   John Keats, *Letter to J.H. Reynolds*

I had said of Christ that he ranks with the poets. That is true. Shelley and Sophocles are his company. But his entire life also is the most wonderful of poems.

Oscar Wilde, *De Profundis*

Poetry should be vital – either stirring our blood by its divine movement, or snatching our breath by its divine perfection. To do both is supreme glory; to do either is enduring fame.

Augustine Birrell, *Obiter Dicta, Mr Browning's Poetry*

The essence of all poetry is to be found, not in high-wrought subtlety of thought, nor in pointed cleverness of phrase, but in the depths of the heart and the most sacred feelings of the men who write.

John Keble, *Keble's Lectures on Poetry*

The touchstone of genuine poetry is that it has the ability, as a secular gospel, to liberate us from the weight of our earthly burden by an inner serenity and an outward sense of well-being.

Johann Wolfgang von Goethe, in Herman J. Weigand, *Wisdom and Experience*

When a poet takes words as his instruments . . . the very sound of the words is now part of the meaning; that meaning can never be apprehended or recovered except by re-hearing physically or in imagination the actual sound of the words . . . Here we are near to a sacrament.

William Temple, *Nature, Man and God*

A poem is the image of life expressed in its eternal truth. There is this difference between a story and a poem, that a story is a catalogue of detached facts, which have no other bond of connexion than time, place, circumstance, cause and effect; the other is the creation of actions according to the unchangeable forms of human nature, as existing in the mind of the creator, which is itself the image of all other minds.

Percy Bysshe Shelley, *Prose, A Defence of Poetry*

The most beautiful poem there is, is life – life which discerns its own story in the making, in which inspiration and self-consciousness go together and help each other, life which knows itself to be the world in little, a repetition in miniature of the divine universal poem. Yes, be man; that is to say, be nature, be spirit, be the image of God, be what is greatest, most beautiful, most lofty in all the spheres of being, be infinite will and idea, a reproduction of the great whole.

Henri Frédéric Amiel, *Amiel's Journal*

What is a Poet? To whom does he address himself? And what language is to be expected from him? – He is a man speaking to men: a man, it is true, endowed with more lively sensibility, more enthusiasm and tenderness, who has a greater knowledge of human nature, and a more comprehensive soul, than are supposed to be common among mankind; a man pleased with his own passions and volitions, and who rejoices more than other men in the spirit of life that is in him . . .

William Wordsworth, *Lyrical Ballads*

See also Art, Beauty, Literature, Music, Wonder

85

POWER

Power – ability to do or act; particular faculty of body or mind, vigour, energy; influential person, body or thing

In the Wisdom of Solomon we read of 'the One who shaped him, who breathed an active soul into him, and inspired a living spirit'. Writers, such as Meister Eckhart, believe we are born with a seed or spark of the divine power in the depths of ourselves. An awareness of this power was experienced by the prophets. Micah, for instance, acknowledged he was 'filled with power, with the Spirit of the Lord, and with justice and might'. In the Gospels, we recall the claim of Jesus: 'All authority in heaven and on earth has been given me.' Paul prays for the members of the early church: 'May you be made strong with all the strength that comes from his glorious power, and may you be prepared to endure everything with patience while joyfully giving thanks to the Father, who has enabled you to share in the inheritance of the saints in the light.' Today we have lost sight of the divine power to be found in ourselves. We need to return to that source for a richer experience of life.

∽

. . . he gives power and strength to his people.
Psalm 68.35

I pray that the God of our Lord Jesus Christ, the Father of glory, may give you a spirit of wisdom and of revelation as you come to know him, so that, with the eyes of your heart enlightened, you may know what is the hope to which he has called you, what are the riches of his glorious inheritance among the saints, and what is the immeasurable greatness of his power for us who believe, according to the working of his great power.
Ephesians 1.17–19

Energy is Eternal Delight.
William Blake, 'The Marriage of Heaven and Hell'

Patience and Gentleness is Power.
> Leigh Hunt, 'On a Lock of Milton's Hair'

The power of God is the worship He inspires.
> Alfred North Whitehead, *Science and the Modern World*

Man is a born child, his power is the power of growth.
> Rabindranath Tagore, *Stray Birds*

The strongest man in the world is the man who stands alone.
> Henrik Ibsen, *An Enemy of the People*

Right and Truth are greater than any *Power*, and all Power is limited by Right.
> Benjamin Whichcote, *Moral and Religious Aphorisms*

Life engenders life. Energy creates energy. It is by spending oneself that one becomes rich.
> Sarah Bernhardt, in Cornelia Otis Skinner, *Madam Sarah*

> Self-reverence, self-knowledge, self-control,
> These three alone lead life to sovereign power.
> > Alfred, Lord Tennyson, 'Oenone'

From the summit of power men no longer turn their eyes upward, but begin to look about them.
> J.R. Lowell, *New England Two Centuries Ago*

Concentration is the secret of strength in politics, in war, in trade, in short, in all management of human affairs.
> Ralph Waldo Emerson, *The Conduct of Life, Nature and Other Essays*

To know the pains of power, we must go to those who have it; to know its pleasures, we must go to those who are seeking it: the pains of power are real, its pleasures imaginary.
> C.C. Colton, *Lacon*

We are the wire, God is the current. Our only power is to let the current pass through us. Of course, we have the power to interrupt it and say 'no'. But nothing more.
> Carlo Carretto, *Letters from the Desert*

A non-violent revolution is not a programme of 'seizure of power'. It is a programme of transformation of relationships ending in a peaceful transfer of power.

Mohandas K. Gandhi, *Non-Violence in Peace and War*

Justice without might is helpless; might without justice is tyrannical . . . We must then combine justice and might, and for this end make what is just strong, or what is strong just.

Blaise Pascal, *Pensées*

He [Christ] stimulates us, as other great men stimulate us, but we find a power coming from Him into our lives that enables us to respond. That is the experience that proves Him to be the universal Spirit. It does not happen with others.

William Temple, *Christian Faith and Life*

His power [that of Kahlil Gibran] came from some great reservoir of spiritual life else it could not have been so universal and so potent, but the majesty and beauty of the language with which he clothed it were all his own.

Claude Bragdon, in Kahlil Gibran, *The Prophet*

There is a power which lapses into the human soul, and by that divine power all the faculties of man become competent to do or to be what they cannot do or be when they are left to the laws of society or to the laws of nature.

Henry Ward Beecher, *Proverbs from Plymouth Pulpit*

You have lost the knack of drawing strength from God, and vain strivings after communion of the *solitude à deux* will do nothing for you at this point. Seek contact with Him now in the goodness and splendour which is in other people, in *all* people, for those who have the art to find it.

Evelyn Underhill, *The Letters of Evelyn Underhill*

For man, discovering that knowledge is power, uses that power to dominate. The power within him is not the power of a great personality, the power which is sure and strong and is therefore able to be gentle and tolerant. This is the true power of God, the power of an infinite understanding, and it can only exist in a context of eternity.

Stuart B. Jackman, *The Numbered Days*

Christianity is not, as it is sometimes presented and sometimes practised, an additional burden of observances and obligations to weigh down and increase the already heavy load, or to multiply the already paralysing ties of our life in society. It is, in fact, a soul of immense power which bestows significance, beauty and a new lightness on what we are already doing.

Pierre Teilhard de Chardin, *Le Milieu Divin*

It was at the baptism that the Spirit came upon Jesus with power . . . The Jewish word for Spirit is *ruach*, which is the word which means *wind*. To the Jew there was always three basic ideas of Spirit. The Spirit was *power,* power like a mighty rushing wind; the Spirit was *life,* the very centre and soul and essence of life, the very dynamic of the existence of man; the Spirit was *God*; the power and the life of the Spirit were beyond mere human achievement and attainment. The coming of the Spirit into a man's life was the coming of God.

William Barclay, *The Gospel of John*

See also Influence, Inner Life, Leadership, Presence, Wholeness

86

PRAYER

Prayer – solemn request to God or object of worship; formula used in praying, practice of prayer; entreaty to a person; thing prayed for

I was taught to say my prayers by our school chaplain. He gave us a simple technique in preparing us for confirmation. We were to say our prayers at night, just before going to bed. First we were to start with thanksgiving, giving thanks for the many blessings we enjoyed. Second, we were to move on to confession, owning up to all that had gone wrong in our lives – in thought, word, deed, and omission – ending with an acceptance of God's forgiveness. Third, we were to say the Lord's Prayer. Fourth, we were to pray for other people, especially those who were in any kind of need. Finally we were to pray for ourselves and for our own particular needs. I used this technique for several years, until the time came for a change. Instead of doing all the talking I had to learn to keep quiet and listen. I found this difficult at first. Keeping a journal was a help. Gradually I learnt to reflect, meditate and contemplate.

～

. . . then you will delight in the Almighty, and lift up your face to God. You will pray to him, and he will hear you.

    Job 22.26–27

In the morning, while it was still very dark, he got up and went out to a deserted place, and there he prayed.

    Mark 1.35

Prayer takes place in the heart, not in the head.

    Carlo Carretto, *The Desert in the City*

Prayer is the Divine in us appealing to the Divine above us.

    C.H. Dodd, in William Barclay, *The Letter to the Romans*

Prayer is the nearest approach to God, and the highest enjoyment of Him, that we are capable of in this life.

William Law, *A Serious Call to a Devout and Holy Life*

Prayer is not an old woman's idle amusement. Properly understood and applied, it is the most potent instrument of action.

Mohandas K. Gandhi, *Non-Violence in Peace and War*

You pray in your distress and in your need; would that you might pray also in the fullness of your joy and in your days of abundance.

Kahlil Gibran, *The Prophet*

Prayer, crystallized in words, assigns a permanent wavelength on which the dialogue has to be continued, even when our mind is occupied with other matters.

Dag Hammarskjöld, *Markings*

So true prayer demands that we be more passive than active; it requires more silence than words, more adoration than study, more concentration than rushing about, more faith than reason.

Carlo Carretto, *Letters from the Desert*

Prayer is the responsibility to meet others with *all* that I have, to be ready to encourage the unconditional in the conditional, to expect to meet God in the way, not to turn aside from the way.

John Robinson, *Honest to God*

You pray best when the mirror of your soul is empty of every image except the image of the invisible Father. This image is the Wisdom of the Father, the Word of the Father . . . the glory of the Father.

Thomas Merton, *Thoughts in Solitude*

Lift up your heart to Him, sometimes even at your meals and when you are in company; the least little remembrance will always be acceptable to Him. You need not cry very loud; He is nearer to us than we are aware of.

Brother Lawrence, *The Practice of the Presence of God*

In our Lord's teaching about petitionary prayer there are three main principles. The first is confidence, the second is perseverance and the third, for lack of a better word, I will call correspondence with Christ.

William Temple, *Christian Faith and Life*

Prayer should never be regarded as a science or reduced to a system – that ruins it, because it is essentially a living and personal relationship, which tends to become more personal and also more simple, as one goes on.

Evelyn Underhill, in Charles Williams, *The Letters of Evelyn Underhill*

Prayer places our understanding in the divine brightness and light and exposes our will to the warmth of heavenly love. There is nothing that so effectually purges our understanding of its ignorance and our will of its depraved affections.

St Francis de Sales, *Introduction to the Devout Life*

Do not forget to say your prayers. If your prayer is sincere, there will be every time you pray a new feeling containing an idea in it, an idea you did not know before, which will give you fresh courage; you will then understand that prayer is education.

Fyodor Dostoyevsky, *The Brothers Karamazov*

The Lord's prayer is the prayer above all prayers, a prayer which the most high Master taught us, wherein are comprehended all spiritual and temporal blessings, and the strongest comforts in all trials, temptations, and troubles, even in the hour of death.

Martin Luther, *Table-Talk*

Believe and trust that as it is easy for you to breathe the air and live by it, or to eat and drink, so it is easy and even still easier for your faith to receive all spiritual gifts from the Lord. Prayer is the breathing of the soul; prayer is our spiritual food and drink.

John of Cronstadt, in G.P. Fedatov, *A Treasury of Russian Spirituality*

Prayer is a fundamental style of thinking, passionate and compassionate, responsible and thankful, that is deeply rooted in our humanity and that manifests itself not only among believers but also among serious-minded people who do not profess any religious faith.

John Macquarrie, *Paths in Spirituality*

Love to pray – feel the need to pray often during the day and take the trouble to pray. If you want to pray better, you must pray more. Prayer enlarges the heart until it is capable of containing God's gift of himself. Ask and seek and your heart will grow big enough to receive him and keep him as your own.

Mother Teresa, in Kathryn Spink, *In the Silence of the Heart*

God will always answer our prayers; *but He will answer them in His way*, and His way will be the way of perfect wisdom and of perfect love. Often if He answered our prayers as we at the moment desire, it would be the worst thing possible for us, for in our ignorance we often ask for gifts which would be our ruin.

William Barclay, *The Gospel of Matthew*

See also Action, Adoration, Contemplation, Listening, Meditation

87

PRESENCE

Presence – being present; real presence, place where person is

There was a time when I tended to think of God miles above the sky and therefore absent from everyday living. Christ was seen primarily as someone who lived nearly two thousand years ago and distanced from us by time. My eyes were opened to the presence of God by an experience recorded by Joseph Estlin Carpenter. One afternoon he went for a walk in the country. He had not gone far before he became conscious of the presence of someone else. He was unable to describe it. He felt he had as direct a perception of the being of God all about him, as if he were with a friend. For him, it was an act of spiritual apprehension. This experience never happened to him again but the effects never left him. The sense of a direct relation to God then generated in his soul became a part of his habitual thought and feeling. I am also indebted to Brother Lawrence, a Carmelite lay brother of the seventeenth century. He developed a form of prayer called *The Practice of the Presence of God*. Perhaps we should take a leaf out of his book and learn to practise the presence of God.

My presence will go with you, and I will give you rest.
  Exodus 33.14

I am with you always, to the end of the age.
  Matthew 28.20

Faith is the realization of an invisible presence of truth.
  Henry Ward Beecher, *Proverbs from Plymouth Pulpit*

Though God be everywhere present, yet He is only present to Thee in the deepest, and most central Part of thy Soul.
  William Law, *The Spirit of Prayer*

Drench your spirit in the palpitating consciousness of the Presence! Then let an astonished world behold the resultant change.

F.W. Boreham, *A Late Lark Singing*

Speak to Him thou for He hears, and Spirit with Spirit can meet –
Closer is He than breathing, and nearer than hands and feet.

Alfred, Lord Tennyson, 'The Higher Pantheism'

The doctrine of the presence of God, to be realized here and now, should give to the habitually unhappy both the light to see what Christian hope is all about and the grace to act upon this light.

Hubert van Zeller, *Considerations*

The time of business does not with me differ from the time of prayer; and in the noise and clatter of my kitchen, while several persons are at the same time calling for different things, I possess God in as great tranquillity as if I were upon my knees at the Blessed Sacrament.

Brother Lawrence, *The Practice of the Presence of God*

It is easier to attain knowledge of this presence by personal experience, than by reading books, for it is life and love, strength and light, joy and peace to a chosen soul. A soul that has once experienced it cannot therefore lose it without pain; it cannot cease to desire it, because it is so good in itself, and brings such comfort.

Walter Hilton, *The Ladder of Perfection*

The presence of God which sanctifies our souls is the indwelling of the Blessed Trinity, who take up their abode in the depths of our hearts when we submit to the divine will; for the presence of God that results from contemplation effects this intimate union in us only in the same way as other things which are part of God's design.

Jean-Pierre de Caussade SJ, *Self-Abandonment to the Divine Providence*

The practice of the presence of God may involve very many hours of hard work; but the reward is great; for this is the joy that no man can take from us; this is the faith which is the human side of divine grace, an experiment which is becoming an experience, a foretaste and assurance of the rest remaineth for the people of God.

W.R. Inge, *Personal Religion and the Life of Devotion*

Practise . . . the presence of God . . . Let us thus think often that our only business in this life is to please God, that perhaps all besides is but folly and vanity . . . Let us think of Him perpetually. Let us put all our trust in Him . . . We cannot have too much in so good and faithful a Friend, Who will never fail us in this world or in the next.

    Brother Lawrence, *The Practice of the Presence of God*

What Christians claim in 'Christian experience' is not to pick up a body of wrought-out knowledge on the cheap, and to have a pat reply to all the mysteries of the universe, but to be aware of a Presence . . . As the Christian responds to the Presence and ventures forward, he becomes acquainted with a Person – holy, loving and merciful, and One who proves His personal care over all who turn to Him in trust.

    W.E. Sangster, *Give God a Chance*

At the same time they became conscious by degrees of an usual yearning of the soul for stillness and solitude, and for a rest and quietness in which all the natural powers are hushed and silent. And their hearts seem to them to be drawn away into a region where all external things become distasteful, and pass into forgetfulness. And they are drawn sweetly and gently in the hidden power of love, to God Himself, and *awaken to a sense of His presence.*

    Gerhard Tersteegen, in Frances Bevan, *Sketches of the Quiet of the Land*

. . . to live in the Presence of God is the way to perfection. We never depart from that way, but by losing sight of God, and forgetting our dependence upon Him. God is the Light by which we see, and the end at which we should aim. In all the business and events of life we should consider only the order of His Providence, and we shall maintain a sense of His Presence in the midst of our business, as long as we have no other intention in performing it, but purely that of obeying Him.

    François de la M. Fénelon, *Spiritual Thoughts for Busy People*

It is the presence of God which makes anywhere heaven or hell or what we call purgatory. The presence of God is the heaven of those who love His presence; the presence of God is the hell of those who do not love His presence; and the presence of God is the sweet purification of the penitent who longs to be worthy of His presence. The presence of God is everywhere, and it is our reaction to it which makes us either good or peaceful people, or rebellious, defiant people, or penitent, learning people.

    Father Andrew SDC, *The Symbolism of the Sanctuary*

In those rare glimpses of Christ's own life and prayer which the Gospels vouch-safe for us, we always notice the perpetual reference to the unseen Father; so much more vividly present to Him than anything that is seen. Behind that daily life into which He entered so generously, filled as it was with constant appeals to His practical pity and help, there is ever the sense of that strong and tranquil Presence, ordering all things and bringing them to their appointed end; not with a rigid and mechanical precision, but with the freedom of a living, creative, cherishing thought and love.

    Evelyn Underhill, *Abba*

What if it be true that the key to the correct understanding of the Second Coming is indeed to be found in John's Gospel in the words which tell how Father and Son will come and make their dwelling in the loving and obedient heart? (John 14.23). The cosmic upheaval may well stand for the destruction of the old life and the creation of the new when Christ enters into life. The judgement may well stand for the confrontation of the soul with Christ. The blessedness may well stand for the new life which is the life lived in Christ.

    William Barclay, *The Plain Man Looks at the Apostles' Creed*

See also Divinity, Experience, Glory, Inner Life, Power

88

PRIDE

*P**ride – overweening opinion of one's own qualities, merits etc;
arrogant bearing or conduct; exalted position, consciousness of
this, arrogance; also proper pride – a sense of what befits one's position, preventing one from doing an unworthy thing*

The Gurkhas are a good illustration of a proper sense of pride. They have an honourable outlook on life and an infectious enthusiasm for their work. They are reputed to be the smartest soldiers in the world, both on and off parade. They have a well-deserved reputation for loyalty, cheerfulness and bravery. I remember an occasion when a rifleman was picked up for a fault in his arms drill. Late that evening he was hard at work, ironing out the fault. He, like the others, had a proper sense of pride which insisted on doing a good job and producing top quality work. I was very privileged to serve with them. We all know of instances of the other kind of pride. For the writer of Ecclesiasticus, the beginning of human pride is to forsake the Lord, and to turn one's heart away from one's Maker. We then tend to get caught up in an inordinate self-love, and we succumb to pride.

∽

The beginning of human pride is to forsake the Lord; the heart has withdrawn from its Maker.

Ecclesiasticus 10.12

. . . he has scattered the proud in the thoughts of their hearts. He has brought down the powerful from their thrones.

Luke 1.51–52

His own opinion was his law.

William Shakespeare, *Henry VIII*

Self-blinded are you by your pride.
> Alfred, Lord Tennyson, 'The Two Voices'

The whole trouble is that we won't let God help us.
> George Macdonald, *The Marquis of Lossie*

Pride is over-estimation of oneself by reason of self-love.
> Benedict Spinoza, *Spinoza's Ethics and de Intellectus Emendatione*

Evil can have no beginning, but from pride; nor any end, but from humility.
> William Law, in Stephen Hobhouse, *Selected Mystical Writings of William Law*

Pride is therefore pleasure arising from a man's thinking too highly of himself.
> Benedict Spinoza, *Spinoza's Ethics and de Intellectus Emendatione*

A *Proud* man hath no *God*: for he hath put God down, and set Himself up.
> Benjamin Whichcote, *Moral and Religious Aphorisms*

Pride: ignorant presumption that the qualities and status of the organism are due to merit.
> A.R. Orage, *On Love*

Intellectual pride inflicts itself upon everybody. Where it dwells there can be no other opinion in the house.
> Cardinal Manning, *Pastime Papers*

Pride, like the magnet, constantly points to one object, self; but, unlike the magnet, it has no attractive pole, but at all points repels.
> C. C. Colton, *Lacon*

Perverted pride is a great misfortune in men; but pride in its original function, for which God created it, is indispensable to a proper manhood.
> Henry Ward Beecher, *Proverbs from Plymouth Pulpit*

There are two states or conditions of pride. The first is one of self-approval, the second one of self-contempt. Pride is seen probably at its purest in the last.
> Henri Frédéric Amiel, *Amiel's Journal*

Every good thought that we have, every good *action* that we do, lays us open to pride, and exposes us to the assaults of vanity and self-satisfaction.
> William Law, *A Serious Call to a Devout and Holy Life*

He that is proud eats up himself: pride is his own glass, his own trumpet, his own chronicle and whatever praises itself, but in the deed, devours the deed in the praise.

William Shakespeare, *Troilus and Cressida*

Now, if this thought that you deliberately conjure up, or harbour, and dwell lovingly upon, is natural worth or knowledge, charm or station, favour or beauty – then it is *Pride*.

The Cloud of Unknowing

As all things are God's, so all things are to be used and regarded as the things of God. For men to abuse things on earth, and live to themselves, is the same rebellion against God, as for angels to abuse things in Heaven; because God is just the same Lord of all on earth, as He is the Lord of all in Heaven.

William Law, *A Serious Call to a Devout and Holy Life*

We need to avoid pride. Pride destroys everything. That's why Jesus told his disciples to be meek and humble. He didn't say contemplation is a big thing – but being meek and humble with one another. If you understand that, you understand your vocation. To live his way is the key to being meek and humble.

Mother Teresa, in Brother Angelo Devananda, *Jesus, the Word to Be Spoken*

> Of all Causes which conspire to blind
> Man's erring Judgement, and misguide the Mind,
> What the weak Head with strongest Byass rules,
> Is *Pride*, the *never-failing Vice of Fools*.
>
> Alexander Pope, 'An Essay on Criticism'

The self-centred or self-concerned soul, making itself the object of its contemplation, and seeing all else as related to itself, is trying to feed upon itself. The food may be congenial, but the process is inevitably one of wastage. Such a soul must shrink and shrivel, suffering at last both the pain of unsatisfied hunger and the pain of contraction.

William Temple, *Nature, Man and God*

Nothing hath separated us from God but our own will, or rather our own will is our separation from God . . . The fall of man brought forth the kingdom of this world; sin in all shapes is nothing else but the will of man driving on in a state of self-motion and self-government, following the workings of a nature broken off from its dependency upon, and union with, the divine will. All the evil and misery in the creation arises only and solely from this one cause.

William Law, in Stephen Hobhouse, *Selected Mystical Writings of William Law*

In the last resort there are only two pivots about which human life can revolve, and we are always organizing society and ourselves about one or other of them. They are self and God. In the great book with which the Bible closes, these two principles are set before us under the symbolical figures of the 'Lamb standing, as it had been slain' – the symbol of love that uses sacrifice as its instrument – and the great wild beast, the symbol of self-will or pride, whose instrument is force.

William Temple, *Christian Faith and Life*

See also Doubt, Loneliness, Selfishness, Sin, Worldliness

89

PROGRESS

Progress – forward or onward movement in space, advance, development

Martin Luther King put his finger on a crucial point when he wrote we must work passionately and indefatigably to bridge the gulf between our scientific progress and our moral progress. He went on to add one of the great problems of humanity is that we suffer from a poverty of spirit which stands in glaring contrast to our scientific and technological abundance. The scientific and technological revolutions have been truly impressive, and we have witnessed awe-inspiring progress in both these spheres in the twentieth century. This form of progress can be seen in every technical area of life, but for some reason similar progress has not been forthcoming in the spiritual and moral spheres of life. What I think is now needed is a spiritual and moral revolution, similar to the one we have experienced in science and technology, coming to us through meditation and contemplation.

∽

But the path of the righteous is like the light of dawn, which shines brighter and brighter until full day.
> Proverbs 4.18

I press on towards the goal for the prize of the heavenly call of God in Christ Jesus.
> Philippians 3.14

There's a back'ard current in the world, and we must do our utmost to advance in order just to bide where we be.
> Thomas Hardy, *Desperate Remedies*

Progress in the spiritual life comes from climbing a ladder of which the rungs are made alternately of belief and doubt.
> Edward Patey, *Christian Life Style*

I consider that the way of life in urbanized, rich countries, as it exists today, and as it is likely to go on developing, is probably the most degraded and unillumined ever to come to pass on earth.

Malcolm Muggeridge, *Jesus Rediscovered*

So long as all the increased wealth which modern progress brings goes but to build up great fortunes, to increase luxury and make sharper the contrast between the House of Have and the House of Want, progress is not real and cannot be permanent.

Henry George, *Progress and Poverty*

His test of progress – of the moral worth of his own or any other age – was the *men* it produced. He admired most of all things in this world single-minded and sincere people, who believed honestly what they professed to believe, and lived it out in their actions.

James A. Froude, *Thomas Carlyle*

The whole process of social and civic development is the parallel growth of two things: richness of individual personality with completeness of social intercourse. The development of personality in fellowship is no bad definition of what we mean by progress.

William Temple, *Christian Faith and Life*

Life has lost its controlling unity. The idea of progress has been dissociated from the inspiration of faith. The subsidence of the ancient framework has brought down the overarching roof of certainty that God is regnant in the universe which, for the men of an earlier generation, gave life shelter and significance.

F.R. Barry, *The Relevance of Christianity*

. . . the heart of moral improvement, the heart of moral progress, therefore also of social progress, and the amelioration of this world's bitter condition, is always to be found in worship, worship which is the opening of the heart to the love of God and the exposure of the conscience to be quickened by it.

William Temple, *The Preacher's Theme Today*

We must work passionately and indefatigably to bridge the gulf between our scientific progress and our moral progress. One of the great problems of mankind is that we suffer from a poverty of the spirit which stands in glaring contrast to our scientific and technological abundance. The richer we have become materially, the poorer we have become morally and spiritually.

Martin Luther King, in Coretta Scott King, *The Words of Martin Luther King*

In the great mystics we see the highest and widest development of that consciousness to which the human race has yet attained. We see its growth exhibited to us on a grand scale, perceptible to all men . . . The germ of that same transcendent life, the spring of the amazing energy which enables the great mystic to rise to freedom and dominate his world, is latent in all of us; an integral part of our humanity.

Evelyn Underhill, *Mysticism*

Progress, however, of the best kind, is comparatively slow. Great results cannot be achieved at once; and we must be satisfied to advance in life as we walk, step by step . . . 'to know *how to wait* is the great secret of success'. We must sow before we can reap, and often have to wait long, content meanwhile to look patiently forward in hope; the fruit best worth waiting for often ripening the slowest. But 'time and patience', says the Eastern proverb, 'change the mulberry leaf to satin'.

Samuel Smiles, *Self-Help*

Human progress is neither automatic nor inevitable. Even a superficial look at history reveals that no social advance rolls in on the wheels of inevitability. Every step toward the goal of justice requires sacrifice, suffering, and struggle; the tireless exertions and passionate concern of dedicated individuals. Without persistent effort, time itself becomes an ally of the insurgent and primitive forces of irrational emotionalism and social destruction. This is no time for apathy or complacency. This is a time for vigorous and positive action.

Martin Luther King, in Coretta Scott King, *The Words of Martin Luther King*

Just as it was thought that developing science and technology would bring happiness and progress, there are people today who think that building just, social, economic and political structures will bring happiness and progress.

It is true that better conditions help, but it's illusory to believe that they alone are sufficient. Man doesn't change anything – unless *man himself takes part in these changes* for himself and his brothers. What changes him then is his commitment, his dedication to others. It becomes a spiritual mission at the core of which the believer recognizes the presence of God.

Michel Quoist, *With Open Heart*

A man's ability to be a pioneer of progress, that is, to understand what civilization is and to work for it, depends, therefore, on his being a thinker and on his being free. He must be the former if he is to be capable of comprehending his ideals and putting them into shape. He must be free in order to be in a position to launch his ideals out into the general life. The more completely his activities are taken up in any way by the struggle for existence, the more strongly will the impulse to improve his own condition find expression in the ideals of his thought. Ideals of self-interest then get mixed up with and spoil his ideals of civilization. Material and spiritual freedom are closely bound up with one another. Civilization presupposes free men, for only by free men can it be thought out and brought to realization.

Albert Schweitzer, *The Philosophy of Civilization, The Decay and Restoration of Civilization*

See also Action, Blessedness, Fulfilment, Growing, Transformation

9 0

PURPOSE

*P*urpose – *object, thing intended; fact, faculty, of resolving on something; design or intention*

Louis Lavelle wrote that the object of life is the discovery (by a deepening of the self) of the centre of the self that constitutes our unique and personal essence. He went on to add that most of us miss this by remaining on the surface of things, thinking only in terms of self-aggrandizement. In retrospect, I realize that I lived very much on the surface of things for the first twenty years of my life. At school I worked away to get through 'O' levels, and then specialized in three subjects for 'A' levels. In other areas of life my interest was mainly on sporting achievement. It was only later that I realized this was superficial. Self-aggrandizement was the order of the day. I would do National Service, go to university, get a well-paid job, buy a house and a car, have a family, and so on. I thought this must surely be right because everyone else was doing it. In my twenties I had a change of priorities, due to an evolving Christian faith. Eventually I discovered a real sense of purpose, which has been with me ever since.

I cry to God Most High, to God who fulfils his purpose for me.
Psalm 57.2

With all wisdom and insight he has made known to us the mystery of his will, according to his good pleasure that he set forth in Christ, as a plan for the fullness of time.
Ephesians 1.9–10

What makes life dreary is the want of motive.
George Eliot, *Daniel Deronda*

Purpose is what gives life a meaning . . . A drifting boat always drifts downstream.
Charles H. Parkhurst, *The Pattern in the Mount and Other Sermons*

Man is never happy until his own vague striving has found and fixed its goal.
 Johann Wolfgang von Goethe, *Wilhelm Meister's Apprenticeship*

God has a purpose and it is the function of normal beings to try to comprehend that purpose.
 A.R. Orage, *On Love*

 Make me useful, positive, appreciative, generous.
 Make me live.
 Norman W. Goodacre, 'Layman's Lent'

As individuals, we should sometimes pause and ask ourselves: what is our aim in life? Have we got one at all?
 William Barclay, *The Letters to Timothy and Titus*

Decide who and what you want to be; then pursue your purpose with total concentration until you become what you wish to be.
 Anon

Deeply the Christian believes that beneath all the flux and change of this mortal life, God is seeking to work out a profound purpose.
 W.E. Sangster, *God Does Guide Us*

Continuity of purpose is one of the most essential ingredients of happiness in the long run, and for most men this comes chiefly through their work.
 Bertrand Russell, *The Conquest of Happiness*

We need God, not in order to understand the why, but in order to feel and sustain the ultimate wherefore, to give a meaning to the Universe.
 Miguel de Unamuno, *The Tragic Sense of Life*

How could there be any question of acquiring or possessing, when the one thing needful for man is to *become* – to *be* at last, and to die in the fullness of his being.
 Antoine de Saint-Exupéry, *The Wisdom of the Sands*

Many persons have a wrong idea of what constitutes true happiness. It is not attained through self-gratification but through fidelity to a worthy purpose.
 Helen Keller, *Helen Keller's Journal*

The end of life is not profit, amusement, philosophy, science or religion. It is not even happiness: it is life itself. Life consists in the plenitude of all the organic and mental activities of the body.

Alexis Carrel, *Reflections on Life*

The need for devotion to something outside ourselves is even more profound than the need for companionship. If we are not to go to pieces or wither away, we must all have some purpose in life; for no man can live for himself alone.

Ross Parmenter, *The Plant in My Window*

> The man who consecrates his hours
> By vig'rous effort and honest aim,
> At once he draws the sting of life and death.
>
> Edward Young, *Night Thoughts*

What is the meaning of human life, or, for that matter, of the life of any creature? To know an answer to this question means to be religious. You ask: Does it make any sense, then, to pose this question? I answer: The man who regards his own life and that of his fellow-creatures as meaningless is not merely unhappy but hardly fit for life.

Albert Einstein, *Ideas and Opinions*

This is the true joy in life, the being used for a purpose, recognized by yourself as a mighty one; the being thoroughly worn out before you are thrown on the scrap heap; the being a force of Nature instead of a feverish selfish little clod of ailments and grievances complaining that the world will not devote itself to making you happy.

George Bernard Shaw, *The Complete Bernard Shaw Prefaces*

But it is not the place where you are that is the important thing. It is the intensity of your presence there. It is not the situation that counts. What counts is that you are fully alive in any situation. It is this that puts down roots and then flowers in your life. Availability: that is obedience. That, and looking hard at the place where you are, instead of wanting to work wonders somewhere else.

Neville Cryer, *Michel Quoist*

To accomplish anything you need an interest, a motive, a centre for your thought. You need a star to steer by, a cause, a creed, an idea, a passionate attachment. Men have followed many guiding lights. They have followed Christ, Mahomet,

Napoleon. Something must beckon you or nothing is done, something about which you ask no questions. Thought needs a fulcrum for its lever, effort demands an incentive or an aim.

W. MacNeile Dixon, *The Human Situation*

Life does not need comfort, when it can be offered meaning, nor pleasure, when it can be shown purpose. Reveal what is the purpose of existence and how he may attain it – the steps he must take – and man will go forward again hardily, happily, knowing that he has found what he must have – intentional living – and knowing that an effort, which takes all his energy because it is worth his full and constant concentration, is the only life deserving the devotion, satisfying the nature and developing the potentialities of a self-conscious being.

Anon

See also Commitment, Fulfilment, Hope, Life, Transformation

QUIETNESS

Quietness – silence, stillness; being free from disturbance or agitation or urgent tasks; rest, repose; peace of mind

Ambrose Bierce in his book, *The Devil's Dictionary*, defined noise as a 'stench in the ear'. Noise has become one of the great pollutions of modern time. I know this only too well having spent the last thirty-seven years in the centre of cities. I am also fond of the phrase 'oases of quiet' – those times when we can withdraw, perhaps, from the thick of things, and find moments of quiet to get a sense of perspective and proportion. I have had a busy and active ministry, but have been able to balance this by observing times of quietness. The practice started as an undergraduate. For many years now, I have kept a journal or what might be called a spiritual diary. I regard this as the most valuable thing I have done in my life. I have found it possible to have 'oases of quiet' on a daily basis, on a Sunday and on holiday. In the summer I love to go to an isolated part of the coast and have an extended time of quietness which sets me up for the following year. Through this practice it is possible to experience that rare commodity, quiet, and peace of mind.

In returning and rest you shall be saved; in quietness and in trust shall be your strength.

Isaiah 30.15

. . . let your adornment be the inner self with the lasting beauty of a gentle and quiet spirit, which is very precious in God's sight.

1 Peter 3.4

I am come by a hard way to the quiet of God.

Alistair MacLean, *The Quiet Heart*

Think glorious thoughts of God and serve with a quiet mind.

  Charles Duthrie, *God in His World*

In silence alone does a man's truth bind itself together and strike root.

  Antoine de Saint-Exupéry, *The Wisdom of the Sands*

A happy life must be to a great extent a quiet life, for it is only in an atmosphere of quiet that true joy can live.

  Bertrand Russell, *The Conquest of Happiness*

> Tranquillity! Thou better name
> Than all the family of Fame.
>   Samuel Taylor Coleridge, 'Ode to Tranquillity'

I have discovered that all the unhappiness of men arises from one single fact, that they cannot stay quietly in their own chamber.

  Blaise Pascal, *Pensées*

To go up alone into the mountain and come back as an ambassador to the world, has ever been the method of humanity's best friends.

  Evelyn Underhill, *Mysticism*

The quiet of quiet places is made quieter by natural sounds. In a wood on a still day the quiet is increased by the whisper of the trees.

  Mark Rutherford, *Last Pages from a Journal*

Altogether it will be found that a quiet life is characteristic of great men, and that their pleasures have not been of the sort that would look exciting to the outward eye.

  Bertrand Russell, *The Conquest of Happiness*

Unhappy, unfulfilled people, who find it difficult to care, are going to be the people interested in wars, fast cars, consumer fads in ridiculous variety, in conflict and in competition and in all the hectic and feverish pursuit of a lost security – not in those things which make for quietness of heart and mind.

  Roy Stevens, *Education and the Death of Love*

Christ's existence was ruled by a great silence. His soul was 'listening'. It was given over to the needs of others. In his innermost being he was silent, not asserting himself, detached. He did not grasp at anything in the world. Thus he overcame in his life the power of habit and daily routine, of dullness and fatigue, and created within himself a carefree tranquillity, a place for every encounter.

Ladislaus Boros, *In Time of Temptation*

> Drop thy still dews of quietness,
> Till all our strivings cease;
> Take from our souls the strain and stress,
> And let our ordered lives confess
> The beauty of thy peace.
>
> John Greenleaf Whittier, 'The Brewing of Soma'

Violence is not strength, noisiness is not earnestness. Noise is a sign of want of faith, and violence is a sign of weakness.

By quiet, modest, silent, private influence we shall win. 'Neither strive nor cry nor let your voice be heard in the streets', was good advice of old, and is still. I have seen many a movement tried by other method of striving and crying and making a noise in the streets, but I have never seen one succeed thereby, and never shall.

Charles Kingsley, *Daily Thoughts*

Many people today look for silence, solitude and peace. They dream of places where they can rest, away from the daily hassles of living which tear them apart, exhaust them and leave them dissatisfied, wounded and bleeding – and always alone.

But they won't necessarily find peace and quiet waiting for them in other places. There is a place within us where quiet reigns – the centre, our heart of hearts. There we can find him who is the plenitude of silence. But who will guide us there? We must learn the way.

Michel Quoist, *With Open Heart*

. . . we simply need quiet time in the presence of God. Although we want to make all our time for God, we will never succeed if we do not reserve a minute, an hour, a morning, a day, a week, a month, or whatever period of time for God and God alone.

This asks for much discipline and risk-taking because we always seem to have something more urgent to do and 'just sitting there' and 'doing nothing' often disturbs us more than it helps. But there is no way around this. Being useless and silent in the presence of our God belongs to the core of all prayer.

Henri J.M. Nouwen, in Robert Durback, *Seeds of Hope*

God is a Being, still, and peaceful, dwelling in the still eternity. Therefore should your mind be as a still, clear mountain tarn, reflecting the glory of God as in a mirror, where the image is unbroken and perfect. Avoid, therefore, all that would needlessly disturb or confuse or stir up your natural mind, from without or from within. Nothing in the whole world is worth being disturbed about . . . God is in His holy temple. Let all that is in you keep silence before Him – silence of the mouth, silence of all desires and all thoughts, silence of labour and toil. Oh, how precious and how useful is a still and quiet spirit in the eyes of God.

 Gerhard Tersteegen, in Frances Bevan, *Sketches of the Quiet in the Land*

See also Contemplation, Contentment, Meditation, Peace, Serenity

9 2

RELATIONSHIPS

*R*elationships – what one person or thing has to do with another,
R way in which one stands or is related to another

The Swiss psychologist C.G. Jung once wrote the love problem is part of humanity's heavy toll of suffering, and nobody should be ashamed that he must pay his tribute. Over the years I have found Jung's words helpful, especially in the wake of broken relationships. I have also been helped in my understanding of the nature of relationships by some words of R.E.C. Browne. In *The Ministry of the Word* he wrote in the sphere of human relationships there are no rules to be found for knowing the appropriate behaviour in a particular situation. Perhaps this helps us to understand why relationships are so difficult. No fixed guidance to follow. One thing I am learning from my experience of relationships is to be honest, in thoughts and in feelings. This is difficult, and sometimes painful, but it can prevent much stress and strain later on in our relationships.

⌖

Set me as a seal upon your heart, as a seal upon your arm; for love is strong as death . . . Many waters cannot quench love, neither can floods drown it. If one offered for love all the wealth of one's house, it would be utterly scorned.
  Song of Solomon 8.6–7

Love is patient; love is kind; love is not envious or arrogant or rude. It does not insist on its own way; it is not irritable or resentful; it does not rejoice in wrong-doing, but rejoices in the truth. It bears all things, believes all things, hopes all things, endures all things. Love never ends.
  1 Corinthians 13.4–8

The emotionally crippled person is always the produce of a love gone wrong.
  Michel Quoist, *With Open Heart*

An intimate relationship between people not only asks for mutual openness, but also for mutual respectful protection of each other's uniqueness.

Henri J.M. Nouwen, *Reaching Out*

A man needs something which is more than friendship and yet is not love as it is generally understood. This something nevertheless a woman only can give.

Mark Rutherford, *Last Pages from a Journal*

Good judgment in our dealings with others consists not in seeing through deceptions and evil intentions but in being able to waken the decency dormant in every person.

Eric Hoffer, *The Passionate State of Mind*

When a person loves, all that is in his power is invested with a sense of purpose, as available for the other, or becomes a cause or occasion of gratitude, as received as gift from the other.

W.H. Vanstone, *Love's Endeavour, Love's Expense*

I like direct and simple relations with people, and dread complex, subtle, intricate relations – and above all *claims*. One gives, and does the best one can, but the moment that *claims* come in, the atmosphere is uneasy.

A.C. Benson, *Extracts from the Letters of Dr A.C. Benson to M.E.A.*

> Talk not of wasted affection, affection never was wasted;
> If it enrich not the heart of another, its waters, returning
> Back to their springs, like the rain, shall fill them full of refreshment.
>
> Henry Wadsworth Longfellow, 'Evangeline'

I have often wondered why it is that men should be so fearful of new ventures in social relationships . . . Most of us fear, actually fear, people who differ from ourselves, either up or down the scale.

David Grayson, *The Friendly Road*

There is hardly anything that can make one happier than to feel that one counts for something with other people. What matters here is not numbers, but intensity. In the long run, human relationships are the most important thing in life.

Dietrich Bonhoeffer, *Letters and Papers from Prison*

We discover, perhaps to our astonishment, that our greatest moments come when we find that we are not unique, when we come upon another self that is very like our own. The discovery of a continent is mere idle folly compared with this discovery of a sympathetic other-self, a friend or a lover.

    J.B. Priestley, *All About Ourselves and Other Essays*

The woman is increasingly aware that love alone can give her her full stature, just as the man begins to discern that spirit alone can endow his life with its highest meaning. Fundamentally, therefore, both seek a psychic relation one to the other; because love needs the spirit, and the spirit, love, for their fulfilment.

    C.G. Jung, *Contributions to Analytical Psychology*

True relationship with others involves humility of attitude, refusal to treat others as things or slaves, refusal to pass judgement upon them, acceptance of their limitations and culpability, readiness to welcome and to listen to what they have to say, respect for their uniqueness, progressive understanding of their mystery, trust in what they can become, stimulation of their spiritual progress, appreciation of both the value and insufficiency of ethical norms and moral virtues.

    Emil Rideau, in George Appleton, *Journey for a Soul*

The first [danger] is that a man lives for himself alone, deciding everything in the light of his own advantage, disregarding the rights and needs of his fellow-men. The second [danger] is that we should think of people impersonally, in the mass, with numbers rather than names, thinking of them as cast in the same mould, with no individuality of their own. Each man wants value in himself, thinking of others in the same way. Neither individualism or collectivism is the right way of human relationships.

    George Appleton, *Journey for a Soul*

The sexual act is not a mere pleasure of the body, a purely carnal act, but is a means by which love is expressed and life perpetuated. It becomes evil, if it harms others or if it interferes with a person's spiritual development, but neither of these conditions is inherent in the act itself. The act by which we live, by which love is expressed and the race continued is not an act of shame or sin. But when the masters of spiritual life insist on celibacy, they demand that we should preserve singleness of mind from destruction by bodily desires.

    Sir Sarvepalli Radhakrishnan, *Mahatma Gandhi*

If we think about it, we find our life *consists* in this achieving of a pure relationship between ourselves and the living universe about us. This is how I 'save my soul' by accomplishing a pure relationship between me and another person, me and other people, me and a nation, me and a race of men, me and the animals, me and the trees or flowers, me and the earth, me and the skies and sun and stars, me and the moon: an infinity of pure relations, big and little, like the stars of the sky: that makes our eternity, for each one of us, me and the timber I am sawing, the lines of force I follow; and the dough I knead for bread, me and the very motion with which I write, me and the bit of gold I have got.

D.H. Lawrence, *The Phoenix*

To drive home the close parallel between the sexual act and the mystical union with God may seem blasphemous today. Yet the blasphemy is not in the comparison, but in the degrading of the one act of which man is capable that makes him like God both in the intensity of his union with his partner and in the fact that by this union he is a co-creator with God. All the higher religions recognize the sexual act as something holy; hence the condemnation of adultery and fornication under all circumstances. These acts are not forbidden because they are demonstrably injurious on rational grounds; they are forbidden because they are a desecration of a holy thing, they are a misuse of what is most godlike in man.

R.C. Zaehner, *Mysticism Sacred and Profane*

See also Acceptance, Awareness, Character, Compassion, Friendship

RESURRECTION

Resurrection – rising from the dead, especially the resurrection of Christ; rising again of people at the last day; revival from disuse of inactivity

Three observations have helped me to believe in the resurrection of Christ. The first comes from some words of Martin Luther, writing about nature: 'Our Lord has written the promise of the resurrection, not in books alone, but in every leaf in springtime.' The second comes from some words of Emil Brunner, the Swiss theologian: 'You believe in the Resurrection, not because it is reported by the Apostles but because the Resurrected One Himself encounters you in a living way.' I would like to link this statement with the experience of Archbishop Anthony Bloom, recorded in the last quotation of this section. The third follows on from the Genesis story of the creation of humanity, and the life of Christ. When we are open and receptive to the grace of God it is possible to experience a 'resurrection', a *re-surrection* – a rising of the divine from the depths of ourselves. These observations have helped me to a belief in the historic resurrection.

⤸

For I know that my Redeemer lives, and that at the last he will stand upon the earth; and after my skin has been thus destroyed, then in my flesh I shall see God.

Job 19.25–26

Were not our hearts burning within us while he was talking to us on the road, while he was opening the scriptures to us?

Luke 24.32

Christian theology has never suggested that the 'fact' of Christ's resurrection could be known apart from faith.

Alan Richardson, *History Sacred and Profane*

Jesus' resurrection makes it impossible for man's story to end in chaos – it has to move inexorably towards light, towards life, towards love.

Carlo Carretto, *The Desert in the City*

The Resurrection is not a miracle like any other. It is a unique manifestation within this world of the transition God makes for us out of this way of being into another.

Austin Farrer, *Saving Belief*

What is more difficult, to be born or to rise again; that what has never been should be, or that what has been should be again? Is it more difficult to come into existence than to return to it?

Blaise Pascal, *Pensées*

The Christian doctrine is a doctrine not of immortality but of Resurrection. The difference is profound. The method of all non-Christian systems is to seek an escape from the evils and misery of life. Christianity seeks no escape, but accepts these at their worst, and makes them the material of its triumphant joy. That is the special significance in this connection of the Cross and Resurrection of Jesus Christ.

William Temple, *Nature, Man and God*

You ask, 'What is the Good?' I suppose God Himself is the Good; and it is this, in addition to a thousand things, which makes me feel the absolute certainty of a resurrection, and a hope that this, our present life, instead of being an ultimate one, which is to decide our fate for ever, in which man's faculties are so narrow and cramped, his chances (I speak of millions, not of units) of knowing the Good so few, that he may have chances hereafter, perhaps continually fresh ones, to all eternity.

Charles Kingsley, *Daily Thoughts*

The New Testament promises us that our physical body shall be transmuted into a spiritualized body, like the body of the risen Christ, released from the domination of the material, the spatial and the temporal. Yet in some mysterious way it will be recognizable perhaps with its most significant features, as the nail-marks and the spear-wound on our Lord's resurrection body. We may think of the body as a life-long comrade, who will survive death and in some spiritualized form be our comrade still.

George Appleton, *Journey for a Soul*

The Christian belief is that after death individuality will survive, that you will still be you and I will still be I. Beside that we have to set another immense fact. To the Greek the body could not be consecrated. It was matter, the source of all evil, the prison-house of the soul. But to the Christian the body is not evil. Jesus, the Son of God, has taken this human body upon him and therefore it is not contemptible because it has been inhabited by God. To the Christian, therefore, the life to come involves the total man, body and soul.

William Barclay, *The Letters to the Corinthians*

Without the Resurrection the Christian movement would have petered out in ignominy, and there would have been no Christianity. It is not too much to say that without the Resurrection the phenomenon of Christianity in the apostolic age and since is scientifically unaccountable. It is also true to say that without the Resurrection Christianity would not be itself, as the distinctiveness of Christianity is not its adherence to a teacher who lived long ago but its belief that 'Jesus is Lord' for every generation through the centuries.

Michael Ramsey, in Margaret Duggan, *Through the Year with Michael Ramsey*

Jesus revealed God to them and became so utterly the central form that they were clinging to Him. But that could not go on for ever. They had to make a painful transition to a new relationship in which they clung to Him as something within their own lives, and not just as a nostalgic kind of thing. The great story that marks this transition is that of Jesus saying to Mary Magdalen on the Resurrection Day: 'Do not cling to Me, as in the past. It really is Me, but you and my other followers are passing on to a new relationship of a very tremendous kind.'

Michael Ramsey, in Gerald Priestland, *Priestland's Progress*

The friends of Jesus saw him and heard him only a few times after that Easter morning, but their lives were completely changed. What seemed to be the end proved to be the beginning; what seemed to be a cause for fear proved to be a cause for courage; what seemed to be defeat proved to be victory; and what seemed to be the basis for despair proved to be the basis for hope. Suddenly a wall becomes a gate, and although we are not able to say with much clarity or precision what lies beyond the gate, the tone of all that we do and say on our way to the gate changes drastically.

Henri J.M. Nouwen, in Robert Durback, *Seeds of Hope*

. . . Paul never said that we would rise with the body with which we died. He insisted that we would have a spiritual body. What he really meant was that a man's *personality* would survive. It is almost impossible to conceive of personality without a body, because it is through the body that the personality expresses itself. What Paul is contending for is that after death the individual remains. He did not inherit the Greek contempt of the body but believed in the resurrection of the whole man. He will still be himself, he will survive as a person.

William Barclay, *The Letters to the Corinthians*

While I was reading the beginning of St Mark's Gospel, before I reached the third chapter, I suddenly became aware that on the other side of my desk there was a presence. And the certainty was so strong that it was Christ standing there that it has never left me. This was the real turning-point. Because Christ was alive and I had been in his presence I could say with certainty that what the Gospel said about the crucifixion of the prophet of Galilee was true, and the centurion was right when he said 'Truly he is the Son of God' . . . I became absolutely certain within myself that Christ is alive and that certain things existed. I didn't have all the answers, but having touched that experience, I was certain that ahead of me there were answers, visions, possibilities.

Anthony Bloom, *School for Prayer*

See also Cross, Experience, Grace, Hope, Presence

94

REVELATION

*R*evelation – *disclosing of knowledge, to man by divine or super-natural agency; knowledge so disclosed*

In the opening verses of the Bible we read of God creating 'the heavens and the earth . . . and the Spirit of God was moving over the face of the waters'. As a result of these words I expect to see some evidence of the creator in the creation. Consequently nature has always been an important source of revelation for me. The opening words of John's Gospel point us to a revelation in the person of Jesus Christ: 'In the beginning was the Word, and the Word was with God, and the Word was God . . . And the Word became flesh and dwelt among us, full of grace and truth; we have beheld his glory, glory as of the only Son from the Father.' Consequently the Gospels have always been for me an important media of revelation. I have also found the saints an important source of revelation of God as experienced in their lives. Close allies are other people, and art, music, poetry, literature, drama, philosophy, science, etc. All these are potential sources of revelation. Mention must also be made of worship, the sacraments, and an open and receptive form of prayer.

In the beginning when God created the heavens and the earth, the earth was a formless void and darkness covered the face of the deep, while a wind from God swept over the face of the waters.

Genesis 1.1–2

They who have my commandments and keep them are those who love me; and those who love me will be loved by my Father, and I will love them and reveal myself to them.

John 14.21

The world is charged with the grandeur of God.

Gerard Manley Hopkins, 'God's Grandeur'

Man is the revelation of the Infinite, and it does not become finite in him. It remains the Infinite.

Mark Rutherford, *More Pages from a Journal*

If you only say, you have a Revelation from God; I must have a Revelation from God too, before I can believe you.

Benjamin Whichcote, *Moral and Religious Aphorisms*

The one obvious, unmistakable manifestation of the Deity is the law of good and evil disclosed to men by revelation.

Leo Tolstoy, *Anna Karenina*

Instead of complaining that God had hidden Himself, you will give Him thanks for having revealed so much of Himself.

Blaise Pascal, *Pensées*

For each truth revealed by grace, and received with inward delight and joy, is a secret murmur of God in the ear of a pure soul.

Walter Hilton, *The Ladder of Perfection*

The first and most important fact that we can know about God is ever this: *we* know nothing of Him, except what He Himself has revealed to us.

Emil Brunner, *Our Faith*

That which we really know about God, is not what we have been clever enough to find out, but what the Divine Charity has secretly revealed.

Evelyn Underhill, *The School of Charity*

My own mind is the direct revelation which I have from God and far least liable to mistake in telling his will of any revelation.

Ralph Waldo Emerson, *The Heart of Emerson's Journals*

The knowledge of man is as the waters, some descending from above, and some springing from beneath: the one informed by the light of nature, the other inspired by divine revelation.

Francis Bacon, *The Advancement of Learning*

God is revealed as the God of love, and henceforth every morally good act, that is, every act formed by charity, is a revelation of God. Every word of truth and love, every hand extended in kindness, echoes the inner life of the Trinity.

Gabriel Moran FSC, *Theology of Revelation*

One of the mistakes which men sometimes make is to identify God's revelation *solely* with the Bible. That would be to say that since about AD 120, when the latest book in the New Testament was written, God has ceased to speak, that since then there has been no more revelation from God. God's Spirit is *always* revealing Himself. It is true that God's supreme and unsurpassable revelation came in Jesus Christ; but Jesus is not a figure in a book. He is a living person, and in Him God's revelation goes on. God is still leading us into a greater and greater realization of what Jesus means . . .

William Barclay, *The Gospel of John*

In nature we find God; we do not infer from Nature what God must be like, but when we see Nature truly, we see God self-manifested in and through it. Yet the self-revelation so given is incomplete and inadequate. Personality can only reveal itself in persons. Consequently it is specially in Human Nature – in men and women – that we see God.

William Temple, *Nature, Man and God*

Love, whether in its most exalted form as the love between husband and wife, or in the less ardent experience of affection and sympathy, unlocks the doors of our prison-house and reveals to us something of the breadth and length and depth and height of the spiritual world which surrounds us. In various degrees, all cordial human intercourse is a liberation and an enhancement of our personality; it is a channel of revelation.

W.R. Inge, *Personal Religion and the Life of Devotion*

For two reasons the event in which the fullness of revelation is given must be the life of a Person: the first is that the revelation is to persons who can fully understand only what is personal; the second is that the revelation is of a personal Being, who accordingly cannot be adequately revealed in anything other than personality. Moreover, if the Person who is Himself the revelation is to be truly adequate to that function, He must be one in essence with the Being whom He reveals.

William Temple, *Nature, Man and God*

It is quite wrong to think of God's revelation as being confined to what we might call theological truth. The theologians and the preachers are not the only persons who are inspired . . . When a great poet delivers to men a great message in words which defy time, he is inspired . . . A great musician is inspired . . . When a scientist discovers something which will help the world's toil and make life better for men, when a surgeon discovers a new technique which will save men's lives and ease their pain, when someone discovers a new treatment, a new drug, which will bring life and hope to suffering humanity, that is a revelation from God. It actually happens in a way that we can see.

William Barclay, *The Gospel of John*

See also Aspiration, Holy Spirit, Inspiration, Jesus Christ, Light

95

SAINTS

Saints – the holy people of God

I grew up with a rather jaundiced view of saints. I spotted a few of them in stained-glass windows in churches. They looked cold and severe in demeanour, and thin and emaciated in body. The turning-point came in meeting a real live saint. I was surprised to be confronted by a warm and loving person. He was outgoing and fully alive. His disposition was kindly and sympathetic. His bright shining eyes were evidence of an inner energy and enthusiasm. He was radiant. I wonder how he got to be like that? Something of the divine in him coming alive, nurtured by prayer and worship, and finding an outlet in service? I began to look around and discovered several more. I came to call them my 'heroes' and 'heroines'. Indirectly they have been an enormous help to me. In times of difficulty, I have thought about my 'heroes' and 'heroines' and immediately felt much better. Whatever else was happening in the world, they were quietly getting on with things – their lives giving ample evidence of God. The experience of the saints has also provided me with an invaluable source of inspiration.

As for the holy ones in the land, they are the noble, in whom is all my delight.
  Psalm 16.3

. . . called to be saints, together with all those who in every place call on the name of our Lord Jesus Christ, both their Lord and ours.
  1 Corinthians 1.2

To pray is to open oneself to the possibility of sainthood, to the possibility of becoming set on fire by the Spirit.
  Kenneth Leech, *True Prayer*

[373]

The holiness of the saints is the restored image of God in them.
> Benedicta Ward, in Alan Richardson and John Bowden, *A New Dictionary of Christian Theology*

The heroes, the saints and sages – they are those who face the world alone.
> Norman Douglas, *An Almanac*

Grace is indeed needed to turn a man into a saint, and he who doubts it does not know what a saint or a man is.
> Blaise Pascal, *Pensées*

The saint is essentially someone who communicates and radiates the character of God, his love, his joy, his peace.
> Kenneth Leech, *True Prayer*

The loving acceptance of the saints is never mistaken by sinners as condoning their sins. Rather it lifts them to new aspirations.
> Anon

God creates out of *nothing*, wonderful, you say: yes, to be sure, but he does what is still more wonderful: he makes saints out of sinners.
> Søren Kierkegaard, *The Journals of Søren Kierkegaard*

They may have had their trials too – failing health, declining years, the ingratitude of men – but they have endured as seeing Him who is invisible.
> Benjamin Jowett, *College Sermons*

The power of the Soul for good is in proportion to the strength of its passions. Sanctity is not the negation of passion but its order . . . Hence great Saints have often been great sinners.
> Coventry Patmore, *The Rod, the Root and the Flower*

They were men of intense religious faith, of marked mystical type, characterized by interior depth of experience, but at the same time they were men of scholarship, breadth and balance.
> Rufus M. Jones, *Spiritual Reformers in the 16th and 17th Centuries*

We may allow that the saints are specialists, but they are specialists in a career to which all Christians are called. The difference between them and us is a difference in degree, not in kind.
> Evelyn Underhill, in John Stobbart, *The Wisdom of Evelyn Underhill*

This man is known by five signs. First, he never complains. Next, he never makes excuses: when accused, he leaves the facts to vindicate him. Thirdly, there is nothing he wants in earth or heaven but what God wills himself. Fourthly, he is not moved in time. Fifthly, he is never rejoiced: he is joy itself.

Meister Eckhart, in Franz Pfeiffer, *Meister Eckhart*, translated by C. de B. Evans

The saint is God's greatest work. All the world's 'great' men seem small beside the saint. The great statesman, the great writer, the great soldier may be far above us, but he remains altogether of our world. The great saint fills us with awe and seems at times almost a visitor from another sphere.

W.E. Sangster, *The Pure in Heart*

I have met in my life two persons, one a man, the other a woman, who convinced me that they were persons of sanctity. Utterly different in character, upbringing and interests as they were, their affect on me was the same. In their presence I felt myself to be ten times as nice, ten times as intelligent, ten times as good-looking as I really am.

W.H. Auden, *A Certain World*

The eyes of the saint make all beauty holy and the hands of the saint consecrate everything they touch to the glory of God, and the saint is never offended by anything and judges no man's sin because he does not know sin. He knows the mercy of God. He knows that his own mission on earth is to bring that mercy to all men.

Thomas Merton, *Seeds of Contemplation*

The saints are men and women of prayer to whom we owe our deepest revelations of the Supernatural – those who give us real news about God – are never untrained amateurs or prodigies. Such men and women as Paul, Augustine, Catherine, Julian, Ruysbroeck, are genuine artists of eternal life. They have accepted and not scorned the teachings of tradition: and humbly trained and disciplined their God-given genius for ultimates.

Evelyn Underhill, *Man and the Supernatural*

There is after all something in Christian saintliness which eludes analysis. For saintliness is the partial expression, the reflection in the external life, of the hidden man of the heart, who is not fully known even to the saint himself; and it is always imperfect, because it is always going on to perfection. I will not have my portrait painted, said a holy man; for which man do you want to paint? One of them is not worth painting, and the other is not finished yet.

W.R. Inge, *Types of Christian Saintliness*

A saint is not so much a man who realizes that he possesses virtues and sanctity as one who is overwhelmed by the sanctity of God. God is holiness. And therefore things are holy in proportion as they share what He is. All creatures are holy insofar as they share in His being, but men are called to be holy, in a far superior way – by somehow sharing His transcendence and rising above the level of everything that is not God.

Thomas Merton, *The Sign of Jonas*

A saint is a human creature devoured and transformed by love: a love that has dissolved and burnt out those instinctive passions – acquisitive and combative, proud and greedy – which commonly rule the lives of men.

Evelyn Underhill, in John Stobbart, *The Wisdom of Evelyn Underhill*

See also Character, Holiness, Holy Spirit, Love, Mystics

96

SALVATION

Salvation – saving of the soul; deliverance from sin and its consequences and admission to heaven brought about by Christ; acquisition of holiness

William Law gave me a valuable insight into the meaning of salvation: 'There is but one salvation for all mankind,' he wrote, 'and that is the life of God in the soul.' He added that God's intent is to 'introduce or generate His own life, light, and Spirit in them, that all may be so many images, temples and habitations of the Holy Trinity'. Baptism is about cleansing and the birth of the life of God in the soul. We are baptized in the name (nature of) the Father, the Son and the Holy Spirit. The seed or spark of God already in us is triggered off and catalysed. The gifts of the Holy Spirit, latent within us, are brought to life and activated. As we grow and develop we experience the presence of the fruits of the Spirit in our lives. Through prayer and sacrament, our bodies become temples and habitations of the Holy Trinity. I have mentioned previously the presence of the earthly and creaturely in our lives. In the process of salvation, the life of God thus generated in the soul accepts the earthly and creaturely and brings about an integration. A valuable part of our nature, thought to be fallen, is redeemed and salvation – the acquisition of wholeness – gets under way.

The Lord is my strength and my might, and he has become my salvation.
    Exodus 15.2

For you were going astray like sheep, but now you have returned to the shepherd and guardian of your souls.
    1 Peter 2.25

What is most contrary to salvation is not sin but habit.
    Charles Péguy, *Basic Verities*

[377]

Our salvation, thank God! depends much more on His love of us than of our love of Him.

Father Andrew SDC, *Meditations for Every Day*

. . . the man who is saved, made whole, is the man who responds to a vision of God's life in Christ.

Frank Wright, *The Pastoral Nature of the Ministry*

God both represents to us what we are to become and shows us both the way to become it. Union with God is the goal and the love of God is the way.

Don Cupitt, *Taking Leave of God*

Man needs, above all else, salvation. He needs to turn round and see that God is standing there with a rope ready to throw to him if only he will catch it and attach it to himself. Then life can start all over again for him.

Norman W. Goodacre, *Laymen's Lent*

Salvation does not come from not going along, or running away. Nor does it come from letting oneself be carried along without willing. Salvation comes from complete self-surrender, and one's gaze must be directed upon a centre.

C.G. Jung, *The Integration of the Personality*

Christ died to save us, not from suffering, but from ourselves; not from injustice, far less from justice, but from being unjust. He died that we might live – but live as he lives, by dying as he died who died to himself that he might live unto God.

George Macdonald, *Unspoken Sermons*

The believer is one who places a particular kind of interpretation on his past – he sees it as salvation. And he does this, not by selecting from it what suits him; not by ignoring the less pleasant bits. He ignores nothing. He accepts it *all* as the way God brought him; learns from it all, but is bowed down by none of it. His past becomes not the history of failure, but the history of what God has done to him, and for him, and with him.

Henry McKeating, *God and the Future*

It was something in which they were *being saved*. It is interesting to note that in the Greek this is a present tense, and not past. It would be strictly correct to translate it not, 'in which you have been saved', but 'in which you are being saved'. Salvation goes from glory to glory. It is not something which is ever completed in this world. There are many things in this life which we can exhaust, but the meaning of salvation is something which a man can never exhaust.

William Barclay, *The Letters to the Corinthians*

There is but one salvation for all mankind, and that is the life of God in the soul. God has but one design or intent towards all mankind and that is to introduce or generate His own life, light, and Spirit in them, that all may be as so many images, temples and habitations of the Holy Spirit . . . There is not one for the Jew, another for a Christian, and a third for the heathen. No; God is one, human nature is one, salvation is one, and the way to it is one; and that is, the desire of the soul turned to God.

William Law, in Stephen Hobhouse, *Selected Mystical Writings of William Law*

Those who are in the Universities and Churches of men have Christ in their mouths, and they have a measuring-reed by their side – the inhabitants of God's Church on the other hand have the Life of Christ and the testing-standing within themselves. Those who are 'nominal professors' hang salvation on a literal knowledge of the merit secured by Christ's death; the true believer knows that salvation is never a purchase, is never outwardly effected, but is a new self, a new spirit, a new relation to God: 'Man must cease to be what he is before he can come to be another kind of person.'

Rufus M. Jones, *Spiritual Reformers in the 16th and 17th Centuries*

The true aim of the soul is not its own salvation; to make that the chief aim is to ensure its perdition ('Whosoever would save his soul shall lose it' – St Matthew 16.25); for it is to fix the soul on itself as centre. The true aim of the soul is to glorify God; in pursuing that aim it will attain to salvation unawares. No one who is convinced of his own salvation is as yet even safe, let alone 'saved'. Salvation is the state of him who has ceased to be interested whether he is saved or not, provided that what takes the place of that supreme self-interest is not a lower form of self-interest but the glory of God.

William Temple, *Nature, Man and God*

Consider yourself a refractory pupil for whom you are responsible as mentor and tutor. To sanctify sinful nature, by bringing it gradually under control of the angel within us, by the help of a holy God, is really the whole of Christian pedagogy and of religious morals. Our work – my work – consists in taming, subduing, evangelizing and *angelizing* the evil self and in restoring harmony with the good self. Salvation lies in abandoning the evil self in principle, and in taking refuge with the other, the divine self, – in accepting with courage and prayer the task of living with one's own demon, and making it into a less and less rebellious instrument of good.

Henri Frédéric Amiel, *Amiel's Journal*

What every man looks for in life is his own salvation and the salvation of the men he lives with. By salvation I mean first of all the full discovery of who he himself really is. Then I mean something of the fulfilment of his own God-given powers, in the love of others and of God. I mean also the discovery that he cannot find himself in himself alone, but that he must find himself in and through others. Ultimately, these propositions are summed up in two lines of the Gospel: 'If any man would save his life, he must lose it,' and, 'Love one another as I have loved you.' It is also contained in another saying from St Paul: 'We are members one of another.'

Thomas Merton, *No Man Is an Island*

When, therefore, the first spark of a desire after God arises in thy soul, cherish it with all thy care, give all thy heart into it, it is nothing less than a touch of the divine loadstone that is to draw thee out of the vanity of time into the riches of eternity. Get up, therefore, and follow it gladly as the Wise men of the East followed the star from Heaven that appeared before them. It will do for thee as the star did for them: it will lead thee to the birth of Jesus, not in a stable in Bethlehem in Judea, but to the birth of Jesus in the dark centre of thy own fallen soul.

William Law, in Stephen Hobhouse, *Selected Mystical Writings of William Law*

See also Finding God, Freedom, Healing, Transformation, Wholeness

97

SCIENCE AND RELIGION

Science – branch of knowledge; organized body of knowledge that has been accumulated on a subject; one dealing with material phenomena and based mainly on observation, experiment, and induction, as chemistry, biology

Professor Coulson in his book *Science and Christian Belief* wrote: 'To the question, 'What is a primrose?' several valid answers may be given. One person says:

> *A primrose by the river's brim*
> *A yellow primrose was to him,*
> *And it was nothing more.*

'Just that, and no more'. Another person, the scientist, says, 'a primrose is a delicately balanced biochemical mechanism, requiring potash, phosphates, nitrogen and water in definite proportions'. A third person says, 'a primrose is God's promise of spring'. All three definitions are correct. We see here three different approaches to truth – that of the poet, scientist and theologian.' Add to this some words of William Temple, and we have an understanding of the relationship of science and religion. In *Nature, Man and God*, he wrote 'the theologian who quarrels with science on its own ground is but a presumptuous fool. But the scientist who quarrels with theology on its own grounds is no better. If there is mutual respect and common reverence for truth in all its forms there may still be divergence and even what we have called tension; but there will be no quarrel.'

For it is he who gave me unerring knowledge of what exists, to know the structure of the world and the activity of the elements; the beginning and end and middle of times, the alternations of the solstices and the changes of the seasons, the cycles of the year and the constellations of the stars, the natures of animals and the tempers of wild animals, the powers of spirits and the thoughts of human beings, the varieties of plants and the virtues of roots.

Wisdom of Solomon 7.17–20

. . . for 'the earth and its fullness is the Lord's'.

1 Corinthians 10.26

Science without religion is lame, religion without science is blind.

Albert Einstein, *Out of My Later Years*

Science cannot supply faith in a loving God, and a God whom we can love.

Henry Ward Beecher, *Proverbs from Plymouth Pulpit*

Perhaps some day science can explain the world, but it can never explain its meaning.

Michel Quoist, *With Open Heart*

[Evolution] has for many taken the place of God Himself, and bowed Him calmly out of His Own Universe.

G.A. Studdert Kennedy, *Food for the Fed-Up*

Science may have found a cure for most evils; but it has found no remedy for the worst of them all – the apathy of human beings.

Helen Keller, *My Religion*

Science sees everything mechanically, through part of the moving-instinctive centre. It has no answer to human needs in a crisis.

A.R. Orage, *On Love*

Scientists are attempting to come to God head-first. They must come to Him heart-first. Then let their heads interpret what they have found.

Henry Ward Beecher, *Proverbs from Plymouth Pulpit*

The means by which we live have outdistanced the ends for which we live. Our scientific power has outrun our spiritual power. We have guided missiles and misguided man.

Martin Luther King, *Strength to Love*

Anybody who has been seriously engaged in scientific work of any kind realizes that over the entrance to the gates of the temple of science are written the words: *Ye must have faith*. It is a quality which the scientist cannot dispense with.

Max Planck, *Where is Science Going?*

But to the great man of science, science is an art, and he himself is an artist. And his creation is not the less a work of art because it is but a faint and imperfect copy of another – of the supreme work of art which is nature itself.

J.W.N. Sullivan, *Limitations of Science*

It may be that in the practice of religion men have real evidence of the Being of God. If that is so, it is merely fallacious to refuse consideration of this evidence because no similar evidence is forthcoming from the study of physics, astronomy or biology.

William Temple, *Nature, Man and God*

Science cannot solve the ultimate mystery of nature. And that is because, in the last analysis, we ourselves are part of nature and therefore part of the mystery that we are trying to solve. Music and art are, to an extent, also attempts to solve or at least express the mystery. But to my mind the more we progress with either the more we are brought into harmony with all nature itself. And that is one of the great services of science to the individual.

Max Planck, *Where is Science Going?*

Science investigates; religion interprets. Science gives man knowledge which is power; religion gives man wisdom which is control. Science deals mainly with facts; religion deals mainly with values. The two are not rivals. They are complementary. Science keeps religion from sinking into the valley of crippling irrationalism and paralyzing obscurantism. Religion prevents science from falling into the marsh of obsolete materialism and moral nihilism.

Martin Luther King, in Coretta Scott King, *The Words of Martin Luther King*

All science has God as its author and giver. Much is heard of the conflict between science and religion, and of the contrast between sacred and secular. There may be aspects of truth to which religion is the gate, as indeed there are aspects of truth to which particular sciences are the gate. But if there be a Creator, and if truth be one of his attributes, then everything that is true can claim his authorship, and every search for truth can claim his authority.

Michael Ramsey, in Margaret Duggan, *Through the Year with Michael Ramsey*

The simple and plain fact is that the scientific method wins its success by ignoring parts of reality as given in experience; it is perfectly right to do this for its own purposes; but it must not be permitted by a kind of bluff to create the impression that what it ignores is non-existent.

William Temple, *Nature, Man and God*

You will hardly find one among the profounder sort of scientific minds without a religious feeling of his own . . . His religious feeling takes the form of a rapturous amazement at the harmony of natural law, which reveals an intelligence of such superiority that, compared with it, all systematic thinking and acting of human beings is an utterly insignificant reflection. This feeling is the guiding principle of his life and work, in so far as he succeeds in keeping himself from the shackles of selfish desire. It is beyond question closely akin to that which has possessed the religious geniuses of all ages.

Albert Einstein, *Ideas and Opinions*

See also Awareness, Education, Humility, Truth, Wonder

SEEKING

Seeking – making search or inquiry for; anxious to find or get; asking (thing or person) for advice

Several years ago I was on a chalet reading party in the French Alps with a dozen undergraduates. One of our Junior Research Fellows dropped in for a couple of days. He wanted to see as much of Mont Blanc as possible in the limited time available; so the two of us went for a walk by the Bionnassay glacier, up to a place called Le Nid d'Aigle, and back. We had not gone very far before he made a direct request. 'Bill, tell me, what do you believe in?' 'Oh, gosh,' I thought to myself, 'he's so bright, he is never going to believe this.' Anyway I gave him an outline of my vision of faith; of the divine inbreathing of the Genesis story of the creation of humanity; of this being fully worked out in the life of Jesus Christ; of St Paul realizing what Christ had experienced we can all in some measure also experience – something of the presence of the Father in ourselves, the Son, the gifts and fruits of the Holy Spirit. This seemed to strike a chord in him. To my great surprise he found what he had been seeking on our walk in the French Alps. Shortly after this he was baptized and confirmed.

~

. . . and those who seek me diligently find me.
   Proverbs 8.17

. . . search, and you will find.
   Matthew 7.7

Prayer has much more to do with God's search for us than our search for him.
   Christopher Bryant SSJE, *Jung and the Christian Way*

A man travels the world over in search of what he needs and returns home to find it.
   George Moore, *The Brook Kerith*

The search for meaning is richly rewarded when an adolescent can find something that deeply absorbs the talents of his mind and his emotional resources. He then has a passion for life.

Arthur T. Jersild, *The Psychology of Adolescence*

The way to know God is not by mental search, but by giving attention to Jesus Christ. The search for God can end in the contemplation of Jesus Christ, for in Him we see what God is like.

William Barclay, *The Gospel of Matthew*

The Kingdom of God is in you and he who searches for it outside himself will never find it, for *apart from God no one can either seek or find God, for he who seeks God, already in truth has Him.*

Rufus M. Jones, *Spiritual Reformers in the 16ᵗʰ and 17ᵗʰ Centuries*

My only task is to be what I am, a man seeking God in silence and solitude, with deep respect for the demands and realities of his own vocation, and fully aware that others too are seeking the truth in their own way.

Thomas Merton, *Contemplation in a World of Action*

Know that, by nature, every creature seeks to become like God . . . Nature's intent is neither food nor drink, nor clothing, nor comfort, nor anything else in which God is left out. Covertly, nature seeks, hunts, tries to ferret out the track on which God may be found.

Meister Eckhart, *Meister Eckhart*, translated by Raymond B. Blakney

Even in the midst of the lowest pleasures, the most abandoned voluptuary is still seeking God; nay more, as far as regards what is positive in his acts, that is to say in all that makes them an analogue of the true Love, it is God Himself Who, in him and for him, seeks Himself.

Etienne Gilson, *The Spirit of Medieval Philosophy*

I veritably believe that the Religion of the future will be something like this, an awed seeking, an orientation towards the superhuman, the Power behind all; with no permanent dogma, but the use of any and every dogma, when, if only for a day that dogma appears to be either true or a bridgeway towards truth or towards spiritual value, spiritual beauty.

Stephen MacKenna, *Journal and Letters*

There seem times when one can neither help oneself nor anyone else to find what we are all in search of, and it seems impossible to submit or acquiesce. I, as you know, have been in this frame of mind, and can only say that one does go on, though it seems impossible. The only way I think, is to do whatever comes to one, as quietly and fully as one can.

A.C. Benson, *Extracts from the Letters to Dr A.C. Benson*

Hold fast to God and he will add every good thing. Seek God and you shall find him and all good with him . . . To the man who cleaves to God, God cleaves and adds virtue. Thus, what you have sought before, now seeks you; what you once pursued, now pursues you; what once you fled, now flees you. Everything comes to him who truly comes to God, bringing all divinity with it, while all that is strange and alien flies away.

Meister Eckhart, *Meister Eckhart*, translated by Raymond B. Blakney

. . . Seek God and discover Him and make Him a power in your life. Without Him all of our efforts turn to ashes and our sunrises into darker nights. Without Him, life is a meaningless drama with the decisive scenes missing. But with Him we are able to rise from the fatigue of despair to the buoyancy of hope. With Him we are able to rise from the midnight of desperation to the daybreak of joy. St Augustine was right – we were made for God and we will be restless until we find our rest in Him.

Martin Luther King, in Coretta Scott King, *The Words of Martin Luther King*

We must learn to realize that the love of God seeks us in every situation, and seeks our good. His inscrutable love seeks our awakening. True, since this awakening implies a kind of death to our exterior self, we will dread His coming in proportion as we are identified with this exterior self and attached to it. But when we understand the dialectic of life and death we will learn to take risks implied by faith, to make the choices that deliver us from the routine self and open to us the door of a new being, a new reality.

Thomas Merton, *New Seeds of Contemplation*

When is the Search ended? In one sense, it is finished when our hand, stretched out to God in the name of His anointed mediator Jesus Christ, feels an answering grasp and knows that He is there. But in another sense the searching never ends, for the first discovery is quickly follow by another, and that by another, and so it goes on.

To find *that* He is, is the mere starting-point of our search. We are lured on to explore *what* He is, and that search is never finished, and it grows more thrilling the farther one proceeds.

Isobel Kuhn, *By Searching*

If we seek God earnestly, we shall find him – or – rather he will find us. If we ask God humbly to come into our lives, he will indeed come. And he will not do with us what we had expected – still less what we had 'hoped'. We shall find, to our dismay as natural men, that the God whose assistance we remotely invoked is already here, within us, speaking, even commanding; his presence manifested in an immediate and imperative revealing of duty and obligation. We asked him to advise, to help, to strengthen, from afar. He comes to indwell, command, and direct, within.

Harry Blamires, *The Will and the Way*

See also Experience, Finding God, Listening, Meditation, Presence

99

SELF

Self – person's or thing's own individuality or essence, person or thing as object of introspection or reflexive action

Some writers in previous generations have made a distinction between the false self and the real self. The false self is usually made up of a number of elements. First, self-centredness or selfishness, often cunningly disguised. Second, a single-minded pursuit of wealth and what money can buy. Third, a striving for status and success; i.e. an ego trip. Fourth, a quest for happiness and pleasure, often with sexual connotations. In brief, the false self is completely taken up with the 'earthy and creaturely'. The real self is rather different. In this section W.R. Inge enables us to understand the nature of the real self: 'We are potentially all things; our personality is what we are able to realize of the infinite wealth which our divine–human nature contains hidden in its depths.' The real self discovers the 'infinite wealth' of our 'divine–human nature'. This is integrated with the 'earthy–creaturely' and leads to wholeness, at ease with oneself, and with other people. There is now no longer any need for pretence and cut-throat competition.

Keep your heart with all vigilance, for from it flow the springs of life.
Proverbs 4.23

But we have this treasure in clay jars, so that it may be made clear that this extraordinary power belongs to God and does not come from us.
2 Corinthians 4.7

Very often a change of self is needed more than a change of scene.
A.C. Benson, *Extracts from the Letters of Dr A.C. Benson to M.E.A*

He, that has no government of himself, has no Enjoyment of himself.
Benjamin Whichcote, *Moral and Religious Aphorisms*

My business is not to remake myself,
But make the absolute best of what God made.
Robert Browning, 'Bishop Blougram's Apology'

Self-knowledge comes to us only in the dark times, when we are stripped of illusion and naked to truth.
Mary Craig, *Blessings*

Resolve to be thyself; and know that he,
Who finds himself, loses his misery!
Matthew Arnold, 'Self-Dependence'

The true value of a human being is determined primarily by the measure and the sense in which he has attained liberation from the self.
Albert Einstein, *Ideas and Opinions*

Man is made 'in God's image'. God is a 'subsequent relation'. Within this relationship, man is made; through it, he becomes what he is. Out of it, he falls apart.
Michel Quoist, *With Open Heart*

The living self has one purpose only: to come into its own fullness of being, as a tree comes into full blossom, or a bird into spring beauty, or a tiger into lustre.
D.H. Lawrence, *The Phoenix*

Remember that there is but one man in the world, with whom you are to have perpetual contention, and be always striving to exceed him, and that is yourself.
William Law, *A Serious Call to a Devout and Holy Life*

We are potentially all things; our personality is what we are able to realize of the infinite wealth which our divine–human nature contains hidden in its depths.
W.R. Inge, *The Philosophy of Plotinus*

Not in the clamour of the crowded street,
Not in the shouts and plaudits of the throng,
But in ourselves, are triumph and defeat.
Henry Wadsworth Longfellow, 'The Poems'

Learning to know oneself is not just an affair of private introspection. It is also an affair of seeing how others behave and of recognizing and identifying feelings of theirs with feelings of one's own. Each is indispensable to the other.
John S. Brubacher, *Modern Philosophies of Education*

For it is precisely when all the bogus protective structures have collapsed, when the soul is 'pulverized' or nihilated, when it cries out, as the soul of Jesus did, in its helplessness and pain – it is precisely then that God is discovered in the darkness and love shapes itself in the world.   David Anderson, *Simone Weil*

Love of self is the basic sin, from which all others flow. The moment a man makes his own will the centre of life, divine and human relationships are destroyed, obedience to God and charity to men both become impossible. The essence of Christianity is not the enthronement but the obliteration of self.
   William Barclay, *The Letters to Timothy, Titus and Philemon*

Begin to search and dig in thine own Field for this *Pearl of Eternity*, that lies hidden in it; it cannot cost Thee too much, nor canst thou buy it too dear, for it is *All*, and when thou hast found it, thou wilt know, that all which thou hast sold or given away for it, is as mere a Nothing, as a Bubble upon the Water.
   William Law, *The Spirit of Prayer*

But can one actually find oneself in someone else? In someone else's love? Or even in the mirror someone else holds up for one? I believe that true identity is found, as Eckhart once said, by 'going into one's own ground and knowing oneself'. It is found in creative activity springing from within. It is found, paradoxically, when one loses oneself. One must lose one's life to find it.
   Anne Morrow Lindbergh, *Gift from the Sea*

The more man goes out from himself or goes beyond himself, the more the spiritual dimension of his life is deepened, the more he becomes truly man, the more also he grows in likeness to God, who is Spirit. On the other hand, the more he turns inward and encloses himself in self-interest, the less human does he become. This is the strange paradox of spiritual being – that precisely by going out and spending itself, it realizes itself.
   John Macquarrie, *Paths in Spirituality*

Just as we say that we must look at ourselves both as members of the entire world body and in individuals, so, too, I must seek universal truth as well as my own personal truth. These are not contradictory or exclusive truths, they are in harmony. Yet the part of the great truth which is my very own truth is unique to me. My task then is to search for that truth which is mine – which is me, really – find it, and then seize it, make it so conscious a part of my existence that it informs everything that I do.   Harry James Cargas, *Encountering Myself*

See also Acceptance, Image of God, Incarnation, Inner Life, Jesus Christ

SELFISHNESS

Selfishness – deficient in consideration for others, alive chiefly to personal profit or pleasure, actuated by self-interest, that pursuit of pleasure of one kind or another is the ultimate aim of every action

There is a vital point we often miss in reading the Genesis story of the creation of man and woman. It comes out in the sentence: 'That which was fashioned and shaped in the image and likeness of God *was taken from the dust of the earth*'. Interpreted, this means although we have an enormous potential of divine life in the depths of our being, we are at one and the same time earthy and creaturely, and rightly so. This earthy and creaturely side is a valuable source of power and energy. What is needed is an inner integration of these two sides of our nature, leading to a full-blooded person, as worked out in the life of Jesus Christ. This is wholeness – salvation. We have forgotten this and by and large centre ourselves on our earthy and creaturely side and end up in selfishness. The cost is, we dampen down the enormous potential of divine life in the depths of ourselves, and greatly restrict our lives and relationships with others.

And you, do you seek great things for yourself? Do not seek them.
    Jeremiah 45.5

All of them are seeking their own interests.
    Philippians 2.21

One suffers most who is most selfish.
    Taoist saying

The selfish heart deserves the pain it feels.
    Edward Young, *Night Thoughts*

No man is more cheated than the selfish man.

Henry Ward Beecher, *Proverbs from Plymouth Pulpit*

Man seeks his own good at the whole world's cost.

Robert Browning, 'Luria'

The more selfish you are, the more involved life becomes.

Thomas Merton, *The Sign of Jonas*

Perhaps one should not think so much of oneself, though it is an interesting subject.

Norman Douglas, *An Almanac*

Selfish prosperity makes a man a vortex rather than a fountain; instead of throwing out, he learns only to draw in.

Henry Ward Beecher, *Proverbs from Plymouth Pulpit*

Egoism: measuring others by our likes and dislikes – not by their needs but by our preferences.

A.R. Orage, *On Love*

Selfish persons are incapable of loving others, but they are not capable of loving themselves either.

Erich Fromm, *Man for Himself*

Selfish man, who does not want to be selfish – that aspiration for something better, is of God. Worldly man, conscious of spiritual things – that consciousness is of God.

Henry Ward Beecher, *Proverbs from Plymouth Pulpit*

Selfish men may possess the earth, but it is the meek who inherit it, and enjoy it as an inheritance from their heavenly Father, free from all the defilements and perplexities of unrighteousness.

John Woolman, *The Journal of John Woolman*

Every man must decide whether he will walk in the light of creative altruism or the darkness of destructive selfishness. This is the judgment. Life's most persistent and urgent question is, What are you doing for others?

Martin Luther King, in Coretta Scott King, *The Words of Martin Luther King*

I may say that the growth has all been upward toward the elimination of selfishness. I do not mean simply the grosser, more sensual forms, but those subtler and generally unrecognized kinds, such as express themselves in sorrow, grief, regret, envy, etc.

William James, *The Varieties of Religious Experience*

If a man is centred upon himself, the smallest risk is too great for him, because both success and failure can destroy him. If he is centred upon God, then no risk is too great because success is already guaranteed – the successful union of Creator and creature beside which everything else is meaningless.

Morris West, *The Shoes of the Fisherman*

In your excessive self-love you are like a molecule closed in upon itself and incapable of entering easily into any new combination. God looks to you to be more open and more pliant. If you are to enter into him you need to be freer and more eager. Have done, then, with your egoism and your fear of suffering.

Pierre Teilhard de Chardin, *Let Me Explain*

It seems to me that nothing is so important from the point of view of Christianizing society as to recognize that competition is not a thing limited to business. It is a thing that pervades the whole of our life. It is simply organized selfishness, and, as things stand, from the moment we become conscious, almost throughout our lives, the whole influence of our environment is competitive, and suggests that our business is to do the utmost for ourselves in the struggle against other people.

William Temple, *The Kingdom of God*

The great evils of society do not result from the startling and appalling wickedness of some few individuals; they are the result of a few million people like ourselves living together; and if anyone wants to see the picture of his sin, let him look at slums, and wars, and the like. These things have their origin in characters like ours, ready, no doubt, to be generous with superfluities, but in the last resort self-centred with alike that defensiveness and aggressiveness that go with that self-centredness.

William Temple, *The Preacher's Theme Today*

For the self-centred spirit there can be no eternal life. Even if it should exist for ever, its existence could only be an ever deepening chill of death. Because it seeks its satisfaction in itself, where none is to be found, it must suffer an always intenser pang of spiritual hunger, which cannot be allayed until that spirit turns to another source of satisfaction. In the self which it contemplates there can only be successive states. The self is not sufficient to inspire a dedication such as brings purposive unity into life.

William Temple, *Nature, Man and God*

Anyone who from time to time will sit quiet with himself and survey his life and present state will be conscious of failure. He will remember things of which he is now ashamed. He will see his secret selfishness, his carefully controlled ambitions, his secret lusts. He will know the power of temptations – from without and from within. He will recognize times of wilful choice of wrong attitudes and deeds. When he compares himself with the perfection of Jesus, he will realize his need of forgiveness, a fresh start and continuing grace.

George Appleton, *Journey for a Soul*

See also Cross, Loneliness, Pride, Sin, Suffering

101

SERENITY

Serenity – calmness, placidity, tranquillity, unperturbed

C.S. Duthrie, in his book *God in His World*, wrote: 'The serenity relevant for our time is a serenity that does not bypass the turmoil and torment of the atomic age but sends its roots down through the agonies to the life and power of God.' I find this sentence helpful because it fits in with the vision of faith which has evolved for me during the last twenty-five years. Most of us experience elements of turmoil, torment and agonies in everyday life. If we balance this by developing an inner life, we become rooted in the life and power of God, and at times experience serenity. I am very fond of my set of rooms in University College, Oxford. Sometimes I feel surrounded by turmoil, torment and agonies towards the end of a term when people are tired, and yet in spite of this there is an atmosphere of peace in my sitting-room. In these surroundings I can cope with stress and strain provided I tap into my inner resources. In this way I can keep things in perspective. St Augustine wrote: 'You have made us for yourself and our hearts find no peace until they rest in you.' This is what serenity means to me.

$$\backsim$$

. . . he made the storm be still, and the waves of the sea were hushed. Then they were glad because they had quiet, and he brought them to their desired haven.
Psalm 107.29–30

We call those happy who were steadfast.
James 5.11 (RSV)

No one can achieve Serenity until the glare of passion is past the meridian.
Cyril Connolly, *The Unquiet Grave*

All men who live with any degree of serenity live by some assurance of grace.
Reinhold Niebuhr, *Reflections on the End of an Era*

Serenity of Mind, and Calmness of Thought are a better Enjoyment; than any thing without us.

Benjamin Whichcote, *Moral and Religious Aphorisms*

Serene but strong, majestic yet sedate,
Swift without violence, without terror great.

Matthew Prior, 'Carmen Seculare for the Year MDCC'

In Jesus there is the quiet, strong serenity of one who seeks to conquer by love, and not by strife of words.

William Barclay, *The Gospel of Matthew*

We have yet to learn that strength is shown at least as well as by serenity and poise as in strenuous action.

Odell Shepard, *The Joys of Forgetting*

There is certainly something in angling . . . that tends to produce a gentleness of spirit, and a pure serenity of mind.

Washington Irving, *The Sketch-Book*

True contemplative grace gently tranquillizes the personality, giving a wonderful serenity and a calm self-dominion.

William Johnston, *The Mysticism of the Cloud of Unknowing*

An old age, serene and bright
And lovely as a Lapland night.

William Wordsworth, in W.E. Sangster, *The Secret of Radiant Life*

Only a soul full of despair can ever attain serenity and, to be in despair, you must have loved a good deal and still love the world.

Henry Miller, *The Books in My Life*

Whatever helps a person to use his resources productively and reduces his need to live up to a false image of strength and perfection is likely to add to his serenity and freedom from fear.

Arthur T. Jersild, in *Educational Psychology*

A sense of rest, of deep quiet even. Silence within and without. A quietly burning fire. A sense of comfort . . . I am not dazed or stupid, but only happy in this peaceful morning. Whatever may be the charm of emotion, I do not know whether it equals the sweetness of those hours of silent meditation, in which we have a glimpse and foretaste of the contemplative joys of Paradise. Desire and fear, sadness and care, are done away. Existence is reduced to the simplest form, the most ethereal mode of being, that is, to pure self-consciousness. It is a state of harmony, without tension and without disturbance, the dominical state of the soul, perhaps the state which awaits it beyond the grave.

    Henri Frédéric Amiel, *Amiel's Journal*

I am serene because I know thou lovest me.
Because thou lovest me, naught can move me from my peace. Because thou lovest
  me, I am as one to whom all good has come.

    Alistair Maclean, in *God in Our Midst*

> Serene will be our days and bright,
> And happy will our nature be,
> When love is an unerring light,
> And joy its own security.
>
>   William Wordsworth, 'Ode to Duty'

It was one of those moments of total serenity which the spiritual part of me, always aspiring to the heights of philosophical detachment, so often compelled me to seek in the days of my meditative youth; one of those moments when all the materialistic and cynical views of life collapse like pathetic fabrications before the sovereign evidence of life's beauty, meaning and wisdom, and when every man experiences the triumphant feeling of an artist of genius who has just entirely expressed himself.

    Romain Gary, *Promise at Dawn*

Sometimes we meet a person who has a quiet serenity of spirit of which we become quickly conscious; who seems to be unhurried and unworried; uncomplaining about the past, content with the present, unafraid of the future; one who seems to live in another tempo of life, with a stillness that is not a technique but comes from a centre of stillness within himself; one who is relaxed and restful, unself-assertive; whose 'isness' says more than his words, and will validate his words when he speaks of what he has discovered.

    George Appleton, *Journey for a Soul*

It is clear that the western nations . . . know very little of this state of feeling [serenity]. For them life is devouring and incessant activity. They are eager for gold, for power, for dominion; their aim is to crush men and to enslave nature. They show an obstinate interest in means, and have not a thought for the end. They confound being with individual being, and the expansion of the self with happiness, – that is to say, they do not live by the soul; they ignore the unchange-able and the eternal; they live at the periphery of their being, because they are unable to penetrate to its axis. They are excited, ardent, positive, because they are superficial. Why so much effort, noise, struggle, and greed? – it is all a mere stunning and deafening of the self.

Henri Frédéric Amiel, *Amiel's Journal*

See also Acceptance, Contentment, Joy, Peace, Quietness

102

SERVICE

Service – doing of work, or work done, for another or for a community, etc.; assistance or benefit given to someone, readiness to perform this

One of my duties in Nigeria was to teach in a local school – The Good Samaritan School for Handicapped Children. This unique school had been founded, a few years previously, by an elderly missionary couple, Mr and Mrs Patey. The pupils were small in number, but because of their physical and mental disabilities required a great deal of attention. I was impressed by Mr and Mrs Patey. They accommodated the children in their own home, looked after them, fed them, taught them and nursed them, and were on call twenty-four hours a day. Somehow, in spite of all the demands on their time and energy, they remained cheerful and produced a happy atmosphere. A warm friendly spirit pervaded the school – a consequence of costly service. In the end the cost proved to be too great and their health broke down and eventually they had to return to England. Jesus realized the importance of service. He said of himself: 'I am among you as one who serves.' He was also aware of the demands of service and warned his disciples to count the cost beforehand. Even the Good Samaritan needed to share the burden of service with the innkeeper.

Here is my servant, whom I uphold, my chosen, in whom my soul delights; I have put my spirit upon him.

Isaiah 42.1

Worship the Lord your God, and serve him only.

Matthew 4.10

Be useful where thou livest.

George Herbert, 'The Church Porch'

Life is given to us, we earn it by giving it.
  Rabindranath Tagore, *Stray Birds*

They also serve who only stand and wait.
  John Milton, 'Sonnet on His Blindness'

In Jesus the service of God and the service of the least of the brethren were one.
  Dietrich Bonhoeffer, *The Cost of Discipleship*

Great works, do not always lie in our way, but every moment we may do little ones excellently, that is, with great love.
  St Francis de Sales, *On the Love of God*

You have not done enough, you have never done enough, so long as it is still possible that you have something of value to contribute.
  Dag Hammarskjöld, *Markings*

The service of the fruit is precious, the service of the flower is sweet, but let my service be the service of the leaves in its shade of humble devotion.
  Rabindranath Tagore, *Stray Birds*

Nothing I can do, even if I do my best, can be good. As Jesus said, 'We are unprofitable servants, we have done our duty.' Therefore I shall strive to do my best.
  A.R. Orage, *On Love*

Service of man . . . does not replace service of God. But the service of God never excuses from service of man: it is in service to man that service to God is proved.
  Hans Küng, *On Being a Christian*

The giving of self to the service of God is not like making a single offer, handing over a single gift, receiving a single acknowledgement. It is a continued action, renewed all the time.
  Hubert van Zeller, *Considerations*

Abide in me and I in you . . . All truth and depth of devotion, all effectiveness in service springs from this. It is not a theme for words, but for the deeper apprehensions of silence.
  William Temple, *Readings in St John's Gospel*

When a man turns to Him, desiring to serve Him, God directs his attention to the world and its need. It is His will that our service of Him should be expressed as our service to the world, through Him, and for His sake.

Emil Brunner, *The Divine Imperative*

An act of prayer at the heart of every act of service – a self-offering to His purpose so that the action may be His and not our own. That, in its perfection, is the secret of the saints. *I live – yet not I!* Christ is the boundless source of energy and love.

Evelyn Underhill, *The Light of Christ*

The lives of the saints have always been for Christians the reminder that in this life men and women of all kinds, temperaments and cultures have touched the heights of Christian experience and have committed themselves utterly to the service of their fellows.

E.G. Rupp, in Alan Richardson and John Bowden, *A New Dictionary of Christian Theology*

There came to me, as I awoke, the thought that I must not accept this happiness as a matter of course, but must give something in return for it . . . I settled with myself before I got up, that I would consider myself justified in living till I was thirty for science and art, in order to devote myself from that time forward to the direct service of humanity.

Albert Schweitzer, *My Life and Thought*

Everybody can be great. Because anybody can serve. You don't have to have a college degree to serve. You don't have to make your subject and your verb agree to serve. You don't have to know about Plato and Aristotle to serve. You don't have to know Einstein's theory of relativity to serve. You don't have to know the second theory of thermo-dynamics in physics to serve. You only need a heart full of grace. A soul generated by love.

Martin Luther King, in Coretta Scott King, *The Words of Martin Luther King*

What, then, is the service rendered to the world by Christianity? The proclamation of 'good news'. And what is this 'good news'? The pardon of sin. The God of holiness loving the world and reconciling it to Himself by Jesus, in order to establish the kingdom of God, the city of souls, the life of heaven on earth, – here you have the whole of it, but in this is revolution. 'Love one another, as I have loved you'; 'Be ye one with me, as I am one with the Father', for this is life eternal, here is perfection, salvation, joy.

Henri Frédéric Amiel, *Amiel's Journal*

Ah yes, men must learn to serve
not for money, but for life.
Ah yes, men must learn to obey
not a boss, but the gleam of life on the face of a man
who has looked into the eyes of the gods.
Man is only perfectly human
when he looks beyond humanity.

    D.H. Lawrence, 'Service'

See also Commitment, Discipleship, Leadership, Neighbour, Work

103

SIN

Sin – transgression, a transgression against the divine law of principles of morality

Father Andrew has written, 'Sin is that condition in which a man makes himself the centre of his own life, and either ignores God or pushes Him on to the circumference. Fallen human nature is self-centred human nature.' Seen in the context of the Genesis story of the creation of humanity, humans choose to centre themselves on the earthy and creaturely, and ignore the fact they are made in the image and likeness of God. The divine life, latent in the depths of their being, is ignored altogether or pushed out on to the circumference of life. The outcome is a serious condition called sin. This leads to the commission of sins, and to a deadening of real life. Father Andrew goes on to point out: 'The human nature Christ brought to earth is God-centred.' Looking at the life of Christ as revealed in the Gospels we notice he centred his life on God, and brought about an integration of the earthy and creaturely. The outcome was wholeness or salvation. We need to centre our lives on God in like manner, integrating the earthy and creaturely.

&

. . . and be sure your sin will find you out.

Numbers 32.23

. . . since all have sinned and fall short of the glory of God; they are now justified by his grace as a gift, through the redemption that is in Christ Jesus.

Romans 3.23–24

You have ordained and so it is with us, that every soul that sins brings its own punishment upon itself.

St Augustine, *Confessions*

. . . The principle of sin which is man's self-centred desire to secure his independence against God.

G.W.H. Lampe, in A.R. Vidler, *Soundings*

> Know this, O man, the sole root of sin in thee
> Is not to know thine own divinity!
>
> James Rhoades, in Ralph Waldo Trine, *My Philosophy and My Religion*

The worst sin towards our fellow creatures is not to hate them, but to be indifferent to them, that's the essence of inhumanity.

George Bernard Shaw, *The Devil's Disciple*

The appalling thing about sin is that man does not appear to be able to create in that realm, it is always the same old thing man has been doing all along.

J. Neville Ward, *The Use of Praying*

The safest road to Hell is the gradual one – the gentle slope, soft underfoot, without sudden turnings, without milestones, without signposts.

C.S. Lewis, *The Screwtape Letters*

Original sin? It is probably the malice that is ever flickering within us. Seen thus, it is a grievous error for those who manage human affairs not to take original sin into account.

Eric Hoffer, *The Passionate State of Mind*

One shall not kill 'the evil impulse', the passion, in oneself, but one shall serve God *with it*; it is the power which is destined to receive its direction from man.

Martin Buber, *Hasidism*

Sin is something inside our fallen selves trying to come out and be free to hurt. The evil outside ourselves in the fallen world is something which is trying to come in – also to hurt.

Hubert van Zeller, *Considerations*

. . . means the determined or lackadaisical refusal to live up to one's essential humanity. It is the torpid unwillingness to revel in the delights or to share in the responsibilities of being fully human.

Harvey Cox, *God's Revolution and Man's Responsibility*

Whenever you fight against the root of sin in general or any sin in particular, hold fast to this desire, and fix your mind upon Jesus Christ for whom you long rather than upon the sin which you are fighting.

Walter Hilton, *The Ladder of Perfection*

St Paul says that the wages of sin is death, not that God condemns us to death for our sins, but that sin kills the life of the spirit. Sin is a sickness that leads to spiritual death unless it is cured by forgiveness and the soul kept healthy by grace.

George Appleton, *Journey for a Soul*

Sin has always been an ugly word, but it has been made so in a new sense over the last half-century. It has been made not only ugly, but passé. People are no longer sinful, they are only immature or underprivileged or frightened or, more particularly, sick.

Phyllis McGinley, *The Province of the Heart*

The smallest atom of good realized and applied to life, a single vivid experience of love, will advance us much further, will far more surely protect our souls from evil, than the most arduous *struggle* against sin, than the resistance to sin by the severest ascetic methods of chaining the dark passions within us.

Father Yelchaninov, in G.P. Fedotov, *A Treasury of Russian Spirituality*

Over and over again, as we break some rule which seems rather arbitrary and meaningless, we discover the principle which had dictated it. We set in motion the causes and effects from which we understand, for the first time, why there had ever been that prohibition; then it is too late. The discovery is called the Fall of Man.

William Temple, *Christian Faith and Life*

Sin is the putting of self in the centre where God alone should be. Sin is acting from the self instead of from God. It is falling short of the will and glory of God. Often it is more than that – it is setting one's will against God's will, consciously (where guilt is involved) or unconsciously (when the sinful consequences are equally disastrous).

George Appleton, *Journey for a Soul*

I'm very much of a Jungian, and I feel Jung's concept of the dark side in all of us is very near the truth. If we equate that dark side with the Devil, we are not far wrong in our understanding of what the Devil is up to. The interesting thing about the dark side, or the Devil, is that he was a fallen angel – he belongs to God really – and our problem is to reconcile the dark side and make use of its energy. It's always recognized that the Devil is walking up and down the earth, full of energy. In education I used to find the apparently wicked boy was full of it. You've got to understand it, come to terms with it and make use of it. In other words, bring the Devil back into God's Kingdom.

Kenneth Barnes, in Gerald Priestland, *Priestland's Progress*

Eden is on no map, and Adam's fall fits no historical calendar. Moses is not nearer the Fall than we are, because he lived three thousand years before our time. The Fall refers not to some datable aboriginal calamity in the historic past of humanity, but to a dimension of human experience which is always present – namely, that we who have been created for fellowship with God repudiate it continually; and that the whole of mankind does this along with us. Every man is his own 'Adam', and all men are solidarily 'Adam'. Thus, Paradise before the Fall, the *status perfectionis*, is not a period of history, but our 'memory' of a divinely intended quality of life, given to us along with our consciousness of guilt.

J.S. Whale, *Christian Doctrine*

See also Anxiety, Cross, Loneliness, Pride, Selfishness

SOUL

Soul – the spiritual or immaterial part of humans, often regarded as immortal; the moral or emotional or intellectual nature of a person; the meeting-place of God in a person

The Authorized Version of the Bible uses a different terminology in the Genesis story of the creation of humanity from the one we have been using. Genesis 2.7 reads: 'And the Lord God formed man of the dust of the ground, and breathed into his nostrils the breath of life; and man became a living soul.' This was the beginning of the meeting-place of God in humans, fully worked out in the life of our Lord. The lives of the saints, prophets and martyrs testify to the reality of the soul, and are examples of this way of life.

Non-biblical language may help us to understand more about the nature of the soul. Richard Jefferies in *The Story of My Heart*, wrote of a desire for 'a greatness of soul, an irradiance of mind, a deeper insight, a broader hope . . . By the word soul, or psyche, I mean an inner consciousness which aspires.' For Henry Ward Beecher, 'The human soul is God's treasury, out of which He coins unspeakable riches.' This insight points to the role of the priest and the 'cure of souls', enabling people to come to wholeness by drawing out the divine in them. We have now largely abandoned this role through ignorance and unbelief.

～

. . . the one who formed them and inspired them with active souls and breathed a living spirit into them.

Wisdom of Solomon 15.11

For what will it profit them to gain the whole world and forfeit their life? Indeed, what can they give in return for their life?

Mark 8.36–37

What is a soul? The thing that keeps the body alive.

James A. Froude, *Thomas Carlyle*

And it is with the soul that we grasp the essence of another human being, not with the mind, not even with the heart.

Henry Miller, *The Books in My Life*

There is a direct in-shining, a direct in-breathing, a direct in-reaching of the Divine Soul upon the human soul.

Henry Ward Beecher, *Proverbs from Plymouth Pulpit*

We shall know some day that death can never rob us of that which our soul has gained, for her gains are one with herself.

Rabindranath Tagore, *Stray Birds*

When he is in possession of his soul, then will man be fully alive, caring nothing for immortality and knowing nothing of death.

Henry Miller, *The Books in My Life*

The sphere that is deepest, most unexplored, and most unfathomable, the wonder and the glory of God's thought and head, is our own souls!

Henry Ward Beecher, *Proverbs from Plymouth Pulpit*

Love unites the soul with God, and, the more degrees of love the soul has, the more profoundly does it enter into God and the more it is centred in Him.

St John of the Cross, *Living Flame of Love*

I desire a greatness of soul, an irradiance of mind, a deeper insight, a broader hope. Give me power of soul, so that I may actually effect by its will that which I strive for.

Richard Jefferies, *The Story of My Heart*

The soul is a temple; and God is silently building it, by night and by day. Precious thoughts are building it; disinterested love is building it; all-penetrating faith is building it.

Henry Ward Beecher, *Proverbs from Plymouth Pulpit*

God's designs, God's good pleasure, the will of God, the action of God and his grace are all one and the same thing in life. They are God's working in the soul to make it like himself.

Jean-Pierre de Caussade SJ, *Self-Abandonment to Divine Providence*

But with Western man the value of the self sinks to zero. Hence the universal depreciation of the soul in the West. Whoever speaks of the reality of the soul or psyche is accused of 'psychologism'.

C.G. Jung, *The Collected Works of C.G. Jung*

The human soul is God's treasury, out of which He coins unspeakable riches. Thoughts and feelings, desires and yearnings, faith and hope – these are the most precious things which God finds in us.

Henry Ward Beecher, *Proverbs from Plymouth Pulpit*

By the word soul, or psyche, I mean that inner consciousness which aspires. By prayer I do not mean a request for anything preferred to a deity; I mean intense soul-emotion, intense aspiration.

Richard Jefferies, *The Story of My Heart*

By nature the core of the soul is sensitive to nothing but the divine Being, unmediated. Here God enters the soul with all he has and not in part. He enters the soul through the core and nothing may touch that core except God himself.

Meister Eckhart, *Meister Eckhart*, translated by Raymond B. Blakney

> And see all sights from pole to pole,
> And glance, and nod, and bustle by,
> And never once possess our soul
> Before we die.
>
> Matthew Arnold, 'A Southern Night'

It is man's soul that Christ is always looking for. He calls it 'God's Kingdom', and finds it in every one. He compares it to little things, to a tiny seed, to a handful of leaven, to a pearl. That is because one realizes one's soul only by getting rid of all alien passions, all acquired culture, and all external possessions, be they good or evil.

Oscar Wilde, *De Profundis*

Either we have an immortal soul, or we have not. If we have not, we are beasts; the first and wisest of beasts, it may be; but still true beasts. We shall only differ in degree, and not in kind; just as the elephant differs from the slug. But by the concession of all the materialists of all the schools, or almost all, we are not of the same kind as beasts – and this also we say from our own consciousness. Therefore, methinks, it must be the possession of a soul within us that makes the difference.

Samuel Taylor Coleridge, *Table Talk of Samuel Taylor Coleridge*

If we wish to respect men we must forget what they are, and think of the ideal which they carry hidden within them, of the just man and the noble, the man of intelligence and goodness, inspiration and creative force, who is loyal and true, faithful and trustworthy, of the higher man, in short, and that divine thing we call a soul. The only men who deserve the name are the heroes, the geniuses, the saints, the harmonious, puissant, and perfect samples of the race.

    Henri Frédéric Amiel, *Amiel's Journal*

See also Character, Eternal Life, Holy Spirit, Inner Life, Wholeness

105

SUFFERING

Suffering – undergoing pain, loss, grief, defeat, disablement, change, punishment, wrong, etc.

I have been thinking about the carnage of the two World Wars recently. Most forms of suffering pale into insignificance in comparison, except when we ourselves have suffered directly, or have witnessed suffering in another, close by. In the small ways in which I have suffered, I have stopped asking the question, 'Why has this happened to me?' This seems to be the wrong sort of question. The thing has already happened, and that's that. The important question now is: 'How am I going to respond to this suffering, and is it possible to make a creative use of it?' While out in Singapore during National Service I went down with a severe dose of prickly heat, so much so that I was nearly invalided back to England. However the doctor put me on a new, possibly dangerous drug, and ordered me to bed for several days, lying down on my back and keeping perfectly still. I was bored stiff, but learnt important lessons. My mind took over and sorted out a great deal of dross. I was able to return to duties a wiser person.

⸎

The Lord is near to the broken-hearted, and saves the crushed in spirit.
Psalm 34.18

And after you have suffered for a little while, the God of all grace, who has called you to his eternal glory in Christ, will himself restore, support, strengthen and establish you.
1 Peter 5.10

He who suffers much will know much.
Greek proverb

In time of sickness the soul collects itself anew.
Latin proverb

We must somehow believe that unearned suffering is redemptive.
  Martin Luther King, in Coretta Scott King, *The Words of Martin Luther King*

Although the world is full of suffering, it is full also of the overcoming of it.
  Helen Keller, *Optimism*

Deep, unspeakable suffering may well be called a baptism, a regeneration, the initiation into a new state.
  George Eliot, *Adam Bede*

> Know how sublime a thing it is
> To suffer and be strong.
>   Henry Wadsworth Longfellow, 'The Light of Stars'

Understood in its deepest sense, being Christ's follower means suffering that is unendurable to the great majority of mankind.
  C.G. Jung, *Psychology and Alchemy*

I wonder why we suffer so strangely – to bring out something in us, I try to believe, which can't be brought out in any other way.
  A.C. Benson, *Extracts from the Letters of Dr A.C. Benson to M.E.A.*

Shut out suffering, and you see only one side of this strange and fearful thing, the life of man. Brightness, and happiness, and rest – that is not life. It is only one side of life: Christ saw both sides.
  F.W. Robertson, *Sermons*

There are powerful kinds of good that can come into life only where something has gone terribly wrong. That does not justify even the smallest area of life going wrong; it just happens to be one aspect of the composition of things.
  J. Neville Ward, *Friday Afternoon*

. . . The bad things that happen to us in our lives do not have a meaning when they happen. But we can redeem these tragedies from senselessness by imposing meaning on them. In the final analysis, the question is not why bad things happen to good people, but how we respond when such things happen.
  Rabbi H. Kushner, *When Bad Things Happen to Good People*

The mark of the spiritually mature man is that he can endure sorrow without bitterness, bewilderment without fuss, loss without envy or recrimination or self-pity. Above all, whatever the set-backs and misunderstandings, public and private, that he maintains a belief in the essential goodness of mankind.

    Hubert van Zeller, *Considerations*

Only by saying 'Amen' ('So be it') explicitly or implicitly – despite everything – can suffering be endured if not explained. Saying 'Amen' is the translation of the Old Testament noun 'belief' (*heemen*). The world with its enigma, its evil and suffering, can be affirmed because of God. Not otherwise. The mystery of the Incomprehensible in his goodness embraces also the misery of our suffering.

    Hans Küng, *On Being a Christian*

When trouble hits us we can react to it in a variety of ways. We can let it knock us out, so that we lose all hope and stamina. We can rebel and refuse to accept the rightness or merit of it. We can fill our lives with feverish activity so that we have no time to think about it. Or we can accept it – without defeat, rebellion, or evasion – trusting that God will make clear tomorrow what is so difficult to understand today.

    George Appleton, *Journey for a Soul*

Job never found an answer to the problem of unmerited suffering. The problem remained insoluble, but in it he met God. That is where man always meets God. That is where man most frequently meets his fellows. For he is so constituted that he needs problems more than solutions. His soul thrives on questions but grows sickly on answers – especially answers served up by others and, most of all, answers laid down by authority.

    John V. Taylor, *The Go-Between God*

Creative suffering – and this alone is real suffering – is positively non-resistant. It is a spiritual act, not a physical or mental reaction. And we cannot truly perform it until we wholly consent to the situation in which we find ourselves, however painful or disconcerting it may be, regarding it as the price we must pay for spiritual growth. By thus consenting to suffer we learn how to live by dying, how to surrender our existence to our being, until it is informed, more and more, by the eternal light of our essence.

    Hugh L'Anson Fausset, *Fruits of Silence*

Sooner or later suffering, misfortune, trouble come to every life. Some of it comes from our own ignorance, some from our own mistakes, some is a consequence of our own sin. But in almost every life there is a residue which seems inexplicable.

Our Christian faith does not completely explain the mystery of suffering. It teaches us how to deal with suffering. It assures us that God does not will suffering, but he is in it, to redeem it and to turn it into good and blessing. Let us also remember that the perfect life was not exempt from suffering.

George Appleton, *Journey for a Soul*

See also Anxiety, Cross, Death, Depression, Grief

106

TEMPTATION

Temptation – tempting or being tempted, incitement especially to wrongdoing; attractive thing or course of action; archaic putting to the test

While chaplain to University College, London, I went through a testing time and was tempted to leave the ordained ministry. I looked around for openings elsewhere, and was attracted to student counselling, or some form of psychotherapy. Fortunately providence came to my rescue and took me on a three-week tour to America, organized by the London University Church of Christ the King. We began with a week in New York. At the first opportunity I nipped off to a certain bookshop, to buy a copy of *The Choice Is Always Ours*, by Dorothy Berkley Phillips – a book which had been highly recommended to me. Back at the hotel, I quickly realized I had been looking for this book for ten years. By the time we landed at Gatwick, I was back on course with an outline of a new vision of faith. As I look back I value that initial period of testing and temptation. Without that I would never have come across *The Choice Is Always Ours* which has changed the whole course of my life.

My child, when you come to serve the Lord, prepare yourself for testing. Set your heart right and be steadfast, and do not be impetuous in time of calamity. Cling to him and do not depart, so that your last days may be prosperous. Accept whatever befalls you, and in times of humiliation be patient. For gold is tested in the fire, and those found acceptable, in the furnace of humiliation. Trust in him, and he will help you; make your ways straight, and hope in him.

Ecclesiasticus 2.1–6

Stay awake and pray that you may not come into the time of trial; the spirit indeed is willing, but the flesh is weak.

Matthew 26.41

All temptations are founded either in hope or fear.
> Thomas Fuller, *Gnomologia*

Every evil to which we do not succumb is a benefactor.
> Ralph Waldo Emerson, *Essays*

Subdue your appetites . . . and you've conquered human nature.
> Charles Dickens, *Nicholas Nickleby*

Yet temptations often bring great benefits, even if they are disagreeable and a great burden; for in temptation a man is humbled, purified and disciplined.
> Thomas à Kempis, *The Imitation of Christ*

He did not say, 'You will never have a rough passage, you will never be over-strained, you will never feel uncomfortable', but he *did* say 'You will never be overcome.'
> Lady Julian of Norwich, *Revelations of Divine Love*

> No man is tempted so, but may o'ercome,
> If that he has a will to Masterdome.
>> Robert Herrick, 'Temptations'

The habitual conviction of the Presence of God is the sovereign remedy; it supports, it consoles, it calms us. We must not be surprised that we are tempted. We are placed here to be proved by temptation. Everything is temptation to us.
> F. de la M. Fénelon, in B.W. Randolph, *Letters and Reflections*

The story of the Temptations is, of course, a parable of His spiritual wrestlings, told by Himself to His disciples. It represents the rejection, under three typical forms, of all existing conceptions of the Messianic task, which was to inaugurate the Kingdom of God.
> William Temple, *Readings in St John's Gospel*

Temptation in the New Testament means any testing situation. It includes far more than the mere seduction to sin; it covers every situation which is a challenge to and a test of a person's manhood and integrity and fidelity. We cannot escape it, but we can meet it with God.
> William Barclay, *The Gospel of Luke*

Thou know'st that Thou hast formed me,
With Passions wild and strong;
And list'ning to their witching voice
Has often led me wrong.

Robert Burns, 'A Prayer in the Prospect of Death'

Man is not entirely safe from temptation as long as he is alive, because the source of temptation lies within us – we are born in concupiscence. When one trial or temptation leaves us, another takes its place, and we will always have something to endure, because we have lost the blessing of human happiness.

Thomas à Kempis, *The Imitation of Christ*

Ay me, how many perils doe enfold
The righteous man, to make him daily fall?
Were not, that heavenly grace doth him uphold,
And stedfast truth acquit him out of all.

Edmund Spenser, 'The Faerie Queene'

The drunken Rip Van Winkle in Jefferson's play excuses himself for every fresh dereliction by saying, 'I won't count this time!' Well, he may not count it, and a kind Heaven may not count it, but it is being counted none the less. Down among his nerve-cells and fibres the molecules are counting it, registering and storing it up to be used against him when the next temptation comes.

William James, *The Principles of Psychology*

Some of the most difficult and perplexing experiences in life come to us in temptation. We have given ourselves to God; we have begun to pray in earnest; we are trying to order our lives – so far as we can – in accordance with the will of God. And then, when we think that we have made a good start . . . we are suddenly overwhelmed by a storm of temptations. Sins we thought we had overcome renew their attacks, and a host of new and bewildering temptations come upon us. This is both painful and bewildering . . .

Olive Wyon, *On the Way*

In the very overcoming of temptation . . . we may draw out a hidden spiritual sweetness, as the bees suck honey from the thorn-bushes as well as from all other flowers. He who has not been tempted, knows nothing, nor lives as yet, say the wise man Solomon, and the holy teacher St Bernard. We find more than a thousand testimonies in Scripture to the great profit of temptation; for it is the special sign of the love of God towards a man for him to be tempted and yet kept from falling; for thus he must and shall of a certainty receive the crown.

John Tauler, *The History and Life of the Reverend Doctor John Tauler*

There are but two things that we can do against temptations. The first is to be faithful to the light within us, in avoiding all exposure to temptation, which we are at liberty to avoid. I say, all that we are at liberty to avoid, because it does not always depend upon ourselves, whether we shall escape occasions of sin. Those that belong to the situation in life in which Providence has placed us, are not under our control. The other is to turn our eyes to God in moments of temptation, to throw ourselves immediately upon the protection of heaven, as a child, when in danger, flies to the arms of its parent.

F. de la M. Fénelon, in B.W. Randolph, *Letters and Reflections of Fénelon*

See also Anxiety, Doubt, Pride, Sin, Worldliness

107

THANKSGIVING

T hanksgiving – expression of gratitude, especially to God

I shall always remember a sermon preached on the phrase – 'Learn to count your blessings, name them one by one.' I have tried to put this into practice on a daily basis ever since. The first few weeks of being a part-time hospital chaplain at the Bradford Royal Infirmary were particularly difficult and demanding. At the beginning of each week I would visit a hundred sick people and spend a few minutes with each patient. At the end of each session I was physically and mentally exhausted – mainly through concentration. On the way back to the cathedral clergy house I would 'count my blessings'. I would go over the session in the wards. For instance, I had met a man about to have his leg amputated. How thankful I was having both legs functioning properly, and able to walk and run. I had spent a few minutes with a woman who had a constriction in her throat. She had been fed solely on liquids for the last two months. How thankful I was, able to eat solid foods. By the time I had reached home I was well on the road to recovery. William Law has some good advice: 'If anyone would tell you the shortest, surest way to all happiness, and all perfection, he must tell you to make a rule to yourself, to thank and praise God for everything that happens to you.'

∽

But I am like a green olive tree in the house of God. I trust in the steadfast love of God for ever and ever. I will thank you for ever, because of what you have done. In the presence of the faithful I will proclaim your name, for it is good.

Psalm 52.8–9

Thanks be to God for his indescribable gift!

2 Corinthians 9.15

Joy untouched by thankfulness is always suspect.

Theodor Haecker, *Journal in the Night*

Gratitude is a fruit of great cultivation; you do not find it among gross people.

Samuel Johnson, *Boswell's Life of Johnson*

To wake at dawn with a winged heart and give thanks for another day of loving.

Kahlil Gibran, *The Prophet*

Let us, therefore, be thankful for health and a competence; and above all, for a quiet conscience.

Izaak Walton, *The Compleat Angler*

> Let never day nor night unhallow'd pass,
> But still remember what the Lord hath done.
>
> William Shakespeare, *II King Henry VI*

. . . the chief idea of my life . . . the doctrine I should always have liked to teach. That is the idea of taking things with gratitude, and not taking things for granted.

G.K. Chesterton, *Autobiography*

Gratitude was surely implanted in our hearts by our great Creator, and to fail in its observance, is acting against the dictates of conscience and humanity.

Elizabeth Helme, *St Margaret's Cave; or, The Nun's Story*

Thank God, carefully and wonderingly, for your continuing privileges, and for every experience of his goodness. Thankfulness is a soil in which pride does not easily grow.

Michael Ramsey, in Margaret Duggan, *Through the Year with Michael Ramsey*

Cultivate the thankful spirit – it will be to thee a perpetual feast. There is, or ought to be, no such things as small mercies. A really thankful heart will extract motive for gratitude from everything, making the most even of scanty blessings.

Anon

Thank God that those times which strain faith so hard come only occasionally in life. For the most part we travel a sunlit road, and when we are unaware of the love of God it is often because we have not looked for it. To see the evidence of God's mercies you have only to look.

W.E. Sangster, *Westminster Sermons*

. . . I will thank and praise God for the strength of my body enabling me to work, for the refreshment of sleep, for my daily bread, for the days of painless health, for the gift of my mind and the gift of my conscience, for His loving guidance of my mind ever since it first began to think, and of my heart ever since I first began to love.

Edward King, *Sermons and Addresses*

Thank God every morning, when you get up, that you have something to do that day which must be done, whether you like it or not. Being forced to work, and forced to do your best, will breed in you temperance and self-control, diligence and strength of will, cheerfulness and content and a hundred virtues which the idle man never knows.

Charles Kingsley, *Town and Country Sermons*

Would you know who is the greatest saint in the world? It is not he who prays most or fasts most; it is not he who gives most alms, or is most eminent for temperance, chastity or justice; but it is he who is always thankful to God who wills everything that God willeth, who receives everything as an instance of God's goodness, and has a heart always ready to praise God for it . . .

William Law, *A Serious Call to a Devout and Holy Life*

Certainly a marked feature of Christ's character was his perennial gratefulness of spirit. Run through His prayers and you will be surprised how large a place thanksgiving holds in them, how often He gave eager praise for what would have soured you and me, and made us feel quite certain that God had forgotten to be gracious. Did He not take the cup, that awful symbol of things so near and so fearsome, and even then give thanks?

A.J. Gossip, *From the Edge of the Crowd*

If anyone would tell you the shortest, surest way to all happiness, and all perfection, he must tell you to make a rule to yourself, to thank and praise God for everything that happens to you. For it is certain that whatever seeming calamity happens to you, if you thank and praise God for it, you turn it into a blessing. Could you therefore work miracles, you could not do more for yourself than by this thankful spirit; for it heals with a word speaking and turns all that it touches into happiness.

William Law, *A Serious Call to a Devout and Holy Life*

I will thank Him for the pleasures given me through my senses, for the glory of the thunder, for the mystery of music, the singing of birds and the laughter of children. I will thank Him for the pleasures of seeing, for the delights through colour, for the awe of the sunset, the beauty of flowers, the smile of friendship and the look of love; for the changing beauty of the clouds, for the wild roses in the hedges, for the form and beauty of birds, for the leaves on the trees in spring and autumn, for the witness of the leafless trees through the winter, teaching us that death is sleep and not destruction, for the sweetness of flowers and the scent of hay. Truly, O Lord, the earth is full of thy riches!

Edward King, *Sermons and Addresses*

See also Adoration, Contentment, Fulfilment, Happiness, Prayer

108

THINKING

Thinking – considering; being of opinion; forming conception of; exercising the mind otherwise than by passive reception of another's idea, imagining

D.H. Lawrence opens up thinking in his poem on 'Thought':

Thought is the welling up of unknown life into consciousness,
Thought is the testing of statements on the touchstone of the conscience,
Thought is gazing onto the face of life, and reading what can be read,
Thought is pondering over experience, and coming to a conclusion.
Thought is not a trick, or an exercise, or a set of dodges,
Thought is a man in his wholeness wholly attending.

All this sounds rather like reflection. In reflection full use is made of our minds, as in the poem above. Full use is also made of our hearts, meaning our feelings and emotions, our instinct and intuition. Full use is made too of our imagination, and our experience of life. More importantly we open ourselves to what D.H. Lawrence described as 'the welling up of unknown life into consciousness'. Seen this way, thinking can be a great adventure. Let D.H. Lawrence have the final word: 'Thought is a man in his wholeness wholly attending.'

We ponder your steadfast love, O God, in the midst of your temple.
Psalm 48.9

What do you think of the Messiah?
Matthew 22.42

One thought fills immensity.
William Blake, 'Proverbs of Hell'

What is the hardest task in the world? To think.

Ralph Waldo Emerson, *Essays*

Thought feeds itself with its own words and grows.

Rabindranath Tagore, *Stray Birds*

It is wonderful what a breadth of life can be encompassed in a moment's thought.

O.T. Beard, *Bristling with Thorns*

Christianity has need of thought that it may come to the consciousness of its real self.

Albert Schweitzer, *Out of My Life and Thought*

It is thoughts of God's thinking which we need to set us right, and remember, they are not as our thoughts.

W.M. Macgregor, *Jesus Christ the Son of God*

> My own thoughts
> Are my companions.
>
> Henry Wadsworth Longfellow, 'The Masque of Pandora'

Thought that can emerge wholly into feeling, feeling that can merge wholly into thought – these are the artist's highest joy.

Thomas Mann, *Death in Venice*

. . . We must recognize that the whole world is ruled in a wrong spirit, and that a change of spirit will not come from one day to the next. Our expectations must not be for tomorrow, but for the time when what is thought now by a few shall have become the common thought of many. If we have courage and patience, we can think the thought and feel the hopes by which, sooner or later, men will be inspired, and weariness and discouragement will be turned into energy and ardour. For this reason, the first thing we have to do is to be clear in our own minds as to the kind of life we think good and the kind of change that we desire in the world.

Bertrand Russell, *Principles of Social Reconstruction*

As soon as man does not take his existence for granted, but beholds it as something unfathomably mysterious, thought begins.

Albert Schweitzer, *The Teaching of Reverence for Life*

'A' thinks much, but it is always something to be done. The thinking in the Old Testament and the Gospels is of this type.

Mark Rutherford, *Last Pages from a Journal*

No one can fail of the regenerative influence of optimistic thinking, pertinaciously pursued. Every man owns indefeasibly this inlet to the divine.

William James, *The Varieties of Religious Experience*

When we ask the ultimate questions, whether about the direction of our own lives or about the meaning of existence, the outcome of thinking is not an answer but a transformed way of thinking, not propositions to assent to but heightened power of apprehension.

Helen Merry Lynd, *On Shame and the Search for Identity*

I began to think, and to think is one real advance from hell to heaven. All that hellish, hardened state and temper of soul, which I have said so much of before, is but a deprivation of thought; he that is restored to his power of thinking, is restored to himself.

Daniel Defoe, *Moll Flanders*

Elemental thinking is that which starts from the fundamental questions about the relations of man in the universe, about the meaning of life, and about the nature of goodness. It stands in the most immediate connexion with the thinking which impulse stirs in everyone. It enters into that thinking, widening and deepening it.

Albert Schweitzer, *My Life and Thought*

The powers of thought, the vast regions which it can master, the much more vast regions which it can only dimly suggest to imagination, to those whose minds have travelled beyond the daily round an amazing richness of material, an escape from the triviality and wearisomeness of familiar routine, by which the whole of life is filled with interest, and the prison walls of the commonplace are broken down.

Bertand Russell, *Principles of Social Reconstruction*

And, too, Jesus appeals to the mind. Again and again he challenges his hearers to think. He doesn't reveal the truth to them in a kind of tabloid packet to be swallowed whole – 'Shut your eyes and swallow'. No, Jesus challenges his hearers, sowing seeds of truth in their minds and consciences, and then urging them to think out the meaning of it.

Think it out, think it out. It is in this process of thinking it out – together with the love and the will and the imagination – that Jesus and his message are made known.

Michael Ramsey, in Margaret Duggan, *Through the Year with Michael Ramsey*

But those who wish to gain the world by thought must be content to lose it as a support in the present. Most men go through life without much questioning, accepting the beliefs and practices which they find current, feeling that the world will be their ally if they do not put themselves in opposition to it. New thought about the world is incompatible with this comfortable acquiescence; it requires a certain intellectual detachment, a certain solitary energy, a power of inwardly dominating the world and the outlook that the world engenders. Without some willingness to be lonely new thought cannot be achieved. And it will not be achieved to any purpose if the loneliness is accompanied by aloofness, so that the wish for union with others dies, or if intellectual detachment leads to contempt. It is because the state of mind required is subtle and difficult, because it is hard to be intellectually detached yet not aloof, that fruitful thought on human affairs is not common, and that most theorists are conventional or sterile.

Bertrand Russell, *Principles of Social Reconstruction*

See also Intellect, Knowledge, Meditation, Mind, Wisdom

109

TIME

*T**ime – duration; continued existence; progress of this viewed as affecting person or things, past, present and future*

When I was at theological college I went through a minor crisis, and it was to do with 'time'. I had taken on too many commitments, and suddenly everything seemed to go wrong, and my little world collapsed. In trying to rescue the situation, I came across a book written by Max Warren, called *The Master of Time*, and found it helpful. According to him, the 'mastery of time' depended on putting into practice the two main commandments, to love the Lord your God with heart, soul, mind and strength, and to love your neighbour as yourself. Easy to state, but difficult to do, even in a theological college. I put his recommendations into practice, and drastically reduced my commitments. It turned out to be a valuable exercise. Even now I stand back from time to time and prune my activities. We tend to waste so much time in trivia and superficialities.

Remember the sabbath day, and keep it holy. For six days you shall labour and do all your work. But the seventh day is a sabbath to the Lord your God; you shall not do any work.

Exodus 20.8

... because we look not at what can be seen but at what cannot be seen; for what can be seen is temporary, but what cannot be seen is eternal.

2 Corinthians 4.18

Time is the great physician.

Benjamin Disraeli, *Henrietta Temple*

Let every man be master of his time.

William Shakespeare, *Macbeth*

The day is of infinite length for him who knows how to appreciate and use it.

Johann Wolfgang von Goethe, in Ludwig Curtius, *Wisdom and Experience*

We must use time creatively, in the knowledge that the time is always ripe to do right.

Martin Luther King, in Coretta Scott King, *The Words of Martin Luther King*

Life must be measured rather by depth than by length, by thought and action rather than by time.

Sir John Lubbock, *The Pleasures of Life*

The more a person is able to direct his life consciously, the more he can use time for constructive benefit.

Rollo May, *Man's Search for Himself*

Time is lost when we have not lived a full human life, time unenriched by experience, creative endeavour, enjoyment and suffering.

Dietrich Bonhoeffer, *Letters and Papers from Prison*

If time is not to be either hoarded or pressed out of existence it must be spent as possessions are spent; not solely for personal use but for others.

Hubert van Zeller, *Considerations*

Love Jesus, and everything he has is yours. Because he is God, he is maker and giver of time. Because he is Man, he has given true heed to time. Because he is both God and Man he is the best judge of the spending of time.

The Cloud of Unknowing

Man's greatest disease is the consciousness of transience. Nothing is so likely to produce despair as the awareness of the contingency and vanity of life. A powerful and time-honoured cure is to seek a perception of eternity.

Peter Munz, *Problems of Religious Knowledge*

I think I have learned a new view of time – one that brings freedom from many useless anxieties, as Jesus said it would. As the horizon of the future contracts, the importance of 'now' is so much clearer than when there always seemed to be time in hand.

Leslie J. Tizard, *Facing Life and Death*

Time . . . is what keeps the light from reaching us. There is no greater obstacle to God than time. He means not time alone but temporalities: not only temporal things but temporal affections; not only temporal affections but the very taint and aroma of time.

Meister Eckhart, in Franz Pfeiffer, *Meister Eckhart*, translated by C. de B. Evans

All men complain that they haven't enough time. It's because they look at their lives from too human a point of view. There's always time to do what God wants us to do, but we must put ourselves completely into each moment that he offers us.

Michel Quoist, *Prayers of Life*

What is Time? The shadow on the dial, the striking of the clock, the running of the sand, day and night, summer and winter, months, years, centuries – these are but arbitrary and outward signs, the measure of Time, not Time itself. Time is the Life of the soul. If not this, then tell me, what is Time?

Henry Wadsworth Longfellow, 'Hyperion'

Everything is in the mind; time and beyond time, hell and heaven, death and life. The key to understanding is awareness in the now. But awareness of the moment is not a state that comes naturally to man. Usually, if at all, it comes and goes, elusively, with happiness or suffering; it comes with the creative urge, in abstract thought, through the love of God, or the love of creatures.

Anon (on T.S. Eliot's 'Four Quartets')

I don't have the time! We don't have the time!

It's not time. We don't *take* the time. We let life gnaw away at our time, stealing it from us bit by bit. We're slaves, not masters. We must be masters of our time. I must control my life – and the obligations it imposes on me – not the other way round.

Michel Quoist, *With Open Heart*

Today we have no time even to look at each other, to talk to each other, to enjoy each other, and still less to be what our children expect from us, what the husband expects from the wife, what the wife expects from her husband. And so less and less we are in touch with each other. The world is lost for want of sweetness and kindness. People are starving for love because everybody is in such a great rush.

Mother Teresa, in Kathryn Spink, *The Silence of the Heart*

The word 'time' is used in two ways in the New Testament. The first is in the sense of duration, time by the clock or the calendar, a purely impersonal, chronological idea. The second is judged by rightness, ripeness, achievement of purpose, which is determined by reference to God, in his goodwill, in his love and patience. Those who believe in God try to live their lives in chronological time with ever-deepening understanding of God's purpose, God's timelessness and their own keen eye for opportunity.

George Appleton, *Journey for a Soul*

See also Awareness, Eternal Life, Love, Mystics, Worldliness

110

TRANSFORMATION

Transformation – transforming, being transformed, as having undergone a great transformation; change of character, outward appearance

I love the story of the transfiguration – of Jesus going up the mountain with his inner core of disciples, and of being transformed before them. His face, we are told 'shone like the sun'. While an undergraduate I was confronted with something similar. I came across someone transfigured, whose face also 'shone like the sun'. The occasion was a Sunday morning in a church in Oxford. A visiting bishop had come to preach. As soon as I saw him I was taken aback by his appearance. It was as though light were radiating from him. He was vibrantly alive, a picture of health, and full of energy. I listened carefully to what he had to say, but cannot now remember a word he said. The important thing was him – transfigured and transformed – and I knew I wanted to be like that. I took a step of faith. I was never argued into faith but won over at the sight of someone transformed.

⌇

Look to him, and be radiant.
  Psalm 34.5

And all of us, with unveiled faces, seeing the glory of the Lord as though reflected in a mirror, are being transformed into the same image from one degree of glory to another; for this comes from the Lord, the Spirit.
  2 Corinthians 3.18

The central idea in Christianity is not justification, but transfiguration.
  Nicolas Berdyaev, in Donald A. Lowrie, *Christian Existentialism*

Love is the only force capable of transforming an enemy into a friend.
  Martin Luther King, in Coretta Scott King, *The Words of Martin Luther King*

Human souls, transformed by the Spirit of God till they live in the highest qualities, must form a public sentiment that is to be the transforming power among
men.

Henry Ward Beecher, *Proverbs from Plymouth Pulpit*

The process of transforming our inner lives must be expressed in the transformation of our outer life, of the life of the individual as well as that of the community.

Martin Buber, in Aubrey Hodes, *Encounter with Martin Buber*

The highest degree, which the mystics call the transformation or essential and
immediate union with God, is the reality of pure love in which there is no self-
interest.

François de la M. Fénelon, in B.W. Randolph, *Maxims of the Mystics*

It is far more important that one's life should be perceived than that it should be
transformed; for no sooner has it been perceived, than it transforms itself of its
own accord.

Maurice Maeterlinck, *The Treasure of the Humble*

Our day-to-day life is of vital importance as the mystery of transformation is
worked out in us and through us by the power of Christ. No detail is insignificant
because the reassimilation of all creation in Christ is to be complete.

John Main OSB, in Clare Hallward, *The Joy of Being*

But once a man accepts Christ, he has accepted an entirely new set of standards;
he is committed to an entirely new kind of life at his work, in his personal
relationships, in his pleasure, in his conduct, in his speech, in the things which he
allows himself to do.

William Barclay, *The Letters to Timothy and Titus*

The harvest of suffering cannot be reaped until it has been eaten, burnt, digested.
If the suffering is accepted and lived through, not fought against and refused,
then it is completed and becomes transmuted. It is absorbed, and having
accomplished its work, it ceases to exist as suffering, and becomes part of our
growing self.

E. Graham Howe and L. Le Mesurier, *The Open Way*

It is one of the most moving experiences of life to watch a bewildered frightened
human being, starved of friendship and hardly daring to be expectant of it,

blossom out into a happy, trustful and confident personal life as the result of being so welcomed and received. It is of the essence of the Gospel that we are so received in Christ, that His Yes to men is pronounced in such directly personal terms.

Alan Ecclestone, *Yes to God*

Life should be a giving birth to the soul, the development of a higher mode of reality. The animal must be humanized: flesh must be made spirit; physiological activity must be transmuted into intellect and conscience, into reason, justice, and generosity, as the torch is transmuted into life and warmth. The blind, greedy selfish nature of man must put on beauty and nobleness. This heavenly alchemy is what justifies our presence on the earth; it is our mission and our glory.

Henri Frédéric Amiel, *Amiel's Journal*

In his love for someone he brought out that which was peculiar to a person's life, even though it lay hidden under layers of dirt; he loved it out. Therefore many who knew that he saw them and loved them became new persons and experienced the great transformation. His love was not simply a reaction to something lovable, as our love is. His love was creative. It called a 'new creature' into existence.

Helmut Thielicke, *I Believe – The Christian's Creed*

The mainspring of life is in the heart. Joy is the vital air of the soul . . . To make anyone happy, then, is strictly to augment his store of being, to double the intensity of his life, to reveal him to himself, to ennoble him and transfigure him. Happiness does away with ugliness, and even makes the beauty of beauty. The man who doubts it, can never have watched the first gleam of tenderness dawning in the clear eyes of one who loves; – sunrise itself is a lesser marvel.

Henri Frédéric Amiel, *Amiel's Journal*

If the soul is transformed by participation in the divine nature so also must the body be and with the body the whole material universe. God in Christ becomes what we are in order that we might become his 'body'. This transformation of man by the divine life begins even now on earth, but it is only completed when man's body is also transformed by the resurrection.

Bede Griffiths OSB, in Peter Spink, *The Universal Christ*

A fundamental transformation is expected: something like a new birth of man himself, which can be understood only by one who actively takes part in it. It is therefore a transformation which does not come about merely through progress in right thinking for the sake of right action . . . or through the education of man who is fundamentally good . . . Nor is it a transformation through enlightenment . . . According to Jesus, a fundamental transformation is achieved through a man's surrender to God's will.

Hans Küng, *On Being a Christian*

One morning when I was in the wood something happened which was nothing less than a transformation of myself and the world, although I 'believed' nothing new. I was looking at a great, spreading, bursting oak. The first tinge from the greenish-yellow buds was just visible. It seemed to be no longer a tree away from me and apart from me. The enclosing barriers of consciousness were removed and the text came into my mind, *Thou in me and I in thee.* The distinction of self and not-self was an illusion. I could feel the rising sap; in me also sprang the fountain of life uprushing from its roots, and the joy of its outbreak at the extremity of each twig right up to the summit was my own: that which kept me apart was nothing.

Mark Rutherford, *More Pages from a Journal*

See also Fulfilment, Glory, Grace, Healing, Wholeness

III

TRUST

Trust – firm belief in the honesty, veracity, justice, strength, etc., of a person or thing – as our trust is in God

In my early twenties I came to trust in God, and took a simple step of faith. I accepted the contents of the Gospels as substantially true, and the person they revealed – Jesus Christ. In the next two years I put down some roots to fortify this trust. The next major step taken on trust was ordination. The last thirty-six years of ministry have been lived in a background of trust, but what crevasses, hurricanes and minefields. The quotation on trust I most clearly identify with comes from *Mister God, This is Anna*: 'And what a word that is! Define it how you like and I bet you'll miss the main point! It's more than confidence, more than security; it doesn't belong to ignorance or, for that matter, to knowledge either. It is simply the ability to move out of the, "I'm the centre of all things" and to let something or someone take over.' This fits in well with the underlying vision of faith in *The Eternal Vision*. I have consistently pointed out that God in the first instance is a 'presence' to be found in the depths of ourselves. Somehow we have to let go of the insistent claims of the ego for predominance and let this 'something or someone' take over. To this end, this book acts as a skeleton or frame-work of faith, designed to undergird trust. The practice of reflection can be used as an aid to let Anna's 'something or someone' take over, and to foster a spirit of trust.

Those of steadfast mind you keep in peace – in peace because they trust in you.
   Isaiah 26.3

See, I am sending you out like sheep into the midst of wolves; so be wise as serpents and innocent as doves.
   Matthew 10.16

God provides for him that trusteth.
   George Herbert, *Outlandish Proverbs*

Let this be my last word, that I trust in thy love.

Rabindranath Tagore, *Stray Birds*

The recurrent needs of every day are all known to God. A full reliance can be put upon all His promises.

W.E. Sangster, *He Is Able*

You can trust and rest in God simply because He has said, you may and you must.

Henry Ward Beecher, *Proverbs from Plymouth Pulpit*

When we trust as far as we can, we often find ourselves able to trust at least a little further.

Mark Gibbard, *Jesus, Liberation and Love*

The whole of God's being cannot be understood, but enough of it can be understood to trust it.

Henry Ward Beecher, *Proverbs from Plymouth Pulpit*

We have reached that stage in human development when we are able to ask the questions, but are not always able to understand the answers. God expects us to trust His Love.

W.E. Sangster, *He Is Able*

Trust men, and they will be true to you; treat them greatly, and they will show themselves great, though they make an exception in your favour to all their rules of trade.

Ralph Waldo Emerson, *Essays and Representative Men*

In such a world as this, with such ugly possibilities hanging over us all, there is but one anchor which will hold, and that is utter trust in God; let us keep that, and we may yet get to our graves without *misery* though not without *sorrow*.

Charles Kingsley, *Daily Thoughts*

We can trust Him wholly with His world. We can trust Him with ourselves. We are sure He cares far more to make the best of us, and to do the most through us, than we have ever cared ourselves. He is ever trying to make us understand that He yearns to be to us more than aught in the universe besides. That He really wants us, and needs us, is the wonder and strength of our life.

A.W. Robinson, *The Personal Life of the Clergy*

Trust, which is always on the way to being love, must be spontaneous or non-existent. It grows of itself within our hearts as we come to appreciate the character and wisdom of someone whose record we know; and it grows more surely when we come to know personally in actual companionship someone who, the more we know him, inspires in us more trust and confidence in his character and wisdom.

William Temple, *The Hope of a New World*

> In simple trust like theirs who heard
> Beside the Syrian sea
> The gracious calling of the Lord,
> Let us, like them, without a word,
> Rise up and follow thee.
>
> John Greenleaf Whittier, 'The Brewing of Soma'

If you have doubts about the existence of God or misgivings as to the kind of God He is, I do not think your need will be met by argument. It will be met only by an act of trust on your part. You must be willing to be found by the pursuing love of God which will not let you go; to face the challenge which is relentless; to move out fearlessly from your narrow self-centred life into a new, wide, spacious life with Christ at the centre – trusting not in yourself but in the all-sufficient love and power of God.

Leslie J. Tizard, *Facing Life and Death*

Trust thyself: every heart vibrates to that iron string. Accept the place the divine providence has found for you, the society of your contemporaries, the connection of events. Great men have always done so, and confided themselves childlike to the genius of their age, betraying their perception that the absolutely trustworthy was seated at their heart, working through their hands, predominating in all their being. And we are now men, and must accept in the highest mind the same transcendent dignity; and not minors and invalids in a protected corner, not cowards fleeing before a revolution, but guides, redeemers, and benefactors, obeying the Almighty effort, and advancing on Chaos and the Dark.

Ralph Waldo Emerson, *Self-Reliance*

If the universe was created by God and human life planned by God, then we should see principles of goodness and wisdom embedded in both. The writer of the book of Genesis pictures God looking at his creation and finding it good. He is emphatic that man is akin to God, made in the divine image. He is conscious of

[438]

man's ignorance, foolishness and wilfulness, but never does he think of man as being so depraved as not to be able to hear God speaking within himself. There may be a lot of original sin but there is also original goodness to which God and men can appeal. In spite of occasional natural catastrophes, for most of the time we think life is good. So we can trust life, both empirically from experience, and also because we trust the Creator.

George Appleton, *Journey for a Soul*

Over the greater part of the so-called civilized world is spreading a deep distrust, a deep irreverence of every man towards his neighbour, and a practical unbelief in every man whom you do see, atones for itself by a theoretical belief in an ideal human nature which you do not see. Such a temper of mind, unless it be checked by that which alone can check it, namely, the grace of God, must lead towards sheer anarchy. There is a deeper and uglier anarchy. There is a deeper and uglier anarchy than any mere political anarchy – which the abuse of the critical spirit leads to – the anarchy of society and of the family, the anarchy of the head and of the heart, which leaves poor human beings as orphans in the wilderness to cry in vain, 'What can I know? What can I love?'

Charles Kingsley, *Daily Thoughts*

See also Belief, Commitment, Faith, Hope, Joy

TRUTH

Truth – quality or state of being true or faithful

Having spent over thirty years in a university setting I have come across many different kinds of truth – both in the arts and sciences. Our definition above speaks of personal truth. F.W. Robertson, in his *Sermons*, wrote: 'Truth lies in character. Christ did not simply *speak* truth; He was truth: true through and through; for truth is a thing, not of words, but of Life and Being.' The psalmist thought of God desiring truth in the inward being and requested to be taught wisdom in his secret heart. According to the writer of John's Gospel, truth came through Jesus Christ, and his promise was: 'You will know the truth, and the truth will set you free.' A modern writer, Rufus Jones, concisely sums all this up in these marvellous words: 'To find Truth . . . we must break through the outward shell of words and phrases which house it, and by *experience and practice* discover the "inward beauty, life and loveliness of Truth".'

You desire truth in the inward being; therefore teach me wisdom in my secret heart.

    Psalm 51.6

The law indeed was given through Moses; grace and truth came through Jesus Christ. No one has ever seen God. It is God the only Son, who is close to the Father's heart, who has made him known.

    John 1.17–18

Truth . . . loves to be centrally located.

    Herman Melville, *Typee*

Truth is the highest thing that men may keep.

    Geoffrey Chaucer, *The Franklin's Tale*

In the usefulness of truth lies the hope of humanity.
  Norman Douglas, *An Almanac*

Rather than love, than money, than fame, give me truth.
  Henry David Thoreau, *Walden*

The friend of Truth obeys not the multitude *but the Truth*.
  Rufus M. Jones, *Spiritual Reformers in the 16th and 17th Centuries*

Say not, 'I have found the truth', but rather, 'I have found a truth.'
  Kahlil Gibran, *The Prophet*

But it is not enough to possess a truth; it is essential that the truth should possess us.
  Maurice Maeterlinck, *The Treasure of the Humble*

Truth is given, not to be contemplated, but to be done. Life is an action – not a thought.
  F.W. Robertson, *Sermons*

Love of truth asserts itself in the ability to find and appreciate what is good wherever it be.
  Johann Wolfgang von Goethe, in Herman J. Weigand, *Wisdom and Experience*

Truth does not lie beyond humanity, but is one of the products of the human mind and feeling.
  D.H. Lawrence, *The Rainbow*

I think the most important quality in a person connected with religion is absolute devotion to the truth.
  Albert Schweitzer, *Out of My Life and Thought*

> I thirst for truth,
> But shall not drink it till I reach the source.
>   Robert Browning, 'The Ring and the Book'

Ethical axioms are found and tested not very differently from the axioms of science. Truth is what stands the test of experience.
  Albert Einstein, *Out of My Later Years*

'I cannot hear what you say for listening to what you are.' Truth and preaching are both 'truth through personality'.

William Barclay, *The Gospel of Luke*

Truth lies in character. Christ did not simply *speak* truth: He *was* truth: true through and through; for truth is a thing, not of words, but of Life and Being.

F.W. Robertson, *Sermons*

The gospel story, whether historically true or not, could still be regarded as a parable; that is, as a working model, cast in fictitious form, of the way things really are.

Sydney Carter, *Dance in the Dark*

The arrogance of supposing that, what could not be clearly expressed could be cheerfully discarded, has impoverished religion and made lonely men of its mystics and seers.

W.E. Sangster, *The Pure in Heart*

Truth, in a word, is whatever cleanses you. Truth is whatever delights the higher you in you. Truth is whatever summons your spirit to do battle in her service. Truth is whatever makes you or me one with the mind of God.

Alistair MacLean, *The Happy Finder*

When man is, with his whole nature, loving and willing the truth, he is then a live truth. But this he has not originated in himself. He has seen it and striven for it, but not originated it. The one originating, living, visible truth, embracing all truths in all relations, is Jesus Christ. He is true; he is the live Truth.

George Macdonald, *Unspoken Sermons*

Truth is the perfect correlation of mind and reality; and this is actualized in the Lord's Person. If the Gospel is true and God is, as the Bible declares, a Living God, the ultimate truth is not a system of propositions grasped by a perfect intelligence, but is a Personal Being apprehended in the only way in which persons are ever fully apprehended, that is, by love.

William Temple, *Readings in St John's Gospel*

From my youth I have held the conviction that all religious truth must in the end be capable of being grasped as something that stands to reason. I, therefore, believe that Christianity, in the contest with philosophy and with other religions, should not ask for exceptional treatment, but should be in the thick of the battle of ideas, relying solely on the power of its own inherent truth.

Albert Schweitzer, *Christianity and the Religions of the World*

. . . the truth which Jesus brings to us shows us the real values of life. The fundamental question to which every man has consciously or unconsciously to give an answer is: 'To what am I to give my life?' 'Am I to give it to a career? Am I to give it to the amassing of material possessions? Am I to give it to pleasure? Am I to give it to the obedience and to the service of God?' The truth which Jesus brings enables us to get our scale of values right; it is in His truth that we see what things are really important and what things are not.

William Barclay, *The Gospel of John*

See also Character, Experience, Integrity, Mind, Wisdom

UNDERSTANDING

Understanding – comprehending, perceiving the meaning of, grasping mentally, perceiving the significance or explanation or cause or nature of, knowing how to deal with, having insight

One of our undergraduates was reputed to be a very brilliant geologist. I was curious to know what constituted his brilliance, so asked his tutor about him. He paused for a moment and recalled the experience of a recent tutorial. He had been teaching him a new area of study. The undergraduate was not only able to understand it completely first time round, but was two steps ahead of the tutor in the course of his instruction. It was as if he had an intuitive knowledge of the entire subject, the tutor merely confirming what he already knew. This was one area of his brightness, the ability to assimilate new material quickly. The other was his capacity to understand the significance of what he had learnt and to make imaginative leaps. These two areas of understanding, working together, constituted his brilliance. So much for understanding an academic discipline, but what about something even more complex – understanding oneself and other people.

⤻

. . . I will light in your heart the lamp of understanding, which shall not be put out.

2 Esdras 14.25

I want their hearts to be encouraged and united in love, so that they may have all the riches of assured understanding and have the knowledge of God's mystery, that is, Christ himself, in whom are hidden all the treasures of wisdom and knowledge.

Colossians 2.2–3

What one has not experienced, one will never understand in print.

Isadora Duncan, *My Life*

The highest of all is not to understand the highest but to act upon it.
    Søren Kierkegaard, in Harold Loukes, *The Quaker Contribution*

The real thing is to understand, and love that you may understand.
    J.B. Yeats, *Letters to His Son, W.B. Yeats and Others*

All the glory of greatness has no lustre for people who are in search of understanding.
    Blaise Pascal, *Pensées*

A clear understanding of God makes one want to follow the direction of things, the direction of oneself.
    André Gide, *The Journals of André Gide*

To understand a matter properly, a man must dominate it, instead of allowing it to dominate him.
    Ernest Hello, *Life, Science, and Art*

That which enables us to know and understand aright in the things of God, must be a living principle of holiness within us.
    John Smith the Platonist, *Select Discourses*

If one is master of one thing and understands one thing well, one has at the same time insight into and understanding of many things.
    Vincent van Gogh, *Dear Theo: An Autobiography of Vincent van Gogh*

You never really understand a person until you consider things from his point of view . . . until you climb into his skin and walk around in it.
    Harper Lee, *To Kill a Mockingbird*

Understanding a person does not mean condoning; it only means that one does not accuse him as if one were God or a judge placed above him.
    Erich Fromm, *Man for Himself*

We are apt to outgrow our teachers in wisdom, but whoever has helped us to a larger understanding is entitled to our gratitude for all time.
    Norman Douglas, *An Almanac*

Of course, *understanding* of our fellow-beings is important. But this understanding becomes fruitful only when it is sustained by sympathetic feeling in joy and sorrow.
    Albert Einstein, *Ideas and Opinions*

The language of the mystics cannot, of course, match that of science or reason. Yet, in a world craving for evidence from real life, it will remain one of the means through which our contemporaries can find God.

René Voillaume, *The Need for Contemplation*

I want, by understanding myself, to understand others. I want to be all that I am capable of becoming . . . This all sounds very strenuous and serious. But now that I have wrestled with it, it's no longer so. I feel happy – deep down. *All is well.*

Katherine Mansfield, *Journal of Katherine Mansfield*

Actually, of course, few people in this world see what is going on about them. Nobody really sees until he understands, until he can create a pattern into which the helter-skelter of passing events fits and makes a significance. And for this sort of vision a personal death is required . . . Nobody sees with his eyes alone; we see with our souls.

Henry Miller, *The Cosmological Eye*

For the rights of understanding to be valid one must venture out into life, out on the sea and lift up one's voice, even though God hears it not, and not stand on the shore and watch others fighting and struggling – only then does understanding acquire its *official sanction*, for to stand on one leg and prove God's existence is a very different thing from going on one's knees and thanking him.

Søren Kierkegaard, *The Journals of Kierkegaard*

The greatest gift that any human being can give to another is the gift of under-standing and of peace. To have someone to whom we can go at any time, and know that they will not laugh at our dreams, or misunderstand our confidences is a most wonderful thing. To have somewhere to go to where the tensions of life are relaxed in peace is a lovely thing. It is open to us all to make our own homes like that. This is something which does not cost money, and which does not need lavish and costly hospitality. It costs only the understanding heart.

William Barclay, *The Gospel of John*

The comprehension of life, of its living flow is beyond conceptual thought, which, in the very effort to comprehend, arrests, divides and falsifies it. Life can be understood only by living. To understand any living thing you must, so to say, creep within; and feel the beating of its heart. Every creature knows at least enough about the world to support its own existence there. The intellect seems to stand in its own light, reducing all it contemplates to the shadowiness of its self-chosen concepts, and by its own confession we can know nothing more than these, its peculiar creation. Life lies too deep to be penetrated by them. It is an island fortress. You cannot march into it on your two feet of logic and mathematics.

W. MacNeile Dixon, *The Human Situation*

See also Acceptance, Awareness, Compassion, Faith, Truth

114

VISION

Vision – act of faculty of seeing, things seen in dream or trance; thing seen in the imagination, imaginative insight; statesmanlike foresight

I have never seen a vision in a dream or in a trance. My visions have been more down-to-earth, involving the imagination and imaginative insight. Thomas Traherne once wrote: 'And thus you have a Gate, in the prospect even of this world, whereby you may see into God's Kingdom.' In one sense these words could have been written of *The Eternal Vision*. This book acts as a gate through which one can 'see' a prospect (of a vision) of this world, and of God's kingdom. In mulling over the contents of this compilation the imagination is stimulated, and through imaginative insight we 'see' things not previously 'seen'. We discover the main part of the vision in the lives and writings of poets, novelists, playwrights, philosophers, theologians, artists, musicians, historians, scientists, psychologists, statesmen, etc. up to the present day. We bring reflection into play and open up a 'prospect even of this world', whereby we 'may see into God's Kingdom'.

⸰⸎

. . . the oracle of one who hears the words of God, and knows the knowledge of the Most High, who sees the vision of the Almighty.

Numbers 24.15–16

. . . I was not disobedient to the heavenly vision.

Acts 26.19

And thus you have a Gate, in the prospect even of this world, whereby you may see into God's Kingdom.

Thomas Traherne, *Centuries*

The true poet is all the time a visionary and whether with friends or not, as much alone as a man on his death bed . . .

    J.B. Yeats, *Letters to His Son, W.B. Yeats and Others*

Golden hours of vision come to us in this present life, when we are at our best, and our faculties work together in harmony.

    Charles Fletcher Dole, *The Hope of Immortality*

The simple vision of pure love, which is marvellously penetrating, does not stop at the outer husk of creation; it penetrates to the divinity which is hidden within.

    Malaval, in Evelyn Underhill, *Mysticism*

An eternal trait of men is the need for vision and the readiness to follow it; and if men are not given the right vision, they will follow wandering fires.

    Sir Richard Livingstone, *On Education*

A mere dream, a vague hope may be more potent than certainty in a lesser matter. The faintest vision of God is more determinative of life than a gross earthly certainty.

    Mark Rutherford, *More Pages from a Journal*

The spirit of the world, the great calm presence of the Creator, comes not forth to the sorceries of opium or of wine. The sublime vision comes to the pure and simple souls in a clear and chaste body.

    Ralph Waldo Emerson, *The Poet, from Essays and Representative Men*

> I have seen the vision,
> the vision of mine own revealing itself,
> coming out from within me.
>
>   Rabindranath Tagore, *The Religion of Man*

This made it more likely that he had seen a vision; for instead of making common things look commonplace, as a false vision would have done, it had made common things disclose the wonderful that was in them.

    George Macdonald, *Cross Purposes and the Shadows*

Now, this state of 'spiritual unrest' can never bring you to a state of vision, of which the essential is peace. And struggling to see does not help one to see. The light comes, when it does come, rather suddenly and strangely I think. It is just like falling in love; a thing that never happens to those who are always trying to do it.

Evelyn Underhill, edited by Charles Williams, *The Letters of Evelyn Underhill*

The normal limits of the human vision are not the limits of the universe. There are other worlds than that which our senses reveal to us, other senses than those which we share with the lower animals, other forces than those of material nature. If we have faith in the soul, then the supernatural is also a part of the natural.

Sir Sarvepalli Radhakrishnan, *Indian Philosophy*

Religion is the vision of something which stands beyond, behind, and within, the passing flux of immediate things; something which is real, and yet waiting to be realized; something which is a remote possibility, and yet the greatest of present facts; something that gives meaning to all that passes, and yet eludes apprehension; something whose possession is the final good, and yet is beyond all reach; something which is the ultimate ideal, and the hopeless quest. The immediate reaction of human nature to the religious vision is worship.

Alfred North Whitehead, *Science and the Modern World*

The nature of the mind is such that the sinner who repents and makes an act of faith in a higher power is more likely to have a blissful visionary experience than is the self-satisfied pillar of society with his righteous indignations, his anxiety about possessions and pretensions, his ingrained habits of blaming, despising and condemning.

Aldous Huxley, *Heaven and Hell*

Most of us go through life with eyes half shut and with dull minds and heavy hearts, and even the few who have had those rare moments of vision and awakening fall back quickly into somnolence. It is good to know that the ancient thinkers required us to realize the possibilities of the soul in solitude and silence and transform the flashing and fading moments of vision into a steady light which could illumine the long years of life.

Sir Sarvepalli Radhakrishnan, *Indian Philosophy*

There are analagous moments when one suddenly sees the glory of people. On some unforgettable evening one's friend is suddenly seen as the unique, irreplaceable, and utterly delightful being that he is. It is as if he had been freshly created. One is no longer concerned with his relations to oneself, with his *pragmatic* value. He exists wholly in his own right; his significance is eternal, and the essential mystery of his being is as fathomless as that of God Himself.

J.W.N. Sullivan, *But for the Grace of God*

Religion has emerged into human experience mixed with the crudest fancies of barbaric imagination. Gradually, slowly, steadily the vision recurs in history under nobler form and with clearer expression. It is the one element in human experience which persistently shows an upward trend. It fades and then recurs. But when it renews its force, it recurs with an added richness and purity of content. The fact of the religious vision, and its history of persistent expansion, is our one ground for optimism. Apart from it, human life is a flash of occasional enjoyments lighting up a mass of pain and misery, a bagatelle of transient experience.

Alfred North Whitehead, *Science and the Modern World*

See also Aspiration, Imagination, Inspiration, Kingdom of God, Light

I I 5

VOCATION

Vocation – divine call to, or sense of fitness for a career or occupation; employment, trade, profession

Occasionally people ask me – why did I become ordained? My answer is that in my early twenties, I took a step of faith and made a commitment. Two years later, I went on a long train journey and read a book entitled *Margaret* by James Davidson Ross. 'Margaret' was a fifteen-year-old schoolgirl, the life and soul of the party, and a person of faith. She came home one day not feeling very well. At first she was thought to be suffering from flu, but eventually an aggressive cancer was diagnosed, and she had not long to live. I was very moved by the way Margaret faced up to her ordeal. She accepted it all in faith. Visitors who came to cheer her up found the roles reversed and she was cheering them up. As I read the book I became convinced the Holy Spirit was at work in her life, and that she was 'living in the power of the resurrection'. By the time the train reached Paddington I had already decided to live my life in like manner. After a few days I became aware of a little voice inside me asking, 'If this is so important to you, shouldn't you be actively engaged in spreading this, rather than just living it for yourself?' I was unable to avoid this searching challenge, and shortly afterwards offered myself for ordination.

Before I formed you in the womb I knew you, and before you were born I consecrated you; I appointed you a prophet to the nations.

Jeremiah 1.5

You did not choose me but I chose you. And I appointed you to go and bear fruit, fruit that would last.

John 15.16

The test of a vocation is the love of the drudgery it involves.

Logan Pearsall Smith, *Afterthoughts*

God has a task for every one of us, which is made to measure for us.
   William Barclay, *The Gospel of Matthew*

There is a specialty of work in the world for each man. But man must search for it, for it will not hunt the man.
   Henry Ward Beecher, *Proverbs from Plymouth Pulpit*

Vocation is not the exceptional prerogative of a few specially good or gifted people . . . All men and women are called to serve God.
   F.R. Barry, *Vocation and Ministry*

Do not despise your situation; in it you must act, suffer, and conquer. From every point on earth we are equally near to heaven and to the infinite.
   Henri Frédéric Amiel, *Amiel's Journal*

All things are produced plentifully and easily and of a better quality when one man does one thing which is natural to him and at the right time, and leaves other things.
   Plato, *The Republic of Plato*

If a man could take his choice of all the lives that are possible on earth, there is none so much to be desired for its joy-producing quality as a truly self-denying, consecrated Christian life.
   Henry Ward Beecher, *Proverbs from Plymouth Pulpit*

Whatever work you do for a living, it must be a form of service of some kind, for no one will pay you for your work if he does not want it done. What makes all the difference is what you are thinking of first and foremost, as you consider the spirit and temper in which you carry out your work. Is it your livelihood, or is it God's service? The work in itself is both. But which do you think of first? Nothing would bring nearer the promised day of God than that all Christian people should enter on their profession in the spirit of those who regard it as their chief sphere of serving God.
   William Temple, *Christian Faith and Life*

God's principal job is *to make man*: 'Let us make man in our image.' So, to work at 'making man' – developing, helping and protecting him – is to join God in his essential plan, working to realize his project.
   Michel Quoist, *With Open Heart*

Vocation today means also to understand the hard but stupendous mission of the church, now more than ever engaged in teaching man his true nature, his end, his fate, and in revealing to the faithful the immense riches of the charity of Christ.

Mother Teresa, in Brother Angelo Devananda, *Jesus, the Word to Be Spoken*

His vocation is to become fully human himself by helping others to achieve a deeper, fuller, humanity by all means available. This is what Christians are for, and at this time perhaps we are able to see our vocation as part of the universal striving towards a more complete understanding and living of human life.

Rosemary Haughton, *On Trying to Be Human*

There are so few people who become what they have it in them to be. It may be through lethargy and laziness, it may be through timidity and cowardice, it may be through lack of discipline and self-indulgence, it may be through the involvement in second-bests and byways. The world is full of people who have never realized the possibilities which are in them.

William Barclay, *The Gospel of John*

Each man has his own vocation. The talent is the call. There is one direction in which all space is open to him. He has faculties silently inviting him thither to endless exertion. He is like a ship in a river: he runs against obstructions on every side but one; on that side all obstruction is taken away, and he sweeps serenely over a deepening channel into an infinite sea.

Ralph Waldo Emerson, *Spiritual Laws*

What are you going to do with your lives? To choose your career for selfish reasons is a worse sin, than, let us say, committing adultery, for it is the withdrawal of the greater part of your time and energy from the service of God. Of course you are not going to be turned out of a club for doing it, but you will turn yourself out of the fellowship of Christ by doing it.

William Temple, *Christian Faith and Life*

There is a will for career as well as for character. There is a will for *where* – in what place, viz., in this town or another town – I am to become like God, as well as *that* I am to become like God. There is a will for where I am to be, and what I am to be, and what I am to do to-morrow. There is a will for what scheme I am to take up, and what work I am to do for Christ, and what business arrangements to make, and what money to give away. This is God's private will for me, for every step I take, for the path of life along which He points my way: God's will for my *career*.

Henry Drummond, *The Greatest Thing in the World*

[454]

But if you are in doubt how you may best lay out your life, and if you are quite clear in your acceptance of Jesus Christ as your Saviour and your God, then the mere circumstances of the time constitute a call to the Church's direct service in its ministry which you must face; for there is no sphere of life in which a man can more certainly lay out all talents in the service of God. It will call for every capacity; it will bring you into touch with human beings in every conceivable relation. There is no life so rich or so full of all those joys which come from serving people at the point of their greatest need.

William Temple, *Christian Faith and Life*

See also Commitment, Discipleship, Listening, Obedience, Service

WHOLENESS

Wholeness – in good health, in sound condition, intact; thing complete in itself, organic unity, complete system, total make up of parts

A few years ago I was leading a morning session, and one of the participants asked me what I was trying to do in my work. I said in reply I was trying to bring about some form of wholeness unique to each individual person. The emphasis of my work is on the 'God within' seen primarily as Father, Son, and the gifts and fruits of the Holy Spirit. Reflection is rather like 'practising the presence of God' to quote a phrase used by Brother Lawrence, a seventeenth-century Carmelite lay brother. In silent reflection we open ourselves to experiencing something of the presence of God. Some find it helpful to think of reflection as a listening form of prayer, in which great use is made of the mind and heart (feelings), as well as intuition and imagination. Reflection is mainly about the cure of souls, enabling people to come to wholeness through the releasing of the divine in them. As D.H. Lawrence wrote in *The Phoenix*: 'To be alive, to be man alive, to be whole man alive: that is the point.'

I will give thanks to you, O Lord my God, with my whole heart, and I will glorify your name for ever.

Psalm 86.12

Your faith has made you well.

Matthew 9.22

When we rejoice in our fulness, then we can part with our fruits with joy.

Rabindranath Tagore, *Stray Birds*

Wholeness demands relationship – with man or with God, and often with both together.

Monica Furlong, *Travelling In*

I wished for all things that I might enjoy life, and was granted life that I might enjoy all things.

Anon

'Holy', 'Healthy', 'Whole' – they all come from the same root and carry different overtones of the same meaning.

Aldous Huxley, *Island*

There is no such thing as an immortal work of art. There is one art – the greatest of all, the art of making a complete human being of oneself.

A.R. Orage, *On Love*

But this work may not be accomplished in one moment of conversion; it is not the work of one day, but of much time, much sweat, much labour, according to the grace of God that pitieth and the zeal of man that willeth and runneth.

William of St Thierry, *The Golden Epistles of Abbot William of St Thierry*

The cure for all the illness of life is stored in the inner depth of life itself, the access to which becomes possible when we are alone. This solitude is a world in itself, full of wonders and resources unthought of. It is so absurdly near, yet so un-approachably distant.

Rabindranath Tagore, *Letters to a Friend*

I keep on saying Our Lord was the first psychiatrist, with a penetrating awareness of human beings ten times better than psychological theory. And finally, what He did on the Cross was to take all the human ingredients and transform them into both a human wholeness and a divine wholeness. Only Christ could achieve that. What our Lord could do was to take the fulness of being divine and transform it in terms which we could understand.

Jack Dominion, in Gerald Priestland, *Priestland's Progress*

Above all, the individual should aim at fullness and wholeness of development. Every human being is confronted with the task of growing up, of building a personality out of the raw materials of his infant self. A rich and full personality, in moral and spiritual harmony with itself and with its destiny, one whose talents are not buried and whose wholeness transcends its conflicts, is the highest creation of which we have knowledge, and in its attainment the individual possibilities of the evolutionary process are brought to supreme fruition.

Sir Julian Huxley, *Religion Without Revelation*

Many of us do not grow an inner health and maturity as we grow in bodily health, mental ability and control over outside things. Few of us devote to the study of God and his will the same time and application that we give to worldly studies and professional training. The writers of the New Testament frequently lament the lack of maturity in the Christians for whom they are writing. That spiritual maturity is essential for inner health, right attitudes and right decisions and is creative for a dimension of life beyond the physical and the material

George Appleton, *Journey for a Soul*

Faith is not just conformity. It is *life*. It embraces all the realms of life, penetrating into the most mysterious and inaccessible depths not only of our unknown spiritual being but even of God's own hidden essence and love. Faith, then, is the only way of opening up the true depths of reality, even of our own reality. Until a man yields himself to God in the consent of total belief, he must inevitably remain a stranger to himself, an exile from himself, because he is excluded from the most meaningful depths of his own being: those which remain obscure and unknown because they are too simple and too deep to be attained by reason.

Thomas Merton, *New Seeds of Contemplation*

Yesterday I met a whole man. It is a rare experience but always an illuminating and ennobling one. It costs so much to be a full human being that there are very few who have the enlightenment or the courage to pay the price . . . One has to abandon altogether the search for security, and reach out to the risk of living with both arms. One has to embrace the world like a lover, and yet demand no easy return of love. One has to accept pain as a condition of existence. One has to court doubt and darkness as the cost of knowing. One needs a will stubborn in conflict, but apt always to the total acceptance of every consequence of living and dying.

Morris West, *The Shoes of the Fishermen*

When scientific specialization has almost reached the point where a different surgeon is required to remove each tonsil, a key question hangs in the air of our time. When the specialists have taken Man apart, who is to put him together again? Who will see him steadily and whole as a person who lives, loves, sins and dies? I would contend that it is the preacher and only the preacher who addresses Man in his wholeness, the totality of his being. In this world of specialists, the preacher is an unashamed generalizer. With breathtaking audacity, he states truths which are cosmic in sweep and yet apply to any individual, anywhere at any time.

Colin Morris, *The Word and the Words*

When a man ignores the 'spiritual life' it means that, however brilliant, well-intentioned, decent, a man may be, he is really only half-alive; his life is incomplete, unfulfilled; for he has not found the clue to the meaning of life. He is unaware of the need for 'wholeness' or 'integration' which is felt by so many people, even without any reference to what they would call 'religion' . . .

It is our conviction, as Christians, that man was made for 'wholeness' – that every part of his nature is so ordered that it cannot find fulfilment unless all is co-ordinated and integrated into a whole; this can only happen – even in a very general and imperfect way – as the whole personality is unified to serve *one* end: 'Who keeps one end in view, makes all things serve.' In other words: we have been created for God, and we are lost, empty and restless until we come to our senses, and come home to our Father.

Olive Wyon, *On the Way*

See also Fulfilment, Healing, Holiness, Presence, Salvation

WILL

Will – faculty by which a person decides to conceive himself as deciding upon and initiating action; power of determining one's choice of action independently of causation, doing the will of God, God's will

When I was a teenager at school, sometimes I would get up early and go to a communion service in the Lady Chapel. In those days we used the Book of Common Prayer, and one of the offertory sentences which registered with me was: 'Not every one that saith unto me, Lord, Lord, shall enter into the kingdom of heaven, but he that doeth the will of my Father which is in heaven.' When I took a deeper step of commitment in my early twenties these words challenged me even more forcibly, and brought about a determination to do 'the will of my Father' at all costs. In retrospect this developing attitude of 'all or nothing' influenced me in going forward to ordination. Some of William Barclay's words put over my feelings at the time concisely: 'The one great principle was that in all things a man must seek God's will and that, when he knows it, he must dedicate his whole life to the obeying it.' Well, the step to ordination was taken, but how difficult it has been to do God's will in the succeeding years. Help has been found in these words of Jesus: 'Anyone who resolves to do the will of God will know whether the teaching is from God, or whether I am speaking on my own.'

I delight to do your will, O my God; your law is within my heart.
  Psalm 40.8

. . . not my will, but yours be done.
  Luke 22.42

In His will is our peace.
  Dante Alighieri, *The Divine Comedy*

The unconquerable Will.

John Milton, 'Paradise Lost'

Today, more than ever, we need to pray for the light to know the will of God, for the love to accept the will of God, for the way to do the will of God.

Mother Teresa, in Brother Angelo Devananda, *Jesus, the Word to Be Spoken*

The one great principle was that in all things a man must seek God's will and that, when he knows it, he must dedicate his whole life to the obeying it.

William Barclay, *The Gospel of Matthew*

Great things are not done by impulse, but by a series of small things brought together. And great things are not something accidental, but must certainly be *willed*.

Vincent van Gogh, *Dear Theo: An Autobiography of Vincent van Gogh*

He [Christ] hangs all true acquaintance with divinity upon the doing of God's will: 'If any man will do His will, he shall know of the doctrine, whether it be of God' (John 7.17).

John Smith the Platonist, *Select Discourses*

He gave man the power to thwart his will, that, by means of that same power, he might come at last to do his will in a higher kind and way than would otherwise have been possible.

George Macdonald, *Unspoken Sermons*

This is certain, that there is no peace but in the will of God. God's will is our peace and there is no other peace. God's peace is perfect freedom and there is no other freedom.

Father Andrew SDC, *The Life and Letters of Fr Andrew SDC*

. . . the will of God cannot be simply read off from facts or events but must be discerned, must be found through insight, through the kindling of the heart and the illumining of the mind that occur on the spiritual adventure.

John S. Dunne, *The Reasons of the Heart*

The one complete cure for the sense of frustration and futility is to know and do the will of God. Everyone to whom this becomes a reality is at once supplied with a purpose in life and one which covers the whole of life.

William Temple, *The Hope of a New World*

God's will does not waver. Nor can it be manipulated. From all that we have said hitherto, from the concrete requirements of Jesus himself, it should already have become clear that God wills nothing for himself, nothing for his own advantage, for his greater glory. God wills nothing but man's advantage, man's true greatness and his ultimate dignity. This then is God's will: *man's well-being.*

Hans Küng, *On Being a Christian*

The night of prayer which preceded Jesus's selection of the twelve apostles was focussed, we must surely believe, upon the kingdom and the power and the glory of God rather than on any short-list of candidates. It was communion and submission and adoration, renewing and clarifying the human body and mind and soul of Christ, which led, quite incidentally, to that sure knowledge of the next step he had to take in doing his Father's will.

John V. Taylor, *The Go-Between God*

The spiritual life, the Christian life does not consist in developing a strong will capable of compelling us to do what we do not want. In a sense, of course, it is an achievement to do the right things when we really wish to do the wrong ones, but it remains a small achievement. A mature spiritual life implies that our conscious will is in accordance with the words of God and has remoulded, transformed our nature so deeply, with the help of God's grace, that the totality of our human person is only one will.

Anthony Bloom, *The Essence of Prayer*

There is a clue in the Gospel of John in the saying of Jesus, 'I have food to eat which you do not know' . . . 'My food is to do the will of him who sent me, and to accomplish his work.' There is a sense here of relating to other human beings out of a fullness rather than an emptiness . . . As one passes from the languishing to the love it becomes possible to relate to others out of a fullness. The will of God is no longer what happens to one but is something to be done, as is this saying of Jesus, something to be accomplished.

John S. Dunne, *The Reasons of the Heart*

God's will is not just goodwill towards men in the sense of a benevolent disposition, though it is certainly that. It is a determined, dynamic force, working to achieve his purpose, ceaselessly opposed to evil, constantly countering the mistaken or sinful moves of men, always ready to guide those who take his will as the purpose of their lives, immediately generous to supply more than abundant grace to carry it out. 'Thy will be done!' is a cry of glad acceptance of the rightness, goodness and love of God. 'Thy will be done' is an equally joyful conviction.

George Appleton, *Journey for a Soul*

'I will arise and go to my Father', and so develop in itself the highest *Divine* of which it is capable – the will for the good against the evil – the will to be one with the life whence it has come, and in which it still is – the will to close the round of its procession in its return, so working the perfection of reunion – to shape in its own life the ring of eternity – to live immediately, consciously, and active-willingly from its source, from its own very life – to restore to the beginning the end that comes of that beginning – to be the thing the maker thought of when he willed, ere he began to work its being.

George Macdonald, *Unspoken Sermons*

See also Commitment, Contemplation, Love, Meditation, Obedience

118

WISDOM

Wisdom – being wise, (possession of) experience and knowledge together with the power of applying them critically or practically, sagacity, prudence, common sense

'For wisdom will come into your heart'. So wrote the author of the book of Proverbs on the source of wisdom. If we want to see this fully worked out in a life we can go to the New Testament. In the Gospels some of those who heard our Lord's teaching were astonished, saying, 'Where did this man get all this? What is the wisdom given to him?' A modern writer, Christopher Bryant, wrote: 'It is part of the Christian spiritual tradition that God dwells in the centre of every man, an unseen, largely unknown Strength and Wisdom, moving him to be human, to grow and to expand his humanity to the utmost of its capacity.' We have found that being open and receptive in reflection is one of the best ways of growing in wisdom. In reflection we use the mind as far as it will go. We also use the 'heart' – our feelings and emotions, our instinct and intuition. Great use is also made of the imagination, and our experience of life. A full use can also be made of these quotations.

My mouth shall speak wisdom; the meditation of my heart shall be understanding.
Psalm 49.3

Who is wise and understanding among you? Show by your good life that your works are done with gentleness born of wisdom.
James 3.13

Wisdom cometh by suffering.
Aeschylus, *Agamemnon*

God waits for man to regain his childhood in wisdom.
Rabindranath Tagore, *Stray Birds*

The wisdom of the wise is an uncommon degree of common sense.

W.R. Inge, in Sir James Marchant, *Wit and Wisdom of Dean Inge*

Wisdom lies more in – affection and sincerity – than people are apt to imagine.

George Eliot, *Middlemarch*

Only when we offer our minds to God do we receive the illumination of his wisdom.

Bede Griffiths OSB, in Peter Spink, *The Universal Christ*

There is a deep wisdom inaccessible to the wise and prudent but disclosed to babes.

Christopher Bryant SSJE, *The Heart in Pilgrimage*

Some hold . . . that there is a wisdom of the Head, and that there is a wisdom of the Heart.

Charles Dickens, *Hard Times*

Common sense mellowed and experienced is wisdom; and wisdom in its ripeness is beauty.

A.R. Orage, *On Love*

The true sage is not he who sees, but he who, seeing the furthest, has the deepest love for mankind.

Maurice Maeterlinck, *Wisdom and Destiny*

> Wisdom is oftimes nearer when we stoop
> Than when we soar.
>
> William Wordsworth, 'The Excursion'

Accumulated knowledge does not make a wise man. Knowledgeable people are found everywhere, but we are cruelly short of wise people.

Michel Quoist, *With Open Heart*

Wisdom is the knowledge of truth in its inmost reality, expression of truth, arrived at through the rectitudes of our own soul. Wisdom knows God in ourselves and ourselves in God.

Thomas Merton, *Thoughts in Solitude*

And we shall be truly wise if we be made content; content, too, not only with what we can understand, but, content with what we do not understand – the habit of mind which theologians call – and rightly – faith in God.

Charles Kingsley, *Health and Education*

By 'a new nativity' – initiated by obedient response to the inward Light . . . of God the indwelling Spirit – he may put on the new man, created after the likeness of God, and become the recipient of heavenly Wisdom springing up within him from the Life of the Spirit.

Rufus M. Jones, *Spiritual Reformers in the 16th and 17th Centuries*

The Wisdom of God is working through all created life, and far and wide is the sustainer and the inspirer of the thought and the endeavour of men. The Church will therefore reverence every honest activity of the minds of men; it will perceive that therein the Spirit of God is moving, and it will tremble lest by denying this, in word or in action, it blaspheme the Spirit of God.

Michael Ramsey, *The Gospel and the Catholic Church*

Aristotle defined *sophia*, wisdom, as knowledge of the most precious things. Cicero defined it as knowledge of things both human and divine. *Sophia* was a thing of the searching intellect, of the questing mind, of the reaches of the thoughts of men. *Sophia* is the answer to the eternal problems of life and death, and God and man, and time and eternity.

William Barclay, *The Letters to the Galatians and Ephesians*

> Here is the test of wisdom,
> Wisdom is not finally tested in schools,
> Wisdom cannot be pass'd from one having it to another not having it,
> Wisdom is of the soul, is not susceptible of proof, is its own proof.
>> Walt Whitman, 'Song of the Open Road'

> What is the price of Experience? do men buy it for a song?
> Or wisdom for a dance in the street? No, it is bought, with the price
> Of all that a man hath, his house, his wife, his children.
> Wisdom is sold in the desolate market place where none come to buy,
> And in the wither'd field where the farmer ploughs for bread in vain.
>> William Blake, 'Vale or the Four Zoas'

The whole secret of remaining young in spite of years, and even of gray hairs, is to cherish enthusiasm in oneself, by poetry, by contemplation, by charity, – that is, in fewer words, by the maintenance of harmony in the soul. When everything is in its right place within us, we ourselves are in equilibrium with the whole work of God. Deep and grave enthusiasm for the eternal beauty and the eternal order, reason touched with emotion and a serene tenderness of heart – these surely are the foundations of wisdom.

Henri Frédéric Amiel, *Amiel's Journal*

Wisdom is not cheaply won. It is achieved through hard sacrifice and discipline, through the endurance of conflict and pain. It is the perfection of human living, the ceaseless straining of the human soul to pierce through the crushing body, the distracting intellect, the selfish will, and to apprehend the unsheathed spirit. It is intent living, the most fruitful act of man by which he tries to reach reality behind the restless stream of nature and his own feelings and desires. The destiny of the human soul is to realize its oneness with the supreme.

Sir Sarvepalli Radhakrishnan, *Eastern Religions and Western Thought*

See also Intellect, Knowledge, Mind, Thinking, Truth

119

WONDER

Wonder – emotion excited by what surpasses expectation or experience or seems inexplicable, surprise mingled with admiration or curiosity or bewilderment

One morning I went into University College, London (where I used to work) and was hailed excitedly by one of our postgraduates. 'Hey, Bill, have you got a moment? Come and look at this.' I was ushered into his laboratory and invited to look down a microscope. What I saw was what I took to be a shell of the most perfect proportions – something of real beauty. I responded enthusiastically, 'Yes,' he said, 'it is wonderful, isn't it. But do you know what it is?' 'Well, it looks to be a rather lovely shell.' 'Yes, you are partly right, but last week we took it to be merely a grain of sand which we've dredged up from the North Sea. Under the microscope, we've discovered it's a shell. That's very significant, isn't it. Maybe there is something to be said for your Creator God after all.' I left his laboratory feeling rather excited. Even in that microscopic shell there was a sense of order and design. Nature still remains a great source of wonder to me.

❧

For it was you who formed my inward parts; you knit me together in my mother's womb. I praise you, for I am fearfully and wonderfully made. Wonderful are your works; that I know very well.

Psalm 139.13–14

And all spoke well of him, and were amazed at the gracious words that came from his mouth.

Luke 4.22

To be surprised, to wonder, is to begin to understand.

José Ortega Y Gasset, *The Revolt of the Masses*

The idea of God that man has in his being is the wonder of all wonders.
  Rabindranath Tagore, *Sadhana*

Worship is transcendent wonder; wonder for which there is no limit or measure.
  Thomas Carlyle, *Heroes and Hero-Worship*

Philosophy begins in wonder. And, at the end, when philosophic thought has done its best, the wonder remains.
  Alfred North Whitehead, *Modes of Thought*

Truth sees God: wisdom gazes on God. And these produce a third, a holy, wondering delight in God, which is love.
  Lady Julian of Norwich, *Revelations of Divine Love*

Wonder and love are caught, not taught; and to catch them we must be in an atmosphere where we are sure to find the germs.
  Evelyn Underhill, in John Stobbart, *The Wisdom of Evelyn Underhill*

The wonder and curiosity which welcomes what is new and regards it not as threatening but enriching life – that wonder and curiosity is God.
  H.A. Williams CR, *The True Wilderness*

There is nothing that is so wonderfully created as the human soul. There is something of God in it. We are infinite in the future, though we are finite in the past.
  Henry Ward Beecher, *Proverbs from Plymouth Pulpit*

Wonder is the highest thing in man, and if the ultimate phenomenon sets him wondering he should be content: he can be aware of nothing higher and he should seek nothing beyond: here is the limit.
  Johann Wolfgang von Goethe, in Emil Ludwig, *The Practical Wisdom of Goethe*

Wonder . . . is essentially an 'opening' attitude – an awareness that there is more to life than one has yet fathomed, an experience of new vistas in life to be explored as well as new profundities to be plumbed.
  Rollo May, *Man's Search for Himself*

The first and fundamental wonder is existence itself. That I should be alive, conscious, a person, a part of the whole, that I should have emerged out of nothingness, that the Void should have given birth, not merely to things, but to me.
  W. MacNeile Dixon, *The Human Situation*

It is wonder that prompts the mind to examine its environment – and at first the elementary wonder how to make the best of it; but the enquiry ends in the wonder of awe, before that which, the more it is understood, by so much the more transcends our understanding.

William Temple, *Nature, Man and God*

Then there is the appeal of Jesus to the imagination, to the sense of wonder. How often we read in the gospel story that the people wondered at what Jesus did and said! They marvelled – the wondering imagination.

Jesus evokes that sense of wonder, and isn't it perhaps that sense of wonder which is a large part of what we call worship, and which really makes the difference between what is only an ethical allegiance, and what is religion?

Michael Ramsey, in Margaret Duggan, *Through the Year with Michael Ramsey*

The most beautiful experience we can have is the mysterious. It is the fundamental emotion which stands at the cradle of true art and science. Whoever does not know it and can no longer wonder, no longer marvel, is as good as dead, and his eyes are dimmed. It was the experience of mystery – even if mixed with fear – that engendered religion. A knowledge of the existence of something we cannot penetrate, our perceptions of the profoundest reason and the most radiant beauty, which only in their most primitive forms are accessible to our minds – it is this knowledge and this emotion that constitutes true religiosity.

Albert Einstein, *Ideas and Opinions*

No man or woman begins to live a full life until they realize they live in the presence of something greater, outside and beyond themselves. Self-consciousness truly means that you are standing over against that other than yourself and you cannot be living in truth. Wonder is at the base of true living, and wonder leads to worship and after that the great other than self; it is yet kin to you, you are one with it. Then you begin to live more completely and realize the kinship between you and nature, that out of nature you came and are part and parcel with it, this brings nearer faith which is self-conscious life (opposed to birds, trees, etc.), reaching out to perfection.

G.A. Studdert Kennedy, *The New Man in Christ*

And when the wonder has gone out of a man he is dead . . . When all comes to all, the most precious element in life is wonder. Love is a great emotion, and power is power. But both love and power are based on wonder. Love without wonder is a sensational affair, and power without wonder is mere force and compulsion.

The one universal element in consciousness which is fundamental to life is the element of wonder . . .

Plant consciousness, insect consciousness, fish consciousness, all are related by one permanent element, which we may call the religious element inherent in all life, even in a flea: the sense of wonder. That is our sixth sense. And it is the *natural* religious sense.

D.H. Lawrence, *Phoenix II*

See also Adoration, Freedom, Imagination, Joy, Worship

WORK

*W*ork – *expenditure of energy, striving, application of effort to some purpose; task to be undertaken; employment, especially of earning money by labour; laborious occupation*

'Work hard, play hard, pray hard, and then you will be happy.' This was the advice I was given on arriving at school. For the next seven years I put these words into practice, and found I was very happy. My first work experience was in the army, while doing National Service. As a private soldier the advice I received was somewhat different from the advice received at school. On the first day we were taught by the corporals never to volunteer for anything, and the next day we received instructions from them on the gentle art of skiving. While at university I had some valuable work experience in a bacon factory during a long vacation. The pigs were slaughtered at one end of a production line, and I was at the far end of the production line, stacking sides of bacon into a huge refrigerator, and doing something (I've forgotten precisely what) with the heads of pigs. I was incredibly bored as the job made no demands on my mind whatsoever. After a few weeks I came to the conclusion the secret of work was interest in the job – and enjoyment while doing it

The Lord God took the man and put him in the garden of Eden to till it and keep it.
  Genesis 2.15

We must work the works of him who sent me.
  John 9.4

Work is not the curse, but drudgery is.
  Henry Ward Beecher, *Proverbs from Plymouth Pulpit*

The real essence of work is concentrated energy.
  Walter Bagehot, *Biographical Studies*

A man can be so busy making a living that he forgets to make a life.
  William Barclay, *The Gospel of Matthew*

It is a good sign where a man is proud of his work or his calling.
  Henry Ward Beecher, *Proverbs from Plymouth Pulpit*

Certainly work is not always required of a man. There is such a thing as a sacred idleness, the cultivation of which is now fearfully neglected.
  George Macdonald, *Wilfred Cumbermede*

Blessed be the man whose work drives him. Something must drive men; and if it is wholesome industry, they have no time for a thousand torments and temptations.
  Henry Ward Beecher, *Proverbs from Plymouth Pulpit*

The most important motive for work in the school and in life is the pleasure of work, pleasure in its results and the knowledge of the value of the result to the community.
  Albert Einstein, *Out of My Later Years*

I don't like work – no man does – but I like what is in the work, – the chance to find yourself. Your own reality – for yourself, not for others – what no other man can ever know.
  Joseph Conrad, *Heart of Darkness, in Youth, a Narrative and Two Other Stories*

There is no right more universal and more sacred, because lying so near to the root of existence, than the right of men to their own labour.
  Henry Ward Beecher, *Proverbs from Plymouth Pulpit*

Every citizen should have a voice in the conduct of the business or industry which is carried on by means of his labour, and the satisfaction of knowing that his labour is directed to the well-being of the community.
  William Temple, *Christianity and the Social Order*

Love work: for if thou dost not want it for food, thou mayst for physic. It is wholesome for thy body, and good for thy mind. It prevents the fruits of idleness, which many times come of nothing to do, and leads too many to do what is worse than nothing.

William Penn, *Fruits of Solitude*

The world demands work. Work is needed for the mere maintenance of life; more work is needed for the maintenance of a particular level of civilization; still more work is needed if we look to the future and aim at giving later generations better chances of fuller life.

Sir Julian Huxley, *Religion Without Revelation*

The story is relevant here of the somewhat pompous parson leaning over the gate with the farmer, viewing a fine crop of barley. 'It is wonderful,' said the parson, 'what can be done when you and God get together.' 'Aye,' said the farmer, 'but you should have seen this field last year when God had it all to Himself.'

George Macleod, *Only One Way Left*

Capitalism is an evil thing, because it is based on what is called enlightened self-interest, and that is a baptismal name for selfishness. Poverty is a crime. The Church has been very specific on other matters. It hasn't hesitated to speak arbitrarily on most intimate affairs like sex. I don't see why it should restrict its particularity to those and not extend them to the world of the unemployed.

Lord Soper, in Gerald Priestland, *Priestland's Progress*

The problem set before us is to bring our daily task into the temple of contemplation and ply it there, to act as in the presence of God, to interfuse one's little part with religion. So only can we inform the detail of life, all that is passing, temporary, and insignificant, with beauty and nobility. So may we dignify and consecrate our meanest of occupations. So may we feel that we are paying our tribute to the universal work and the eternal will. So are we reconciled with life and delivered from the fear of death. So we are in order and in peace.

Henri Frédéric Amiel, *Amiel's Journal*

Commitment does not stop with contemplation. It seeks issue at work. For the God discovered thus is a God at work, reconciling the world to Himself. And those who worship in spirit and truth find themselves called to a ministry of reconciliation. A world unfinished and broken is to be made whole. Ultimately, it is God, not we, who must heal it, but in our small measure, we may be co-labourers with God. That is our calling. Worship sends us out to work. But work in turn, through frustration or consummation, may continually tend again toward worship, wherein illumination and renewal are to be found. Such, in part, is man's way toward God.

Robert Lowry Calhoun, *God and the Common Life*

No work done by any man, however great, will really prosper unless it has a distinct religious backing. But what is Religion? I for one would answer: 'Not the Religion you will get after reading all the scriptures of the world. Religion is not really grasped by the brain, but a heart grasp.'

Religion is a thing not alien to us. It has to be evolved out of us. It is always within us: with some, consciously so; with others, quite unconsciously. But it is always there. And whether we wake up this religious instinct in us through outside assistance or by inward growth, no matter how it is done, it has got to be done, if we want to do anything in the right manner, or to achieve anything that is going to persist.

Mohandas K. Gandhi, in C.F. Andrews, *Mahatma Gandhi's Ideas*

See also Action, Discipleship, Kingdom of God, Progress, Service

I 2 I

WORLDLINESS

Worldliness – temporal, earthly, exclusively or preponderantly concerned with or devoted to the affairs of this life, especially the pursuit of wealth or pleasure, prudence in advancing one's own interests

I wonder if I am correct in discerning three forms of worldliness in our day and age. First, there is material wealth. Money and what money can buy seem to be crucially important for most people. Second, there is success and status. Our sense of identity often comes by having made it to the top. Third, there are relationships, with sex having a high profile. I would counter these forms of worldliness by regarding women and men as made primarily in the image and likeness of God.

Three consequences seem to follow from this. First, there is wealth. This is not to be found primarily in cash, but in the human personality, and in realizing one's gifts and talents. Second, there is success and status. Our sense of identity would come primarily in realizing our status as a child of God, and not just in having made it to the top. Third, there are relationships. First get our inner relatedness with God established, and then our outer relationships will naturally follow, with sex finding its rightful, valuable place. There will then be no need to worship it to excess, and exploit people. We shall be in the world, but not of it.

&

He will judge the world with righteousness, and the peoples with his truth.
Psalm 96.13

For what will it profit them if they gain the whole world and forfeit their life?
Matthew 16.26

The kingdom of this world is 'human society as it organizes itself apart from God'.
Leslie J. Tizard, *Facing Life and Death*

Those who set out to serve both God and Mammon soon discover that there is no God.

    Logan Pearsall Smith, *Afterthoughts*

> Where wealth and freedom reign contentment fails,
> And honour sinks where commerce long prevails.
>   Oliver Goldsmith, 'The Traveller'

The character of worldly men is shaped by the influence of the love of property, of power, of influence, of praise, and the love of animal indulgence – not by the right, the true, the noble.

    Henry Ward Beecher, *Proverbs from Plymouth Pulpit*

This secular world – formerly regarded as 'this' world, the wicked world *par excellence*, a neopagan world – today is not only taken into account in Christendom, but largely consciously approved and assisted in its development.

    Hans Küng, *On Being a Christian*

The world expresses itself in magnificence, the spirit in magnanimity. The one means making big, inflating. The other means greatness (or openness) of mind, heart, soul. It is the difference between false and true generosity.

    Hubert van Zeller, *Considerations*

Most people are kept from a true sense and taste of religion, by a regular kind of sensuality and indulgence, than by gross drunkenness. More men live regardless of the great duties of piety, through too great a concern for worldly goods, than through direct injustice.

    William Law, *A Serious Call to a Devout and Holy Life*

The things which most often happen in life and are esteemed as the greatest good of all, as may be gathered from their works, can be reduced to these three headings: to wit, Riches, Fame, and Pleasure. With these three the mind is so engrossed that it cannot scarcely think of any other good.

    Benedict Spinoza, *Spinoza's Ethics and De Intellectus Emendatione*

> The world is too much with us; late and soon,
> Getting and spending, we lay waste our powers:
> Little we see in Nature that is ours;
> We have given our hearts away, a sordid boon!
>   William Wordsworth, 'The World Is too much with Us'

The so-called 'real world'; the world which psychiatrists and social scientists and tycoons in advertising firms want us to adjust to and be at home in. That world saps our integrity and eats up our whole personality, giving us not freedom to do what we really want to do but a whole set of false wants and artificial and quite unnecessary 'needs'.

   Geoffrey Preston OP, *Hallowing the Time*

The world [is] the sum of created being, which belongs to the sphere of human life as an ordered whole, considered apart from God, and in its moral aspect represented by humanity . . . It is easy to see how the thought of an ordered whole relative to man and considered *apart* from God passes into that of the ordered whole *separated* from God.

   B.F. Westcott, *The Gospel According to St John*

The 'worldly' man is not necessarily the depraved man. He is the man who is misled into treating the world's goods as absorbing ends in themselves, and so misses the awareness of meaning and purpose beyond them.

   The 'unworldly' man is not necessarily the devout man, or the man with conscious concern for God or for heaven. He is the man who is not absorbed in the world's goods or dominated by them, for there is in him an imagination or a simplicity or a humility or a care for persons which hints at something beyond. His unworldliness is properly seen not in any neglect of the world, but in the nature of his care for it.

   Michael Ramsey, in Margaret Duggan, *Through the Year with Michael Ramsey*

There is so much frustration in the world because we have relied on gods rather than God. We have genuflected before the god of science only to find that it has given us the atomic bomb, producing fears and anxieties that science can never mitigate. We have worshipped the god of pleasure only to discover that thrills play out and sensations are short-lived. We have bowed before the god of money only to learn that there are such things as love and friendship that money cannot buy and that in a world of possible depressions, stock market crashes, and bad business investments, money is a rather uncertain deity. These transitory gods are not able to save or bring happiness to the human heart. Only God is able. It is faith in Him that we must rediscover.

   Martin Luther King, in Coretta Scott King, *The Words of Martin Luther King*

The world . . . is a co-operative society with limited liability, existing for purely secular and chiefly selfish ends, some of which can only be realized by combined action, preying on the weakness of others, and exploiting their moral as well as physical and economic weakness. If its victims are trampled on, or if they are tempted to take part in iniquities the guilt of which is spread and distributed over a large number of persons, the world disclaims all responsibility. Like the Chief Priests to the remorseful Judas, it says, 'What is that to us? See thou to that.' All who take part in practical work, especially in political or semi-political work, but also in business or commerce, know how extremely difficult it is not to be caught in the toils of this ubiquitous and intricate machinery; they know how difficult it is to win any sort of success without soiling our hands and straining our consciences.

W.R. Inge, *Personal Religion and the Life of Devotion*

See also Anxiety, Power, Pride, Selfishness, Temptation

122

WORSHIP

Worship – reverent homage or service paid to God; acts, rites or ceremonies of honour and respect, adoration and devotion

Over the years I have greatly enjoyed church music, and listening to anthems, feel to be close to the spirit of worship. For the most part I find formal worship difficult, and was greatly helped in my understanding by a sentence from J. Neville Ward's book, *Five for Sorrow, Ten for Joy*. In this book he wrote: 'Institutional religion will always exasperate us because it is carried on in the words and deeds of inadequate and sinful human beings.' Anthony Bloom has also enabled me to understand another difficulty with formal worship. In *Living Prayer*, he wrote: 'One of the reasons why communal worship or private prayer seems to be so dead or so conventional, is that the act of worship, which takes place in the heart, communicating with God, is too often missing. Every expression, either verbal or in action, may help, but they are only expressions of what is essential, namely, a deep silence of communion . . . If we want to worship God, we must first of all learn to feel happy, being silent together with him.' In the silence of reflection we try to worship God in spirit and truth.

O come, let us worship and bow down, let us kneel before the Lord our Maker! For he is our God.

Psalm 95.6–7

But the hour is coming, and is now here, when the true worshippers will worship the Father in spirit and truth, for the Father seeks such as these to worship him. God is spirit, and those who worship him must worship in spirit and truth.

John 4.23–24

Wonder . . . is the basis of Worship.

Thomas Carlyle, *Sartor Resartus*

We *Worship* God best; when we Resemble Him most.
> Benjamin Whichcote, *Moral and Religious Aphorisms*

Without worship you shrink; it's as brutal as that . . .
> Peter Shaffer, *Equus*

But the purpose of all worship is the same: to offer praise to God for his grace and glory.
> Alan Richardson, in Alan Richardson and John Bowden, *A New Dictionary of Christian Theology*

So long as the letter is the servant of the spirit and not its master, the spirit gives life to the letter. Hence public worship. Hence vocal prayer.
> Hubert van Zeller, *Considerations*

. . . worship is a communing, the opening of human life to God, the response to grace, the growing up into union with God, who has made us for himself.
> John Macquarrie, *Paths in Spirituality*

This alone is true worship – the giving to God of body, soul and spirit ('ourselves, our souls and bodies') with all that they need for their full development, so that He may take and use them for His purpose.
> William Temple, *Citizen and Churchman*

When our Lord told the Samaritan woman that worship of the Father should be in spirit and in truth he was not ruling out considerations of place, ceremonial, formulas. He was saying that these factors were useless unless animated by spirit and truth.
> Hubert van Zeller, *Considerations*

. . . a spiritual discipline must be freely accepted and embraced if it is to be fully effective . . . worship must be a free response of love rather than a homage exacted.
> John Macquarrie, *Paths in Spirituality*

What else can a lame old man as I am do but chant the praise of God? If, indeed, I were a nightingale I should sing as a nightingale, if a swan, as a swan; but as I am a rational creature I must praise God. This is my task, and I do it: and I will not abandon this duty, so long as it is given me; and I invite you all to join in this same song.
> Epictetus, in Witney J. Oates, *The Stoic and Epicurean Philosophers*

For worship is the submission of all our nature to God. It is the quickening of the conscience by His holiness; the nourishment of mind with His truth; the purifying of imagination by His beauty; the opening of the heart to His love; the surrender of will to His purpose – and all of this gathered up in adoration, the most selfless emotion of which our nature is capable.

William Temple, *Readings in St John's Gospel*

The true worship, the really spiritual worship, is the offering of one's body, and all that one does every day with it, to God. Real worship is not the offering of elaborate prayers to God; it is not the offering to God of a liturgy, however noble, and a ritual, however magnificent. *Real worship is the offering of everyday life to God.* Real worship is not something which is transacted in a church; real worship is something which sees the whole world as the temple of the living God, and every common deed an act of worship.

William Barclay, *The Letter to the Romans*

The word 'worship' comes from an old English word meaning worthship – giving to God his true worth as Creator, Redeemer, and indwelling Spirit. Worship is man's response to these divine activities. As we realize the greatness, the goodness and the 'allness' of God, we forget ourselves and our hearts break forth in praise. Yet worship is not just an expression in words or music of feeling, but the outgoing of our hearts and the acceptance of God as the governing reality of our lives. He becomes our chiefest good and our lives are henceforth offered to him in loving obedience.

George Appleton, *Journey for a Soul*

Abide in me, and I in you. The whole phrase has an imperative tone: let there be mutual indwelling. *Abide in me*, of which the consequence will be that I shall abide in you . . .

All forms of Christian worship, all forms of Christian discipline, have this as their object. Whatever leads to this is good; whatever hinders this is bad; whatever does not bear on this is futile. This is the life of the Christian: *Abide in me and I in you.* All truth and depth of devotion, all effectiveness in service spring from this. It is not a theme for words but for the deeper apprehensions of silence.

William Temple, *Readings in St John's Gospel*

The worship of God is itself the inner core of Christian spirituality: the heart, the mind, and the will, directed towards the glory of God as man's goal. Every time that a Christian lifts up his soul to God in desire towards him he is, however faintly, realizing that fellowship with the Creator for which he was created, and he is, in a tiny and yet significant way, anticipating the goal of heaven. Thus regarded, spirituality is no escape from the world. It is lived out in all the complexities of our social life, in family, city, country, industry, culture, joy, sorrow, for it is the spirituality of a man, and a man is involved in all these things. It is inseparable from service, love, duty, the moulding of the common-life. Yet in deep-down essence it is the spirit of worship.

Michael Ramsey, in Margaret Duggan, *Through the Year with Michael Ramsey*

. . . worship can be a continuously creative thing. It means coming from the world, from the squalor, the hunger, the misery, the heartbreak, for the act of acknowledging again the love and kingship of God. It means ascending the hill of the Lord to receive again His pardon, to receive again the bread and wine of life, to offer obedience again and find the strength for it, to bring all that has been learned and suffered at the crossroads of life to God for His dealing. But it does not mean a permanent lodging in the cathedrals and churches where worship in community is offered. It means going back from the hour of worship to the arena of the world's life and the place of man's need only to discover that God to whom the worship was offered is the contemporary friend and partner to farmer and healer, teacher and preacher and all others who for the love of God and man seek to meet man's need.

Leonard Hurst, *Hungry Men*

See also Adoration, Church, Contemplation, Meditation, Thanksgiving

NOTES

Acceptance

1. NRSV.
2. NRSV.
3. Anon.
4. Martin Luther King, in Coretta Scott King, *The Words of Martin Luther King*, William Collins Sons and Co. 1986, p. 25.
5. John S. Dunne, *The Reasons of the Heart*, SCM Press 1978, p. 26.
6. Michel Quoist, *With Open Heart*, translated by Colette Copeland, Gill and Macmillan 1983, p. 183.
7. Oscar Wilde, *De Profundis, The Works of Oscar Wilde*, edited by G.F. Maine, William Collins Sons and Co. 1948, p. 866.
8. Arthur T. Jersild, *The Psychology of Adolescence*, The Macmillan Co. 1963, p. 34.
9. Peter G. van Breemen SJ, *As Bread that Is Broken*, Dimension Books 1978, p. 9.
10. *Theologia Germanica*, translated by Susanna Winkworth, Stuart and Watkins 1966, p. 53.
11. van Breemen, *As Bread that Is Broken*, p. 9.
12. Richard Wilhelm and C.G. Jung, *The Secret of the Golden Flower*, Routledge and Kegan Paul 1972, p. 126.
13. van Breemen, *As Bread that Is Broken*, p. 9.
14. Paul Tillich, *The Shaking of the Foundations*, SCM Press 1949, p. 162.
15. van Breemen, *As Bread that Is Broken*, p. 9.

Action

1. NRSV.
2. NRSV.
3. Francis Thompson, '*Shelley*', *The Works of Francis Thompson*, Burns and Oates 1913, vol. III, p. 2.
4. Marcus Aurelius, *The Meditations of Marcus Aurelius*, translated by Jeremy Collier, Walter Scott n.d., p. 25.
5. Benjamin Whichcote, *Moral and Religious Aphorisms*, century X, no. 912, Elkin Mathews and Marrot 1930.
6. Dietrich Bonhoeffer, *Letters and Papers from Prison*, William Collins Sons and Co. 1963, p. 158.
7. A.C. Benson, *Extracts from the Letters of Dr A.C. Benson to M.E.A.*, Jarrold Publishing 1927, p. 6.
8. Dag Hammarskjöld, *Markings*, translated by Leif Sjoberg and W.H. Auden, Faber and Faber 1964, p. 108.
9. Henry Ward Beecher, *Proverbs from Plymouth Pulpit*, Charles Burnet and Co. 1887, p. 151.
10. Nicolas Berdyaev, *Christianity and Class War*, translated by Donald Attwater, Sheed and Ward 1933, p. 50.
11. Charles Péguy, *Basic Verities*, translated by Ann and Julian Green, Kegan Paul, Trench, Trubner and Co. 1943, p. 51.

12. Anon.
13. Johann Wolfgang von Goethe, in Ludwig Curtius, *Wisdom and Experience*, translated by Hermann J. Weigand, Routledge and Kegan Paul 1949, p. 210.
14. William Blake, 'Jerusalem', *The Complete Writings of William Blake*, edited by Geoffrey Keynes, Oxford University Press 1974, p. 672.
15. George Eliot, *Adam Bede*, Virtue and Co. 1908, vol. 1, p. 318.
16. Basil Hume OSB, *To Be a Pilgrim*, St Paul Publications 1984, p. 157.
17. George Eliot, 'Stradivarius', *The Works of George Eliot*, Virtue and Co. 1913, vol. XVIII, *Jubal and Other Poems*, p. 218.
18. Mother Teresa, in Brother Angelo Devananda, *Jesus, the Word to Be Spoken*, William Collins Sons and Co. 1990, p. 8.
19. Florence Higham, said of F.D. Maurice, in *Frederick Denison Maurice*, SCM Press 1947, p. 126.
20. John Macmurray, *Creative Society*, SCM Press 1935, p. 88.
21. James Martineau, *Endeavours after the Christian Life: Discourses*, Longmans, Green, Reader and Dyer 1876, p. 90.

Adoration

1. NRSV.
2. NRSV.
3. Kenneth Leech, *True Prayer*, Sheldon Press 1980, p. 119.
4. Evelyn Underhill, *The Love of God*, Mowbray 1953, p. 136.
5. Ernest Hello, *Life, Science, and Art*, R. and T. Washbourne 1913, p. 158.
6. John V. Taylor, *The Go-Between God*, SCM Press 1973, p. 45.
7. William Wordsworth, 'It is a Beauteous Evening', *The Poetical Works of William Wordsworth*, edited by E. de Selincourt and Helen Darbishire, Oxford at the Clarendon Press 1954, vol. III, *Miscellaneous Sonnets*, p. 17.
8. Vida D. Scudder, *The Privilege of Age*, J.M. Dent and Sons 1939, p. 30.
9. Pierre Teilhard de Chardin, *Le Milieu Divin*, William Collins Sons and Co. 1960, p. 117.
10. John Macquarrie, *Paths in Spirituality*, SCM Press 1972, p. 6.
11. de Chardin, *Le Milieu Divin*, p. 188.
12. William Temple, *The Hope of a New World*, SCM Press 1940, p. 30.
13. J. Neville Ward, *The Use of Praying*, Epworth Press 1967, p. 28.
14. Thomas F. Green, *Preparation for Worship*, (Swarthmore Lecture), George Allen and Unwin Publishers 1952, p. 17.
15. Evelyn Underhill, *The Golden Sequence*, Methuen and Co. 1932, p. 162.
16. Olive Wyon, *On the Way*, SCM Press 1958, p. 101.
17. Underhill, *The Golden Sequence*, p. 165.

Anxiety

1. NRSV.
2. NRSV.
3. Alfred, Lord Tennyson, 'Enoch Arden', *The Works of Alfred Lord Tennyson*, Macmillan Publishers 1898, p. 128.
4. Ralph Waldo Emerson, *Letters and Social Aims, Addresses, The Works of Ralph Waldo Emerson, vol. III, Society and Solitude*, edited by George Sampson, George Bell and Sons 1906, p. 147.
5. A.C. Benson, *Extracts from the Letters of Dr A.C. Benson to M.E.A.*, Jarrold Publishing 1927, p. 69.
6. Henry Ward Beecher, *Proverbs from Plymouth Pulpit*, Charles Burnet and Co. 1887, p. 18.
7. Benson, *Extracts from the Letters of Dr A.C. Benson to M.E.A.*, p. 60.
8. Author unknown.
9. Thomas Merton, *No Man Is an Island*, Burns and Oates 1974, p. 197.
10. Mark Rutherford, *Last Pages from a Journal*, Oxford University Press 1915, p. 257.
11. Richard Foster, *The Celebration of Discipline*, Hodder and Stoughton 1982, p. 77.
12. Rutherford, *Last Pages from a Journal*, p. 308.

13. Thomas Merton, *Thoughts in Solitude*, Burns and Oates 1958, p. 71.
14. Anthony Bloom, *The Essence of Prayer*, Darton, Longman and Todd 1989, p. 116.
15. Rollo May, *Man's Search for Himself*, George Allen and Unwin 1953, p. 44.
16. Geoffrey Harding, in George Appleton, *Journey for a Soul*, William Collins Sons and Co. 1976, p. 114.
17. E. Stanley Jones, *Growing Spiritually*, Hodder and Stoughton 1954, p. 45.
18. Lilian Whiting, *Lilies of Eternal Peace*, Gay and Hancock 1908, p. 17.
19. Rutherford, *Last Pages from a Journal*, p. 290.
20. Lilian Whiting, *The Life Radiant*, Gay and Bird 1904, p. 320.

Art

1. NRSV.
2. NRSV.
3. Henry Wadsworth Longfellow, 'Hyperion', George Routledge and Sons 1887, p. 196.
4. John Ruskin, *The Two Paths*, George Allen 1905, p. 57.
5. Henry Ward Beecher, *Proverbs from Plymouth Pulpit*, Charles Burnet and Co. 1887, p. 223.
6. Thomas Carlyle, *Latter-Day Pamphlets*, Chapman and Hall 1899, p. 271.
7. Amy Lowell, *Tendencies in Modern American Poetry*, The Macmillan Co. 1917, p. 7.
8. Henri Frédéric Amiel, *Amiel's Journal*, translated by Mrs Humphry Ward, Macmillan and Co. 1918, p. 249.
9. A. Clutton Brock, *The Ultimate Belief*, Constable and Co. 1916, p. 101.
10. Mohandas K. Gandhi, in C.F. Andrews, *Mahatma Gandhi's Ideas*, George Allen and Unwin 1929, p. 332.
11. Wassily Kandinsky, *Concerning the Spiritual in Art*, translated by M.T.H. Sadler, Dover Publications 1977, p. 54.
12. Ludwig Lewisohn, *The Modern Drama*, B.W. Huebsch 1915, p. 109.
13. John Ruskin, *The Stones of Venice*, edited by Jan Morris, Faber and Faber 1981, p. 233.
14. Robert Henri, *The Art Spirit*, compiled by Margery A. Ryerson, J.B. Lippincott and Co. 1960, p. 66.
15. Henry Wadsworth Longfellow, 'Michel Angelo', *The Poetical Works of Longfellow*, Humphrey Milford, Oxford University Press 1913, part 1, section 3, p. 793.
16. Alexander Solzhenitsyn, *One Word of Truth: The Nobel Speech in Literature*, The Bodley Head 1970, p. 5.
17. Nathaniel Hawthorne, *The Marble Faun*, The Bobbs-Merrill Co. 1971, p. 324.
18. Robert Bridges, 'The Testament of Beauty', Oxford at the Clarendon Press, iii. 1058, p. 126.
19. Joseph Conrad, *The Nigger of the 'Narcissus'*, J.M. Dent and Sons 1929, p. viii.
20. Henri, *The Art Spirit*, p. 15.
21. Sir Joshua Reynolds, *Sir Joshua Reynolds' Discourses*, Kegan Paul, Trench and Co. 1883, p. 247.

Aspiration

1. NRSV.
2. NRSV.
3. Henry Wadsworth Longfellow, 'The Masque of Pandora', *The Poetical Works of Longfellow*, Humphrey Milford, Oxford University Press 1913, p. 688.
4. William Wordsworth, 'Devotional Incitements', 'Poems of the Imagination', no. XLVI, *The Poetical Works of William Wordsworth*, edited by E. de Selincourt, Oxford at the Clarendon Press 1944, vol. II, p. 313.
5. Francis Bacon, *The Advancement of Learning*, Cassell and Co. 1905, p. 156.
6. Johann Wolfgang von Goethe, *Faust*, translated by Bayard Taylor, Sphere Books 1974, part 1, 'Prologue in Heaven', l.328.
7. Michel Quoist, *With Open Heart*, translated by Colette Copeland, Gill and Macmillan 1983, p. 66.
8. Sir Philip Sidney, 'Leave Me, O Love', *The Poems of Sir Philip Sidney*, edited by William A. Ringler, Jr, Oxford at the Clarendon Press 1962, p. 161.

9. Robert Louis Stevenson, *Familiar Studies of Men and Books, Virginibus Puerisque, Selected Poems*, William Collins Sons and Co. 1956, p. 293.
10. John Milton, *Of Education, Complete Works of John Milton*, Oxford University Press 1959, vol. 11, p. 385.
11. Richard Jefferies, *The Story of My Heart*, Macmillan and Co. 1968, p. 142.
12. Hubert van Zeller, *Considerations*, Sheed and Ward 1974, p. 84.
13. Rufus M. Jones, in H. Loukes, *The Quaker Contribution*, SCM Press 1965, p. 91.
14. Stephen MacKenna, *Journal and Letters*, Constable and Co. 1936, p. 276.
15. Matthew Arnold, 'Stanzas from the Grande Chartreuse', *The Poems of Matthew Arnold*, edited by Kenneth Allott, Longmans, Green and Co. 1965, xii.67, p. 288.
16. Alfred, Lord Tennyson, 'Idylls of the King, Guinevere', *The Poems of Tennyson*, edited by Christopher Ricks, Longmans, Green and Co. 1969, No. 474, l.652, p. 1741.
17. Lecomte du Nöuy, *Human Destiny*, Longmans, Green and Co. 1947, p. 178.
18. Albert Einstein, *Out of My Later Years*, Thames and Hudson 1950, p. 9.
19. Raynor C. Johnson, *A Pool of Reflections*, Hodder and Stoughton 1975, p. 143.

Awareness

1. NRSV.
2. NRSV.
3. Edward Bellamy, *Looking Backwards*, Alvin Redman 1948, p. 111.
4. Michel Quoist, *With Open Heart*, translated by Colette Copeland, Gill and Macmillan 1983, p. 168.
5. William Barclay, *The Gospel of Matthew*, The Saint Andrew Press 1987, vol. 1, p. 280.
6. Eric Hoffer, *The Passionate State of Mind*, Martin Secker and Warburg 1956, p. 76.
7. *The Cloud of Unknowing*, translated by Clifton Wolters, Penguin Books 1971, p. 66.
8. F.R. Barry, *The Relevance of Christianity*, James Nisbet and Co. 1932, p. 75.
9. Sir Thomas Browne, *Christian Morals, The Works of Sir Thomas Browne*, edited in 4 volumes by Geoffrey Keynes, Faber and Faber 1964, vol. 1, p. 254.
10. George Eliot, *Middlemarch*, Penguin Books 1985, p. 226.
11. Margaret Bondfield, *What Life Has Taught Me*, edited by Sir James Marchant, Odhams Press 1948, p. 27.
12. Charles Kingsley, *Daily Thoughts*, Macmillan Publishers 1884, p. 103.
13. Frank Wright, *The Pastoral Nature of the Ministry*, SCM Press 1980, p. 34.
14. Helmut Thielicke, *I Believe – The Christian's Creed*, translated by John W. Doberstein and M. George Anderson, William Collins Sons and Co. 1969, p. 35.
15. J. Neville Ward, *The Use of Praying*, Epworth Press 1967, p. 25.
16. Bondfield, *What Life Has Taught Me*, p. 27.
17. Thomas Merton, *Conjectures of a Guilty Bystander*, Burns and Oates 1968, p. 274.

Beauty

1. AV.
2. NRSV.
3. William Shakespeare, *Othello*, act V.i.19.
4. Henry Ward Beecher, *Proverbs from Plymouth Pulpit*, Charles Burnet and Co. 1887, p. 101.
5. Harry Emerson Fosdick, *As I See Religion*, SCM Press, 1932, p. 128.
6. Rabindranth Tagore, *Stray Birds, Collected Poems and Plays of Rabindranath Tagore*, Macmillan and Co. 1936, CXCV, p. 312.
7. Richard Jefferies, *Pageant of Summer*, Chatto and Windus 1911, p. 39.
8. George Macdonald, *The Marquis of Lossie*, Everett and Co. 1912, p. 68.
9. Ralph Waldo Emerson, *Essays and Representative Men, The Works of Ralph Waldo Emerson*, edited by George Sampson, George Bell and Sons 1906, vol. 1, p. 191.
10. Kahlil Gibran, *Sand and Foam*, William Heineman 1927, p. 23.
11. Beecher, *Proverbs from Plymouth Pulpit*, p. 187.
12. Nicolas Berdyaev, *Christian Existentialism*, selected and translated by Donald A. Lowrie, George Allen and Unwin 1965, p. 323.

13. Henri Frédéric Amiel, *Amiel's Journal*, translated by Mrs Humphry Ward, Macmillan and Co. 1918, p. 68.
14. Friedrich Schiller, *Essays, Aesthetical and Philosophical*, George Bell and Sons 1875, p. 4.
15. A.C. Benson, *Extracts from the Letters of Dr A.C. Benson to M.E.A.*, Jarrold Publishing 1927, p. 77.
16. Percy Bysshe Shelley, 'Hymn to Intellectual Beauty', *The Complete Poems of Percy Bysshe Shelley*, Oxford University Press 1935, verse 11, p. 526.
17. H.G. Wells, *The History of Mr Polly*, Thomas Nelson and Sons 1910, p. 321.
18. Maurice Maeterlinck, *Wisdom and Destiny*, translated by A. Sutro, George Allen 1898, p. xiii.
19. Henry Wadsworth Longfellow, 'Evangeline, Part the First', *The Poetical Works of Longfellow*, Humphrey Milford, Oxford University Press 1913, p. 144, l.59.
20. Johann Wolfgang von Goethe, *Wilhelm Meister's Year of Apprenticeship*, translated by H.M. Waidson, John Calder (Publishers) 1978, vol. II, p. 74.
21. Alan Seeger, 'An Ode to Natural Beauty', *Poems*, Constable and Co. 1917, p. 4.
22. Fyodor Dostoyevsky, *Letters of Fyodor Michailovitch Dostoyevsky to His Family and Friends*, translated by Ethel Colburn Mayne, Peter Owen, pp. 71 and 142.

Belief

1. NRSV.
2. NRSV.
3. W.B. Yeats, in Samuel H. Miller, *The Great Realities*, Longmans, Green and Co. 1956, p. 112.
4. Thomas Fuller, *Gnomologia*, Stearne Brock 1773, p. 71.
5. Carlo Carretto, *Summoned by Love*, translated by Alan Neame, Darton, Longman and Todd 1977, p. 35.
6. William James, *The Will to Believe*, Longmans, Green and Co. 1904, p. 62.
7. F.R. Barry, *Secular and Supernatural*, SCM Press 1969, p. 36.
8. Ralph Waldo Emerson, *Essays and Representative Men, The Works of Ralph Waldo Emerson*, edited by George Sampson, George Bell and Sons 1906, vol. 1, p. 453.
9. Mark Rutherford, *Last Pages from a Journal*, Oxford University Press 1915, p. 318.
10. Dag Hammarskjöld, *Markings*, translated by Leif Sjoberg and W.H. Auden, Faber and Faber 1964, p. 95.
11. David Sheppard, *Bias to the Poor*, Hodder and Stoughton 1983, p. 151.
12. Brother Lawrence, *The Practice of the Presence of God*, A.R. Mowbray and Co. 1977, p. 19.
13. Hugh Redwood, *Residue of Days*, Hodder and Stoughton 1958, p. 20.
14. William Temple, *The Hope of a New World*, SCM Press 1940, p. 107.
15. Pierre Teilhard de Chardin, *Le Milieu Divin*, William Collins Sons and Co. 1960, p. 129.
16. William Barclay, *The Gospel of John*, The Saint Andrew Press 1965, vol. 2, p. 177.
17. William Law, in Stephen Hobhouse, *Selected Mystical Writings of William Law*, Rockliff 1948, p. 32.
18. John Baillie, *Invitation to Pilgrimage*, Oxford University Press 1942, p. 18.
19. Fyodor Dostoyevsky, *The Brothers Karamazov*, translated by David Magarshack, Penguin Books 1963, vol. 1, p. 275.
20. W.E. Sangster, *These Things Abide*, Hodder and Stoughton 1939, p. 78.
21. Benjamin Franklin, *The Private Correspondence of B. Franklin*, printed for Henry Colburn 1817, p. 131.

Blessedness

1. NRSV.
2. NRSV.
3. Thomas Carlyle, *Past and Present,* Ward, Lock and Co., lxxx, p. 136.
4. Thomas Carlyle, *Sartor Resartus*, Ward, Lock and Co., lxxx, p. 128.
5. Henry David Thoreau, *Walden*, The New American Library of World Literature Inc 1960, p. 149.
6. Edward Young, *Night Thoughts,* Thomas Nelson 1841, p. 210.

7. William Barclay, *The Gospel of Matthew*, The Saint Andrew Press 1987, vol. 1, p. 100.
8. John Burchhardt, *The Civilization of the Renaissance in Italy*, Harper and Brothers, Publishers, 1958, p. 516.
9. Henry Ward Beecher, *Proverbs from Plymouth Pulpit*, Charles Burnet and Co. 1887, p. 170.
10. Izaak Walton, *The Compleat Angler*, Macmillan and Co. 1906, p. 174.
11. Beecher, *Proverbs from Plymouth Pulpit*, p. 136.
12. *Theologia Germanica*, translated by Susanna Winkworth, Stuart and Watkins 1966, p. 48.
13. Carroll E. Simcox, *The Promises of God*, Dacre Press, A. and C. Black 1958, p. 91.
14. William Law, *The Spirit of Love and the Spirit of Prayer*, edited by Sidney Spencer, James Clarke and Co. 1969, p. 165.
15. Sir John Lubbock, *The Pleasures of Life*, Macmillan Publishers 1891, p. 5.
16. Henri Frédéric Amiel, *Amiel's Journal*, translated by Mrs Humphry Ward, Macmillan and Co. 1918, p. 188.
17. Anon.

Character

1. AV.
2. NRSV.
3. William Shakespeare, *Hamlet*, act I.iii.78.
4. Alexander Pope, *An Essay on Man*, Cassell and Co. 1905, 'Epistle IV', p. 52.
5. Henry Ward Beecher, *Life Thoughts*, Alexander Strahan and Co. 1895, p. 95.
6. Johann Wolfgang von Goethe, *Torquato Tasso, 1709*, act I. ii. 66.
7. Ralph Waldo Emerson, *Society and Solitude: Letters and Social Aims: Addresses*, The Works of Ralph Waldo Emerson, edited by George Sampson, George Bell and Sons, vol. III 1906, p. 381.
8. Henry Ward Beecher, *Proverbs from Plymouth Pulpit*, Charles Burnet and Co. 1887, p. 122.
9. Henri Frédéric Amiel, *Amiel's Journal*, translated by Mrs Humphry Ward, Macmillan and Co. 1918, p. 47.
10. Thomas Jefferson, *The Writings of Thomas Jefferson*, Taylor and Maury 1854, vol. IV, p. 476.
11. Beecher, *Proverbs from Plymouth Pulpit*, p. 150.
12. Hubert van Zeller, *Considerations*, Sheed and Ward 1974, p. 13.
13. Beecher, *Proverbs from Plymouth Pulpit*, p. 43.
14. Helen Keller, *Helen Keller's Journal*, Michael Joseph 1938, p. 66.
15. Beecher, *Proverbs from Plymouth Pulpit*, p. 164.
16. John Cowper Powys, *Autobiography*, Macdonald and Co. 1967, p. 376.
17. Father Andrew SDC, *A Gift of Light*, elected and edited by Harry C. Griffith, A.R. Mowbray and Co. 1968, p. 84.
18. William Temple, *Christian Faith and Life*, SCM Press 1963, p. 43.
19. Beecher, *Proverbs from Plymouth Pulpit*, p. 166.
20. John Smith the Platonist, *Select Discourses*, Cambridge at the University Press 1859, p. 401.
21. W.R. Inge, *Personal Religion and the Life of Devotion*, Longmans, Green and Co. 1924, p. 59.
22. Samuel Smiles, *Self-Help*, S.W. Partridge and Co. 1912, p. 285.

Cheerfulness

1. NRSV.
2. NRSV.
3. Thomas Fuller, *Gnomologia*, Stearne Brock 1733, p. 43.
4. Ralph Waldo Emerson, *Essays and Representative Men, The Works of Ralph Waldo Emerson*, edited by George Sampson, George Bell and Sons, vol. 1, 1906, p. 353.
5. Joseph Addison, *The Works of Joseph Addison*, edited and published by Henry G. Bohn 1856, vol. III, p. 363.
6. Ralph Waldo Emerson, *The Conduct of Life, Nature, and Other Essays*, J.M. Dent and Sons 1911, p. 279.
7. Anon.
8. William Shakespeare, *The Winter's Tale*, act IV.iii.125.

9. Addison, *The Works of Joseph Addison*, vol. II, p. 153.

10. A.C. Benson, *Extracts from the Letters of Dr A.C. Benson to M.E.A.*, Jarrold Publishing 1927, p. 19.

11. Charlotte Brontë, *Shirley*, Clarendon Press 1979, p. 43.

12. Henry Ward Beecher, *Proverbs from Plymouth Pulpit*, Charles Burnet and Co. 1887, p. 20.

13. Addison, *The Works of Joseph Addison*, vol. III, p. 356.

14. Francois de la M. Fénelon, in Mrs Follen, *Extracts from the Writings of Fénelon*, Edward T. Whitfield 1850, p. 233.

15. Charles Kingsley, *Daily Thoughts*, Macmillan Publishers 1884, p. 227.

16. Michael Ramsey, in Margaret Duggan, *Through the Year with Michael Ramsey*, Hodder and Stoughton 1975, p. 81.

17. William Wordsworth, 'London, 1802', l.9, 'Poems Dedicated to National Independence and Liberty', no. XIV, *The Poetical Works of William Wordsworth*, edited by E. de Selincourt, Oxford at the Clarendon Press 1954, vol. III, p. 131.

18. Anne Frank, *The Diary of Anne Frank*, Pan Books 1954, p. 175.

19. W.E. Sangster, *Westminster Sermons*, Epworth Press 1960, vol. 1, *At Morning Worship*, p. 4.

Christian

1. NRSV.

2. NRSV.

3. Edward Young, *Night Thoughts*, Thomas Nelson 1841, p. 64.

4. Tertullian, *The Writings of Tertullian*, Hamilton and Co. 1869, vol. 1, Apology no.17, p. 87.

5. Sir Richard Livingstone, *On Education*, Cambridge at the University Press 1954, p. 133.

6. Henry Ward Beecher, *Life Thoughts*, Alexander Strahan and Co. 1859, p. 135.

7. Samuel Taylor Coleridge, *Letters of Samuel Taylor Coleridge*, edited by Ernest Hartley Coleridge, William Heineman 1895, vol. 11, Letter No. 209, p. 775.

8. E. Stanley Jones, *Growing Spiritually*, Hodder and Stoughton 1954, p. 188.

9. John A.T. Robinson, *The Roots of a Radical*, SCM Press 1980, p. 55.

10. Hans Küng, *On Being a Christian*, translated by Edward Quinn, William Collins Sons and Co. 1977, p. 380.

11. Henry Ward Beecher, *Proverbs from Plymouth Pulpit*, Charles Burnet and Co. 1887, p. 171.

12. Henri J.M. Nouwen, *The Wounded Healer*, Doubleday 1979, p. 99.

13. Izaak Walton, *The Compleat Angler*, The Nonesuch Press 1929, p. 18.

14. Henry McKeating, *God and the Future*, SCM Press 1974, p. 58.

15. C.G. Jung, *Memories, Dreams, Reflections*, William Collins Sons and Co. 1971, p. 236.

16. Rufus M. Jones, *Spiritual Reformers in the 16th and 17th Centuries*, Macmillan and Co. 1914, p. 170.

17. Mark Rutherford, *Last Pages from a Journal*, Oxford University Press 1915, p. 266.

18. Jones, *Spiritual Reformers in the 16th and 17th Centuries*, p. 46.

19. David Brown, *God's Tomorrow*, SCM Press 1977, p. 55.

Church

1. NRSV.

2. NRSV.

3. Henry Ward Beecher, *Proverbs from Plymouth Pulpit*, Charles Burnet and Co. 1887, p. 109.

4. Cardinal Leon Joseph Suenens, *A New Pentecost?*, translated by Francis Martin, Darton, Longman and Todd 1975, p. 1.

5. Paul Oestreicher, in Hans Jurgen Schultz, *Conversion to the World*, SCM Press 1967, p. 32.

6. Henry Ward Beecher, *Proverbs from Plymouth Pulpit*, Charles Burnet and Co. 1887, p. 200.

7. W.A. Visser 'T Hooft, *The Renewal of the Church*, SCM Press 1956, p. 23.

8. Daniel Jenkins, *Christian Maturity and the Theology of Success*, SCM Press 1976, p. 67.

9. Hans Küng, *On Being a Christian*, translated by Edward Quinn, William Collins Sons and Co. 1977, p. 285.

10. Beecher, *Proverbs from Plymouth Pulpit*, p. 198.

11. J.H. Oldham, *Life is Commitment*, SCM Press 1953, p. 95.
12. Colin Morris, *The Hammer of the Lord*, Epworth Press 1973, p. 10.
13. H.E. Root, in A.R. Vidler, *Soundings*, Cambridge at the University Press 1962, p. 6.
14. Paul Tillich, *On the Boundary*, William Collins Sons and Co. 1967, p. 67.
15. F.R. Barry, *Secular and Supernatural*, SCM Press 1969, p. 33.
16. Thomas Merton, *Contemplative Prayer*, Darton, Longman and Todd 1973, p. 144.
17. Alec R. Vidler, *God's Demand and Man's Response*, John Hermitage, The Unicorn Press 1938, p. 102.
18. Norman Goodall, *The Local Church*, Hodder and Stoughton 1966, p. 28.
19. George Appleton, *Journey for a Soul*, William Collins Sons and Co. 1976, p. 166.
20. Monica Furlong, *With Love to the Church*, Hodder and Stoughton 1965, p. 22.

Commitment

1. NRSV.
2. NRSV.
3. Hans Küng, *On Being a Christian*, translated by Edward Quinn, William Collins Sons and Co. 1977, p. 286.
4. William Law, *A Serious Call to a Devout and Holy Life*, J.M. Dent and Co. 1898, p. 8.
5. E. Stanley Jones, *Mastery*, Hodder and Stoughton 1956, p. 45.
6. E. Stanley Jones, *The Word Became Flesh*, Hodder and Stoughton 1964, p. 343.
7. John Keats, *The Letters of John Keats*, Oxford University Press, 'To James Augustus Hessey, Friday 9th Oct. 1818', editor, Maurice Buxton Forman, number 90, 1952, p. 221.
8. Thomas Merton, *Thoughts in Solitude*, Burns and Oates 1958, p. 17.
9. Küng, *On Being a Christian*, p. 291.
10. William Temple, *Readings in St John's Gospel*, first and second series, Macmillan and Co. 1947, p. 161.
11. John V. Taylor, *The Go-Between God*, SCM Press 1973, p. 98.
12. John Macquarrie, *In Search of Humanity*, SCM Press 1982, p. 157.
13. Paul Tournier, *Escape from Loneliness*, translated by John S. Gilmour, SCM Press 1962, p. 111.
14. C.S. Lewis, *Mere Christianity*, William Collins Sons and Co. 1961, p. 164.
15. Rabindranath Tagore, *Gitanjali*, Macmillan and Co. 1971, p. 42.

Compassion

1. NRSV.
2. NRSV.
3. Antoine de Saint-Exupéry, *The Wisdom of the Sands*, translated by Stuart Gilbert, Hollis and Carter, 1952, p. 98.
4. Baron Friedrich von Hügel, *Letters to a Niece*, J.M. Dent and Sons 1929, p. xiv.
5. Fyodor Dostoyevsky, *The Idiot*, translated by David Magarshack, Penguin Books 1983, p. 248.
6. Blaise Pascal, *Pensées*, translated by W.F. Trotter, Random House, Inc. 1941, p. 176.
7. Mary Craig, *Blessings*, Hodder and Stoughton 1979, p. 61.
8. Henri J.M. Nouwen, *The Wounded Healer*, Doubleday 1979, p. 41.
9. William Temple, *Readings in St John's Gospel*, first and second series, Macmillan and Co. 1947, p. 160.
10. L. Blum, in James F. Childress and John Macquarrie, *A New Dictionary of Christian Ethics*, SCM Press 1986, p. 109.
11. Henri J.M. Nouwen, *The Way of the Heart*, Darton, Longman and Todd 1981, p. 34.
12. James F. Childress, in Childress and Macquarrie, *A New Dictionary of Christian Ethics*, p. 109.
13. Bertrand Russell, *The Impact of Science on Society*, George Allen and Unwin 1968, p. 84.
14. John Milton, 'Paradise Lost', *The Poems of John Milton*, Clarendon Press 1900, book III, l.138, p. 231.
15. Eric Hoffer, *The Passionate State of Mind*, Martin Secker and Warburg 1956, p. 69.
16. Anthony Bloom, *Living Prayer*, Darton, Longman and Todd 1966, p. 16.
17. A co-worker, in Kathryn Spink, *A Chain of Love*, SPCK 1984, p. 113.

Contemplation

1. NRSV.
2. NRSV.
3. Ernest Dimnet, *What We Live By*, Jonathan Cape 1932, p. 195.
4. Meister Eckhart, in Franz Pfeiffer, *Meister Eckhart*, translated by Raymond B. Blakney, Harper and Row, 1941, p. 111.
5. St John of the Cross, *The Complete Works of Saint John of the Cross*, translated and edited by E. Allison Peers, Burns, Oates and Washbourne 1953, vol. II, 27,5, p. 326.
6. Ralph Waldo Emerson, *Miscellaneous Pieces, The Works of Ralph Waldo Emerson*, edited by George Sampson, George Bell and Sons Ltd 1906, vol. IV, p. 431.
7. Stephen MacKenna, *Journal and Letters*, Constable and Co. 1936, p. 120.
8. Michael Ramsey, *Canterbury Pilgrim*, SPCK 1974, p. 60.
9. William Wordsworth, 'Prelude', Book Fifth, l.3.
10. Lady Julian of Norwich, *Revelations of Divine Love*, Penguin Books 1976, p. 71.
11. Thomas Merton, *Elected Silence*, Hollis and Carter 1949, p. 368.
12. Richard Harries, in Alan Richardson and John Bowden, *A New Dictionary of Christian Theology*, SCM Press 1985, p. 121.
13. Thomas Merton, *The Waters of Silence*, Hollis and Carter 1950, p. 14.
14. Iris Murdoch, *The Sovereignty of Good Over Other Concepts*, Cambridge University Press 1967, p. 34.
15. George Gissing, *The Private Papers of Henry Rycroft*, J.M. Dent and Sons 1964, p. 134.
16. Aldous Huxley, *The Perennial Philosophy*, Chatto and Windus 1974, p. 259.
17. Thomas Merton, *New Seeds of Contemplation*, Burns and Oates 1962, p. 1.
18. Michael Ramsey, in *Spirituality for Today*, edited by Eric James, SCM Press 1968, p. 139.
19. Merton, *New Seeds of Contemplation*, p. 1.

Contentment

1. NRSV.
2. NRSV.
3. English proverb.
4. Edmund Spenser, 'The Faerie Queene', edited by J.C. Smith, Oxford at the Clarendon Press 1964, book 1, canto 1, st.xxxv, l.4, p. 13.
5. Robert Greene, 'Farewell to Folly' 1587, st.ii, l.12
6. Thomas Fuller, *Gnomologia*, Stearne Brock 1733, p. 68.
7. Izaak Walton, *The Compleat Angler*, The Nonesuch Press 1929, p. 191.
8. Henry Ward Beecher, *Proverbs from Plymouth Pulpit*, Charles Burnet and Co. 1887, p. 178.
9. W.E. Sangster, *The Secret of Radiant Life*, Hodder and Stoughton 1957, p. 19.
10. Old proverb.
11. Beecher, *Proverbs from Plymouth Pulpit*, p. 26.
12. John Dryden, 'The Wife of Bath, Her Tale', *The Poems of John Dryden*, edited by James Kinsley, Oxford at the Clarendon Press 1958, vol. IV, l.466, p. 1715.
13. C.S. Lewis, *They Stand Together*, The Letters of C.S. Lewis, to Arthur Greeves (1914–63), edited by Walter Hooper, William Collins Sons and Co. 1979, p. 161.
14. Albert Einstein, *Out of My Later Years*, Thames and Hudson 1950, p. 12.
15. Alban Goodier SJ, *The School of Love*, Burns and Oates and Washbourne 1920, p. 68.
16. Henry Fielding, *Joseph Andrews*, J.M. Dent and Sons 1910, p. 173.
17. William Shakespeare, *King Henry VI*, part III, act III.i.62.
18. Beecher, *Proverbs from Plymouth Pulpit*, p. 224.
19. Spenser, 'The Faerie Queene', book VI canto IX, st.xxix, l.6.
20. Charles Cotton, 'The Retirement', *Poems*, chosen and edited by J.R. Tutin, published by the editor 1903, p. 16.
21. William E. Channing, 'My Symphony', *A Series of Miscellaneous Illustrated Cards* 1902, p. 37.
22. Winston S. Churchill, *Thoughts and Adventures*, Thornton Butterworth 1932, p. 19.

Courage

1. NRSV.
2. NRSV.
3. German proverb.
4. Thomas Bailey Aldrich, *The Stillwater Tragedy*, David Douglas 1886, vol. 1, p. 172.
5. Søren Kierkegaard, *The Journals of Søren Kierkegaard*, a selection edited and translated by Alexander Dru, Oxford University Press 1938, p. 87.
6. Rollo May, *Man's Search for Himself*, George Allen and Unwin 1953, p. 224.
7. Thomas Carlyle, *Boswell's Life of Johnson, The Works of Thomas Carlyle*, Chapman and Hall 1899, *Critical and Miscellaneous Essays*, vol. III, p. 123.
8. A.D. Sertillanges OP, *The Intellectual Life*, translated by Mary Ryan, The Mercier Press 1948, p. 157.
9. D.H. Lawrence, *The Selected Letters of D.H. Lawrence*, edited by Diana Trilling, Farrar, Straus and Cudahy 1958, p. 243.
10. Anon.
11. William Barclay, *The Gospel of Matthew*, The Saint Andrew Press 1975, vol. II, p. 37.
12. Carlo Carretto, *Letters from the Desert*, translated by Rose Mary Hancock, Darton, Longman and Todd 1972, p. 130.
13. C.S. Lewis, in Cyril Connelly, *The Unquiet Grave*, Hamish Hamilton 1945, p. 75.
14. Thomas Carlyle, *Corn-Law Rhymes, The Works of Thomas Carlyle*, Chapman and Hall 1899, *Critical and Miscellaneous Essays*, vol. III, p. 147.
15. Graham Greene, *The Heart of the Matter*, William Heinemann 1959, p. 61.
16. Rollo May, *Man's Search for Himself*, George Allen and Unwin 1953, p. 229.
17. Paul Tillich, *The Courage to Be*, Nisbet and Co. 1952, p. 28.
18. W. MacNeile Dixon, *The Human Situation*, Edward Arnold and Co. 1937, p. 89.
19. Rainer Maria Rilke, *Letters to a Young Poet*, translated by Reginald Snell, Sidgwick and Jackson 1945, p. 38.
20. Tillich, *The Courage to Be*, 1952, p. 14.
21. W.E. Sangster, *These Things Abide*, Hodder and Stoughton 1939, p. 157.
22. Thomas Traherne, *The Way to Blessedness*, the spelling and punctuation by Margaret Bottrall, The Faith Press 1962, p. 178.

Cross

1. NRSV.
2. NRSV.
3. Anon.
4. Rufus M. Jones, *Spiritual Reformers in the 16th and 17th Centuries*, Macmillan and Co. 1914, p. 250.
5. William Law, in Stephen Hobhouse, *Selected Mystical Writings of William Law*, Rockliff 1948, p. 99.
6. Thomas à Kempis, *The Imitation of Christ*, translated by Betty I. Knott, William Collins Sons and Co. 1979, p. 196.
7. Simone Weil, *Gravity and Grace*, Routledge and Kegan Paul 1972, p. 30.
8. Michel Quoist, *Prayers of Life*, translated by Anne Marie de Commaile and Agnes Mitchell Forsyth, Gill and Macmillan 1963, p. 5.
9. Aldous Huxley, *The Perennial Philosophy*, Chatto and Windus 1974, p. 113.
10. George Reindorp, in Gerald Priestland, *Priestland's Progress*, BBC Worldwide 1982, p. 79.
11. John Donne, 'Holy Sonnets, XIV', *Poetical Works*, edited by Sir Herbert Grierson, Oxford University Press 1977, xiv, p. 299.
12. John Tauler, *The Following of Christ*, translated by J.R. Morell, Burns and Oates 1886, p. 175.
13. Jones, *Spiritual Reformers in the 16th and 17th Centuries*, p. 194.
14. William Law, in Sidney Spencer, *The Spirit of Prayer and the Spirit of Love*, James Clarke and Co. 1969, p. 167.
15. George Appleton, *Journey for a Soul*, William Collins Sons and Co. 1976, p. 178.

16. D.H. Lawrence, 'Pheonix', *The Complete Poems of D.H. Lawrence*, edited by Vivian de Sola Pinto and Warren Roberts, William Heinemann 1967, vol. 2, p. 728.

Death

1. NRSV.
2. NRSV.
3. French proverb.
4. Leonardo da Vinci, *The Notebooks of Leonardo da Vinci*, edited by Edward McCurdy, vol. 1, Jonathan Cape 1977, p. 65.
5. J. Neville Ward, *Five for Sorrow, Ten for Joy*, Epworth Press 1971, p. 83.
6. Erich Fromm, *Man for Himself*, Routledge and Kegan Paul 1975, p. 162.
7. Dag Hammarskjöld, *Markings*, translated by Leif Sjoberg and W.H. Auden, Faber and Faber 1964, p. 136.
8. Rabidrananth Tagore, *Stray Birds, Collected Poems and Plays of Rabindranath Tagore*, Macmillan and Co. 1936, xcix, p. 299.
9. John S. Dunne, *The Reasons of the Heart*, SCM Press 1978, p. 61.
10. J. Neville Ward, *Friday Afternoon*, Epworth Press 1982, p. 131.
11. Thomas Mann, *The Magic Mountain*, translated by H.T. Lowe-Porter, Penguin Books 1983, p. 200.
12. A.C. Benson, *Extracts from the Letters of Dr A.C. Benson to M.E.A.*, Jarrold Publishing 1927, p. 22.
13. Norman Goodall, *The Local Church*, Hodder and Stoughton 1966, p. 18.
14. Rabindranath Tagore, *Gitanjali*, Macmillan and Co. 1971, p. 83.
15. William Temple, *Readings in St John's Gospel*, first and second series, Macmillan and Co. 1947, p. 147.
16. Nicolas Berdyaev, *The Destiny of Man*, translated by Natalie Duddington, Geoffrey Bles: The Centenary Press 1937, p. 156.
17. J. Neville Ward, *Friday Afternoon*, Epworth Press 1982, p. 103.
18. William Barclay, *The Gospel of John*, The Saint Andrew Press 1965, vol. 2, p. 38.
19. Jean Vanier, *Man and Woman He Made Them*, Darton, Longman and Todd 1985, p. 149.

Depression

1. NRSV.
2. NRSV.
3. Sir Walter Scott, *The Heart of Midlothian*, Oxford University Press 1912, p. 581.
4. Edmund Burke, *Burke's Works*, printed for J. Dodsley, vol. 1, 'Light: On the Sublime and Beautiful', l.17, p. 145.
5. Henry Ward Beecher, *Proverbs from Plymouth Pulpit*, Charles Burnet and Co. 1887, p. 163.
6. Henry Wadsworth Longfellow, 'The Rainy Day', *The Poetical Works of Longfellow*, Humphrey Milford, Oxford University Press 1913, st.iii, l.44, p. 63.
7. A.C. Benson, *Extracts from the Letters of Dr A.C. Benson to M.E.A.*, Jarrold Publishing 1927, p. 14.
8. Matthew Arnold, 'Self-Dependence', *The Poems of Matthew Arnold*, edited by Kenneth Allott, Longmans, Green and Co. 1965, l.31, p. 144.
9. Hubert van Zeller, *Considerations*, Sheed and Ward 1974, p. 25.
10. George Eliot, *Adam Bede*, Virtue and Co. 1908, vol. II, p. 68.
11. Arthur T. Jersild, *The Psychology of Adolescence*, Macmillan Publishers 1963, p. 35.
12. Rollo May, *Man's Search for Himself*, Souvenir Press 1975, p. 24.
13. Murial Spark, *Territorial Rights*, Macmillan Publishers 1979, p. 51.
14. Percy Bysshe Shelley, 'The Revolt of Islam: Dedication: To Mary', *The Complete Poetical Works of Percy Bysshe Shelley*, edited by Thomas Hutchinson, Oxford University Press 1935, st.6, p. 39.
15. van Zeller, *Considerations*, p. 76.
16. Jerome K. Jerome, *Idle Thoughts of an Idle Fellow*, J.M. Dent and Sons 1983, p. 21.

17. David Watson, *You Are My God*, Hodder and Stoughton 1983, p. 190.
18. Rabindranath Tagore, *Gitanjali*, Macmillan Publishers 1971, p. 30.
19. Michel Quoist, *With Open Heart*, translated by Colette Copeland, Gill and Macmillan 1983, p. 173.

Discipleship

1. NRSV.
2. NRSV.
3. William Barclay, *The Gospel of* Matthew, The Saint Andrew Press 1987, vol. 1, p. 234.
4. Dietrich Bonhoeffer, *The Cost of Discipleship*, translated by R.H. Fuller, SCM Press 1956, p. 119.
5. Henry Ward Beecher, *Proverbs from Plymouth Pulpit*, Charles Burnet and Co. 1887, p. 161.
6. Hans Jürgen Schultz, *Conversion to the World*, SCM Press 1967, p. 100.
7. Harry Emerson Fosdick, *The Hope of a New World*, SCM Press 1933, p. 179.
8. William Penn, *The Fruits of Solitude*, A.W. Bennett 1863, p. 13.
9. William Temple, *Readings in St John's Gospel*, first and second series, Macmillan and Co. 1947, p. 225.
10. Mark Rutherford, *Last Pages from a Journal*, Oxford University Press 1915, p. 303.
11. John J. Vincent, *Secular Christ*, Lutterworth Press 1968, p. 77.
12. George Appleton, *Journey for a Soul*, William Collins Sons and Co. 1976, p. 188.
13. Archibald C. Craig, *University Sermons*, James Clarke and Co. 1937, p. 147.
14. William Temple, *Citizen And Churchman*, Eyre and Spottiswoode 1941, p. 65.
15. J.R.H. Moorman, *The Path to Glory*, SPCK and Seabury Press 1960, p. 182.
16. Appleton, *Journey for a Soul*, p. 157.
17. John Macquarrie, *Paths in Spirituality*, SCM Press 1972, p. 116.
18. Moorman, *The Path to Glory*, p. 182.

Divinity

1. NRSV.
2. NRSV
3. Thomas Carlyle, *Sartor Resartus*, Ward, Lock and Co., p. 92.
4. William Shakespeare, *Hamlet*, act V.ii.10.
5. F. Ernest Johnson, *The Social Gospel Re-Examined*, James Clarke and Co. 1942, p. 50.
6. Matthew Arnold, *Written in Emerson's Essays, The Poems of Matthew Arnold*, edited by Kenneth Allott, Longmans, Green and Co. 1965, l.11, p. 53.
7. Henry Ward Beecher, *Proverbs from Plymouth Pulpit*, Charles Burnet and Co. 1887, p. 116.
8. John Smith the Platonist, *Select Discourses*, Cambridge at the University Press 1859, p. 1.
9. Meister Eckhart, in Franz Pfeiffer, *Meister Eckhart*, translated by C. de B. Evans, John M. Watkins 1956, vol. 1, p. 36.
10. Ralph Waldo Emerson, *The Conduct of Life, Nature and Other Essays*, J.M. Dent and Sons 1911, p. 262.
11. Samuel Taylor Coleridge, *Table Talk of Samuel Taylor Coleridge*, George Routledge and Sons, 1884, p. 186.
12. Beecher, *Proverbs from Plymouth Pulpit*, p. 155.
13. Ralph Waldo Emerson, *Essay on History, The Works of Ralph Waldo Emerson*, George Bell and Sons 1960, vol. 1, *Essays and Representative Men*, p. 6.
14. Ralph Waldo Emerson, *Journals*, Constable and Co. 1910, vol. 3, p. 14.
15. Rufus M. Jones, *Spiritual Reformers in the 16th and 17th Centuries*, Macmillan and Co. 1914, p. 322.
16. Max Lerner, *The Unfinished Country*, Simon and Schuster 1959, p. 724.
17. Meister Eckhart, *Meister Eckhart*, translated by Raymond B. Blakney, Harper and Row 1941, p. 74.

Doubt

1. NRSV.
2. NRSV.
3. A.R. Orage, *On Love*, The Janus Press 1957, p. 60.
4. Anon.
5. H.A. Williams CR, *The True Wilderness*, William Collins Sons and Co. 1983, p. 49.
6. Agnes Sanford, *The Healing Light*, Arthur James 1949, p. 52.
7. William Shakespeare, *Troilus and Cressida*, act II.ii.15.
8. Miguel de Unamuno, *The Agony of Christianity*, Payson and Clarke 1928, p. 27.
9. Anthony Bloom, *The Essence of Prayer*, Darton, Longman and Todd 1989, p. 69.
10. Herbert H. Farmer, *The Healing Cross*, Nisbet and Co. 1938, p. 208.
11. St Augustine of Hippo, *Confessions*, translated by R.S. Pine-Coffin, Penguin Books 1964, p. 116.
12. Francis Bacon, *The Advancement of Learning*, Cassell and Co. 1905, p. 38.
13. William Barclay, *The Gospel of John*, The Saint Andrew Press 1965, vol. 2, p. 151.
14. William Shakespeare, *Measure for Measure*, act I.v.78.
15. Paul Tillich, *The Courage to Be*, Nisbet and Co. 1952, p. 115.
16. Alfred, Lord Tennyson, 'The Ancient Sage', *The Poems of Tennyson*, edited by Christopher Ricks, Longmans, Green and Co. 1969, p. 1351.
17. Monica Furlong, *The End of Our Exploring*, Hodder and Stoughton 1973, p. 16.
18. Erich Fromm, *Man for Himself*, Routledge and Kegan Paul 1975, p. 140.
19. *Christian Faith and Practice in the Experience of the Society of Friends*, London Yearly Meeting of the Religious Society of Friends, 1972, number 119, 1911; 1925.

Education

1. NRSV.
2. NRSV.
3. William Hazlitt, *The Plain Speaker, The Collected Works of William Hazlitt*, J.M. Dent and Co. 1903, vol. VII, p. 320.
4. John Milton, *Paradise Regain'd, The Poetical Works of Milton*, edited by Revd. H.C. Beeching, Oxford at the Clarendon Press 1900, p. 495, Book IV, l.327.
5. Herbert Spencer, *Social Statics*, Williams and Norgate 1892, p. 81.
6. Plato, *The Republic of Plato*, translated by B. Jowett, Oxford at the Clarendon Press 1881, p. 110, book IV, 425B.
7. Robert Louis Stevenson, *Familiar Studies of Men and Books, Virginibus Puerisque*, William Collins Sons and Co. 1956, p. 112.
8. Thomas Arnold, *Sermons*, Longmans, Green, and Co. 1878, vol. III, xvi, p. 131.
9. Horace Mann, *Lectures and Reports on Education*, Cambridge, published for the editor 1867, p. 84.
10. Henry Ward Beecher, *Proverbs from Plymouth Pulpit*, Charles Burnet and Co. 1887, p. 76.
11. Roy Stevens, *On Education and the Death of Love*, Epworth Press 1978, p. 136.
12. Michael Ramsey, in Margaret Duggan, *Through the Year with Michael Ramsey*, Hodder and Stoughton 1975, p. 215.
13. John Ruskin, *The Stones of Venice*, edited by Ernest Rhys, J.M. Dent and Co. 1907, vol. III, p. 197.
14. A. Clutton, Brock, *The Ultimate Belief*, Constable and Co. 1916, p. 99.
15. William Temple, *The Hope of a New World*, SCM Press 1940, p. 12.
16. Meister Eckhart, *Meister Eckhart*, translated by Raymond B. Blakney, Harper and Row 1941, p. 236.
17. Martin Thornton, *Spiritual Direction*, SPCK 1984, p. 11.
18. Mark Rutherford, *Last Pages from a Journal*, Oxford University Press 1915, p. 279.
19. Albert Einstein, *Out of My Later Years*, Thames and Hudson 1950, p. 36.
20. William James, *The Letters of William James*, edited by Henry James, Longmans, Green and Co. 1926, p. 253.

Eternal Life

1. NRSV.
2. NRSV.
3. Benedict Spinoza, *Spinoza's Ethics and De Intellectus Emendatione*, J.M. Dent and Sons 1955, p. 214.
4. Herman Melville, *Mardi*, The New American Library of World Literature 1964, p. 516.
5. William Penn, *Fruits of Solitude*, A.W. Bennett 1863, p. 60.
6. Rabindranath Tagore, *Stray Birds, Collected Poems and Plays of Rabindranath Tagore*, Macmillan and Co. 1936, xcvi, p. 299.
7. George Meredith, *Diana of the Crossways*, Archibald Constable and Co. 1909, p. 11.
8. Henry Vaughan, *Silex Scintillans, The Works of Henry Vaughan*, edited by L.C. Martin, Oxford at the Clarendon Press 1957, p. 419.
9. Nicolas Berdyaev, *The Destiny of Man*, translated by Natalie Duddington, Geoffrey Bles: The Centenary Press 1937, p. 189.
10. Leo Tolstoy, *War and Peace*, translated by Rosemary Edmonds, Penguin Books 1969, vol. 1, p. 455.
11. William Barclay, *The Plain Man Looks at the Apostles' Creed*, William Collins Sons and Co. 1967, p. 374.
12. Richard Jefferies, *The Story of My Heart*, Duckworth and Co. 1923, p. 30.
13. Rufus M. Jones, *Spiritual Reformers in the 16th and 17th Centuries*, Macmillan and Co. 1914, p. xxxiv.
14. Henry Ward Beecher, *Proverbs from Plymouth Pulpit*, Charles Burnet and Co. 1887, p. 168.
15. William Temple, *Readings in St John's Gospel*, first and second series, Macmillan and Co. 1947, p. 310.
16. Henri Frédéric Amiel, *Amiel's Journal*, translated by Mrs Humphry Ward, Macmillan and Co. 1918, p. 96.
17. George Appleton, *Journey for a Soul*, William Collins Sons and Co. 1976, p. 212.
18. Friedrich von Hügel, *Eternal Life*, T. and T. Clarke 1913, p. 396.
19. Thornton Wilder, *Our Town*, Longmans, Green and Co. 1964, act III, p. 93.
20. William Barclay, *The Gospel of John*, The Saint Andrew Press 1965, vol. 1, p. 118.

Experience

1. NRSV.
2. NRSV.
3. Dag Hammarskjöld, *Markings*, translated by Leif Sjoberg and W.H. Auden, Faber and Faber 1964, p. 85.
4. Henry Ward Beecher, *Proverbs from Plymouth Pulpit*, Charles Burnet and Co. 1887, p. 173.
5. William Johnston, *The Inner Eye of Love*, William Collins Sons and Co. 1978, p. 81.
6. Beecher, *Proverbs from Plymouth Pulpit*, p. 163.
7. Rufus M. Jones, *Spiritual Reformers in the 16th and 17th Centuries*, Macmillan and Co. 1914, p. 190.
8. William Temple, *Thoughts on Some Problems of the Day*, Macmillan and Co. 1931, p. 25.
9. Helmet Thielicke, *I Believe: The Christian's Creed*, translated by John W. Doberstein and H. George Anderson, William Collins Sons and Co. 1969, p. 11.
10. C.G. Jung, in Jolande Jacobi, *Psychological Reflections*, Routledge and Kegan Paul 1953, p. 322.
11. Jones, *Spiritual Reformers in the 16th and 17th Centuries*, p. xxi.
12. *The Cloud of Unknowing*, translated by Clifton Wolters, Penguin Books 1971, p. 71.
13. Albert Schweitzer, *The Quest of the Historical Jesus*, A. and C. Black 1954, p. 401.
14. George Appleton, *Journey for a Soul*, William Collins Sons and Co. 1976, p. 37.
15. C.G. Jung, *The Stucture and Dynamics of the Psyche, The Collected Works of C.G. Jung*, vol. 8, translated by R.F.C. Hull, Routledge and Kegan Paul 1969, p. 328.
16. C.G. Jung, *Psychology and Religion*, Yale University Press 1960, p. 113.

Faith

1. NRSV.
2. NRSV.
3. John Dryden, 'Religio Laici', *The Poems of John Dryden*, edited by James Kinsley, Oxford at the Clarendon Press 1958, vol. 1, p. 313.
4. William Johnston, *The Inner Eye of Love*, William Collins Sons and Co. 1978, p. 85.
5. C.S. Lewis, *Letters of C.S. Lewis*, edited by W. H. Lewis, Geoffrey Bles 1966, p. 220.
6. Joseph Addison, *The Works of Joseph Addison*, edited and published by Henry G. Bohn 1856, vol. III, p. 484.
7. Giles and Melville Harcourt, *Short Prayers for the Long Day*, William Collins Sons and Co. 1978, p. 18.
8. Charles Parkhurst, *The Pattern and the Mount and Other Sermons*, R.D. Dickinson 1890, p. 57.
9. Benjamin Whichcote, *Moral and Religious Aphorisms*, century XII, no. 1168, Elkin, Mathews and Marrot 1930, p. 136.
10. Said of Edward Wilson, in George Seaver, *Edward Wilson of the Antarctic*, John Murray 1935, p. 104.
11. Lesslie Newbigin, *Honest Religion for Secular Man*, SCM Press 1966, p. 98.
12. Thomas à Kempis, *The Imitation of Christ*, translated by Betty I. Knott, William Collins Sons and Co. 1979, p. 249.
13. Henri Frédéric Amiel, *Amiel's Journal*, translated by Mrs Humphry Ward, Macmillan and Co. 1918, p. 192.
14. Sir William Osler, *Aphorisms from His Bedside Teachings and Writings*, collected by Robert Bennett Bean, edited by William Bennett Bean, Charles C. Thomas 1961, p. 102.
15. William Temple, *Basic Convctions*, Hamish Hamilton 1937, p. 16.
16. J.R. Lowell, *My Study Windows*, George Routledge and Sons 1905, p. 142.
17. Hans Küng, *On Being a Christian*, translated by Edward Quinn, William Collins Sons and Co. 1977, p. 159.
18. John Macquarrie, *Paths in Spirituality*, SCM Press 1972, p. 33.
19. George Santayana, *Interpretations of Poetry and Religion*, Charles Scribner's Sons 1916, p. 95.
20. William Wordsworth, 'The Excursion', *The Poetical Works of William Wordsworth*, vol. V, edited by E. de Selincourt and Helen Darbishire, Oxford at the Clarendon Press, 1959, iv. 1294, p. 150.
21. George Macdonald, *Unspoken Sermons*, first series, Alexander Strahan 1867, p. 25.
22. Evelyn Underhill, in John Stobbart, *The Wisdom of Evelyn Underhill*, A.R. Mowbray and Co. 1951, p. 18.
23. William Temple, *The Preacher's Theme Today*, SPCK 1936, p. 31.
24. Dietrich Bonhoeffer, *Letters and Papers from Prison*, William Collins Sons and Co. 1963, p. 125.

Finding God

1. NRSV.
2. NRSV.
3. Thomas à Kempis, *The Imitation of Christ*, translated by Betty I. Knott, William Collins Sons and Co. 1979, p. 41.
4. Blaise Pascal, *Pensées*, translated by W.F. Trotter, Random House 1941, p. 7.
5. Mark Rutherford, *Last Pages from a Journal*, Oxford University Press 1915, p. 274.
6. Rufus M. Jones, *Spiritual Reformers in the 16th and 17th Centuries*, Macmillan and Co. 1914, p. 187.
7. Alfred, Lord Tennyson, 'The Passing of Arthur', *The Works of Alfred Lord Tennyson*, Macmillan and Co. 1898, p. 467.
8. Bede Griffiths OSB, *The Golden String*, The Harvill Press 1954, p. 12.
9. George Macdonald, *Unspoken Sermons*, third series, Longmans, Green and Co. 1889, p. 227.
10. Norman Pittenger, *The Christian Situation Today*, Epworth Press 1969, p. 116.
11. Jones, *Spiritual Reformers in the 16th and 17th Centuries*, p. 52.
12. Morris West, *The Devil's Advocate*, Heinemann/Octopus 1977, p. 168.

13. William Law, in Sidney Spencer, *The Spirit of Prayer*, James Clarke and Co. 1969, p. 44.
14. Michel Quoist, *With Open Heart*, translated by Colette Copeland, Gill and Macmillan 1983, p. 180.
15. René Voillaume, *The Need for Contemplation*, translated by Elizabeth Hamilton, Darton, Longman and Todd 1972, p. 57.

Freedom

1. NRSV.
2. NRSV.
3. Robert Browning, 'Andrea del Sarto', *The Poetical Works of Robert Browning*, Smith, Elder and Co. 1899, vol. 1, l.51, p. 524.
4. John Macmurray, *Freedom in the Modern World*, Faber and Faber 1935, p. 101.
5. W.R. Inge, *The Philosophy of Plotinus*, Longmans, Green and Co. 1948, vol. II, p. 192.
6. Herbert Spencer, *Social Statics*, Williams and Norgate 1892, p. 54.
7. Martin Luther King, in Coretta Scott King, *The Words of Martin Luther King*, William Collins Sons and Co. 1986, p. 51.
8. Al-Ghazali, *Al-Ghazali, The Mystic*, Margaret Smith, Luzac and Co. 1944, p. 106.
9. King, *The Words of Martin Luther King*, p. 58.
10. Nicolas Berdyaev, *The Fate of Man in the Modern World*, translated by Donald A. Lowrie, SCM Press 1935, p. 44.
11. Louis Lavelle, in Paul Foulquié, *Existentialism*, translated by Kathleen Raine, Dennis Dobson 1947, p. 113.
12. Rabindranath Tagore, *Creative Unity*, Macmillan and Co. 1922, p. 133.
13. Edward Carpenter, *Love's Coming-of-Age*, George Allen and Unwin 1923, p. 108.
14. L.S. Thornton CR, *The Common Life of the Body of Christ*, Dacre Press: A. and C. Black 1950, p. 242.
15. Nicolas Berdyaev, *Freedom and the Spirit*, Geoffrey Bles, The Centenary Press 1935, p. 140.
16. Yehudi Menuhin, *Theme and Variations*, William Heinemann 1972, p. 46.
17. Kahlil Gibran, *The Prophet*, Sheldon Press 1970, p. 56.
18. Johann Wolfgang von Goethe, *Faust*, translated by Bayard Taylor, Sphere Books 1974, part 2, act V. vi. 1573, p. 424.
19. Hubert van Zeller, *Praying While You Work*, Burns, Oates and Washbourne 1951, p. 48.
20. George Appleton, *Journey for a Soul*, William Collins Sons and Co. 1976, p. 181.
21. Benedict Spinoza, *Short Treatise on God, Man, and His Well-Being*, translated by A. Wolf, Adam and Charles Black 1910, p. 148.

Friendship

1. NRSV.
2. NRSV.
3. William Shakespeare, *Timon of Athens*, act II.ii.189.
4. Thomas Fuller, *Gnomologia*, Stearne Brock 1733, p. 31.
5. Ralph Waldo Emerson, *Essays*, Bernhard Tauchnitz Edition 1915, p. 147.
6. Hugh Black, *Friendship*, Hodder and Stoughton 1897, p. 43.
7. Emerson, *Essays*, p. 156.
8. William Penn, *Reflections and Maxims, Relating to, the Conduct of Human Life*, A.W. Bennett 1863, p. 23.
9. St Francis de Sales, *Introduction to the Devout Life*, translated and edited by John K. Ryan, Longmans, Green and Co. 1962, p. 186.
10. Ladislaus Boros, *Hidden God*, translated by Erika Young, Search Press 1973, p. 62.
11. C.S. Lewis, *The Four Loves*, William Collins Sons and Co. 1981, p. 52.
12. Penn, *Reflections and Maxims, Relating to, the Conduct of Human Life*, p. 24.
13. Robert Standish, *The Big One Got Away*, Peter Davies 1960, p. 217.
14. Samuel Johnson, *The Rambler, The Yale Edition of the Works of Samuel Johnson*, edited by W.J. Bate and Albrecht B. Strauss, Yale University Press 1969, vol. III, no. 64, p. 341.

15. Vincent van Gogh, *Dear Theo: An Autobiography of Vincent van Gogh*, edited by Irving Stone, Constable and Co. 1937, p. 39.
16. Robert Louis Stevenson, *Across the Plains*, T. Nelson and Sons 1892, p. 274.
17. Mark Rutherford, *Last Pages from a Journal*, Oxford University Press 1915, p. 304.
18. Walt Whitman, 'I Dream'd in a Dream', *The Complete Poems*, edited by Francis Murphy, Penguin Books 1982, l.1, p. 164.
19. Ralph Waldo Emerson, *Essay on Friendship*, Roycrofters 1899, p. 34.
20. Aelred of Rievaux, *De spiritu amicitia* 1:45 (adapted).

Fulfilment

1. NRSV.
2. NRSV.
3. P.J. Bailey, *Festus*, William Pickering 1839, p. 51.
4. Cyril Connolly, *The Unquiet Grave*, Hamish Hamilton 1945, p. 26.
5. Rabindranath Tagore, *Stray Birds, Collected Poems and Plays of Rabindranath Tagore*, Macmillan and Co. 1936, ccciii, p. 326.
6. Thomas Merton, *No Man Is an Island*, Burns and Oates 1974, p. 20.
7. Paul Goodman, *The Community of Scholars*, Random House 1962, p. 175.
8. Henry Miller, *The Wisdom of the Heart*, New Directions Books 1941, p. 87.
9. Tagore, *Stray Birds, Collected Poems and Plays of Rabindranath Tagore*, clix, p. 307.
10. Smiley Blanton, *Love or Perish*, The World's Work (1913) 1957, p. 132.
11. Lewis Mumford, *The Conduct of Life*, Secker and Warburg 1952, p. 291.
12. Anne Morrow Lindbergh, *Bring Me a Unicorn*, A Helen and Kurt Wolff Book 1972, p. 38.
13. A.R. Orage, *On Love*, The Janus Press 1957, p. 54.
14. D.H. Lawrence, *Letter to Catherine Caswell, The Letters of D.H. Lawrence*, edited by George J. Zytaruk and James T. Boulton, Cambridge University Press 1981, vol. 2, 1913–16, 16 July 1916, p. 633.
15. Morton T. Kelsey, *The Other Side of Silence*, SPCK 1977, p. 61.
16. Rollo May, *Man's Search for Himself*, Souvenir Press 1975, p. 238.
17. Phillips Brooks, *Twenty Sermons*, Macmillan and Co. 1897, p. 216.
18. Erich Fromm, *Man For Himself*, Routledge and Kegan Paul 1975, p. 249.
19. William James, *The Varieties of Religious Experience*, William Collins Sons and Co. 1974, p. 491.
20. Robert Burns, 'Second Epistle to J. Lapraik', *The Poems and Songs of Robert Burns*, edited by James Kinsley, Oxford at the Clarendon Press 1968, vol. 1, p. 92.
21. Richard Jefferies, *The Story of My Heart*, Duckworth and Co. 1923, pp. 79 and 86.

Glory

1. NRSV.
2. NRSV.
3. Henry Ward Beecher, *Proverbs from Plymouth Pulpit*, Charles Burnet and Co. 1887, p. 141.
4. St Irenaeus, *Five Books of St Irenaeus Against Heresies*, translated by the Rev. John Keble, James Parker and Co. 1872, book IV, p. 369.
5. Thomas Merton, *The Sign of Jonas*, Sheldon Press 1976, p. 76.
6. Rufus M. Jones, *Spiritual Reformers in the 16th and 17th Centuries*, Macmillan and Co. 1914, p. 287.
7. Meister Eckhart, in Franz Pfeiffer, *Meister Eckhart*, translated by C. de B. Evans, John M. Watkins 1956, vol. 1, p. 287.
8. Henri J.M. Nouwen, *The Way of the Heart*, Darton, Longman and Todd 1981, p. 86.
9. William Barclay, *The Gospel of John*, The Saint Andrew Press 1965, vol. 2, p. 46.
10. Mark Rutherford, *Last Pages from a Journal*, Oxford University Press 1915, p. 263.
11. Benjamin Whichcote, *Moral and Religious Aphorisms*, Elkin, Mathews and Marrot 1930, iv. 321.
12. Bertrand Russell, *Authority and the Individual*, Unwin Paperbacks 1977, p. 21.
13. Anon. In Sir Walter Scott, *Old Mortality*, Oxford University Press 1912, p. 316.

14. D. Columba Marmion, *Christ the Life of the Soul*, Sands and Co. 1922, p. 24.
15. William Temple, *Christian Faith and Life*, SCM Press 1963, p. 34.
16. William Temple, *Basic Convictions*, Hamish Hamilton 1937, p. 29.
17. W.E. Sangster, *Westminster Sermons*, Epworth Press 1961, vol. 2, *At Fast and Festival*, p. 20.
18. Eric Symes Abbott, *The Compassion of God and the Passion of* Christ, Geoffrey Bles 1963, p. 92.
19. John Smith the Platonist, *Select Discourses*, Cambridge at the University Press 1859, p. 417.

God

1. NRSV.
2. NRSV.
3. Joyce Grenfell, *In Pleasant Places*, Macmillan General Books 1983, p. 161.
4. A girl of fourteen.
5. Robert Browning, 'Paracelsus V', *The Poetical Works of Robert Browning*, vol. 1, Smith, Elder, and Co. 1899, p. 61.
6. Emanuel Swedenborg, *The Divine Love and Wisdom*, J.M. Dent and Sons 1914, p. 12.
7. John of Ruysbroeck, *The Adornment of Spiritual Marriage*, translated by C.A. Wynschenk Dom, edited by Evelyn Underhill, John M. Watkins 1951, p. 173.
8. Dennis Potter, *A Lent Talk, The Other Side of the Dark*, Radio 4, March 1978, in Mary Craig, *Blessings*, Hodder and Stoughton 1979, p. 121.
9. Henry Ward Beecher, *Proverbs from Plymouth Pulpit*, Charles Burnet and Co. 1887, p. 142.
10. Izaak Walton, *The Compleat Angler*, Macmillan and Co. 1906, p. 175.
11. John S. Dunne, *The Reasons of the Heart*, SCM Press 1978, p. 24.
12. Rufus M. Jones, *Spiritual Reformers in the 16th and 17th Centuries*, Macmillan and Co. 1914, p. 315.
13. Dietrich Bonhoeffer, *Letters and Papers from Prison*, William Collins Sons and Co. 1963, p. 93.
14. Rufus M. Jones, *Spiritual Reformers in the 16th and 17th Centuries*, Macmillan and Co. 1914, p. 323.
15. Norman Pittenger, *Christology Reconsidered*, SCM Press 1970, p. 21.
16. Leo Tolstoy, *A Confession, the Gospel in Brief, and What I Believe*, translated by Aylmer Maude, Oxford University Press 1940, p. 267.
17. Charlotte Brontë, *Jane Eyre*, Oxford at the Clarendon Press 1969, p. 414.
18. F.C. Happold, *Mysticism*, Penguin Books 1981, p. 65.
19. George Macdonald, 'Without and Within', Longman, Brown, Green and Longman 1855, p. 9.
20. Matthew Arnold, *Literature and Dogma, The Complete Prose Works of Matthew Arnold*, vol. VI, *Dissent and Dogma*, edited by R.H. Super, The University of Michigan Press 1968, p. 171.
21. John Macquarrie, *Paths in Spirituality*, SCM Press 1972, p. 55.
22. F. Max Muller, *Anthropological Religion*, Longmans, Green, and Co. 1892, p. 90.

Goodness

1. NRSV.
2. NRSV.
3. Hindu proverb.
4. Charlotte Brontë, *Jane Eyre*, Oxford at the Clarendon Press 1969, p. 166.
5. Oscar Wilde, *The Picture of Dorian Gray*, Chivers Press 1979, p. 128.
6. Henry Ward Beecher, *Proverbs from Plymouth Pulpit*, Charles Burnet and Co. 1887, p. 107.
7. H.A. Overstreet, *The Enduring Quest*, Jonathan Cape 1931, p. 174.
8. *Theologia Germanica*, translated by Susanna Winkworth, Stuart and Watkins 1966, p. 48.
9. Dag Hammarskjöld, *Markings*, translated by Leif Sjoberg and W.H. Auden, Faber and Faber 1964, p. 87.
10. Walt Whitman, 'Song of the Open Road', *The Complete Poems*, edited by Francis Murphy, Penguin Books 1982, section 5, l.60, p. 181.
11. W. Somerset Maugham, *The Summing Up*, Bernhard Tauchnitz 1938, p. 242.
12. John Dryden, 'The Satires of Juvenal', *The Poems of John Dryden*, Oxford at the Clarendon Press 1958, vol. II, p. 720, 'The Tenth Satyr', l.1.

13. George Meredith, *The Ordeal of Richard Feverel*, The Times Book Club 1912, p. 210.
14. Edmund Spenser, 'The Shepherd's Calendar: May', *Spenser Poetical Works*, edited by J.C. Smith and E. de Selincourt, Oxford University Press 1943, p. 436.
15. Lady Julian of Norwich, *Revelations of Divine Love*, Penguin Books 1976, p. 67.
16. *Theologia Germanica*, translated by Susanna Winkworth, Stuart and Watkins 1966, p. 84.
17. John Milton, 'Paradise Lost', *The Poetical Works of John Milton*, edited by the Rev. H.C. Beeching, Oxford at the Clarendon Press 1900, Book V, l.71, p. 274.
18. Albert Schweitzer, *Out of My Life and Thought*, Henry Holt and Co. 1949, p. 92.
19. Beecher, *Proverbs from Plymouth Pulpit*, p. 154.
20. William James, *The Will to Believe*, Longmans, Green and Co. 1904, p. 209.
21. George Eliot, *Middlemarch*, edited by W.J. Harvey, Penguin Books 1985, p. 427.
22. Beecher, *Proverbs from Plymouth Pulpit*, p. 96.
23. Leo Tolstoy, *Anna Karenina*, translated by Rosemary Edmonds, Penguin Books 1983, p. 853.
24. Mark Rutherford, *Last Pages from a Journal*, Oxford University Press 1915, p. 319.
25. Rufus M. Jones, *Spiritual Reformers in the 16th and 17th Centuries*, Macmillan and Co. 1914, p. 308.

Grace

1. NRSV.
2. NRSV.
3. Anthony Bloom, *The Essence of Prayer*, Darton, Longman and Todd 1989, p. 25.
4. C.S. Lewis, *Williams and the Arthuriad*, Oxford University Press 1948, p. 156.
5. Brother Lawrence, *The Practice of the Presence of God*, introduction by Dorothy Day, Burns and Oates 1977, p. 51.
6. Henry Ward Beecher, *Proverbs from Plymouth Pulpit*, Charles Burnet and Co. 1887, p. 176.
7. John Milton, 'Paradise Lost', *The Poetical Works of John Milton*, edited by H.C. Beeching, Oxford at the Clarendon Press 1900, viii.488.
8. Rufus M. Jones, *Spiritual Reformers in the 16th and 17th Centuries*, Macmillan and Co. 1914, p. 154.
9. John Osborne, *Luther*, Faber and Faber 1961, II.ii., p. 56.
10. Joachim Jeremias, *New Testament Theology*, SCM Press 1971, vol. 1, p. 178.
11. Blaise Pascal, *Pensées*, translated by W.F. Trotter, Random House 1941, p. 145.
12. Daniel D. Williams, in James F. Childress and John Macquarrie, *A New Dictionary of Christian Ethics*, SCM Press 1986, p. 139.
13. William Temple, *Readings in St John's Gosepl*, First and Second Series, Macmillan and Co. 1957, p. 29.
14. William Temple, *Nature, Man and God*, Macmillan and Co. 1934, p. 485.
15. Thomas à Kempis, *The Imitation of Christ*, translated by Betty I. Knott, William Collins Sons and Co. 1979, p. 175.
16. Richard of Saint-Victor, *Selected Writings on Contemplation*, translated by Clare Kirchberger, Faber and Faber 1957, p. 111.
17. A.C. Benson, *Extracts from the Letters of Dr A.C. Benson to M.E.A.*, Jarrold Publishing 1927, p. 60.
18. Richard of Saint-Victor, *Selected Writings on Contemplation*, p. 205.
19. Paul Tillich, *The Shaking of the Foundations*, Penguin Books 1962, p. 163.
20. Williams, in Childress and Macquarrie, *A New Dictionary of Christian Ethics*, p. 254.
21. Thomas à Kempis, *The Imitation of Christ*, p. 202.
22. Walter Hilton, *The Ladder of Perfection*, translated by Leo Sherley-Price, Penguin Books 1957, p. 146.
23. C.S. Lewis, *Letters of C.S. Lewis*, edited by W.H. Lewis, Geoffrey Bles 1966, p. 250.
24. John Macquarrie, *The Humility of God*, SCM Press 1978, p. 9.

Greatness

1. NRSV.
2. NRSV.
3. Thomas Fuller, *Gnomologia*, Dublin 1732, No. 1759, p. 67.
4. Henri Frédéric Amiel, *Amiel's Journal*, translated by Mrs Humphry Ward, Macmillan and Co. 1918, p. 137.
5. Seneca, *Epistulae Morales*, Richard M. Gummere, William Heinemann, vol. II, p. 285.
6. Edmund Burke, *Speeches and Letters on American Affairs*, J.M. Dent and Sons 1961, p. 51.
7. Dr Harvey Cushing, in *Dialogues of Alfred North Whitehead*, recorded by Lucien Price, Max Reinhardt 1954, p. 47.
8. Theodor Haecker, *Journal in the Night*, translated by Alexander Dru, Harvill Press 1950, p. 37.
9. William Barclay, *The Gospel of Matthew*, The Saint Andrew Press 1987, vol. 1, p. 278.
10. Barclay, *The Gospel of Matthew*, vol. 1, p. 111.
11. Thomas Carlyle, *Sartor Resartus*, Chapman and Hall 1840, 'Lectures on Heroes', p. 206.
12. William Shakespeare, *Twelfth Night*, act II.v.48.
13. G.K. Chesterton, *Charles Dickens*, Methuen and Co. 1906, p. 8.
14. Barclay, *The Gospel of Matthew*, vol. 1, p. 279.
15. J.R. Lowell, 'Sonnet No. 6', *The Poetical Works of James Russell Lowell*, Ward, Lock and Co. 1911, p. 110.
16. Carlyle, *Sartor Resartus*, p. 127.
17. Phillips Brooks, *Sermons*, Richard D. Dickinson 1879, p. 14.
18. E.B. Browning, 'Rhyme of the Duchess May', *Elizabeth Barrett Browning's Poetical Works*, Smith, Elder, and Co. 1875, vol. 2, st. xi, p. 82.
19. Matthew Arnold, *Sweetness and Light*, *The Complete Prose Works of Matthew Arnold*, vol. V, *Culture and Anarchy*, edited by R.H. Super, Ann Arbor, The University of Michigan Press 1965, p. 96.
20. Henry Ward Beecher, *Proverbs from Plymouth Pulpit*, Charles Burnet and Co. 1887, p. 16.
21. Henri Frédéric Amiel, *Amiel's Journal*, translated by Mrs Humphry Ward, Macmillan and Co. 1918, p. 112.
22. Carlyle, 'Lectures on Heroes', p. 185.
23. Henry Wadsworth Longfellow, 'The Ladder of St Augustine', *The Poetical Works of Longfellow*, Humphrey Milford, Oxford University Press 1858, st.x, l.1, p. 299.

Grief

1. NRSV.
2. NRSV.
3. William Cowper, 'Charity', *The Poetical Works of Cowper*, edited by H.S. Milford, Oxford University Press 1950, p. 79.
4. Adelaide Anne Proctor, *Life in Death and Death in Life,* The Complete Works of Adelaide Anne Proctor, George Bell and Sons 1905, p. 169.
5. William Shakespeare, *King Henry VI*, part III, act II.i.85.
6. English proverb.
7. Benjamin Disraeli, *Endymion*, Longmans, Green, and Co. 1880, p. 42.
8. William Morris, 'Prologue, The Wanderers', *The Earthly Paradise*, vol. 1, Reeves and Turner 1896, p. 5.
9. Confucius, *The Analects of Confucius*, translated by William Edward Soothill, edited by Lady Hosie, Oxford University Press 1937, p. 213.
10. J. Neville Ward, *Friday Afternoon*, Epworth Press 1982, p. 101.
11. Norman Douglas, *An Almanac*, Chatto and Windus in association with Martin Secker and Warburg 1945, p. 11.
12. C.S. Lewis, *A Grief Observed*, Faber and Faber 1961, p. 44.
13. Ward, *Friday Afternoon*, p. 97.
14. Henri Frédéric Amiel, *Amiel's Journal*, translated by Mrs Humphry Ward, Macmillan and Co. 1918, p. 192.

15. Chinese proverb.
16. Maurice Maeterlinck, *Wisdom and Destiny*, translated by Alfred Sutro, George Allen and Sons 1898, p. 113.
17. Henry Ward Beecher, *Proverbs from Plymouth Pulpit*, Charles Burnet and Co. 1887, p. 202.
18. A.C. Benson, *Extracts from the Letters of Dr A.C. Benson to M.E.A.*, Jarrold Publishing 1927, p. 19.
19. Erich Fromm, *Man for Himself*, Routledge and Kegan Paul 1975, p. 190.
20. Benson, *Extracts from the Letters of Dr A.C. Benson to M.E.A.*, p. 18.
21. Robert Southey, *Joan of Arc and Minor Poems*, George Routledge and Co. 1854, p. 9.
22. Beecher, *Proverbs from Plymouth Pulpit*, p. 209.
23. Mary Craig, *Blessings*, Hodder and Stoughton 1979, p. 63.
24. Lord Byron, *Manfred, The Complete Poetical Works*, edited by Jerome J.McGann, Clarendon Press 1986, vol. IV, act 1. sc.i. l.9, p. 53.
25. Johann Wilhelm von Goethe, *To Eckerman, The Practical Wisdom of Goethe*, chosen by Emil Ludwig, George Allen and Unwin Publishers 1933, p. 75.
26. Father Andrew SDC, *A Gift of Light*, selected and edited by Harry C. Griffith, Mowbray 1968, p. 31.

Growing

1. NRSV.
2. NRSV.
3. Anon.
4. Robert Browning, 'Cleon', *The Poetical Works of Robert Browning*, Smith, Elder and Co. 1899, vol. 1, *Men and Women*, l.114, p. 543.
5. Dag Hammarksjöld, *Markings*, translated by Leif Sjoberg and W.H. Auden, Faber and Faber 1964, p. 89.
6. Oscar Wilde, *The Picture of Dorian Gray*, Chivers Press 1979, p. 122.
7. Henry Ward Beecher, *Proverbs from Plymouth Pulpit*, Charles Burnet and Co. 1887, p. 8.
8. George Macdonald, 'Within and Without', Longman, Brown, Green, and Longman 1855, p. 16.
9. Michel Quoist, *With Open Heart*, translated by Colette Copeland, Gill and Macmillan 1983, p. 202.
10. Beecher, *Proverbs from Plymouth Pulpit*, p. 180.
11. Martin Luther King, in Coretta Scott King, *The Words of Martin Luther King*, William Collins Sons and Co. 1986, p. 30.
12. Oscar Wilde, *De Profundis, The Works of Oscar Wilde*, edited by G.F. Maine, William Collins Sons and Co. 1948, p. 860.
13. Mark Rutherford, *Last Pages from a Journal*, Oxford University Press 1915, p. 280.
14. Quoist, *With Open Heart*, p. 133.
15. Aldous Huxley, *Music at Night*, Chatto and Windus 1970, p. 332.
16. Rutherford, *Last Pages from a Journal*, p. 256.
17. Harry Emerson Fosdick, *Successful Christian Living*, SCM Press 1938, p. 16.
18. Jean Vanier, *Community and Growth*, Darton, Longman and Todd 1991, p. 105.
19. Rainer Maria Rilke, *Letters to a Young Poet*, translation and commentary by Reginald Snell, Sidgwick and Jackson 1945, p. 13.
20. Vanier, *Community and Growth*, p. 133.

Guidance

1. NRSV.
2. NRSV.
3. Rabindranath Tagore, *Stray Birds, Collected Poems and Plays of Rabindranath Tagore*, Macmillan and Co. 1936, cxlii, p. 305.
4. Basil Hume OSB, *Searching for God*, Hodder and Stoughton 1977, p. 54.
5. William Shakespeare, *King Henry VI*, part II, act II.iii.24.
6. Henry Ward Beecher, *Proverbs from Plymouth Pulpit*, Charles Burnet and Co. 1887, p. 154.

7. W.E. Sangster, *God Does Guide Us*, Hodder and Stoughton 1934, p. 144.
8. Samuel Johnson, Motto for *The Rambler*, *The Yale Edition of the Works of Samuel Johnson*, vol. III, edited by W.J. Bate and Albrecht B. Strauss, Yale University Press 1969, p. 36.
9. A.C. Benson, *Extracts from the Letters of Dr A.C. Benson to M.E.A*, Jarrold Publishing 1927, p. 7.
10. Grace Cooke, *Spiritual Unfoldment*, The White Eagle Publishing Trust 1961, p. 13.
11. Sangster, *God Does Guide Us*, p. 190.
12. John Milton, 'Paradise Lost', *The Works of John Milton*, Columbia University Press 1931, vol. 2, part 1, iii 194, p. 84.
13. William Barclay, *The Letter to the Romans*, The Saint Andrew Press 1969, p. 117.
14. John Burnaby, in A.R. Vidler, *Soundings*, Cambridge at the University Press 1962, p. 235.
15. William Blake, *Epigrams, Verses, and Fragments for the Note Book*, *The Complete Writings of William Blake*, edited by Geoffrey Keynes, Oxford University Press 1974, p. 551.
16. William Temple, *Christian Faith and Life*, SCM Press 1963, p. 57.
17. Gerhard Tersteegen, in Francis Bevan, *Sketches of the Great in the Land*, John F. Shaw and Co. 1891, p. 390.
18. George Appleton, *Journey for a Soul*, William Collins Sons and Co. 1976, p. 207.
19. Herbert Butterfield, *Christianity and History*, George Bell and Sons 1949, p. 145.

Happiness

1. NRSV.
2. NEB.
3. Robert Louis Stevenson, *Virginibus Puerisque*, Chatto and Windus 1906, p. 80.
4. A.R. Orage, *On Love*, The Janus Press 1957, p. 61.
5. Henrik Ibsen, *Rosmersholm*, translated and edited by James Walter McFarlane, Oxford University Press 1960, vol. VI, act III, p. 349.
6. Blaise Pascal, *Pensées*, translated by W.F. Trotter, Random House 1941, p. 154.
7. Samuel Johnson, *The History of Rasselas*, Oxford University Press 1971, p. 48.
8. Robert Louis Stevenson, *Memories and Portraits*, Chatto and Windus 1887, p. 48.
9. Marcus Aurelius, *The Meditations of Marcus Aurelius*, translated by Jeremy Collier, Walter Scott, p. 116.
10. W.R. Inge, in Sir James Marchant, *The Wit and Wisdom of Dean Inge*, Longmans, Green and Co. 1927, p. 55.
11. Gordon S. Wakefield, in *A Dictionary of Christian Spirituality*, SCM Press 1986, p. 68.
12. Henry Ward Beecher, *Proverbs from Plymouth Pulpit*, Charles Burnet and Co. 1887, p. 186.
13. Johann Wolfgang von Goethe, *Wisdom and Experience*, selections by Ludwig Curtius, translated and edited by Hermann J. Weigand, Routledge and Kegan Paul 1949, p. 213.
14. Arthur Helps, *Companions of My Solitude*, George Routledge and Sons 1907, p. 20.
15. Marcus Aurelius, *The Meditations of Marcus Aurelius*, p. 42.
16. Samuel Johnson, *The Rambler*, *The Yale Edition of the Works of Samuel Johnson*, edited by W.J. Bate and Albrecht B. Strauss, Yale University Press 1969, vol. III, p. 225.
17. Thomas Merton, *Elected Silence*, Hollis and Carter 1949, p. 332.
18. Henry Ward Beecher, *Proverbs from Plymouth Pulpit*, Charles Burnet and Co. 1887, p. 22.
19. Alexander Solzhenitsyn, *Cancer Ward*, translated by Nicholas Bethell and David Burg, Penguin Books 1972, p. 290.
20. J.B. Yeats, *Letters to His Son, W.B. Yeats and Others*, Faber and Faber 1944, p. 121.
21. William James, *The Varieties of Religious Experience*, William Collins Sons and Co. 1974, p. 92.
22. Henri Frédéric Amiel, *Amiel's Journal*, translated by Mrs Humphry Ward, Macmillan and Co. 1918, p. 239.
23. Anne Frank, *The Diary of Anne Frank*, Pan Books 1954, p. 137.

Healing

1. NRSV.
2. NRSV.
3. GP in Birmingham, in *Faith in the City*, Church House Publishing 1985, p. 265.
4. William Shakespeare, *Cymboline* act II.ii.11.
5. Henry Ward Beecher, *Proverbs from Plymouth Pulpit*, Charles Burnet and Co. 1887, p. 137.
6. Nathaniel Hawthorne, *The Scarlet Letter*, The Gresham Publishing Co. 1900, p. 90.
7. William Barclay, *The Gospel of Matthew*, The Saint Andrew Press 1987, vol. 1, p. 328.
8. Michel Quoist, *With Open Heart*, translated by Colette Copeland, Gill and Macmillan 1983, p. 66.
9. Beecher, *Proverbs from Plymouth Pulpit*, p. 153.
10. William James, *Essays on Faith and Morals*, Longmans, Green and Co. 1943, p. 235.
11. Beecher, *Proverbs from Plymouth Pulpit*, p. 138.
12. Izaak Walton, *The Compleat Angler*, The Nonesuch Press 1929, p. 193.
13. Francis MacNutt, *Healing*, Ave Maria Press 1977, p. 164.
14. William Temple, *The Preacher's Theme Today*, SPCK 1936, p. 53.
15. D.H.Lawrence, 'Healing', *The Complete Poems of D.H. Lawrence*, edited by Vivian de Sola Pinto and Warren Roberts, William Heinemann 1967, p. 620.
16. George Appleton, *Journey for a Soul*, William Collins Sons and Co. 1976, p. 185.
17. Jean Vanier, *The Broken Body*, Darton, Longman and Todd 1988, p. 135.

Holiness

1. NRSV.
2. NRSV.
3. Thomas Fuller, *Gnomologia*, 1732 Dublin, no. 4924, p. 214.
4. Father Andrew SDC, *The Way of Victory*, A.R. Mowbray and Co. 1938, p. 12.
5. Henry Wadsworth Longfellow, 'Hyperion', George Routledge and Sons 1887, p. 215.
6. Rufus M. Jones, *Spiritual Reformers in the 16th and 17th Centuries*, Macmillan and Co. 1914, p. 148.
7. Jonathan Edwards, *A Treatise Concerning Religious Affections*, Chalmers and Collins 1825, p. 323.
8. Thomas Traherne, *Centuries*, The Faith Press 1969, p. 39.
9. Hugh Montefiore, *Sermons from Great St Mary's*, William Collins Sons and Co. 1968, p. 16.
10. Mother Teresa, in Brother Angelo Devananda, *Jesus, the Word to be Spoken*, William Collins Sons and Co. 1990, p. 49.
11. George Herbert, 'Lent', *The Works of George Herbert*, edited by F.E. Hutchinson, Oxford at the Clarendon Press 1953, p. 87.
12. Henry Ward Beecher, *Proverbs from Plymouth Pulpit*, Charles Burnet and Co. 1887, p. 171.
13. Benjamin Whichcote, *Moral and Religious Aphorisms*, century iii, no. 262, Elkin Mathews and Marrot 1930, p. 32.
14. W.E. Sangster, *The Pure in Heart*, Epworth Press 1954, p. 28.
15. John of Ruysbroeck, *The Seven Steps of the Ladder of Spiritual Love*, translated by F. Sherwood Taylor, Dacre Press 1942, p. 15.
16. Hugh Montefiore, *Confirmation Notebook*, Fifth Edition, SPCK 1985, p. 39.
17. Jonathan Edwards, *A Treatise Concerning Religious Affections*, Chalmers and Collins 1825, p. 349.
18. Fyodor Dostoyevsky, *The Brothers Karamazov*, translated by David Magarshack, Penguin Books 1962, vol. 1, p. 32.
19. W.R. Inge, *Speculum Animae*, Longmans, Green and Co. 1911, p. 50.
20. Henri Frédéric Amiel, *Amiel's Journal*, translated by Mrs Humphry Ward, Macmillan and Co. 1918, p. 155.

Holy Spirit

1. NRSV.
2. NRSV.
3. William Barclay, *The Gospel of John*, The Saint Andrew Press 1965, vol. 2, p. 195.
4. Nicolas Berdyaev, *Christian Existentialism*, selected and translated by Donald A. Lowrie, George Allen and Unwin 1965, p. 39.
5. Henry Ward Beecher, *Proverbs from Plymouth Pulpit*, Charles Burnet and Co. 1887, p. 152.
6. Rufus M. Jones, *Spiritual Reformers in the 16th and 17th Centuries*, Macmillan and Co. 1914, p. 139.
7. Evelyn Underhill, in John Stobbart, *The Wisdom of Evelyn Underhill*, A.R. Mowbray and Co. 1951, p. 8.
8. Norman Goodall, *The Local Church*, Hodder and Stoughton 1966, p. 33.
9. C.C.J. Webb, *Religious Experience*, Oxford University Press 1945, p. 35.
10. Jones, *Spiritual Reformers in the 16th and 17th Centuries*, p. 43.
11. Robert Bridges, *The Spirit of Man*, Longmans, Green and Co. 1973, p. 1.
12. William Temple, *Nature, Man and God*, Macmillan and Co. 1934, p. 446.
13. John Macquarrie, *Paths in Spirituality*, second edition, SCM Press 1992, p. 42.
14. Carroll E. Simcox, *Living the Creed*, Dacre Press: A. and C. Black 1954, p. 116.
15. John V. Taylor, in Gerald Priestland, *Priestland's Progress*, BBC Worldwide 1982, p. 108.
16. Jacob Boehme, *The Aurora*, translated by John Sparrow, John M. Watkins 1914, p. 72.
17. Jones, *Spiritual Reformers in the 16th and 17th Centuries*, p. 217.
18. Lilian Whiting, *Lilies of Eternal Peace*, Gay and Hancock 1908, p. 26.

Hope

1. NRSV.
2. NRSV.
3. William Shakespeare, *The Merry Wives of Windsor*, act II.i.58.
4. Miguel de Unamuno, *The Tragic Sense of Life in Men and in Peoples*, Macmillan and Co. 1921, p. 203.
5. Carlo Carretto, *Summoned by Love*, translated by Alan Neame, Darton, Longman and Todd 1977, p. 116.
6. Samuel Johnson, *Boswell's Life of Johnson*, edited by G.B. Hill, revised by L.F. Powell, Oxford at the Clarendon Press 1934, vol. 1, p. 368.
7. H. Rider Haggard, *She*, William Collins Sons and Co. 1957, p. 199.
8. Carlo Carretto, *The Desert in the City*, translated by Barbara Wall, William Collins Sons and Co. 1983, p. 90.
9. Percy Bysshe Shelley, 'Prometheus Unbound', *The Poetical Works of Percy Bysshe Shelley*, edited by H. Buxton Forman, George Bell and Sons 1892, vol. III, act IV, l.573, p. 257.
10. William Hazlitt, *Characteristics*, *The Collected Works of William Hazlitt*, J.M. Dent and Co. 1902, vol. II, XXXIV, p. 359.
11. Simone Weil, *Gateway to God*, edited by David Raper, with the collaboration of Malcolm Muggeridge and Vernon Sproxton, William Collins Sons and Co. 1974, p. 131.
12. Jürgen Moltmann, *The Open Church*, SCM Press 1978, p. 35.
13. Alexander Pope, 'An Essay on Man', introduction by Henry Morley, Cassell and Co. 1905, epistle 1, p. 18.
14. Hubert van Zeller, *Considerations*, Sheed and Ward 1974, p. 100.
15. William Temple, *Christian Faith and Life*, SCM Press 1963, p. 44.
16. W.R. Inge, *Personal Religion and the Life of Devotion*, Longmans, Green and Co. 1924, p. 54.
17. Hans Küng, *On Being a Christian*, translated by Edward Quinn, William Collins Sons and Co. 1977, p. 311.
18. Walt Whitman, *The Early Poems and the Fiction*, *The Collected Writings of Walt Whitman*, edited by Thomas L. Brasher, New York University Press, Franklin Evans 1963, vol. VI, p. 148.
19. Charles Dickens, *Nicholas Nickleby*, The Gresham Publishing Co. 1904, p. 528.

20. Evelyn Underhill, in John Stobbart, *The Wisdom of Evelyn Underhill*, A.R. Mowbray and Co. 1951, p. 21.
21. Paul Tillich, *The Shaking of the Foundations*, SCM Press 1949, p. 59.
22. Richard Jefferies, *The Pageant of Summer*, Chatto and Windus 1911, p. 10.

Humility

1. NRSV.
2. NRSV.
3. Henri Frédéric Amiel, *Amiel's Journal*, translated by Mrs Humphry Ward, Macmillan and Co. 1918, p. 46.
4. Thomas à Kempis, *The Imitation of Christ*, translated by Betty I. Knott, William Collins Sons and Co. 1979, p. 150.
5. Henry David Thoreau, *Walden*, The New American Library of World Literature 1960, p. 218.
6. William Penn, *Fruits of Solitude*, A.W. Bennett 1863, p. 92.
7. Charlotte Brontë, *Jane Eyre*, Clarendon Press 1969, p. 514.
8. George Bernard Shaw, *The Complete Bernard Shaw Prefaces*, Paul Hamlyn 1965, *St Joan*, p. 622.
9. Johann Wolfgang von Goethe, *Wisdom and Experience*, selected by Ludwig Curtius, translated and edited by Hermann J. Weigand, Routledge and Kegan Paul 1949, p. 189.
10. Iris Murdoch, *The Sovereignty of Good Over Other Concepts*, Routledge and Kegan Paul 1970, p. 103.
11. *The Cloud of Unknowing*, translated by Clifton Wolters, Penguin Books 1971, p. 70.
12. Amiel, *Amiel's Journal*, p. 1.
13. John Bunyan, *The Pilgrim's Progress*, J.M. Dent and Sons 1964, p. 237.
14. Blaise Pascal, *Pensées*, translated by W.F. Trotter, Random House 1941, p. 169.
15. Alfred, Lord Tennyson, 'The Holy Grail', *The Poems of Tennyson*, edited by Christopher Ricks, Longmans, Green and Co. 1969, no. 471, l.445, p. 1674.
16. Izaak Walton, *The Compleat Angler*, Macmillan and Co. 1906, p. 37.
17. Meister Eckhart, in Franz Pfeiffer, *Meister Eckhart*, translated by C. de B. Evans, John M. Watkins 1956, vol. 1, p. 158.
18. Mark Rutherford, *Last Pages from a Journal*, Oxford University Press 1915, p. 301.
19. Henry Ward Beecher, *Proverbs from Plymouth Pulpit*, Charles Burnet and Co. 1887, p. 175.
20. Alfred, Lord Tennyson, 'The Holy Grail', p. 420.
21. Ralph Waldo Emerson, *Spiritual Laws*, *The Works of Ralph Waldo Emerson*, George Bell and Sons 1906, vol.1, *Essays and Representative Men*, p. 87.
22. Oscar Wilde, *De Profundis*, *The Works of Oscar Wilde*, William Collins Sons and Co. 1948, p. 858.
23. William Law, *A Serious Call to a Devout and Holy Life*, J.M. Dent and Sons 1898, p. 245.
24. Al-Ansari, 'The Invocations of Sheikh Abdullah Ansari of Herat', *The Persian Mystics*, translated by Sardar Sir Jogendra Sing, John Murray 1939, p. 39.
25. John Ruskin, *Modern Painters*, George Allen and Sons 1910, vol. III, p. 276.

Ideals

1. NRSV.
2. NRSV.
3. Joseph Conrad, *Chance*, J.M. Dent and Sons 1949, p. 262.
4. George Moore, *Evelyn Innes*, Bernhard Tauchnitz 1898, vol. II, p. 103.
5. G.K. Chesterton, *What's Wrong with the World*, Bernhard Tauchnitz 1910, p. 43.
6. Thomas Carlyle, *Sartor Resartus*, Ward, Lock and Co., p. 131.
7. Yevgeny Yevtushenko, *A Precocious Autobiography*, translated by Andrew H. MacAndrew, Collins and Harvill Press 1963, p. 39.
8. Henry Ward Beecher, *Proverbs from Plymouth Pulpit*, Charles Burnet and Co. 1887, p. 54.
9. William James, *The Varieties of Religious Experience*, William Collins Sons and Co. 1974, p. 258.
10. Beecher, *Proverbs from Plymouth Pulpit*, p. 22.

11. Henry David Thoreau, *Walden*, The New American Library of World Literature, 1960, p. 215.
12. Beecher, *Proverbs from Plymouth Pulpit*, p. 127.
13. L. Falconer, in M.G. Ostle, *The Note Books of a Woman Alone*, J.M. Dent and Sons 1935, p. 228.
14. Beecher, *Proverbs from Plymouth Pulpit*, p. 23.
15. John Oman, *The Natural and the Supernatural*, Cambridge at the University Press 1931, p. 329.
16. Henri Frédéric Amiel, *Amiel's Journal*, translated by Mrs Humphry Ward, Macmillan and Co. 1918, p. 105.
17. Mother Teresa, in Brother Angelo Devananda, *Jesus, the Word to be Spoken*, William Collins Sons and Co. 1990, p. 42.
18. Harry James Cargas, *Encountering Myself*, SPCK 1978, p. 54.
19. Albert Schweitzer, *The Philosophy of Civilization*, Part II, *Civilization and Ethics*, translated by C.T. Campion, A. and C. Black, third English edition, revised by Mrs C.E.B. Russell 1946, p. xvii.
20. Albert Einstein, *Ideas and Opinions*, Souvenir Press (Educational and Academic) 1973, p. 9.
21. Sir Sarvepalli Radhakrishnan, *Eastern Religions and Western Thought*, Oxford University Press 1940, p. 25.

Image Of God

1. NRSV.
2. NRSV.
3. Meister Eckhart, in Franz Pfeiffer, *Meister Eckhart*, vol. 1, translated by C. de B. Evans, John M. Watkins 1956, p. 436.
4. Thomas Traherne, *Centuries*, The Faith Press 1969, p. 9.
5. C.G. Jung, *Aion, The Collected Works of C.G. Jung*, translated by R.F.C. Hull, Routledge and Kegan Paul 1959, vol. 9, part 2, p. 39.
6. Father Andrew SDC, *Meditations for Every Day*, A.R. Mowbray and Co. 1941, p. 352.
7. Sister Elizabeth of the Trinity, *Spiritual Writings*, Geoffrey Chapman 1962, p. 147.
8. George Eliot, *Mill on the Floss*, Virtue and Co. 1908, vol. 2, p. 58.
9. Rufus M. Jones, *Spiritual Reformers in the 16th and 17th Centuries*, Macmillan and Co. 1914, p. xxx.
10. Charles Kingsley, *Daily Thoughts*, Macmillan and Co. 1884, p. 229.
11. William Law, *The Spirit of Love*, edited by Sidney Spencer, James Clarke and Co. 1969, p. 207.
12. John Pulsford, *Quiet Hours*, James Nisbet and Co. 1857, p. 75.
13. Meister Eckhart, *Meister Eckhart*, translated by Raymond B. Blakney, Harper and Row 1941, p. 209.
14. Johann Arndt, *True Christianity*, translated by Peter Erb, SPCK 1979, p. 29.
15. Basil Hume OSB, *To Be a Pilgrim*, St Paul Publications 1984, p. 66.
16. F.W. Faber, *Spiritual Writings*, Thomas Richardson and Son 1859, p. 2.

Imagination

1. NRSV.
2. NRSV.
3. Joseph Joubert, *Pensées and Letters*, George Routledge and Sons 1928, p. 48.
4. Laurens van der Post, *Venture to the Interior*, Penguin Books 1968, p. 26.
5. Percy Bysshe Shelley, *A Defence of Poetry, The Prose Works of Percy Bysshe Shelley*, edited by H. Buxton Forman, Reeves and Turner 1880, vol. III, p. 111.
6. Henry Ward Beecher, *Proverbs from Plymouth Pulpit*, Charles Burnet and Co. 1887, p. 183.
7. Ralph Waldo Emerson, *The Conduct of Life, Nature, and Other Essays*, J.M. Dent and Sons, 1911, p. 298.
8. Henry David Thoreau, *The Journal of Henry D. Thoreau*, edited by Bradford Torrey and Francis H. Allen, Houghton Mifflin Co., Boston, The Riverside Press 1949, vol. II, p. 413.
9. W. Somerset Maugham, *The Summing Up*, Bernhard Tauchnitz 1938, p. 131.
10. J.B. Yeats, *Letters to His Son, W.B. Yeats and Others*, Faber and Faber 1944, p. 87.
11. Thomas Traherne, *Centuries*, The Faith Press 1969, p. 90.

12. Joseph Conrad, *A Personal Record*, J.M. Dent and Sons 1923, p. 25.
13. Katherine Mansfield, in Antony Alpers, *Katherine Mansfield*, Jonathan Cape 1954, p. 296.
14. Beecher, *Proverbs from Plymouth Pulpit*, p. 25.
15. Henry Miller, *The Books in My Life*, Village Press 1974, p. 84.
16. Virginia Woolf, *A Writer's Diary*, edited by Leonard Woolf, The Hogarth Press 1953, p. 67.
17. Max Planck, in F.C. Happold, *Religious Faith and Twentieth-Century Man*, Darton, Longman and Todd 1980, p. 41.
18. Oscar Wilde, *De Profundis*, *The Works of Oscar Wilde*, edited by G.F. Maine, William Collins Sons and Co. 1948, p. 867.
19. John Cowper Powys, *Autobiography*, Macdonald and Co. 1967, p. 436.
20. F.W. Robertson, *Sermons*, Kegan Paul, Trench, Trubner and Co. 1907, First Series, p. 8.
21. W. MacNeile Dixon, *The Human Situation*, Edward Arnold and Co. 1937, p. 65.
22. Henry Ward Beecher, *Royal Truths*, Alexander Strahan and Co. 1862, p. 47.

Incarnation

1. NRSV.
2. NRSV.
3. Pierre Teilhard de Chardin, *Le Milieu Divin*, William Collins Sons and Co. 1960, p. 38.
4. C.S. Lewis, *Mere Christianity*, William Collins Sons and Co. 1961, p. 179.
5. Ugo Betti, *The Burnt Flower-Bed*, Three Plays by Ugo Betti, translated by Henry Read, Victor Gollancz 1956, act II, p. 151.
6. St Irenaeus, *Five Books of St Irenaeus*, translated by the Rev. John Keble, James Parker and Co. 1872, p. 449.
7. St Leo, in F.C. Happold, *Religious Faith and Twentieth-Century Man*, Darton, Longman and Todd 1980, p. 145.
8. Evelyn Underhill, *The Letters of Evelyn Underhill*, edited by Charles Williams, Longmans, Green and Co. 1947, p. 259.
9. Michel Quoist, *With Open Heart*, translated by Colette Copeland, Gill and Macmillan 1983, p. 147.
10. Alan Watts, *Behold the Spirit*, John Murray 1947, p. 244.
11. St Augustine, *City of God*, translated by Henry Bettenson, edited by David Knowles, Penguin Books 1972, p. 431.
12. Kenneth Leech, *True Prayer*, Sheldon Press 1980, p. 13.
13. C.B. Moss, *The Christian Faith*, SPCK 1944, p. 115.
14. Thomas Merton, *Elected Silence*, Hollis and Carter 1949, p. 332.
15. Rufus M. Jones, *Spiritual Reformers in the 16th and 17th Centuries*, Macmillan and Co. 1914, p. 310.
16. A.S. Pringle-Pattison, *The Idea of God*, Oxford University Press 1920, p. 157.
17. George Appleton, *Journey for a Soul*, William Collins Sons and Co. 1976, p. 135.
18. W.R. Inge, *Speculum Animae*, Longmans, Green and Co. 1911, p. 19.
19. Appleton, *Journey for a Soul*, p. 138.

Influence

1. NRSV.
2. NRSV.
3. André Gide, *The Journals of André Gide*, translated by Justin O'Brien, Secker and Warburg 1947, p. 42.
4. Forbes Robinson, *Letters to His Friends*, Spottiswoode and Co. 1904, p. 165.
5. Henry Ward Beecher, *Proverbs from Plymouth Pulpit*, Charles Burnet and Co. 1887, p. 153.
6. George Eliot, *Scenes of Clerical Life, Janet's Repentance*, Oxford University Press 1909, p. 369.
7. Henry Adams, *The Education of Henry Adams*, Constable and Co. 1919, p. 300.
8. Meister Eckhart, *Meister Eckhart*, translated by Raymond B. Blakney, Harper and Row 1941, p. 121.

9. Beecher, *Proverbs from Plymouth Pulpit*, p. 161.
10. William Shakespeare *II King Henry IV*, act V.ii.76.
11. George Seaver (said of Edward Wilson) in *Edward Wilson of the Antarctic*, John Murray 1935, p. 104.
12. Beecher, *Proverbs from Plymouth Pulpit*, p. 153.
13. Henri J.M. Nouwen, *Reaching Out*, William Collins Sons and Co. 1980, p. 59.
14. Charles Kingsley, *Daily Thoughts*, Macmillan and Co. 1884, p. 37.
15. Benjamin Disraeli, *Coningsby*, Peter Davies 1927, p. 129.
16. Hans Küng, *On Being a Christian*, translated by Edward Quinn, William Collins Sons and Co. 1977, p. 63.
17. Charles Kingsley, *Daily Thoughts*, Macmillan and Co. 1884, p. 71.
18. Thomas Merton, *Elected Silence*, Hollis and Carter 1949, p. 371.
19. Anon.
20. Anon.

Inner Life

1. NRSV.
2. NRSV.
3. Henri Frédéric Amiel, *Amiel's Journal*, translated by Mrs Humphry Ward, Macmillan and Co. 1918, p. 114.
4. A.C. Benson, *Extracts from the Letteers of Dr A.C. Benson to M.E.A.*, Jarrold Publishing 1927, p. 67.
5. Amiel, *Amiel's Journal*, p. 114.
6. Rufus M. Jones, *Spiritual Reformers in the 16th and 17th Centuries*, Macmillan and Co. 1914, p. 85.
7. D.H. Lawrence, *The Letters of D.H. Lawrence*, edited by George T. Zytaruk and James T. Boulton, Cambridge University Press, vol. II, 1981, p. 280.
8. Dag Hammarskjöld, *Markings*, translated by Leif Sjoberg and W.H. Auden, Faber and Faber 1964, p. 64.
9. Jones, *Spiritual Reformers in the 16th and 17th Centuries*, p. 97.
10. Norman Douglas, *An Almanac*, Chatto and Windus in association with Martin Secker and Warburg, 1945, p. 59.
11. Henry Drummond, *The Greatest Thing in the World*, William Collins Sons and Co. 1978, p. 169.
12. Christopher Bryant SSJE, *Jung and the Christian Way*, Darton, Longman and Todd 1983, p. 103.
13. Matthew Arnold, 'Mycerinus', *The Poems of Matthew Arnold*, Longmans, Green and Co. 1965, l.108, p. 31.
14. Thomas Kelly, *A Testament of Devotion*, Hodder and Stoughton 1943, p. 31.
15. John Smith the Platonist, *Select Discourses*, Cambridge at the University Press 1859, p. 13.
16. Michel Quoist, *With Open Heart*, translated by Colette Copeland, Gill and Macmillan 1983, p. 31.
17. Edward Burroughs, *The Memorable Works of a Son of Thunder and Consolation* 1672, p. 698.
18. John Pulsford, *Quiet Hours*, James Nisbet and Co. 1857, p. 216.

Inspiration

1. NRSV.
2. NRSV.
3. Henry Ward Beecher, *Proverbs from Plymouth Pulpit*, Charles Burnet and Co. 1887, p. 132.
4. Kahlil Gibran, *Sand and Foam*, William Heinemann 1927, p. 21.
5. C.G. Jung, in Jolandi Jacobi, *Psychological Reflections*, Routledge and Kegan Paul 1953, p. 239.
6. Beecher, *Proverbs from Plymouth Pulpit*, p. 168.
7. Richard Jefferies, *The Story of My Heart*, Macmillan and Co. 1968, p. 1.
8. Beecher, *Proverbs from Plymouth Pulpit*, p. 132.
9. William Law, *The Spirit of Love*, by Sidney Spencer, full text, James Clarke and Co. 1969, p. 206.
10. Beecher, *Proverbs from Plymouth Pulpit*, p. 150.

11. James Tunstead, Burtchaell CSC, in Alan Richardson and John Bowden, *A New Dictionary of Christian Theology*, SCM Press 1985, p. 304.
12. Beecher, *Proverbs from Plymouth Pulpit*, p. 54.
13. George Eliot, *Adam Bede*, Virtue and Co. 1908, vol. 1, p. 168.
14. Plotinus, *The Enneads*, translated by Stephen Mackenna, Faber and Faber 1956, p. 396.
15. Beecher, *Proverbs from Plymouth Pulpit*, p. 170.
16. Esther Harding, *Women's Mysteries*, Pantheon Books 1955, p. 232.
17. Aldous Huxley, *The Perennial Philosophy*, Chatto and Windus 1974, p. 196.
18. Igor Stravinsky, *An Autobiography*, Calder and Boyars 1975, p. 174.
19. Huxley, *The Perennial Philosophy*, p. 135.

Integrity

1. NRSV.
2. NRSV.
3. Latin proverb.
4. Walt Whitman, 'Song of the Broad-Axe', *The Complete Poems*, edited by Francis Murphy, Penguin Books 1982, iv.99, p. 218.
5. William Shakespeare *II King Henry VI*, act III.ii.232.
6. Henry David Thoreau, *Walden*, The New American Library of World Literature 1960, p. 219.
7. Alexis Carrel, *Reflections on Life*, Hamish Hamilton 1952, p. 183.
8. Erich Fromm, *Man for Himself*, Routledge and Kegan Paul 1975, p. 237.
9. Carrel, *Reflections on Life*, p. 41.
10. Randolph Bourne, *Youth and Life*, Constable and Co. 1913, p. 181.
11. G.A. Studdert Kennedy, *By His Friends*, Hodder and Stoughton 1929, p. 63.
12. André Gide, *The Journals of André Gide*, translated by Justin O'Brien, Secker and Warburg 1947, p. 116.
13. Harry James Cargas, *Encountering Myself*, SPCK 1978, p. 67.
14. Nicolas Berdyaev, *The Fate of Man in the Modern World*, translated by Donald A. Lowrie, SCM Press 1935, p. 83.
15. Ordway Tead, *The Art of Leadership*, McGraw-Hill Book Co. 1935, p. 111.
16. Hubert van Zeller, *Leave Your Life Alone*, Sheed and Ward 1973, p. 109.
17. F.W. Robertson, *Sermons*, Kegan Paul, Trench, Trubner and Co. 1907, first series, p. 286.
18. Marcus Aurelius, *The Meditations of Marcus Aurelius*, translated by Jeremy Collier, Walter Scott, p. 186.
19. George Appleton, *Journey for a Soul*, William Collins Sons and Co. 1976, p. 96.

Intellect

1. NRSV.
2. NRSV.
3. *The Cloud of Unknowing*, translated by Clifton Wolters, Penguin Books 1961, p. 55.
4. W. MacNeile Dixon, *The Human Situation*, Edward Arnold and Co. 1937, p. 64.
5. Blaise Pascal, *Pensées*, translated by W.F. Trotter, Random House 1941, p. 6.
6. Harvey Cox, *The Secular City*, SCM Press 1967, p. 228.
7. John Keats, *Letter to J.H. Reynolds*, *The Works of John Keats*, edited by H. Buxton Forman, Reeves and Turner 1883, vol. III, p. 117.
8. Grace Cooke, *Spiritual Unfoldment*, The White Eagle Publishing Trust 1961, p. 113.
9. John Smith the Platonist, *Select Discourses*, Cambridge at the University Press 1859, p. 16.
10. William Temple, *Readings in St John's Gospel*, first and second series, Macmillan and Co. 1947, p. 68.
11. George Macdonald, *Unspoken Sermons*, third series, Longmans, Green and Co. 1889, p. 43.
12. Mark Rutherford, *Last Pages from a Journal*, Oxford University Press 1915, p. 311.
13. C.G. Jung, *Psychological Types*, translated by H. Godwin Baynes, Kegan Paul, Trench, Trubner and Co. 1946, p. 628.
14. Charles Morgan, *The Fountain*, Macmillan and Co. 1932, p. 58.

15. Charles Péguy, *Basic Verities*, translated by Ann and Julian Green, Kegan Paul, Trench, Trubner and Co. 1943, p. 115.
16. William Temple, *Nature, Man and God*, Macmillan and Co. 1934, p. 379.
17. Angelus Silesius, 'Of the Inner Light and Enlightenment', translated by Frederick Franck, Wildwood House 1976, p. 104.
18. Anne Morrow Lindbergh, *The Wave of the Future*, Harcourt, Brace and Co. 1940, p. 6.
19. Alexis Carrel, *Reflections on Life*, Hamish Hamilton 1952, p. 33.

Jesus Christ

1. NRSV.
2. NRSV.
3. William Barclay, *The Gospel of Matthew*, The Saint Andrew Press 1965, vol. 1, p. 234.
4. Anon.
5. Malcolm Muggeridge, *Jesus, the Man who Lives*, William Collins Sons and Co. 1981, p. 31.
6. Henry Ward Beecher, *Proverbs from Plymouth Pulpit*, Charles Burnet and Co. 1887, p. 148.
7. William Barclay, *The Gospel of Matthew*, The Saint Andrew Press 1975, vol. 2, p. 296.
8. D.S. Cairns, *The Riddle of the World*, SCM Press 1937, p. 321.
9. F.W.Robertson, *Lectures and Addresses*, Smith, Elder and Co. 1858, p. 77.
10. Evelyn Underhill, *The Letters of Evelyn Underhill*, edited by Charles Williams, Longmans, Green and Co. 1947, p. 217.
11. C.G. Jung, in F.C. Happold, *Religious Faith and Twentieth-Century Man*, Darton, Longman and Todd 1980, p. 71.
12. H.G. Wells, in Barclay, *The Gospel of Matthew*, vol. 1, p. 87.
13. Thomas Carlyle, *Sartor Resartus*, Ward, Lock and Co., p. 148.
14. Robert Bridges, 'The Testament of Beauty', Oxford at the Clarendon Press 1930, iv. 1399, p. 190.
15. Basil Hume OSB, in Gerald Priestland, *Priestland's Progress*, BBC Worldwide 1982, p. 41.
16. Charles Kingsley, *Daily Thoughts*, Macmillan and Co. 1884, p. 45.
17. Evelyn Underhill, in John Stobbart, *The Wisdom of Evelyn Underhill*, edited by John Stobbart, A.R. Mowbray and Co. 1951, p. 15.
18. Rufus M. Jones, *Spiritual Reformers in the 16th and 17th Centuries*, Macmillan and Co. 1914, p. 244.

Joy

1. NRSV.
2. NRSV.
3. Samuel Taylor Coleridge, 'A Christmas Carol', *Coleridge's Poetical Works*, edited by Ernest Hartley Coleridge, Oxford University Press 1978, st.viii, l.47, p. 340.
4. Richard Baxter, *The Saints' Everlasting Rest*, Blackie and Son 1817, p. 16.
5. Johann Wolfgang von Goethe, *The Practical Wisdom of Goethe*, chosen by Emil Ludwig, Martin Secker and Warburg 1933, *Travels in Italy*, p. 26.
6. John Main OSB, in Clare Hallward, *The Joy of Being*, Darton, Longman and Todd 1989, p. 42.
7. Rabindranath Tagore, *Stray Birds, Collected Poems and Plays of Rabindranath Tagore*, Macmillan and Co. 1936, XVII, p. 289.
8. Harry Williams CR, *The True Wilderness*, William Collins Sons and Co. 1983, p. 111.
9. Mother Teresa, in Malcolm Muggeridge, *Something Beautiful for God*, William Collins Sons and Co. 1983, p. 68.
10. Robert Browning, 'Saul', *The Poetical Works of Robert Browning*, Smith, Elder and Co. 1899, vol. 1, st.ix, l.21, p. 275.
11. Thomas Traherne, *Centuries*, The Faith Press 1969, p. 150.
12. D. Columba Marmion, *Christ in His Mysteries*, Sands and Co. 1924, p. 9.
13. William Temple, *Readings in St John's Gospel*, first and second series, Macmillan 1947, p. 295.
14. John Main OSB, *Moment of Christ*, Darton, Longman and Todd 1984, p. 80.
15. Henry Ward Beecher, *Proverbs from Plymouth Pulpit*, Charles Burnet and Co. 1887, p. 185.

16. Beecher, *Proverbs from Plymouth Pulpit*, p. 170.
17. Janet Erskine Stuart, in Maud Monahan, *Life and Letters of Janet Erskine Stuart*, Longmans, Green and Co. 1922, p. 88.
18. Izaak Walton, *The Compleat Angler*, Macmillan and Co. 1906, p. 15.
19. Rollo May, *Man's Search for Himself*, Souvenir Press 1975, p. 96.
20. William Barclay, *The Letters to the Galations and Ephesians*, The Saint Andrew Press 1958, p. 55.
21. Thomas Wolfe, *The Web and the Rock*, The Sun Dial Press 1940, p. 377.

Kindness

1. NRSV.
2. NRSV.
3. Russian proverb.
4. Alfred, Lord Tennyson, 'Lady Clara Vere de Vere', *The Complete Works of Alfred Lord Tennyson*, Macmillan 1898, p. 49.
5. Proverb.
6. William Barclay, *The Gospel of Matthew*, The Saint Andrew Press 1987, vol. 1, p. 262.
7. Jean Jacques Rousseau, *Emile or Education*, translated by Barbara Foxley, J.M. Dent and Sons 1911, p. 43.
8. F.W. Faber, *Spiritual Conferences*, Thomas Richardson and Son 1859, p. 40.
9. Henri Frédéric Amiel, *Amiel's Journal*, translated by Mrs Humphry Ward, Macmillan and Co. 1918, p. 16.
10. Robert Burns, 'A Winter's Night', *The Poems and Songs of Robert Burns*, edited by James Kinsley, Clarendon Press 1968, vol. 1, l.95, p. 305.
11. Henry Ward Beecher, *Proverbs from Plymouth Pulpit*, Charles Burnet and Co. 1887, p. 154.
12. Olive Schreiner, *The Letters of Olive Schreiner*, edited by S.C. Cronwright-Schreiner, T. Fisher Unwin 1924, p. 48.
13. Amiel, *Amiel's Journal*, p. 146.
14. William Wordsworth, 'Lines Composed a few Miles Above Tintern Abbey', *The Poetical Works of William Wordsworth*, edited by E. de Selincourt, Oxford at the Clarendon Press 1944, vol. II, l.33, p. 260.
15. A.C. Benson, *Extracts from the Letters of Dr A.C. Benson to M.E.A.*, Jarrold Publishing 1927, p. 40.
16. André Gide, *Pretexts, Reflections on Literature and Morality*, selected by Justin O'Brien, Martin Secker and Warburg 1960, p. 313.
17. Attributed to Stephen Grellet.
18. F.W. Faber, *Spiritual Conferences*, Thomas Richardson and Son 1859, p. 22.
19. F.W. Robertson, *Sermons*, Kegan Paul, Trench, Trubner and Co. 1897, second series, p. 293.
20. Mother Teresa, in Kathryn Spink, *In the Silence of the Heart*, SPCK 1983 p. 42.
21. W.E. Sangster, *The Pure in Heart*, Epworth Press 1954, p. 136.

Kingdom Of God

1. NRSV.
2. NRSV.
3. George Macdonald, *Unspoken Sermons*, Longmans, Green and Co., second series 1885, p. 38.
4. William Barclay, *The Gospel of Luke*, The Saint Andrew Press 1964, p. 236.
5. Rudolf Steiner, *Knowledge of the Higher Worlds*, Rudolf Steiner Press 1963, p. 22.
6. Seraphim of Sarov, in G.P. Fedatov, *A Treasury of Russian Spirituality*, Sheed and Ward 1977, p. 277.
7. E. Stanley Jones, *Mastery*, Hodder and Stoughton 1956, p. 199.
8. Lilian Whiting, *Lilies of Eternal Peace*, Gay and Hancock 1908, p. 34.
9. Trevor Beeson, *An Eye for an Ear*, SCM Press 1972, p. 28.
10. George Appleton, *Journey for a Soul*, William Collins Sons and Co. 1976, p. 160.
11. Albert Schweitzer, in E.N. Mozley, *The Theology of Albert Schweitzer*, 'Epilogue: The Conception

of the Kingdom of God in the Transformation of Eschatology', translated by J.R. Coates, A. and C. Black 1950, p. 106.

12. Aldous Huxley, *The Perennial Philosophy*, Chatto and Windus 1974, p. 74.

13. Schweitzer, in Mozley, *The Theology of Albert Schweitzer*, p. 106.

14. George Appleton, *Journey for a Soul*, William Collins Sons and Co. 1976, p. 159.

15. Schweitzer, in Mozley, *The Theology of Albert Schweitzer*, p. 106.

16. Albert Schweitzer, in Charles H. Joy, *An Anthology*, A. and C. Black 1955, p. 110.

Knowledge

1. NRSV.

2. NRSV.

3. Ben Jonson, *Explorata: or, Discoveries*, in Ben Jonson, *The Poems, The Prose Works*, vol. VIII, edited by C.H. Herford, Percy and Evelyn Simpson, Oxford at the Clarendon Press 1947, p. 588.

4. Alfred, Lord Tennyson, 'Locksley Hall', *The Poems of Tennyson*, edited by Christopher Ricks, Longmans, Green and Co. 1969, p. 697.

5. Antoine de Saint-Exupéry, *Flight to Arras*, translated by Lewis Galantiere, William Heinemann 1942, p. 33.

6. Michel Quoist, *With Open Heart*, translated by Colette Copeland, Gill and Macmillan 1983, p. 40.

7. Kathleen Raine, *Defending Ancient Spings*, Oxford University Press 1967, p. 118.

8. William Cowper, 'The Task', *The Poetical Works of Cowper*, edited by H.S. Milford, Oxford University Press 1950, p. 221.

9. Thomas Carlyle, *Sartor Resartus*, 'Lectures on Heroes', Chapman and Hall 1840, p. 227.

10. Charles Kingsley, *Daily Thoughts*, Macmillan and Co. 1884, p. 151.

11. Hermann Hesse, *If the War Goes on*, translated by Ralph Manheim, Pan Books 1974, p. 54.

12. Rufus M. Jones, *Spiritual Reformers in the 16th and 17th Centuries*, Macmillan and Co. 1914, p. xviii.

13. Bede Griffiths OSB, in Peter Spink, *The Universal Christ*, Darton, Longman and Todd 1990, p. 44.

14. Harry James Cargas, *Encountering Myself*, SPCK 1978, p. 120.

15. Francis Bacon, *The Advancement of Learning*, Cassell and Co. 1905, p. 38.

16. Cargas, *Encountering Myself*, p. 120.

Leadership

1. NRSV.

2. NRSV.

3. André Maurois, *The Art of Living*, The English Universities Press 1940, p. 160.

4. Henry Miller, *The Wisdom of the Heart*, New Directions Books 1941, p. 46.

5. John Eskine, *The Complete Life*, Andrew Melrose 1945, p. 134.

6. Ordway Tead, *The Art of Leadership*, McGraw-Hill Book Co. 1935, p. 98.

7. Ralph Waldo Emerson, *The Conduct of Life, Nature, and Other Essays*, J.M. Dent and Sons 1911, p. 175.

8. Philip Massinger, *The Bondman, The Plays of Massinger*, Alfred Thomas Crocker 1868, act 1. sc.iii, p. 102.

9. Henry Miller, *The Wisdom of the Heart*, New Directions Books 1941, p. 122.

10. Tead, *The Art of Leadership*, p. 115.

11. J.B. Yeats, *Letters to His Son, W.B. Yeats and Others*, Faber and Faber 1944, p. 218.

12. Jean Vanier, *Community and Growth*, Darton, Longman and Todd 1991, p. 220.

13. Sir John Glubb, *The Fate of Empires and Search for Survival*, William Blackwood and Sons 1978, p. 39.

14. Robert Browning, 'The Lost Leader', *The Poetical Works of Robert Browning*, Smith, Elder and Co. 1899, vol. 1, st.i, l.12, p. 249.

15. Vanier, *Community and Growth*, p. 219.

16. Tead, *The Art of Leadership*, p. 115.

17. Albert Einstein, (written of Mahatma Gandhi), *Ideas and Opinions*, Souvenir Press (Educational and Academic) 1973, p. 7.
18. Tead, *The Art of Leadership*, p. 87.

Life

1. NRSV.
2. NRSV.
3. C.G. Jung, in Jolande Jacobi, *Psychological Reflections*, Routledge and Kegan Paul 1953, p. 185.
4. Alexis Carrel, *Reflections on Life*, translated by Antonia White, Hamish Hamilton 1952, p. 76.
5. Dag Hammarskjöld, *Markings*, translated by Leif Sjoberg and W.H. Auden, Faber and Faber 1964, p. 63.
6. Llewelyn Powys, *Impassioned Clay*, Longmans, Green and Co. 1931, p. 94.
7. Evelyn Underhill, *The Letters of Evelyn Underhill*, edited by Charles Williams, Longmans, Green and Co. 1947, p. 219.
8. Hubert van Zeller, *Considerations*, Sheed and Ward 1974, p. 69.
9. W. MacNeile Dixon, *The Human Situation*, Edward Arnold and Co. 1937, p. 50.
10. William Shakespeare, *All's Well that Ends Well*, act IV.iii.68.
11. Rufus M. Jones, *Spiritual Reformers in the 16th and 17th Centuries*, Macmillan and Co. 1914, p. 38.
12. George Bernard Shaw, *Mrs Warren's Profession*, *The Complete Plays of Bernard Shaw*, Paul Hamlyn 1965, Act 11, p. 75.
13. D.H. Lawrence, *The Selected Letters of D.H. Lawrence*, edited by Diana Trilling, Farrar, Straus and Cudahy 1958, p. 210.
14. Harry Emerson Foskick, *On Being a Real Person*, Harper and Row 1943, p. 77.
15. Father Andrew SDC, *The Way of Victory*, A.R. Mowbray and Co. 1938, p. 146.
16. Thomas Carlyle, *Past and Present*, Ward, Lock and Co., p. 198.
17. R.L. Smith, in Paul Rowntree Clifford, *Man's Dilemma and God's Answer*, Broadcast talks, SCM Press 1964, p. 73.
18. Frederick von Hugel, *Letters to a Niece*, J.M. Dent and Sons 1929, p. xi.
19. John S. Dunne, *The Reasons of the Heart*, SCM Press 1978, p. 123.
20. Ralph Waldo Emerson, *The Heart of Emerson's Journals*, edited by Bliss Perry, Constable and Co. 1927, p. 79.

Light

1. NRSV.
2. NRSV.
3. Samuel Johnson, *The History of Rasselas*, Oxford University Press 1971, p. 124.
4. Henry Wadsworth Longfellow, 'To a Child', *The Poetical Works of Longfellow*, Oxford University Press 1913, p. 126.
5. Ralph Waldo Emerson, *Self-Reliance*, *The Works of Ralph Waldo Emerson*, George Bell and Sons 1906, vol. 1, *Essays and Representative Men*, p. 23.
6. Meister Eckhart, *Meister Eckhart*, translated by Raymond B. Blakney, Harper and Row 1941, p. 101.
7. Rufus M. Jones, *Spiritual Reformers in the 16th and 17th Centuries*, Macmillan and Co. 1914, p. 219.
8. St Augustine, *Confessions*, translated by R.S. Pine-Coffin, Penguin Books 1964, p. 260.
9. Walt Whitman, 'Hast Never Come to Thee an Hour', *The Complete Poems*, edited by Francis Murphy, Penguin Books 1982, p. 303.
10. Thomas Traherne, *Centuries*, The Faith Press 1969, p. 129.
11. Louise M. Haskins, 'God Knows', quoted by King George VI in a Christmas Broadcast, 25 December 1939.
12. Jones, *Spiritual Reformers in the 16th and 17th Centuries*, p. 345.
13. Charles Kingsley, *Daily Thoughts*, Macmillan and Co. 1884, p. 259.
14. Hubert van Zeller, *Considerations*, Sheed and Ward 1974, p. 51.

15. Jones, *Spiritual Reformers in the 16th and 17th Centuries*, p. 159.
16. William Barclay, *The Gospel of John*, The Saint Andrew Press 1965, vol. 2, p. 13.
17. Albert Schweitzer, *Memoirs of Childhood and Youth*, translated by C.T. Campion, George Allen and Unwin 1924, p. 90.

Listening

1. NRSV.
2. NRSV.
3. John Keble, *The Christian Year*, edited by Ernest Rhys, J.M. Dent and Sons 1914, p. 72.
4. Anon.
5. Martin Buber, *I and Thou*, translated by Walter Kaufman, T. and T. Clark 1971, p. 26.
6. Anon, heard on the radio.
7. Rabindranath Tagore, *Stray Birds, Collected Poems and Plays of Rabindranath Tagore*, Macmillan and Co. 1936, p. 288.
8. Dag Hammarskjöld, *Markings*, translated by Leif Sjoberg and W.H. Auden, Faber and Faber 1964, p. 35.
9. Simone Weil, *Waiting on God*, translated by Emma Craufurd, William Collins Sons and Co. 1974, p. 106.
10. Carlo Carretto, *Letters from the Desert*, translated by Rose Mary Hancock, Darton, Longman and Todd, Orbis Books 1972, p. 40.
11. Hammarskjöld, *Markings*, p. 34.
12. Stephen MacKenna, *Journal and Letters*, Constable and Co. 1936, p. 260.
13. Mark Rutherford, *More Pages from a Journal*, Oxford University Press 1910, p. 223.
14. Michel Quoist, *With Open Heart*, translated by Anne Marie de Commaile and Agnes Mitchell Forsyth, Gill and Macmillan 1963, p. 2.
15. Hubert van Zeller, *Considerations*, Sheed and Ward 1974, p. 88.
16. Dan Billany and David Dowie, *The Cage*, Longmans, Green and Co. 1949, p. 158.
17. Dr Cyril H. Powell, *Secrets of Answered Prayer*, Arthur James 1858, p. 123.
18. William Barclay, *The Gospel of John*, The Saint Andrew Press 1974, vol. 1, p. 225.
19. Quoist, *With Open Heart*, p. 159.
20. Erich Fromm, *Man for Himself*, Routledge and Kegan Paul 1975, p. 161.
21. Mother Mary Clare SLG, *Encountering the Depths*, Darton, Longman and Todd 1981, p. 33.

Literature

1. NRSV.
2. NRSV.
3. Henry Ward Beecher, *Proverbs from Plymouth Pulpit*, Charles Burnet and Co. 1887, p. 102.
4. Erza Pound, *How to Read*, Desmond Harmsworth 1931, p. 21.
5. E.M. Forster, *Howard's End*, Penguin Books 1981, p. 127.
6. Beecher, *Proverbs from Plymouth Pulpit*, p. 129.
7. Norman Douglas, *An Almanac*, Chatto and Windus in association with Secker and Warburg 1945, p. 31.
8. Rebecca West, *Ending in Earnest*, Doubleday, Doran and Co. 1931, p. 77.
9. Henry Wadsworth Longfellow, *Kavanagh, The Writings of Henry Wadsworth Longfellow*, George Routledge and Sons, vol. II, p. 366.
10. John Dryden, *Essay on Dramatic Poesy, The Works of John Dryden*, general editor, H.T. Swedenberg, Jr, University of California Press 1971, vol. XVII, *Prose 1668–1691*, l.20, p. 55.
11. J.B. Yeats, *Letters to His Son, W.B. Yeats and Others*, Faber and Faber 1944, p. 53.
12. Mark Rutherford, *Last Pages from a Journal*, Oxford University Press 1915, p. 280.
13. Henry David Thoreau, *Walden*, The New American Library of World Literature 1960, p. 74.
14. Hermann Hesse, in Volker Michels, *Reflections*, translated by Ralph Manheim, Jonathan Cape 1977, p. 109.
15. Beecher, *Proverbs from Plymouth Pulpit*, p. 128.
16. William E. Channing, *Self-Culture*, Dutton and Wentworth, 1838, p. 40.

17. Benjamin Disraeli, *Coningsby*, Peter Davies 1927, p. 129.
18. E.M. Forster, *Anonymity, An Enquiry*, Leonard and Virginia Woolf at the Hogarth Press 1925, p. 16.

Loneliness

1. NRSV.
2. NRSV.
3. William Wordsworth, 'Prelude', book third, l.210.
4. Dag Hammarskjöld, *Markings*, translated by Leif Sjoberg and W.H. Auden, Faber and Faber 1964, p. 85.
5. Erich Fromm, *The Art of Loving*, George Allen and Unwin 1974, p. 14.
6. John S. Dunne, *The Reasons of the Heart*, SCM Press 1978, p. 50.
7. Henri J.M. Nouwen, *Reaching Out*, William Collins Sons and Co. 1980, p. 29.
8. Alfred, Lord Tennyson, 'The Holy Grail', *The Poems of Tennyson*, edited by Christopher Ricks, Longmans, Green and Co. 1969, *The Idylls of the King*, no. 471, p. 1673.
9. Antoine de Saint-Exupéry, *The Wisdom of the Sands*, translated by Stuart Gilbert, Hollis and Carter 1952, p. 224.
10. C.S. Lewis, *The Four Loves*, William Collins Sons and Co. 1960, p. 7.
11. Paul Tillich, *The Eternal Now*, SCM Press 1963, p. 11.
12. Stephen Neill, *The Church and Christian Union*, Oxford University Press 1968, p. 279.
13. John S. Dunne, *The Church of the Poor Devil*, SCM Press 1983, p. 18.
14. Henri J.M. Nouwen, in Robert Durback, *Seeds of Hope*, Darton, Longman and Todd 1989, p. 12.
15. Nouwen, *Reaching Out*, 1980, p. 35.
16. D.H. Lawrence, *Loneliness, The Complete Poems of D.H. Lawrence*, edited by Vivian de Sola Pinto and Warren Roberts, William Heinemann 1967, vol. II, p. 610.
17. Nouwen, in Durback, *Seeds of Hope*, p. 12.
18. Hubert van Zeller, *Considerations*, Sheed and Ward 1974, p. 23.
19. Harry James Cargas, *Encountering Myself*, SPCK 1978, p. 108.
20. van Zeller, *Considerations*, p. 18.

Longing

1. NRSV.
2. NRSV.
3. Rabindranath Tagore, *Stray Birds, Collected Poems and Plays of Rabindranath Tagore*, Macmillan and Co. 1936, LXXXVIII, p. 298.
4. Henry Ward Beecher, *Proverbs from Plymouth Pulpit*, Charles Burnet and Co. 1887, p. 116.
5. J.R.Lowell, 'Longing', *The Poetical Works of James Russell Lowell*, Ward, Lock and Co. 1911, p. 94.
6. Elizabeth Bassett, *The Bridge is Love*, Darton, Longman and Todd 1981, p. 31.
7. Richard Chevenix Trench, *Notes on the Parables of Our Lord*, Pickering and Inglis 1953, p. 400.
8. John L. Casteel, *Rediscovering Prayer*, Hodder and Stoughton 1955, p. 13.
9. John S. Dunne, *The Reasons of the Heart*, SCM Press 1978, p. 112.
10. Anon.
11. Origen, in G.W. Butterworth, *Origen on First Principles*, SPCK 1936, p. 149.
12. Elizabeth Bassett, *The Bridge is Love*, Darton, Longman and Todd 1981, p. 31.
13. Miguel de Cervantes Saavedra, *The Life of Don Quixote and Sancho*, translated by Homer P. Earle, Alfred A. Knopf 1927, p. 33.
14. Bassett, *The Bridge is Love*, p. 31.
15. Edward Wilson, in George Seaver, *Edward Wilson of the Antarctic*, John Murray 1935, p. 46.

Love

1. NRSV.
2. NRSV.
3. E.B. Browning, 'Aurora Leigh', *Elizabeth Barrett Browing's Poetical Works*, Smith, Elder and Co. 1873, vol. V, first book, p. 39.
4. *The Cloud of Unknowing*, John M. Watkins 1956, p. 77.
5. Benjamin Disraeli, *Sybil or the Two Nations*, Peter Davies 1927, p. 354.
6. W. Somerset Maugham, *The Summing Up*, Bernhard Tauchnitz 1938, p. 312.
7. Father Andrew SDC, *Seven Words from the Cross*, A.R. Mowbray and Co. 1954, p. 32.
8. Kahlil Gibran, *The Prophet*, William Heinemann 1970, p. 24.
9. William Temple, *Christian Faith and Life*, SCM Press 1963, p. 106.
10. Gibran, *The Prophet*, p. 11.
11. Charles Morgan, *The Fountain*, Macmillan 1932, p. 211.
12. Mark Rutherford, *More Pages from a Journal*, Oxford University Press 1910, p. 244.
13. Henry Ward Beecher, *Proverbs from Plymouth Pulpit*, Charles Burnet and Co. 1887, p. 106.
14. Thomas à Kempis, *The Imitation of Christ*, translated by Betty I. Knott, William Collins Sons and Co. 1963, p. 117.
15. Beecher, *Proverbs from Plymouth Pulpit*, p. 180.
16. Mark Rutherford, *Last Pages from a Journal*, Oxford University Press 1915, p. 283.
17. Gibran, *The Prophet*, p. 12.
18. Rufus M. Jones, *Spiritual Reformers in the 16th and 17th Centuries*, Macmillan and Co. 1914, p. 96.
19. Thomas à Kempis, *The Imitation of Christ*, p. 118.
20. Lady Julian of Norwich, *Revelations of Divine Love*, edited by Grace Warrack, Methuen and Co. 1949, p. 202.
21. Fyodor Dostoyevsky, *The Brothers Karamazov*, translated by David Magarshack, Penguin Books 1963, vol. 1, p. 375.
22. Edward Wilson, in George Seaver, *The Faith of Edward Wilson*, John Murray 1949, p. 15.
23. Martin Buber, in Aubrey Hodes, *Encounter with Martin Buber*, Allen Lane, The Penguin Press 1972, p. 66.

Marriage

1. NRSV.
2. NRSV.
3. William Penn, *Fruits of Solitude*, A.W. Bennett 1863, part 1, no. 79, p. 19.
4. Coventry Patmore, *The Rod, the Root and the Flower*, The Grey Walls Press 1950, p. 215.
5. Henrik Ibsen, *The League of Youth*, edited and translated by James Walter McFarlane and Graham Orton, Oxford University Press 1963, vol. IV, act IV, p. 99.
6. Russian proverb.
7. Thomas Hardy, *Jude the Obscure*, Macmillan Publishers, 1924, p. 325.
8. Antoine de Saint-Exupéry, *The Wisdom of the Sands*, translated by Stuart Gilbert, Hollis and Carter 1952, p. 152.
9. Hubert van Zeller, *Considerations*, Sheed and Ward 1974, p. 94.
10. Antoine de Saint-Exupéry, *Wind, Sand and Stars*, translated by Lewis Galantiere, William Heinemann 1939, p. 268.
11. Count Hermann Keyserling, *The Book of Marriage*, Harcourt, Brace and Co. 1926, p. 286.
12. Patmore, *The Rod, the Root and the Flower*, 'Aurea Dicta', cxxxv, p. 51.
13. C.G. Jung, *Contributions to Analytical Psychology*, translated by H.G. and Cary F. Baynes, Kegan Paul, Trench, Trubner and Co. 1928, p. 193.
14. C.S. Lewis, *A Grief Observed*, Faber and Faber 1961, p. 18.
15. van Zeller, *Considerations*, p. 93.
16. Søren Kierkegaard, *Training in Christianity*, translated by Walter Lowrie, Princeton University Press 1942, p. 71.
17. Penn, *Fruits of Solitude*, p. 19.

18. Keyserling, *The Book of Marriage*, p. 290.
19. A young housewife.
20. Henry Van Dyke, *Little Rivers*, David Nutt 1903, p. 132.
21. J. Neville Ward, *Five for Sorrow, Ten for Joy*, Epworth Press 1971, p. 17.
22. van Zeller, *Considerations*, p. 94.
23. W.C. Willoughby, *Race Problems in the New Africa*, Clarendon Press 1923, p. 104.
24. Bertrand Russell, *Marriage and Morals*, George Allen and Unwin 1976, p. 203.

Meditation

1. NRSV.
2. NRSV.
3. William Temple, *The Preacher's Theme Today*, SPCK 1936, p. 60.
4. Isaac Disraeli, *Literary Character of Men of Genius*, edited by The Earl of Beaconsfield, Frederick Warne and Co. 1881, p. 131.
5. Lawrence LeShan, *How to Meditate*, Turnstone Press 1983, p. 9.
6. Thomas Merton, *Thoughts in Solitude*, Burns and Oates 1958, p. 41.
7. Richard Challoner, in Gordon Wakefield, *A Dictionary of Christian Spirituality*, SCM Press 1986, p. 85.
8. Madam Guyon, *A Method of Prayer*, James Clarke and Co. 1902, p. 9.
9. Anthony Bloom, *Living Prayer*, Darton, Longman and Todd 1966, p. 52.
10. Morton T. Kelsey, *The Other Side of Silence*, SPCK 1977, p. 83.
11. George Appleton, *Journey for a Soul*, William Collins Sons and Co. 1976, p. 38.
12. John Main OSB, in Clare Hallward, *The Joy of Being*, Darton, Longman and Todd 1989, p. 26.
13. Kelsey, *The Other Side of Silence*, p. 31.
14. John Main OSB, *Moment of Christ*, Darton, Longman and Todd 1984, p. 31.
15. George Trevelyan, *A Vision of an Aquarian Age*, Coverture 1977, p. 87.
16. Kelsey, *The Other Side of Silence*, p. 65.

Mind

1. NRSV.
2. NRSV.
3. Henri Matisse, in Francoise Gilot and Carlton Lake, *Life with Picasso*, Thomas Nelson and Sons 1965, p. 245.
4. Henry Ward Beecher, *Proverbs from Plymouth Pulpit*, Charles Burnet and Co. 1887, p. 26.
5. Joseph Conrad, *Heart of Darkness*, J.M. Dent and Sons 1923, p. 96.
6. William Temple, *Christian Faith and Life*, SCM Press 1963, p. 36.
7. Edmund Spenser, 'The Faerie Queene', *The Works of Edmund Spenser*, The Johns Hopkins Press, 1961, book VI, XI. xxx.1, p. 109.
8. Beecher, *Proverbs from Plymouth Pulpit*, p. 153.
9. Michel Quoist, *With Open Heart*, translated by Colette Copeland, Gill and Macmillan 1983, p. 135.
10. Sir John Lubbock, *The Pleasures of Life*, Macmillan and Co. 1904, part II, p. 250.
11. Alfred North Whitehead, in Lucien Price, *Dialogues of Alfred North Whitehead*, recorded by Lucien Price, Max Reinhardt 1954, p. 160.
12. Beecher, *Proverbs from Plymouth Pulpit*, p. 147.
13. William Temple, *Basic Convictions*, Hamish Hamilton 1937, p. 78.
14. Hubert van Zeller, *Considerations*, Sheed and Ward 1974, p. 67.
15. George Appleton, *Journey for a Soul*, William Collins Sons and Co. 1976, p. 18.
16. W.E. Sangster, *The Secret of Radiant Life*, Hodder and Stoughton 1957, p. 174.
17. Beecher, *Proverbs from Plymouth Pulpit*, p. 30.
18. William Barclay, *The Letter to the Romans*, The Saint Andrew Press 1969, p. 167.
19. Roy Stevens, *Education and the Death of Love*, Epworth Press 1978, p. 138.
20. Appleton, *Journey for a Soul*, p. 19.

Money

1. NRSV.
2. NRSV.
3. George Herbert, *Outlandish Proverbs, The Works of George Herbert*, edited by F.E. Hutchinson, Oxford at the Clarendon Press 1945, no. 591, p. 341
4. Thomas Fuller, *Gnomologia*, published in Dublin 1732, p. 68.
5. Samuel Johnson, *The Vanity of Human Wishes*, The Yale Edition of the Works of Samuel Johnson, Yale University Press 1964, volume VI, 'Poems', p. 92.
6. Benjamin Franklin, *Poor Richard's Almanack*, Taurus Press 1962, p. 4.
7. Thomas Fuller, *Gnomologia*, Stearne Brock 1733, p. 172.
8. H.G. Wells, *Kipps*, Thomas Nelson and Sons 1909, p. 260.
9. Henry Ward Beecher, *Proverbs from Plymouth Pulpit*, Charles Burnet and Co. 1887, p. 8.
10. Norman Douglas, *An Almanac*, Chatto and Windus in association with Secker and Warburg 1945, p. 2.
11. Oliver Goldsmith, 'The Deserted Village', *Collected Works of Oliver Goldsmith*, edited by Arthur Friedman, Oxford at the Clarendon Press 1966, vol. IV, l.51, p. 289.
12. Beecher, *Proverbs from Plymouth Pulpit*, p. 36.
13. John Ruskin, *The Crown of Wild Olives*, George Allen and Sons 1910, p. 46.
14. Michel Quoist, *Prayers of Life*, translated by Anne Marie de Commaile and Agnes Mitchell Forsyth, Gill and Macmillan 1963, p. 23.
15. Arthur Schopenhauer, in W.H. Auden, *A Certain World*, Faber and Faber 1971, p. 266.
16. Martin Luther King, in Coretta Scott King, *The Words of Martin Luther King*, William Collins Sons and Co. 1986, p. 21.
17. Izaak Walton, *The Compleat Angler*, The Nonesuch Press 1929, p. 17.
18. John Woolman, *The Journal of John Woolman*, Edward Marsh 1857, p. 16.
19. Beecher, *Proverbs from Plymouth Pulpit*, p. 27.
20. Carlo Carretto, *Letters from the Desert*, translated by Rose Mary Hancock, Darton, Longman and Todd 1972, p. 81.
21. Arthur Koestler, *Darkness at Noon*, translated by Daphne Hardy, Jonathan Cape 1980, p. 257.
22. W.E. Sangster, *He Is Able*, Hodder and Stoughton 1936, p. 124.
23. William Law, *A Serious Call to a Devout and Holy Life*, J.M. Dent and Co. 1898, p. 88.
24. William Temple, *Christian Faith and Life*, SCM Press 1963, p. 131.

Morals

1. NRSV.
2. NRSV.
3. Henry David Thoreau, *The Journal of Henry D. Thoreau*, vol. IV, edited by Bradford Torrey and Francis H. Allen, Houghton Mifflin Co., Boston, The Riverside Press 1949, p. 128.
4. Henry Ward Beecher, *Proverbs from Plymouth Pulpit*, Charles Burnet and Co. 1887, p. 96.
5. J.A. Froude, *Short Stories on Great Subjects*, Longmans, Green and Co. 1907, vol. IV, p. 265.
6. Matthew Arnold, *Literature and Dogma, The Complete Prose Works of Matthew Arnold*, vol. VI, *Dissent and Dogma*, edited by R.H. Super, The University of Michigan Press 1968, p. 180.
7. Robert Louis Stevenson, *Across the Plains*, T. Nelson and Sons 1892, p. 276.
8. Aldous Huxley, *The Doors of Perception*, Harper and Row 1970, p. 43.
9. William Penn, *Fruits of Solitude*, A.W. Bennett 1863, p. 67.
10. Beecher, *Proverbs from Plymouth Pulpit*, p. 97.
11. Bertrand Russell, *Authority and the Individual*, George Allen and Unwin Publishers 1949, p. 111.
12. Thomas Jefferson, *The Writings of Thomas Jefferson*, Taylor and Maury 1854, vol. IV, p. 476.
13. William Penn, *Fruits of Solitude*, A.W. Bennett 1863, p. 68.
14. Walter Lippman, *A Preface to Politics*, Ann Arbor Publications 1962, p. 152.
15. Ernest Hemingway, *Death in the Afternoon*, Jonathan Cape 1968, p. 11.
16. Norman Vincent Peale, *Man, Morals and Maturity*, World's Work 1970, p. 77.
17. F.R. Barry, *The Relevance of Christianity*, James Nisbet and Co. 1932, p. 8.

18. D.H. Lawrence, 'Immorality', *The Complete Poems of D.H. Lawrence*, edited by Vivian de Sola Pinto and Warren Roberts, William Heinemann 1967, vol. II, p. 836.
19. William Boyd Carpenter, *The Witness to the Influence of Christ*, Constable and Co. 1905, p. 59.
20. Percy Bysshe Shelley, *A Defence of Poetry*, *The Prose Works of Percy Bysshe Shelley*, vol. III, edited by H. Buxton Forman, Reeves and Turner 1880, p. 111.
21. William Temple, *Nature, Man and God*, Macmillan 1934, p. 196.
22. William Temple, *Christian Faith and Life*, SCM Press 1963, p. 60.
23. Anon.

Music

1. NRSV.
2. NRSV.
3. C.M. Widor, in Charles R. Joy, *Music in the Life of Albert Schweitzer*, selections from his writings translated and edited by Charles R. Joy, A. and C. Black 1953, p. 157.
4. Robert Browning, 'Balaustion's Adventure', *The Poetical Works of Robert Browning*, Smith, Elder and Co. 1899, vol. 1, p. 631.
5. William Law, in Stephen Hobhouse, *Selected Mystical Writings of William Law*, Rockliff 1948, p. 631.
6. Thomas Carlyle, *Sartor Resartus*, 'Lectures on Heroes', Chapman and Hall 1840, p. 246.
7. Ludwig von Beethoven, in *Thayer's Life of Beethoven*, revised and edited by Elliot Forbes, Princeton University Press 1970, p. 494.
8. Richard Wagner, *Beethoven*, translated by Edward Dannreuther, William Reeves 1880, p. 1.
9. Henry Ward Beecher, *Proverbs from Plymouth Pulpit*, Charles Burnet and Co. 1887, p. 11.
10. Walter de la Mare, 'Music', *The Complete Poems of Walter de la Mare*, Faber and Faber 1969, p. 199.
11. Beecher, *Proverbs from Plymouth Pulpit*, p. 28.
12. Carlyle, *Sartor Resartus*, 'Lectures on Heroes', p. 247.
13. Sir Thomas Browne, *Religio Medici*, *The Works of Sir Thomas Browne*, edited by Geoffrey Keynes, Faber and Faber 1964, vol. 1, p. 84.
14. Joanna Field, *A Life of One's Own*, Chatto and Windus 1934, p. 29.
15. Henry Peacham, *The Compleat Gentleman*, Da Capo Press, Theatrum Orbis Terrarum 1968, p. 104.
16. Plato, *The Republic of Plato*, translated by B. Jowett, Oxford at the Clarendon Press 1881, book III, 401D, p. 85.
17. Aaron Copeland, *Music and Imagination*, Harvard University Press 1977, p. 1.
18. H.L. Kirk, *Pablo Casals: A Biography*, Hutchinson and Co. 1974, p. 187.
19. Heinrich Heine, in Jacques Barzun, *Pleasures of Music*, Michael Joseph 1952, p. 268.
20. Etty Hillesum, *A Diary 1941–43*, translated by Arnold J. Pomerans, Jonathan Cape 1983, p. 62.

Mystics

1. NRSV.
2. NRSV.
3. Henri Frédéric Amiel, *Amiel's Journal*, translated by Mrs Humphry Ward, Macmillan and Co. 1918, p. 80.
4. Lewis Mumford, *The Conduct of Life*, Secker and Warburg 1952, p. 57.
5. William Johnston, *The Inner Eye of Love*, William Collins Sons and Co. 1978, p. 20.
6. William Barclay, *The Letters to the Corinthians*, The Saint Andrew Press 1988, p. 256.
7. Havelock Ellis, *Selected Essays*, J.M. Dent and Sons 1936, p. 186.
8. Gerhard Tersteegen, in Frances Bevan, *Sketches of the Quiet in the Land*, John F. Shaw and Co. 1891, p. 396.
9. Gerald Bullett, *The English Mystics*, Michael Joseph 1950, p. 17.
10. John V. Taylor, *The Go-Between God*, SCM Press 1973, p. 225.
11. Evelyn Underhill, in John Stobbart, *The Wisdom of Evelyn Underhill*, A.R. Mowbray and Co. 1951, p. 22.

12. Samuel Butler, in Gerald Bullett, *The English Mystics*, Michael Joseph 1950, p. 227.
13. Thomas Merton, *The Waters of Silence*, Hollis and Carter 1950, p. 20.
14. Aldous Huxley, *The Perennial Philosophy*, Chatto and Windus 1974, p. 345.
15. Underhill in Stobbart, *The Wisdom of Evelyn Underhill*, p. 23.
16. Rufus M. Jones, *Spiritual Reformers in the 16th and 17th Centuries*, Macmillan and Co. 1914, p. 133.
17. Albert Einstein, in Lincoln Barnett, *The Universe and Dr Einstein*, Victor Gollancz 1949, p. 95.
18. C.K. Chesterton, *Orthodoxy*, The Bodley Head 1935, p. 46.

Neighbour

1. NRSV.
2. NRSV.
3. C.S. Lewis, *The Great Divorce*, William Collins Sons and Co. 1982, p. 84.
4. George Herbert, *Outlandish Proverbs*, *The Works of George Herbert*, edited by F.E. Hutchinson, Oxford at the Clarendon Press 1972, no.10, p. 321.
5. George Macdonald, *Unspoken Sermons*, first series, Alexander Strahan 1867, p. 214.
6. Benjamin Whichcote, *Morals and Religious Aphorisms* 1930, century II, no.122, p. 16.
7. Norman Douglas, *An Almanac*, Chatto and Windus in association with Martin Secker and Warburg 1945, p. 10.
8. Martin Luther King, *Strength to Love*, William Collins Sons and Co. 1980, p. 29.
9. St Teresa of Avila, *Interior Castle*, *Complete Works of St Teresa of Jesus*, translated by E. Allison Peers, Sheed and Ward 1978, p. 261.
10. Charles Kingsley, *Daily Thoughts*, Macmillan Publishers 1884, p. 59.
11. Macdonald, *Unspoken Sermons*, p. 210.
12. C.S. Lewis, *The Screwtape Letters*, Chivers Press 1983, p. 58.
13. Hans Küng, *On Being a Christian*, translated by Edward Quinn, William Collins Sons and Co. 1977, p. 256.
14. Albert Schweitzer, *Memoirs of Childhood and Youth*, translated by C.T. Campion, George Allen and Unwin 1924, p. 95.
15. Martin Luther King, in Coretta Scott King, *The Words of Martin Luther King*, William Collins Sons and Co. 1986, p. 24.
16. Fyodor Dostoyevsky, *The Brothers Karamazov*, translated by David Magarshack, Penguin Books 1963, vol. 1, p. 61.
17. Eric Hoffer, *The Passionate State of Mind*, Martin Secker and Warburg 1956, p. 54.
18. George Appleton, *Journey for a Soul*, William Collins Sons and Co. 1976, p. 60.
19. Vatican Council II, *The Conciliar and Post Conciliar Documents*, 1981 edition, General Editor, Austin Flannery OP, Fowler Wright Books, p. 928.

Obedience

1. NRSV.
2. NRSV.
3. George Macdonald, *The Marquis of Lossie*, Everett and Co. 1912, p. 207.
4. P.T. Forsyth, *Positive Preaching and the Modern Mind*, Independent Press 1949, p. 32.
5. John J. Vincent, *Secular Christ*, Lutterworth Press 1968, p. 199.
6. Henry Suso, in St Alphonsus de Liguori, *On Conformity with the Will of God*, translated by the Rev. James Jones, Catholic Truth Society 1892, p. 7.
7. George Macdonald, *Unspoken Sermons*, second series, Longmans, Green and Co. 1885, p. 22.
8. Henry Ward Beecher, *Proverbs from Plymouth Pulpit*, Charles Burnet and Co. 1887, p. 179.
9. Father Andrew SDC, *A Gift of Light*, selected and edited by Harry C. Griffith, A.R. Mowbray and Co. 1968, p. 89.
10. Paul Oestreicher, in Hans Jürgen Schultz, *Conversion to the World*, SCM Press 1967, p. 12.
11. Beecher, *Proverbs from Plymouth Pulpit*, p. 206.
12. Henry David Thoreau, *Walden*, The New American Library of World Literature 1960, p. 216.
13. Sister Madeleine OSA, *Solitary Refinement*, SCM Press 1972, p. 49.

14. Alistair MacLean, *The Quiet Heart*, Allenson and Co. 1940, p. 186.
15. J.R.H. Moorman, *The Path to Glory*, SPCK 1960, p. 54.
16. Hans Küng, *On Being a Christian*, translated by Edward Quinn, William Collins Sons and Co. 1977, p. 244.
17. Jeremy Taylor, *Holy Living*, abridged by Anne Lamb, The Langford Press 1970, p. 85.
18. Küng, *On Being a Christian*, p. 246.
19. William Temple, *Thoughts on Some Problems of the Day*, Macmillan and Co. 1931, p. 28.
20. Moorman, *The Path to Glory*, p. 54.

Other Faiths

1. NRSV.
2. NRSV.
3. William Blake, 'All Religions Are One', *Complete Writings*, edited by Geoffrey Keynes, Oxford University Press 1974, p. 98.
4. Raimundo Panikkar, *The Unknown Christ of Hinduism*, Darton, Longman and Todd 1981, p. 168.
5. William Penn, *Fruits of Solitude*, A.W. Bennett 1863, p. 63.
6. Simone Weil, *Gateway to God*, William Collins Sons and Co. 1974, p. 147.
7. George Appleton, *Journey for a Soul*, William Collins Sons and Co. 1976, p. 71.
8. Bede Griffiths OSB, in Peter Spink, *The Universal Christ*, Darton, Longman and Todd 1990, p. 10.
9. Leo Tolstoy, *Anna Karenina*, translated by Rosemary Edmonds, Penguin Books 1983, p. 851.
10. Mother Teresa, in Kathryn Spink, *In the Silence of the Heart*, SPCK 1983, p. 81.
11. Sri Ramakrishna, *Ramakrishna: Prophet of New India*, translated by Swami Nikhilananda, Rider and Co. 1951, p. 163.
12. Appleton, *Journey for a Soul*, p. 70.
13. Griffiths in Spink, *The Universal Christ*, p. 33.
14. F.C. Happold, *The Journey Inwards*, Darton, Longman and Todd 1974, p. 128.

Patience

1. NRSV.
2. NRSV.
3. John Dryden, 'The Hind and the Panther', *The Poems of John Dryden*, edited by James Kinsley, Oxford at the Clarendon Press 1958, vol. II, *The Third Part*, l.839, p. 525.
4. Ben Johnson, *Volpone*, edited by C.H. Herford and Percy Simpson, Oxford at the Clarendon Press 1965, vol. V, act II, sc.ii, p. 50.
5. George Macdonald, *Weighed and Wanting*, Sampson Low, Marston, Searle and Rivington 1882, vol. III, p. 191.
6. Thomas Fuller, *Gnomologia*, Stearne Brock 1733, p. 164.
7. E B. Browning, 'Aurora Leigh', *Elizabeth Barrett Browning's Poetical Works*, Smith, Elder, and Co. 1873, vol. V, *Third Book*, p. 96.
8. John Ruskin, *The Two Paths*, George Allen 1905, p. 179.
9. Henry Wadsworth Longfellow, 'Evangeline', *The Poetical Works of Longfellow*, Humphrey Milford, Oxford University Press 1913, *Part the Second*, l.160, p. 156.
10. Norman Douglas, *An Almanac*, Chatto and Windus in association with Martin Secker and Warburg 1945, p. 26.
11. Anon.
12. J.R. Lowell, 'Columbus', *The Poetical Works of James Russell Lowell*, Ward, Lock and Co. 1911, p. 58.
13. Anon.
14. A.C. Benson, *Extracts from the Letters of Dr A.C. Benson to M.E.A*, Jarrold Publishing 1927, p. 7.
15. John Ruskin, *Ethics of the Dust*, George Allen and Sons 1907, p. 61.
16. Thomas à Kempis, *The Imitation of Christ*, translated by Betty I. Knott, William Collins Sons and Co. 1979, p. 129.

17. Francois de la M. Fénelon, *Spiritual Thoughts for Busy People*, SPCK 1894, p. 80.
18. George Macdonald, *Unspoken Sermons*, third series, Longmans, Green and Co. 1889, p. 227.
19. William Shakespeare, *The Merchant of Venice*, act IV.i.9.
20. William Penn, *Fruits of Solitude*, A.W. Bennett 1863, p. 36.
21. W.E. Sangster, *The Pure in Heart*, Epworth Press 1954, p. 129.
22. Hermann Hesse, in Volker Michels, *Reflections*, translated by Ralph Manheim, Jonathan Cape 1977, p. 58.
23. F.W. Faber, *Growth in Holiness*, Thomas Richardson and Son 1855, p. 148.

Peace

1. NRSV.
2. NRSV.
3. Walt Whitman, 'The Sleepers', *The Complete Poems*, edited by Francis Murphy, Penguin Books 1982, l.147, p. 447.
4. George Herbert, *Outlandish Poems*, *The Works of George Herbert*, edited by F.E. Hutchinson, Oxford at the Clarendon Press 1972, no.733, p. 345.
5. St Augustine, *Confessions*, translated by R.S. Pine-Coffin, Penguin Books 1964, p. 232.
6. William Wordsworth, 'The Excursion', book III, l.382, *The Poetical Works of William Wordsworth*, edited by E. de Selincourt, Oxford at the Clarendon Press 1959, vol. IV, p. 861.
7. Hubert van Zeller, *Leave Your Life Alone*, Sheed and Ward 1973, p. 103.
8. Thomas à Kempis, *The Imitation of Christ*, translated by Betty I. Knott, William Collins Sons and Co. 1979, p. 87.
9. Johann Wolfgang von Goethe, *Wisdom and Experience*, selected by Ludwig Curtius, translated and edited by Herman J. Weigand, Routledge and Kegan Paul 1949, p. 295.
10. John Ruskin, *The Eagle's Nest*, George Allen and Sons 1910, p. 222.
11. Father Yelchaninov, in G.P. Fedatov, *A Treasury of Russian Spirituality*, Sheed and Ward 1977, p. 445.
12. Hubert van Zeller, *Considerations*, Sheed and Ward 1974, p. 43.
13. John Macquarrie, *The Concept of Peace*, SCM Press 1973, p. 81.
14. Søren Kierkegaard, *The Journals of Søren Kierkegaard*, selected, edited and translated by Alexander Dru, Oxford University Press 1938, p. 85.
15. Bede Griffiths OSB, in Peter Spink, *The Universal Christ*, Darton, Longman and Todd 1993, p. 25.
16. Matthew Arnold, 'Lines written in Kensington Gardens', l.37, *The Poems of Matthew Arnold*, edited by Kenneth Allott, Longmans, Green and Co. 1965, p. 257.
17. Henry Ward Beecher, *Proverbs from Plymouth Pulpit*, Charles Burnet and Co. 1887, p. 169.
18. John Tauler, *The History and Life of the Reverend Doctor John Tauler*, translated by Susanna Winkworth, Smith, Elder and Co. 1857, p. 381.
19. Bede Griffiths OSB, *Return to the Centre*, William Collins Sons and Co. 1976, p. 136.
20. William Barclay, *The Gospel of John*, The Saint Andrew Press 1974, vol. 2, p. 199.

Perseverance

1. NRSV.
2. NRSV.
3. A.C. Benson, *Extracts from the Letters of Dr A.C.Benson to M.E.A.*, Jarrold Publishing 1927, p. 41.
4. John Buchan, *Montrose*, Oxford University Press 1957, p. 423.
5. William Shakespeace, *Troilus and Cressida*, act III.iii.150.
6. A.R. Orage, *On Love*, The Janus Press 1957, p. 61.
7. Robert Herrick, 'Hesperides: Seek and Find', *The Poetical Works of Robert Herrick*, Oxford University Press 1915, p. 311.
8. Mark Rutherford, *Last Pages from a Journal*, Oxford University Press 1915, p. 316.
9. William Makepeace Thackeray, *The Virginians*, Smith, Elder, and Co. 1894, p. 761.
10. Benson, *Extracts from the Letters of Dr A.C. Benson to M.E.A.*, p. 14.
11. Oliver Wendell Holmes, in Max Lerner, *The Mind and Faith of Justice Holmes*, Little, Brown and Co. 1945, p. 425.

12. William Barclay, *The Letters to Timothy and Titus*, The Saint Andrew Press 1965, p. 283.
13. André Gide, *The Journals of André Gide*, translated by Justin O'Brien, Secker and Warburg 1929, vol. IV, p. 71.
14. Right Hon. Lord Avebury, *Essays and Addresses*, Macmillan and Co. 1903, p. 276.
15. Johann Wolfgang von Goethe, in Emil Ludwig, *The Practical Wisdom of Goethe*, George Allen and Unwin 1933, p. 159.
16. William Barclay, *The Letters to the Corinthians*, The Saint Andrew Press 1988, p. 143.
17. Samuel Smiles, *Self-Help*, S.W. Partridge and Co. 1912, p. 53.
18. Barclay, *The Letters to the Corinthians*, p. 212.
19. Ordway Tead, *The Art of Leadership*, McGraw-Hill Book Co. 1935, p. 92.

Philosophy

1. NRSV.
2. NRSV.
3. English proverb.
4. Henry Miller, *The Wisdom of the Heart*, New Directions Books 1941, p. 93.
5. Nicolas Berdyaev, *Christian Existentialism*, selected and translated by Donald A. Lowrie, George Allen and Unwin 1965, p. 119.
6. Clement of Alexandria, *The Miscellanies*, *The Writings of Clement of Alexandria*, translated by the Rev. William Wilson, T. and T. Clark 1867, p. 368.
7. Henry Ward Beecher, *Proverbs from Plymouth Pulpit*, Charles Burnet and Co. 1887, p. 152.
8. Ralph Waldo Emerson, *The Works of Ralph Waldo Emerson*, George Bell and Sons 1906, vol. 1, *Essays and Representative Men*, 'Essay on the Over-Soul', p. 143.
9. Bertrand Russell, *Principles of Social Reconstruction*, George Allen and Unwin 1971, p. 168.
10. Henry David Thoreau, *Walden*, The New American Library of World Literature 1960, p. 15.
11. William Temple, *Nature, Man and God*, Macmillan and Co. 1934, p. 520.
12. William James, *Prgamatism*, Longmans, Green and Co. 1943, p. 4.
13. Temple, *Nature, Man and God*, p. 45.
14. A. Clutton Brock, *The Ultimate Belief*, Constable and Co. 1916, p. 9.
15. Russell, *Principles of Social Reconstruction*, p. 168.
16. Sir Sarvepalli Radhakrishnan, *Indian Philosophy*, George Allen and Unwin 1923, p. 44.
17. Russell, *Principles of Social Reconstruction*, p. 168.

Poetry

1. NRSV.
2. NRSV.
3. J.B. Yeats, *Letters to His Son, W.B. Yeats and Others*, Faber and Faber 1944, p. 105.
4. Percy Bysshe Shelley, *A Defence of Poetry*, *The Prose Works of Percy Bysshe Shelley*, edited by H. Buxton Forman, Reeves and Turner 1880, vol. III, p. 138.
5. Thomas Carlyle, *Sartor Resartus*, 'Lectures on Heroes', Chapman and Hall 1840, p. 247.
6. Yeats, *Letters to His Son, W.B. Yeats and Others*, p. 150.
7. John Keble, *Lectures on Poetry*, vol. 1, lecture 1, Oxford at the Clarendon Press, p. 22.
8. Henry Wadsworth Longfellow, *Kavanagh*, *The Writings of Henry Wadsworth Longfellow*, George Routledge and Sons, vol. II, p. 367.
9. Yeats, *Letters to His Son, W.B. Yeats and Others*, p. 212.
10. Thomas Merton, *New Seeds of Contemplation*, Burns and Oates 1962, p. 85.
11. Cyril Connolly, in Stephen Spender, *The Making of a Poem*, Hamish Hamilton 1955, in a review of Keats' Collected Letters, p. 26.
12. Francis Bacon, *The Advancement of Learning*, Cassell and Co. 1905, p. 79.
13. John Keats, *Letter to J.H. Reynolds*, *The Works of John Keats*, edited by H. Buxton Forman, Reeves and Turner 1883, vol. III, p. 113.
14. Oscar Wilde, *De Profundis*, *The Works of Oscar Wilde*, William Collins Sons and Co. 1948, p. 868.
15. Augustine Birrell, *Obiter Dicta*, Mr Browning's Poetry, Elliot Stock 1884, p. 92.

16. John Keble, *Keble's Lectures on Poetry*, translated by E.K. Francis, Oxford at the Clarendon Press 1912, vol. II, p. 201.

17. Johann Wolfgang von Goethe, in Ludwig Curtius, *Wisdom and Experience*, translated and edited by Hermann J. Weigand, Routledge and Kegan Paul 1949, p. 246.

18. William Temple, *Nature, Man and God*, Macmillan and Co. 1934, p. 484.

19. Percy Bysshe Shelley, *Prose, A Defence of Poetry, The Works of Percy Bysshe Shelley*, edited by Roger Ingpen and Walter E. Peck, Ernest Benn 1930, vol. VII, p. 115.

20. Henri Frédéric Amiel, *Amiel's Journal*, translated by Mrs Humphry Ward, Macmillan and Co. 1918, p. 28.

21. William Wordsworth, *Lyrical Ballads, The Poems of William Wordsworth*, edited by Nowell Charles Smith, Methuen and Co. 1908, vol. III, Preface to the second edition of *Lyrical Ballads*, p. 490.

Power

1. NRSV.

2. NRSV.

3. William Blake, 'The Marriage of Heaven and Hell', *The Complete Writings of William Blake*, edited by Geoffrey Keynes, Oxford University Press 1974, p. 149.

4. Leigh Hunt, 'On a Lock of Milton's Hair', *The Poetical Works of Leigh Hunt*, edited by H.S. Milford, Oxford University Press 1923, p. 247.

5. Alfred North Whitehead, *Science and the Modern World*, The New American Library 1964, p. 172.

6. Rabindranath Tagore, *Stray Birds, Collected Poems and Plays of Rabindranath Tagore*, Macmillan and Co. 1936, p. 290.

7. Henrik Ibsen, *An Enemy of the People*, translated and edited by James Walter McFarlane, Oxford University Press 1960, vol. VI, p. 126.

8. Benjamin Whichcote, *Moral and Religious Aphorisms*, Elkin, Mathews and Marrot 1930, no.34, p. 5.

9. Sarah Bernhardt, in Cornelia Otis Skinner, *Madam Sarah*, Michael Joseph 1967, p. xvi.

10. Alfred, Lord Tennyson, 'Oenone', *The Poems of Tennyson*, edited by Christopher Ricks, Longmans, Green and Co. 1969, p. 392.

11. J.R. Lowell, *New England Two Centuries Ago*, in *Among My Books*, J.M. Dent and Sons 1914, p. 182.

12. Ralph Waldo Emerson, *The Conduct of Life, Nature and Other Essays*, J.M. Dent and Sons 1911, p. 186.

13. C.C. Colton, *Lacon*, William Tegg 1866, p. 243.

14. Carlo Carretto, *Letters from the Desert*, translated by Rose Mary Hancock, Darton, Longman and Todd 1972, p. 19.

15. Mohandas K. Gandhi, *Non-Violence in Peace and War*, Navajivan Publishing House, vol. II, 1949, p. 8.

16. Blaise Pascal, *Pensées*, translated by W.F. Trotter, Random House 1941, p. 103.

17. William Temple, *Christian Faith and Life*, SCM Press 1963, p. 45.

18. Claude Bragdon, in Kahlil Gibran, *The Prophet*, William Heinemann 1923, introduction.

19. Henry Ward Beecher, *Proverbs from Plymouth Pulpit*, Charles Burnet and Co. 1887, p. 155.

20. Evelyn Underhill, *The Letters of Evelyn Underhill*, edited by Charles Williams, Longmans, Green and Co. 1947, p. 98.

21. Stuart B. Jackman, *The Numbered Days*, SCM Press 1954, p. 31.

22. Pierre Teilhard de Chardin, *Le Milieu Divin*, William Collins Sons and Co. 1960, p. 43.

23. William Barclay, *The Gospel of John*, The Saint Andrew Press 1965, vol. 1, p. 66.

Prayer

1. NRSV.

2. NRSV.

3. Carlo Carretto, *The Desert in the City*, translated by Barbara Wall, William Collins Sons and Co. 1983, p. 23.

4. C.H. Dodd, in William Barclay, *The Letter to the Romans*, The Saint Andrew Press 1969, p. 116.
5. William Law, *A Serious Call to a Devout and Holy Life*, J.M. Dent and Co. 1898, p. 78.
6. Mohandas K. Gandhi, *Non-Violence in Peace and War*, Navajivan Publishing House 1949, vol. II, p. 77.
7. Kahlil Gibran, *The Prophet*, William Heinemann 1970, p. 78.
8. Dag Hammarskjöld, *Markings*, translated by Leif Sjoberg and W.H. Auden, Faber and Faber 1964, p. 97.
9. Carlo Carretto, *Letters from the Desert*, translated by Rose Mary Hancock, Darton, Longman and Todd 1972, p. 55.
10. John Robinson, *Honest to God*, SCM Press 1963, p. 100.
11. Thomas Merton, *Thoughts in Solitude*, Burns and Oates 1958, p. 91.
12. Brother Lawrence, *The Practice of the Presence of God*, A.R. Mowbray and Co. 1977, p. 47.
13. William Temple, *Christian Faith and Life*, SCM Press 1963, p. 115.
14. Evelyn Underhill, in Charles Williams, *The Letters of Evelyn Underhill*, Longmans, Green and Co. 1947, p. 271.
15. St Francis de Sales, *Introduction to the Devout Life*, Longmans, Green and Co. 1962, p. 54.
16. Fyodor Dostoyevsky, *The Brothers Karamazov*, translated by David Magarshack, Penguin Books 1963, vol. I, p. 375.
17. Martin Luther, *Table-Talk*, translated and edited by William Hazlitt, George Bell and Sons 1895, p. 125.
18. John of Cronstadt, in G.P. Fedatov, Sheed and Ward 1977, p. 354.
19. John Macquarrie, *Paths in Spirituality*, SCM Press, 1992, second edition, p. 30.
20. Mother Teresa, in Kathryn Spink, *In the Silence of the Heart*, SPCK 1983, p. 17.
21. William Barclay, *The Gospel of Matthew*, The Saint Andrew Press 1965, vol. I, p. 275.

Presence

1. NRSV.
2. NRSV.
3. Henry Ward Beecher, *Proverbs from Plymouth Pulpit*, Charles Burnet and Co. 1887, p. 183.
4. William Law, *The Spirit of Prayer*, edited by Sidney Spencer, full text, James Clarke and Co., 1969, p. 44.
5. F.W. Boreham, *A Late Lark Singing*, Epworth Press 1945, p. 160.
6. Alfred, Lord Tennyson, 'The Higher Pantheism', *The Poems of Tennyson*, edited by Christopher Ricks, Longmans, Green and Co. 1969, no. 353, l.11, p. 1205.
7. Hubert van Zeller, *Considerations*, Sheed and Ward 1974, p. 100.
8. Brother Lawrence, *The Practice of the Presence of God*, A.R. Mowbray and Co. 1977, p. 23.
9. Walter Hilton, *The Ladder of Perfection*, translated by Leo Sherley-Price, Penguin Books 1957, p. 233.
10. Jean-Pierre de Caussade SJ, *Self-Abandonment to the Divine Providence*, William Collins Sons and Co. 1972, p. 42.
11. W.R. Inge, *Personal Religion and the Life of Devotion*, Longmans, Green and Co. 1924, p. 32.
12. Brother Lawrence, *The Practice of the Presence of God*, p. 50.
13. W.E. Sangster, *Give God a Chance*, Epworth Press 1968, p. 104.
14. Gerhard Tersteegen, in Frances Bevan, *Sketches of the Quiet of the Land*, John F. Shaw and Co. 1891, p. 384.
15. Francois de la M. Fénelon, *Spiritual Thoughts for Busy People*, SPCK 1894, p. 85.
16. Father Andrew SDC, *The Symbolism of the Sanctuary*, A.R. Mowbray and Co. 1927, p. 18.
17. Evelyn Underhill, *Abba*, Longmans, Green and Co. 1940, p. 12.
18. William Barclay, *The Plain Man Looks at the Apostles' Creed*, William Collins Sons and Co. 1967, p. 197.

Pride

1. NRSV.
2. NRSV.
3. William Shakespeare, *Henry VII*, act IV.ii.37.
4. Alfred, Lord Tennyson, 'The Two Voices', *The Works of Alfred Lord Tennyson*, Macmillan and Co. 1898, p. 31.
5. George Macdonald, *The Marquis of Lossie*, Everett and Co. 1912, p. 91.
6. Benedict Spinoza, *Spinoza's Ethics and de Intellectus Emendatione*, J.M. Dent and Sons 1955, p. 134.
7. William Law, in Stephen Hobhouse, *Selected Mystical Writings of William Law*, Rockliff 1948, p. 107.
8. Spinoza, *Spinoza's Ethics and de Intellectus Emendatione*, p. 102.
9. Benjamin Whichcote, *Moral and Religious Aphorisms*, Elkin, Mathews and Marrot 1930, ix, 801, p. 90.
10. A.R. Orage, *On Love*, The Janus Press 1957, p. 60.
11. Cardinal Manning, *Pastime Papers*, Burns and Oates 1892, p. 27.
12. C.C. Colton, *Lacon*, William Tegg 1866, p. 248.
13. Henry Ward Beecher, *Proverbs from Plymouth Pulpit*, Charles Burnett and Co. 1887, p. 26.
14. Henri Frédéric Amiel, *Amiel's Journal*, translated by Mrs Humphry Ward, Macmillan and Co. 1918, p. 45.
15. William Law, *A Serious Call to a Devout and Holy Life*, J.M. Dent and Co. 1898, p. 246.
16. William Shakespeare, *Troilus and Cressida*, act II.iii.156.
17. *The Cloud of Unknowing*, translated by Clifton Wolters, Penguin Books 1971, p. 68.
18. Law, *A Serious Call to a Devout and Holy Life*, p. 39.
19. Mother Teresa, in Brother Angelo Devananda, *Jesus, the Word to Be Spoken*, William Collins Sons and Co. 1990, p. 20.
20. Alexander Pope, 'An Essay on Criticism', *The Poems of Alexander Pope*, vol. 1, *Pastoral Poetry and An Essay on Criticism*, edited by E. Audra and Aubrey Williams, Methuen and Co. 1961, p. 263.
21. William Temple, *Nature, Man and God*, Macmillan and Co. 1934, p. 421.
22. Law in Hobhouse, *Selected Mystical Writings of William Law*, pp. 25 and 29.
23. William Temple, *Christian Faith and Life*, SCM Press 1963, p. 132.

Progress

1. NRSV.
2. NRSV.
3. Thomas Hardy, *Desperate Remedies*, Macmillan and Co. 1918, p. 450.
4. Edward Patey, *Christian Life Style*, A.R. Mowbray and Co. 1976, p. 113.
5. Malcolm Muggeridge, *Jesus Rediscovered*, William Collins Sons and Co. 1982, p. 52.
6. Henry George, *Progress and Poverty*, Kegan Paul and Co. 1881, p. 9.
7. James A. Froude, *Thomas Carlyle*, Longmans, Green and Co. 1884, vol. II, p. 77.
8. William Temple, *Christian Faith and Life*, SCM Press 1963, p. 96.
9. F.R. Barry, *The Relevance of Christianity*, Nisbet and Co. 1932, p. 14.
10. William Temple, *The Preacher's Theme Today*, SPCK 1936, p. 60.
11. Martin Luther King, in Coretta Scott King, *The Words of Martin Luther King*, William Collins Sons and Co. 1986, p. 67.
12. Evelyn Underhill, *Mysticism*, Methuen and Co. 1912, p. 532.
13. Samuel Smiles, *Self-Help*, S.W. Partridge and Co. 1912, p. 54.
14. King, *The Words of Martin Luther King*, 1986, p. 59.
15. Michel Quoist, *With Open Heart*, translated by Colette Copeland, Gill and Macmillan 1983, p. 186.
16. Albert Schweitzer, *The Philosophy of Civilization, The Decay and Restoration of Civilization*, translated by C.T. Campion, A. and C. Black 1932, p. 16.

Purpose

1. NRSV.
2. NRSV.
3. George Eliot, *Daniel Deronda*, J.M. Dent and Sons 1964, vol. II, p. 580.
4. Charles H. Parkhurst, *The Pattern in the Mount*, R.D. Dickinson 1890, p. 8.
5. Johann Wolfgang von Goethe, *Wilhelm Meister's Apprenticeship*, *The Practical Wisdom of Goethe*, chosen by Emil Ludwig, Secker and Warburg 1933, p. 26.
6. A.R. Orage, *On Love*, The Janus Press 1957, p. 54.
7. Norman W. Goodacre, 'Laymen's Lent', A.R. Mowbray and Co. 1969, p. 33.
8. William Barclay, *The Letters to Timothy and Titus*, The Saint Andrew Press 1965, p. 225.
9. Anon.
10. W.E. Sangster, *God Does Guide Us*, Hodder and Stoughton 1934, p. 30.
11. Bertrand Russell, *The Conquest of Happiness*, George Allen and Unwin 1984, p. 48.
12. Miguel de Unamuno, *The Tragic Sense of Life*, Macmillan and Co. 1921, p. 152.
13. Antoine de Saint-Exupéry, *The Wisdom of the Sands*, translated by Stuart Gilbert, Hollis and Carter 1952, p. 127.
14. Helen Keller, *Helen Keller's Journal*, Michael Joseph 1938, p. 64.
15. Alexis Carrel, *Reflections on Life*, Hamish Hamilton 1952, p. 131.
16. Ross Parmenter, *The Plant in My Window*, Geoffrey Bles 1951, p. 39.
17. Edward Young, *Night Thoughts*, Thomas Nelson 1841, p. 17.
18. Albert Einstein, *Ideas and Opinions*, Souvenir Press (Educational and Academic) 1973, p. 11.
19. George Bernard Shaw, *The Complete Bernard Shaw Prefaces*, Paul Hamlyn 1965, p. 163.
20. Neville Cryer, *Michel Quoist*, Hodder and Stoughton 1977, p. 53.
21. W. MacNeile Dixon, *The Human Situation*, Edward Arnold and Co. 1937, p. 34.
22. Anon.

Quietness

1. NRSV.
2. NRSV.
3. Alistair MacLean, *The Quiet Heart*, Allenson and Co. 1940, p. 25.
4. Charles Guthrie, *God in His World*, Independent Press 1955, p. 43.
5. Antoine de Saint-Exupéry, *The Wisdom of the Sands*, translated by Stuart Gilbert, Hollis and Carter 1952, p. 45.
6. Bertrand Russell, *The Conquest of Happiness*, George Allen and Unwin 1984, p. 52.
7. Samuel Taylor Coleridge, 'Ode to Tranquillity', *Coleridge's Poetical Works*, edited by Ernest Hartley Coleridge, Oxford University Press 1978, p. 360.
8. Blaise Pascal, *Pensées*, translated by W.F. Trotter, Random House 1941, p. 48.
9. Evelyn Underhill, *Mysticism*, Methuen and Co. 1912, p. 210.
10. Mark Rutherford, *Last Pages from a Journal*, Oxford University Press 1915, p. 273.
11. Russell, *The Conquest of Happiness*, p. 49.
12. Roy Stevens, *Education and the Death of Love*, Epworth Press 1978, p. 127.
13. Ladislaus Boros, *In Time of Temptation*, translated by Simon and Erika Young, Burns and Oates 1968, p. 18.
14. John Greenleaf Whittier, 'The Brewing of Soma', *The Poetical Works of John Greenleaf Whittier*, Macmillan and Co. 1874, p. 457.
15. Charles Kingsley, *Daily Thoughts*, Macmillan and Co. 1884, p. 139.
16. Michel Quoist, *With Open Heart*, translated by Colette Copeland, Gill and Macmillan 1983, p. 65.
17. Henri J.M. Nouwen, in Robert Durback, *Seeds of Hope*, Darton, Longman and Todd 1989, p. 70.
18. Gerhard Tersteegen, in Frances Bevan, *Sketches of the Quiet in the Land*, John F. Shaw and Co. 1891, p. 400.

Relationships

1. NRSV.
2. NRSV.
3. Michel Quoist, *With Open Heart,* translated by Colette Copeland, Gill and Macmillan 1983, p. 36.
4. Henri J.M. Nouwen, *Reaching Out,* William Collins Sons and Co. 1980, p. 32.
5. Mark Rutherford, *Last Pages from a Journal,* Oxford University Press 1915, p. 261.
6. Eric Hoffer, *The Passionate State of Mind,* Martin Secker and Warburg 1956, p. 70.
7. W.H. Vanstone, *Love's Endeavour, Love's Expense,* Darton, Longman and Todd 1978, p. 45.
8. A.C. Benson, *Extracts from the Letters of Dr A.C. Benson to M.E.A.,* Jarrold Publishing 1927, p. 12.
9. Henry Wadsworth Longfellow, 'Evangeline', *The Poetical Works of Longfellow,* Humphrey Milford, Oxford University Press 1913, 'Part the Second', l.55, p. 158.
10. David Grayson, *The Friendly Road,* Andrew Melrose 1946, p. 117.
11. Dietrich Bonhoeffer, *Letters and Papers from Prison,* edited by Eberhard Bethge, translated by R.H. Fuller, SCM Press 1967, second revised edition, p. 212.
12. J.B. Priestley, *All About Ourselves and Other Essays,* William Heinemann 1956, p. 232.
13. C.G. Jung, *Contributions to Analytical Psychology,* translated by H.G. and Cary F. Baynes, Kegan Paul, Trench, Trubner and Co. 1928, p. 185.
14. Emid Rideau, in George Appleton, *Journey for a Soul,* William Collins Sons and Co. 1976, p. 26.
15. Appleton, *Journey for a Soul,* 1976, p. 27.
16. Sir Sarvepalli Radhakrishnan, *Mahatma Gandhi,* George Allen and Unwin 1949, p. 18.
17. D.H. Lawrence, *The Phoenix,* edited by Edward D. McDonald, William Heinemann 1936, p. 528.
18. R.C. Zaehner, *Mysticism Sacred and Profance,* Oxford University Press 1967, p. 152.

Resurrection

1. NRSV.
2. NRSV.
3. Alan Richardson, *History Sacred and Profane,* SCM Press 1964, p. 206.
4. Carlo Carretto, *The Desert in the City,* translated by Barbara Wall, William Collins Sons and Co. 1983, p. 103.
5. Austin Farrer, *Saving Belief,* Hodder and Stoughton 1964, p. 83.
6. Blaise Pascal, *Pensées,* translated by W.F. Trotter, Random House 1941, p. 77.
7. William Temple, *Nature, Man and God,* Macmillan and Co. 1934, p. 461.
8. Charles Kingsley, *Daily Thoughts,* Macmillan and Co. 1884, p. 171.
9. George Appleton, *Journey for a Soul,* William Collins Sons and Co. 1976, p. 16.
10. William Barclay, *The Letters to the Corinthians,* The Saint Andrew Press 1988, p. 141.
11. Michael Ramsey, in Margaret Duggan, *Through the Year with Michael Ramsey,* Hodder and Stoughton 1975, p. 71.
12. Michael Ramsey, in Gerald Priestland, *Priestland's Progress,* BBC Worldwide 1982, p. 111.
13. Henri J.M. Nouwen, in Robert Durback, *Seeds of Hope,* Darton, Longman and Todd 1989, p. 137.
14. Barclay, *The Letters to the Corinthians,* p. 141.
15. Anthony Bloom, *School for Prayer,* Darton, Longman and Todd 1970, p. xi.

Revelation

1. NRSV.
2. NRSV.
3. Gerard Manley Hopkins, 'God's Grandeur', *The Poems of Gerard Manley Hopkins,* Oxford University Press 1967, p. 66.
4. Mark Rutherford, *More Pages from a Journal,* Oxford University Press 1910, p. 251.
5. Benjamin Whichcote, *Moral and Religious Aphorisms,* Elkin Mathews and Marrot 1930, p. 51.
6. Leo Tolstoy, *Anna Karenina,* translated by Rosemary Edmonds, Penguin Books 1983, p. 851.

7. Blaise Pascal, *Pensées*, translated by W.F. Trotter, Random House 1941, p. 98.
8. Walter Hilton, *The Ladder of Perfection*, translated by Leo Sherley-Price, Penguin Books 1957, p. 252.
9. Emil Brunner, *Our Faith*, translated by John W. Rilling, Charles Scribner's Sons 1936, p. 11.
10. Evelyn Underhill, *The School of Charity*, Longmans, Green and Co. 1956, p. 12.
11. Ralph Waldo Emerson, *The Heart of Emerson's Journals*, edited by Bliss Perry, Constable and Co. 1927, p. 53.
12. Francis Bacon, *The Advancement of Learning*, Cassell and Co. 1905, p. 81.
13. Gabriel Moran FSC, *Theology of Revelation*, Burns and Oates 1967, p. 127.
14. William Barclay, *The Gospel of John*, The Saint Andrew Press 1974, vol. II, p. 227.
15. William Temple, *Nature, Man and God*, Macmillan and Co. 1934, p. 266.
16. W.R. Inge, *Personal Religion and the Life of Devotion*, Longmans, Green and Co. 1924, p. 16.
17. Temple, *Nature, Man and God*, 1934, p. 319.
18. Barclay, *The Gospel of John*, vol. II, p. 227.

Saints

1. NRSV.
2. NRSV.
3. Kenneth Leech, *True Prayer*, Sheldon Press 1980, p. 36.
4. Benedicta Ward, in Alan Richardson and John Bowden, *A New Dictionary of Christian Theology*, SCM Press 1985, p. 518.
5. Norman Douglas, *An Almanac*, Chatto and Windus in association with Martin Secker and Warburg 1945, p. 13.
6. Blaise Pascal, *Pensées*, translated by W.F. Trotter, Random House 1941, p. 165.
7. Kenneth Leech, *True Prayer*, Sheldon Press 1980, p. 36.
8. Anon.
9. Søren Kierkegaard, *The Journals of Søren Kierkegaard*, edited and translated by Alexander Dru, Oxford University Press 1938, p. 59.
10. Benjamin Jowett, *College Sermons*, edited by W.H. Fremantle, John Murray 1895, p. 317.
11. Coventry Patmore, *The Rod, the Root and the Flower*, 'Aurea Dicta', Grey Walls Press 1950, p. 51.
12. Rufus M. Jones, *Spiritual Reformers in the 16th and 17th Centuries*, Macmillan and Co. 1914, p. 336.
13. Evelyn Underhill, in John Stobbart, *The Wisdom of Evelyn Underhill*, Mowbray 1951, p. 30.
14. Meister Eckhart, in Franz Pfeiffer, *Meister Eckhart*, vol. 1, translated by C. de B. Evans, John M. Watkins 1956, p. 327.
15. W.E. Sangster, *The Pure in Heart*, Epworth Press 1954, p. 96.
16. W.H. Auden, *A Certain World*, Faber and Faber 1971, p. 331.
17. Thomas Merton, *Seeds of Contemplation*, Anthony Clarke Books 1972, p. 20.
18. Evelyn Underhill, *Man and the Supernatural*, Methuen and Co. 1927, p. 211.
19. W.R. Inge, *Types of Christian Saintliness*, Longmans, Green and Co. 1915, p. 92.
20. Thomas Merton, *The Sign of Jonas*, Sheldon Press 1976, p. 262.
21. Underhill in Stobbart, *The Wisdom of Evelyn Underhill*, p. 30.

Salvation

1. NRSV.
2. NRSV.
3. Charles Péguy, *Basic Verities*, translated by Ann and Julian Green, Kegan Paul, Trench, Trubner and Co. 1943, p. 181.
4. Father Andrew SDC, *Meditations for Every Day*, A.R. Mowbray and Co. 1941, p. 164.
5. Frank Wright, *The Pastoral Nature of the Ministry*, SCM Press 1980, p. 16.
6. Don Cupitt, *Taking Leave of God*, SCM Press 1980, p. 9.
7. Norman W. Goodacre, *Laymen's Lent*, A.R. Mowbray and Co. 1969, p. 31.

8. C.G. Jung, *The Integration of the Personality*, Kegan Paul, Trench, Trubner and Co. 1941, p. 158.
9. George Macdonald, *Unspoken Sermons*, Longmans, Green and Co. 1889, Third Series, p. 96.
10. Henry McKeating, *God and the Future*, SCM Press 1974, p. 8.
11. William Barclay, *The Letters to the Corinthians*, The Saint Andrew Press 1988, p. 143.
12. William Law, in Stephen Hobhouse, *Selected Mystical Writings of William Law*, Rockliff 1948, p. 102.
13. Rufus M. Jones, *Spiritual Reformers in the 16th and 17th Centuries*, Macmillan and Co. 1914, p. 147.
14. William Temple, *Nature, Man and God*, Macmillan and Co. 1934, p. 390.
15. Henri Frédéric Amiel, *Amiel's Journal*, translated by Mrs Humphry Ward, Macmillan and Co. 1918, p. 70.
16. Thomas Merton, *No Man Is an Island*, Burns and Oates 1974, p. xiv.
17. Law in Hobhouse, *Selected Mystical Writings of William Law*, p. 102.

Science And Religion

1. NRSV.
2. NRSV.
3. Albert Einstein, *Out of My Later Years*, Thames and Hudson 1950, p. 26.
4. Henry Ward Beecher, *Proverbs from Plymouth Pulpit*, Charles Burnet and Co. 1887, p. 118.
5. Michel Quoist, *With Open Heart*, translated by Colette Copeland, Gill and Macmillan 1983, p. 196.
6. G.A. Studdert Kennedy, *Food for the Fed-Up*, Hodder and Stoughton 1921, p. 34.
7. Helen Keller, *My Religion*, Hodder and Stoughton 1927, p. 162.
8. A.R. Orage, *On Love*, The Janus Press 1957, p. 57.
9. Henry Ward Beecher, *Proverbs from Plymouth Pulpit*, Charles Burnet and Co. 1887, p. 138.
10. Martin Luther King, *Strength to Love*, William Collins Sons and Co. 1980, p. 74.
11. Max Planck, *Where is Science Going?*, translated and edited by James Murphy, George Allen and Unwin 1933, p. 214.
12. J.W.N. Sullivan, *Limitations of Science*, Chatto and Windus 1933, p. 266.
13. William Temple, *Nature, Man and God*, Macmillan and Co. 1934, p. 11.
14. Planck, *Where is Science Going?*, p. 217.
15. Martin Luther King, in Coretta Scott King, *The Words of Martin Luther King*, William Collins Sons and Co. 1986, p. 63.
16. Michael Ramsey, in Margaret Duggan, *Through the Year with Michael Ramsey*, Hodder and Stoughton 1975, p. 147.
17. Temple, *Nature, Man and God*, p. 216.
18. Albert Einstein, *Ideas and Opinions*, Souvenir Press (Educational and Academic) 1973, p. 40.

Seeking

1. NRSV.
2. NRSV.
3. Christopher Bryant SSJE, *Jung and the Christian Way*, Darton, Longman and Todd 1983, p. 105.
4. George Moore, *The Brook Kerith*, William Heinemann 1927, p. 121.
5. Arthur T. Jersild, *The Psychology of Adolescence*, The Macmillan Co. 1963, p. 10.
6. William Barclay, *The Gospel of Matthew*, The Saint Andrew Press 1975, vol. II, p. 17.
7. Rufus M. Jones, *Spiritual Reformers in the 16th and 17th Centuries*, Macmillan and Co. 1914, p. 24.
8. Thomas Merton, *Contemplation in a World of Action*, Unwin Paperbacks 1980, p. 231.
9. Meister Eckhart, *Meister Eckhart*, translated by Raymond B. Blakney, Harper and Row 1941, p. 167.
10. Etienne Gilson, *The Spirit of Medieval Philosophy*, translated by A.H.C. Downes, Sheed and Ward 1950, p. 274.
11. Stephen MacKenna, *Journal and Letters*, Constable and Co. 1936, p. 206.
12. A.C. Benson, *Extracts from the Letters of Dr A.C. Benson to M.E.A.*, Jarrold Publishing 1927, p. 15.

13. Eckhart, *Meister Eckhart*, p. 7.
14. Martin Luther King, in Coretta Scott King, *The Words of Martin Luther King*, William Collins Sons and Co. 1986, p. 64.
15. Thomas Merton, *New Seeds of Contemplation*, Burns and Oates 1962, p. 13.
16. Isobel Kuhn, *By Searching*, Overseas Missionary Fellowship (IHQ) 1990, p. 93.
17. Harry Blamires, *The Will and the Way*, SPCK 1957, p. x.

Self

1. NRSV.
2. NRSV.
3. A.C. Benson, *Extracts from the Letters of Dr A.C. Benson to M.E.A.*, Jarrold Publishing 1927, p. 64.
4. Benjamin Whichcote, *Moral and Religious Aphorisms*, Elkin Mathews and Marrot 1930, p. 30.
5. Robert Browing, 'Bishop Blougram's Apology', *The Poetical Works of Robert Browning*, Smith, Elder, and Co. 1897, vol. 1, p. 533.
6. Mary Craig, *Blessings*, Hodder and Stoughton 1979, p. 104.
7. Matthew Arnold, 'Self-Dependence', edited by Kenneth Allott, Longmans, Green and Co. 1965, l.31, p. 144.
8. Albert Eistein, *Ideas and Opinions*, Souvenir Press (Educational and Academic) 1973, p. 12.
9. Michel Quoist, *With Open Heart*, translated by Colette Copeland, Gill and Macmillan 1983, p. 41.
10. D.H. Lawrence, *The Phoenix*, edited by Edward D. McDonald, William Heinemann 1936, p. 714.
11. William Law, *A Serious Call to a Devout and Holy Life*, J.M. Dent and Sons 1898, p. 288.
12. W.R. Inge, *The Philosophy of Plotinus*, Longmans, Green and Co. 1918, vol. 1, p. 248.
13. Henry Wadsworth Longfellow, 'The Poems', *The Poetical Works of Longfellow*, Humphrey Milford, Oxford University Press 1913, p. 717.
14. John S. Brubacher, *Modern Philosophies of Education*, McGraw-Hill Book Co. 1969, p. 9.
15. David Anderson, *Simone Weil*, SCM Press 1971, p. 61.
16. William Barclay, *The Letters to Timothy, Titus and Philemon*, The Saint Andrew Press 1987, p. 184.
17. William Law, *The Spirit of Prayer*, full text, edited by Sidney Spencer, James Clarke and Co. 1969, p. 44.
18. Anne Morrow Lindbergh, *Gift from the Sea*, Chatto and Windus 1974, p. 68.
19. John Macquarrie, *Paths in Spirituality*, SCM Press 1972, p. 45.
20. Harry James Cargas, *Encountering Myself*, SPCK 1978, p. 14.

Selfishness

1. NRSV.
2. NRSV.
3. Taoist saying.
4. Edward Young, *Night Thoughts*, Thomas Nelson 1841, p. 8.
5. Henry Ward Beecher, *Proverbs from Plymouth Pulpit*, Charles Burnet and Co. 1887, p. 191.
6. Robert Browning, 'Luria', *The Poetical Works of Robert Browning*, vol. 1, Smith, Elder and Co. 1899, act 1, p. 441.
7. Thomas Merton, *The Sign of Jonas*, Sheldon Press 1976, p. 102.
8. Norman Douglas, *An Almanac*, Chatto and Windus in association with Martin Secker and Warburg 1945, p. 60.
9. Henry Ward Beecher, *Proverbs from Plymouth Pulpit*, Charles Burnet and Co. 1887, p. 49.
10. A.R. Orage, *On Love*, The Janus Press 1957, p. 60.
11. Erich Fromm, *Man for Himself*, Routledge and Kegan Paul 1975, p. 131.
12. Beecher, *Proverbs from Plymouth Pulpit*, p. 154.
13. John Woolman, *The Journal of John Woolman*, Edward Marsh 1857, p. 311.
14. Martin Luther King, in Coretta Scott King, *The Words of Martin Luther King*, William Collins Sons and Co. 1986, p. 17.

15. William James, *The Varieties of Religious Experience*, William Collins Sons and Co. 1974, p. 136.
16. Morris West, *The Shoes of the Fisherman*, William Heinemann 1963, p. 296.
17. Pierre Teilhard de Chardin, *Let Me Explain*, William Collins Sons and Co. 1970, p. 137.
18. William Temple, *The Kingdom of God*, Macmillan Publishers 1912, p. 96.
19. William Temple, *The Preacher's Theme Today*, SPCK 1936, p. 52.
20. William Temple, *Nature, Man and God*, Macmillan and Co. 1934, p. 424.
21. George Appleton, *Journey for a Soul*, William Collins Sons and Co. 1976, p. 121.

Serenity

1. NRSV.
2. RSV.
3. Cyril Connolly, *The Unquiet Grave*, Hamish Hamilton 1945, p. 13.
4. Reinhold Niebuhr, *Reflections on the End of an Era*, Charles Scribner's Sons 1936, p. 284.
5. Benjamin Whichcote, *Moral and Religious Aphorisms* 1930, century III, no.280.
6. Matthew Prior, 'Carmen Seculare for the Year MDCC', *The Poetical Works of Matthew Prior*, edited by Charles Cowden Clarke, William P. Nimmo 1868, p. 116.
7. William Barclay, *The Gospel of Matthew*, The Saint Andrew Press 1975, vol. II, p. 37.
8. Odell Shepard, *The Joys of Forgetting*, George Allen and Unwin 1928, p. 22.
9. Washington Irving, *The Sketch-Book*, George Newnes 1902, vol. 11, p. 226.
10. William Johnston, *The Mysticism of the Cloud of Unknowing*, Anthony Clarke Books 1978, p 265.
11. William Wordsworth, in W.E. Sangster, *The Secret of Radiant Life*, Hodder and Stoughton 1957, p. 14.
12. Henry Miller, *The Books in My Life*, Village Press 1974, p. 59.
13. Arthur T. Jersild, in *Educational Psychology*, edited by Charles E. Skinner, Staples Press 1952, p. 93.
14. Henri Frédéric Amiel, *Amiel's Journal*, translated by Mrs Humphry Ward, Macmillan and Co., p. 263.
15. Alistair Maclean, in *God in Our Midst*, Triangle/SPCK 1989, p. 27.
16. William Wordsworth, 'Ode to Duty', *The Poetical Works of William Wordsworth*, edited by E. de Selincourt and Helen Darbishire, Oxford at the Clarendon Press 1958, vol. IV, p. 84.
17. Romain Gary, *Promise at Dawn*, Michael Joseph 1962, p. 26.
18. George Appleton, *Journey for a Soul*, William Collins Sons and Co. 1976, p. 99.
19. Amiel, *Amiel's Journal*, p. 263.

Service

1. NRSV.
2. NRSV.
3. George Herbert, 'The Church Porch', *The Works of George Herbert*, edited by F.E. Hutchinson, Oxford at the Clarendon Press 1972, p. 19.
4. Rabindranath Tagore, *Stray Birds*, *Collected Poems and Plays of Rabindranath Tagore*, Macmillan and Co. 1936, lvi, p. 294.
5. John Milton, 'Sonnet on His Blindness', *John Milton: Complete Shorter Poems*, edited by John Carey, Longmans Group 1971, 83, Sonnet XVI, l.14, p. 328.
6. Dietrich Bonhoeffer, *The Cost of Discipleship*, revised and abridged edition, SCM Press 1959, p. 118.
7. St Francis de Sales, *On the Love of God*, Methuen and Co. 1902, p. 94.
8. Dag Hammarskjöld, *Markings*, translated by Leif Sjoberg and W.H. Auden, Faber and Faber 1964, p. 135.
9. Rabindranath Tagore, *Stray Birds*, *Collected Poems and Plays of Rabindranath Tagore*, Macmillan and Co. 1936, ccxvii, p. 315.
10. A.R. Orage, *On Love*, The Janus Press 1957, p. 61.
11. Hans Küng, *On Being a Christian*, translated by Edward Quinn, William Collins Sons and Co. 1977, p. 253.

12. Hubert van Zeller, *Considerations*, Sheed and Ward 1974, p. 124.
13. William Temple, *Readings in St John's Gospel*, first and second series, Macmillan and Co. 1947, p. 258.
14. Emil Brunner, *The Divine Imperative*, translated by Olive Wyon, Lutterworth Press 1942, p. 189.
15. Evelyn Underhill, *The Light of Christ*, Longmans, Green and Co. 1944, p. 94.
16. E.G. Rupp, in Alan Richardson and John Bowden, *A New Dictionary of Christian Theology*, SCM Press 1985, p. 441.
17. Albert Schweitzer, *My Life and Thought*, translated by C.T. Campion, George Allen and Unwin 1933, p. 103.
18. Martin Luther King, in Coretta Scott King, *The Words of Martin Luther King*, William Collins Sons and Co. 1986, p. 17.
19. Henri Frédéric Amiel, *Amiel's Journal*, translated by Mrs Humphry Ward, Macmillan and Co. 1918, p 147.
20. D.H. Lawrence, 'Service', *The Complete Poems of D.H. Lawrence*, edited by Vivian de Sola Pinto and Warren Roberts, William Heinemann 1967, vol. II, p. 650.

Sin

1. NRSV.
2. NRSV.
3. St Augustine, *Confessions*, translated by R.S. Pine-Coffin, Penguin Books 1964, p. 33.
4. G.W.H. Lampe, in A.R. Vidler, *Soundings*, Cambridge at the University Press 1962, p. 186.
5. James Rhoades, in Ralph Waldo Trine, *My Philosophy and My Relgion*, George Bell and Sons 1926, p. 27.
6. George Bernard Shaw, *The Devil's Disciple*, *The Complete Plays of Bernard Shaw*, Paul Hamlyn 1965, act II, p. 230.
7. J. Neville Ward, *The Use of Praying*, Epworth Press 1967, p. 45.
8. C.S. Lewis, *The Screwtape Letters*, William Collins Sons and Co. 1960, p. 65.
9. Eric Hoffer, *The Passionate State of Mind*, Secker and Warburg 1956, p. 70.
10. Martin Buber, *Hasidism*, The Philosophical Library 1948, p. 71.
11. Hubert van Zeller, *Considerations*, Sheed and Ward 1974, p. 49.
12. Harvey Cox, *God's Revolution and Man's Responsibility*, SCM Press 1969, p. 40.
13. Walter Hilton, *The Ladder of Perfection*, translated by Leo Sherley-Price, Penguin Books 1957, p. 109.
14. George Appleton, *Journey for a Soul*, William Collins Sons and Co. 1976, p. 122.
15. Phyllis McGinley, *The Province of the Heart*, The World's Work (1913) 1962, p. 35.
16. Father Yelchaninov, in G.P. Fedotov, *A Treasury of Russian Spirituality*, Sheed and Ward 1977, p. 461.
17. William Temple, *Christian Faith and Life*, SCM Press 1963, p. 65.
18. Appleton, *Journey for a Soul*, p. 122.
19. Kenneth Barnes, in Gerald Priestland, *Priestland's Progress*, BBC Worldwide 1982, p. 72.
20. J.S. Whale, *Christian Doctrine*, Cambridge University Press 1942, p. 52.

Soul

1. NRSV.
2. NRSV.
3. James A. Froude, *Thomas Carlyle*, Longmans, Green, and Co. 1884, vol. 2, p. 35.
4. Henry Miller, *The Books in My Life*, Village Press 1974, p. 212.
5. Henry Ward Beecher, *Proverbs from Plymouth Pulpit*, Charles Burnet and Co. 1887, p. 153.
6. Rabindranath Tagore, *Stray Birds*, *Collected Poems and Plays of Rabindranath Tagore*, Macmillan and Co. 1936, cccxii, p. 327.
7. Miller, *The Books in My Life*, p. 193.
8. Beecher, *Proverbs from Plymouth Pulpit*, p. 27.
9. St John of the Cross, *Living Flame of Love*, translated by E. Allison Peers, Image Books 1962, p. 40.

10. Richard Jefferies, *The Story of My Heart*, Macmillan and Co. 1968, p. 8.
11. Henry Ward Beecher, *Proverbs from Plymouth Pulpit*, Charles Burnet and Co. 1887, p. 31.
12. Jean-Pierre de Caussade SJ, *Self-Abandonment to Divine Providence*, translated by Algar Thorold, William Collins Sons and Co. 1972, p. 37.
13. C.G. Jung, *The Collected Works of C.G. Jung*, translated by R.F.C. Hull, Routledge and Kegan Paul 1953, vol. XII, p. 8.
14. Beecher, *Proverbs from Plymouth Pulpit*, p. 31.
15. Richard Jefferies, *The Story of My Heart*, Duckworth and Co. 1923, p. 143.
16. Meister Eckhart, *Meister Eckhart*, translated by Raymond B. Blakney, Harper and Row 1941, p. 97.
17. Matthew Arnold, 'A Southern Night', *The Poems of Matthew Arnold*, edited by Kenneth Allott, Longmans, Green and Co. 1965, p. 460.
18. Oscar Wilde, *De Profundis*, *The Works of Oscar Wilde*, William Collins Sons and Co. 1948, p. 870.
19. Samuel Taylor Coleridge, *Table Talk of Samuel Taylor Coleridge*, George Routledge and Sons 1884, p. 33.
20. Henri Frédéric Amiel, *Amiel's Journal*, translated by Mrs Humphry Ward, Macmillan and Co. 1918, p. 247.

Suffering

1. NRSV.
2. NRSV.
3. Greek proverb.
4. Latin proverb.
5. Martin Luther King, in Coretta Scott King, *The Words of Martin Luther King*, William Collins Sons and Co. 1986, p. 67.
6. Helen Keller, *Optimism*, George G. Harrop 1903, p. 17.
7. George Eliot, *Adam Bede*, J.M. Dent and Sons 1960, p. 409.
8. Henry Wadsworth Longfellow, 'The Light of Stars', *The Poetical Works of Longfellow*, edited by Humphrey Milford, Oxford University Press 1913, p. 4.
9. C.G. Jung, *Psychology and Alchemy*, *The Collected Works of C.G. Jung*, vol. XII, translated by R.F.C. Hull, Routledge and Kegan Paul 1953, p. 22.
10. A.C. Benson, *Extracts from the Letters of Dr A.C. Benson to M.E.A.*, Jarrold Publishing 1927, p. 13.
11. F.W. Robertson, *Sermons*, fifth series, Kegan Paul, Trench, Trubner and Co. 1890, p. 17.
12. J. Neville Ward, *Friday Afternoon*, Epworth Press 1982, p. 97.
13. Rabbi H. Kushner, *When Bad Things Happen to Good People*, Pan Books 1982, p. 142.
14. Hubert van Zeller, *Considerations*, Sheed and Ward 1974, p. 122.
15. Hans Küng, *On Being a Christian*, translated by Edward Quinn, William Collins Sons and Co. 1977, p. 299.
16. George Appleton, *Journey for a Soul*, William Collins Sons and Co. 1976, p. 51.
17. John V. Taylor, *The Go-Between God*, SCM Press 1973, p. 146.
18. Hugh L'Anson Fausset, *Fruits of Silence*, Abelard-Schuman 1963, p. 197.
19. Appleton, *Journey for a Soul*, p. 50.

Temptation

1. NRSV.
2. NRSV.
3. Thomas Fuller, *Gnomologia*, Stearne Brock 1733, p. 21.
4. Ralph Waldo Emerson, 'Compensation', *Essays*, Bernhard Tauchnitz 1915, p. 84.
5. Charles Dickens, *Nicholas Nickleby*, The Gresham Publishing Co. 1904, p. 36.
6. Thomas à Kempis, *The Imitation of Christ*, translated by Betty I. Knott, William Collins Sons and Co. 1979, p. 53.
7. Lady Julian of Norwich, *Revelations of Divine Love*, translated by Clifton Wolters, Penguin Books 1976, p. 185.

8. Robert Herrick, 'Temptations', *The Poetical Works of Robert Herrick*, edited by F.W. Moorman, Oxford at the Clarendon Press 1915, p. 389.

9. F. de la M. Fénelon, in B.W. Randolph, *Letters and Reflections of Fénelon*, A.R. Mowbray and Co. 1906, p. 93.

10. William Temple, *Readings in St John's Gospel*, first and second series, Macmillan and Co. 1947, p. xxvi.

11. William Barclay, *The Gospel of Luke*, The Saint Andrew Press 1965, p. 146.

12. Robert Burns, 'A Prayer in the Prospect of Death', edited by James Kinsley, *The Poems and Songs of Robert Burns*, Oxford at the Clarendon Press 1968, vol. 1, p. 20.

13. Thomas à Kempis, *The Imitation of Christ*, p. 53.

14. Edmund Spenser, 'The Faerie Queene', edited by J.C. Smith, Oxford at the Clarendon Press 1964, p. 95.

15. William James, *The Principles of Psychology*, Macmillan and Co. 1890, vol. 1, p. 127.

16. Olive Wyon, *On the Way*, SCM Press 1958, p. 55.

17. John Tauler, *The History and Life of the Reverend Doctor John Tauler*, translated by Susanna Winkworth, Smith, Elder and Co. 1857, p. 404.

18. Fénelon in Randolph, *Letters and Reflections of Fénelon*, p. 93.

Thanksgiving

1. NRSV.

2. NRSV.

3. Theodor Haecker, *Journal in the Night*, translated by Alexander Dru, The Harvill Press 1950, p. 1.

4. Samuel Johnson, *Boswell's Life of Johnson*, vol. V, edited by G.B. Hill, revised by L.F. Powell, Oxford at the Clarendon Press 1950, p. 232.

5. Kahlil Gibran, *The Prophet*, William Heinemann 1970, p. 15.

6. Izaak Walton, *The Compleat Angler*, Macmillan and Co. 1906, p. 172.

7. William Shakespeare, *II King Henry VI*, act II.i.85.

8. G.K. Chesterton, *Autobiography*, Hutchinson and Co. 1969, p. 330.

9. Elizabeth Helme, *St Margaret's Cave; or, The Nun's Story*, printed for Earle and Hemet 1801, vol. 2, p. 141.

10. Michael Ramsey, in Margaret Duggan, *Through the Year with Michael Ramsey*, Hodder and Stoughton 1975, p. 82.

11. Anon.

12. W.E. Sangster, *Westminster Sermons*, Epworth Press 1961, vol. 2, *At Fast and Festival*, p. 140.

13. Edward King, *Sermons and Addresses*, Longmans, Green and Co. 1911, p. 37.

14. Charles Kingsley, *Town and Country Sermons*, Macmillan and Co. 1868, p. 99.

15. William Law, *A Serious Call to a Devout and Holy Life*, J.M. Dent and Co. 1898, p. 231.

16. A.J. Gossip, *From the Edge of the Crowd*, T. and T. Clark 1925, p. 37.

17. Law, *A Serious Call to a Devout and Holy Life*, p. 231.

18. Edward King, *Sermons and Addresses*, Longmans, Green and Co. 1911, p. 37.

Thinking

1. NRSV.

2. NRSV.

3. William Blake, 'Proverbs of Hell', *The Complete Writings of William Blake*, edited by Geoffrey Keynes, Oxford University Press 1974, p. 151.

4. Ralph Waldo Emerson, 'Intellect', *Essays*, Bernhard Tauchnitz Edition 1915, p. 191.

5. Rabindranath Tagore, *Stray Birds*, *Collected Poems and Plays of Rabindranath Tagore*, Macmillan and Co. 1936, clxix, p. 308.

6. O.T. Beard, *Bristling with Thorns*, The Gregg Press 1968, p. 400.

7. Albert Schweitzer, *Out of My Life and Thought*, Henry Holt and Co. 1949, p. 236.

8. W.A. Macgregor, *Jesus Christ the Son of God*, T. and T. Clark 1907, p. 99.

9. Henry Wadsworth Longfellow, 'The Masque of Pandora', *The Poetical Works of Longfellow*, Humphrey Milford, Oxford University Press 1913, p. 688.

10. Thomas Mann, *Death in Venice*, translated by H.T. Lowe-Porter, Penguin Books 1978, p. 52.
11. Bertrand Russell, *Principles of Social Reconstruction*, George Allen and Unwin 1971, p. 155.
12. Albert Schweitzer, *The Teaching of Reverence for Life*, Peter Owen 1965, p. 33.
13. Mark Rutherford, *Last Pages from a Journal*, Oxford University Press 1915, p. 272.
14. William James, *The Varieties of Religious Experience*, William Collins Sons and Co. 1974, p. 119.
15. Helen Merry Lynd, *On Shame and the Search for Identity*, Routledge and Kegan Paul 1958, p. 251.
16. Daniel Defoe, *Moll Flanders*, Arandar Books 1946, p. 245.
17. Albert Schweitzer, *My Life and Thought*, translated by C.T. Campion, George Allen and Unwin 1933, p. 260.
18. Bertrand Russell, *Principles of Social Reconstruction*, George Allen and Unwin 1971, p. 114.
19. Michael Ramsey, in Margaret Duggan, *Through the Year with Michael Ramsey*, Hodder and Stoughton 1975, p. 24.
20. Russell, *Principles of Social Reconstruction*, p. 155.

Time

1. NRSV.
2. NRSV.
3. Benjamin Disraeli, *Henrietta Temple*, John Lane, The Bodley Head 1906, p. 430.
4. William Shakespeare, *Macbeth*, act III.i.48.
5. Johann Wolfgang von Goethe, in Ludwig Curtius, *Wisdom and Experience*, translated and edited by Hermann J. Weigand, Routledge and Kegan Paul 1949, p. 216.
6. Martin Luther King, in Coretta Scott King, *The Words of Martin Luther King*, William Collins Sons and Co. 1986, p. 33.
7. Sir John Lubbock, *The Pleasures of Life*, Macmillan and Co. 1881, p. 109.
8. Rollo May, *Man's Search for Himself*, George Allen and Unwin 1953, p. 259.
9. Dietrich Bonhoeffer, *Letters and Papers from Prison*, William Collins Sons and Co. 1963, p. 134.
10. Hubert van Zeller, *Considerations*, Sheed and Ward 1974, p. 60.
11. *The Cloud of Unknowing*, translated by Clifton Wolters, Penguin Books 1971, p. 56.
12. Peter Munz, *Problems of Religious Knowledge*, SCM Press 1959, p. 129.
13. Leslie J. Tizard, *Facing Life and Death*, George Allen and Unwin 1959, p. 162.
14. Meister Eckhard, in Franz Pfeiffer, *Meister Eckhart*, translated by C. de B. Evans, John M. Watkins 1956, vol. 1, p. 237.
15. Michel Quoist, *Prayers of Life*, translated by Anne Marie de Commaile and Agnes Mitchell Forsyth, Gill and Macmillan 1963, p. 76.
16. Henry Wadsworth Longfellow, 'Hyperion', George Routledge and Sons 1887, p. 123.
17. Anon. (on T.S. Eliot's 'Four Quartets').
18. Michel Quoist, *With Open Heart*, translated by Colette Copeland, Gill and Macmillan 1983, p. 137.
19. Mother Teresa, in Kathryn Spink, *In the Silence of the Heart*, SPCK 1983, p. 42.
20. George Appleton, *Journey for a Soul*, William Collins Sons and Co. 1976, p. 221.

Transformation

1. NRSV.
2. NRSV.
3. Nicolas Berdyaev, in Donald A. Lowrie, *Christian Existentialism*, George Allen and Unwin 1965, p. 248.
4. Martin Luther King, in Coretta Scott King, *The Words of Martin Luther King*, William Collins Sons and Co. 1986, p. 18.
5. Henry Ward Beecher, *Proverbs from Plymouth Pulpit*, Charles Burnet and Co. 1887, p. 161.
6. Martin Buber, in Aubrey Hodes, *Encounter with Martin Buber*, Allen Lane, The Penguin Press 1972, p. 83.
7. Francois de la M. Fénelon, in B.W. Randolph, *Maxims of the Mystics*, translated by W.W. Williams, A.R. Mowbray and Co. 1909, p. 104.

8. Maurice Maeterlinck, *The Treasure of the Humble*, translated by Alfred Sutro, George Allen, 1897, p. 185.
9. John Main OSB, in Clare Hallward, *The Joy of Being*, Darton, Longman and Todd 1989, p. 9.
10. William Barclay, *The Letters to Timothy and Titus*, The Saint Andrew Press 1965, p. 245.
11. E.Graham Howe and L. le Mesurier, *The Open Way*, Methuen and Co. 1939, p. 180.
12. Alan Ecclestone, *Yes to God*, Darton, Longman and Todd 1975, p. 116.
13. Henri Frédéric Amiel, *Amiel's Journal*, translated by Mrs Humphry Ward, Macmillan and Co. 1918, p. 285.
14. Helmut Thielicke, *I Believe – The Christian's Creed*, translated by John W. Doberstein and H. George Anderson, William Collins Sons and Co. 1969, p. 90.
15. Amiel, *Amiel's Journal*, p. 104.
16. Bede Griffiths OSB, in Peter Spink, *The Universal Christ*, Darton, Longman and Todd 1990, p. 27.
17. Hans Küng, *On Being a Christian*, translated by Edward Quinn, William Collins Sons and Co. 1977, p. 249.
18. Mark Rutherford, *More Pages from a Journal*, Oxford University Press 1910, p. 182.

Trust

1. NRSV.
2. NRSV.
3. George Herbert, *Outlandish Proverbs*, *The Works of George Herbert*, edited by F.E. Hutchinson, Oxford at the Clarendon Press 1972, p. 345.
4. Rabindranath Tagore, *Stray Birds*, *Collected Poems and Plays of Rabindranath Tagore*, Macmillan and Co. 1936, cccxxv, p. 329.
5. W.E. Sangster, *He is Able*, Hodder and Stoughton 1936, p. 42.
6. Henry Ward Beecher, *Proverbs from Plymouth Pulpit*, Charles Burnet and Co. 1887, p. 173.
7. Mark Gibbard, *Jesus, Liberation and Love*, A.R. Mowbray and Co. 1982, p. 55.
8. Beecher, *Proverbs from Plymouth Pulpit*, p. 145.
9. W.E. Sangster, *He Is Able*, Hodder and Stoughton 1936, p. 23.
10. Ralph Waldo Emerson, *Essays and Representative Men*, *The Works of Ralph Waldo Emerson*, edited by George Sampson, George Bell and Sons 1906, vol. 1, p. 128.
11. Charles Kingsley, *Daily Thoughts*, Macmillan and Co. 1884, p. 239.
12. A.W. Robinson, *The Personal Life of the Clergy*, Longmans, Green and Co. 1902, p. 157.
13. William Temple, *The Hope of a New World*, SCM Press 1940, p. 28.
14. John Greenleaf Whittier, 'The Brewing of Soma', *The Poetical Works of John Greenleaf Whittier*, Macmillan and Co. 1874, p. 457.
15. Leslie Tizard, *Facing Life and Death*, George Allen and Unwin 1959, p. 73.
16. Ralph Waldo Emerson, *Self-Reliance*, *The Works of Ralph Waldo Emerson*, George Bell and Sons 1906, vol. 1, *Essays and Representative Men*, p. 24.
17. George Appleton, *The Journey of a Soul*, William Collins Sons and Co. 1976, p. 84.
18. Kingsley, *Daily Thoughts*, p. 165.

Truth

1. NRSV.
2. NRSV.
3. Herman Melville, *Typee*, Heron Books 1968, p. 203.
4. Geoffrey Chaucer, *The Franklin's Tale*, G. Routledge and Co. 1838, p. 319.
5. Norman Douglas, *An Almanac*, Chatto and Windus in association with Martin Secker and Warburg, 1945, p. 37.
6. Henry David Thoreau, *Walden*, The New American Library of World Literature 1960, p. 219.
7. Rufus M. Jones, *Spiritual Reformers in the 16th and 17th Centuries*, Macmillan and Co. 1914, p. 90.
8. Kahlil Gibran, *The Prophet*, William Heinemann 1970, p. 66.
9. Maurice Maeterlinck, *The Treasure of the Humble*, translated by Alfred Sutro, George Allen 1897, p. 187.

10. F.W. Robertson, *Sermons,* first series, Kegan Paul, Trench, Trubner and Co. 1893, p. 289.
11. Johann Wolfgang von Goethe, in Ludwig Curtius, *Wisdom and Experience,* translated and edited by Hermann J. Weigang, Routledge and Kegan Paul 1949, p. 212.
12. D.H. Lawrence, *The Rainbow,* Cambridge University Press 1989, p. 317.
13. Albert Schweitzer, *Out of My Life and Thought,* translated by C.T. Campion, Henry Holt and Co. 1949, p. 249.
14. Robert Browning, 'The Ring and the Book', *The Complete Poetical Works of Robert Browning,* Ohio University Press 1988, vol. 8, vi. 2038, p. 156.
15. Albert Einstein, *Out of My Later Years,* Thames and Hudson 1950, p. 115.
16. William Barclay, *The Gospel of Luke,* The Saint Andrew Press 1964, p. 79.
17. Robertson, *Sermons,* p. 286.
18. Sydney Carter, *Dance in the Dark,* William Collins Sons and Co. 1980, p. 26.
19. W.E. Sangster, *The Pure in Heart,* Epworth Press 1954, p. 3.
20. Alistair MacLean, *The Happy Finder,* Allenson and Co. 1949, p. 71.
21. George Macdonald, *Unspoken Sermons,* third series, Longmans, Green and Co. 1889, p. 79.
22. William Temple, *Readings in St John's Gospel,* first and second series, Macmillan and Co. 1947, p. 230.
23. Albert Schweizer, *Christianity and the Religions of the World,* translated by Joanna Powers, George Allen and Unwin 1924, p. 18.
24. William Barclay, *The Gospel of John,* The Saint Andrew Press 1965, vol. 2, p. 25.

Understanding

1. NRSV.
2. NRSV.
3. Isadora Duncan, *My Life,* Sphere Books 1968, p. 60.
4. Søren Kierkegaard, in Harold Loukes, *The Quaker Contribution,* SCM Press 1965, p. 9.
5. J.B. Yeats, *Letters to His Son, W.B. Yeats and Others,* Faber and Faber 1944, p. 136.
6. Blaise Pascal, *Pensées,* translated by W.F. Trotter, Random House 1941, p. 277.
7. Andre Gidé, *The Journals of André Gide* 1894, translated by Justin O'Brien, Martin Secker and Warburg 1947, p. 41.
8. Ernest Hello, *Life, Science, and Art,* R. and T. Washbourne 1913, p. 106.
9. John Smith the Platonist, *Select Discourses,* Cambridge at the University Press 1859, p. 3.
10. Vincent van Gogh, *Dear Theo: An Autobiography of Vincent van Gogh,* edited by Irving Stone, Constable and Co. 1937, p. 28.
11. Harper Lee, *To Kill a Mockingbird,* Pan Books 1981, p. 35.
12. Erich Fromm, *Man for Himself,* Routledge and Kegan Paul 1975, p. 237.
13. Norman Douglas, *An Almanac,* Chatto and Windus in association with Martin Secker and Warburg 1945, p. 82.
14. Albert Einstein, *Ideas and Opinions,* Souvenir Press (Educational and Academic) 1973, p. 53.
15. René Voillaume, *The Need for Contemplation,* translated by Elizabeth Hamilton, Darton, Longman and Todd 1972, p. 58.
16. Katherine Mansfield, *Journal of Katherine Mansfield,* edited by John Middleton Murry, Constable and Co. 1927, p. 251.
17. Henry Miller, *The Cosmological Eye,* New Directions 1939, p. 282.
18. Søren Kierkegaard, *The Journals of Kierkegaard,* Harper and Row 1959, p. 68.
19. William Barclay, *The Gospel of John,* The Saint Andrew Press 1974, vol. 2, p. 93.
20. W. MacNeile Dixon, *The Human Situation,* Edward Arnold 1937, p. 64.

Vision

1. NRSV.
2. NRSV.
3. Thomas Traherne, *Centuries,* The Faith Press 1969, p. 71.
4. J.B. Yeats, *Letters to His Son, W.B. Yeats and Others,* Faber and Faber 1944, p. 179.

5. Charles Fletcher Dole, *The Hope of Immortality*, Houghton Mifflin Co., The Riverside Press 1906, p. 59.
6. Malaval, in Evelyn Underhill, *Mysticism*, Methuen and Co. 1912, p. 305.
7. Sir Richard Livingston, *On Education*, Cambridge at the University Press 1954, p. 151.
8. Mark Rutherford, *More Pages from a Journal*, Oxford University Press 1910, p. 220.
9. Ralph Waldo Emerson, *The Poet*, from *Essays and Representative Men*, *The Works of Ralph Waldo Emerson*, George Bell and Sons 1906, vol. 1, p. 213.
10. Rabindranath Tagore, *The Religion of Man*, George Allen and Unwin 1931, p. 117.
11. George Macdonald, *Cross Purposes and the Shadows*, Blackie and Son, 1891, p. 62.
12. Evelyn Underhill, edited by Charles Williams, *The Letters of Evelyn Underhill*, Longmans, Green and Co. 1947, p. 51.
13. Sir Sarvepalli Radhakrishnan, *Indian Philosophy*, George Allen and Unwin 1931, vol. II, p. 373.
14. Alfred North Whitehead, *Science and the Modern World*, Cambridge at the University Press 1932, p. 238.
15. Aldous Huxley, *Heaven and Hell*, Chatto and Windus 1956, p. 52.
16. Radhakrishnan, *Indian Philosophy*, p. 373.
17. J.W.N. Sullivan, *But for the Grace of God*, Jonathan Cape 1932, p. 133.
18. Alfred North Whitehead, *Science and the Modern World*, Cambridge at the University Press 1932, p. 238.

Vocation

1. NRSV.
2. NRSV.
3. Logan Pearsall Smith, *Afterthoughts*, Constable and Co. 1931, p. 54.
4. William Barclay, *The Gospel of Matthew*, The Saint Andrew Press 1965, vol. 2, p. 19.
5. Henry Ward Beecher, *Proverbs from Plymouth Pulpit*, Charles Burnet and Co. 1887, p. 48.
6. F.R. Barry, *Vocation and Ministry*, James Nisbet and Co. 1958, p. 8.
7. Henri Frédéric Amiel, *Amiel's Journal*, translated by Mrs Humphry Ward, Macmillan and Co. 1918, p. 45.
8. Plato, *The Republic of Plato*, translated by B. Jowett, Oxford at the Clarendon Press 1881, p. 49.
9. Beecher, *Proverbs from Plymouth Pulpit*, p. 165.
10. William Temple, *Christian Faith and Life*, SCM Press 1963, p. 107.
11. Michel Quoist, *With Open Heart*, translated by Colette Copeland, Gill and Macmillan 1983, p. 49.
12. Mother Teresa, in Brother Angelo Devananda, *Jesus, the Word to Be Spoken*, William Collins Sons and Co. 1990, p. 89.
13. Rosemay Haughton, *On Trying to Be Human*, Geoffrey Chapman 1966, p. 33.
14. William Barclay, *The Gospel of John*, The Saint Andrew Press 1965, vol. 1, p. 40.
15. Ralph Waldo Emerson, *Spiritual Laws*, *Essays*, Bernhard Tauchnitz 1915, p. 120.
16. Temple, *Christian Faith and Life*, p. 44.
17. Henry Drummond, *The Greatest Thing in the World*, William Collins Sons and Co. 1978, p. 291.
18. Temple, *Christian Faith and Life*, p. 139.

Wholeness

1. NRSV.
2. NRSV.
3. Rabindranath Tagore, *Stray Birds*, Indian edition, Macmillan and Co. 1941, p. 42.
4. Monica Furlong, *Travelling In*, Hodder and Stoughton 1971, p. 64.
5. Anon.
6. Aldous Huxley, *Island*, Chatto and Windus 1962, p. 92.
7. A.R. Orage, *On Love*, The Janus Press 1957, p. 59.
8. William of St Thierry, *The Golden Epistles of Abbot William of St Thierry*, Sheed and Ward 1930, p. 45.

9. Rabindranath Tagore, *Letters to a Friend*, George Allen and Unwin 1928, p. 55.
10. Jack Dominion, in Gerald Priestland, *Priestland's Progress*, BBC Worldwide 1982, p. 82.
11. Sir Julian Huxley, *Religion Without Revelation*, C.A. Watts and Co. 1967, p. 168.
12. George Appleton, *Journey for a Soul*, William Collins Sons and Co. 1976, p. 110.
13. Thomas Merton, *New Seeds of Contemplation*, Burns and Oates 1962, p. 106.
14. Morris West, *The Shoes of the Fisherman*, William Heinemann 1983, p. 204.
15. Colin Morris, *The Word and the Words*, Epworth Press 1975, p. 15.
16. Olive Wyon, *On the Way*, SCM Press 1958, p. 30.

Will

1. NRSV.
2. NRSV.
3. Dante Alighieri, *The Divine Comedy*, translated by Charles S. Singleton, Princeton University Press, Bollingen Series, LXXX 1977, vol. 1, 'Paradisio', iii.85.
4. John Milton, 'Paradise Lost', *The Poetical Works of John Milton*, edited by the Rev. H.C. Beeching, Oxford at the Clarendon Press 1900, book 1, p. 184.
5. Mother Teresa, in Brother Angelo Devananda, *Jesus, the Word to Be Spoken*, William Collins Sons and Co. 1990, p. 98.
6. William Barclay, *The Gospel of Matthew*, The Saint Andrew Press 1965, vol. 1, p. 127.
7. Vincent van Gogh, *Dear Theo: An Autobiography*, edited by Irving Stone, Constable and Co. 1937, p. 187.
8. John Smith the Platonist, *Select Discourses*, Cambridge at the University Press 1859, p. 9.
9. George Macdonald, *Unspoken Sermons*, Third Series, Longmans, Green and Co. 1889, p. 229.
10. Father Andrew SDC, *The Life and Letters of Fr Andrew SDC*, Mowbray 1948, p. 121.
11. John S. Dunne, *The Reasons of the Heart*, SCM Press 1978, p. 21.
12. William Temple, *The Hope of a New World*, SCM Press 1940, p. 114.
13. Hans Küng, *On Being a Christian*, translated by Edward Quinn, William Collins Sons and Co. 1977, p. 251.
14. John V. Taylor, *The Go-Between God*, SCM Press 1973, p. 231.
15. Anthony Bloom, *The Essence of Prayer*, Darton, Longman and Todd 1989, p. 61.
16. John S. Dunne, *The Reasons of the Heart*, SCM Press 1978, p. 13.
17. George Appleton, *Journey for a Soul*, William Collins Sons and Co. 1976, p. 234.
18. George Macdonald, *Unspoken Sermons*, Second Series, Longmans, Green and Co. 1885, p. 168.

Wisdom

1. NRSV.
2. NRSV.
3. Aeschylus, *Agamemnon*, translated by Herbert Weir Smyth, William Heinemann 1952, p. 19.
4. Rabindranath Tagore, *Stray Birds, Collected Poems and Plays of Rabindranath Tagore*, Macmillan and Co. 1936, ccxciv, p. 325.
5. W.R. Inge, in Sir James Marchant, *Wit and Wisdom of Dean Inge*, selected and arranged by Sir James Marchant, Longmans, Green and Co. 1927, p. 112.
6. George Eliot, *Middlemarch*, J. M. Dent and Sons 1959, vol. 2, p. 77.
7. Bede Griffiths OSB, in Peter Spink, *The Universal Christ*, Darton, Longman and Todd 1990, p. 7.
8. Christopher Bryant SSJE, *The Heart in Pilgrimage*, Darton, Longman and Todd 1980, p. 98.
9. Charles Dickens, *Hard Times*, The Gresham Publishing Co. 1904, p. 155.
10. A.R. Orage, *On Love*, The Janus Press 1957, p. 60.
11. Maurice Maeterlinck, *Wisdom and Destiny*, translated by Alfred Sutro, George Allen 1898, p. 38.
12. William Wordsworth, 'The Excursion', *The Poetical Works of William Wordsworth*, edited by E. de Selincourt and Helen Darbishire, Oxford at the Clarendon Press 1959, vol. V, book III, l.231, p. 82.
13. Michel Quoist, *With Open Heart*, translated by Colette Copeland, Gill and Macmillan 1983, p. 50.
14. Thomas Merton, *Thoughts in Solitude*, Burns and Oates 1958, p. 64.

15. Charles Kingsley, *Health and Education*, W. Isbister and Co. 1874, p. 194.
16. Rufus M. Jones, *Spiritual Reformers in the 16th and 17th Centuries*, Macmillan and Co. 1914, p. 150.
17. Michael Ramsey, *The Gospel and the Catholic Church*, Longmans, Green and Co. 1936, p. 125.
18. William Barclay, *The Letters to the Galatians and Ephesians*, The Saint Andrew Press 1958, p. 95.
19. Walt Whitman, 'Song of the Open Road', *The Complete Poems*, edited by Francis Murphy, Penguin Books 1982, section 6, l.77, p. 182.
20. William Blake, 'Vale or the Four Zoas', *The Complete Writings of William Blake*, edited by Geoffrey Keynes, Oxford University Press 1974, p. 290.
21. Henri Frédéric Amiel, *Amiel's Journal*, translated by Mrs Humphry Ward, Macmillan and Co. 1918, p. 95.
22. Sir Sarvepalli Radhakrishna, *Eastern Religions and Western Thought*, Oxford University Press 1940, p. 96.

Wonder

1. NRSV.
2. NRSV.
3. José Ortega Y Gasset, *The Revolt of the Masses*, George Allen and Unwin 1932, p. 12.
4. Rabindranath Tagore, *Sadhana*, Macmillan Publishers 1930, p. 48.
5. Thomas Carlyle, *Heroes and Hero-Worship*, Ward, Lock 1841, p. 8.
6. Alfred North Whitehead, *Modes of Thought*, Cambridge University Press 1938, p. 232.
7. Lady Julian of Norwich, *Revelations of Divine Love*, Penguin Books 1976, p. 130.
8. Evelyn Underhill, in John Stobbart, *The Wisdom of Evelyn Underhill*, Mowbray 1951, p. 11.
9. H.A. Williams CR, *The True Wilderness*, William Collins Sons and Co. 1983, p. 111.
10. Henry Ward Beecher, *Proverbs from Plymouth Pulpit*, Charles Burnet and Co. 1887, p. 31.
11. Johann Wolfgang von Goethe, in Emil Ludwig, *The Practical Wisdom of Goethe*, George Allen and Unwin Publishers 1933, To Ekermann 1829, p. 91.
12. Rollo May, *Man's Search for Himself*, George Allen and Unwin 1953, p. 212.
13. W. MacNeile Dixon, *The Human Situation*, Edward Arnold 1937, p. 75.
14. William Temple, *Nature, Man and God*, Macmillan Publishers 1934, p. 156.
15. Michael Ramsey, in Margaret Duggan, *Through the Year with Michael Ramsey*, Hodder and Stoughton 1975, p. 24.
16. Albert Einstein, *Ideas and Opinions*, Souvenir Press (Educational and Academic) 1973, p. 11.
17. G.A. Studdert Kennedy, *The New Man in Christ*, edited by the Dean of Worcester, Hodder and Stoughton 1932, p. 132.
18. D.H. Lawrence, *Phoenix II*, William Heinemann 1968, p. 598.

Work

1. NRSV.
2. NRSV.
3. Henry Ward Beecher, *Proverbs from Plymouth Pulpit*, Charles Burnet and Co. 1887, p. 37.
4. Walter Bagehot, *Biographical Studies*, edited by Richard Holt Hutton, Longmans, Green, and Co. 1907, p. 370.
5. William Barclay, *The Gospel of Matthew*, The Saint Andrew Press 1976, vol. 11, p. 296.
6. Beecher, *Proverbs from Plymouth Pulpit*, p. 36.
7. George Macdonald, *Wilfred Cumbermede*, Hurst and Blackett, 1872, vol. III, p. 169.
8. Beecher, *Proverbs from Plymouth Pulpit*, p. 58.
9. Albert Einstein, *Out of My Later Years*, Thames and Hudson 1950, p. 35.
10. Joseph Conrad, *Heart of Darkness, in Youth, a Narrative and Two Other Stories*, J.M. Dent and Sons 1923, p. 37.
11. Beecher, *Proverbs from Plymouth Pulpit*, p. 37.
12. William Temple, *Christianity and the Social Order*, Penguin Books 1942, p. 73.

13. William Penn, *Fruits of Solitude*, A.W. Bennett 1863, p. 16.
14. Sir Julian Huxley, *Religion without Revelation*, C.A. Watts and Co. 1967, p. 140.
15. George Macleod, *Only One Way Left*, The Iona Community 1956, p. 29.
16. Lord Soper, in Gerald Priestland, *Priestland's Progress*, BBC Worldwide 1982, p. 54.
17. Henri Frédéric Amiel, *Amiel's Journal*, translated by Mrs Humphry Ward, Macmillan and Co. 1918, p. 224.
18. Robert Lowry Calhoun, *God and the Common Life*, The Shoe String Press 1954, p. 240.
19. Mohandas K. Gandhi, in C.F. Andrews, *Mahatma Gandhi's Ideas*, George Allen and Unwin 1929, p. 101.

Worldliness

1. NRSV.
2. NRSV.
3. Leslie J. Tizard, *Facing Life and Death*, George Allen and Unwin 1959, p. 111.
4. Logan Pearsall Smith, *Afterthoughts*, Constable and Co. 1931, p. 29.
5. Oliver Goldsmith, 'The Traveller', *Collected Works of Oliver Goldsmith*, vol. IV, edited by Arthur Friedman, Oxford at the Clarendon Press 1966, p. 252.
6. Henry Ward Beecher, *Proverbs from Plymouth Pulpit*, Charles Burnet and Co. 1887, p. 44.
7. Hans Küng, *On Being a Christian*, translated by Edward Quinn, William Collins Sons and Co. 1977, p. 28.
8. Hubert van Zeller, *Considerations*, Sheed and Ward 1974, p. 10.
9. William Law, *A Serious Call to a Devout and Holy Life*, J.M. Dent and Co. 1898, p. 85.
10. Benedict Spinoza, *Spinoza's Ethics and De Intellectus Emendatione*, J.M. Dent and Sons 1955, p. 227.
11. William Wordsworth, 'The World Is too much with Us', *The Poetical Works of William Wordsworth*, edited by E. de Selincourt and Helen Darbishire, Oxford at the Clarendon Press 1954, vol. III, p. 16.
12. Geoffrey Preston OP, *Hallowing the Time*, Darton, Longman and Todd 1980, p. 32.
13. B.F. Westcott, *The Gospel According to St John*, John Murray 1908, vol. 1, pp. 14 and 64.
14. Michael Ramsey, in Margaret Duggan, *Through the Year with Michael Ramsey*, Hodder and Stoughton 1975, p. 123.
15. Martin Luther King, in Coretta Scott King, *The Words of Martin Luther King*, William Collins Sons and Co. 1986, p. 63.
16. W.R. Inge, *Personal Religion and the Life of Devotion*, Longmans, Green and Co. 1924, p. 79.

Worship

1. NRSV.
2. NRSV.
3. Thomas Carlyle, *Sartor Resartus*, Ward, Lock and Co., p. 52.
4. Benjamin Whichcote, *Moral and Religious Aphorisms*, Number 248, Elkin, Mathews and Marrot 1930.
5. Peter Shaffer, *Equus*, Longman 1983, II.xxv, p. 67.
6. Alan Richardson, in Alan Richardson and John Bowden, *A New Dictionary of Christian Theology*, SCM Press 1985, p. 605.
7. Hubert van Zeller, *Considerations*, Sheed and Ward 1974, p. 86.
8. John Macquarrie, *Paths in Spirituality*, SCM Press 1972, p. 21.
9. William Temple, *Citizen and Churchman*, Eyre and Spottiswoode 1941, p. 43.
10. van Zeller, *Considerations*, p. 87.
11. Macquarrie, *Paths in Spirituality*, p. 20.
12. Epictetus, in Witney J. Oates, *The Stoic and Epicurean Philosophers*, Random House 1940, p 253.
13. William Temple, *Readings in St John's Gospel*, first and second series, Macmillan and Co. 1947, p. 68.
14. William Barclay, *The Letter to the Romans*, The Saint Andrew Press 1969, p. 169.

15. George Appleton, *Journey for a Soul*, William Collins Sons and Co. 1976, p. 215.
16. Temple, *Readings in St John's Gospel*, p. 258.
17. Michael Ramsey, in Margaret Duggan, *Through the Year with Michael Ramsey*, Hodder and Stoughton 1975, p. 75.
18. Leonard Hurst, *Hungry Men*, The Livingstone Press 1955, p. 107.

ACKNOWLEDGEMENTS

We would like to thank all those who have given us permission to reproduce extracts from publications in this book, as indicated in the list below. Every effort has been made to trace copyright ownership. The publisher would be grateful to be informed of any omissions.

Michel Quoist, *With Open Heart*, 1983, translated by Colette Copeland, by permission of the publishers, Gill and Macmillan Ltd. Michel Quoist, *Prayers of Life*, 1963, translated by Anne Marie de Commaile and Agnes Mitchell Forsyth, Gill and Macmillan Ltd. Basil Hume OSB, *To Be a Pilgrim*, 1984, by permission of St Pauls Press (formerly St Paul Publications). Albert Schweitzer, *The Teaching of Reverence for Life*, 1965, Peter Owen Ltd, London. Sir Sarvepalli Radhakrishnan, *Eastern and Western Thought*, 1940, reprinted by permission of Oxford University Press. Andrew Seth Pringle-Pattison, *The Idea of God in the Light of Recent Philosophy*, 1917, reprinted by permission of Oxford University Press. John Baillie, *Invitation to Pilgrimage*, 1942, reprinted by permission of Oxford University Press. Stephen Neill, *The Church and Christian Union*, 1968, reprinted by permission of Oxford University Press. R.C. Zaehner, *Mysticism Sacred and Profane*, 1957, reprinted by permission of Oxford University Press. Iris Murdoch, *The Sovereignty of Good Over Other Concepts*, 1967, reprinted by permission of Cambridge University Press. John Oman, *The Natural and the Supernatural*, 1931, Cambridge at the University Press, permission granted by Cambridge University Press. Sir Richard Livingstone, *On Education*, 1954, Cambridge at the University Press, permission granted by Cambridge University Press. J.H. Whale, *Christian Doctrine*, 1942, Cambridge University Press, permission granted by Cambridge University Press. Alfred North Whitehead, *Modes of Thought*, 1938, Cambridge University Press, permission granted by them. Alfred North Whitehead, *Science and the Modern World*, 1932, The New American Library, 1964, permission granted by Cambridge University Press. A.R. Vidler, *Soundings*, 1962, Cambridge at the University Press, permission granted by Cambridge University Press. Cyril H. Powell, *Secrets of Answered Prayer*, 1958, Arthur James Ltd. Agnes Sanford, *The Healing Light*, 1949, Arthur James Ltd. Alan Watts, *Behold the Spirit*, 1947, John Murray (Publishers) Ltd. C.S. Lewis, *The Screwtape Letters,* © C.S. Lewis Pte, Ltd. 1942. C.S. Lewis, *Mere Christianity*, © C.S. Lewis Pte, Ltd. 1942, 1943, 1944, 1952. C.S. Lewis, *They Stand Together*, © C.S. Lewis Pte, Ltd. 1979. C.S. Lewis, *The Four Loves*, © C.S. Lewis Pte. Ltd, 1960. C.S. Lewis, *The Great Divorce*, © C.S. Lewis, 1946. Extracts reprinted by permission. Rosemary Haughton, *On Trying to Be Human*, Geoffrey Chapman, 1966, by permission of The Continuum International Publishing Group Ltd. Sister Elizabeth of the Trinity, *Spiritual Writings*, 1962, Geoffrey Chapman, by permission of The Continuum International Publishing Group Ltd. Martin Buber, *I and Thou*, translated by Walter Kaufman, 1971, T&T Clark, by permission of The Continuum International Publishing Group Ltd. W.M. Macgregor, *Jesus Christ the Son of God*, 1907, T&T Clark, by permission of The Continuum International Publishing Group Ltd. A.J. Gossip, *From the Edge of the Crowd*, 1925, T&T Clark, by permission of The Continuum International Publishing Group Ltd. Mark Gibbard, *Liberation and Love*, 1982, A.R. Mowbray and Co., by permission of The Continuum International Publishing Group Ltd. Father Andrew SDC, *The Life and Letters of Fr Andrew* SDC, 1948, A.R. Mowbray and Co., by permission of The Continuum International Publishing Group Ltd. Father Andrew SDC, *A Gift of Light*, selected and edited by Harry C. Griffith, 1968, A.R. Mowbray and Co., by permission of The Continuum International Publishing Group Ltd. Father Andrew SDC, *The Symbolism of the Sanctuary*, 1927, A.R. Mowbray and Co., by permission of The Continuum International Publishing Group Ltd. Father Andrew SDC, *The Seven Words from the Cross*, 1954, A.R. Mowbray and Co., by permission of The Continuum International Publishing Group Ltd. Father Andrew SDC, *The Way of Victory*, 1938, A.R. Mowbray and Co., by permission of The Continuum International Publishing Group Ltd. Father Andrew SDC, *Meditations for Every Day*, 1941, A.R.

ACKNOWLEDGEMENTS

Mowbray and Co., by permission of The Continuum International Publishing Group Ltd. Evelyn Underhill, *The Love of God*, 1953, A.R. Mowbray and Co., by permission of The Continuum International Publishing Group Ltd. Evelyn Underhill, in John Stobbart, editor, *The Wisdom of Evelyn Underhill*, 1951, A.R. Mowbray and Co., by permission of The Continuum International Publishing Group Ltd. Edward Patey, *Christian Life Style*, 1976, A.R. Mowbray and Co., by permission of The Continuum International Publishing Group Ltd. Norman W. Goodacre, *Laymen's Lent*, 1969, A.R. Mowbray and Co., by permission of The Continuum International Publishing Group Ltd. Rabindranath Tagore, *Letters to a Friend*, © 1928, George Allen and Unwin, permission given by HarperCollins Publishers Ltd. Rabindranath Tagore, *The Religion of Man*, © 1931, George Allen and Unwin, permission given by HarperCollins Publishers Ltd. Norman Pittenger, *The Christian Situation Today*, © Epworth Press, used by permission of Methodist Publishing House. W.E. Sangster, *The Pure in Heart*, © Epworth Press, used by permission of Methodist Publishing House. W.E. Sangster, *Westminster Sermons*, Volume 1, 1960, and Volume 2, 1962, © Epworth Press, used by permission of Methodist Publishing House. J. Neville Ward, *The Use of Praying*, 1967, © Epworth Press, used by permission of Methodist Publishing House. J. Neville Ward, *Five for Sorrow, Ten for Joy*, 1971, © Epworth Press, used by permission of Methodist Publishing House. J. Neville Ward, *Friday Afternoon*, 1982, © Epworth Press, used by permission of Methodist Publishing House. W.E. Sangster, *Give God a Chance*, 1968, © Epworth Press, used by permission of Methodist Publishing House. F.W. Boreham, *A Late Lark Singing*, 1945, © Epworth Press, used by permission of Methodist Publishing House. Roy Stevens, *Education and the Death of Love*, 1978, © Epworth Press, used by permission of Methodist Publishing House. Colin Morris, *The Hammer of the Lord*, Epworth Press, 1973, © Epworth Press, used by permission of Methodist Publishing House. Colin Morris, *The Word and the Words*, 1975, © Epworth Press, used by permission of Methodist Publishing House. Henri J.M. Nouwen, *Reaching Out*, William Collins Sons and Co., © 1880, reprinted by permission of HarperCollins Publishers Ltd. Albert Schweitzer, *Christianity and the Religions of the World*, 1924, translated by Joanna Powers, George Allen and Unwin, permission granted by HarperCollins Publishers Ltd. Leslie J. Tizard, *Facing Life and Death*, 1959, George Allen and Unwin, permission granted by HarperCollins Publishers Ltd. Sir Sarvepalli Radhakrishnan, *Mahatma Gandhi: Essays and Reflections*, 1949, George Allen and Unwin Publishers Ltd, permission granted by HarperCollins Publishers Ltd. Joseph Joubert, *Pensées and Letters*, 1928, George Routledge and Sons Ltd, permission granted by Thomson Publishing Services, North Way, Andover, Hants, SP10 5BE. Richard Wilhelm and C.G. Jung, *The Secret of the Golden Flower*, (extract from a former patient), 1972, Routledge and Kegan Paul, permission granted by Thomson Publishing Services. C.G. Jung, *The Collected Works of C.G. Jung*, Volume 12, 1953, translated by R.F.C. Hull, Routledge and Kegan Paul, permission granted by Thomson Publishing Services. C.G. Jung, *The Structure and Dynamics of the Psyche*, The Collected Works of C.G. Jung, Volume 8, 1969, translated by R.F.C. Hull, Routledge and Kegan Paul, permission granted by Thomson Publishing Services. C.G. Jung, *Psychological Reflections*, 1953, Routledge and Kegan Paul Ltd, permission granted by Thomson Publishing Services. C.G. Jung, *Aion*, The Collected Works of C.G. Jung, Volume 9, Part 2, 1959, translated by R.F.C. Hull, Routledge and Kegan Paul, permission granted by Thomson Publishing Services. C.G. Jung, *Psychology and Alchemy*, The Collected Works of C.G. Jung, 1953,Volume 12, translated by R.F.C. Hull, Routledge and Kegan Paul, permission granted by Thomson Publishing Services. Simon Weil, *Gravity and Grace*, 1972, Routledge and Kegan Paul, permission granted by Thomson Publishing Services. Helen Mary Lynd, *On Shame and Search for Identity*, 1958, Routledge and Kegan Paul Ltd, permission granted by Thomson Publishing Services. Erich Fromm, *Man for Himself*, 1975, Routledge and Kegan Paul, permission granted by Thomson Publishing Services. Ernest Hemingway, *Death in the Afternoon*, 1968, Jonathan Cape Ltd, reprinted by permission of The Random House Group Ltd. Arthur Koestler, *Darkness at Noon*, 1980, Jonathan Cape, reprinted by permission of The Random House Group Ltd. Thomas Merton, *Contemplative Prayer*, 1973, Darton Longman and Todd, permission granted by the publisher. Alan Ecclestone, *Yes to God*, 1975, Darton, Longman and Todd, permission granted by the publisher. Anthony Bloom, *School for Prayer*, 1970, Darton, Longman and Todd, permission granted by the publisher. Anthony Book, *The Essence of Prayer*, 1989, Darton, Longman and Todd, permission granted by the publisher. John Main OSB, *The Joy of Being*, selection by Clare Hallward, 1989, Darton, Longman and Todd, permission granted by the publisher. John Main OSB, *Moment of Christ*, 1984, Darton, Longman and Todd, permission granted by the publisher. Carlo Corretto, *Letters from the Desert*, 1972, translated by Rose Mary Hancock, Darton, Longman and Todd, permission granted by the publisher. Henri J.M. Nouwen, *The Way of the Heart*, 1981, Darton, Longman and Todd Ltd, permission granted by the

ACKNOWLEDGEMENTS

publisher. Henri J.M. Nouwen, *Seeds of Hope*, 1989, edited by Robert Durback, Darton, Longman and Todd Ltd, permission granted by the publisher. Hubert van Zeller, *Praying While You Work*, 1951, Burns, Oates and Washbourne, permission granted by The Continuum International Publishing Group Ltd. Thomas Merton, *Conjectures of a Guilty Bystander*, 1968, Burns and Oates Ltd, permission granted by The Continuum International Publishing Group Ltd. Thomas Merton, *No Man Is an Island*, 1974, Burns and Oates, permission granted by The Continuum International Publishing Group Ltd. Thomas Merton, *Thoughts in Solitude*, 1958, Burns and Oates, permission granted by The Continuum International Publishing Group Ltd. Thomas Merton, *New Seeds of Contemplation*, 1962, Burns and Oates Ltd, permission granted by The Continuum International Publishing Group Ltd. Alban Goodier SJ, *The School of Love*, 1920, Burns and Oates and Washbourne, permission granted by The Continuum International Publishing Group Ltd. Ladislaus Boros, *In Time of Temptation*, 1968, translated by Simon and Erika Young, Burns and Oates Ltd, permission granted by The Continuum International Publishing Group Ltd. Gabriel Moran FSC, *The Theology of Revelation*, 1967, Burns and Oates, permission granted by The Continuum International Publishing Group Ltd. Lewis Mumford, *The Conduct of Life*, 1952, Secker and Warburg, used by permission of The Random House Group Limited. André Gide, *The Journals of André Gide*, 1894, translated by Justin O'Brien, Secker and Warburg, 1947, used by permission of The Random House Group Limited. Virginia Woolf, *A Writer's Diary*, 1953, edited by Leonard Woolf, The Hogarth Press, used by permission of the executors of the Virginia Woolf Estate and The Random House Group Limited. Yevgeny Yevtushenko, *A Precocious Autobiography*, 1963, translated by Andrew R. MacAndrew, Collins and Harvill Press, used by permission of The Random House Group Limited. A.D. Sertillanges OP, *The Intellectual Life*, 1948, translated by Mary Ryan, The Mercier Press, permission granted by The Mercier Press. Wassily Kandinsky, *Concerning the Spiritual in Art*, 1977, translated by M.T.H, Sadler, Dover Publications, permission given by Dover Publications. William Barclay, *The Plain Man Looks at the Apostles Creed*, 1967, William Collins Sons and Co. Ltd, permission given by The Estate of William Barclay. C.G. Jung, *Memories, Dreams, Reflections*, 1971, William Collins Sons and Co., permission granted by HarperCollins Publishers Ltd. Sydney Carter, *Dance in the Dark* (originally *Rock of Doubt*) 1980, William Collins Sons and Co., permission granted by HarperCollins Publishers Ltd. William Johnston, *The Inner Eye of Love*, 1978, William Collins Sons and Co., permission granted by HarperCollins Publishers Ltd. Giles and Melville Harcourt/Hugh Montefiore, *Short Prayers for the Long Day/Sermons from Great St. Mary's*, 1978, William Collins Sons and Co., permission granted by HarperCollins Publishers Ltd. Rabbi H. Kushner, *When Bad Things Happen to Good People*, 1982, Pan Books, permission granted by Pan Macmillan. Stephen MacKenna, *Journal and Letters*, 1936, Constable and Co. Ltd, reproduced by kind permission of Constable and Robinson Publishing Ltd. Logan Pearsall Smith, *Afterthoughts*, 1931, Constable and Co. Ltd, reproduced by kind permission of Constable and Robinson Publishing Ltd. A. Clutton Brock, *The Ultimate Belief*, 1916, Constable and Company, reproduced by kind permission of Constable and Robinson Publishing Ltd. F.R. Barry, *Vocation and Ministry*, James Nisbet and Co. Ltd, 1958. F.R. Barry, *The Relevance of Christianity*, James Nisbet and Co. Ltd, 1932. Paul Tillich, *The Courage To Be*, James Nisbet and Co. Ltd, 1952. Herbert Farmer, *The Healing Cross*, James Nisbet and Co. Ltd, 1938. C.M. Vidor, in Charles R. Joy, *Music in the Life of Albert Schweitzer, Selections from His Writings*, translated and edited by Charles R. Joy, 1953, A. and C. Black, by kind permission of A. and C. Black (Publishers) Ltd. Norman Goodall, *The Local Church*, Hodder and Stoughton, 1960, reproduced by permission of Hodder and Stoughton Limited. Mary Craig, *Blessings*, Hodder and Stoughton, 1979, reproduced by permission of Hodder and Stoughton Limited. David Watson, *You Are My God*, Hodder and Stoughton, 1983, reproduced by permission of Hodder and Stoughton Limited. Raynor C. Johnson, *A Pool of Reflections*, Hodder and Stoughton, 1983, reproduced by permission of Hodder and Stoughton Limited. Richard Foster, *The Celebration of Discipline*, Hodder and Stoughton, 1982, reproduced by permission of Hodder and Stoughton Limited. Neville Cryer, *Michel Quoist*, Hodder and Stoughton, 1977, reproduced by permission of Hodder and Stoughton Limited. Austin Farrer, *Saving Belief*, Hodder and Stoughton, 1964, reproduced by permission of Hodder and Stoughton Limited. W.E. Sangster, *He Is Able*, Hodder and Stoughton, 1936, permission granted for this and the next three books, by Dr Paul Sangster. W.E. Sangster, *God Does Guide Us*, Hodder and Stoughton, 1934. W.E. Sangster, *These Things Abide*, Hodder and Stoughton, 1939. W.E. Sangster, *The Secret of Radiant Life*, Hodder and Stoughton, 1957. Hugh Redwood, *Residue of Days*, Hodder and Stoughton, 1958, reproduced by permission of Hodder and Stoughton Limited. David Sheppard, *Bias to the Poor*, Hodder and Stoughton, 1983, reproduced by permission of Hodder and Stoughton Limited. Norman

ACKNOWLEDGEMENTS

Goodall, *The Local Church*, Hodder and Stoughton, 1966, reproduced by permission of Hodder and Stoughton Limitied. W. MacNeile Dixon, *The Human Situation*, Edward Arnold (Publishers) Ltd, 1937. Lesslie Newbigin, *Honest Religion for Secular Man*, SCM Press, 1966, this and the next 48 entries, reproduced by permission from SCM Press. Peter Munz, *Problems of Religious Knowledge*, SCM Press, 1959. Florence Higham, said of F.D. Maurice, in *Frederick Denison Maurice*, SCM Press, 1947. John Macmurray, *Creative Society*, SCM Press, 1935. Olive Wyon, *On The Way*, SCM Press, 1958. F.R. Barry, *Secular and Supernatural*, SCM Press, 1969. Frank Wright, *The Pastoral Nature of the Ministry*, SCM Press, 1980. Harry Emerson Fosdick, *As I See Religion*, SCM Press, 1932. Harry Emerson Fosdick, *Successful Christian Living*, SCM Press, 1938. Harry Emerson Fosdick, *The Hope of a New World*, SCM Press, 1933. D.S. Cairns, *The Riddle of the World*, SCM Press, 1937. Trevor Beeson, *An Eye for an Ear*, SCM Press, 1972. R.L. Smith, *Life Made Possible by the Gospel*, in Paul Rowntree Clifford, *Man's Dilemma and God's Answer*, Broadcast Series, SCM Press, 1944. Sister Madeleine OSA, *Solitary Refinement*, SCM Press, 1972. Stuart B. Jackman, *The Numbered Days*, SCM Press, 1954. Alan Richardson, *History Sacred and Profane*, SCM Press, 1964. Don Cupitt, *Taking Leave of God*, SCM Press, 1980. David Anderson, *Simone Weil*, SCM Press, 1971. John Macquarrie, *The Humility of God*, SCM Press, 1978. William Temple, *Christian Faith and Life*, SCM Press (1931), reissued 1963. Norman Pittenger, *Christology Reconsidered*, SCM Press, 1970. Joachim Jeremias, *New Testament Theology*, Volume 1, SCM Press, 1971. Jürgen Moltmann, *The Open Church*, SCM Press, 1978. Harvey Cox, *God's Revolution and Man's Responsibility*, SCM Press, 1969. Harvey Cox, *The Secular City*, SCM Press, 1967. William Temple, *The Hope of a New World*, SCM Press, 1940. John S. Dunne, *The Reasons of the Heart*, SCM Press, 1978. John S. Dunne, *The Church of the Poor Devil*, SCM Press, 1983. John Macquarrie, *Paths in Spirituality*, SCM Press, 1972. John Macquarrie, *The Concept of Peace*, SCM Press, 1973. John Macquarrie, *In Search of Humanity*, SCM Press, 1982. John V. Taylor, *The Go-Between God*, SCM Press, 1973. Paul Tillich, *The Shaking of the Foundations*, SCM Press, 1949. Paul Tillich, *The Eternal Now*, SCM Press, 1963. Dietrich Bonhoeffer, *Letters and Papers from Prison*, The Enlarged Edition, SCM Press, 1971. Dietrich Bonhoeffer, *The Cost of Discipleship*, translated by R.H. Fuller, SCM Press, 1959. Nicolas Berdyaev, *The Fate of Man in the Modern World*, translated by Donald A. Lowrie, SCM Press, 1935. John A.T. Robinson, *The Roots of a Radical*, SCM Press, 1980. Henry McKeating, *God and the Future*, SCM Press, 1974. David Brown, *God's Tomorrow*, SCM Press, 1977. Paul Oestreicher, Introduction to Hans Jürgen Schultz, *Conversion to the World*, SCM Press, 1967. W.A. Visser't Hooft, *The Renewal of the Church*, SCM Press, 1956. Daniel Jenkins, *Christian Maturity and the Theology of Success*, SCM Press, 1976. J.H. Oldham, *Life is Commitment*, SCM Press, 1953. Hans Jürgen Schultz, *Conversion to the World*, SCM Press. Paul Tournier, *Escape from Loneliness*, translated by John S. Gilmour, SCM Press, 1962. Michael Ramsey, *The Idea of the Holy and the World Today*, in *Spirituality for Today*, edited by Eric James, SCM Press, 1968. Alan Richardson and John Bowden, *A New Dictionary of Christian Theology*, SCM Press, 1983. James F. Childress, in *A New Dictionary of Christian Ethics*, James F. Childress and John Macquarrie, SCM Press, 1986. Gordon S. Wakefield in *A Dictionary of Christian Spirituality*, edited by Gordon S. Wakefield, SCM Press, 1986. Harry Williams CR, *The True Wilderness*, William Collins Sons and Co. Ltd, 1983, reprinted by permission of Constable and Robinson Ltd. Graham Greene, *The Heart of the Matter*, William Heinemann, 1959, by permission of David Higham Associates Limited. Hubert van Zeller, *Leave Your Life Alone*, Sheed and Ward, 1973, permission granted by The Continuum International Publishing Group Ltd. Hubert van Zeller, *Considerations*, Sheed and Ward, 1974, permission granted by The Continuum International Publishing Group Ltd. Nicolas Berdyaev, *Christianity and Class War*, translated by Donald Attwater, Sheed and Ward, 1933, permission granted by The Continuum International Publishing Group Ltd. Etienne Gilson, *The Spirit of Medieval Philosophy*, translated by A.H.C. Downes, Sheed and Ward, 1950, permission granted by The Continuum International Publishing Group Ltd. G.P. Fedatov, *A Treasury of Russian Spirituality*, Sheed and Ward, 1977, permission granted by The Continuum International Publishing Group Ltd. G.K. Chesterton, *Charles Dickens*, Methuen and Co., 1906, permission given by A.P. Watt Ltd on behalf of the Royal Literary Fund. J.B. Priestley, *All About Ourselves and Other Essays*, William Heinemann Ltd, 1956 (© J.B. Priestly 1956) by permission of PFD on behalf of the Estate of J.B. Priestley. Malcolm Muggeridge, *Jesus Rediscoved*, William Collins Sons and Co. Ltd, 1982, by permission of David Higham Associates Ltd. Carroll E. Simcox, *Living the Creed*, Dacre Press/ A. and C. Black, 1954, permission given by A. and C. Black Publishers Ltd. Carroll E. Simcox, *The Promises of God*, Dacre Press/ A. and C. Black, 1958, permission given by A. and C. Black Publishers Ltd. Albert Schweitzer, *The Quest of the Historical Jesus*, A. and C. Black, 1954,

ACKNOWLEDGEMENTS

permission given by A. and C. Black Publishers Ltd. Albert Schweitzer, in E.N. Mozley, *The Theology of Albert Schweitzer*, translated by J.R. Coates, A. and C. Black, 1950, permission given by A. and C. Black Publishers Ltd. Albert Schweitzer, *The Philosophy of Civilization, Part 11, Civilization and Ethics*, translated by C.T. Campion, Third English Edition, revised by Mrs C.E.B. Russell, 1946, permission given by A. and C. Black Publishers Ltd. Albert Schweitzer in Charles H. Joy, *An Anthology*, A. and C. Black, 1955, permission given by A. and C. Black Publishers Ltd. L.S. Thorton CR, *The Common Life in the Body of Christ*, Dacre Press/ A. and C. Black, 1950, permission given by A. and C. Black Publishers Ltd. Thomas Kelly, *A Testament of Devotion*, Hodder and Stoughton, 1943, reproduced by permission of William Neill-Hall Ltd. Anne Morrow Lindbergh, *Gift from the Sea*, Chatto and Windus Ltd, 1974, used by permission of The Random House Group Limited. John Macquarrie, *Paths in Spirituality*, SCM Press, 1972, 1992, reprinted with permission by Morehouse Publishing, Harrisburg Pennsylvania. Bede Griffiths, *Return to the Center*, Templegate Publishers (templegate.com) 1977. Hermann Hesse, in Volker Michels, *Reflections*, translated by Ralph Manheim, Jonathan Cape, 1977, © Suhrkamp Verlag, permission granted by them. Mother Teresa, *Jesus, The Word to Be Spoken*, compiled by Fr. Angelo Devananda Scolozzi M.C.111.O. – William Collins Sons and Co. Ltd, 1990 – permission sentence from *Jesus, The Word to Be Spoken*, Mother Teresa, compiled by Fr Angelo Devanande Scolozzi M.C.111.O © 1998 by Servant Publications. Published by Servant Publications, P.O. Box 8617, Ann Arbor, Michigan, 48107. Used with permission. Aaron Copeland, *Music and Imagination*, Harvard University Press, 1977, reprinted by the permission of the publisher from *Music and Imagination: The Charles Eliot Norton Lectures 1951–1952* by Aaron Copeland, Cambridge, Mass.: Harvard University Press, © 1952 by the President and Fellows of Harvard College, © renewed 1980 by Aaron Copeland. George Moore, *Evelyn Innes*, Volume 11, Bernhard Tauchnitz, 1898. Hans Küng, *On Being a Christian*, translated by Edward Quinn, William Collins Sons and Co., 1977, permission granted by Professor Dr Hans Küng. André Gide, *The Journals of André Gide*, translated by Justin O'Brien, Secker and Warburg, 1947. Dag Hammarskjöld, *Markings*, translated by Leif Sjöberg and W.H. Auden, Faber and Faber, 1964, permission granted by Faber and Faber Ltd. C.S. Lewis, *A Grief Observed*, Faber and Faber, 1961, permission granted by Faber and Faber Ltd. W.H. Auden, *A Certain World*, Faber and Faber, 1971, permission granted by Faber and Faber Ltd. André Maurois, *The Art of Living*, The English Universities Press, 1940, permission granted 'L'Art de Vivre' © Heritiers André Maurois – Paris. W. Somerset Maugham, *The Summing Up*, Bernhard Tauchnitz, 1938, permission granted by A.P. Watt Ltd on behalf of the Royal Literary Fund. G.K. Chesterton, *Orthodoxy*, 1935, The Bodley Head, permission granted by A.P. Watt Ltd on behalf of the Royal Literary Fund. G.K. Chesterton, *What's Wrong with the World*, Bernhard Tauchnitz, 1910, permission granted by A.P. Watt Ltd on behalf of the Royal Literary Fund. Bertrand Russell, *Principles of Social Reconstruction*, George Allen and Unwin, 1971, permission granted by Taylor and Francis Books (Unwin Hyman). Bertrand Russell, *The Conquest of Happiness*, 1984, George Allen and Unwin Ltd, 1984, permission granted by Taylor and Francis Books (Unwin Hyman). Bertrand Russell, *The Impact of Science*, George Allen and Unwin Publishers Ltd, 1968, permission granted by Taylor and Francis Books (Unwin Hyman). Bertrand Russell, *Authority and the Individual*, Unwin Paperbacks, 1977, permission granted by Taylor and Francis Books (Unwin Hyman). Bertrand Russell, *Marriage and Morals*, George Allen and Unwin Publishers Ltd, 1976, permission granted by Taylor and Francis Books (Unwin Hyman). John Cowper Powys, *Autobiography*, Macdonald and Co., (Publishers), 1967, by permission of the Estate of John Cowper Powys. Henri J.M. Nouwen, *Seeds of Hope*, edited by Robert Durback, Darton, Longman and Todd, 1989, permission is granted by Doubleday, a division of Random House Inc. Norman Douglas, *An Almanac*, Chatto and Windus in association with Martin Secker and Warburg Ltd, 1945, permission granted by The Society of Authors as the Literary Representative of the Estate of Norman Douglas. Arthur Koestler, *Darkness at Noon*, translated by Daphne Hardy, Jonathan Cape, 1980, USA, English language right granted by Peters Fraser and Dunlop Ltd, on behalf of the Estate of Arthur Koestler. John C. Vincent, *Secular Press*, Lutterworth Press, 1968, permission granted by James Clarke and Co. Ltd. Emil Brunner, *The Divine Imperative*, translated by Olive Wyon, Lutterworth Press, 1942, permission granted by James Clarke and Co. Ltd. Ernest Johnson, *The Social Gospel Re-Examined*, James Clarke and Co. Ltd, 1942, permission granted by James Clarke and Co. Ltd. Thomas Merton, *Seeds of Contemplation*, Anthony Clarke Books, 1972, permission granted by The Merton Legacy Trust. Yehudi Menuhin, *Theme and Variations*, William Heinemann, 1972, permission given by The Estate of Yehudi Menuhin. Malcolm Muggeridge, Mother Teresa in, *Something Beautiful for God*, William Collins Sons and Co. Ltd, 1983, permission granted by The Zondervan Corporation.

[551]

ACKNOWLEDGEMENTS

Albert Schweitzer, *Out of My Life and Thought: An Autobiography*, translated by C.T. Campion, Henry Holt and Co., 1949. H.L. Kirk, *Pablo Casals: A Biography*, Hutchinson and Co. (Publishers), 1974, © H.L. Kirk, permission granted by A.M. Heath and Co. Ltd. Eric Hoffer, *The Passionate State of Mind*, Martin Secker and Warburg Ltd, © 1956, reprinted by permission of Curtis Brown, Ltd. Monica Furlong, *Travelling In*, Hodder and Stoughton Ltd, © 1971, permission granted by Sheil L and Associates Ltd. Monica Furlong, *The End of Our Exploring*, Hodder and Stoughton, © 1973, permission granted by Sheil Land Associates Ltd. André Gide, *Pretexts, Reflections on Literature and Morality*, selected by Justin O'Brien, Martin Secker and Warburg Ltd, 1960, permission granted. English translation © 1959 by Meridian Books, Inc. Originally published in French as *Pretextes and Nouveaux Pretextes* by Mercure de France. Reprinted by permission of Georges Borchardt, Inc., for Mecure de France. Anne Morrow Lindbergh, *Gift from the Sea*, Chatto and Windus Ltd, 1974, permission credit line – from *Gift from the Sea*, by Anne Morrow Lindbergh, © 1955, 1975, renewed 1983, used by permission of Pantheon Books, a division of Random House, Inc. E. Stanley Jones, *The Word Became Flesh*, Hodder and Stoughton, 1964, © 1963, Abington Press – used by permission. Thomas Merton, *Contemplation in a World of Action*, George Allen and Unwin Ltd, 1971, permission granted by Thomson Publishing Services – on behalf of Taylor and Francis Books (publisher). *Christian Faith and Practice in the Experience of the Society of Friends*, Yearly Meeting of the Religious Society of Friends in Britain, 1972, Number 119, 1911: 1925, permission granted by The Religious Society of Friends in Britain. George Trevelyan, *A Vision of the Aquarian Age*, Coverture, 1977, by permission of Catriona Tyson. Winston S. Churchill, *Thoughts and Adventures*, Thornton Butterworth Ltd, 1932, reproduced with permission of Curtis Brown Ltd, London on behalf of Winston S. Churchill, © Winston S. Churchill 1932. William Barclay, *New Testament Daily Bible Study Commentaries*, The Saint Andrew Press, permission given by the estate of William Barclay. Ezra Pound, 'How to Read' from *The Literary Essays of Ezra Pound*, © Ezra Pound 1935, reprinted by permission of New Directions Publishing Corp. Excerpt from Lewis Mumford, *The Conduct of Life*, © 1951 and renewed 1979, reprinted by permission of Harcourt Inc. Excerpt from Virginia Woolf, *A Writer's Diary*, © 1954 Leonard Woolf and renewed 1982 by Quentin Bell and Angelica Garnett, reprinted by permission of Harcourt Inc. Excerpt from C.S. Lewis, *The Four Loves*, © 1960 Helen Joy Lewis and renewed Arthur Owen Barfield, reprinted by permission of Harcourt Inc. Excerpt from Antoine de Saint-Exupéry, *Wind, Sand and Stars*, © renewed 1967 by Lewis Galantiere, reprinted by permission of Harcourt Inc. Pierre Tielard de Chardin, *Le Milieu Divin*, William Collins Sons and Co. © 1960, by permission of Editions du Seuil. W.R. Inge, *The Philosophy of Plotinus*, Longmans, Green and Co., 1948, permission granted by Pearson Education Ltd. W.R. Inge, *Personal Religion and the Life of Devotion*, Longmans, Green and Co., 1924, permission granted by Pearson Education Ltd. W.R. Inge, *Types of Christian Saintliness*, Longmans, Green and Co., 1915, permission granted by Pearson Education Ltd. W.R. Inge, *Speculum Animae*, Longmans, Green and Co., 1911, permission granted by Pearson Education Ltd. W.R. Inge, *The Wit and Wisdom of Dean Inge*, compiled by Sir James Marchant, Longmans, Green and Co.,1927, permission granted by Pearson Education Ltd. Lecomte du Nöuy, *Human Destiny*, Longmans, Green and Co., 1947, permission granted by Pearson Education Ltd. Evelyn Underhill, *The Light of Christ*, Longmans, Green and Co., 1944, permission granted by Pearson Education Ltd. Evelyn Underhill, *The School of Charity*, Longmans, Green and Co., 1956, permission granted by Pearson Education Ltd. Evelyn Underhill, *The Letters of Evelyn Underhill*, edited by Charles Williams, Longmans, Green and Co., 1947, permission granted by Pearson Education Ltd. Evelyn Underhill, *Abba*, Longmans, Green and Co., 1940, permission granted by Pearson Education Ltd. Janet Erskine Stuart, in Maud Monahan, *Life and Letters of Janet Erskine Stuart*, Longmans, Green and Co., 1922, permission granted by Pearson Education Ltd. Llewelyn Powys, *Impassioned Clay*, Longmans, Green and Co., 1931, permission granted by Pearson Education Ltd. Dan Billany and David Dowie, *The Cage*, Longmans, Green and Co., 1949, permission granted by Pearson Education Ltd. W.B. Yeats, in Samuel H. Miller, *The Great Realities*, Longmans, Green and Co., 1956, permission granted by Pearson Education Ltd. Thornton Wilder, *Our Town*, Longmans, Green and Co., 1964, permission granted by Pearson Education Ltd. Michael Ramsey, *The Gospel and the Catholic Church*, Longmans, Green and Co., 1936, permission granted by Pearson Education Ltd. Peter Shaffer, *Equus*, Longmans, Green and Co., 1983, permission granted by Pearson Education Ltd. Ordway Tead, *The Art of Leadership*, McGraw-Hill Book Co., 1935, permission granted by McGraw-Hill Education. Clement G.J. Webb, *Religious Experience*, Oxford University Press, 1944, with permission.

INDEX OF AUTHORS